POLICE
ORGANIZATION
AND
MANAGEMENT

NINTH EDITION

By
V. A. LEONARD, Ph.D. (Late)
and
HARRY W. MORE, Ph.D.

New York, New York
FOUNDATION PRESS
2000

COPYRIGHT © 1951, 1964, 1971, 1974, 1978, 1982, 1987, 1993 FOUNDATION PRESS
COPYRIGHT © 2000 By FOUNDATION PRESS

11 Penn Plaza, Tenth Floor
New York, NY 10001
Phone (212) 760–8700
Fax (212) 760–8705

ISBN 1–56662–813–X

TEXT IS PRINTED ON 10% POST
CONSUMER RECYCLED PAPER

Dedicated to the professional ideals and philosophy of August Vollmer, Dean of American Chiefs of Police, who was directly responsible for the publication of the First Edition of POLICE ORGANIZATION AND MANAGEMENT in 1951.

*

PREFACE

For the ninth time in forty-nine years the authors bring to the academic community and the American police scene a land mark textbook and reference work that presents principles and procedures in the organization and management of the police enterprise. The ninth edition of POLICE ORGANIZATION AND MANAGEMENT provides in addition, an accounting of the tremendous advances in technology and consideration of social imperatives that have come upon the scene since the appearance of the last edition. As this Nation enters the millennium it is like entering into a New World compared to the middle of the last century. In fact, we have seen significant technological advances in wireless communications that have revolutionized police relationships with members of the community. Computers are a vital part of the American police scene and software has altered considerably the criminal investigative process, and the handling of traffic accidents. Unfortunately we have not made the same level of advancements in the social arena that impacts every aspect of police services. Of great significance are the greater openness of many law enforcement agencies and the inclusion of the public in efforts to improve neighborhood quality of life. The World Wide Web provides information about police departments, to members of the public, that alters their working relationship. Numerous footnotes include Web sites as a means of keeping faculty and students up to date one new developments.

Community policing and problem solving have come of age. Continuation of this movement can only be looked upon as an opportunity to depart from the isolationism that has long characterized American law enforcement. To improve the quality of life is not just an empty phrase it is a philosophical underpinning that must permeate every aspect of community policing. In this light what we previously knew as effectiveness and efficiency are being redefined. In this current edition an effort has been made to allude to the community policing throughout the text. This concept is so important that two new chapters have been added that relate directly to this concept—Chapter 8, CHANGE: A Reality of Organizational Life, and Chapter 10, Groups: Dynamics of Team Behavior.

This volume is dedicated to the senior author, the late V.A. Leonard, a native of Cleburne, TX, who, after a short illness, died on October 28, 1984, in Denton, TX. His death ended a career in police operations, communications, administration, and education that spanned six decades. He was truly a pioneer in the field, not only in his professional accomplishments but also in his outstanding academic achievements. V.A., or Doc as his students knew him, left a legacy of criminal justice literature that included authorship or co-authorship of 32 books on the administration of justice, ranging from records to research. He contributed to numerous professional journals and recruited authors and edited manuscripts for 38 volumes in the Police Science Series. A signal contribution to the literature was his classical work, *Police Communications Systems*, published in 1938.

Mentor to many during his long carrier as founder, developer, and director of the Police Science and Administration Department at Washington State University, he had a profound influence on students entering the police service. He served as professor and chairman for 17 years. A singular and highly significant contribution was the founding of the first chapter of Alpha Phi Sigma, the criminal justice honor society.

ACKNOWLEDGEMENTS

Numerous individuals and organizations contribute to this book during the preparation on the ninth edition by either providing information or granting permission for materials used in their publications. Special thanks is extended to the following individuals:

Frederick Herzberg, Cummins Engines Distinguished Professor Emeritus; Major P.M. Shepard, Commander, Field Support Section, Miami Police Department; Captain Genny May, Operational Development, Louisiana State Police; Dennis E. Nowicki, Chief of Police, Charlotte-Mecklenburg Police Department; Robert G. Norman, Chief of Police, Foster City Police Department; Carlo P. Garzona, Health Communications Director, The Hope Heart Institute, Seattle, WA; Thomas R. Guequierre, Lieutenant, Whitewater Police Department; Barbara Raymond, Program Coordinator, Seattle Police Department; Charles H. Ramsey, Chief of Police, Metropolitan Police Department; John E. Radeleff, Lieutenant, Contract Law Enforcement, Los Angeles County Sheriff's Office; Jerrold Olandi, The Olandi Group, Bellevue, WA; James D. Sewell, Regional Director, Florida Department of Law Enforcement; Gulf Publishing Company; Steven R. Belcher, Chief of Police, Santa Cruz Police Department; Colonel John F. Bardelli, Division of State Police, State of Connecticut; Jesse N. Graybill, Lieutenant Colonel, Chief, Field Operations Bureau, Maryland State Police; McGraw-Hill Companies; California Management Review; Sergeant Edward J. Kosmerl, Jr., Reading Police Department; George Mitchell, Major/Director, Planning and Research Division, Baltimore Police Department; Eugenia E. Gratto, Deputy Director of Communications, Police Executive Research Forum; Jay W. Lorsch, Harvard University; Dell Publishing; Charles C. Thomas, Publisher; Mitchell Yanak, Inspector, Commanding Officer, Philadelphia Police Department; Dallas Police Department; Sacramento Police Department; Bernard C. Parks, Chief of Police Los Angeles Police Department; ESRI Developers; Charles A. Moose, Chief of Police, Portland Police Bureau; Tucson Police Department; Brad Gagnepin, Captain, Pima County Sheriff's Department; Ed Pecinovsky, Senior Consultant, Center for Leadership Development, POST, State of California; Brigitte W. Wittel, NIJ/NCJRS Coordinator, US Department of Justice; American Psychological Association; Law Enforcement News; Neil Miller, Sheriff, Buffalo Sheriff's Department, Kearney, NE; Lt. David Kiniller, San Jose Police Department; John Wiley, & Sons; Richard F. Kitterman, Jr., Commission on Accreditation for Law Enforcement Agencies, Inc.; Macmillan; Boston Police Department;

ACKNOWLEDGEMENTS

American Bar Association; Charles E. Samarra, Chief of Police, Alexandria Police Department; Susan Birrell, National Crime Prevention Council, and Marsha J. Martello, National Tactical Training Officers Association.

Additional thanks are extended to the many police departments that have seen fit to provide extensive material on the Internet. These Web sites have a great deal of information that gives one insight into the operations and management of contemporary police agencies.

SUMMARY OF CONTENTS

*

TABLE OF CONTENTS

xiii

*

TABLE OF FIGURES

TABLE OF FIGURES

TABLE OF TABLES

POLICE
ORGANIZATION
AND
MANAGEMENT

*

Chapter 1

ORGANIZATIONAL THEORY: Foundations of Management

Learning Objectives

1. Identify the five types of managerial skills.
2. Describe the major characteristics of the ideal bureaucracy.
3. List the major schools of management thought.
4. Write a short essay describing scientific management.
5. Compare functional management and scientific management.
6. Discuss the implications of the Hawthorne studies.
7. List the five basic considerations when viewing management as a system.
8. Define systems.
9. Contrast POSDCORB and functional management.
10. Identify the major properties of the contingency management model.
11. List the key elements of community policing.
12. Describe the role of the beat officer under community policing.
13. Compare the ideal bureaucracy with community policing.

Since the creation of law enforcement agencies in this nation police administrators have selected varying approaches to managing and organizing police departments. The primary mechanisms of social control in contemporary society have come under increased scrutiny in the past decades and evidence of stress is noticeable in the management of law enforcement agencies. The police system is government's primary instrument of social control; therefore, the police who are highly visible have been the recipients of a veritable plethora of criticisms. The manifestations of deviant and disruptive behavior have called forth age-old "repression v. anarchy" discussions that are divorced from reason in their rhetoric and burdened with self-serving perceptions of reality and justice.

While there is currently a downtrend in crime rates there is still a great deal of faultfinding directed toward the police. Hardly a day can go by without the police being subjected to tirades of those who have traditionally opposed the police as a social control entity. This is especially true for those who have a political agenda. The basic police responsibilities have traditionally required a face-to-face confrontation with complex social and behavioral issues as they have been forced to deal with the ills of society. The importance of a well-informed and systematic management of police agencies has never been more important. This is especially true as changes in our society occur at an increasingly rapid pace. Currently many police agencies are undergoing expeditious change in order to meet the need of society.

Police organizations are becoming increasingly sensitive and responsive to the changes occurring in society. The problems of organizational communication and coordination in a changing environment and assimilation of technological advancements demands a unique arrangement of manpower and functions if police agencies are to continue to provide adequate public service. Integrated insight into behavioral sciences, organizational theory, and the dynamics of change can provide the theoretical framework for an action oriented management style that will meet the policing needs of a democratic society. If change and complex issues are to be dealt with properly, law enforcement management should reflect (methodically) innovative yet enlightened approaches. Models of law enforcement management must attempt a bridge between conceptual and street reality to move toward planned, sequential, and integrated strategies of goal-realization. To accomplish this, administrators must be well-trained in organizational theory the change process, management skills, and have an in-depth understanding of specific police activities. Managers need skills, a philosophical framework, functional knowledge, and a change-agent perspective. In addition, the law enforcement manager must give special attention to developing an awareness of organizational behavior with specific consideration of the cause and consequences of internal and external change-agents. Police executives are increasingly concerned with improving their own effectiveness. Managerial skills are essential to the fulfillment of this aspiration, accomplished only by:

- An awareness of current management theories and their relationship to classical and neoclasscal management techniques.
- An acknowledgment of the importance of the processes of management, consideration of conceptual aspects of organization with a commitment to administrative models.
- Acquiring knowledge of the tactical and strategical considerations of resource utilization.
- The application of management audit concepts to law enforcement agencies, and an awareness of the change process.

The theoretical aspects of management provide a necessary frame of reference for an adequate understanding of the evolution of police management. Management theory is still in a transitional state, as noted by recent developments such as decision theory, operations research, systems management, and contingency management. Scholars have attempted to classify concepts into a varying number of categories. With these workable categories in mind, various authors and practitioners have made significant contributions in recent years, and in part, social scientists have led the way in the development of management theory. Developments in business management have had a great deal of influence on police management.

The contemporary police manager should become familiar with the theorists who have had an impact on police administration. The early police writers were strongly influenced by these theorists. A thorough understanding of their contribution to management theory provides a theoretical framework for the study and analysis of management. In fact, each major development in behavioral sciences has soon found its way into the police literature. The major schools of management thought include the ideal bureaucracy, scientific management, functional management, human relations, systems, contingency, POSDCORB, and community policing (see figure 1–1). In many instances the schools are not mutually exclusive, but allow for the treatment of management's divergent points of view and belief systems.

Figure 1–1

Management Theory Continuum

Ideal Bureaucracy
Scientific Management
Functional Management
POSDCORB
Human Relations
Systems
Contingency
Community Policing

Ideal Bureaucracy

Max Weber is regarded as the founder of the systematic analysis of bureaucracy. His works on the subject have led to numerous studies that presented an in-depth analysis of this concept. Many authors who apply their skills to police administration have been negligent by not reviewing Weber's vital contribution. The core of his bureaucratic theory (best illustrated by the concepts of administrative regulations, rational legal authority, and the criteria for individual office holders) has dominated the management of many of our police departments.

Weber identified the characteristics of bureaucracy to include three essential attributes. First, the routine activities were distributed in the organization in a fixed way and were identified as official duties. Second, commensurate authority essential for the accomplishment of duties was to be distributed to officials. Lastly, provision was made for the regular and continuous fulfillment of these duties.[1] In his study of

1. H.H. Gerth and C. Wright Mills, from *Max Weber: essays in Sociology,* New York, Oxford University Press, p. 196.

organizations, Weber found that the principal hierarchical authority was evident in governmental, ecclesiastical and private enterprises. He also pointed out that authority was vested in the office (not the individual).[2] Accordingly a bureaucracy needed a staff who prepared and maintained official records. Today these functions are performed by accountants, administrative assistants and staff experts. [3]

Weber viewed training as an essential prerequisite to effective performance both in public as well as private structures. He felt that management was a full-time job and his postulation of this characteristic was in response to the practice of considering management as a secondary activity.[4] He expressed the position that the reduction of office management to rules was deeply inherent in its nature. It presupposed the need for regulating matters abstractly. He viewed this process as being in sharp contrast to the bestowing of individual favors and privileges under patrimonialism. Unfortunately for many years' police managers were political appointees and came and went with changes in political machines. Without question the political process and interference is still evident in a number of departments.[5]

The ideal type of bureaucracy, defined by Weber, had legal norms established by agreement based upon the rational values of the typical person occupying an office and the application of norms to a specific case. The bureaucracy followed legal precepts and principles within this context. Weber identified the following fundamental categories of rational legal authority:

- A continuous organization of official functions circumscribed by rules.

- A explicit sphere of competence.

- The principle of hierarchy.

- Rules may be technical or norms.

- Administrative duties are separate from personal responsibilities.

- A complete absence of appropriation for the incumbent of a managerial position.

- Administrative acts, decisions, and rules formulated and recorded in writing.

- Legal authority can be exercised in a wide variety of different forms.[6]

2. *Ibid.*, 197.

3. *Ibid.*, p. 198.

4. *Ibid.*

5. Office of Justice Programs, *The Challenge of Crime in a Free Society: Looking Back Looking Forward*, Washington, DC, 1997, pp. 1–180.

6. Max Weber, *The Theory of Social and Economic Organization,* translated by A. M. Hendeson and Talcott Parsons. Edited by Talcott Parsons. Copyright © 1947, copyright renewed 1975 by Talcott Parsons, Reprinted with permission of The Free Press, a Division of Simon & Schuster, Inc. 1947, pp. 19–21.

Weber emphasized that a rational, legal administrative staff could function in all kinds of situations and contexts. A staff exercising its legal authority was viewed as the most important mechanism in the administration of everyday affairs. In addition, he believed that the administrative staff should consist of appointed officials.[7] In general, Max Weber was of the opinion that the ideal bureaucracy was technically capable of attaining the highest degree of efficiency. Such a monocratic type of bureaucracy was viewed as the most rational means of accomplishing imperative control of human beings. The superiority of bureaucratic administration was the result of the dominant role of technical knowledge. This is the feature that makes bureaucracy rational, and is the key characteristic of the ideal bureaucracy.

Weber's concepts of bureaucracy permeate the managerial style employed by many contemporary police managers. Most managers have "risen from the ranks," consequently have spent most of their life in a bureaucratic organization.[8] For the most part, few chiefs of police have had the benefit of modern executive development training, an innovative process that most certainly would introduce the police executive to behavioral and systems aspects of management. It is small wonder then, when one views the total police field, that the management of police agencies reflects Weber's ideal bureaucracy. Police organizations hold sacred the concepts of rationality, hierarchy, specialization and positional authority, but this stranglehold is slowly loosening as an increasing number of police managers have become versed in behavioral aspects of management.

Scientific Management

In the study of management thought it is imperative that serious consideration be given to the works of Frederick Taylor. The "father of scientific management," He was responsible for the unifying of the mechanisms of management and the creation of an underlying management philosophy that dominated American industry for many years.[9] Scientific management has a philosophical foundation resulting in the combination of four fundamental principles of management:

- The development of a true science.

- Scientific selection of the worker.

- Scientific education and development of workers.

- Intimate friendly cooperation between management and personnel.[10]

Taylor identified task management or scientific management, as being in contradistinction to "initiative and incentive" management

7. *Ibid.*, pp. 21–22.

8. Tony L. Jones, "Autocratic vs. People–Minded Supervisor", *Law and Order,* May 1998, Vol. 46, No. 5, pp. 32–36.

9. Frederick W. Taylor, *Scientific Management,* New York: Harper & Brothers, 1947, pp. 129–130.

10. *Ibid.,* p. 130.

which was prevalent at the turn of the century. The latter management style emphasized such financial plans as piecework, premium-pay and the bonus-plan. Task management as perceived by its founder required two to five years before it could be successfully implemented into a working environment.

Taylor concluded that the essence of scientific management involved a complete mental revolution by both management and the worker. The employees had to revitalize their attitudes toward work, their fellow workers and their employers. Conversely management had to change their attitude toward duties, workers, fellow managers, and all of their daily problems. Without this comprehensive mental revolution, scientific management does not exist.[11]

Taylor's major works "Principles of Scientific Management" was published in the first part of the twentieth century. It immediately became the subject of controversy. Organized labor viewed it as a "sweat shop" technique and was instrumental in generating congressional concern. In Taylor's testimony before a Special House Committee at the beginning of the last century he presented his views on scientific management, that are best summarized as constituting:

- Science, not rule of thumb.
- Harmony not discords.
- Cooperation not individualism.
- Maximum output in place of restricted output.
- The development of each man to his greatest efficiency and prosperity.[12]

Scientific management has been condemned as a mechanistic-oriented management philosophy, but its detractors have ignored its awareness of and support for workers.[13] In contrast to Weber's emphasis on the ideal bureaucracy and Taylor's on specific management techniques, the functional approach took an entirely different tact and expressed its concern for management concepts. The most prominent contributor in this area was Henri Fayol. He published a comprehensive theory of management and opened the door to the development of the functional school of thought and breathed clarity into the muddled thinking on the nature of top management.[14]

Functional Management

Fayol initially published a monograph in French in the early part of the last century, but it was not published in the United States until the middle of the last century.[15] In analyzing activities that he believed

11. *Ibid.,* p. 27.
12. *Ibid.,* p. 140.
13. *Ibid.,* p. 145.
14. Claude S. George, Jr., *The History of Management Thought,* Englewood Cliff, NJ, Prentice Hall, Inc., 1968, p. 106.

15. Leonard J. Kazmier, *Principles of Management,* Third Edition, New York, McGraw–Hill, 1974, p. 8.

imperative accomplishments in all organizations, Fayol identified the most important activity as management. He pointed out that management activity consisted of the following five components:

- Planning.
- Organizing.
- Commanding.
- Coordination.
- Controlling.[16]

Complementary to the above indicated management activities was the principles of management that are set forth in the following figure.

Figure 1–2

Principles of Management

- Work is divided into component parts allowing for specialization.
- Authority should be balanced with responsibility
- Discipline includes obedience, application, energy and respect.
- Unity of command provides that subordinates should receive orders from one superior.
- Unity of direction requires that each objective should have only one plan.
- Subordination of Individual Interest to general interest.
- Remuneration of personnel on an equitable basis.
- One central point should have control over all of the parts.
- Unbroken chain of managers from top to bottom.
- A well-chosen place for everything and everything in its place.
- Equity should dominate and tempered with justice and fairness.
- Plans should be well thought out before they are executed.
- The group should work as a team and every member should work to accomplish organizational goals (esprit de corps).

Source: Gerald H. Graham, *Management: The Individual, The Organization, The Process,* First Edition, by © 1975. Reprinted with permission of South–Western College Publishing, a division of International Thompson Publishing.

Fayol's contribution to management thought was most significant. It presented several revolutionary aspects considered important to the development of management thought. Consideration was initially given to the concept that management, as a unique body of knowledge, was definitely germane to all forms of group activity consequently it demonstrated the universality of management.

At the same time it proved to be a comprehensive theory of management surpassing prior theories. The impact of functional management on police departments is readily apparent when one analyzes current management practices in a number of departments. The application of principles is especially evident in the early writings on police management by Leonard F. Fuld and Elmer D. Graper.[17] Formal

---

16. George, *op. cit.,* p. 108.

17. See such writers as: Leonard F. Fuld, *Police Administration,* New York,

structural relationships, as depicted by the organizational chart, were viewed as a prerequisite to the attainment of organizational goals. The police executive accomplished his management task by performing such functions as planning, organizing, staffing, directing and controlling. The primary emphasis of functional management was on things and techniques rather than the human element. The principles of management were viewed as inviolable. If a manager applied the standards, then success would surely be attained as indicated in the following figure.

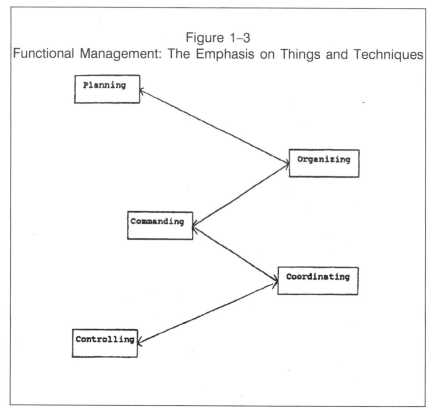

Figure 1–3
Functional Management: The Emphasis on Things and Techniques

Fayol concerned himself with top management in an organization; later writers emphasized the individual—thus giving rise to the human relation's movement. This is especially noteworthy because it reinforced an increasing interest in a concern for the individual. Up to now the primary interest was in the organization and the attainment of organizational goals.

POSDCORB

A refinement of the concept of functional management occurred when Luther Gulick released a paper as part of a larger work (Papers on the Science of Administration).[18] In the paper he presented the

G.P. Putnam's Sons, 1909; and Elmer D. Graper, *American Police Administration,* New York, The Macmillian Co., 1921.

18. Luther Gulick, "Notes on the Theory of Organization," cited in Lu-

acronym POSDCORB that is set forth in the following figure.

Figure 1–4

POSDCORB

P	PLANNING sets forth what needs to be accomplished and methods of achieving identifiable goals.
O	ORGANIZING is the process of developing an authority structure.
S	STAFFING refers t all of the personnel functions ranging from recruiting to training.
D	DIRECTING is the process of decision-making, creation of policies, and providing leadership.
CO	COORDINATING is the process of providing for interaction between units.
R	REPORTING requires keeping everyone informed through inspection, records, and research.
B	BUDGETING involves every aspect of fiscal control.

Because of its simplicity POSDCORB won immediate acceptance in business and public administration. This was soon followed by law enforcement that saw in it a concise rendition of the essential element of the managerial process. It promptly held a conspicuous place in police training programs as well as police literature. It was offered as a partial panacea for the reformation of police administration and held a noticeable place in consulting reports recommending the reorganization of police departments.

Human Relations

Numerous individuals are identified with the human relation's movement, but most management experts have selected Elton Mayo as the founder of this field. He was a consultant on the research project conducted at the Hawthorne plant of Western Electric in the later part of the 1920's and the early 1930's. This was the initial use of a behavioral science approach to management problems.[19]

The *Hawthorne Studies* were inspired by experiments completed by company engineers who were attempting to determine the effects of differing levels of illumination on the performance of workers.[20] Utilizing the scientific method of inquiry, both "test" and "control" groups were included in the research design. The "test" group was subjected to varying levels of lighting and it was found that production increased regardless of the level of illumination. At the same time the researchers

ther Gulick and L. Urwick, Editors, *Papers on the Science of Administration*, New York, Institute of Public Administration, Augustus M. Kelley, 1937, pp. 32–41. Reprinted with permission of the publisher,1969.

19. Kazmier, *op. cit.*, p. 11.

20. Henry L. Tossi and Stephen J. Carroll, *Management: Contingencies, Structure, and Process*, Chicago, St. Clair Press, 1976, p. 46.

were amazed to find that production increased in the "control" group.[21]

The researchers were of the opinion that the important variable was not illumination, but the fact that the participants were enjoying human contact and attention. It seemed that the workers were responding in a way that the experimenters desired—enjoying being the center of attention.[22] Thus, the term "Hawthorne Effect" has been used to describe such circumstances. Following this initial experimentation, a research team initiated the comprehensive *Hawthorne Studies*. This inquiry concentrated on employees who were members of the first relay assembly group. Work conditions were altered extensively to include changes in work breaks, length of workday, humidity and temperature. As each change was made, productivity was measured. The changes in the environment were instituted over a two-year period and extended to such variables as an incentive wage plan if the group production increased. The nature of supervision was such that it emphasized humanitarian aspects and undivided attention to employees. The hypotheses for the two-year study were drawn and accounted for an increase in productivity due to: (1) improved work methods, (2) reduction in fatigue with changes in rest periods and shorter hours, (3) reduction in monotony, (4) effect of wage incentives, and (5) effect of the method of supervision.[23]

The researchers rejected the hypotheses except for the two that related to wages and supervision, and these were subjected to further research.[24] In the second phase of the study Elton Mayo and his associates tested the effects of wage incentives on a group of workers. Production increased by 13 percent. After a relatively short period of time the study was terminated because of the objections of other plant workers. The last hypothesis (concerned with supervision) was tested on a group of workers, but over an extended period of time, supervision was found to be an unimportant variable.[25] The five hypotheses were rejected and the researchers concluded that employee behavior was a consequence of their reaction to a social system rather than any single factor. Mayo and his associates then interviewed workers over an extended period of time concluding:

- Morale improves when an opportunity is provided for grievances.

- Complaints cannot be considered as statements of fact.

- Workers are influenced by factors external to the job.

- Worker satisfaction is influenced by how a worker views his social status.[26]

The last major area of study was in the bank wiring observation room of the Hawthorne plant. This experiment lasted for 61/2 months

21. George, *op. cit.,* p. 129.
22. Tossi and Carroll, *op. cit.,* p. 47.
23. *Ibid.,* p. 48.
24. George, *op. cit.,* p. 129.
25. Tossi and Carroll, *op. cit.*
26. *Ibid.*

and involved a number of men especially chosen for the study. The participants were assured that information obtained from the study would not jeopardize them. All of the men were in their twenties and only one had some college education. Group piecework was the system of pay for the participants and each worker was paid an hourly rate plus a bonus based upon production. Observers found that behavior differed from job descriptions. For example, workers assisted each other—when someone fell behind in his work, a faster worker exchanged jobs with the slower worker. Numerous types of gambling occurred such as craps, pool and cards and the men shared food at lunch breaks. The observers found that the employees controlled the rate of production, as a group, and that they were well aware of what was an acceptable level of production.[27]

The researchers concluded that behavior at work could not be understood without considering the informal organization of the group and the relation of the informal organization to the total social organization.[28] The men had adopted a definite code of good behavior, revealed by what the men said and, in different degrees, by what they did. Even the worker who did not live up to the code knew what it was. The code suggested that one should not turn out too much work. If you do, you are a "rate-buster." The code also said that one should not turn out too little work. If you do, you are a "chiseler." Another key element was that one should not tell a supervisor anything that would react to the detriment of an associate. If you do, you are a "squealer." Additionally, one should not attempt to maintain social distance or act officious. If you are an inspector, for example, you should not act like one.[29] With the Hawthorne studies, the foundation was laid for a strong emphasis on human relations. While these studies and others have had critics, it must be acknowledged that the emphasis on the work group dominated management research for several decades. It became accepted that a work culture existed and that the needs of the individual had to be considered as well as the need for productivity.

Systems

In recent years many administrative theorists have strived to apply systems concepts to management. C. West Churchman points out that in order for one to view management as a system, it is best to follow five basic considerations:

- The total system objective and, more specifically, the performance measures of the whole system.

- The system's environment i.e. the fixed constraints.

- The resources of the system.

27. Tossi, *ibid.*, p. 102.

28. F.J. Roethlisberger and William J. Dickson, *Management and the Work-* *er,* Cambridge, Mass., Harvard University Press, 1939, p. 551.

29. *Ibid.,* p. 522.

- The components of the system, their activities, goals and measures of performance.

- The management of the system.[30]

This series of "thinking steps" provides for a logical analysis of one's reasoning and is actually a process for checking and rechecking one's reasoning. The term "system" is subject to numerous definitions ranging from simple to complex. At the elementary level, it suggests a consideration of the whole rather than parts.[31] The dictionary definition states that a system is an orderly combination or arrangement of parts, into a whole, especially, such combination according to some rational principle. More technical definitions abound in the literature—typically:

- A system in general can be defined as an established arrangement of components, which leads to the attainment of particular objectives according to plan.[32]

- System is a network of related procedures developed according to an integrated scheme for performing major activity.[33]

For the sake of simplicity a system may be defined as a set of objects, either fixed, or mobile, and all relationships that may exist between the objects. All systems are composed of sub-systems and are members of a higher system.[34] Notwithstanding the variance in definitions it is readily apparent that the common elements of the systems can readily be identified as input, throughput, and output. A simplified police system is illustrated in figure 1–5 where "input" is *what* occurs as illustrated by a law violation or a public safety occurrence requiring an agency response. "Throughput" is the *operations,* which prescribes how the agency will respond and lastly the "output" reflects the *satisfactory accomplishment* of the task that can range from the resolution of a crime to solving a problem involving quality of life.

30. C. West Churchman, *The Systems Approach,* New York, Dell Publishing Co., a Division of Random House, Inc. Copyright © 1968, 1979, pp. 29–30, by C. West Churchman. Used by permission of Delacorte Press, a division of Random House, Inc.

31. Kazmier, *op. cit.,* p. 478.

32. *Ibid.*

33. R.F. Neuschel, *Management by System,* New York, McGraw–Hill, Inc., 1960, p. 10.

34. Kenneth Heathington and Gustaue Rath, "The Systems Approach In Traffic Engineering," *Traffic Engineering,* June 1967, p. 71. For additional discussions see: Charles Zwick, *Systems Analysis and Urban Planning,* Santa Monica, Rand Corporation, 1967; David I. Cleland and William R. King, *Management: A Systems Approach,* New York, McGraw–Hill, 1972, and Van Cort Hare, *Systems Analysis: A Diagnostic Approach,* New York, Harcourt Brace and World, 1967. Brett F. Woods, "Systems Management: An Overview," *Law and Order,* Vol. 28 No. 9, September 1980.

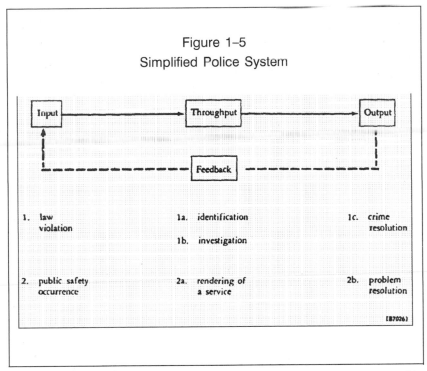

Figure 1–5
Simplified Police System

The systems approach directs its attention to inter-relationship and the hierarchy of sub-systems. It is a rational structure for complex problem solving and views both the micro and macro aspects of an organization. Systems analysis is a tool for the creation of a conceptual model and the following steps (see figure 1–6) should be followed:

- Define the desired goals.
- Develop alternative means for realizing the goals.
- Develop resource requirements for each alternative.
- Design a model for determining outputs of each alternative.
- Establish measurements of effectiveness for evaluating alternatives.[35]

These steps provide a comprehensive process for viewing police organizations. It allows for an emphasis on the sub-systems and the inter-relationship of each unit. It is a theoretical framework for organizational analysis. Systems theory is still evolving, but as pointed out by Kast and Rosensweig, it "provides a relief from the limitations of more mechanistic approaches and a rationale for rejecting 'principles' based on relatively 'closed-system' thinking."[36]

35. Ernst K. Nillsson, "Systems Analysis Applied to Law Enforcement," *Allocations of Resources in the Chicago Police Department,* Washington, Law Enforcement Assistance Administration, March 1972, p. 6.

36. Fremont E. Kast and James E. Rosenzweig, "General Systems Theory: Applications for Organization and Management," *Academy of Management Journal,* December 1972, p. 447.

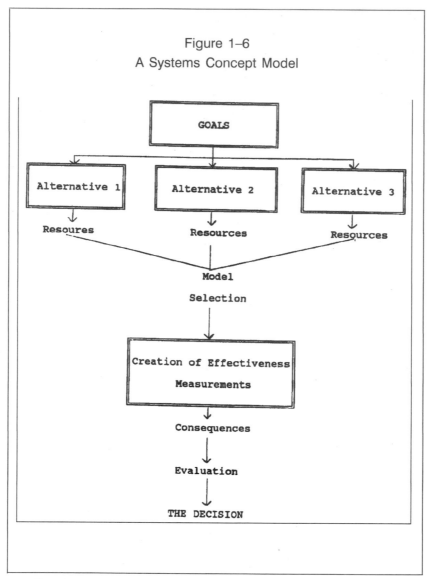

Figure 1–6
A Systems Concept Model

The departure from closed systems analysis is relatively unique in police management. For many years' police managers viewed the police enterprise as essentially a closed system. In terms of rationalizing professionalization, the executive limited interchange between the organization and the environment. This is not to suggest that the police were a totally closed system, but by limiting input and the acquisition of total system energy, the police system suffered a limited input from other sub-systems within criminal justice and from other elements of the larger society. Systems management presents itself as a challenge of the future and an acknowledgment of the inter-dependence of all systems in our environment. Systems management is not a panacea for the police administrator, but it is a frame of reference for viewing the complexity of police organizations.

Contingency

An integrative framework for management theory evolved in the middle of the last century as a result of a number of studies in England and later in this country. During that era, the management field was sharply divided between supporters of one of the previously discussed management theories. The administrative advocates argued that the behaviorists were "ivory tower" theorists and ignored reality. Critics of the "principles" approach postulated that the individual and group dynamics were being ignored and there were many ways to manage successfully.[37]

Two experts fittingly summarized this new approach by pointing out that rather than searching for the one best way to do something, theorists have moved to examining organizational functions, the needs of employees, and the nature of confronting external pressures. This process became known as the contingency theory of organization.[38] The contingency approach is, in actuality, a blend of different approaches. Fundamental to this method is the fact that there is no one best way for analyzing a job or organization, managing people in a variety of different kinds of organizations, or achieving change in an organization.[39] The number and *kind* of managerial responses vary considerably and it is only after the situation has been comprehensively analyzed that a responding process can be implemented.

A contingency model includes the following four major properties:

- Environmental.

- Individual.

- Organizational.

- Group.[40]

An awareness of the patterns of relationships between the above areas permits a manager to design an organization and/or a motivational program in such a way that it will be most effective in a given situation. The thrust of the contingency approach is such that the behavior of individuals and groups becomes a known quantity. Environmental properties are readily identified resulting in the development of managerial practices and organizational responses to specific situations (see figure 1–7).

37. Tossi and Carroll, *op. cit.*

38. Jay W. Lorsch and Paul R. Lawrence, editors, *Studies in Organizational Design,* Homewood, Illinois, Irwin and Dorsey Press, 1970, p. 1.

39. Don Hellriegel and John W. Slocum, Jr., *Organizational Behavior Contingency Views,* St. Paul, West Publishing Co., 1976, p. 5.

40. *Ibid.,* p. 7.

Figure 1-7

Major Properties of the Contingency Model

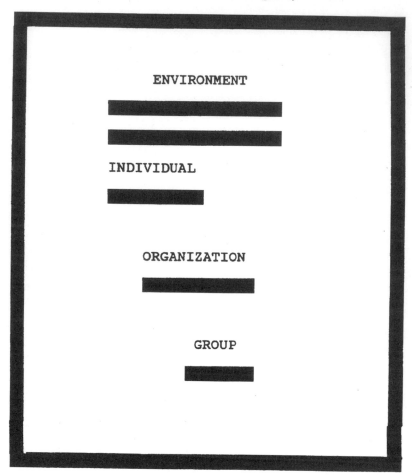

Community

A prominent theory being invoked is community policing It is more than a program—it is an operational philosophy permeating every facet of a police organization.[41] It is more than a style of policing. It is a means of managing a police department based on underlying value statements. These statements provide a foundation on which the department can respond to the needs of the community.[42] It is a process that has profoundly altered the idea of professional policing. In place of a finely honed military operation, or a top-heavy bureaucracy, the new ideal police agency works at the community level to affect crime and disorder, seeks cooperation with local citizens, and provides

41. Jerome H. Skolnick and David H. Bayley, *Community Policing: Issues and Answers Around the World,* Washington, D.C., National Institute of Justice, 1988, p. 16.

42. Jerald R. Vaughn, "Community Oriented Policing You Can Make it Happen," *Law and Order,* June 1991, Vol. 39, No. 6, p. 35.

substantial discretion to local officers who are responsible for identifying problems and solving them.[43] In the Tucson Police Department operating under a geo-based patrol plan the average officer had at least 266 hours annually to problem solving as a benefit to the community through designed policing activities.[44]

Fundamental to community policing is the creation of the values of policing. Citizens are involved in the decision-making process as the value statements develop from joint discussions. At this stage the discussions revolve around the quality of neighborhood life with an emphasis on safety factors. Another key element of community policing is an emphasis on results. Problem solving permeates the process based on the techniques of problem identification, problem analysis and finally problem resolution. This element requires a rethinking of the department's approach to the crime problem and public safety (see figure 1–8).

Figure 1–8

Key Elements of Community Policing

Problem Solving Orientation
Value Statements
Accountability
Decentralization
Power Sharing
Beat Revision
Empowerment of Beat Officers
Empowerment of Citizens

Central to the transition from traditional policing models to the community policing model is the sharing of power. This requires the police to share power to the point that a real partnership is created. Active citizen participation is essential and police officers and citizens must work together to solve community problems.[45] Quiescent public involvement inhibits the process, and every possible effort must be made to maximize citizen contribution. The rallying point is teamwork. The police and citizens must work together to attain specified goals.[46]

Accountability under community policing is dual in nature. Officers are accountable not only to the police department, but also to the public. They must keep abreast of neighborhood needs by being continuously involved in the identification of neighborhood concerns, desires,

43. Office of Justice Programs, *op. cit. 148.*

44. City of Tucson, *Adopted Budget Operating Detail, Fiscal Year 1989–1999,* Volume II, Tucson, AZ, Tucson Police Department, 1998–1999, p. 158.

45. Lee P. Brown, *Community Policing: A Practical Guide For Police Offi-* *cials,* Washington, D.C., National Institute of Justice, 1989, pp. 5–7.

46. Lee P. Brown, "Policing in the '90s: Trends, Issues and Concerns," *The Police Chief,* March 1989, Vol. LVI-II, No. 3, p. 21.

and priorities. Two-way communications, between the police and the community, coupled with the identification of problems will lead to eventual problem resolution. As understanding evolves, officers and members of the community begin to work as a real team to solve community problems.

An additional element of community policing is the need for the police department to become more decentralized. It calls for a change in the traditional bureaucratic view of management with an emphasis on flattening the organization. Additionally, there is an encouragement of horizontal and vertical interaction and a definitive decentralization of authority. [47]At some point knowledge, instead of rank, proves to be the catalyst for problem solving. Roles change as problems change as participation in the decision-making process grows.[48] Organizational rigidity will become a thing of the past as the underlying elements of community policing are applied and permeate every corner of the organization.

Another fundamental element of community policing is redesigning beat boundaries. Natural neighborhood boundaries become the guiding criteria, not boundaries meeting the arbitrary needs of the police department. Again it has to be pointed out that the public participates in the identification of neighborhood boundaries. Each identifiable neighborhood becomes a beat.[49] The role of the beat officer is unique under the theory of community policing Officers shift their focus from the dual roles of patrolling the streets and report taking to a role requiring work with neighborhood citizens to solve community problems. The beat officer becomes a manager not just a responder to bureaucratic demands of the police department. Beat officers become involved in the decision-making process. Problem identification done jointly with members of the community leads to the development of programs to resolve problems. The beat officer becomes a real part of the community and works to improve the quality of life in the neighborhood. Permanently assigned to a beat, the officer becomes familiar with local citizens placing them in an excellent position to identify resources that can be used to resolve problems.[50]

Management theory is not an entity unto itself. It is dynamic in nature and the organization conditions and reconditions it, along with the members of the organization, the community it serves, and the political process. Community policing is a new approach to dealing with the crime problem and the wellness of the community. It is not completely defined, but it is being increasingly adopted by all sizes of police departments and in all parts of the United States. Over time it

47. Jihong Zhao, *Why Organizations Change: A Study of Community–Oriented Policing,* Washington, DC, Police Executive Research Forum, 1996, p. 7.

48. Brown, *op. cit.* 1989, p. 5.

49. *Op. cit.*

50. Timothy N. Oettmeir and Lee P. Brown, "Developing a Neighborhood–Oriented Policing Style," in Jack R. Greene and Stephen D. Mastrofski, Editors, *Community Policing: Rhetoric or Reality,* New York, Praeger, 1988, p. 129.

will be refined to the point where the public will be better served, and the police will integrate the community into the department.

Case Study

Chief Sandra C. Thompson

Chief Thompson has recently been appointed to head the Lima Police Department having received an appointment after a nationwide search and given a five-year contract. She has been in office less than a month and she is still in the process of conceptualizing the charge that she was given when she was appointed. The department has been very traditional in its approach to crime and emphasized response time and answering calls for service. The para-military model prevails and the organization is top heavy. Additionally, a number of sworn personnel perform clerical activities and only 52 percent of the officers are assigned to patrol activities. This is well below the national average wherein 63.7 percent of full-time sworn personnel are assigned to patrol and respond to calls for service. One of the charges that have been given to the new chief is to move toward the concept of community policing and to restructure the department. Another charge is to place more officers on the street. The city has a community relations division with five officers assigned to it and supervised by a deputy chief. This unit was created at a time when community relations was in vogue. Additionally, the chief had been charged with developing a five-year plan to meet these objectives.

The community has a population of 242,000 and there are 266 sworn police officers and 63 civilians in the police department. The city is adjacent to a large metropolitan area on the West Coast. The community has four major shopping areas and extensive light industry. In the department 74.2 percent of the officers are White, 8.2 percent are African American, 14.3 percent are Hispanic, and 3.3 percent are Asian. The ethnicity of the department is similar to that of the community. Additionally 92.1 percent of the officers are male and the remainder female. The crime rate is similar to that in cities of the same relative size.

> If you were Chief Thompson what would you do first to change from a bureaucratic organization to one that stresses community policing? Why? What would you do to restructure the department? In order to fulfill your mission what would you put into your five-year plan? Why?

For Further Reading

John Bizzack, Management *for the 1990s: A Practitioner's Road Map*, Second Edition, Springfield, IL, Charles C. Thomas, 1995, pp. 1–33.

Presents a number of forecasts for the 21st century regarding their impact on law enforcement. The author believes that there is a possibility that law enforcement might be overwhelmed by sophisticated crimes and that investigator might not have the technical skills needed to cope with high-tech crime. He suggests that by 2005 economic depression will be identified as the major factor in the incident of traditional crime. He forecasts that by 2025 the majority of law enforcement executives will have a leadership style that has an proactive goal orientation. He suggests that the police will not be professionalized until the year 20050.

Jean Johnson, "Americans' Views on Crime and Law Enforcement," *National Institute of Justice Journal,* Washington, DC, National Institute of Justice, September 1997, pp. 9–14.

Discusses the public's concerns about crime and the fact that they seem to be somewhat independent of the actual crime rate. There are deeply held public fears developed over decades that may be slow to dissipate even in the best of circumstances. Reviews opinion research that strongly suggests that the public is concerned about protecting the rights of the accused and redressing wrongs done to victims and society. Reviews public opinion polls about confidence in the police.

Office of Justice Programs, *The Challenge of Crime in a Free Society: Looking Back and Looking Forward,* Washington, DC, U.S. Department of Justice, 1997,pp. 1–180.

Thirty years ago the President's Commission released a report that heralded an era of attention to crime and criminal justice identifies accomplishment of the Commission administration to include an increased professionalism in various criminal justice occupations, improved collection of information and data on the justice system, and a better understanding of the justice system. Suggests that insufficient attention has been paid to prevention and too much emphasis on prison construction.

Cicero Wilson, "Economic Shifts That Will Impact Crime Control and Community Revitalization, *What Can the Federal Government Do To Decrease Crime and Revitalize Communities?"* Washington, DC, Office of Justice Programs and Executive Office for Weed and Seed, 1998, pp. 1–105.

Reviews three general trends that will influence the American economic landscape in the 21st century and will have a special impact on crime rates and the success of efforts to revitalize distressed communities. The trends include increases in populations with higher than average risk of participating in crime, increases in the number of high-poverty communities, and the continued reliance on ineffective programs and policies to promote family self-efficiency and revitalize distressed communities.

Chapter 2

POLITICS AND MANAGEMENT:
Dynamic Interaction

Learning Objectives

1. Discuss why it is important to oppose federalization of the American police.
2. Describe the impact of patronage on law enforcement.
3. Write a short essay describing how federal law enforcement influences local departments.
4. Compare the mayor-council and commission types of local government.
5. Identify the elements of a city manager plan.
6. List ten members of the community you would interview when assessing local corruption.
7. Describe the importance of service organizations to the political process.
8. Write a short essay describing business and trade groups that function as an interest group.
9. List ten issues that can be included in a memorandum of understanding (MOU).
10. Discuss the evolution of collective bargaining in the police field.
11. Describe the relationship between the police and the media.
12. List five minority groups who can influence a law enforcement agency.
13. Compare left-winged and right-winged domestic militant groups.
14. Describe the nature of politics in the justice system.

Police administration operates in a political environment. As one of the principal line agencies of government, it must be located at some point in the organizational structure of government (either at the federal, state or local level). The nature of the controls exercised over the police differs with the level of government. In a democratic society the question of control assumes considerable importance and can serve as a barometer of public attitude toward the police. Earlier efforts to divorce the police from politics isolated the police from the community and it can be readily suggested that this eventually resulted in a rift that lead to less effective enforcement of the laws and the failure to solve community problems. What it meant was that the police did not serve the public but themselves.

Because of the inadequacies of some local and state agencies the possibility of a national police force has been mentioned on occasion. But with the extraordinary inefficiencies and inadequacies demonstrated (in recent years) by federal law enforcement organizations in Ruby Ridge[1], and the misconduct in the FBI laboratory,[2] this prospective trend has diminished. This support lessened even more with the release of the Department of Treasury report of "the good O' Boys roundup."[3] and the Waco incident.[4] The specter of a federal police force is no longer an issue and hopefully will remain dormant. The idea of one all-powerful and omnipotent law enforcement agency is abhorrent to many.

Another alternative advanced by proponents in the President's Crime Commission in 1967 calling for consolidation of records and communications, but this had not occurred with any great frequency. Nor has the problem of police training been rectified since that time. In the 30 years since the initial report that had 34 recommendations on policing numerous positive changes have occurred. For example, every state has a training commission, more minority group members are employed in law enforcement, and laboratory services are available for nearly all agencies.[5] Even with the progress that has occurred in the last century a great deal needs to be done before law enforcement can be described as a true profession.

In the United States where the principle of local autonomy reigns supreme, state, county and city police forces function in a condition of comparative independence. There have been few encroachments except in times of excessive corruption. Although the city and county are creatures of the state under state constitutions, these local jurisdictions operate with limited interference from above. One significant exception to this has been the creation of such organizations as Peace Officers Standards and Training Commissions (POST) that are in every state. Through this vehicle training standards delineate what has to be taught and funding insures compliance. Nationwide the Commission on

1. Subcommittee on Terrorism, *Ruby Ridge,* Washington, DC, Senate Committee on the Judiciary, 1996, pp. 1–154.

2. Michael R. Bromwich, *The FBI Laboratory: An Investigation into Laboratory Practices and Alleged Misconduct in Explosive–Related and Other Cases,* Washington, DC, Office of the Inspector General, U.S. Department of Justice, April 1997,pp. 1–517.

3. Department of the Treasury, *Department of the Treasury Report of the Good O'Boys Roundup policy Review,* Washington, DC, Department of the Treasury, April 1996, pp. 1–22–.

4. U.S. Department of Justice, *Report to the Deputy Attorney General on the Events at Waco, Texas, February 28 to April 19, 1993,* Redacted Version, Washington, DC, U.S. Department of Justice, October 8, 1993, pp. 1–348; David B. Kopel and Paul H. Blackman, *No More Wacos: What's Wrong With Federal Law Enforcement and How to Fix It,* Amherst, NY, Promenthus Books, 1997, pp. 224–291.

5. Office of Justice Programs, *The Challenge of Crime in a Free Society: Looking Back and Looking Forward,* Washington, DC, U. S. Department of Justice, June 19, 1997, pp. 1–180.

Accreditation for Law Enforcement Agencies established standard in 1983 and numerous agencies have participated in this process thus local and state agencies have placed themselves under voluntary scrutiny.[6]

All together police administration in the United States is only rarely exposed to any serious pressure above that of the local appointing authority, such as the Mayor, City Manager, or Director of Public Safety. The police operate largely under the principle that *Main Street* has the intelligence and resources to meet its problem and suggestions from the state capitol or from either end of Pennsylvania Avenue are out of order, except when largess is such that interference become acceptable. Federal purse strings have done much to erode local autonomy and increase federal control over lower political entities. Typical of this was a proposal by the federal government to impose a lower and uniform blood-alcohol level for drunken driving. The leverage of federal grants will be used to persuade states to adopt a level of .08 as the standard for drinking while driving.[7]

The latest research identified 18,769 publicly funded state and local law enforcement agencies operating in the United States. These included 13,578 general-purpose local police departments, 3,008 sheriffs' departments and offices, and 49 primary state police agencies. The remanding agencies were special-purpose police departments i.e. school, transit. The local police agencies employed 521,985 persons on a full time basis and of this number sworn officers with general arrest powers constitute 79 percent of the total. Most of the agencies are small with half employing fewer than 10 sworn officers. Additionally, 2,245 of the departments had only one officer.[8] This seems to be a desire of even the smallest hamlet to have its own police department. An example of one of these small departments is illustrated by the retirement of the chief of police from a small town. The chief was the only member of the police department. After his retirement his home telephone number was no longer listed for the "police," and law enforcement services, under contract, became the responsibility of the sheriff's department.[9]

While law enforcement remains primarily a local function in the United States there are numerous federal agencies exercising law enforcement powers. The latest count identified 60 agencies with 74,493 full-time employees with arrest and firearms authority.[10] Fiscal

6. Commission on Accreditation Law Enforcement Agencies, *Standards for Law Enforcement Agencies,* Fairfax, VA, Fourth Edition, Commission on Accreditation for Law Enforcement Agencies, 1999, pp. 1–1 to 84–3.

7. *The Arizona Daily Star,* "Clinton Calls for Stricter Drunken-driving Level," December 27, 1998, A5.

8. Brian A. Reaves and Andrew L. Goldberg, *Census of State and Local Law Enforcement Agencies, 1996,* Washington, DC, Bureau of Justice Statistics, June 1998, pp. 1–15.

9. *San Jose Mercury News.* "One–Man Police Department Retire," June 15, 1992, 7A.

10. Kathleen Maguire and Ann L. Pastore, Editors, *Sourcebook of Criminal*

support of federal law enforcement agencies comes at a considerable expense. Recently the annual expenditure for federal police protection was 8,069,000 (in thousands)[11]. Federal law enforcement continues to expand its jurisdiction as illustrated by recent laws governing computer crimes, background checks on purchasers of long rifles, and specified crimes committed at abortion clinics. If the public hue is loud enough or a special interest group powerful enough a new law can enter the statute books because of congressional response to constituent pressure. Another example, of attempting to solve a problem by passing a law was the enactment of a terrorism bill that resulting in the hiring of some 2,000 FBI agents to confront the specter of the Militia and international terrorism. The press in its coverage of the Militia, Oklahoma City, the Centennial Olympic Park bombing, and the bombing of the World Trade Center contributed directly to an unprecedented expansion of the powers of the federal government as it related to terrorism.

Political Reality

Politics are a "given" in the realm of law enforcement and this is true at every governmental level. One need only reflect on presidential elections and this statement becomes a reality. From President Lyndon B. Johnson down to the pending campaign, crime has been a major issue. Typical of this was President George Bush's campaign against violent crime and drugs. Some charge that a significant issue in the 1988 presidential election was the Willie Horton case. President Bush attacked his opponent, Michael Dukakis, for the early release of Horton (a convicted sexual offender) from prison.[12] The opposition claimed it raised the specter of racism because Horton was African–American. Some claim it helped the president to be elected. In presidential elections, controlling crime, and law and order rank right up with other factors such as the economy and unemployment. This attitude toward crime presents politicians with a partial platform serving many very well. As an issue it has helped candidates attain or remain in political office. George Bush said he always remembers the freedom from fear as the last, but often forgotten, of President Franklin D. Roosevelt's original Four Freedoms. He rightly reminded us—"When we ask what kind of society we hope to pass on to our children it is clear our goal must be a Nation in which law-abiding citizens are safe and feel safe."[13]

In the 1996 presidential campaign Bill Clinton set forth a platform on crime control that put the Republican platform to shame. Clinton

Justice Statistics–1997, Washington, D.C., Bureau of Justice Statistics, 1998, p. 4.

11. *Ibid.*

12. David C. Anderson, *Crime and Politics of Hysteria*, New York, Random House, *1995, pp. 2–45.*

13. U.S. Department of Justice, *Attorney General's Summit on Law Enforcement Responses to Violent Crime: Public Safety in the Nineties*, Washington, D.C., Bureau of Justice Statistics, 1988, p. 1.

could best be described as a Democrat in Republican clothes, when it came to the issue of crime. He beat the Republicans at every turn setting forth a real law and order platform. When crimes occurred in schools he supported the use of metal detectors, searching student automobiles, searching lockers, and the wearing of uniforms. Sensitive to political winds Bill Clinton supported and signed numerous crime control initiatives. When signing these bills into law he surrounded himself with uniformed police officers as a means of demonstrating to the public that he was really concerned about the enforcement of laws and that he supported police officers. Never passing up a political opportunity Clinton took credit for putting 100,000 police officers on the street although that total was never attained and there is some reason to believe that some of these positions will disappear when federal funding ceases in the future. Federal grants supporting this type of program were matching and after three years the political entity assumed full costs. During his second term President Clinton has continued to place himself in the spotlight championing a strong justice platform including support for community policing.

At the local level, crime and politics are linked in many ways. Over the years crime has been a significant election issue. Politically it can be described as a question of policy or patronage. A politician must, in many instances, propose to control and reduce crime. This is especially true when the populace views crime as important to them. Many people are fearful of becoming a crime victim.[14] Nightly we see reports about crimes on television. Newspapers normally place crime on the front page. In some instances, the fear of crime controls our lives and limits the things we do. When a particularly heinous crime or civil disturbance occurs, the mass media follow it closely. In response, the sale of locks and weapons increases markedly, and citizens enroll in weapons training classes. It is easy then to see why crime becomes an election issue. Politicians get on the band wagon and gain supporters by proposing crime control policies.

In one study, the two major issues in local politics over an extended period were "law and order" and "leadership."[15] The task of the politician is to convince voters a proposed crime control policy will work. If the public is concern about crime, the politician becomes concerned—and rightly so. The advantage a politician has with crime, as an issue is that it is difficult to define. Generally, the average citizen views it narrowly. In one instance, it is a concern for sexual offenses, in other instances it can be burglaries, drive by shootings or the protection of clients entering abortion clinics. Its amorphous nature makes crime a political issue election after election. Putting more "cops" on beats, building more jails, and throwing the book at perpetrators easily

14. Jean Johnson, "Americans' Views on Crime and Law Enforcement," *National Institute of Justice Journal*, Washington, DC, National Institute of Justice, 1998, p. 10.

15. Anne Heinz, Herbert Jacob, and Robert L. Lineberry, Editors, *Crime in City Politics*, New York, Longman, 1983, pp. 2–3.

becomes the cry of the moment. Who can forget the "three strikes and your out" slogan championed by many politicians. In spite of the importance of crime as a political issue and the policy response to it, the crime rate even though it has gone down remains an unsolvable problem and a perennial political issue.

For many years patronage was practiced in American cities. When a new party entered office, it was common to have a clean sweep in the police department. Friends and supporters received appointments and members of the opposition party were terminated. In many instances, twenty-five percent of the city employees are sworn officers. The numbers involved makes it a ready source for patronage appointments and the clear cut result is an expansion one's political power base. It was not until the efficiency movement and civil service reform that patronage became less significant. In fact, it altered the scene in a significant way. Officers could not be dismissed without cause. As civil service rules and regulations became common, the shift was from patronage to influence. Politicians worked to obtain special assignments for those they favored. Becoming a detective or getting a "cushy" appointment depended upon "juice" not skill or ability. As recent as forty years ago in Newark, New Jersey, political interference within the police department was constant. In Philadelphia the Commissioner used the department to intimidate rival politicians. In Minneapolis, Minnesota removal of the chief of police occurred every time a new mayor assumed power.[16] For many years, in Boston, appointment of the commissioner of police was by the governor not the mayor. This was the result of an ethnic political conflict between the aristocrats and the Irish over who would control the city.[17]

In the latter part of the last century the former Chief of Police of San Francisco, allegedly ordered the seizure of newspapers that carried an unfavorable article. After a Police Commission hearing, the mayor fired the Chief. Other departments, supported by civil service reform, have worked diligently to isolate themselves from political interference. Numerous chiefs' of police have found it advantageous to avoid the political process, as much as possible, and strive to remain politically neutral. The professional era of law enforcement fostered this approach, but it served to isolate chief executive officers from the political process that is the lifeblood of the public administration process. Others have taken the opposite approach and acquired political power rivaling or exceeding political incumbents. It is a difficult tight rope to walk, but it has allowed a number of chiefs to remain in office. Some chiefs have retired and entered the political arena. Typical of these are the former mayors of San Francisco, and Campbell, California. Also a former chief of police in Los Angeles, Edward Davis, became a state Senator. Daryl Gates, controversial former chief of police of Los Angeles stated he might run for a position on the city council, but this never

16. *Ibid.,* p. 16.

17. Herbert Jacobs, *The Frustration of Policy,* New York, Little, Brown & Company, 1984, p. 10.

occurred. Lee Brown, the current mayor in Houston, TX was the former chief of police in that city, and at one time was the US Drug Czar and prior to that the Commissioner of Police in New York City. It would seem that survival as a chief executive in a law enforcement agency prepares one for the political arena.

Federal influence and control are considerable. Especially notable are the services of the Federal Bureau of Investigation in the operation of the national fingerprint bureau, The DNA data bank, the offering of in-service training programs, especially the National Academy, and the availability to local police forces of it's forensic capabilities. Notably, federal agencies have considerable political impact because they control the pursue strings. Funds are disbursed by the Office of Justice Programs and support a wide range of activities as set forth in figure 2–1. A review of the items suggests there is something for everyone who has a concern for controlling crime. This includes anti-drug abuse, state criminal alien assistance, juvenile justice, crime victims, missing children, and public safety officers' benefits. The budgetary allocation for 1998 was $3,733,066 (in thousands of dollars). The largest segment of the funding went to state and local correctional facilities.[18] Funding of new jails, supports the law and order position of "lock them up and throw the key away." The awarding of funds by federal agencies is, in many instances, caught up in the political process and the perceived need to support differing constitutes. For example, in a study of the use of deadly force by the police, two major ethnic units and a university received grants. Each of these groups had a major concern in this area and a federal administrator admitted awards granted had serious political undertones.

18. Maguire and Pastore, *op. cit.*, p. 15.

Figure 2-1

Allocation of Fund by the Office
of Justice Programs

Anti-drug abuse formula
Anti-drug abuse discretionary
State and local correctional facilities grants
Televised testimony of child abuse victims
State criminal alien assistance program
Criminal records upgrade
Drug courts
Juvenile justice formula grants
Crime victims funds
Child abuse investigation and prosecution
Court appointed special advocates
Judicial child abuse training
Juvenile justice programs
Missing children
Regional information sharing system
White collar crime information center
Public safety officers' benefits program
Research, evaluation, and demonstration programs
Justice statistical programs
High intensity drug trafficking areas
Missing Alzheimer's program
State prison drug treatment
Law enforcement block grants
DNA identification State grants
Motor vehicle theft prevention
Terrorism training
Violence against women training program
Development of counterterrorism technology
National sexual offender registry
Juvenile justice block grants
Telemarketing fraud prevention.

Source: Kathleen Maguire and Ann L. Pastore, Editors, *Sourcebook of Criminal Justice Statistics–1997,* Washington, DC, Bureau of Justice Statistics, 1998, p.15.

Typical of the efforts to extend federal control over local law enforcement were the efforts of one US senator. After hearings on federal remedies concerning police brutality one senator introduced legislation to limit federal assistance in certain instances. He proposed not funding cities with populations exceeding 100,000 unless they had a policy establishing a "potential problem officer early warning system." The Rodney King case in Los Angeles, California precipitated this action [19]and is typical of techniques used to extend control over local

19. Charles J. Ogletree, Jr., Mary Prosser, Abbe Smith, and William Talley, Jr., *Beyond the Rodney King Story: An Investigation of Police Conduct in Minority Communities,* Boston, Northeastern University Press, 1995, pp. 1–198.

law enforcement departments.[20] In the first part of the last decade several congressmen introduced a bill to strength the federal response to police misconduct. The bill stated:

> It shall be unlawful for any government authority, or any agent thereof, or any person acting on behalf of a governmental authority, to engage in a pattern or practice of conduct by law enforcement officers depriving rights, privileges, or immunities, secured or protected by the Constitution or laws of the United States.[21]

This act died in committee, but it illustrates the continuing effort of some to exert additional controls over the varying levels of law enforcement. Additional efforts can be anticipated in the future as long as the centrist movement remains viable.

Influence of Governmental Patterns upon Police Service

The organization of American police departments has passed through several stages in an evolutionary process, characterized in the beginning by a plurality of official controls. Early in the process this administrative pattern took the form of a committee of members of the city council who supervised the police. By diffusing responsibility and mingling it with the councilmen's interests in other matters, it encouraged corrupt political controls, favoritism, and extravagance. The inefficiency, which it produced soon, led to the appearance of a separate police board somewhat independent of the council. Members of this body were appointed by the mayor or elected by popular vote, in some cases on a non-partisan basis. Whether bi-partisan or non-partisan, both plans violated a basic principle of organization by placing executive control in a plural agency. Neither an army nor a police force can deliver effective service under plural leadership, or under the leadership of a committee.

Recognition of the need for unity of command and centralized executive control over the police mounts when realizing the work of maintaining law and order in a city, large or small, is a highly complicated and difficult enterprise. These duties cannot be successfully performed by a group of well-intentioned citizens who give only there spare time and thought to the task. Operating a police department is altogether different from maintaining a public library or a school system. Experience both in Europe and in the United States has demonstrated the indispensability of the single executive possessing final authority and accepting undivided responsibility for the administration of a crime fighting organization.

A gradual implementation of this basic principle of organization in the American police field is closely related to the evolution of municipal government itself. It may be best understood within the frame of

20. Cheryl Anthony Epps, "House Hearings Focus on Police Brutality," *The Police Chief,* June 1992, Vol. LIX, No. 6, p. 14.

21. House of Representatives, *Police Accountability Act of 1991,* H.R. 2972, 102D Congress, and 1st Session, July 23, 1991, pp.–1–2.

reference of five major forms of present-day municipal organization, the Mayor–Council plan, the Commission plan, and the Council–Manager plan, Town Meeting and Representative Town Meeting. The position of the police department in the administrative pattern is of the greatest importance. Without sound administrative structure at the top, a police organization cannot be administered and controlled efficiently and honestly. The type of administrative climate the police find themselves compelled to function within may cripple the line capability of the organization, or on the other hand may foster a high degree of competence and efficiency.

Mayor–Council

The traditional pattern of municipal organization is the Mayor and Council form. Under this plan, the members of the Council are elected. They represent the political aspect of local government and in a democracy, provide the opportunity for the flow of control and responsibility between government and the electorate. The Council constitutes the chief legislative and policy making body. Through its ordinance power, subject to constitutional and statutory provisions including the city charter, the Council carries out its legislative functions; when within its authority, its enactment has the force of law and is binding upon administration and the electorate. In addition to legislative and policy making functions, the Council in common with most legislative bodies, holds the purse strings and exercises control over appropriations. In one community the chief of police made the decision to decriminalize the theft of fuel from gas stations, but the city council took the position that this was a policy making decision and not within the preview of the administrative duties of the chief of police. The city council then moved to decriminalize the offense. This is a neat way to reduce the crime rate—redefine it!

The Mayor–Council plan reflects the traditional separation of powers between the executive and legislative branches of government. There are two types of government under this system. One is the strong mayor-council system and the other the weak mayor-council system. In the strong mayor city the candidates run for office and usually set forth a specific platform. But no two cities are exactly alike. In cities like Boston San Francisco, and Atlanta the mayor runs the show. In Houston and Indianapolis the mayors have a lesser amount of power. This may be because they face more frequent elections and these cities are not as homogeneous as other cities.[22]

Normally, a strong mayor has considerable political authority. For example, this official can veto ordinances, prepare budgets, and appoint personnel to administrative positions. These powers are considerable and it allows a strong mayor to function as the "boss." In many

22. Jacob Herbert, *The Frustration of Policy,* New York, Little, Brown & Co., 1984, p. 12.

communities other members of the city council represent either a specific geographical area or they are elected at large. In recent years there has been a trend to neighborhood or area representation. Courts have held that minority neighborhoods must have representation. In the classical arrangement, a strong mayor selects and appoints the chief of police. There is a high turnover rate for chief of police and the mayor can influence the type of law enforcement provided. Through the appointment power, the mayor's influence expands exponentially. The longer an incumbent is in office, the greater the amount of accumulated power. The mayor and the chief each have an agenda to follow and each is a vital component of the political process.[23]

In the weak mayor-council city, significant formal power is not incumbent to the position. In some situations it is largely ceremonial. The mayor attends city functions requiring city representation. It can be to open a new shopping center or highway. It can be at dinners where one eats "chicken and creamed peas" while presenting the key to the city to visiting dignitaries. There is usually high visibility, but limited formal power. In some situations other factors serve to expand the power base. For example, Richard Daley (1950s to 1970s) as mayor of Chicago served as a weak mayor, but his power was considerable. He was the head of the county Democratic party and was a true boss running a political machine. His power was sufficient to give him influence at the national level.[24] Another example of a city with a weak mayor system is Minneapolis, where the real power resides with the council. The council appoints the individual who administers the city. It is apparent that American cities have a wide variety of political structural arrangements. Diversity is the hallmark of municipal government.[25] In recent years, the mayor-council plan has lost ground to the city manager plan, especially in small and middle-sized cities. Since 1991 the city manager plan has prevailed in the majority of communities surveyed. However, in large cities the strong mayor system remains dominant with 35.2 percent of American cities utilizing some form of the mayor-council plan.

Figure 2–2

Governmental Patterns

Type	Reporting Cities	Percentage
Mayor–Council	1,605	35.2
Council–Manager	2,207	48.5
Commission	101	1.4
Town Meeting	214	4.7
Representative Town Meeting	24	0.5
	4,151	

23. Richard D. Bingham, *Managing Local Government: Public Administration in Practice,* Newbury Park, CA., Sage Publications, Inc., 1991, p. 40.

24. *Ibid.*

25. Jacob, *op. cit.*

Source: From Tari Renner and Victor S. De Santis, "Municipal Form of Government: Issues and Trends." Reprinted with permission of the International City/County Management Association, 777 North Capitol Street, NE, Suite 500, Washington, DC, *The Municipal YearBook—1998*, IC/CMA, 1998, table A5/2, p. 31.

The history of police administration in the United States is largely an account of the failures of the Mayor–Council form of municipal government. As often as not, the Mayor is a figurehead while the line departments of government are dominant and even corrupted by legislative interference. The Mayor as an elected official, is a politician who must depend on the political campaign for retention of office. Yielding first to one pressure group and then to another, this office too often becomes headquarters for the dispensing of patronage, favors and gratuities undermining the administration of line departments and reducing public service to the level of graft or incompetence. Police administration is the first to suffer in this type of situation. Morale and discipline experience a decline; sound personnel administration becomes an impossibility and the quality of management deteriorates to a point where public officers are unworthy of their responsibility. It was under such conditions of incompetence in local government that new forms of municipal administration were born.

The Commission Plan

At the beginning of the last century Galveston, TX, was one of the most miserably governed cities in the United States. Enjoying a low tax rate, operations were financed largely through increasing the bonded indebtedness. Department heads were elected and municipal government was run largely for personal profit. Then in that year, a great tidal wave inundated the city resulting in the loss of life and destruction of property. It was a tremendous crisis demanding brains and energy; municipal officials could furnish neither. The distinguishing feature of the Commission Plan was its combining both the legislative and administrative functions of government in an all-powerful body of five members chosen by popular election. As a group, the Commission constituted the legislative and policy-making body of local government; singly, each Commissioner was the administrative head of one or more municipal departments. Thus, the Commissioner of Public Safety exercised administrative control over the Police and Fire Departments.

The plan had the initial advantage of making a clean break with traditional political ties; in an atmosphere of emergency, it put a new concentration of powers in new hands. Perhaps the challenge of the task, as much as the change in forms, accounted for the early success of the plan in Galveston. Almost overnight the city became one of the best-governed cities in the nation. Featured in the public press, the commission form of municipal government was hailed by students of municipal affairs as the reform bringing light out of darkness and ending the dominion of the professional politicians. This was good news for police administration. Within seventeen years the total number of commission-governed cities had reached five hundred. This form of local government became known as the "Des Moines Plan" after its adoption by that city. It was the finalization of a typical commission form of government.[26] Variations in structure are found around the country, but the essential ingredients of the commission plan include:

- The concentration of legislative and executive powers in a small group elected at large on a nonpartisan ballot.
- The collective responsibility of the commission to pass ordinances and control the purse strings.
- The individual responsibility of each commissioner to head a city department, such as public works, finance, and public safety.
- The selection of the mayor from among the commissioners but reducing the office to that of ceremonial leadership.[27]

Although the Commission plan held forth-considerable promise for a new era in police administration at the beginning, subsequent events exposed it as a new device for corrupt exploitation. The dual role of the individual commissioner as both legislator and administrator opened wide the door for illegitimate influence and pressure, and made police administration more vulnerable than ever before to the sinister forces in the community whose interests are opposed to those of the public, of even greater significance. Additionally, it restored plural command over the police force, which had been previously demonstrated to be a violation of sound organizational procedure.

A typical dispute occurring between a public safety commissioner and a chief of police happened in Collinsville, IL. Only one month after being hired, Commissioner Michael Fischer accused the chief of not following his orders. The Chief, David Niebur, stated the Commissioner constantly interfered with the running of the department. The Commissioner had tried to remove the Chief on four occasions. In a primary election, Fischer did not receive enough votes to be placed on the general election ballot. The Commissioner felt the negative press describing the battle between the two contributed to his defeat.[28]

Council Manager or City Manager Plan

The Council–Manager plan was originally devised and promoted by the National Short Ballot Organization, as a part of its effort to make government more responsible by reducing the number of elective offices. The first city to adopt its "commission-manager" or Council–Manager plan was Sumter, South Carolina, in 1912 and the first large city to do so was Dayton, Ohio. This new pattern provided an outstand-

26. Bingham, *op. cit.*, p. 41.
27. Jack C. Plano and Milton Greenberg, *The American Political Dictionary*, Fifth Edition, New York, Holt, Rinehart and Winston, p. 442.

28. *Law Enforcement News*, "Feud Ends in TKO" March 15, 1991, p. 4.

ing demonstration of efficiency in the administration of public affairs. Other cities soon followed the example of Dayton in the march toward better management of cities. In the 1960s the International City/County Management Association, reacting to the changes in local government, recognized that some communities appointed administrators who did not function under a traditional council-manager plan. Communities functioning in this manner are "general management municipalities." This type of administrator is eligible for full membership in IC/CMA.[29]

Managers under both systems are selected because of relevant education and experience. The IC/CMA does not require a specific preparation for entry into these fields. It relies on demonstrated competence in the field with significant management responsibility and authority.[30] A city manager is responsible for working with the governing body. Managers seem to be successful when they work diligently developing a working relationship with the council. Whenever possible a "good" manager makes sure the elected body receives credit for achievements.[31] The relationship between a city council and a city manager can erode for various reasons. Recently the majority of a newly elected city council fired a city manager in Hayward California. The manager had served for three and one-half years. Political insiders felt the dismissal occurred because of a power struggle between the mayor and the manager. It was a question of two strong-willed individuals being unable to agree on significant issues.[32]

The City Manager plan borrows its methods of organization from modern business. Under this arrangement, the City Council functions in much the same manner as the board of directors in a corporate enterprise. The Council determines public policies and chooses the city manager to carry them out. The manager is a technical expert in the field of management who is placed in charge of every phase of municipal administration. Once chosen, this individual is given wide administrative control with authority to select subordinates, including the executive heads of the departments of municipal government. The City Manager plan has served to produce trained administrators for a supremely technical job of public management and has given American City government its first professional touch. The plan has, from the beginning, been consistently opposed by the professional politicians and pressure groups whose interests are not in harmony with the development of high standards in the public service. With variations the essentials of this plan consist of:

29. ICCMA, *op. cit.*, p. xiii.

30. *Ibid*, p. 3.

31. International City Management Association, *The Effective Local Government Manager*, Washington D.C., ICCMA, 1983, p. 50.

32. Dennis Akizuki, "New Council Majority Fires Hayward Manager," *San Jose Mercury News*, June 18, 1992, p. 4B.

- A small council or commission of five or seven members elected at large on a nonpartisan ballot, with power to make policy and to hire and fire the manager.

- A professionally trained manager (with authority to hire and fire subordinates) who is responsible to the council for efficient administration of the city.

- A mayor chosen separately from within the council, but with no executive functions. The council must refrain from bypassing the manager by interfering with the subordinates or in the details of administration. Conversely the manager must follow the policies outlined by the council. A merit system for selection of employees is generally used under this plan.[33]

While an efficient police service can be developed within the framework of the Mayor–Council or the Commission Plan, it is patent the City Manager form fosters professionalization in the various municipal departments. A professional administrator with full managerial power and responsibility would, by the very nature of training and position, endeavor to place at the head of each department the most capable individual available. Hence, the City Manager would obviously be interested in the appointment of a Chief of Police qualified for the delivery of a professional grade of management, and then delegate to this subordinate, the powers and responsibilities required for the proper exercise of the functions of this important position.

External control of the force is thus turned into legitimate channels, with the police chief executive responsible directly to the city manager alone. With the complete separation of the legislative and administrative functions of government provided by this pattern of municipal organization, political interference with police administration is reduced to a minimum. Under this form of administrative control, police administration finds itself in a professional atmosphere where it is less likely to be burdened by the inhibitions, which in the past have retarded the professionalization of this branch of the public service.

Town Meeting

Direct democracy is the principle of the open town meeting in six New England States. Such meeting are generally held annually. Prior to the meeting selectmen present a warrant that includes notification of the time, place, and agenda. Any citizen can attend the meeting but voting is limited to registered voters. Those eligible to vote can do so on articles under consideration or they can cast a vote for election candidates. Selectmen may include in a warrant any article they feel the town meeting should consider. Officials, boards, commissions, or committees may submit articles for consideration. Additionally voters are allowed to initiate petitions to place an article before the town meeting.

33. Plano and Greenberg, *op. cit.*, p. 115.

Selectmen can also call for a vote when appropriate. It has been generally found that attendance at town meeting is somewhat sparse, and when the population of a town exceeds 25,000 it can be considered less than an effective process.[34] The representative town meeting is a variation that has received increasing attention Wherein members of a community elect someone to represent them.

Pressure Groups

It is a basic principle of democratic government that administration must be responsive to public control. This is especially true of police administration because of the unique powers with which it is entrusted. Basic, also, is the fact that such control must find expression through formal channels of governmental structure, descending vertically from the people by way of the ballot box through the legislative body to the appointing officer, and through this person to the police chief executive. It is likewise essential for responsibility to flow vertically upward from the police to the appointing authority, and continue on to the legislature and finally to the people. These controls should be out in the open where they are exposed to observation and appraisal.

Violation of this fundamental principle of organization is undoubtedly responsible for many of the ills and growing pains afflicting local government in general and police administration in particular. Violations take the form of pressures and controls generated by special interest groups; they are usually brought to bear upon the weakest point or points in the organizational structure. The point of vulnerability may be the officer on the beat, the "gold braid" of the department, the police chief executive, the Mayor, the City Council, or a combination of two or more of these officials. It depends somewhat upon the form of local government, but usually when illegitimate controls are effectively exercised upon police administration, one or more members of the legislative body are parties to the illicit operation.

The pressure of special interest groups influences all persons in public life. They constitute a sort of phantom fourth branch of government. In every type of government, pressure groups are a normal part of the social and political process. They offer to a considerable extent, effective avenues for the expression of public opinion. In a democratic society characterized by representative government, simultaneously with freedom of speech and expression, they have the almost unbridled opportunity to influence decision-making. Within a community the chief of police is at the focal point of local law enforcement. It is a highly complex job requiring the chief to convey, to many interests, the enforcement policy of the department. It is a most difficult task to constantly inform the many constituencies existing in a community. The effectiveness with which this is accomplished is a measure of the

34. Joseph E. Zimmerman, "The New England Town Meeting: Lawmaking By Assembled Voters," *in International City/County Management Associ-ation,* Municipal Yearbook—1998, Washington, DC, International City/County Management Association, 1998, pp. 25–28.

competence of the chief of police. Figure 2–3 depicts a variety of pressure or interest groups that must be considered. When this task is performed with a high degree of effectiveness the power, status, and influence of the chief is extended. When it is accomplished poorly it can lead to the dilution of the chief's power or in some instances removal from office.

Information is power. A chief must be aware of the need to share information with interested parties. It can be a difficult task. The chief must be especially aware of the objectives, demands, strategy, and tactics of interest groups. It calls for seeking answers to; What is it that the group wants? What will they do to attain their objective? Is there opposition to what is wanted? Answers will vary from group to group and from community to community. The most successful chiefs develop the capacity to work in a highly charged political environment. Developing this skill is an art and it would seem it is something that can only be acquired over time. Unfortunately there is no formula for developing the skills needed to work with interest groups.[35]

It requires a chief to work with divergent, and at times demanding groups. It requires a careful analysis of problems and eventually getting interest groups to seek problem resolution with a minimum of conflict. Police administration is surrounded by a constellation of social forces in the community possibly approaching from any point of the compass to influence policy and administrative decisions. It is appropriate, therefore, to explore the nature and objectives of these special groups and their potential impact on the police enterprise.

Politics

Although the strength of political party organization varies considerably from one city to another, the political machine continues as a corrupter of government and as a direct threat to sound public management in many American municipalities. This is not so much an indictment of the so-called "machine" as it is a reflection of failure on the part of responsible citizens to exercise a participating interest in the affairs of local government. The inevitable result is that a small minority gains control. Generally bankrupt on issues, political party organization in many cities depends for cohesion and loyalty upon the number of positions in the public service that can be distributed to the faithful. In fact, adherents of the spoil doctrine point unashamedly to the contributions of the patronage system in maintaining party discipline and as a means to aid in financing the elaborate party machinery seemingly necessary under our form of government. "It is sometimes argued," states Pfeiffer, "that there must be some patronage for the political officers to dispense to their campaign workers; that American democracy relies upon the party system, which in turn relies upon the spoils of office to keep it going." "This is a fallacy, which should be blasted before its cancerous growth goes farther on its malignant way.

35. ICMA, *op. cit.,* p. 36.

If American democracy is based on loot, its foundations are dangerously weak. It has been proved quite definitely that citizens actuated only by the highest civic motives can organize in the interests of professional public administration."[36]

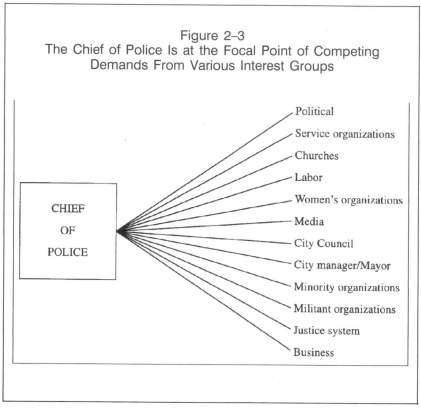

Figure 2–3
The Chief of Police Is at the Focal Point of Competing Demands From Various Interest Groups

- Political
- Service organizations
- Churches
- Labor
- Women's organizations
- Media
- City Council
- City manager/Mayor
- Minority organizations
- Militant organizations
- Justice system
- Business

CHIEF OF POLICE

One former chief of police in addressing the issue of political influence pointed out: Every cop who wanted to get ahead had his "hook"—or as they say in New York, his "rabbi". Everyone owed his success to a politician.[37] It is necessary to accept the fact that policing in America is political. The desire to be apolitical is unattainable and, at the least, utopian. Local government thrives on the political process and the police are a vital part of that process.[38]

This does not mean the police have to be part of the spoils system, in fact they should be apart from it. Politics is never going to be a simon-pure endeavor. Like it or not, the dynamics of the political system is such that the political *boss* must be able to reward followers.[39] Two observers of the political process (one a federal judge and the

36. John M. Pfiffner, *Municipal Administration,* The Ronald Press Company, New York, 1940, pp. 31–32.

37. James F. Ahern, *Police in Trouble,* New York, Hawthorn Books, Inc., 1972, p. 97.

38. Herman Goldstein, *Policing a Free Society,* Cambridge, Mass., Ballinger Publishing Co., 1977, p. 141.

39. Fred J. Cook, *American Political Bosses and Machines,* New York, Franklin Watts, Inc., 1983, p. 145.

other a prosecutor) have pointed out that the colossal corruption of powerful political machines (unless it is stopped and the participants punished) will eventually tear American society apart.[40] The relationships between the police and politics are numerous and complex. There is a continuing exchange of influences, pressures and power plays between the police and society. Unfortunately corruption occurs at every level of government. It involves politicians and law enforcement officers. Corruption can destroy the bond of trust essential between law enforcement and the public.[41] In our society citizens expect officers and officials to perform their duties with a high standard of integrity.[42] When corruption occurs the bond of trust is ruptured.[43]

Corruption is not limited to its most egregious and sensational form—cash for an official favor. Corruption includes all of the circumstances in which the public officeholder or government employee sacrifices or sells all or part of his judgment on matters within the official purview in return for personal gain. Corruption thus defined includes a direct bargain—cash (or securities, a share in a business venture, or the promise of a future job on the outside) in exchange for official action or implied. Such arrangements—frequently described as conflicts of interest—include any and all circumstances in which the officeholder or government employee is or may become the beneficiary of favor from persons with business that comes before the officeholder in an official capacity. Such conflicts of interest often involve the officeholder whose business or professional pursuits any official conduct.

Finally, corruption, as defined here, may flow from the electoral process itself. The payment, or promised payment, of campaign contributions in return for official conduct constitutes a bribe. Moreover, dependence on a source of campaign funding probably represents the more pervasive and constant monetary shackle on the judgment and action of the elected official. The federal government selected municipal corruption prevention (as a topic for training) as one of the most effective strategies for dealing with corruption. Figure 2–4 is a partial checklist identifying indicators allowing one to conduct an assessment of the integrity–maintenance and corruption-risk condition of local government.

40. *Ibid.*

41. New York City, Commission to Combat Police Corruption, *Performance Study: the Internal Affairs Bureau Command Center,* New York, New York City, 1997, pp. 1–63.

42. Richard Girgenti, Michael Boxer, Jill Konviser; and others. *Report to the New York City Commission to Combat Police Corruption: the New York City Police Department Random Integrity Testing Program,* New York, NY, KPMG Peat Marwick LLP, 1996, PP 1–18.

43. Otis E. Cooksey, "Corruption: A Continuing Challenge for Law Enforcement," *FBI Law Enforcement Bulletin,* September 1991, Vol. 60, No. 9, pp. 5–9.

Figure 2–4

Integrity Checklist—Policy Toward
Corruption

A "no" answer to any question indicates a deficiency; the jurisdiction does not have all of the tools needed to combat corruption. A simple and informal assessment of corruption in a community can be accomplished by talking to:

- Taxi drivers.
- Newspaper reporters.
- Chamber of commerce members and staff.
- Lawyers.
- Clergy.
- Bar owners and bartenders.
- Law enforcement officers (local, state, and federal).
- Hotel help.
- Homeowners association members.
- Contractors.

Ask Them:

Can I fix a ticket?
Where can I place a bet?
Who is the best zoning attorney?
How do I get a civil service position?
Can I get a girl for my room?
Who runs the gambling?
Who really controls this city?
Is this a good place to live?
How extensive is the drug problem?
What are the politics of this city?
How do I get a liquor license?
Is it difficult to open a business?
Whom do I see if I want to bid on a city contract?
How good is the Police Department?

Source: Henry S. Dogin, *Maintaining Municipal Integrity, Participants Handbook,* Washington, DC, USGPO, 1980, pp. 61–61.

It is impossible to measure precisely the extent of corruption in America today. But the presence of one especially virulent species—the influence of organized crime syndicates on public officials—has been better documented than most. When police administration finds itself operating under corrupt external controls, law enforcement becomes a mockery. Police operations become defensive in character. The primary concern of the police and their confederates is to "prevent the heat from being turned on." Sporadic vice raids are properly arranged and given wide publicity in order to appease moralists and give the impression that all is well. Outbreaks of major crime are vigorously investigated; even corrupt administration is embarrassed by the robbery and murder of law—abiding citizens because it is fully aware of the limits to public tolerance. But a relaxed administration attracts to the community more than its share of criminal parasites and spawns increased criminal activity on a menacing scale. The system fosters high crime rates and soon the officials can be confronted with an epidemic of crime. Line capability is decimated under such conditions and the department cans no longer discharge its functions in protecting the citizens of the community against criminal attack. Morale and discipline fades into oblivion and the organization become demoralized and helpless. Community sentiment becomes aroused. Even a corrupt press may be unable to stem the advance of reform.[44]

Figure 2–5

Recent Alleged Charges of Corruption
By the Police
Event

- The chief of police of West New York, NJ Police Department and eight other former or current officers were charged with collecting hundreds of thousands of dollars in bribes and kickbacks from illegal gambling operations, prostitution, and after-hours liquor sales.
- In Ohio forty-four officers were arrested in drug-related corruption cases. The officers were from the Cuyahoga County Sheriff's Office, the Cleveland Police Department, Cleveland Heights Police Department, and the East Cleveland Police Department.
- A supervisor from the North Carolina Highway Patrol was fired after he was linked to a man convicted of running a huge interstate stolen-property ring.
- Two former detectives of the Boston Police Department admitted to engaging in a string of crimes that included stealing more than $200,000 and taking bribes in exchange for recommending lenient sentences.
- After being exposed by the editor of the Democratic Reporter in Linden, AL, the Sheriff was arrested and plead guilty to extortion. He was sentenced to 27 years. He received an additional 27-month sentence when he plead guilty to soliciting a bribe and failing to pay state income taxes.

Sources: Law Enforcement News, "Police Force Allegedly Run as Criminal Enterprise;" *Law Enforcement News,* January 15, 1998, 2.; Richard G. Rivera, "Dropping a Dime: One Cop's Insider Account of the Investigation of a Criminal Enterprise Disguised as a New Jersey Police Department," *Law Enforcement News,* February, 14/28, 1998, 11; Law Enforcement News, "Two Fired, One Demoted in NCHP Scandal," *Law Enforcement News,* February 14/28, 1998. 11; Arizona Daily Star, "Two Ex-cops Admit Graft, Stealing $200,000," *Arizona Daily Star,* Sunday, March 8, 1998, A9, and Rick Bragg, "Crusading Journalists Defeat Corrupt Sheriff," *San Jose Mercury News,* Friday, June 5, 1998, 25A.

Recent years have witnessed considerable gain in the elimination of corrupt external influence on police administration, but as soon as this assumption is accepted a department somewhere in this Nation is scandalized by corruption.[45] The FBI conducts vigorous investigations

---

44. Leonard, *op. cit.*

45. Frank Anechiarico and James B. Jacobs, *The Pursuit of Absolute Integri-*

of police corruption as noted by the fact that from 1994 to 1997, 508 officers were convicted of Federal corruption-related charges.[46] Experts know that few American police departments can claim complete freedom from illegitimate pressures. Every competent survey of municipal police organization and administration has revealed their presence, and on occasion their influence upon the administration of police affairs. Symptomatic of this pathological condition are the short tenure and frequent replacement of the police chief executive, low quality of management, defective organization, departmental cliques, substandard personnel resources, and a general failure to ascertain and apply the tested tools and procedures of modern police administration.

Service Organizations

Input to local police administration expresses itself in many different forms. Occasionally it is well intentioned but frequently it is ill conceived and misguided. The constellation of service club organizations and associations that characterize the American scene in every city may affect the quality of police administration for good or for evil. These organizations, as a rule, exert a constructive influence in municipal affairs, but they are not infrequently shortsighted, and may even be prostituted to the selfish ends of an individual or a group. Most service clubs attempt to remain politically neutral. They should also remember that political neutrality is an absolute prerequisite of successful police organization. Service clubs and organizations can do much to promote civic pride and civic improvement by demanding of the City Council, the conditions that foster a professional police service.

Such organizations will usually have a very narrow orientation or interest when they interact with law enforcement. While it varies from group to group, they can prove to be quite influential in local politics. If the issue is of interest, these groups can form a vital alliance with law enforcement. In fact, some chiefs will join certain clubs or associations in order to keep in touch with the community and to develop a personal power base. Figure 2–6 lists the clubs present in a community.

ty: How Corruption Control Makes Government Ineffective, Chicago, University of Chicago Press, 1996, pp. 1–94.

46. *Law Enforcement News,* "Anticorruption Policies Re-examined as Feds Bust Multi-agency Protection Racket," January 31, 1998, 1 and 8A.

Figure 2–6

Clubs, Organizations and Associations
in a Typical Community

Kiwanis Club	Eagles	Alano Club
Rotary	Lions	German Heritage
Elks Lodge	Moose Lodge	
American Legion	Knights of Columbus Hall	
Masonic Temple	Grange	
Native Sons	Japanese American Citizens League	
Filipino Community	Veterans of Foreign Wars	
Japanese American Citizens League	Nuclear Weapons Freeze	
Resource Center for Non Violence	Disabled American Veterans	

Religious Organizations

The churches in a community represent a potential pressure group of considerable proportions. If their members are aroused, their influence can be a controlling factor in administrative policy determination. The voting power of the active church members in an average city is more than sufficient to elect or defeat council members. However, churches are rarely able to mobilize their effective strength and present a united front. Furthermore, church membership includes a fair cross—section of most interest groups in a community, which complicates any effort to pool their resources on issues that are other than neutral in character.

Nevertheless, the influence of churches in municipal affairs should not be underestimated. A person's thinking can be shaped by the impact of the principles enunciated by the Man of Galilee, and a transformation in viewpoint by an individual may have important implications at the ballot box. Furthermore, crusading ministers have not infrequently stirred communities to action by messages from the pulpit. Where economy in government and a low tax rate form the basis for current issues, churches will not ordinarily become too greatly concerned. However, if vice is rampant and corruption the rule, and if these conditions are quite apparent, churches may take a definite stand. In some communities religious groups have taken a strong stand against legalized gambling on the other hand the Catholic church is well know for its support of bingo enterprises. A chief who is attuned to the ground swell in a community over a specific issue can look for support from religious groups. Figure 2–7 lists religious organizations in a town on the West Coast.

Figure 2-7

Religious Organizations

Assemblies of God	Bahai'I Faith	Baha'I Faith
Christ Lutheran	Fundacion San Pablo De Colores	Pray Inc.
Hope Haven Network	Koinonia Conference	TEC Ministries Inc.
Quaker Friend	Bible Church	International Society for Krishna

Canterbury Foundation	Seventh–Day Adventists
Subud	Taungpulu Kaba–Aye Monastery
Temple Or Tiqvah jkfir	Unity Temple
American Jewish Renewal	
Varjrayana Foundation	Valley Churches Valley Missions
Vision Ministries	Voice for Life
Word Growth Institute	

Business and Trade

In most communities business members participate actively in the Chamber of Commerce and other agencies promoting community welfare and growth. They can be from a wide range of businesses such as departments store, electronics firms, utility companies, small-businesses, real estate brokers, and manufacturing. Many of these individuals will have enough interest in the community to run for public office. Others will readily serve on public boards, commissions, and task forces. In this way leaders of the business community can have a direct impact on community improvement. Generally, business leaders will support physical improvements in the community and improvements in public management.[47] In many areas corporations have loaned executives to conduct management studies of public agencies.

The chief of police, in most parts of the United States, can involve the private sector in a broader public safety role. This requires the chief to think across multi-jurisdictional lines in terms of the difference between corporate and public decision-making. Increasingly, businesses are employing professional security managers. This can serve as the foundation for a more positive working relationship between the public and private sectors. Characteristic of the improved working relationships is the creation in some police departments of specialized units to investigate computer crimes in corporations. Investigators work closely with their counterparts in private enterprise. Typical of these is the police department in San Jose, CA., High–Technology Crimes Detail. This unit handles the following types of cases:

- Burglary/theft of computer parts and components.
- Trade secrets.
- Cellular phone fraud.
- Fraudulent access to computer information systems.
- "Internet" crimes
- Sales/possession of stolen computer components.

47. IC/CMA, *op. cit.,* p. 37.

- Crimes related to and involving the procurement/use of high technology equipment.[48]

Officers assigned to the detail work closely with the computer industry. In addition, they provide technical support to other units with the forensic search, seizure, and preservation of electronic data obtained from suspects or at crime scenes.

An exemplary case of cooperation between business and law enforcement is the Sheriff's Advisory Board of Santa Clara, County, San Jose, CA, that is a non-political and non-profit volunteer organization. Formed in 1980 there are approximately 150 business and community leaders who are members of the Board. Sine it was founded over $200,000 has been contributed to provide a safer working environment for the men and women of the Sheriff's Office. Funds have been used to support D.A.R.E., purchase Hi Tech items, and purchase police dogs.[49] The following figure lists the business and trade organizations in a typical community.

Figure 2–8

Business and Trade Organizations

Agriculture	Associated General Contractors
Certified Organic Farmers	Better Business Bureau
Chamber of Commerce	Downtown Arts & Retail Alliance
Downtown Association	Sunbelt World Trade Association
South Mall Association	Women in Building and Design
Women in Construction– National Association	

Labor

The police labor movement in the United States spawned a pressure group of no mean proportions, especially as far as police management is concerned. Organized labor has attempted penetration of police departments in many sections of the country. With the growth in cities, police departments hired new personnel on a substantial scale. Naturally these new members became intensely interested in conditions of service, including adjustment of working hours, pension and retirement benefits, protection of tenure, wage increases and other benefits. Members of police forces came together early in fraternal societies or clubs, and through this medium, exchanged information, carried on social activities for themselves and their families, and established benefits to aid fellow officers or their dependents. Such social or fraternal clubs exist today in many jurisdictions. In some departments they have accomplished much good and have contributed greatly to the morale of

---

48. San Jose Police Department, *High Technology Crimes Detail. San Jose, CA,* 10/10/98, www/http.sjpd.org/hitech.html.

49. Jim Arata, *Sheriff's Advisory Board of Santa Clara County,* San Jose, CA, Sheriff's Office, 7/02/97, www/http://claraweb.co.santa-clara.ca.us/sheriff/sab.htm.

the force. In other departments on occasion, they have been used to accomplish the selfish ends of malcontents in the organization and have left in their wake, dissension and a negative impact upon departmental morale and efficiency.

With the phenomenal development of labor union organization in industry since the beginning of the last century, police personnel in a number of departments, where administration was weak and ineffective, sensed the possibility of applying union mechanisms to their problems. Labor organizers also saw in the police forces of the nation new sources of revenue and an opportunity for a new extension of power and influence. They probably were not unmindful of the advantages that would accrue from control of the force during clashes between labor and management in industrial disputes.

Today, the record shows that the police employee organization is no myth. They have rapidly become a significant factor in the relationships between police personnel and police management. Police administrators would be overlooking their responsibility if they choose to ignore the activity of these organizations. Chiefs of Police who are caught up in the mainstream of these developments must be prepared to initiate programs which will neutralize the need for militancy, so these organizations can address their energies toward constructive goals, including the professionalization of the police services. Otherwise, the executive branch must be prepared to cope with the consequences that may result from the intrusion of a police employee organization or a union between police management and the man on the beat. Table 2–1 lists some of the types of employee organizations by city size.

Table 2–1

TYPE OF POLICE EMPLOYEE ORGANIZATIONS BY CITY SIZE

	City Size (000's)						Total
Affiliated with:	10–25	25–50	50–100a	100–250b	250–500	500–1000	1000 Plus	
Fraternal Order of Police	12	7	19	17	8	5	1	69
Police Benevolent Association	4	1	7	7	0	0	1	20
AFSCME*	1	2	1	3	0	0	0	7
State Organization	6	3	14	4	0	1	0	28
Local Independent	13	7	21	7	1	6	1	56
Joint	11	12	39	27	12	5	2	108
Total	47	32	101	65	21	17	5	288

a. In addition one city reported affiliation with the Teamsters.
b. In addition one city reported affiliation with the International Union of Operating Engineers.
* Union-affiliated in some states (AFL–CIO)—The American Federation of State, County and Municipal Employees.

In a major study of law enforcement agencies with 100 or more officers out of 831 respondents to a survey 39 percent stated the police department allowed membership in non-police unions, 422 of the agencies had police unions, and 88 percent of the departments had members in police associations. It immediately becomes clear that the police have accepted representatives to deal with the chief of police and city administration. [50]Another organization is the International Conference of Police Associations (ICPA) that was charted by the AFL–CIO. This organization has some 100 locals and seven State Councils with a membership of approximately 20,000 police officers. Its goal is to bring officers into the main stream of the labor movement, Another organization is the International Brotherhood of Police Officers (IBPO) that is affiliated with the Service Employees International Union. The IBPO represents 38,000 officers who are members of 175 chapters.

Collective bargaining as a personnel tool or mechanism has characterized the scene in business and industry for many years. The Wagner Act and the Taft–Hartley Act passed by Congress in 1935 and 1947 respectively, created mandatory guidelines for business and industry employers and labor unions to follow in the move toward improved conditions of employment. Public service employees were not too slow in recognizing the advantages they might accrue in the approach to employment benefits through the use of the collective bargaining process.[51]

Collective bargaining is defined as a process through which an employer and employees (represented usually by a non-union police employee organization) negotiate a formal agreement with respect to salaries, hours of duty, and terms and conditions of service. One area of some confusion in the collective bargaining process is the determination of which questions or issues are bargainable and which are not. State legislation usually classifies these issues somewhat as follows:

- Compensation—including salaries, overtime pay, nightshift differential, court appearance pay and longevity pay.

- Manpower allocation—hours worked weekly, hours per shift, shift assignment, numbers of men per car, and work assignments.

- Disciplinary matters—matters pertaining to disciplinary action.

- Promotional procedures—rules and regulations relating to promotion within the department.

In recent years interest-based bargaining has received increasing attention. It is a non-adversarial process wherein both sides address problems not personalities. In fact, at the beginning both sides agree to prohibit yelling fighting and personal attacks, and negotiators are

50. Brian A. Reaves and Andrew L. Goldberg, *Law Enforcement Management and Administrative Statistics, 1997: Data for Individual State and Local Agencies with 100 or More Officers,* Washington, DC, Office of Justice Programs, September 1999, p.p. xiv.

51. John H. Burpo, "Improving Police Agency and Employee Performance Through Collective Bargaining," *The Police Chief,* February 1974, Vol. XLI, No. 2, p. 36.

mandated to address issues with problem solving techniques.[52] The Memorandum of Understanding (MOU) carefully spells out bargainable issues. The MOU also delineates the unnegotiable. For example, in the City of Los Angeles, matters that cannot be grieved include:

- An impasse in meet and confer.

- Transfers, promotions, promotional examinations, and probationary employee terminations. These matters are not grievable or arbitrable whether or not said matters involve discipline.

- Any other matter involving discipline is not grievable or arbitrable.

- A determination of the fitness of an employee to carry a concealable firearm on or off duty is not grievable or arbitrable.[53]

The matters are not grievable or arbitrable are dealt with by general appeal procedures or administrative appeal procedures when it involves discipline for permanent and probationary employees. Following appeal procedures can make transfers and promotion appeals, and promotional examinations can be appealed to the Civil Service Commission. When the grievance involves carrying of a firearm, the appeal is to the Chief of Police with the final administrative level being the Police Commission. This still leaves many issues that can be included in an MOU. It ranges from such things as working hours to bereavement leave. A typical list of items included in an MOU appears in figure 2–10. Management and labor develop an MOU through collective negotiation. Once finalized the MOU covers a period ranging from one to three years. If, during that period, there is a need for revision the two parties negotiate a sidebar agreement. This agreement normally involves issues not addressed in the initial contract. In other instances, the sidebar can clarify issues.[54]

52. Mark Johnson, "Problem-solving Policing Comes to Contract Talks: Interest–Based Bargaining Shows Merit," *Law Enforcement News,* May 15, 1995, p. 6.

53. City of Los Angeles, *Memorandum of Understanding No. 24, Jointly Submitted to the City Council Regarding the Police Officer. Lieutenant and Below Representation Unit,* Los Angeles, CA., City of Los Angeles, 1994, pp. 7–8.

54. City of Los Angeles, *Letter of Agreement for the Detective Work Hours Pilot Program and Clarification of Specified Articles Relating to the Police Officers, Lieutenant and Below Representation Unit,* Los Angeles, City of Los Angeles, 1995, pp. 1–11.

Figure 2–9

Issues That Can be Included In a
Memorandum of Understanding

Working Hours	Overtime
Accumulated Overtime	Court Time
Compensation for Firearms Qualification	Compensation for Medical Examinations
Off Duty Week-end-holiday Premiums	Uniform, Maintenance and Training Allowance
Vacations	Vacation Pay
Holidays and Holiday Premiums	Sick Leave Benefits
Family Illness	Bereavement Leaves
Health Insurance	Dental Insurance
Life Insurance	Salaries
Marksmanship Bonuses	Longevity Pay
Seniority for Vacations	Rights Representation
Overtime Compensation for Meeting Supervisors	P.O.S.T. Certificate Bonus
Hazards Pay	Notice to Correct Deficiencies
Advanced notice	Pay plan
Employee rights	City rights
Substance Tests	Death Benefits
Military Leave	Educational Incentive Pay
Standby Assignment	Light Duty
Work Out of Class	Jury Leave

Source: City of Milpitas, *Memorandum of Understanding, The City of Milpitas and the Milpitas Police Officers Association,* January 1, 1996–December 31, 1998, Milpitas, City of Milpitas, pp. 1–42.

An area of genuine concern to those who are knowledgeable about the bargaining process is that the chief of police is excluded. This usually leaves it in the hands of the city manager or someone designated to negotiate for the city. It is felt this deprives the community from utilizing the knowledge and skills of the one individual who should be involved in negotiating with those representing members of the police department.[55] Judicial decisions have denied the application of the union mechanism (the right to strike) in the police forces of this country. When by law or by mutual consent the union is denied the most fundamental of the traditional instruments for achieving its purposes (the strike) there is very little advantage offered to police officers by membership in national unions.

The unionization of a police force usually can be traced to inadequacies of management. It can be repeated again that in the majority of cases where union penetration of police forces has occurred, it has been a measure of desperation by personnel faced with intolerable conditions of service for which they could secure little redress from indifferent city officials. A vigorous administration will spare no effort in gaining for

55. Allen H. Andrews, Jr., "Structuring the Political Independence of the Police Chief," in William A. Geller, Editor, *Police Leadership in America,* Chicago, IL, American Bar Foundation, 1985, p. 18.

its personnel all the privileges and benefits consistent with the integrity of operations. This includes terms of compensation, days off, sick leave, vacation, hours of duty, pensions and other conditions of service. Indeed, it has been demonstrated that under this type of administrative policy, employees find little occasion to look elsewhere for assistance in the solution of their problems.[56]

Women's Organizations

Conscientious police administrators will welcome the day when women's organizations may become more articulate in matters, which concern the standards of local government. It is a serious mistake to underestimate the potential power of women in the realm of public affairs, particularly when the welfare of their children is at stake. It is equally hazardous to assume that women's organizations will be content to confine their efforts to embroidery contests and book reviews when environmental hazards and other forces in the community continue as a threat to youth welfare. Prophetic of the role of women in the community affairs is the observation that among the most devastating things that could happen to mar an otherwise pleasant day for the average city hall official would be the secretary's announcement that a delegation of women were waiting in the reception room.

If there is any single women's organization that has achieved the position of preeminence as a pressure group, it is Mothers' Against Drunk Drivers (MADD) that was founded by a small group of women in 1980. It can into existence as the result of a drunk driver who killed a 13–year-old-girl. The hit-and-run driver had been out of jail for only two days after another hit-and-run drunk driving crash and had three previous drunken driving arrests and two convictions. The defendant was allowed to plea bargain to vehicular manslaughter. Starting in California, it soon had the "impact of a hammer," and currently has 600 chapters nationwide. MADD lobbied state legislative bodies resulting in Driving while Intoxicated (DWI) laws that had stiffer penalties. Local groups of mothers became court watchers and tracked the sentencing records of judges, publicizing the records of lenient judges. There are few interest groups in the United States that have had such a forceful impact over a short period of time.[57]

Other organizations have come to the front as women have taken an aggressive posture in ensuring their proper handling of problem. Community participation and community involvement are increasingly common. Numerous cities have a commission working for the betterment of women in the workplace and the community. A wide range of women's organizations focuses on different aspect women's needs. This includes such groups as the National Organization for Women (NOW),

---

56. Walt H. Sirene, "Management: Labor's Most Effective Organizer," *FBI Law Enforcement Bulletin,* January 1981, Vol. 50, No. 1, p. 4.

57. MADD, *About MADD,* Dallas, TX, 1/1/99, http:www.madd.org/ABOUT MAD/DEFAULT.shtml.

the League of Women Voters, and Women against Rape. While the latter organization has a very special interest, other groups work for increased participation and rewards for women.

More women are serving on municipal and county task forces and committees and an increasing number of women chair those units. The numbers of women who serve as members of city councils and mayors have increased dramatically. Major cities such as San Francisco, CA., Houston, TX, and San Jose, CA. have had women serve as mayor. Women hold higher administrative positions in private enterprise and every level of government. Notably, women have served as chiefs of police in major cities such as Atlanta, Portland, Houston, Austin, and Tucson and sheriff of Santa Clara County, CA.

It is anticipated, in the future, that women will become more aggressive in their demands for effective government, especially law enforcement. This will focus on sexual assault abortion rights, sexual discrimination in the work place, and rape cases. Women also have realized the importance of organizing and working through pressure groups to achieve specified objectives. A further expectation is that women will be more apt to work for the good of the community and pursue broader social needs. Women are an untapped resource and chief executive officers should look to them for support.

Media

The power of the press has not been underestimated. The newspapers of a community or city can "make or break" a police department. Among the external controls conditioning police administration, the press plays a commanding role. Front page stories, or editorials or cartoons—occasionally all three—may be published with the hope that pressure will convince the city officials that something must be done. Diversions of police manpower and equipment, not infrequently in flagrant violation of sound principles of organization and administration, often result in the media forcing the police department to change. The police feel they must placate the newspapers or suffer the consequences of loss of power and prestige.

Police headquarters is one of the most prolific sources of news in any city or community. In the larger communities and cities, newspapers may maintain one or more police reporters at headquarters on a 24–hour basis. Police-press relationships are important. It has been demonstrated over and over again that through a mutual policy of confidence and cooperation, the ends of both news reporting and police administration can be served in a most effective manner. It is seldom that a newspaper reporter has violated the confidence of a Police Chief in, for example, a sensitive case where premature publicity could prejudice or disrupt the investigation.

Police management and its personnel have a tendency on occasion to ignore the good effect of the press and the results that can be achieved through a sound policy of cooperation with the press. The editorial policy of every newspaper supports good law enforcement. Usually, the men and women who write editorials have had broad experience in dealing with the police. Most of the nation's successful editors have served as police reporters at one time or another and many have never forgotten the experience. One editor has suggested that if they were not news reporters, many of them would be police officers.

Journalists' work under constant pressure to comply with deadlines, so their coverage of a story might not be what it should be. Usually there is little time to check back and verify aspects of a story. Additionally, the reporter might not be knowledgeable about law enforcement procedures or terminology. There is also a tendency to simplify a story to meet the needs of editors and readers. Space in a newspaper is precious and the media must control it to insure a competitive newspaper. Law enforcement should respond to media needs by providing honest, straightforward responses to requests for information. Cooperation, whenever possible, should be timely to allow reporters and TV crews to comply with tight deadlines. As much information as possible should be provided to simplify the media's task. Names, titles, and addresses should be spelled out to insure accuracy. Beyond these easy steps, the key is to make oneself available and to simplify the media's acquisition of information.[58] Some departments have taken TV crews with them when conducting a raid, but it is believed that this is nothing but a publicity stunt and the negatives of such a policy far out weigh the positives.

Police departments should have a police-media relations policy that satisfies the public's right to know, that protects individual rights, and at the same time opens up the agency to public scrutiny. In recent years the creation of Internet web sites by a few departments has served as a vehicle for providing the media and citizens with vital information about police operations. It is a trend that must be expanded and become on e of the primary goals of law enforcement.

Minority Groups

Minority groups are a potent and viable pressure group in many communities throughout the nation. Historically they have had minimal influence, but in recent years they have become an important aspect of the political and social processes of community life. This ethnicity is quite apparent and is a specific manifestation of America's race problem. With increasing frequency, minority groups are demanding more citizen participation in the governance of our cities as indicated by the tendency in some communities for neighborhood control of the police or the demand for a police review board. It is a strong movement in certain cities; police administrators must be pre-

58. Marshal S. Cook, "How to Handle the Press," *Law and Order,* September 1991, Vol. 39, No. 9, pp. 88–89.

pared to deal with demands from African–Americans, Mexican–Americans, Asian–Americans and other ethnic groups. In almost every community there are chapters of national organizations interested in minority civil rights. This includes the:

- National Association for the Advancement of Colored People (NAACP).
- Urban League.
- Japanese American Citizens League.
- Mexican American–Legal Defense League.
- National Alliance of Black Organizations.
- National Alliance of Spanish–Speaking People for Equality.
- National Alliance against Racist and Political Repression.

The chief of police should be prepared to deal with these organizations. It is essential that a line of communications be kept open with each active chapter. This can be done by attending meetings, accepting speaking engagements, and possibly by becoming a member of various organizations.[59] One innovative chief dealt with interests groups and the community at large by having an open door policy that allowed anyone to see him without an appointment. This simple communications bridged the gap between the chief and members of the community.

Militant Groups

Militant activists and agitators can also be described as a pressure group. While there is considerable confusion about the goals or purposes of groups on the far left and right, they certainly have had an impact on our society that is proportionately far beyond their number. Alienated from society, members of such groups make unrealistic demands on our nation. The diverse elements of the far left, typified by the alienated young, expound a special understanding of America's problems; however, their only solution seems to be destruction rather than a resolution of the problem. Some of these radicals pose a special law enforcement problem because rhetoric has been replaced by destructive actions. Expressive activities of left-wing groups are not as frequent as they were several years ago, but they still remain a threat.

At the other end of the spectrum, the reactionary right-wingers have left a significant imprint on our Nation. In the last decade the Oklahoma City bombing brought into sharp focus such extremism These groups take positions that are anti-government, anti-tax, and anti-Semitic.[60] Normally, white supremacy is at the top of their agenda. Many of the organizations on the far right operate through political

59. IC/CMA, *op. cit.*, p. 38.

60. Klanwatch, *Two Years After: The Patriot Movement Since Oklahoma City,* Montgomery, AL, Projects of the Southern Poverty Law Center, 1997, pp. +1–45.

involvement within the established system. The preponderance of their activity is verbal and is protected by the First Amendment right of free speech. Other groups operate outside of the political process and become members of the militia or patriot movement. Many members of the militia believe that there will be open conflict with the federal government and in preparation for such a conflict they stockpile weapons and conduct paramilitary training.[61]

Figure 2–10

Domestic Militant Groups

Ku Klux Klan (KKK)	Posse Comitatus
Skinheads	White Knights of Liberty
New Order Knights	Covenant, Sword and Arm of
White Aryan Resistance	the Lord
Jewish Direct Action	Animal Liberation Front
The Order	EPB–Macheteros
Organization of Volunteers	Evan Mecham Eco–Terrorist
for the Puerto Rican	International Conspiracy
Revolution	Japanese Red Army
Earthy Night Action Group	Earth First

Special interest terrorism concerns itself with explicit interest resolution rather than far-reaching political change. They include groups attentive to animal rights, environmental issues, or Hawaiian independence. Through violent criminal activity these groups hope to change public attitudes toward specific issues as a result this distinguishes them from traditional law abiding interest groups. Consequently these groups will continue to be of interest to law enforcement agencies.

Justice System

As a part of the climate in which police administration operates, it must be noted that the police are a major component of the criminal justice system. Within the system, the police are in orbit with two other major agencies, the judiciary and correctional administration, in addition to a host of social service agencies, in a many-faceted and somewhat dubious approach to the clientele of the system—the criminal offender. The operational interdependence of the police, the judiciary and corrections involves impact, each on the other, and this must be taken into account in order to understand fully the total environment in which the police function. The courts have a definitive and crucial impact on law enforcement. Judges are definitely political. In many states, they must be elected. Governors appoint some and even if it is from a list of attorneys selected by the bar association it is, in reality, part of an well-orchestrated political system. Most selected candidates have the correct party affiliation or an acceptable legal philosophy.

---

61. Federal Bureau of Investigation, *Terrorism in the United States, 1996,* Washington, DC, Federal Bureau of Investigation, 1997, pp. 1–26.

Active involvement in politics is normally a prerequisite for appointment, as is knowing the right people. District Attorney's assume their position after running for election. In some instances they do not have to list a party affiliation, but the prosecutor's office is obviously an integral part of the political process. To campaign takes money, time and effort. In reality, other candidates seldom upset the incumbent district attorney. The position has also proven to be a stepping stone to the governor's office in many states. In recent years, candidates for the position of district attorney have engaged in "negative" campaigning. Mud slinging is the way to get to the top.

Traditionally, sheriffs have attained office via the elective process. Because of the political process, sheriffs believe they are more responsive to their constituency. In most counties the Sheriff can usually remain in office as long as desired. Unless there is a real scandal, the incumbent is elected time and again. This close political tie to the community can have negative consequences. In one county the sheriff allowed minority civilians access to criminal records. When this became known, it proved to be very embarrassing. The same sheriff had a policy of not booking celebrities when stopped for driving while intoxicated (DWI). This clearly reflected favoritism rather than treating everyone equally under the law.

Needless to say, the district attorney or the sheriff can be elected politically and still perform with great skill and equity. In would seem to be highly variable and depends upon the integrity of the incumbent. Professionalism can overcome the negatives that are part of the current political process. Within the justice system the heads of the major components are clearly political actors, and some assume a politically high profile. It is seldom possible for a chief or head of another component to remain totally aloof from politics. It is evident that political influences on the police are both external and internal in nature. The influence will vary from city to city and from state to state but it is readily apparent the police are not apolitical but are actually immersed in the political process.

Case Study

Assistant Chief Jerome Alexander

Jerome Alexander has been the Chief of Staff of the Oakdale Police Department for five years. In this position he is responsible for the daily operations of the police department and three deputy chiefs report directly to him. During the last three years he has been responsible for the implementation of community policing and the reorganization of the department. Internally there has been considerable opposition to these changes. The most vocal opposition was from the police union. During the last year opposition has waned as the result of extensive communications with all personnel and the creation of a number of tasks forces that have worked on the implementation program. The police union is concerned that the reorganization will weaken its power and has worked informally to impede the implementation of the reorganization.

So far a newsletter has been developed in order to enhance communications, monthly meetings have been set up with the police union, other meetings have been held with every major unit in the department, and Chief Alexander has instituted an open door police and meets with officers and civilians at their convenience. While this latter technique has been time consuming it is generally believed that it has defused a number of complaints and is definitely worth while. Currently one task force is working on criteria for the evaluation of personnel when the shift is made to community policing. Another task force is working on a new training curriculum, and the third on revising the departments management system.

The city has a population of 592,000 consisting of a number of differing ethnic groups. The most vocal group consists of Mexican–Americans. They have a strong interest in the development of job opportunity, and reducing conflict in neighborhoods. The city is a transportation hub for the area. It has a major railroad center, and a large airport. Additionally, the city has two major shopping centers and considerable light industry. The department has 781 sworn positions and 92 civilian positions. It has a major problem with illegal drugs, and auto theft. In recent years bank robberies have become more prevalent. The city has just purchased a new communications system that will enhance the department's ability to provide better services.

A relatively new city manager, who has been on the job for nine months, has a strong interest in community policing and has closely monitored the progress of the reorganization. Since his appointment he has contacted the chief of police several time each week about specific issues that are clearly operational issues rather than policy issues. During the last three months the city manager has bypassed the chief and brought his inquiries directly to Assistant Chief Alexander. This has created a difficult situation for Alexander and he feels very strongly that the city manager should deal directly with the chief.

What would be the first thing you would do? Why? Would you discuss the problem with the chief, the city manager or both? Why? If you were Alexander would you refuse to consult with the city manager? What are the implications of violating the chain of command? What are the political implications?

For Further Reading

Leonhard Felix Fuld, *Police Administration*, New York, Putnam, 1909, pp. 1–275.

In the first part of the twentieth century this author presented a very critical study of police organization in the United States. He was faultfinding of police commissions and boards. He followed a traditional management approach to the evaluation of police departments and suggested that it was absolutely necessary for a department to be headed by a strong executive. He identified numerous problems in American policing ranging from the elimination of non-police duties to the elimination of politics from police administration.

Anne Heinz, Herbert Jacob, and Robert L. Lineberry, Editors, *Crime in City Politics,* New York, Longman,1983, pp. 2–129.

In a study over a 31-year period the authors determined that in local politics law and order played a significant part in the governance of communities. The text describes how crime is an election issue year after year, and how politicians use crime issues to their advantage. Analyzes the political aspect of crime in major cities throughout the Nation and the allegiance and involvement of the police in the political process. Of special interest is the discussion of the importance of crime control to local politicians.

George L. Kelling and Mark H. Moore, *The Evolving Strategy of Policing,* Washington, DC, National Institute of Justice, November 1988, pp. 1–11.

Discusses the development of police management by dividing the history of policing into three distinctive eras: political, reform, and community policing. The political era is identified as one characterizing the police as having closed ties with the political process through the beginning of the nineteenth century. In the reform movement politics were rejected as the source of legitimacy and authorization. In the community policing era there has been a redefining of the major functions of the police with a consultative relationship with the members of the community.

Joseph F. Zimmerman, "The New England Town Meeting: Lawmaking by Assembled Voters," *The Municipal Yearbook—1998,* Washington, DC, International city/County Management Association, 1998, 32–41.

The author reviews the history of town meetings and how it assess issues under consideration. Consideration is also given to the attendance at town meeting and its impact on the democratic process. Some of these communities have adopted a budget committee that conducts a year-round study of town finances and problems and provides voters with the data needed to make informed decisions. Additionally, some communities have a planning board that advises the town on issues involving land use and zoning. The author suggests that this type of government has coped successfully with serious problems and should do so in the future.

Chapter 3

ADAPTIVE MANAGEMENT: Integrating the Individual Into the Organization

Learning Objectives

1. Describe why numerical strength is of importance to police administrators.
2. List the four key elements of adaptive management.
3. Define eustress.
4. Identify the three categories of goals for stress programs.
5. Write a short essay describing life changes at work.
6. List eight of the factors that create stress.
7. Describe the importance of integrity as an essential aspect of adaptive management.
8. Identify the fundamental elements of a philosophy of policing.
9. Distinguish between a goal and an objective.
10. List the strategic goals of the Sacramento Police Department.
11. Describe the goals of the Tucson Police Department crime prevention program.
12. Identify the elements of a positive view of conflict.
13. List the three types of conflict.
14. Write a short essay describing the different types of resolution techniques.
15. Describe the attributes of a healthy police organization.

For years police management was viewed as a necessary evil and was of little concern to the dynamic of the political process in municipal and state agencies. In response to changing social conditions and demands for more effective service police executives could no longer just occupy a position hoping that nothing would occur that might impact negatively on their pension. and eventual retirement. The history of police management is such that its development has followed the professionalization of management in private enterprise and public administration. Management has risen from a position of vagueness to a predominant location in our system of justice. It conditions and reconditions every police organization by transmitting value and meaning. It is a positive vehicle that arranges material and human resources into a configuration that directs all efforts toward goal attainment. To do less is to ignore the mandate for effective management. Above all laissez-faire management must be rejected. If results are to be attained, management must acknowledge the importance of the individual but at the same time, organizational goals must remain dominant. The reality is that the patrol officer has become the focal point of the organization and all staff services should be directed toward supporting line services and community policing efforts.

Positive management of the police organization is the only way that the absolute strength of—*the line* can be maximized to achieve departmental goals. The totality of this text is based on the concept of *adaptive management* stressing process theory. Management is viewed as a distinct on-going process including all activities focusing on the identification, refinement, and attainment of objectives by the effective application of resources. This definition is dynamic. It is uni-directional, allowing for a definitive application of process theory. Consequently it visualizes managing in terms of what managers actually do to be effective.[1]

Performance

In the march toward professionalization, most observers, including the police themselves on occasion, have overlooked *line performance* as the basic point of departure. This oversight has resulted in a loss of perspective and a general failure to recognize the relationship between organization and the attainment of police objectives. An accelerated professional tempo in the American police services requires the application of patterns of organization and administration based upon the dynamics of performance in field operations. Operating strength in the line merits acceptance as a controlling factor of high validity in the organization and administration of a police department. Referred to in the text as "line power," or "line capability," it concerns the quality and effectiveness of performance at the point in police organization where the delivery of police service is actually made—*the line.*

The line operations of a police department are directed toward the execution of plans in the field where contact is made with police objectives. Line performance is, therefore, the point at which the investment in organization and administration comes to a focus and it is at this point that the return on the expenditure of public funds for police service may be measured. Line performance is a product of the kind and amount of work performed in the effort to realize police objectives. The quality and quantity of power available in the line determine maximum work standards. Thus, line power is an expression of the competence exercised in the field operations of a department. It

1. Mervin Kohn, *Dynamic Managing,* Menlo Park, Cummings Publishing Co., 1977, p. 21.

is contingent upon the resources available to the enterprise (in terms of personnel and equipment) and the manner in which they are articulated through organization and leadership by following the process theory of management.

For many years the numerical strength of police departments has been a matter of acute concern to police administrators throughout the United States. The question has aroused a corresponding solicitude by municipal management and the average citizen (who obviously is interested in the amount and quality of police service that can be delivered to him as a taxpayer). It is apparent that police costs per capita have risen during the past decades to the point of causing serious concern. A major and continuing problem is the erosion of the numerical strength of line units because of the assignment of personnel to administrative and specialized organizational entities. In one state the departments with 100 or more sworn officers had from 57 to 92 percent of the officers assigned to patrol. One would have to question why so few are assigned to such as critical task in some of these larger departments.[2]

Budgetary constraints over the years indicate increases in the mere numerical strength of American police departments are not forthcoming hence the need for more effective managerial strategies. The universal appeal of past police administration (for more manpower) is changing to a demand for better manpower. The erroneous assumption that numerical strength is a commanding determinant insofar as crime rates are concerned, is going into the discard. Supporters of this fallacy contend that a high correlation exists between the numerical strength of a police organization and its criminal caseload, and point to the need for increased payroll expenditures. There is, however, a general failure to recognize the distinction between numerical strength and absolute strength. Line performance and the awareness of the importance of *the line* are essential ingredients of adaptive management.

The process approach provides a useful frame of reference and foundation for the theoretical analysis of police organization and management. This *must* be considered basic in a scientific approach to the problems of the police enterprise and their solution. It also brings into sharp focus the role of managerial functions that must be present in order to fuse life and purpose into the inanimate structure of organization, giving it thrust toward the achievement of the departmental mission, goals and objectives.

The hierarchical structure of a police organization is certainly not completely void of redeeming values. The concepts of principles of organization; organization by major purpose, and line and staff, are as

2. Brian A. Reaves and Andrew L. Goldberg, *Law Enforcement Management and Administrative Statistics, 1997: Data for Individual State and Lo-* *cal Agencies with 100 or More Officers,* Washington, DC, Office of Justice Programs, 1999, p. 121.

viable in police organizations today as they were In the past thirty years. If tasks are to be accomplished, it must be through such time-honored managerial processes as organizing, planning, directing and controlling. Humanism as a *panacea* for police management must be rejected, but the police executive should create an adaptive organizational climate. This should be a strategy directing organizational efforts toward managing rather than eliminating organizational conflict. Efforts to totally eliminate conflict have generally proven to be ineffective.

Elements of Adaptive Management

Adaptive management accepts conflict as a normal consequence of the collective pursuit of organizational goals. It is an integrative management style based upon an acceptance of bureaucratic organization, with an awareness of its good and bad features including the acknowledgment that the organization cannot meet all employee needs. Such a managerial style presupposes that the individual will adjust to the organization for varying reasons.

Central to the concept of *adaptive management* is the belief that traditionalism in management does not have to be dehumanizing and detrimental to police employees. At the same time, the importance of the individual must be acknowledged for management is the act of working with and through individuals and groups to attain organizational goals. Adaptive management has six fundamental elements as indicated in figure 3–1. Goals are used as the unifying force directing and guiding all organizational activities.

Figure 3–1
Fundamental Elements of Adaptive Management
Goal Orientation Conflict Management Eustress Philosophical Foundation Integrity Importance of the Individual

Eustress (positive stress) is utilized as a means of assimilating the individual into the organization, and conflict management becomes the process by which integration is reinforced. This concept is graphically illustrated in figure 3–2. A unific motivational model has been identified as positive stress. First it must be acknowledged that conflict in an organization is not necessarily bad. A certain degree of stress, based upon competing value structures between the individual and the organization, can in many instances provide a working environment leading to greater attainment of organizational goals. With our limited knowledge of human behavior it would undoubtedly be best to accept the diversity of personalities in police organizations as a given, and work toward creating an organizational climate acknowledging different orientations to work. Stress becomes the bond integrating the individual into the organization.

Eustress

Organizationally induced stress is a positive approach to the achievement of goals and provides for the accommodation of adjusted individual goals. Stress is perceived as the nonspecific response of the body to any demand placed upon it.[3] It is understandable from this definition that stress can be either pleasant or unpleasant. Hans Selye, the father of stress, has coined the word *eustress* meaning "good stress."[4] This approach presupposed that an individual can and must take a positive view of various life events. One's attitude can determine whether an experience is perceived as pleasant or unpleasant. Adopting a positive attitude can convert negative stress into *eustress,* the result being a gratifying life style and positive feelings about the work environment.[5] Eustress can only be viewed as the opposite of unpleasant stress and a normal process of the body's functioning—an essential ingredient of living.[6] This is a key process where in one should always look at the rewards to be gained from life events. It is very easy to take the few that an event is negative, and it takes a great deal of concentration to look at the positive aspect of any event. Cynicism seems to be a by product of much of police work.[7]

3. Hans Selye, *Stress Without Distress,* New York, J.B. Lippincott Company 1975, p. 14.

4. Laurence Cherry, "On The Real Benefit of Eustress," *Psychology Today,* March 1978, Vol. 11, No. 2, p. 63.

5. *Ibid.*

6. Karl Albrecht, *Stress and the Manager,* Englewood Cliffs, NJ, Prentice–Hall, 1979, p. 60.

7. Ellen Kirschman, "Organizational Stress–Looking for Love in All the Wrong Places," *The Police Chief,* October 1998, Vol. LXV, No. 10, pp. 127–134.

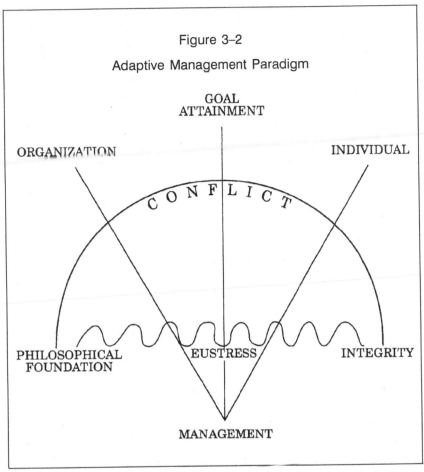

Figure 3–2

Adaptive Management Paradigm

Stress can definitely be harmful, but it can also be helpful, in fact—essential to normal life. Total freedom from stress, according to Selye, can only come in death. In fact, he perceived stress as the "spice of life."[8] Adaptive management utilizes stress as a means of dealing with employee response to the ecology of the organization. Every effort is made to create a social environment based on an awareness of employee reaction to the organization. Employee attitudes and morale are considered. Thus the quality of working life becomes the central theme.[9] Every individual in the organization has a different amount of adaptation energy [10]and organizationally oriented departments can accommodate individual stress levels.

Effective stress programs have to be tailored to the needs and characteristics of a particular police department. The characteristics of stress programs vary considerably. The mission statements of stress

8.   Selye, *op. cit.,* p. 83.
9.   Albrecht, *op. cit.,* p. 135.
10.   Selye, *op. cit.,* p. 78.

programs can be divided into three categories of goals:
- Individual.
- Organizational.
- Community.

Goals that are individual in orientation articulate programs designed to provide help and assist troubled officers. Other orientations vary to include

That of the Behavioral Science Unit of the Tucson Police Department that defines two goals for its stress management program. The primary goal is to help the Chief of Police achieve the community mission of "protecting and serving." The unit also provides a range of rehabilitative services to police officers. Another variation is the Rochester Police Department that has a stress program with the stated goal of providing for organizational readiness.[11] Typical of the trend in this field is the criteria set forth for selecting a stress program provider (See figure 3–3).

Figure 3–3
Guidelines For Selecting a Stress
Program Provider

Administrators can consider taking the following precautions in making the selection of a stress program provider:

- Interview each possible candidate.
- Visit each provider's office to ensure that it is accessible, private, and comfortable.
- Look for staff qualifications such as professional credentials, license to practice, years of experience, and experience with law enforcement agencies.
- Ask for a proposed program budget and explanation of costs.
- Ask to see the provider's malpractice insurance papers.
- Ask for and check references.
- Ask for a detailed account of
  - what services the individual or group ill provide.
  - how often clients will be able to use these services.
  - Whether the provider or a backup will be available 24 hours a day and at critical incident scenes.
  - Where services will be provided.
  - How program use will be encouraged.
  - What referral methods will be used.
  - How the provider will protect client confidentiality.
  - How the provider will maintain program records and assess program effect.
  - How the provider will meet special departmental needs.

Source: Peter Finn and Julie Esselman Tomz, *Developing a Law Enforcement Stress Program for Officers and Their Families,* Washington, DC, Office of Justice Programs, March 1997, p. 43.

An awareness of the consequences of stress is important to the health of every officer and the quality of working life within the

11. *Ibid,* p. 30.

organization. It is important to understand that an event or situation does not cause stress, but how we mentally react to any given event. Stress programs must acknowledge that there is a strong relationship between the amount of change in people's lives and their risk of injury and illness. The more change in one's life the greater the amount of energy, physical and mental, needed to adapt to the change. Within the work environment when an unplanned change occurs (e.g., change of assignment) one can choose to overreact or the change can be looked upon positively and taken in stride by "rolling with the punch."[12]

If it is impossible to fight or flee from a problem, consider flowing with it. Experts have concluded that there are two ways to remove distress in ones life. One way is to change your surroundings, your time schedule, or your activities. An officer can ask for a change of assignment, a different shift or request special training as a means of preparing for a special assignment. In other words "The other way is to allow pleasant demands to be placed upon the body rather than unpleasant demands. Do something different, get out of the rut." One cannot avoid stress altogether, but it is possible for one to learn how to keep distress to a minimum.[13] Management should acknowledge that what is stressful for one employee might not be stressful for another. One employee can react to any isolated event by "flipping out" and another views all of the positive aspects of the event and take everything in stride without becoming truculent. Stress is not abstract it is created by each of us. Stress is dependent upon how one interprets situations and how one relates to the environment around them.

This tells management that if ones mind creates stress then the mind can decrease stress. If management is instituting a major policy change it should consider carefully the potential impact of the policy change. During the planning changes for the proposed change as many people as possible should be involved in the decision-making process so as to reduce the stress that will be created by the change.[14] In other words apply the adaptive management process of participative interaction. Another important consideration is that too little stress can really create boredom on the job consequently it can be as unproductive as too much stress. The goal is to have an ideal level of stress that stimulates life so as to maximize health, happiness, and productivity. Figure 3–4 lists work life events created by change that management must acknowledge and that each worker must cope with from the above list it can be readily seen that some life changes will prove to be more stressful than others are. Certainty to be fired is a greater live change than to be promoted. Or to be transferred is less stressful than

12. Hope, *Adapting to Stress—Start Taking Charge*, Kalamazoo, MI, Hope Publications. 1998, p.5.

13. The Hope Heart Institute, *Stress–Simple Steps to end Distress*, Seattle, WA, The Hope Heart Institute, 1998, p. 1.

14. Jennifer M. Brown and Elizabeth A. Campbell, *Stress and Policing: Sources and Strategies,* New York, John Wiley & Sons, 1994, pp. 59–77.

to be changed to a new type of work. Changes in the workplace can be compounded by life changes occurring in ones personal life such as well-being, social, economic or family. A person's attitude toward work appears to be a critical factor in good health. An individual who enjoys work is less likely to suffer health problems than someone who does not work very hard and dislikes their work.

Figure 3–4
Life Changes At Work

- Change to a new type of work.
- Change in work hours/conditions.
- Change in your responsibilities at work.
  more responsibilities.
  fewer responsibilities.
  promotion.
  demotion.
  transfer.
- Troubles at work.
  with your supervisor.
  with co-workers.
  with persons under your supervision.
  other work troubles.
- Major organizational adjustment.
- Retirement.
- Loss of Job.
  laid off.
  fired.
- Correspondence course to help in your work.

Source: Modified from Hope, Adapting to Stress–Start Taking Charge, Kalamazoo, MI, Hope Publications, 1998, p. 5.

Management can build self-confidence in its employees by creating an atmosphere where employees are allowed to take charge. Employees must be considered as valuable and worthy of the respect of others. They should be encouraged to accept new challenges and when and if there are temporary setbacks they should be viewed as stepping stones to strengthen character and resolve. Officers should be taught to think of problems as opportunities in disguise. Adaptive management creates a working environment wherein negative consequences of any situation are minimized and the concern is for what should have been done rather than what could have been done. Every event or situation should be viewed as part of a learning process and an action plan should be developed that deal with each problem.[15] Occupational stressors abound in the workplace of everyone and law enforcement is definitely no exception. Management must constantly deal with a Wide range of work time situations that require constant attention. These are listed in figure 3–5.

15. *Ibid,* pp. 1–27.

Figure 3–5

Factors That Create Stress

- The feeling that one does not have much control over the situation at work.
- Close supervision.
- Pressures created by workload.
- Repetitive and routine duties.
- Working as a member of a team.
- Work dull and unchallenging.
- Working under pressure.
- Limited opportunity to be creative.
- Work has a tremendous social value.
- Work shows nothing tangible for your efforts.
- Work requires perfection and accuracy.

Source: Modified from Hope, *Adapting to Stress–Start Taking Charge,* Kalamazoo, MI, Hope Publications, 1998, p. 5.

Adaptive management reacts to the stress syndrome by creating a climate fostering and maximizing individual control over job activities and outputs.[16] One of the modifiers of this process is the adaptation of the individual to the necessity of working for the attainment of organizational goals. The other is the need for managers within the police system to change from a power orientation to a participative managerial style. This is a key interrelationship predicated on a continuing adjustment between the individual and management. It is never a static process but dynamic and responsive to a changing organizational culture.

Philosophical Foundation

Adaptive management becomes truly functional when the police develop and implement programs based on a philosophy firmly imbedded in a democratic value system. All activities in which a department engages must be limited to those protecting and extending the rights guaranteed to each citizen by the Constitution of the United States. A police department should have a departmental statement of philosophy that guides the operations of the agency. One police executive set forth a comprehensive statement of policing philosophy as set forth in figure 3–6.

Figure 3–6

Philosophy of Policing

The Police Department prides itself in serving all people within its community by meeting by meeting their requirements for policing in a free and fluid society. The ability to do so requires the police department to be constantly aware of the needs of those they serve and to be accountable to them, yet remain independent from unsavory influence.

---

16. Richard H. Davis, editor, *Stress and the Organization,* Los Angeles, The University of Southern California Press, 1979, p. 13.

Police service is characterized by a commitment to safeguard lives and property, maintaining the attributes of positive life, and insuring that constitutional rights are preserved. This responsibility requires the primary emphasis of our efforts be directed toward the prevention of criminality, the identification and apprehension of those who violate the rights of others, and the preservation of peace. Last— but not least the police must provide other desired municipal police services in order to assist those in need. Quality of life in the neighborhoods of cities is extremely important.

We believe those who knowingly commit criminal acts with wanton disregard for the rights of others should be prosecuted to the fullest extent of the law. However, if mitigating circumstances are such that counseling, diversion, or referral to other resources would accomplish the mission of crime prevention, then these alternatives should be considered. In essence, the "letter of the law" should be followed for those who knowingly and deliberately flaunt society's legal statutes while the "spirit of the law" should remain as the basic criteria for carrying out the police mission.

All in all, we recognize we must provide a wide range of public service, which requires preparedness, endurance, bravery, understanding, compassion, and a desire to serve, in addition to the unyielding pursuit to curtail the criminal element and improve the quality of life. Also, in rendering decisions, which affect police, operations, we must consider what is best for the community over the desires of the Department and its individual members.

Source: Gary E. Brown, Chief of Police, *Philosophy of the San Clement Police Department*, ND, mimeographed.

Such a philosophical statement provides a base for policing a democracy. It takes a constant adjustment and readjustment to the events that confront a police department. A sordid crime, the kidnapping of a young person or a case of child abuse can tighten the emotional string of even the hardest administrator or line officer. While the crises of life tend to blunt emotional response it seems that there is always some event that penetrates to one's soul. Notwithstanding our Nation expects a professional response from the police in every conceivable situation.[17] It also demands a commitment to the community. In recent years more and more police departments are following the "broken widows" theory that provides for the strict enforcement of minor street crimes such as public drunkenness makes the streets available to law-abiding citizens.[18] All of this sets the framework for improving the quality of life in a community. Lastly, this philosophical statement clearly acknowledges the interrelationship between the department, the community and each departmental member.

Integrity

When adaptive management is functional the chances for organizational success are greatly increased. This is especially true when

17. Patrick J. Solar, "Changing Organizational Culture–Monitoring and Developing Professional Officer Skills," *Law And Order,* May 1998, Vol. 46, No. 5, pp. 22–27.

18. James Q. Wilson, and George L. Kelling, "Broken Windows: The Police and Neighborhood Safety," *Atlantic Monthly*, 1982, Vol. 249, 29–38.

integrity is considered to be a key value of the organization. Integrity prevails when every individual in the organization supports organizational changes that allow for the implementation of adaptive management. A manager under this system must be a good communicator, support the concept that everyone should be a team player, and should endorse the involvement of everyone in the problem-solving process. When employees are given information needed in the decision-making process and supported by a facilitative organizational culture effective decision-making will be enhanced and the overall operation will prove to be more viable. Adaptive management allows for a total awareness of individual abilities, level of knowledge, and varying attitudes and opinions. All of this can prove to be a demanding process, but it is predicated upon the necessity of management maintaining a leadership role that is positive and forthright. Individuals within the organization respond to this because they become fully aware of the fact that the decision making process is predicated on absolute organizational integrity.

Adaptive management can only come into existence when the organization is committed to a participatory program. This means the quasi-military organization of the traditional police department must be relegated to the past and shared decision-making must prevail. Successful implementation is possible when communications are maximized and the reality of true participation becomes apparent. Employees must be informed and fully aware of contemplated changes. Additionally, officers should be involved in the preparation of plans for implementation. Participation should occur at the earliest possible stages of the planning process. At this time they should be given information on the total process. This should occur before employees are assigned to taskforces, and every officer should be completely aware of organizational goals. It is also essential that employees receive training in the skills needed to guarantee success. This includes leadership and conflict resolution training. Such a transition cannot be mandated by executive fiat it requires a continuing flow of information through every possible media to include the dissemination of information at rollcall, and the utilization of newsletters and bulletins. A truly innovative adaptive management program has numerous values. A key value is integrity. It is a yardstick for trust, competence, professionalism, and confidence. Deep within every human being is the subconscious ability to interpret behavior and events as a mark of integrity or a violation of trust. Integrity provides a basis for trust between the officer-officer relationship and the officer-supervisor relationship. When trust is exists within an organization it engenders loyalty and truthfulness. As a core value integrity is an essential ingredient of adaptive management.[19]

19. Stephen J. Gaffigan, and Phyllis P. McDonald, *Police Integrity: Public Service with Honor,* Washington, DC, National Institute of Justice, January 1997, pp. 1–14.

Goals

The police departments of this nation are responsible for performing a multitude of tasks, many of which include functions other than the enforcement of criminal law. After a careful analysis of the concept of police intervention, this pattern of functional response to varying community needs has evolved over the years with limited benefit. Consequently, law enforcement departments have reacted to immediate community needs, see figure 3–7. Through the years, they have even accepted responsibility for numerous activities and tasks—such as tax collection ambulance services, and animal control.

Figure 3–7

Standard 1–2.2: Major Current Responsibilities of the Police

In assessing appropriate objectives and priorities for police service, local communities should initially recognize that most police agencies are currently given responsibility, by design or default, to:
(a) identify criminal offenders and criminal activity and, where appropriate, to apprehend offenders and participate in subsequent court proceedings;
(b) reduce the opportunities for the commission of some crimes through preventive patrol and other measures;
(c) aid individuals who are in danger of physical harm;
(d) protect constitutional guarantees;
(e) facilitate the movement of people and vehicles;
(f) assist those who cannot care for themselves;
(g) resolve conflict;
(h) identify problems that are potentially serious law enforcement or governmental problems.
(i) create and maintain a feeling of security in the community;
(j) promote and preserve civil order; and
(k) To provide other services on an emergency basis.

Source: The American Bar Association, (1980), ABA Standards for Criminal Justice, Second Edition, "Standard 1–2.2: Major Current Responsibilities of Police,: Volume 1, Chapter: *The Urban Police Function.*" *Copyright © 1980,* American Bar Association. Reprinted by permission, all rights reserved.

In recent years the surge of criminal activity, the occurrence of extended order-maintenance situations, and the need for resolving conflict has resulted in community pressures to extend the range of police services. Accordingly, there is an apparent need to identify and designate priorities to police responsibilities. Thus the basic beliefs and value system becomes the foundation for the setting of organizational goals, the police policy-makers must take into account the interacting modifiers affecting the characteristics of the community.[20] One of these problems is crime as modified by the factors of politics, and social, economic and psychological conditions. In addition, there is a strong external environment influencing the police organization including other criminal justice agencies such as probation, parole, courts, district attorney, defense attorney and law enforcement agencies. Each of

20. Robert Goodall, "Management by Objectives, A Conceptual Application for the Police," *The Police Journal,* April 1974, Vol. XLVIII, No. 2, p. 180.

these criminal justice agencies affects the police performance by their own policies, procedures, resources, and operations. An analysis of the internal state of the agency itself is essential, in order to pinpoint modifiers such as style, philosophy, mission, and organizational resources. All of these factors influence, to a varying degree, the creation of an optimal objective model that emphasizes organizational effectiveness and allows for the attainment of objectives. Such a model provides a frame of reference for maximal organizational response as well as opportunity for self-actualization.

The establishment and accomplishment of goals and objectives follow such similar paths that the words "goal" and "objective" are often interchanged. Authorities generally agree that "goal" is a more general term than "objective":

Goal—A statement of broad direction, general purpose or intent.

Objective—A desired accomplishment which can be measured within a given time frame and under specifiable conditions.

Fundamental to the establishment of all goals and objectives is a perception of the problems encountered or anticipated by the agency. Clear definition and careful analysis of the factors generating the problem may clearly indicate possible solutions and suggest appropriate goals and objectives. On the other hand, the failure to perceive or to understand a problem may lead to the establishment of goals or objectives that could be nonproductive or even counter-productive.[21]

Neither the police chief executive nor the unit commander can, alone, establish goals and objectives. All employees within the agency, particularly employees at the executive level, can contribute to the understanding of the problem. These employees have face-to-face contact with members of the community and are coping with problems in the field. They, in turn, will understand the problems to be met only through contact and discussion of the problems with members of the community. Obtaining input from within the agency requires an atmosphere that encourages all employees, regardless of rank, to submit ideas. Such an atmosphere must be genuine; it must start at the top and permeate the entire agency. Employees should understand that their evaluation of the problem, their analysis of cause, and their suggestions of possible solutions are all needed. One major police agency has formalized this process by establishing task forces composed of personnel of all ranks, with emphasis on the lower ranks, to work out solutions to problems in certain areas. The agency has succeeded in creating the desired atmosphere.[22]

Other agencies of government often are a good source of ideas and assistance, as are community and service organizations. In order to

21. National Advisory Commission on Criminal Justice Standards and Goals, *Police* (Washington: U.S. Government Printing Office, 1973, pp. 49–50).

22. *Ibid.*, p. 50.

obtain a response that is representative of the community, the police agency should take care to solicit input from private as well as official sources. Additionally, and of utmost importance, is the requirement set out in the first standard of this report that the goals and objectives of the police department must be directed by the policies of the governing body that provide formal authority for the police function.

Community meetings can be valuable for providing private input, although in some cases there is a disappointingly small number of people involved in community activity. Furthermore, those responding have not always been representative of the community, and in some cases response from community meetings does not always reach the top levels of the police agency. The last is always a risk if command personnel do not attend the community meetings.

Notwithstanding the difficulties of obtaining community input, it must be done because the fundamental purpose of law enforcement is *service* to the public through crime prevention and improving the quality of life this cannot be accomplished without public support. One police agency expresses this position as indicated in figure 3–8.

Figure 3–8

Strategic Goals of the Sacramento
Police Department

- To focus department resources on the detection and apprehension of criminals and to assist in their prosecution and control.
- To manage the traffic flow in our City streets so that we may lessen vehicle collisions that result in fatalities, personal injuries, and property damage.
- To educate Sacramento's citizens in crime prevention techniques and services that can be useful self-crime fighting tools.
- To work in partnership with the entire community to resolve crime-related problems in neighborhoods.
- To implement an on going strategic planning process that will assist the Department in managing its future.
- To provide a work environment that is conducive to employee growth and development while ensuring the provision of high quality, efficient, and cost effective services.
- With concern and compassion, continue to improve the quality of service we deliver to victims and witnesses of crime.

Source: Sacramento Police Department, *Strategic Goals–FY 1994–FY 2003,* Sacramento, CA, November 11, 1998, http://www.sacpd.org/strategic_goals.html.

The identification of goals for a police agency should not be taken lightly and can prove to be a time-consuming process when maximum input is sought from all of the external forces and from the internal organizational environment. An examination of each principal police goal must identify the actual nature of the activities and the basis for police intervention.

To identify criminal offenders and criminal activity and, where appropriate, to apprehend offenders and participate in

later court proceedings. This specific goal is truly traditional in nature and constitute what many justice scholars would argue is the most consequential contribution to public order that is the specific control of conduct prohibited by appropriate legislative entities. It involves the identification of individuals suspected of committing a criminal transgression and processing them through the justice system. It also involves the investigative process that involves interviewing or interrogating subjects, e.g. victims, witnesses, and suspects. Additionally, it includes the collection, processing and analysis of physical evidence, and taking into custody those responsible for the commission of an offense. Lastly it involves the preparation of the case for presentation in court. A considerable amount of police work involves responding to information provided by citizens advising that a crime has occurred. It is clearly not a proactive process. The police also become involved in the investigation of a whole range of criminal activities committed over a period of time without an official agency becoming aware of it. This is true, for example, of offenses such as fraud, loan sharking, environmental crimes, computer crimes, and fraudulent business practices. In some instances, criminal actions are only investigated after a complaint is filed. On the other hand, because of political or social pressures, the police have created investigative units to investigate certain crime. This has occurred in areas such as repeat offenders, domestic violence, missing children, bias-related, and environmental crimes.[23]

To reduce the opportunities for the commission of some crimes through preventive patrol and other measures. This goal has is fast becoming highly significant for law enforcement agencies. This is especially true with the increasing emphasis by more and more departments as they implement a community-policing mode. Many years ago the late Chief of Police of Berkeley, California, August Vollmer, the father of modern police administration, stated, "I have spent my life enforcing the law. It is a stupid procedure and will never succeed until supplemented by preventive measures." [24]With a large portion of police resources devoted to the enforcement function, the American people are slowly becoming aware of its being a futile approach to a significant social problem. Enforcement has definitely been given a fair trial! Police agencies are becoming increasingly involved in the area of prevention as noted by the fact that in one recent survey of police departments, employing 100 or more officers, 76 percent were found to have specialized units dealing with community crime prevention. [25]

23. Brian A. Reaves, and Andrew L. Goldberg, *Law Enforcement Management and Administrative Statistics, 1997, Data for Individual State and Local Agencies with 100 or more Officers,* Washington, DC, Office of Justice Programs, 1999, pp. 264–293.

24. August Vollmer, *Community Coordination,* Berkeley, Coordinating Councils, Inc. 1939, pp. 1–32.

25. Reaves and Goldberg, op. cit., p. xix.

Prevention programs vary considerably agency to agency but generally considerable effort is given to informational activities and prevention seminars. During one fiscal year one police department listed the following goals for its partnership with the community:

- Placing officers in local middle schools and around high schools to reinforce community values, to act as role models for youth, and to deter gang-related or other inappropriate behaviors.

- Provide Gang Resistance Education And Training (G.R.E.A.T.) To elementary school children to reduce gang enrollment as the children become adolescents.

- Working with schools to share information about potential problems.

- Working collaboratively with social service agencies to stop the cycle of domestic violence within families.

- Investigating crime to identify, prosecute and penalize those who are threatening families and young people.[26]

For years most agencies have operated a variety of programs to include Neighborhood watch, operation identification, security surveys, child abuse prevention, rape prevention, police athletic leagues and child fingerprinting. One of the most popular programs is operation D.A.R.E. (drug abuse resistance program). This is true in spite of the fact that evaluation of the program indicates that it is effective for a short period of time but it does not have a lasting impact. [27]

To aid individuals who are in danger of physical harm. The role of the police in this area is unique, and clearly distinctive. It in no way conflicts with other objectives. The police have a legal mandate to protect members of society. This involves a wide range of activities from assisting those in eminent danger, to rescuing individuals from burning buildings, to securing hazardous substance areas. It also includes rescuing a drowning person, controlling traffic at the scene of an accident, and preventing someone from committing suicide. Additionally the police play a major role during natural disasters. Fires, floods, tornadoes, and earthquakes ravage various sections of our nation frequently. The recent tornadoes in Oklahoma and Kansas with the loss of many lives clearly illustrates the extraordinary demands that can be placed on law enforcement during major disasters.

To protect constitutional rights. As public officials, police officers, at the time of their appointment take an oath to uphold the Constitution of the United States and the Constitution and laws in their state of employment. In the past, many police officers have

26. City of Tucson, *Adopted Budget, Operating Detail, Fiscal Year 1998–99* Volume II, Tucson, AZ, 1998, p. 146.

27. Arthur G. Sharp, "Is DARE a Sacred Lamb?" *Law and Order*, April *1998*, Vol. 46, No. 4, pp. 42–50, and Eamon Clifford, "Taking a Bite Out of Crime–Why Not More Cops in Clown Suits," *Law and Order*, April 1998, Vol. 46, No. 4., p. 51.

objected to court decisions curbing or restricting their powers to deal with crime and offenders. This has left them feeling the Constitution and the Bill of Rights served to protect the offender at the expense of society.

With the beginning of civil disobedience and major disturbances caused by the Vietnam conflict, the police have revised the way they deal with such events. Today the police protect the constitutional rights of citizens of every spectrum of our society. Currently, in various cities throughout the nation, the police are protecting the rights of the homeless to sit-in and demonstrate. They also protect the rights of homosexuals, to advocate their rights, and even such a disparate group as the Ku Klux Klan (KKK), to the objections of numerous special interest groups. They are also protecting those who support and oppose abortion, and law enforcement agencies are making increasing use of court orders and injunctions to maintain order and protect the rights of demonstrators. The following Figure describes the action taken in the Madesen case by a State court. The decision prohibited anti-abortion protesters from demonstrating in certain places and in certain ways outside of an abortion clinic.

Figure 3–9

Injunction Prohibiting Anti–Abortion Protestors

Protestors are prohibited from the following:

- Demonstrating at, all times, within 36 feet of the clinic's property line.
- Singing, chanting, whistling, shouting, yelling, using sound amplification equipment or other sounds or images observable to or within earshot of the patients inside the clinic during certain times and during surgical procedures.
- Approaching at all times, any person seeking services of the clinic, unless the person indicated a desire to communicate by approaching the protestors.
- Approaching, demonstrating, or using sound equipment, at all times, within 300 feet of the residences of clinic staff.

Source: William U. McCormick, "Supreme Court Cases 1993–1994 Term," *FBI Law Enforcement Bulletin,* October, October 1994, Vol. 63, No. 10, pp. 27–32.

During the review of this case, the Supreme Court of the United States in Madesen v. Women's Health Center, Inc., 114 S. Ct. 2516 (1994) held that the State had significant government interests in imposing the injunction. It also felt there was a need to protect women's freedom to seek lawful medical services, ensuring public safety and order, providing for the free flow of traffic, and promoting residential safety. Overall the Court accepted the primary content of the injunction while rejecting some specifics. The causes change over the years, and the police are becoming increasingly aware of the need to take a positive role in ensuring every citizen constitutional rights are fully protected. In 1998 a federal court responding to a case filed under the Racketeer Influenced and Corrupt Organizations Act (RICO) found that anti-abortion protest organizers used threats and violence to shut down clinics and the abortion organizers were ordered to pay a fine 0f $258,000 in a class-action suit [28]

To facilitate the movement of people and vehicles. In urban America, the ability to move freely and easily from one location to another is an objective few persons are accomplishing. For many years the police and traffic engineers have played an important part in creating a system allowing everyone to move freely and as rapidly as possible from one part of a community to another. Traffic units created in many cities have performed such activities as directing traffic, investigating accidents, and enforcing the traffic code, promoting safety, regulating parking, and controlling pedestrians.

In some cities police administrators, concerned with facilitating the movement of people and vehicles, have assigned a substantial portion of police resources to traffic units. Unfortunately this has reduced the ability of the agency to accomplish other goals and care must be taken to balance the allocation of resources against community needs. The police have a dominant role in regulating traffic by utilizing motor vehicle codes specifying in minute detail, the rules of the road. A majority of larger law enforcement agencies maintain computerized files on traffic citations, accidents, stolen vehicles, and vehicle registration. Sixty-six percent of agencies with 100 or more officers have created special units to deal with drunken drivers.[29]

To accomplish it's mission the South Traffic Division of the Los Angeles Police Department created several goals to include:

- Reduce the year-to-date hit-and-run traffic collisions by 5%.

- Reduce the year-to-date number of fatalities and injuries suffered in traffic collisions by 10%.

- Reduce the year-to-date frequency of driving under the influence (DUI) related traffic collisions by 15%.

- Maintain an overall clearance rate for hit-and-run crimes by 58%.[30]

In recent years another aspect of this goal has entered the picture and that is carjackings. During a four year period about 49,000 completed or attempted nonfatal carjackings took place. In about one-half of the incidents the offender was successful in taking the victim's motor

28. *Arizona Daily Star,* "Jury Invokes Mob Law in Dealing Major Loss to Abortion Protestors," Tuesday, April 21, 1998, 4A.

29. *Ibid.,* pp. 229–239.

30. Los Angeles Police Department, *South Traffic Mission Statement and*

Goals, City of Los Angeles, Los Angeles Police Department, 2/9/99. p. 1. http://www.lapdonline.org/community/op_south_bureau/ south_traffic_division/south_traffic_4.htm2/9/99.

vehicle. In these cases about seven out of ten completed carjackings involved firearms. During each of the four years studied U.S. attorneys filed an average of 229 carjacking cases in U.S. district courts.[31]

To help those who cannot care for themselves. Police officers constantly come into contact with those who need some type of aid. The aged, the impaired, the physically disabled, the youthful, the mentally ill, alcoholics, and those addicted to drugs, are examples of those who constantly come to the attention of the police. Frequently, the initial involvement is the consequence of that person's criminal offense such as public intoxication or trespassing. It also includes attempted suicide or traffic violations. Since the police are readily available 24 hours a day, they assume (in many instances) certain tasks simply because they are the only governmental agent available.

In some cities when the temperature reaches a level close to freezing, a special program becomes operational and the police transport the homeless to shelters. They also remove the inebriated from the streets so they will not freeze to death. In addition, the police eliminate individuals from the street who engage in behavior that can prove to be harmful to themselves or others. This is especially true of individuals who exhibit signs of serious mental disorder. The police are becoming a major mental health resource, perhaps even more so in recent years as a result of deinstitutionalization. Generally, police officers do not rely excessively on conventional mental health resources and arrests are relatively rare. Informal dispositions prove to be the disposition of choice. Most police officers, based on prior experience, know precisely how to respond in order to soothe the mentally disoriented person without medication or hospitalization. Police officers have and will continue to play a pivotal role in the mental health process.[32]

A unique approach to proving assistance to those in need is the Sunshine Division of the Portland Police Bureau. This unit headed by a police sergeant and a program coordinator has helped needy families with emergency food and clothing for 73 years. The $400,000 per year budget and all food and clothing are contributed by citizens and businesses. The division is a non-profit organization, 501 c 3, and all donations are tax deductible.[33]

To resolve conflict. Many police officers spend more time resolving conflict and disputes than they spend in enforcing the criminal law. While the frequency will vary from community to community, the types of conflict include family disputes, conflict between neighbors, barking dogs, landlord and tenant disputes and disagreements between merchants and customers. Formerly termed nuisance calls the police are

---

31. Patsy Klaus, *Carjackings in the United States, 1992–1996,* Special Report, Washington, DC, Bureau of Justice Statistics, March 1999, pp. 1–4.

32. Linda A. Teplin, *Keeping the Peace: Parameters of Police Discretion in Relation to the Mentally Ill,* Washington, DC, National Institute of Justice, 1986, pp.1–37.

33. Wayne Kuechler, Sergeant, *Sunshine Division,* Portland, OR, Portland Police Department, 11/6/98. pp. 1–2. http://www.teleport.com/ppssd/.

becoming increasingly aware that handling these calls in a professional manner is essential to the maintenance of order in the community. Of genuine concern is, many of these incidents can escalate into violent confrontations. For many years some police departments ignored family conflict. Now however, many police officers receive special training in crisis intervention counseling. In agencies with more than 100 or more officers 63 percent have created specialized domestic violence units.[34] Increasingly, the police are becoming a significant part of a domestic violence response team by working with other agencies. This team can include a social worker, a member of the clergy, shelter personnel, and mental health experts.[35] These teams have functioned successfully when a program protects the victim and helps them to cope with the situation. When prosecution proves necessary members of the team help the victim to deal with the justice system. In recent years the police have acknowledged the problem of domestic violence within its own ranks, and have moved to aggressively investigate incidents of domestic violence by police officers.[36]

To identify potentially serious law enforcement or governmental problems. The police are in an excellent position to identify problems as they occur and bring them to the attention of the appropriate governmental entity. It is quite common for legislative units to require police departments to report broken street lights, holes in streets, defective sidewalks, leaking water mains, shrubs obscuring traffic signs, inoperative or malfunctioning traffic lights, and toxic emissions. In recent years the police have participated in the investigation of environmental cases. This has involved offenses such as improper dumping, or disposal of solid hazardous, medical/infectious or other wastes, and improper hauling/transportation of wastes.[37]

The police also report any situation impacting negatively on the welfare and safety of the community. The police have found they are in an excellent position to identify the problems plaguing the community. They can then work for the resolution of the problem by referring complaints to the appropriate agency and, when appropriate, aid in problem resolution. One department takes the position that they must become social activists and act as social change agents in order to foster positive change resulting in a better living environment.[38] It is increasingly common for officers to work with representatives from a variety of city agencies and offices. It can include officials from planning, fire,

34. Reeves and Smith, *Ibid.*

35. John A. Brown, Peter C. Unsinger, and Harry W. More, *Law Enforcement and Social Welfare: The Emergency Response,* Springfield, IL, Charles C. Thomas, 1992, p. 10.

36. Katherine Mader, *The Report of the Domestic Violence Task Force,* Los Angeles, CA, Los Angeles Police Department, 1997, p.45.

37. Jeremy Travis, *Environmental Crime Protection: Results of a National Survey,* Washington, DC, U.S. Department of Justice, 1994, pp. 1–11.

38. Joseph A. Santoro, "A Department's Role as a Social Activist," *Law And Order,* May 1993, Vol. 41, No. 5, pp. 63–66.

streets, or the city attorney's office to improve neighborhood conditions and eradicate specific problems.[39]

To create and maintain a feeling of security in the community. The police in this nation are the primary governmental unit for insuring a degree of tranquillity in a community and the police have not taken this commitment lightly. For many years the police have taken the position that they had the sole responsibility to control and suppress crime, and they have looked with disdain at others who have wanted to assume some responsibility in this area. Citizens who take reasonable precautions for their own protection have, historically, expected to engage in their ordinary daily activities without being endangered or becoming the subject of criminal attack.

Although crime has dropped markedly in recent years the fear of crime is as much a problem as crime itself. In a nationwide survey, 20 percent of the respondents had a great deal of confidence in the ability of the police to protect them from violent crime. Thirty percent had quite a lot of confidence and 39 percent had not very much confidence. The remainder of the respondents (9 percent) had none at all.[40] Through the years, the police have dealt with this problem by preventive patrol in an effort to create omnipresence and provide the community with a feeling of security. In recent years consideration has been given to the concept of broken windows which postulates that when consideration is given to the environment and its improvement it has a significant impact on members of the community and their feeling of security and safety. One factor was to deal with neighborhood disorder such as untended property, disorderly people, drunks, and obstreperous youths—all of which create fear in citizens and attract predators. Community policing has begun to address this goal and if it proves to be successful it will go a long way toward maintaining a feeling of security within neighborhoods. The Sacramento Police Department, in fulfilling this goal, assists the community in establishing drug free zones in targeted areas, parks, schools, public housing developments and other areas where drug trafficking and alcohol availability problems exist. The department also works diligently in expanding the neighborhood revitalization program, that focuses on the underlying physical and social conditions that contribute to the prevalence of drugs and gangs.[41]

To promote and preserve civil order. Civil disorder is not new in our Nation. It seems that almost periodically a major disturbance has occurred that required a police response. Sometimes it has been necessary for the national guard and/or federal troops to intervene in

39. Ronald W. Glensor, and Ken Peek, "Implementing Change: Community-Oriented Policing and Problem-Solving," *FBI Law Enforcement Bulletin*, 1996, Vol. 74, No. 7, pp. 14–21.

40. Kathleen Maguire and Ann. L. Pastore, *Sourcebook of Criminal Justice Statistics–1996*, Washington, DC, Bureau of Justice Statistics, 1997, p. 127.

41. Sacramento Police Department, *Safe Streets*, Sacramento, CA, Sacramento Police Department, 11/19/98, pp. 1–2. http://www.otan.dni.us/cdlpo/111o/safe/success.html.

an effort to restore order. Incidents of this nature included occurrences such as the Draft Riots during the early part of last century and most notably, the civil disturbances over the Vietnam War. The need for preserving public order is not new. Actually, a modern police agency came into existence in England because rioting and civil disorders occurred frequently. At that time, the parochial police forces were unable to control the acts of civil disobedience. With the occurrence of acts of civil disobedience, many police departments responded by creating tactical units. These units cope with critical temporary situations. They permit an overwhelming concentration of police power at a particular time and place to meet a specific problem, such as, disorderly crowds or riotous situations.

The emphasis on this goal remains of interest to many in our communities but it has lessened somewhat because of the reduction in the number of major disorders. There is a clear-cut need for agencies to have response plans that reduce the likelihood of minor disturbances evolving into widespread civil disorder.[42] Although in Miami, during the last decade there were five significant conflicts (with a loss of property and life) in reaction to the use of deadly force. Another major incident occurred in Los Angeles during the spring of 1992. Rioting started when four white police officers were acquitted in the videotaped beating of Rodney King.[43] This riot was the deadliest in the twentieth century.[44] In 1996 in St. Petersburg, FL, a riot broke out when officers stopped a speeding vehicle with two black men inside and the incident resulted in the eventual death of the 18–year old driver of the vehicle. The riot involved 200 people raged through a night as police strived to contain the violence.

In 1999, in New York City, an unarmed man was shot 19 times by four white police officers. These officers fired a total of 41 rounds at the 22–year-old street peddler who was from Guinea in West Africa. This shooting became a rallying point for activists and weeks following the incident rallies were held throughout Manhattan and the Bronx with up to 1,500 protestors in attendance. Numerous protestors were arrested for disorderly conduct. The four officers entered pleaded innocent to second-degree murder and the trial is pending. [45].

To provide other services on an emergency basis. Through the years, the police have stepped in to fill voids in our governmental response, to needs of members of the community. In most instances there has been no one else to turn to. Readily available for a wide

42. Dean DeJong, "Civil Disorder: Preparing for the Worst," *FBI Law Enforcement Bulletin, March* 1994 Vol. 66, No. 3, pp. 1–7.

43. Charles J. Ogletree, Jr., Mary Prosser, Abbe Smith, and William Talley, Jr. *Beyond the Rodney King Story– An Investigation of Police Misconduct in Minority Communities,* Boston, Northeastern University, 1994, pp. 1–198.

44. Scott McCartney, "Reeling LA Struggles to Recover from Deadly Force," *The Arizona Daily Star,* 1992, p. 1., and Daryl F. Gates, *Chief,* New York, Bantam Books, pp. 428–430.

45. *The Arizona Daily Star,* "4 N.Y. Cops Face charges of Murder in Shooting," Thursday, April 1, 1999, A–7.

range of calls for help, the police have controlled minor fires, and administered first aid. In addition, they have delivered babies, impounded stray animals, and created rescue units that are utilized to find lost children and hikers. When the volume of such services become excessive, alternative arrangements have been made in some communities. Other agencies (either public or private) have taken over such functions as animal control, and emergency service. In the future it is anticipated that other governmental and non-governmental will be created to assume some of these tangential activities

Through the years the police have searched for a way to articulate their mission and it can be seen from the above discussion that it has been accomplished with some difficulty and variance. Goals and objectives in England started out with a serious consideration of the relationship of the police to the community and then shifted to a patronage system, then to an internalization of goals with an overriding professional model of policing. With the eleven distinctive functions, articulated by the American Bar Association study, gave greater consideration to specific objectives a number of which reflected a greater concern of individual and community needs.

There is no single list of goals used by law enforcement agencies. They vary considerably, especially in terms of implementation. The Boston Police Department used another approach when identifying goals. When defining the values of the department it also created a list of goals. The values listed in Figure 3–10 serve as a guide for policy making. Additionally, the values are taught in the recruit training program. Values also provide a foundation for the creation of departmental goals. Values are becoming increasingly common in law enforcement.

Figure 3–10

Values of the Boston Police Department
Guarantee the constitutional rights of all citizens.
Maintain the highest standards of honesty and integrity.
Promote the professionalism of Boston police personnel.
Enhance the working relationship between the department and the neighborhoods.
Improve the quality of life in our neighborhoods.

Developed over 18 months, the Boston Police Department goals, after input from citizens, command personnel, and a mayor's management committee. The goals were to:

- Improve the delivery of police services to the neighborhoods.

    a. Implement the neighborhood based patrol program.

    b. Enhancement of the 911 response system.

    c. Expansion of drug enforcement and education.

    d. Additional traffic enforcement.

- Arrange for tools needed to effectively deliver police services.

    a. Continue hiring and promotions.

    b. Open new neighborhood stations.

    c. Improve personnel support services.

    d. Upgrade supervision and training.

- Maintain a strong working relationship with the neighborhoods.

    a. Expand crime prevention programs.

    b. Expand educational efforts.[46]

It can readily be seen, over the last three decades, the defining of goals has shifted from an enforcement posture. Currently, emphasis is on community service and the resolution of problems. Equally important, there has been a shift to a greater consideration of the quality of life within the organization and the general community.

Conflict Management

Earlier in this chapter, there was a discussion concerning "positive stress." A close associate of this term is "conflict"—an expression being viewed as increasingly valuable (if not absolutely essential) to organizational growth. Conflict is pervasive not only in our society, but also in police agencies. It is something each manager must acknowledge so it is necessary to learn the skills that will successfully manage conflict. It is not just a question of conflict resolution, but of conflict management. Conflict is not just always negative. It can prove to be the stimulus leading to solving complex police problems. Conflict is an integral component of every organizational setting of any size. The police manager with a traditionalist bent, view conflict as harmful and clearly a signal that the organization or members of the organization are in trouble. Consequently, the traditionalist makes every effort to avoid conflict or refused to acknowledge its existence.[47] The progressive police manager currently views conflict as something that should be managed. Also, under appropriate circumstances, management (see figure 3–11) should generate conflict.

46. Richard M. Ayres, *Preventing Law Enforcement Stress: The Organizational Response,* Alexandria, VA, The National Sheriff's Association, 1990, p. 44.

47. James A.F. Stoner, *Management,* Englewood Cliffs, NJ: Prentice–Hall, 1982, p. 407, and Thomas K. Capozzoli, "Conflict Resolution–A Key Ingredient in Successful Teams," *Supervision,* December 1995, Vol. 56, No. 12, PP 3–5.

Figure 3–11

The Positive View of Conflict
Conflict is normal.
Conflict exists in every organization.
Conflict can either contribute or detract to goal attainment.
Conflict is neither inherently functional nor dysfunctional.
People change and grow personally from conflict.
Conflict enhances creative problem solving.
Conflict can result in a solution to a problem.
Conflict increases the involvement of everyone involved.
Conflict builds cohesiveness.
Conflict effects performance.
Conflict can be managed.
Conflict can be intrapersonal.
Conflict can be interpersonal.
Conflict can be intragroup.
Conflict can be intergroup.
Conflict can be interorganizational.
Conflict can be intraorganizational.

Conflict need not be harmful or debilitating. When managed properly, conflict provides a stimulus for the attainment of departmental goals and enhances individual and organizational performance. It enhances organizational effectiveness and allows for ingenious and positive decision making. Conflict can force a manager to search for a solution that becomes the basis for innovation and positive change within the department.[48]

Usually, the problem analysis process can make changes more acceptable. Conflict can force the organization to deal with it and not avoid it. It focuses organizational means, time, and money, on the problem at hand, and conserves scarce resources. An additional byproduct of managed conflict is the creation of an organizational ecology that emphasizes the psychological well being of employees. There is a reduction of resentment while anxiety, and tension lessens. Over time, as organizational members realize that when conflict is confronted positively and responsibly a supportive and trusting relationship evolves. There is a need for police managers to seek a level of conflict maximizing its impact. This allows for the attainment of organizational goals and its members an opportunity to maintain their personal integrity. Organizational life acknowledges the existence of six types of conflict. Three of these seem to prevail in police organizations. Each of these is discussed in figure 3–7. Conflict can occur between any two individuals, but most often it involves a superior/subordinate relationship. It can occur because of a lack of understanding of departmental rules and regulation. Or it can be the difficulty of balancing organizational and personal needs. A supervisor may feel it is necessary to provide close supervision, while the officer feels it is unnecessary and overtly restrictive. A worldwide study found that of 60 cultures, Ameri-

48. *Ibid*, p. 408.

can is the most individualistic. The supervisor must work diligently at creating a team out of a number of highly individualistic officers. This proves to be fertile ground for conflict.[49]

Figure 3–12

Distinction Between Types of Conflict

Individuals

Officers are taught to take command in each and every situation, consequently their relationships with other officers, supervisors, and commanders can become troublesome. When an officer's freedom and discretion are reduced, frustration occurs and it can easily escalate into serious conflict.

Groups and Groups

Law enforcement agencies, of even medium size, are complex in nature. Subunits, such as an investigative division, have pursued their unit goals without any consideration of departmental goals. Patrol and investigative units have operated autonomously as if they were separate departments. Specialization is another element exacerbating conflict.

Individuals and Groups

Conflict can occur a number of ways within a police organization. Unions may vie for control of the collective bargaining process to the detriment of organizational members. Social groups, within the organization, may exclude members for various reasons. Individuals who violate organizational norms may isolate and reject norm violators.

Quite plainly, conflict can be as simple as a personality difference between two individuals. The intensity of any conflict varies because of the way individuals interpret each situation, its importance, inhibitors, and constraining variables. Carried to its extreme, the subordinate views the supervisor as the arbiter of bureaucratic control and suppressor of freedom.[50]

As groups within an organization become cohesive, they tend to develop distinct characteristics. Norms come into existence based on attitudes, values and beliefs. Standards evolve and social interaction serves as the base for the development of group guidelines for the way work assignments should be handled. Specialization reinforces group autonomy and quickly isolates bureaus on the same level. In some departments, officers in such bureaus as Technical Services and Administrative Services isolate themselves from officers who work the streets. Also within the group, specialization can further isolate subunits such as within an Investigative Bureau. A homicide unit can perceive itself as an elite unit compared to a general crimes unit.

49. Michael F. Brown, "The Sergeant's Role in a Modern Law Enforcement Agency," *The Police Chief*, May 1992, Vol. LIX, No. 5, p. 20.

50. Daniel Robey, *Designing Organizations*, Homewood, IL, Richard D. Irwin, 1982, p. 151.

Resources can be vied for and cooperation ignored or slighted. Incidents have occurred where vital information is withheld from other units within a department.

Notably, organizational structure affects the nature and level of cooperation between members of an organization. As organizational subunits develop, differential integration becomes difficult. Consequently, the need to create positive interchange between subunits presents management with a real challenge. Through the years managers have used integrative devices such as liaison, and definitive rules and procedures to improve communications between specialized units. Other attempts include the utilization of teams, task forces, and matrix structure.[51]

Another area of concern is the conflict occurring between individuals and groups. Usually such conflicts involve the application of norms within the organization. Individuals may violate group-shared expectations. One of these is the "Code of Silence," where an officer never turns against another officer. It is a by-product of the philosophy that espousing "the officer is against all others (the brass as well as the public)". There are many instances, throughout the United States, where officers have refused to report other officers involved in acts of corruption.

In other instances, conflict occurs between individuals and groups when work norms evolve. It generally involves some aspect of the amount of work that should be done. For example, how long should an officer take for a disturbing the peace call. Norms also identify what should be included in a daily report. Studies have shown there is little reality between the things an officer does on the street compared to what is reported. Sometimes, group norms create guidelines defining what should be brought to the attention of the "brass." Some groups then ostracize violating officers by excluding them from group social activities. Perhaps dysfunctional conflict may occasionally be present, but conflict cannot always be viewed as destructive.

Management has a vital role in identifying conflict—the inevitable entity that is a consequence of interpersonal and intergroup reactions on a day-to-day working basis. Management cannot eliminate dissension, hence it must accept this unavoidable process, and strive to deal with it to the advantage of the organization. In some instances, conflict must actually be created! Conflict is actually a sign of a healthy organization. A *good* manager should not work toward the elimination of conflict but do everything possible to insure it is brought out into the open and dealt with properly.[52]

51. Joseph J. Staft, "Effects of Organizational Design on Communications Between Patrol and Investigative Function (Conclusion)," *FBI Law Enforcement Bulletin,* June 1980, Vol. 49, No. 6, pp. 20–26.

52. Robert Townsend, *Further Up The Organization,* New York, Alfred A. Knopf, 1984, p. 39.

Conflict is defined as any kind of opposition or antagonistic inter-action between two or more parties.[53] It can only be perceived as existing in varying degrees of intensity and is best viewed on a continuum from low to high. Conflict demands a response and the dominant task of management is to create an environment in which conflict serves as a productive function. Additionally, the managerial task is to focus on inconsistencies of work tasks, faulty communications, and other hindrances to organizational effectiveness.[54]

Conflict can readily be classified into the general categories of communications, structure, and personal behavior. Communicative conflicts are prevalent in many agencies and in most instances arise from semantic difficulties, simple misunderstandings, or noise entropy that occurs in all channels of communications (because of our inability to assimilate facts.) Structural conflict occurs when the degree of specialization in an agency is extensive, there are multi-levels within the organization, or when the size of the agency is such that conflict is inevitable. Personal behavior is the last conflict element and is reflective of the fact that as individuals we are each different because of our attitudes, value systems and personal variance.[55]

Reduction of Conflict

The reduction of conflict can only be implemented after the source is determined and one of the techniques listed in figure 3–13 is selected and applied. The effectiveness of each technique varies with the situation and any single technique should not be viewed as more effective than another. Experts do believe, however, that problem solving is the preferred method when there are communicative conflicts and value differences are more responsive to an authoritative command.[56] Change does not occur spontaneously; it is the inevitable consequence of conflict. One expert views conflict as the catalyst of change.[57]

Figure 3–13

Resolution Techniques
- Problem Solving.
- Dominance of Goals.
- Allocation of Resources.
- Avoidance.
- Smoothing.
- Compromise.
- Structural Alteration.
- Command.
- Altering the Human Component.

---

53. Stephen P. Robbins, "Conflict Management and Conflict Resolution are not Synonymous Terms," *California Management Review,* Winter 1978, Vol. XXI, No. 2, p. 67.

54. Eleanor Phillips and Ric Cheston, "Conflict Resolution: What Works?" *California Management Review,* Summer 1979, Vol. XXI, No. 4, p. 83.

55. Robbins, *op. cit.,* p. 72.

56. Robbins, *op. cit.,* p. 74.

57. Robbins, *op. cit.,* p. 69.

Adopted and modified from: Stephen P. Robbins, "Conflict Management and Conflict Resolution are not Synonymous Terms," *California Management Review,* Winter 1978, Vol. XXI, No. 2, p. 73.

As change occurs, it stimulates conflict requiring the individual and the organization to adapt. Without conflict management, the organization limits its ability to provide needed public services. A posture of status quo must be rejected and functional conflict must be accepted as the life-blood of the organization.[58] A reasonable amount of conflict creates an organizational climate resulting in creative decision-making. Research supports the position that conflict is positively related to productivity.[59] Conflict can be both functional and dysfunctional—the manager must strive to support conflict that enhances the achievement of organizational goals. Conversely the manager must direct attention to the eradication of dysfunctional or destructive forms of conflict.[60]

Police organizations have been created to provide services and attain a set of goals—hence the well being of the employee is secondary to organizational welfare. Functional conflict is not defined by individuals or groups, but by management. Conflict can only be dysfunctional if it impedes or stops organizational goal attainment.[61] This means that the way employees view conflict will have an important impact on the agency and the central thesis is that conflict is always functional if it furthers the objectives of the organization.

A Healthy Organization

The truly healthy police organization is fully aware of why it exists. It is conversant with where it is going and what it has to do to get there. It is goal oriented and focuses on what has to be done to be operationally successful. Once the goals are articulated they become a basis guide for the every activity that the agency performs. Every goal articulated by a department must be assessable. Typically departments have articulated abstract goals such as–'to serve and protect.' What is need is a goals that is truly measurable.[62] Another attribute of the healthy police organization is that the organization makes a strong effort to really know the citizens of the community. In some departments tracking citizens' concerns regarding crime in their community, their level of involvement in public safety issues, and their attitudes

58. *Ibid.*

59. Thomas K. Capozzoli, "Conflict Resolution–A Key Ingredient in Successful Teams," *Supervision,* December 1995, Vol. 56, No. 12, pp. 3–5.

60. Robbins, *op. cit.,* p. 70.

61. Jenney Waller, Derek Allen and Andrew Burns, *The T.Q.M. Toolkit—A* *Guide to Practical Techniques for Total Quality Management,* London, Kogan Page, 1998, p. 24.

62. Jeremy Travis, *Measuring What Matters Part Two: Developing Measures of What the Police Do,* Washington, DC, National Institute of Justice, November 1997, pp. 1–15.

toward the police is a measurement that has been accomplished periodically.[63]

Another attribute of a healthy police organization is that they are fully aware of the wide range of calls for service to include, incidents dispatched, self-initiated calls, and referral calls. A responsive department is aware of changes in services to include trends. Crime can now be tracked at the division level with the installation and implementation of the Crime Analysis and Mapping Information Network (CAMIN). This allows crime analysts to create maps of various criminal activities in the city, their division, or focus in one area, such as a few city blocks. The analysis of self-initiated calls is of special interest to police management inasmuch as it reflects proactive efforts of line officers.[64] Of additional interest to management is the utilization of problem solving efforts as measured against previously identified objectives. In one community the standard of allowing officers to have 35 percent of their time allocated to problem solving is stated as a departmental objective and reflects the desire to increase problem solving efforts. Thus resource analysis becomes integral part of the adaptive management process. Problems are addressed based on work with other agencies, businesses and the community to address specific crime problems through the use of a signed agreement where each party is responsible for specific objectives and timelines.[65]

When a department sanctions problem solving all officers must be willing and able to try new approaches, push the limits and learn from mistakes, They must be able to turn theory into reality by taking risks and making important decisions. The truly effective law enforcement agency permits officers to make meaningful decisions about what they will do and how they will do it. An organization's best members will emerge because the agency's philosophy and support systems encourage them, celebrate their successes and nurse them through their occasional failures.[66]

The healthy police agency demonstrates a unique ability to communicate with personnel. Constant efforts are made to improve morale and job satisfaction. Personnel are fully aware of the values and mission of the department and the efforts needed to achieve operational goals. Employees are surveyed semi-annually as a means of identifying areas of concern that should be addressed. This is especially true as management must accept the challenge of providing adequate resources and training so officers can successfully accomplish assigned tasks. Additionally, the department must constantly improve the way that the agency addresses its workload, provides services to customers,

63. Portland Police Bureau, *Portland Police Bureau on Line,* November 6, 1998, http://www.teleport.com/(police/index.html).

64. *Ibid,* pp. 19–20.

65. *Ibid,* p.27.

66. Charles W. Bennett, Jr., "Innovation and Community Policing: Managing and Profiting From Failure," *Community Policing Exchange,* November/December 1998, Phase VI, No. 23, pp. 1 and 4.

and meets community need. The underlying variable of organizational viability is the ability to communicate effectively.[67] This chapter has set the theme for the remainder of the text. Subsequent chapters focus on key managerial imperatives that condition and recondition the working environment of a police department.

Case Study

Assistant Chief Roland Larson

In preparation for the new millennium, the Drake Police Department has been asked by the city manager to prepare a strategic five-year plan that will address the numerous issues that will confront the department in the future. The agency is in its second year of a community-policing program that has been less than successful. The latest community assessment report indicates that there is still need to improve communications with the community, that police personnel feel they need more training in problem-solving, that the public is becoming increasingly concerned with public safety issues, and calls for service are not answered as rapidly as desired. The Chief of Police has assigned Assistant Chief Roland Larson to set up a task force to prepare the five-year plan. The department serves an urban community of and has 274 sworn personnel and 42 civilians. Fifty-two percent of the personnel are unformed whose regularly assigned duties include responding to calls for service. The department has specialized units to include: bias-related crimes, community crime prevention, drunk drivers, environmental crimes, repeat offenders, and victim assistance.

Patrol personnel, in numerous instances, have offered resistance to the new policing approach with its emphasis on improving the quality of life in the community. They express the belief that community policing was instituted by executive fiat. There is a general feeling that the needs of the officers have been ignored. Line officers feel that they have been told to solve neighborhood problems but not given the time or tools to be effective. Conflict varies within the department and seems to be concentrated in the line unit. This is in contrast to the investigative division and staff units that have readily accepted the change, but feel that there is a lack of coordination with the line unit. The police union, that represents the majority of personnel in the department, has remained neutral over the issue of community policing, but is becoming increasingly restless as the patrol units continues to express grave concerns about training and implementation of community policing.

How would you go about creating the task force? What personnel would you ask to become members of the task force? How would you deal with conflict within the specialized units of the department? What resolution technique would you think might be most promising? Why?

---

67. Travis, *op. cit., p. 5.*

For Further Reading

Jennifer M. Brown and Elizabeth A. Campbell, *Stress and Policing: Sources and Strategies,* New York, John Wiley & Sons, 1994, 59–78.

> Comprehensive discussion of how stress might produce adverse effect in the individual. Includes a discussion of the three main types of adverse effects: impaired job performance, psychological problems, and physical health problems. Of special interest are the discussions of intraindividual and interorganizational factors of stress. Points out that officers engaged in different types of duties are thought to have different patterns of exposures to stressors.

Thomas K. Capozzoli, "Conflict Resolution–A Key Ingredient in Successful Teams," *Supervision,* December 1955, Vol. 56, No. 12., pp. 3–5.

> Points out that productive conflict resolution involves learning how to disagree over issues and situations and coming up with a solution that can benefit the whole team. Lists the constructive aspects of conflict, and describes the causes of conflict. Sets forth six steps that can be utilized to resolve conflict. The author also reviews the nature of conflict.

Ellen Kirschman, "Organizational Stress–Looking for Love in all the Wrong Places," *The Police Chief,* October 1998, Vol. LXV, No. 10, pp. 127–135.

> Lists 15 causes of organizational stress ranging from inadequate training to poor leadership. Presents a list of things that a police family can do if organizational stress hits at home. Describes the impact of the bureaucracy on officers in disciplinary matters and the failure of management to support officers. Includes a case study of the impact of departmental policy and the stress it produces.

Patrick J. Solar, "Changing Organizational Culture–Monitoring and Developing Professional Officer Skills," *Law and Order,* May 1998, Vol. 46, No. 5, pp. 22–27.

> The author discusses the utilization of an instrument to measure officer behavior through the perception of others. Suggests that the quality based system of evaluation of officers builds trust and confidence. Identifies those who can be used as raters, and how to utilize the results. Describes nine steps that must be followed when creating a rating instrument. Of special interest is the belief of the officer that the appraisal system serves to reinforce desired behavior and improve the relationship between officers and members of the community.

Chapter 4

COMMUNITY–ORIENTED POLICING & PROBLEM SOLVING (COPPS): Responding to Community Needs

Learning Objectives

1. Identify the changes that have occurred and prompted law enforcement to alter its relationship with the public.

2. Define community policing.

3. Describe the nature of resistance to community policing.

4. List six features that best describe "traditional policing."

5. Write a short essay describing what can be done to insure the success of community policing.

6. List seven terms used to describe community-policing efforts.

7. Describe values management.

8. Identify the type of organizational support that can be used when institution community policing.

9. Compare the Alexandria and the Baltimore value statements.

10. List six of the values for the Buffalo Sheriff's Department.

11. Write a short essay describing what activities a problem-oriented policing agency should consider doing.

12. List the four stages of SARA.

13. Describe the process of scanning.

14. Identify the four goals of surveying.

Numerous police department throughout the country have taken up the challenge of altering the relationship between the department and members of the community. Through the years law enforcement has responded to the demands for change by altering its operational mode in varying ways. We have seen the reality of the reform movement, professionalization, the community-relations movement[1], team policing, directed patrol, preventive patrol, and saturation patrol. During the last 20 years technological innovations have revolutionized the way police departments have responded to the demand for controlling

1. Willard M. Oliver, *Community-oriented Policing: A Systematic Approach to* *Policing,* Upper Saddle River, NJ, Prentice–Hall, 1998, 1–444.

91

crime. This trend had included computer aided dispatching (CAD), geographic information systems (GIS), advanced vehicle location (AVL), global positioning systems (GPS). These are just a few of the space age technologies that have had a significant effect on the operations of police departments. Another area of significance has been the sophisticated computer software programs created for law enforcement to include applications to staffing, scheduling, and deployment of personnel, and traffic control device inventory (TCDI) systems. There are also programs that can compile investigative information to track sex offenders required by Megan's Law, crisis management, information management and critical incident/emergency planning capabilities.

All of these have had a meaningful impact on the management of police departments, but none proved to be exceptionally effective in altering the crime problem. In fact, most of these programs were never evaluated. During the last decade community policing has become the catch phase of the struggle to diminish crime.[2] It has been a topic that has caught the imagination of the media, the police profession and the darling of the political process. It has grabbed headlines throughout the nation and the President of the United States has extolled its virtues in every corner of the Nation. As part of this and for political reason the President has seen it necessary to announce grants from the U.S. Department of Justice COPS grant program,[3] and the President has appeared with uniformed law enforcement at every photo opportunity. Who can argue against putting 1000,000 more officers on the street of the cities and hamlets of the Nation. An additional and significant impact has been the implementation of the Violent Crime Control and Law Enforcement Act of 1994 to deal with an unacceptable level of crime. More than 30 billion dollars over a period of six years has been allocated to agencies throughout the Nation. Some of the best known components of the Act have been its criminal provisions. This includes the ban on assault weapons, tougher sentencing through expansion of the death penalty and creation of a federal "three-strikes" law.[4]

Politics is an important part of policing and it has been alleged that Chicago created a community-policing program for political reasons. Political leaders felt that this type of program would address not only crime, but also racial and fiscal issues. It was anticipated that if community policing were successful it would insure reelection.[5] Community policing has gained momentum as police and community leaders have searched for a means of providing better police services and

2. Jerome H. Skolnick, and David H. Bayley, *Community Policing: Issues and Practices Around the World*, Washington, DC, 1988, U.S. Department of Justice, pp.

3. John Hoffman, "COPS Grants,: An Appraisal After Three Years," *Law and Order*, November 1998, Vol. 46, No. 11, pp. 71–75

4. National Institute of Justice, *Criminal Justice Research Under the Crime Act–1955 to 1996.*, Washington, DC, National Institute of Justice, September 1997 p. 1.

5. Wesley G. Skogan and Susan M. Hartnett, *Community Policing: Chicago Style* New York, Oxford University Press, 1997, pp. 1–258.

being more responsive to the desire to improve the quality of life within communities. The Community Policing Consortium extols its virtues, [6] participants at conferences discuss the topic in depth, and special training prepares participants to implement problem-solving programs. The detractors are few and far between, but there are those who feel that over time these programs will cease to exist. Unfortunately this unique process has reached the point where it is almost a game of one-upmanship as police leaders describe their community policing programs.

In the past the community relations unit was a status symbol. It was an indicator that the agency was responding to the needs of the community, and was part of the vanguard of professional law enforcement. One can only wonder if community policing in some cities is a hollow effort to keep up with what is a momentous shift in policing. Others view it as the ideology underpinning of the agency, suggesting that it provide the reason for the existence of the department. Philosophically it can be a significant change in the provision of police services.[7] At the least it is semantical gamesmanship and at the most it requires radical and lasting change, wherein personnel work with the community in determining the delivery system for police services.[8] Community policing is not a quick fix. If it is to be successful it demands a long-term and believed commitment. It should not be sold as a cure-all and there must be practical expectation as to its potential to improve the quality of life in neighborhoods.[9] Surveys indicate that roughly two out of three police agencies in major jurisdictions report that they have adopted some form of community policing. On the other hand other research shows that three out of four police agencies that claim to be engaged in community policing do not allow the community a voice in identifying, prioritizing or solving problems.[10]

Defining Community Policing

Unfortunately, there is a lack of consensus in defining community policing. Some view it as the need to emphasize a traffic program, a gun tip program, a gang control program, citizens on patrol, development of a citizen police academy, a youth project, or a business survey projects. Any one these programs can be a part of a community policing problem-solving effort but this is true only if it is the result of the

---

6. John Hoffman, "Community Policing Consortium, *Law and Order*," May 1997, Vol. 45, No. 5, pp. 126–128. The Consortium can be reached at www.communitypolicing.org.

7. Michael L. Birzer, "Police Supervision in the 21st Century," *FBI Law Enforcement Bulletin*, June 1996, Vol. 65, No. 6, pp. 6–10, and Michael J. Heidingsfield, Michael J., "Community Policing: Chief's Definition," *Law and Order*, 1997, Vol. 45, No. 10, p.196.

8. Robert Trojanowicz, and Bonnie Bucqueroux, *Community Policing: How to Get Started*, Second Edition, 1998, Cincinnati, OH, pp. 1–166.

9. Bureau of Justice Assistance, *Understanding Community Policing: A Framework for Action*, Washington, DC, 1994a, pp. 1–69.

10. Bucqueroux, "Community Policing is Alive and Well," *Community Policing Exchange*, Washington, DC, Community Policing Consortium, 1995, p. 5.

direct participation and support of the community.[11] Other departments create a special police unit [12]similar to those created when community relations and team policing were in vogue.

Defining community policing proves to be somewhat difficult because it means different things to different people.[13] Despite definitional limitations[14] it seems appropriate at this point to suggest a working definition of community policing and this is set forth in figure 4.1. Key elements of this definition include: (1) officers working pro-actively at problem-solving, (2) consideration given to the need for a partnership with the community (3) the causes of crime and fear are addressed, and (4) other community issues become of concern. If this definition is to have true meaning it has to serve as a philosophical base for the officers involved in the community policing process. Each officer must accept the fact that the department needs assistance in order to maximize the public safety effort. Community policing is democracy in action and the essence of our republican type of government. It requires the active partnership of local government, civic and business leaders, public and private agencies, residents, churches, school and service groups.[15] Everyone that shares a concern for the welfare of the neighborhood should bear accountability for safeguarding that welfare.

Figure 4.1

Definition of Community Policing
Community policing is a philosophy, management style, and organizational strategy that promotes pro-active problem-solving and police community partnerships to address the causes of crime and fear as well as other community issues.

Adopted from California Attorney General's Crime Prevention Center, *COPPS–Community Oriented Policing and Problem Solving*, Sacramento, CA 1992, p. 3. http://caag.state.ca.us/caldojvl/cjlibrary/cops.htm.

Community policing is a mind set wherein the department believes that the public is a vital component of the process and the public supports and understands the mission values, and role of the police department.[16] Community policing provides officers with an opportunity to move closer to the community. It is a process wherein the police

---

11. Bonnie Bucqueroux, *op. cit.*, p. 5.

12. Marty L. West, "Gaining Employee Support for Community Policing," *Law and Order*, April 1997, Vol. 45, No. 4, pp. 51–53.

13. Arthur J. Lurigio, and Dennis P. Rosenbaum, "Community Policing: Major Issues and Unanswered Questions," in M.L. Dantzker, Editor, *Contemporary Policing: Personnel, Issues, & Trends*, Newton, MA, Butterworth–Heinemann, 1997, pp. 195–211.

14. Police Executive Research Forum, *Themes and Variations in Community Policing,—Case Studies in Community Policing*, Washington, DC, Police Executive Research Forum, 1996, pp. 3–4.

15. Bureau of Justice Assistance, op. cit., p. 16.

16. Heidingsfield, *op. cit.*

become organizers, coordinators, and communicators.[17] Community policing, if it is to be successful, demands radical change over time, if there is to be a significant alteration in the way the organization attains goals. If change is to occur it has to be leader centered and engendered.[18] The historical nature of police work, with its quasi-military orientation, mandates the need for change to emanate from top management.[19] The values of community policing must be communicated to every level and everyone in the organization.[20] It is a transitional process wherein the chief executive officer removes barriers that impede change, fostering the development of a culture in which actions contrary to traditional working methods are stimulated.[21]

In community policing, top management must articulate the values of community policing and communicate them to every level and everyone in the organization.[22] The police become an integral part of the community culture and members of the community help in defining future priorities and distributing resources. It is democracy in action. Active participation is required of everyone who has an interest in the welfare of the community.[23] It differs substantially from traditional models of policing and places considerable power and authority at the lowest level of the organization. Line officers and supervisors are the recipient of this significant shift of power and authority.

Under the professional model of policing officers responded, toke a report, and moved on. The citizen's problems remained. Drug pushers, prostitutes, and gang members reappear right after the police left. While the specifics might vary unquestionably the most traditional approaches to controlling crime and protecting society have failed. This nation, especially the metropolitan areas are changing and in some instances so rapidly as to defy reality. In one West Coast city to keep up with the changing ethnic composition of the population has recruiters actively searching for candidates who are fluent in Cantonese, Mandarin, Tagalog, Cambodian, Korean, Spanish and Vietnamese. In a southeastern city, at one time the largest ethnic group was Anglo–American. It is now the smallest ethnic group. Latinos now constitute

17. David C. Couper, "Seven Seeds for Policing," *FBI Law Enforcement Bulletin,* March 1994, Vol. 63, No. 3, pp. 8–11,

18. Jayne Seagrave, "Accounting for Police Resistance to Change: The Benefits of Integrating (Theoretical) Police Subculture Literature with (Pragmatic) Organizational Culture Literature," *Western Criminologist,* Spring 1994, Official Newsletter of the Western Society of Criminology, pp. 5–8.

19. T.R. Moselle, "Community Policing–Is It Really Working," *Journal of California Law Enforcement,* 1997, Vol. 31, No. 1, pp. 23–32.

20. Gary B. Schobel, Thomas A. Evans, and John L. Daly, "Does It Reduce Crime, or Just Displace It?" *The Police Chief,* August 1997, Vol. LXIV, No. 8, pp. 64–71.

21. Oliver, *op. cit., pp. 32–91.*

22. Terrence Pierce, "community Policing: How One Department Sizes It Up," *The Police Chief,* August 1997, Vol. LXIV, No. 8, pp. 78–79.

23. Bureau of Justice Assistance, *Working as Partners with Community Groups,* Washington, DC, Office of Justice Programs, 1994b, pp. 3–7.

62.5 percent of the population and African–Americans, 27.4 percent.[24] Changes like this creates the potential for cultural conflict and misunderstandings between the public and the police. In order to meet the challenge of the changing population many departments have, in the interest of diversity, strived to recruit personnel so as to reflect a changing society.

There are of course other rapid social changes clearly altering our values and life style. Single parent families dominate in many homes. Divorce continues to alter the composition of families. More and more females are entering the job market and new terms evolve like "latchkey children." These and other social changes create a constantly changing society so the police must also change. Hence the police must react to a changing society. Developing new approaches is difficult. The traditional (professional) style of policing is the dominant model used by many departments today. Unfortunately, this mode of policing is resistant to change and viewed by some as obsolete.

Resistance to Community Policing

Community policing has confronted many pitfalls and triumphed, but there are many rocks in the roadway before it will be accepted and achieve what the drumbeaters describe as community policing. "Change shock" is realistic and one should anticipate resistance. When management apprises personnel of a pending change to community policing there will be those who resist the change and others who will favor its implementation. There are also those who will be indifferent to the new process and roll with the punch. On of the major obstacles to community policing is the bureaucracy itself. In fact, it has been concluded that there has been little organizational structural change since the implementation of community policing.[25] This statement is supported by a study of the organizational structure of large police department for the period from 1987 through 1993 it was determined that there was only minimal change and no significant difference between agencies that practiced community policing and those that did not.[26]

The style of policing used by a department can impede if not destroy efforts to bring about a viable community policing effort. Many parts of the professional police model are at odds with the concept perceived as community policing. Primary emphasis on arrests, issuing citations, and responding to calls for service can be incompatible with community policing. The traditional bureaucracy governing police agencies is the antithesis of the organizational arrangement needed to

24. Gale Research, *Cities of the United States,* The South, Third Edition, Detroit, MI, Gale Research, 1998, Vol. 1, pp. 121–123.

25. Jihong Zhao and Quint Thurman, *The Nature of Community Policing Innovations: Do the Ends Justify the Means?* Washington, DC, Police Executive Research Forum, 1996, p.16.

26. Edward R. Maguire, "Structural Change in Large Municipal Police Organizations During the Community Policing Era," *Justice Quarterly,* 1997, Vol. 14, No. 3, pp. 547–576.

deal adequately with the new philosophy of policing. In the past, top management generated reams of regulations, and policies controlling the conduct of officers to lessen potentially negative response to departmental activities. Every new incident sent managers to desktop computers to create a policy-limiting officer's discretion. For example, there are many situations where innocent individuals are injured or killed when the police are in "hot pursuit." For this reason numerous departments have developed restrictive policies. Usually, police managers strive to issue all encompassing policies maximizing control, and mandating compliance. For example, in one department the policy manual states, "fingernails shall be neatly trimmed and cleaned prior to reporting for duty and shall be maintained clean throughout the watch." This is rather explicit, to say the least.[27]

As every new problem occurs, headquarters responds with a flurry of activity and new additions to the departmental manual. Headquarters "controls-controls-controls" as policies develop in the abstract. In many instances, the line is unaware of something even being a problem until a General Order comes from top managers or the chief.[28] The experience many police departments have had with team policing and community relations units are real "food for thought," based on varying amounts of resistance to these programs. Many were political window dressing and essentially programs with limited substance. It was perceived as something that had to be done to pacify politicians, activists, and detractors of law enforcement. Officers assigned to community relations units were viewed as officers playing political games and the term "plastic cops" became prevalent. Detractors felt that real police work occurred on the streets not in meeting with members of the community. Many of the community relation programs have waned as time has passed. What was once perceived as a critical problem or issue became less important as it no longer had strong political or activistic support.

At one time, team policing seemed a way to provide employees with greater job satisfaction and improve services to the community. However, like other innovations, the promises did not materialize. In one study of seven cities it was never fully implemented. Cincinnati began team policing in a downtown sector with a minimal increase in the number of personnel. The team assigned to the sector handled all calls except homicides. Officers attended crime prevention meetings providing crime control information. The results were discouraging. Members of the community did not feel any safer. Burglaries were less frequent, but the rest of the crime rate remained about the same. Reviewers of the program believe several applicable conditions were ignored. The department retained the traditional measurement tools, such as arrests and suspicious stops. However officers were required to

27. Harry W. More and O.R. Shipley, *Police Policy Manual—Personnel,* Springfield, IL, Charles C. Thomas, 1987, p. 168.

28. Malcolm K. Sparrow, *Implementing Community Policing,* Washington, DC, National Institute of Justice, November 1988, p. 4.

spend more time with citizens without measurement of this activity. Additionally, making team leaders who were lieutenants ("mini-chiefs") threatened the authority and power of higher level administrators.[29] Efforts to start community policing can meet similar obstacles. The dominant policing style in the United States remains traditional and many of its aspects can, if ignored, prove inimical to community policing.

Organizational Rigidity

This nation's policing, for more than 40 years, was a traditional model that was a definite improvement over its predecessor. The earlier model were described as politically involved, and one where corruption was widespread. Traditional policing was looked upon as part of the professionalization movement and for some time it served the varying communities well. It had several features that set it apart as a reformation process:

- Preventative patrol was a widely accepted tactic.
- Rapid response was a key police priority.
- Random patrol was utilized by some departments.
- The primary function was crime control.
- Fundamental authority for the police came from the law.
- Organizationally, centralization was the desirable structural response.
- Relationship to the community was distant.
- Central dispatch responded to demands for police service.[30]

In the beginning the professional model of policing was looked upon by police reformers as the panacea for all of the ills of policing. It was hoped that corruption would cease to exist and political interference would wane. Police services were to be provided in an impartial manner and without question the police existed for the sole purpose of fighting crime. Over time the reform movement resulted in the police being separated from the citizens that it served. This style of policing was not as successful as its proponents wanted it to be. The nation became torn apart by riots and protests in the 1960s and the 1970s. The police found they could not control riots—let alone prevent them. Responding to the turmoil, study commissions abounded—ranging from a study of the riots to the creation of standards and goals. Authorities questioned time-honored techniques, such as, random pa-

29. Charles E. Silverman, *Criminal Violence,* New York, Vintage, 1978, pp. 339–340.

30. George L. Kelling and Mark H. Moore, *The Evolving Strategy of Policing,* Washington, DC, National Institute of Justice, November, 1988, pp. 1–13, and Joseph E. Brann, Craig Calhoun, and Paul Wallace, "A Change in Policing Philosophy," in Daniel E. Lungren, *COPPS: Community Oriented Policing & Problem Solving,* Washington, DC, National Institute of Justice, November 1992, pp. 43–46.

trol, saturation patrol, and rapid response. Slowly, it became obvious that more police officers and advanced technology did little to reduce actual crime or the fear of crime. Some departments began to experiment with varying techniques designed to reduce crime. Collectively, these programs showed the importance of involving the community in the response to the problem of crime.

Experimentation and the quasi-military nature of policing inhibited, and in some instances, defeated the successful implementation of new programs. Superimposing innovative programs on police departments designed for another type of policing almost insured the defeat of those programs. The philosophies were incompatible. Because of new program testing managers felt threatened because they either lost or perceived a loss of power. Furthermore, the evaluation of some of these programs was weak, and even nonexistent in some instances. Police managers vigorously sought funding of programs not only for the monies, but the prestige in law enforcement circles. These and other factors combined to impede the effective implementation of many programs. If nothing else, they learned that change in law enforcement is difficult and not easily accomplished.[31] Police executives began to acknowledge the need for a new philosophy of policing.[32]

Community Policing Today

Community policing, whatever that means, is the "go-go" phrase of the day. If an agency does not operate within such a framework it is outdated and probably outmoded. The term community policing encompasses a broad range of activities, and programs. It is a term having a different meaning to everyone who uses it. It is "all things to all people." The variety of programs identified, as community policing is truly bewildering if not mindboggling. To get on the bandwagon some agencies call whatever they are doing—community policing. If an officer gets out of a police vehicle to talk with a citizen it is community policing. By executive fiat, every officer in one department became a "community police officer." Why bother with the creation of value philosophy or train officers in the new concepts? Some view it as just another community relation's ploy, or an effort to generate a positive public image. Two experts stated the term community policing applies to a variety of programs. This includes neighborhood watch, mini-and shopfront-police stations, and liaison with gay communities. Other examples include, foot patrol, village constables, or strategies for reducing the fear of crime. In another instance a department with a victim and notification program identified it as community policing. Figure 4–2 lists some factors that reinforce the possibility for successful beginning implementation of a community-policing program.

31. Jihong Zhao, Quint C. Thurman and Nicholas P. Lovrich, "Community-Oriented Policing Across the US: Facilitators and Impediments to Implementation," *American Journal of Policing, 1996*, Vol. 14, No. 1, pp. 11–28.

32. *Ibid.,* p. 4.

Figure 4-2

Tips for Insuring That Community
Policing Will Succeed
- Provide for adequate officer discretion.
- Maximize community input.
- Involve all level in the planning process.
- Create flexible policies.
- Involve middle managers in all aspects of community policing.
- Rewards non-traditional duties, such as, problem solving, application of evaluation techniques, and the creation and development of community groups.
- Allow those participating in community policing activities to act outside of the chain of command.
- Institute organizational flexibility.
- Confront efforts to sabotage the program.
- Measure qualitative and quantitative impacts.
- Allow for two-way communications.

The literature on community policing abounds with different terms. A few of the examples appear in figure 4-3 that illustrates the variety of terms used in different departments.

Figure 4-3
Terms used to Describe Community Policing
- Community policing.
- Community-oriented policing.
- Problem-oriented policing.
- Problem-solving policing.
- Community-based policing.
- Community-oriented police enforcement (C.O.P.E.).
- Community patrol officer program (C.P.O.P.).
- Community policing partnership program.
- Neighborhood-oriented policing.
- Citizen contact patrol.
- Directed area response team (D.A.R.T.).
- Community Mobilization Project (CMP).
- Chicago Alternative Policing Strategy (CAPS).
- Community–Oriented Policing & Problem Solving (COPPS).
- Neighborhood Police Teams (NPTS)
- Community Oriented Policing/Problem Oriented Policing (COP/POP)

Each of these terms suggests a different approach for dealing with community problems. On the surface they do little to reflect philosophical underpinnings or a comprehensive operational response. At the least, it illustrates a variety of approaches with the goal of showing the public that the police are doing something different. By implication, these programs suggest a new relationship between the police and the public. It alters the relationship, allowing the opening of two-way communications. There is a belief that the public has a significant part to play in making a community safer. Additionally, arrangements occur for placing accountability and responsibility. Jerome H. Skolnick and David H. Bayley point out that some of these parts might be present, but it does not necessarily result in community policing. New programs may not actually become a reality, reorganization may occur, but strategies remain the same. Also the organizational goals may stay the same even when the agency has developed new value statements.[33] Another difficulty is that in some situations administrators introduce multiple, conflicting goals.[34]

Pursuit of Excellence through Values

Even though they might not be expressed, every organization has values. They can be explicit or vague, broad or narrow, mundane or challenging to the imagination, meaningful or insignificant, they can be written or just understood. Values are not usually as explicit as rules and regulations. They are of a higher order expressing a fundamental belief system. They give breath and spirit to an organization. They are the lifeblood guiding the behavior of every employee. The more they express the true reason for the existence of the organization, the greater their importance. They are the reason the organization exists. On the other hand the value system can become entangled with the reality of how the organization actually operates rather than how it should operate. In this instance the values can be just a "bunch of words" rather than guiding the organization. In one agency the "rat pack," several officers who habitually used physical force, created their own code of conduct and style of policing. They perceived themselves as the saviors of the community. In other agencies, jokes and pranks can express the true value system—usually at odds with the values expressed by management. When such implicit value conflict with explicit value negativism prevails, employees distrust each other, and the organization "just exists." Morale is usually low, and cynicism along with excessive "bitching" dominates the interaction between employees. This in turn impacts negatively on the relationship the agency has with members of the community.[35]

Two authorities expressed this dichotomy most succinctly by pointing to mayors and city managers that often give their police executives a dual set of objectives. Such as "clean up the gangs in the park" and "don't break the law in doing it." The executive actually means "don't tell me about it if you must break the law."[36] Managers, to be effective, must work diligently to reduce and eventually discard ambiguous

---

33. *Ibid.*, p. 3.

34. Richard J. De Paris, *Neighborhood Team Policing: Organizational Opportunities and Obstacles*, Washington, DC, Police Executive Research Forum, 1997, pp. 1–52.

35. Robert Wasserman and Mark H. Moore, *Values in Policing*, Washington, D.C., National Institute of Justice, November 1988, p. 1.

36. *Ibid.*, p. 3.

messages with a double meaning. First, the working relationship between mayors and/or city managers must be such that dual objectives are totally unacceptable. Second, every employee must be aware of the absolute necessity for managerial and workplace values being the same. There is no room for disparity between explicit and implicit values. The values expressed by management must be an integral part of every aspect of the organization and totally integrated into its culture. Rules, regulations, and policies must each reflect organizational values. Personnel actions must express value orientations whether for promotional or disciplinary reasons. Balancing each managerial decision against the expressed managerial values is imperative. When doing this the department can meet challenges and handle change forcefully as it strives for excellence. Successful implementation of value management can prove to be an exceptional way of controlling an organization.

When properly implemented, value management materially influences administrative decision-making. The advantage is, management's comportment becomes highly predictable. Presented with such stability, employees have a tendency to use discretion more judiciously. This occurs because they have greater confidence in the contributions they are making to the department and the community. The advantage emanating from this is, there is less need for strong managerial control.[37] When expressing values they can be either specific or abstract. Either way they serve as a springboard for creating commitment from the community and employees. They clarify the abstract and give meaning to the organization. They can strongly influence the actions of employees. For this reason they should be of definite concern to every progressive police manager. In highly viable organizations managers clearly focus on shared values. These managers actually perform in the context of the expressed value system. Influencing each decision, values are constantly expressed and used. Consequently managers who strive for excellence must work diligently reinforcing and expressing organizational values.

Some view value statements as being too abstract—even just platitudes. This is unwarranted criticism. Whether statements sound like the preamble to the Constitution or not is beside the point. The needed ingredient is something providing guidance to the organization, fostering continuity of performance, and expressing accountability. A key to viable values is those expressing and specifically defining the individuality of the organization. Every employee wants to feel they are part of a unique department. A special sense of organizational identity fosters commitment. The working environment becomes something more than putting in time for a paycheck. When supervisors and managers constantly remind employees of underlying organizational values, employees know that value statements guide organizational actions. When most employees actually "feel" the reality of value statements permeating every facet of the organization, its decision-

37. *Ibid.*

making process, reaction to change, and organizational commitment becomes a reality. In other words, the values guide individual behavior. Internally, values provide impetus for statements like—this is the way we do things around here. For example, when relationships with the community are given priority officers immediately notice attitudinal changes when dealing with the public. Then specific values start to become a distinguishing characteristic of the department. Every action taken by personnel at every level of the organization is influenced by the values. It becomes the reason for existence.

A key is to find the qualities really important in an organization. When actions taken by the Chief of Police reinforce and are consistent with organizational values, it sends a message to everyone in the department. If the Chief says one thing and does another, the value system deteriorates and other criteria dominate. Members of the organization can become confused as value statements become meaningless. Police managers on down to first line supervisors must constantly interpret and reinforce the value basis of the organization. Any one of these levels providing only lip service to the value system can weaken its application and possibly cause it to become dysfunctional. Some police executives extend value statements by creating value-based rules. This process includes defining rules and regulations to include the code of conduct as a logical extension of values. Under each value the applicable rules serve to clarify and set forth specific guidelines.[38]

Organizational Support

If values are to be an integral part of the working pattern of a police department, they must first institute organizational support. This requires the creation of programs setting forth-organizational values. For example, newly hired officers should be fully aware of the importance of values within the department. This starts during the initial interview of potential candidates when the value system of the organization is discussed at length. The candidate is asked to respond to "situations," allowing the panel to interpret the candidates suitability and how well they would enforce the law. After hiring the candidate this value testing is pursued during the "Chief's interview." During such a conference, the prospective officer receives a copy of the departments value statement. After the candidate reads it, a detailed review takes place in which important details are emphasized. At this time the Chief points out that all elements of the statement guides the performance of every member of the department. Every employee must abide by the standards set forth in the value statement. After these preliminaries the new officer officially swears to uphold the value statement at a departmental meeting.[39]

38. Thomas Guequierre, "Value–Based Rules: Practicing What You Preach," *The Police Chief,* October 1995, Vol. LXII, No. 10, pp. 120–129.

39. Robert G. Norman, Chief of Police, *Organizational Values: A Vision Becomes Reality (One Man's Perspective),* Foster City, CA., (unpublished), February, 1992, p. 3.

Additional reinforcement of departmental values is present in a community policing promotional system. Since in most law enforcement agencies, promotion comes from within the organization there is a minimal dilution of organizational values. Promotions depend in large upon annual reviews. This process analyzes behavior, in terms of how values are applied. It selects individuals committed to organizational values. Hence one's behavior translates to more positive consideration when promotion occurs. Informal rewards are also very important. Acknowledgment comes to those who consistently perform within the framework of organizational values when they receive preferred assignments or are sent to special training programs.

Organizational members soon learn the type of behavior and traits needed to succeed. Management can also stress the importance of values by publicly recognizing officers whose accomplishments are attuned to the departmental value system. For example, an officer can be given an award for successful starting a crime prevention program significantly reducing the occurrence of specified crimes or incidents. Another example is how the Foster City Police Department handles their career expectation process. In the final stage of the promotional process, the highest rated candidates are invited to a "Career Expectation Panel." This panel consists of the chief of police, a lieutenant, a sergeant, and a police officer. Each panel member tells the candidate their expectations for a person holding the sought after rank. Typically, they refer to the articulated standards of the departments value statement extensively during the discussion. After the presentations the candidate may ask any questions of the panelists to clarify any of the expressed expectations. Then the candidate has two days to consider departmental expectations and decide if they are attainable. At the second meeting, the candidate accepts or rejects the promotion.[40]

A management audit is another means of reinforcing the importance of departmental values. Each employee meets with three managers to discuss privately how effective the agency applies basic values. Each officer may comment candidly on whether or not each of the elements is being enforced by the agency. Additionally, each individual is allowed to discuss confidentially any personnel issues adversely affecting the mission of the agency. After the meeting there are two reports prepared. The first is confidential and contains specific personnel issues and recommendations for addressing real or perceived problems. The second report is more comprehensive and covers all findings and recommendations. It serves as a planning guide for the management team and provides a starting point for the next management audit.[41]

Value Statements

A value statement reflects the style of policing used in a specific community. An agency emphasizing a professional policing model will

40. *Ibid.*   **41.** *Ibid.,* p. 4.

have the tendency to enforce the "letter of the law" rather than the "spirit of the law." Arrests and the issuance of citations will be the dominant method used to resolve conflict. This is far removed from a style of policing emphasizing service instead of enforcement. The service orientation stresses crime prevention, resolving community disputes, and solving problems. The values of community policing express an entirely different approach for dealing with crimes and problems in a community. Normally these values concern two elements. The administration and the employees of the agency, and the community along with other governmental agencies. Jointly these elements come to a consensus about the nature of the police function and police agency operation. As police executives discussed values, it became clear they were not out of place to involve the community in determining the cities' policing style.[42] This a significant shift from the professional model of policing and for many years such a concept would have been viewed as unadulterated heresy. Positive relating to the community will only come after the police have established a relationship of trust with the community. Such a process takes time, especially in communities where internal conflict exists or where relations with the police have been severely strained.[43]

The Houston Police Department experimented with community policing because it was concerned with the tendency for police agencies to institute specific programs and see them go by the board after a short time. They were also concerned with the difficulty of moving from a traditional policing style to one emphasizing the community and its needs. Departmental leadership decided to carry out community policing in two stages. Phase 1 was very traditional. It involved the implementation of specific programs as separate entities. It did not involve the entire department or affect the total community for a period of five years. Phase 2 involved the total department. Programs were started along with a comprehensive change in the style of policing. There were values established emphasizing problem solving and collaboration with the community. For example, there was a redesigning of beats reflecting natural neighborhood boundaries. This 2-phase program enabled the department to:

- Break down barriers to change.

- Educate leaders and rank-and-file members on the merits of community policing.

- Reassure the rank-and-file the community policing concepts under consideration were an outgrowth of programs already in place.

- Address problems on a small scale before making the full change.

42. *Ibid.*   **43.** Bureau of Justice Assistance, *op. cit., p. 5.*

- Reduce the likelihood that members of the department would reject the concept.

- Demonstrate the benefit to the public and elected officials.

- Provide a training ground for community policing.

- Create advocates among those persons who would become community–policing trainers.[44]

Value statements vary considerably depending upon the degree the agency wants to move toward community policing. In some departments considerable consideration is given to community involvement while in others it is somewhat limited. Figures 4–4 through 4–7 illustrate the range of value statements. Some give greater emphasis to employees and others to the community. Some are rather specific and others very general. For example, the Alexandria Police Department has 8 major value areas with many sub-sets. The Baltimore Police Department has a mission statement and eight standards of performance. It also has five items that specify member's responsibilities. The Buffalo County Sheriff's Department has a mission statement and ten value statements. The basic values of the Foster City Police Department are very specific and consider such aspects as the role of the courts. There is a tailoring of each set of values. They reflect the views of the community and the managerial view of policing.

44. Brown, *op. cit.,* p. 5.

Figure 4–4
Foster City Police Department Basic Values

I. Integrity is basic to the accomplishment of the law enforcement mission. Both personal and organizational integrity is essential to the maintenance of the F.C.P.D. This means that we:
  - ★ Insure that accurate reporting occurs at all levels;
  - ★ Promote and recognize ethical behavior and actions;
  - ★ Value the reputation of our profession and agency, yet promote honesty over loyalty to the Department;
  - ★ Openly discuss both ethical and operational issues that require change; and,
  - ★ Collectively act to prevent abuses of the law and violation of civil rights.

II. Due to the dynamic nature of our profession, the F.C.P.D. values innovation from all levels of the Agency. This means we:
  - ★ Reward and recognize those who contribute to the development of more effective ways of providing the policing service;
  - ★ Strive to minimize conflict which negatively impacts our work product, yet we support the constructive airing and resolution of differences in the name of delivering quality police services;
  - ★ Listen to and promote suggestions emanating from all levels of the Department; and
  - ★ Wish to promote an atmosphere that encourages prudent risk taking, and that recognizes that growth and learning may be spawned by honest mistakes.

III. The law enforcement profession is recognized as somewhat close and fraternal in nature. The F.C.P.D. reflects this tradition, yet supports community involvement and on-going critical self appraisal by all its members. This means we:
  - ★ Encourage employees to socialize with employees and community members alike to promote the reputation of the Agency;
  - ★ Promote programs that improve the relationship between our members and the community at large;
  - ★ Report and confront employees who violate laws and the basic values of the organization; and,
  - ★ Promote and discuss the positive aspects of the Agency and its product throughout the community.

IV. The provision of law enforcement services is a substantial expense to the taxpayer. The F.C.P.D. is obligated to provide the highest quality of police service for the resources expended. This means that we:
  - ★ Regularly assess the cost vs. benefits of the various programs of the Agency;
  - ★ Require a standard of professional performance for all members of the Department;
  - ★ Administer the Departmental funds in a prudent, cost-effective manner;
  - ★ Publicly acknowledge and praise employees that excel at their jobs; and,
  - ★ Support and encourage employees in their pursuit of higher education.

V. Law enforcement, in the course of performing its primary mission, is required to deal with both dangerous and difficult situations. The F.C.P.D. accepts this responsibility and supports its members in the accomplishment of these tasks. This means that we:
  - ★ Review and react to an individual's performance during such an event based upon the totality of the circumstances surrounding their decisions and actions;
  - ★ Encourage all employees, as the situation permits, to think before they act;
  - ★ Take all available steps and precautions to protect both the City's and employees' interest in incidents that provide either danger or civil exposure;
  - ★ Keep our supervisor informed of any incident or pending action that jeopardizes either the reputation of the Agency or an individual employee;
  - ★ Attempt, conditions permitting, to reason with individuals in the enforcement setting prior to resorting to the use of physical force; and,
  - ★ Recognize that it is our duty to prevent, report, and investigate crimes, together with the apprehension and the pursuit of vigorous prosecution of lawbreakers. We also recognize that it is the domain of the court to punish individuals convicted of crimes.

Source: Correspondence from Robert C. Norman, Chief of Police, Foster City, CA, November 4, 1998.

Figure 4–5
Baltimore Police Department—Values

MISSION

The mission of the Baltimore Police Department, in partnership with the Baltimore community, is to protect and preserve life and protect property, to understand and serve the needs of the city's neighborhoods, and to improve the quality of life by building capacities to maintain order, recognize and resolve problems, and apprehend criminals in a manner consistent with the law and reflective of shared community values.

STANDARDS OF PERFORMANCE/VALUES THAT GUIDE OUR ACTIONS

Our Highest Commitment is Protecting Life

We consider protecting life our highest priority. Our firearms policy reflects the commitment to protect life; we only use fatal force when it is absolutely necessary to save the life of a person or officer, or prevent serious bodily injury when no other options are available.

We are Committed to Provide High Quality Public Service

We believe all people should have access to police service. We care about public satisfaction with the type of police service they receive. We seek to employee individuals who desire to serve the community.

We Treat People with Respect and Sensitivity

As policing professionals, we seek to ensure every person will be treated with dignity, fairness and respect, without regard to race, religion, sex, sexual orientation, national origin or handicapped condition. We will always protect individuals' Constitutional rights.

We Adhere to Democratic Values in Performing Our Mission

We view the protection of the democratic way of life as an important part of our mission. We never violate the law in pursuit of police objectives.

We are Responsive to Community and Neighborhood Priorities

Community Policing is our primary policing strategy. Our relationship with the community is that of a partnership, jointly working to solve neighborhood problems. Our commitment to a community partnership means we will involve the community in determining neighborhood policing strategies and tactics, which impact their lives. We are committed to ensure that the personnel composition of the department—at all levels—reflects the multi-cultural diversity of our community.

We are Accountable to the Community for our Actions

Recognizing the authority placed with us by the community, we expect to be accountable for our actions. The department will objectively investigate citizen complaints and share with the community an analysis of the results of these administrative investigations into our actions. We will be open and honest in our dealings with the media.

We Care about our Employees' Job Satisfaction

Every employee is a valuable member of the department. We are committed to assisting in the development of our employee's professional and personal competencies. We recognize the employees' needs are important to enhance their performance. In discipline, our emphasis is on developing and reinforcing positive behavior.

We Maintain the Highest Level of Integrity in all our Actions

Reflecting the public trust placed in us, we avoid even the appearance of impropriety or conflict of interest. We never use our position for personal gain or the gain of people associated with us.

MEMBERS' RESPONSIBILITIES

The Values explained above form the basis for new policing in Baltimore. Values are meaningless unless they are accompanied by a real commitment throughout the organization that service match the value standards that have been set forth.

- **Widely disseminate** these values throughout the community and the department so that every citizen and every police officer with whom you interact, is aware of their existence.
- **Reflect and show** these values in everything you write, including speeches and in awards and commendations for members and citizens.
- **Challenge and encourage** the public and fellow members to come forth when they believe a value standard has been violated, no matter who the violator may be.
- **Be committed and adhere to** these values. All members will be committed and adhere to these values, and shall be held strictly accountable for compliance.
- **Make** these values part of our recruitment and training programs.

Source: Correspondence from George Mitchell, Major/Director, Planning and Research Division, Baltimore Police Department dated October 8, 1998.

Figure 4–6

Mission and Values of the Buffalo County
Sheriff's Department

Mission Statement

The mission of the Buffalo County Sheriff's Department is to enhance the quality of life in our county by working cooperatively with the public and within the framework of the U.S. Constitution to enforce law, preserve the peace, reduce fear and provide for a safer environment for all of our citizens.

Sheriff's Department Values

The Sheriff's Department will involve the communities and the people of the county in all policing activities that directly affect the quality of life.

The Sheriff's Department will maintain crime prevention as its primary goal, while vigorously pursuing those who commit crimes.

The Sheriff's Department will ensure that its policing strategies will preserve and advance democratic values.

The Sheriff's Department will structure service delivery in a manner as to reinforce the strengths of the county, communities and rural areas.

The Sheriff's Department will encourage public input regarding the development of policies that directly affect the quality of life.In Buffalo County.

The Sheriff's Department will manage its resources carefully and effectively.

The Sheriff's Department will seek input of employees into matters that affect job satisfaction and effectiveness.

The Sheriff's Department will maintain the highest levels of integrity and professionalism in all its members and its activities.

The Sheriff's Department will seek to provide stability, continuity and consistency in all departmental operations.

The Sheriff's Department will conduct themselves both personally and professionally in a manner that is above reproach by the people of the communities and county it servers.

Source: Neil Miller, Sheriff, Buffalo County, Kearney, NE, http://lec.kearney.net/sheriff.html. 10\12\1998.

Figure 4–7

Alexandria Police—These are Our Values

The Alexandria Police Department exists to serve the community by protecting life and property; by preventing crime; by enforcing the laws; and by maintaining order for all citizens.

Central to our mission are the values that guide our work and decisions, and help us contribute to the quality of life in Alexandria.

Our values are characteristics or qualities of worth. They are non-negotiable. Although we may need to balance them, we will never ignore them for the sake of expediency or personal preference.

We hold our values constantly before us to teach and remind the community and us we serve, of our ideals. They are the foundation upon which our policies, goals and operations are built.

In fulfilling our mission, we need the support of citizens, elected representatives and City officials in order to provide the quality of service our values commit us to providing.

We, the men and women of the Alexandria Police Department, value:

HUMAN LIFE
LAWS AND CONSTITUTION
EXCELLENCE
ACCOUNTABILITY
COOPERATION
PROBLEM–SOLVING
OURSELVES

HUMAN LIFE

We value human life and dignity above all else.
Therefore:
> We give first priority to situations that threaten life.
> We use force only when necessary.
> We treat all persons with courtesy and respect.
> We are compassionate and caring.

INTEGRITY

We believe integrity is the basis for communities trust.
Therefore:
> We are honest and truthful.
> We are consistent in our beliefs and actions.
> We hold ourselves to high standards of moral and ethical conduct.
> We are role models for the community.

LAWS AND CONSTITUTION

We believe in the principles embodied in our Constitution. We recognize the authority of Federal, State and local laws.
Therefore:
> We respect and protect the rights of all citizens.
> We treat all persons fairly and without favoritism.
> We are knowledgeable of the law.
> We enforce the law.
> We obey the law.

EXCELLENCE

We strive for personal and professional excellence.
Therefore:

We do our best.

We have a vision for the future.

We seek adequate resources; staffing, facilities, equipment, training, salaries, benefits.

We recruit and hire the best people.

We train and develop our employees to their highest potential.

We are committed to fair and equitable personnel practices.

We provide organizational mobility.

We recognize and reward good performance.

We support reasonable risk-taking and are tolerant of honest mistakes.

We are receptive to new ideas and to change.

We work toward realistic, mutually agreed upon goals.

We meet nationally recognized law enforcement standards.

We lead by example.

ACCOUNTABILITY

We are accountable to each other and to the citizens we serve who are the sources of our authority.
Therefore:

We communicate openly and honestly among ourselves and with the community.

We understand the importance of community values and expectations.

We are responsive to community concerns.

We acknowledge our mistakes and are open to constructive criticism.

We manage our resources effectively.

We thoroughly investigate complaints against our employees.

COOPERATION

We believe that cooperation and teamwork will enable us to combine our diverse backgrounds, skills and styles to achieve common goals.
Therefore:

We work as a team.

We understand our role in achieving Department and City goals and objectives.

We share our responsibility to serve the citizens of Alexandria with many other agencies and organizations.

We strive to understand those who disagree with us.

We seek the help and cooperation of others.

We seek to resolve conflicts.

We rely on community support and involvement.

PROBLEM–SOLVING

We are most effective when we help identify and solve community problems.
Therefore:

We work to anticipate and prevent problems.

We give a high priority to preventing crime and helping citizens feel safe.

We actively seek opinions and ideas from others.

We plan, analyze and evaluate.

We recognize that crime is a community problem.

We listen to problems and complaints with empathy and sensitivity.

We seek innovative solutions.

OURSELVES

We are capable, caring people who are doing important and satisfying work for the citizens of Alexandria.
Therefore:

    We respect, care about, trust and support each other.
    We enjoy our work and take pride in our accomplishments.
    We are disciplined and reliable.
    We keep our perspective and sense of humor.
    We balance our professional and personal lives.
    We consult the people who will be affected by our decisions.
    We have a positive, "can-do" attitude.
    We cultivate our best characteristics: initiative, enthusiasm, creativity, patience, competence, and judgment.

Source: Correspondence from Charles E. Samarra, Chief of Police, City of Alexandria, VA, dated December 16, 1998.

Problem–Solving Policing

Police departments have, in some instances, instituted community policing along with problem-solving (oriented) policing. These are not incompatible. In fact they are highly complementary. Numerous crime prevention programs are part and parcel of community policing. The key element is the importance of working with the community. On the other hand, problem-oriented policing is concerned with such elements as the careful identification of a problem, and devising means to resolve it. Both of these represent innovative approaches for dealing with the issues of crime and striving to find ways to deal with community problems.[45]

Herman Goldstein was the first one to emphasize the need for the police to become problem-oriented rather than incident-oriented. It was his position that the police should develop the capacity to diagnose solutions to recurring crime and disorder problems. Social issues need to be analyzed, and the police must work with others when devising solutions. An effort must be made to identify the most feasible and least costly program. Finally the police should monitor these programs.[46]

Community–Oriented Policing and Problem Solving (COPPS) is accomplished most effectively if police executives complete the 12

45. Malcolm K. Sparrow, "Information Systems: A Help or Hindrance in the Evolution of Policing?" *The Police Chief,* April 1991, Vol. LVIII, No. 4, p. 26–27.

46. Skolnick and Bayley, *op. cit.,* p. 17.

principles listed in figure 4–8. Several themes thread their way through this style of policing. First, an emphasis is placed on increasing the effectiveness, by dealing with problems consuming the time of patrol and investigations. Second, there has to be a reliance on the expertise and creativity of line officers when studying problems and arriving at recommendations. Finally, the department involves the community, to make sure their needs are taken into consideration.

Figure 4–8

What a Problem–Oriented Policing Agency Should Do

- Reassesses who is responsible for public safety and redefines the roles and relationships between the police and the community.
- Requires shared ownership, decision making, and accountability, as well as sustained commitment from both the police and the community.
- Establishing new public expectations of and measurement standards for police effectiveness (e.g., from solely 911 response time and arrest/crime statistics to include quality of service, customer (community) satisfaction, responsiveness to community defined issues, and cultural sensitivity).
- Increase understanding and trust between police and community members.
- Empowers and strengthens community-based efforts.
- Requires constant flexibility to respond to all emerging issues.
- Requires an on-going commitment to develop long-term and pro-active programs/strategies to address the underlying conditions that cause community problems.
- Requires knowledge of available community resources and how to access and mobilize them, as well as the ability to develop new resources within the community.
- Requires buy-in of the top management of the police and other local government agencies, as well as a sustained personal commitment from all levels of management and other key personnel.
- Decentralize police services/operations/management, relaxes the traditional "chain of command," and encourages innovation and creative problem solving by all—thereby making greater use of the knowledge, skill and expertise throughout the organization without regard to rank.
- Shifts the focus of police work from responding to individual incidents to addressing problems identified by the community as well as the police, emphasizing the use of problem-solving approaches to supplement traditional law enforcement methods.
- Requires commitment to developing new skills through training. (e.g., problem-solving, networking, conflict resolution, cultural competency/literacy).

Source: Daniel E. Lungren, *Community Oriented Policing & Problem Solving, Sacramento, CA,* Attorney General's Office, State of California, November 1992, pp. 3–4.

A key characteristic of the modern approach to policing is a positive orientation to problem solving. It involves more than responding to calls for service. It is a matter of viewing incidents from a community perspective to resolve the problem not just simply handling an incident. Problem-oriented policing shifts police efforts from a reactive to a proactive[47] response to crime wherein officers work with residents to prevent crime.[48]

A cooperative effort includes citizens, business, police departments, and other agencies work together to identify problems and apply appropriate problem-solving strategies. The central thesis of problem-oriented policing is that underlying incidents that police respond to are more general problems which, in order to be resolved, require a different type of response than do the incidents that are indicative of the problems. Problem solution requires analysis of the incidents by persons knowledgeable of the context in which they are occurring, followed by creative brainstorming about and experimentation with possible responses.[49] While problem-oriented policing theoretically can be conducted in the absence of community-oriented policing it is an excellent method of achieving the goals of community-oriented policing. This is why the model that is proposed in this chapter combines both under the term—community oriented policing and problem solving (COPPS).[50]

This process is a proactive philosophy that promotes the concept that incidents consuming patrol and investigative time can best be dealt with more effectively when consideration is given to underlying problems. It also assumes that the expertise and creativity of line officers are reliable sources when developing solutions to problems. Finally if problem solving in the community is to be successful the police must work with the public to insure they're addressing the real needs of citizens.

Detectives and line officers are the ones who can use the problem-solving approach. It allows them to identify, analyze, and respond, continuously to the underlying causes prompting citizens to request police services. It is not a one-shot project or program, but a comprehensive process for identifying, addressing, and resolving problems. It is a strategy consisting of four stages called SARA:

SCANNING—Identifying the problem;

ANALYSIS—Learning the problem's causes, scope, and effects;

RESPONSE—Acting to alleviate the problem; and,

47. Robert R. Friedmann, *Community Policing,* England, Harvester Wheatsheaf, 1992, pp. 186–188.

48. Police Executive Research Forum, *op. cit., pp. 1–6.*

49. Mary Ann Wycoff and Wesley K. Skogan, *Community Policing in Madison: Quality from the Inside Out,* Washington, DC, National Institute of Justice, 1993, pp. 9–10.

50. Richard J. De Paris, "Organizational Leadership and Change Management:

"Removing Systems Barriers to Community–Oriented Policing and Problem Solving," *The Police Chief,* December *1998,* Vol. LXV, No. 12, pp. 68–76.

ASSESSMENT—Determining whether the response worked.[51]

On identification of a problem actions can be taken to collecting information about the problem. This in turn leads to a detailed analysis of the information. The final stage shows whether the actions had the desired effect on the problems.

Scanning. Instead of relying upon legal terms such as robbery, burglary or petty theft to guide a response, officers analyze specific offenses in a broader context and address them as problems. Then these problems are dealt with according to their impact on the neighborhood or the community. For example, a police incident such as "auto theft" might be a part of a "chop" operation (cutting up an automobile into salable or usable parts). A series of "house burglaries" might in reality be a school "truancy problem."

Scanning initiates the problem solving process. In a truly problem-oriented police department every member scans for problems and brings the problem to the attention of a supervisor. With everyone involved no one can assume that it is someone else's responsibility. In other words passing the buck becomes somewhat limited. Some officers are better than others at identifying problems. Some accept the new process as a challenge and others find it is extra work avoidable at all costs. Other officers are reluctant to identify problems because they might be stuck with working on the problems. Over time objections, such as those mentioned above can be overcome as officer become more accustomed to the problem solving process. The objectives of the scanning process include:

- Looking for problems.

- Initial identification of possible problems.

- Initial analysis to determine if the problem exists and whether a detailed analysis is needed.

- Prioritizing of problems and assignment of personnel

Agency personnel have numerous sources that can be used to identify problems, but in many instances officers will initially rely upon there own experience to identify problems. Most officers are cautious about announcing the identification of a problem until they truly felt that a problem actually existed. This usually means that problems have been rejected before bringing the problem to the attention of others. The problem solving process consists of four parts reflected in figure 4–9.

51. William Spelman and John E. Eck, *Problem Oriented Policing*, Research in Brief, Washington, DC, National Institute of Justice, 1987, pp. 1–10.

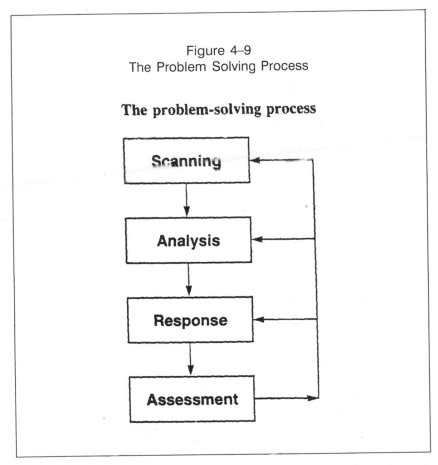

Figure 4–9
The Problem Solving Process

Source: William Spelman, and John E. Eck, *Problem-Oriented Policing,* Research in Brief, Washington, DC, National Institute of Justice, 1987, p. 4.

Analysis. After identification of the problem, the officers assigned should collect information from every conceivable source even remotely related to the problem. This includes private as well as public sources. For example, it can include information from neighborhood associations, and neighborhood watch groups. Other sources include elected officials or the news media as well as information from other law enforcement or governmental agencies. Officers can use a checklist to insure all the needed information is collected. The three areas of concern include:

- Actors involved in the problem, including victims, and offenders;

- Specific incidents including the sequence of events, and the physical contact involved in the incidents; and

- The responses by the community and institutional entities.

Figure 4–10

Checklist for the Analysis of a Problem

ACTORS

Victims

> Lifestyle
> Security measures taken
> Victimization history
> This victimization

Offenders

> Identity and physical description
> Lifestyle, education, employment
>   history, medical history
> Criminal history

Third parties

> Personal data
> Connection to victimization
> Nature of involvement
> Expectations for police action

INCIDENTS

Sequence of events

> Target of act
> Type of tools used by offenders
> Events preceding act
> Event itself
> Events following criminal act

Physical contact
Chronology

> Location
> Access control
> Surveillance

Social context

> Likelihood and probable actions of
> witnesses
> Attitude of residents toward neigh-
> borhood

RESPONSES

Community

> Neighborhood affected by problem
> City as a whole
> People outside the city
> Groups

Institutional

> Criminal justice agencies
> Other public agencies
> Mass media
> Business sector

Source: William Spelman and John E. Eck, *Problem Oriented Policing,* Research in Brief, Washington, DC: National Institute of Justice, 1987, pp. 5–6.

All the information gathered serves as a foundation for developing a thorough understanding of the real problem. This serves as a base for identifying causes and developing options for its resolution. The checklist reminds officers of areas and topics open to consideration. Implicit in the list is potential sources of information that might not have been covered under the "scanning" part of the assessment process. During "analysis" emphasis is given to external information sources such as: consulting with citizens, business leaders, community associations, and other community groups.

When utilizing the checklist officers will not normally collect information from all of the sources listed, but only from those directly related to the problem under consideration. Another qualifier is the time the officer has available to search for an appropriate response to the problem under consideration. There is a tendency for officers to identify the response to the problem before completing the analysis and if and when this occurs options might be eliminated from consideration.

Response. This stage requires initiative by the officer, as different solutions are identified and the best solution is selected and implemented. Involving outside agencies having resources and expertise seldom available within the police agency increases the potential solutions to a problem. This stage involves working with individuals, businesses, and private agencies. It also requires the officer to work with public agencies such as the probation department, health department, public works, and the social service department. All of these sources are important because other agencies and entities can come up with responses that fall outside of the normal expertise possessed by law enforcement agencies. Combined resources can prove to be the most effective response to the problem being studied. Officers striving to find a solution to a problem should have a free rein for discovering the answer. In one city the only restriction was, the solution had to be legally, financially, administratively, and politically possible. Solutions to problems can be organized into five responses:

- Total problem elimination;
- Material reduction of the problem;
- Reduction of the harm caused by the problem;
- Dealing with the problem with the best possible solution; and
- Removable of the problem from police consideration.[52]

When a solution becomes apparent implementation should occur immediately or incrementally depending upon the circumstances. Some problems are subject to immediate solution, because they are minor in nature or involve a few people. Other solutions might involve broad social issues that require a complex response.

Assessment. This is the final stage and it involves measuring how well the program performed? Was it effective? The agency and the community work together to answers these questions. Possibly the

52. *Ibid.*

initial analysis was flawed, or the wrong response was elected. The process of assessment can provide an officer with the information needed to determine success. For some situations "assessment" is quite simple and the results obvious. In other situations it is complex and may involve the collection of complex data. Surveys [53] are becoming increasingly common and can be used to achieve four goals:

- Gathering information on the public's attitudes toward police
- Detect and analyze problems in neighborhoods or among special population groups.
- Evaluate problem-solving efforts and other programs.
- Control crime and reduce fear of crime.[54]

When evaluating a problem solving program multiple surveys can prove to be most effective. For example, before-and-after surveys can be used to determine changes in citizen's fear of crime as a result of a police intervention. Problem-solving units of the Baltimore County Police Department routinely use this technique to gauge their effectiveness. Another area where surveys are most useful is environmental. Recording and analyzing the environmental characteristics of a problem area can use environmental surveys used at each stage of the problem-solving process, from scanning through assessment. They help an officer analyze the nature of a problem by identifying what factors contribute to the crime and pointing to incivilities in the problem area. Used before and after implementing a problem-solving effort, environmental surveys enable the officer to measure the effectiveness of the effort.[55]

Typical of what can be done is the approach used by the City of Fort Lauderdale, FL. This community was plagued with a rising drug-related murder rate. Poor living conditions and an accompanying low quality of life also troubled the inner-city area where the murders occurred. Encountering this problem, the police department studied the issues, concluding there was a need for a "code enforcement team." This involved the integration of officers/members of the police department, the fire department, and the building and zoning department. This allowed the unit to combine the city's full regulatory and police powers to patrol the area together. The team worked to reduce and prevent criminal activity and to bring commercial and residential structures into compliance. The ultimate goal was to improve the quality of life within the community.

During one year the team inspected some 2,500 dwellings. This resulted in the issuance of some 21,600 citations for violations. Sixty

53. Cheryl Simrell King, Kathryn M. Feltey, and Bridget O'Neill Sursel, "The Question of Participation: Toward Authentic Public Participation in Public Administration," *Public Administration Review,* July/August 1998, Vol. 58, No. 4, pp. 317–327.

54. Bureau of Justice Assistance, *A Police Guide to Surveying Citizens and Their Environment,* Washington, DC, US Department of Justice, 1993, pp. 1–41.

55. *Ibid.*

dwellings were boarded-up or demolished.-The team also completed a 6–month action plan to clean up a 15–square block area of the city. This is an outstanding example of a unified approach to problem solving. Using the model of the "code enforcement team" the police department has developed other programs with city departments, the business community, and the neighborhood associations.[56]

The City of Albuquerque following the same pattern created an interagency team to enforce city codes against delinquent properties. This team included an investigator, a housing inspector, a zoning inspector, and a fire inspector. Working together the team performed comprehensive inspections for violations. This approach was so successful that a second team was created and the city was divided into two inspection zones.[57] In California excellent use has been made of the eviction code to displace criminal elements from rental properties. State law makes it illegal to knowingly rent to drug dealers. [58]Cities have also been successful in changing building codes that makes home burglaries more difficult. Police officers conduct inspection of every new structure to ensure that the security section of the building code is met.[59]

Problem solving and community policing exists in a variety of forms throughout the United States. Its final form and its viability remain open to question in the minds of some. One question is can police departments successfully change from the professional model emphasizing centralization, control, and detachment from the community? In time this question will be answered as more and more departments experiment with this new policing philosophy.[60]

A partial answer is that change may be occurring faster than many thought would be possible. In a survey of departments with more than 100 sworn officers it was found that 55 percent of the responding agencies (651) had a formally written community policing plan and 68 percent had community policing units with personnel assigned full-time. Additionally 72 percent of the responding agencies had community substations.

56. Joseph M. Donisi, "Ft. Lauderdale's Code Enforcement Team", *FBI Law Enforcement Bulletin,* March 1992, Vol. 61, No. 3, pp. 24–25.

57. Tony Lesce, "Code Enforcement Teams–Inter-agency Inspections Target Abandoned Building," *Law and Order,* September 1995, Vol. 43, No. 9, pp. 93–95.

58. Drew Bessinger, "Using the Civil Eviction Process," *Law and Order,* August *1997,* Vol. 46, No. 8, pp. 69–70.

59. John Hoffman, "Building Codes Help Reduce Burglaries," *Law And Order,* October 1998, Vol. 46, No. 10, pp. 149–151.

60. John C. Eck and Denis P. Rosenbaum, "The New Police Order: Effectiveness, Equity, and Efficiency in Community Policing," in Dennis P. Rosenbaum, Editor, *The Challenge of Community Policing: Testing the Promises,* Thousand Oaks, CA, Sage Publications, 1994, pp. 1–18.

Figure 4–11
Percent of Agencies Engaging in Selected Community Policing
Activities During a Twelve Month Period

| Activity | Local Law Enforcement Agency | | | |
	County	Municipal	Sheriff	State
Engaged in SARA-type solving problems	57%	59%	43%	41%
Assigned detectives based on geographical Areas/beats	67	41	53	35
Formed problem-solving partnerships through contracts/written agreement	57	68	59	33
Patrol officers responsible for specific geographic areas/beats	97	89	87	57
Included problem-solving projects in criteria for evaluating patrol officers	40	35	31	20
Trained citizens in community policing	67	69	60	27

Source: Brian A. Reaves and Andrew L. Goldberg, *Law Enforcement Management and Administrative Statistics, 1997: Data for Individual State and Local Agencies with 100 or More Officers,* Washington, DC, Bureau of Justice Statistics, April 1999, p. xx.

Figure 4–11 lists data regarding the nature of community policing activities that were engaged in during a one-year period. It is evident that significant strides have been made in community policing and it is entirely possible that it is a managerial process that has come to pass. Of special importance is the inclusion of criteria for evaluating officers on their problem-solving activities. Once more departments include this activity as an integral part of community policing it clearly enhances the viability of the total process.

Case Study

Captain Richard Yu–Seng

Richard Ye–Seng has been in the Bayside Police Department for 15 years. He previously worked in another department for two years and transferred laterally. Chang has a degree in criminology, is currently enrolled in a masters in Public Administration program. He anticipates graduation within one year. He is a very outgoing person, has a good sense of humor. He is well liked by his peers and the officers under his command. He is currently in charge of the Uniformed Division after assuming that position two years ago. Prior to that time he was the head of SWAT. Members of the department anticipated that he would eventually become the Chief of Police. Yu–Seng is a second generation American but has never learned to speak his native tongue, although his grandparents speak Mandarin Chinese fluently. He is married and has three children. He has resided in Bayside since he joined the department.

The department is just in the process of beginning a community-policing program and training is scheduled for part of his Division. The Uniformed Division will conduct as pilot study, to last two years, to test the viability of the community policing concept. During the first six months of the program two teams, one on the day shift and the other on the swing shift, will have completed the forty-hour required training course. Supervisory personnel will be given additional training in problem solving. The target area selected was the Oxford Apartments that is ten blocks from the central business district. The City Housing Department has taken over the apartment that has 312 units. The complex is located amid middle-income incomes and low-to middle-income apartments. A major highway is adjacent to the west-side of the area and a major shopping complex is six blocks away. The condition of the complex has deteriorated in recent years. The grounds are littered with broken glass and trash. Children do not use the playground, and disabled vehicles fill many of the parking spaces in front of the buildings. The occupancy rate of the complex is 68 percent.

Residential burglary has increased dramatically along with thefts from automobiles. The major highway is utilized to enter the area, commit a crime, and exit. Numerous calls have been received from the complex regarding drug activity. A citizens committee, supported by local churches, has demanded action and the City Council supports the concept of community policing.

The first order of business is to meet with the citizens committee. What would be the agenda be for the meeting? After creating an agenda what else would you do? Would you invite anyone else to the meeting? Why? What departmental, city and community resources would you expect would be involved in the scanning phase? Why? What would you do to analyze the problem? Why? Would you conduct a survey? If so what kind?

For Further Reading

Aragon, Randall and Richard E. Adams, "Community–Oriented Policing—Success Insurance Strategies." *FBI Law Enforcement Bulletin*, December 1997, *Vol. 66, No. 12.*

> Presents an excellent discussion of how *a* police department moved slowly from a traditional policing model to a community-oriented approach. Recommends that the organization built a positive organizational culture and implemented Total Quality Management principles. Presents twenty different strategies for supporting the implementation and continued success of community policing. These strategies range from the development of a mission statement to the introduction of community oriented policing to an target-specific area.

Safir, Howard, "Goal–Oriented Community Policing: The NYPD Approach." *The Police Chief*, December 1997, Vol. LXIV, No. 12, pp. 32–39.

> Reviews the application of the problem-solving mechanism for reducing crime and improving neighborhood conditions. Supports the position that problem-solving principles must be steadily and aggressively applied on an agency-wide basis. Recommends that police executives need to cede some degree of power and authority to empower and enhance the discretion of front-line officers and middle managers. Emphasizes the importance of utilizing Comp-Stat (Computerized Statistics) and the promotion of managerial accountability as a means of fostering the implementation of goal-oriented community policing.

Trojanowicz, Robert and Bonnie Bucqueroux, Community Policing: How to Get Started. Second Edition, Cincinnati, OH: Anderson Publishing Co., 1998, pp. 1–182.

> A landmark publication in community policing this book contains sections ranging from theory and definition of community policing to the actual duties of the officer, and how to evaluate officers. The discussion of theory is especially useful if one is to understand the concepts underlying community policing. Of special interest is the section on supervision that includes a wide range of topics such as: internal functions, sources of resistance, external relationships, and measurable activities performed by a first-line supervisor. The section on sources of resistance will prove useful when a supervisor is involved in the implementation of community policing.

Bureau of Justice Assistance, *A Police Guide to Surveying Citizens and Their Environment,* Monogram, Washington, DC, US Department of Justice, October 1993, pp. 1–99.

> This monogram offers a basic practical introduction to two types of surveys that police can find useful: 1)community, and 2) physical environment. It presents a basic practical introduction to the principles of survey methods for police practitioners with no experience or education in survey research in particular or research methods in general. It also introduces readers to the language of survey research. Additionally, it contains several samples of surveys.

Chapter 5

THE ORGANIZATIONAL ENVIRONMENT:
Motivational Considerations

Learning Objectives

1. Described a self-actualized individual.
2. List the five needs identified by Maslow.
3. Write a short essay describing growth needs.
4. Compare E.R.G. theory and Acquired Needs Theory.
5. Utilizing the motivation-hygiene theory list five motivators.
6. Describe the key elements of Theory Y.
7. Contrast Maslow and Herzberg.
8. List the four managerial features present by Likert.
9. Describe the immaturity-maturity continua.
10. Write a short essay describing theory Z.
11. Compare the theory of sensitivity with the theory of values.
12. List ten fundamental motives.

If there is any task that confronts and confounds management it is the successful accomplishment of tasks through the efforts of others. Officers respond to the work environment differently. Additionally, they condition and recondition the organizational culture. Each individual has different skills, abilities, and needs, that must be integrated into the organization in order to achieve defined goals. Another variable the manager must consider is the group process. Research clearly indicates the group process (employees working with others) affects individual behavior. The total managerial process is highly complex. The ultimate goal of a manager is to blend the individual into the organization so there is a minimum of negative entropy. It is an established fact that participative management is increasing, but the key to its success has not yet been found. How much participation is desirable? Who should participate in the decision-making process? What elements of the managerial process should be subjected to participative consideration? Can one truly empower others? None of these questions have been answered, but they are basic to the transition of management from a simplistic consideration of managerial fiats to a position that reflects an eclectic approach to management.

Need Hierarchy

Maslow's studies emphasized mental health and his research concentrated on the very best human beings he could find.[1] Emphasis was placed on studying man as an entity—or the holistic approach. Self-actualizing (SA) individuals are a small percentage of the total population (a fraction of one percent.)[2] The self-actualized person had a more harmonious personality whose perceptions were less distorted by desires, anxieties, fears, hopes, false optimism, or pessimism.[3] The superior individual was usually sixty years of age or older and the most universal characteristic was the ability to see life clearly.[4] The self-actualized person was found to be creative, risk-taking and possessing a low degree of self-conflict. The S–A person has a healthy attitude toward work. It is enjoyable and actually becomes play.[5] From his analysis of self-actualized individuals, Maslow created a theory of human motivation. "The human being is motivated by a number of basic needs which are species-wide, apparently unchanged, and genetic or instinctual in origin."[6]

The five needs identified by Maslow were of the hierarchical type and these are set forth in figure 5–1. Physiological needs are the strongest and are the fundamental needs to sustain life—food, shelter, sex, air, water and sleep. He believed that throughout life the human being always desires something. He is a wanting animal and "rarely reaches a state of complete satisfaction except for a short time. As one desire is satisfied, another pops up to take its place."[7] Once the basic physical needs are fulfilled, the *safety* needs emerge. These needs are essentially the need for reasonable order and stability. Freedom from being anxious and insecure dominates this set of *safety* needs, generally satisfied in the healthy adult.[8]

With the fulfillment of the *physiological* and *safety* needs, there emerges the belongingness and love need. Maslow states that, "*man* will hunger for affectionate relations with people, for a place in a group, and that he will strive with great intensity to achieve this goal."[9] He identified two categories of *esteem* needs. The first was *self-esteem*, which includes the desire for confidence, competence, achievement, independence and freedom. The second category was *respect from* others and includes the concepts of prestige, recognition, acceptance, status and reputation.[10] Assuming the reasonable gratification of

1. Frank G. Goble, *The Third Force: The Psychology of Abraham Maslow,* New York, Pocket Book, 1970, p. 15.

2. *Ibid.,* p. 32.

3. Abraham H. Maslow, *Motivation and Personality,* New York, Harper and Rowe, 1954, p. 181.

4. Abraham H. Maslow, *Toward a Psychology of Being,* New York, Van Nostrand, 1962, p. 118.

5. Globe, *op. cit.,* p. 30.

6. *Ibid.,* p. 38.

7. Maslow, *op. cit.*

8. Globe, *op. cit.,* p. 40.

9. *Ibid.*

10. *Ibid.,* p. 42.

the previous needs, Maslow states "what man *can* be, he *must* be."[11] This is self-actualization that is personal awareness of the need for growth, development and utilization of potential.

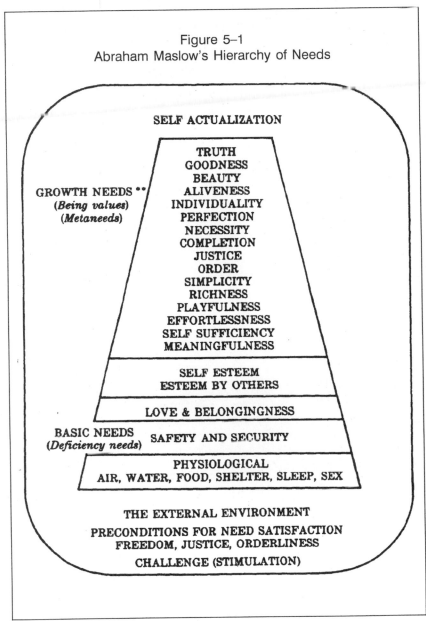

Figure 5–1
Abraham Maslow's Hierarchy of Needs

SELF ACTUALIZATION

GROWTH NEEDS **
(Being values)
(Metaneeds)

TRUTH
GOODNESS
BEAUTY
ALIVENESS
INDIVIDUALITY
PERFECTION
NECESSITY
COMPLETION
JUSTICE
ORDER
SIMPLICITY
RICHNESS
PLAYFULNESS
EFFORTLESSNESS
SELF SUFFICIENCY
MEANINGFULNESS

SELF ESTEEM
ESTEEM BY OTHERS

LOVE & BELONGINGNESS

BASIC NEEDS
(Deficiency needs)   SAFETY AND SECURITY

PHYSIOLOGICAL
AIR, WATER, FOOD, SHELTER, SLEEP, SEX

THE EXTERNAL ENVIRONMENT
PRECONDITIONS FOR NEED SATISFACTION
FREEDOM, JUSTICE, ORDERLINESS
CHALLENGE (STIMULATION)

* Source: Frank G. Globe, *The Third Force: The Psychology of Abraham Maslow,* New York, Pocket Books (Grossman Publisher, Inc.), 1970, p. 52. Reprinted with permission of Pocket Books/Simon & Schuster.

** Growth needs are all of equal importance (not hierarchial).

11. Maslow, *op. cit.*

These fundamental needs are usually identified and evolve into the indicated hierarchical arrangement. But Maslow cautions there are many exceptions. The categories overlap and are not entirely precise. He suggests it is the unsatisfied needs that influence behavior. Once a need has been gratified, it has limited effect on motivation. Since his initial research, Maslow discovered a new list of needs identified, as *growth* needs as compared to the previously identified basic needs. He felt the higher needs utilized the basic needs as a foundation. The higher or *growth* needs were:

- Wholeness.
- Perfection.
- Completion.
- Justice.
- Aliveness.
- Richness.
- Simplicity.
- Beauty.
- Goodness.
- Uniqueness.
- Effortlessness.
- Playfulness.
- Truth.
- Self-sufficiency.[12]

Maslow found that the *growth* needs were interrelated and when defining one value it is necessary to use the other values. These values cannot be separated and everyone reflects the highest need category. The hierarchy-of-needs theory has many supporters and has been extended to the problems of job motivation and management. Maslow was convinced of the practicality of McGregor's *Theory Y. He* expressed the belief that with *healthy* workers, *Theory Y* management would be more productive than Theory X.[13] Maslow cautioned that we should not make the mistake of thinking good working conditions would transform all people into self-actualized individuals.[14]

The hierarchy of needs theory assumes that the job performance of officers and the successful completion of tasks is controlled by three basic principles. The first is *countervailing needs* that views human beings as social individuals who can be viewed as multidimensional. Individuals have the capacity to prioritize needs and satisfy higher and lower needs concurrently. The second is *satisfaction deficit* that de-

12. Globe, *op. cit.,* pp. 47–48.
13. Globe, *ibid.,* p. 99.
14. For a detailed study of Maslow's management views see: Abraham H.

Maslow, *Eupsychian Management,* Illinois, Irwin–Dorsey, 1965.

scribes a state where unsatisfied human needs bring into being a state of uneasiness. As a consequence one acts to satisfy those needs. *Progression* is the final principle and eludes to the fact that needs are hierarchical in nature. When a lower level need is satisfied the next highest need comes into play. When a need is not satisfied individuals behavior becomes focused on a goal that directs effort toward fulfillment. When needs are not satisfied they act as motivators. As one moves through the hierarchy and a need is gratified progression up the hierarchy occurs. From a managerial stand point this means that the lowest level of unsatisfied needs motivates officers. With this in mind self actualization can be sought after once one has adequately satisfied the four lower needs. It should be kept in mind that this process is modified by the natural tendency to increase one's expectations after need satisfaction. In which case officers recycle to one of the lower needs when the adequate level is defined upward or when need satisfaction is jeopardized.[15] An officer who joins a small department might seek a lateral transfer as a means of improving his/her level of compensation. Another officer might seek promotion as a means of dealing with a satisfaction deficit.

Management should strive to identify the unfulfilled needs of personnel. Once these are determined it provides a frame of reference for understanding why officers perform as they do. If officers find it necessary to obtain a second job in order to meet basic survival needs it can have a negative impact on job performance. Management has an obligation to provide officers with adequate financial compensation to meet their survival needs, a safe environment to meet security needs, a working environment that fulfills social needs, and a non-monetary reward system that meets ego-esteem needs. Administrators should opt for a system wherein officers can have a reasonable expectation to engage in meaningful work, become self sufficient, and express their individuality. [16]As fundamental needs are satisfied and the need structure is altered self-actualized comes into play. This suggests that management should place a strong emphasis on employee development. To ignore the creation of a positive working environment is to lay a negative foundation that tolerates ineffectiveness, and inefficiency. When growth needs are part of a personnel development system there is a reduction in absenteeism, diminished interpersonal conflict, and improved morale.

E.R.G. Theory

On the surface Maslow's theory appears to have a great deal of substance, but it has never been validated. At the same time it holds a prominent place in the minds of organizational humanists. A number

15. David A. Tansik, Richard B. Chase, and Nicholas J. Aquilano, *Management: A Life Cycle Approach,* Homewood, IL, Richard D. Irwin, 1980, pp. 5-90.

16. David H. Holt, *Management: Principles and Practices, Englewood Cliffs, NJ, Prentice-Hall,* 1987, pp. 32-78.

of individuals have made an effort to alter the hierarchy of needs in such a way as to make it more useful in explaining human behavior. Adaptations of this nature are known as content theory. The best known of such theories is E.R.G. that Clayton Alderfer developed. This theory reduces the five human needs to three with the assumption that these three are operative in every human being:

- **Existence Needs.** This area encompasses the following needs that include physiological, safety and security. Combined into one category it includes the things that sustain life, such as, food, water, sex, air, shelter, and sleep. It also includes the need that each of us has for being free of insecurity and anxiousness. These latter are usually fulfilled through employment.

- **Relatedness Needs.** These needs involve the social arena. Mankind has a fundamental need to belong to a group and have reciprocal relationships with others. There also is a need to have an affectionate relationship with others. It is a question of belonging to a group or sharing something needed.

- **Growth Needs.** These needs are psychosocial in origin. It is the process of developing a feeling of net worth (self-esteem), and actual fulfillment (self-actualization). The satisfaction of growth needs creates an atmosphere where individuals manifest a high level of self-confidence. These needs sanction an individual to challenge tasks, and develop skills needed to master tasks.

A distinguishing characteristic of E.R.G. theory is that it is not hierarchical in nature. Any one of the three may dominate without the fulfillment of the others. For example, growth needs can prevail rather than existence needs.[17] There is absolutely no need to satisfy one need before moving to the next that is true in Maslow's hierarchy. As a consequence it is difficult to say what motivated someone to do something under certain circumstances. E.R.G. theory has on three principles. These are:

- need-escalation.

- satisfaction-progression.

- frustration-regression.

These make it a lot easier to understand and distinguishes it from Maslow's need hierarchy. The first is the **need-escalation principle.** It holds that the less a human need is satisfied the greater the desire to fulfill that need. Thus when a desire exists it becomes a significant motivator. The second is the **satisfaction-progression principle.** It holds that when lower level needs become satisfied the desire to attain higher order needs evolves. In fact, satisfaction of the lower needs creates a much stronger desire for the higher level needs. The third is the **frustration-regression principle.** It is different from other

17. Clayton P. Alderfer, *Existence, Relatedness, and Growth: Human Needs* *in Organizational Setting*, New York, Free Press, 1972, p. 182.

principles because it reverses the process. If the higher level needs are satisfied at a low level the chances are greater that additional emphasis will be placed on satisfying lower needs. For example, an individual might desire to fulfill relatedness or existence needs.

From a managerial view point there is definitely a dynamic interaction between how people perceive needs and the actual fulfillment of needs. It suggests that greater emphasis on lower needs will satisfy employees when an organization is unable to fulfill higher order needs. For example, when employees have to perform tasks that are not demanding and not allowed to operate at full capacity managers can work to improve such things as general working conditions. In one police department the organization believed its low attrition rate, high number of applicants, lack of problems with educational requirements, and limited problems attracting minority candidates was because of two factors. The department had excellent working conditions and an outstanding salary and benefits package. It boiled down to one thing. The organizational atmosphere was such that it was a "good place to work."[18]

Acquired Needs Theory

Another approach to identify and measure human needs was developed by psychologists who used the Thematic Appreciation Test (TAT) in their research. Subjects looked at photographs and recorded what they saw. From the data the researchers concluded that there were three basic human drives. These three needs were defined as:

- **Need for achievement.** Every individual has a fundamental need to achieve (nAch). This means that each person wants to be competent. It also involves solving problems, and performing complex tasks. Additionally, each person wants to make a meaningful contribution to the department.

- **Need for affiliation.** Human beings have a fundamental need to interact with others, and develop an affiliation with a group (nAff). This need is unquenchable. Each of us wants to have a meaningful and continuing social relationship with others.

- **Need for power.** Human beings have a basic need to influence or control someone else's behavior and to do this they strive to acquire power (nPower). Acquired power becomes "positive power" when the acquirer intertwines the ability to influence others with the goal of attaining organizational objectives.

It is the position of researchers in this area that the three needs exist in everyone all of the time. These needs, nAch, nAff, and nPower will vary from person to person in term of their intensity, and one need will dominate over others. The dominant need is what motivates the

18. Richard M. Ayers, *Preventing Law Enforcement Stress: The Organization's Role,* Alexandria, VA, The National Sheriffs' Association, 1990, p. 21.

employee.[19] These needs are acquired over time. Each individual modifies them because of their personality, background and values. It is important that managers identify their own dominant need. This allows managers to respond to the difference found in each employee. Managers with a nPower need normally function most effectively because they are comfortable when influencing others to achieve departmental objectives. Managers who have a nAch need are those who would rather do it themselves. Finally, managers with a nAff need are more comfortable interacting socially with employees and foster participation, camaraderie, and communications over directing or telling employees what to do.

There is considerable similarity and overlapping between this theory and those proposed by Maslow and Alderfer. Figure 5–2 presents the three theories in juxtaposition as a means of facilitating their comparison. It shows the complexity of the motivation process and illustrates the need for additional research in this area. A manager should become as familiar as possible with each theory in order to better understand human behavior. The key is to remember that at our present level of knowledge we are in a position to realize the variability of the human equation and work to improve our knowledge of why employees behave the way they do. Under the adaptive management concept the reason for the creation of law enforcement agencies is to achieve goals that make communities safer. Motivational theories provide a vehicle for organizational goal attainment.

Figure 5–2		
Comparison of Motivational Theories		
NEED HIERARCHY THEORY	**E.R.G. THEORY**	**ACQUIRED NEEDS THEORY**
Self-actualization	Growth	Achievement
Self esteem and esteem by others		
Love and belongingness	Relatedness	Affiliation
Safety and security Physiological	Existence	Power

Motivation—Hygiene Theory

Frederick Herzberg and his collaborators developed the concept of motivation versus hygiene. The major thrust of this research was to investigate whether different factors were responsible for bringing

19. David H. Holt, *Management:* Cliffs, NJ, Prentice–Hall, 1987, p. 312.
Principles and Practice, Englewood

about job satisfaction or dissatisfaction.[20] In sum, "What do people want from their job?" was the central question for the investigation. The researchers reviewed the literature and found a total of 155 studies purportedly answering this significant question.[21] The literature review indicated different results were achieved when the research design was concerned with what made workers happy with their jobs as opposed to studies emphasizing factors leading to job dissatisfaction. Respondents, who were happy with their jobs, most often described factors related to tasks, to specific events indicating successful work performance, and to a potential for professional growth.[22]

Figure 5–3	
Motivational–Hygiene Theory	
Motivators	**Hygiene**
Advancement	Policies and Administration
Responsibility	Supervision—technical
Work itself	Salary
Recognition	Supervision—interpersonal relations
Achievement	Working conditions

Conversely, when respondents reported feelings of unhappiness, the factors identified were not associated with the job itself, but with conditions external to task accomplishment.[23] Factors involved in these situations were identified as *hygiene,* because they acted in a manner similar to medical hygiene. Herzberg viewed supervision, interpersonal relations, physical working conditions, salary, company policies, administrative practices, benefits and job security, as hygiene factors (see figure 5–3).[24]

If *hygiene* factors reach an unacceptable low level among employees, then job dissatisfaction occurs. However, Herzberg emphasizes that the reverse does not hold true.

The factors leading to positive job attitudes are those satisfying the individual's need for self-actualization in work. Unquestionably, the factors relating to the accomplishment of a job and the factors defining the job context serve as employee goals, but the fundamental nature of the motivating qualities are essentially different. The job factors are designated as the "motivators" as opposed to the extra-job factors that are labeled as the factors of hygiene.[25] Both types of factors meet employee needs, but primarily the *motivators* result in job satisfaction.

20. Frederick Herzberg, Bernard Mausner and Barbara Snyderman, *The Motivation to Work,* Second Edition, New York, John Wiley and Sons, Inc., 1959, p. 57.

21. *Ibid.,* p. 107.

22. *Ibid.,* p. 113.

23. *Ibid.*

24. *Ibid.*

25. *Ibid.,* p. 114.

Motivators (which lead to satisfaction) include advancement, responsibility, work itself, recognition and achievement (see figure 5–4).[26]

Herzberg focused his research on motivators and encouraged management to create a work environment emphasizing *satisfiers* rather than *dissatisfiers*.[27]

At this point it is helpful to compare the theories of Maslow and Herzberg. As evident in figure 5–5 there are immediate similarities and at the same time, there are features exhibiting differences. Maslow suggests that any of the needs he has identified can become motivators while Herzberg states there are several very specific motivators and others that he identified as hygiene factors.[28]

In the application of either theory to law enforcement, there is limited evidence of their viability. Empirical studies are needed, relating motivational factors to actual performance and the attainment of organizational objectives. Furthermore, it is quite evident that both theories do not allow adequately for individual differences in motivation. For example, one person can be highly receptive to the probability of receiving a promotion, but someone else may be threatened by such a prospect. One can ask whether Herzberg's initial research based on the study of accountants and engineers or Maslow's study of the very "best" human beings has any application whatsoever to law enforcement. Until such studies are completed there is all the more reason to accept the mandate of *adaptive management* presupposing that the individual will adjust to the organization for varying reasons.

Theory X—Theory Y

One of the most influential studies was accomplished by Douglas McGregor, the results of which appeared in *The Human Side of Enterprise*.[29] It was his position that all management acts were based on specific assumptions, generalizations and hypotheses. McGregor suggests that the characteristics of behavior and employees' attitudes are in response to the manifestations of the manager's concept of the job and fundamental assumptions about human nature.[30] If a manager holds workers in relatively low esteem, the manager actually sees himself as a member of a small elite group possessing special abilities

26. Paul Hersey and Kenneth H. Blanchard, *Management of Organizational Behavior,* Second Edition, Englewood Cliffs, New Jersey, Prentice–Hall, Inc., 1972, p. 58.

27. For additional works referring to motivation, see: William J. Bopp, "Hawthorne Revisited," *The Police Chief* April 1978, Vol. XLV, No. 4, pp. 81–83; James A. Conser, "Motivational Theory Applied to Law Enforcement Agencies" *Journal of Police Science and Administration,* September 1979, Vol. 7, No. 3, pp. 285–291, and Gary W. Cordner, "A

Review of Work Motivational Theory and Research for the Police Manager," *Journal of Police Science and Administration,* September 1978, Vol. 6, No. 3, pp. 286–292.

28. J.G. Hunt and J.W. Hill, "The New Look in Motivational Theory for Organizational Research," *Human Organization,* 1969, Vol. 28, No. 2, p. 476.

29. Douglas McGregor, *The Human Side of Enterprise,* New York, McGraw–Hill Book Company, 1960, pp. 23–49.

30. *Ibid.,* p. 139.

and the bulk of the human race as rather limited. Such a manager assumes that most workers are inherently lazy, desire to have someone take care of them and actually want strong leadership. This type of manager sees people as prepared to take advantage of the work situation unless they are subjected to firm direction and positive control.[31]

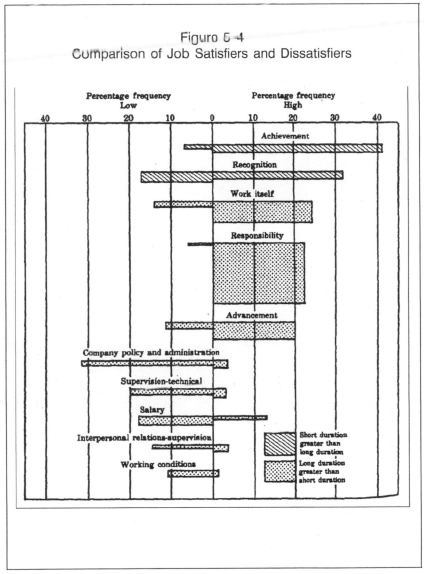

Figure 5-4
Comparison of Job Satisfiers and Dissatisfiers

Adapted from: Frederick Herzberg, et al., *The Motivation to Work,* New York, John Wiley and Sons, Inc., 1969, p. 81, Reprinted with permission of Frederick Herzberg.

31. *Ibid.*

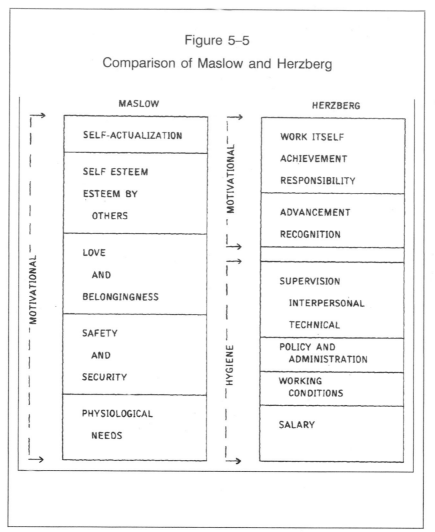

Figure 5–5

Comparison of Maslow and Herzberg

Adapted and modified from: J.G. Hunt and J.W. Hill, "The New Look in Motivational Theory for Organizational Research," *Human Organization,* Vol. 28, No. 2, 1969 cited in, *A Study of Organizational Leadership,* Harrisburg, PA.

In short, such a manager holds to Theory X. This theoretical orientation reflects itself in numerous ways in a manager's daily behavior toward subordinates. Theory X leads to an unusual emphasis on control. Procedures and techniques are created for directing employees, determining whether the task has been accomplished, and for administering rewards and punishments.[32] The assumptions about human nature that portray the traditional view of Theory X are:

- The average human being has an inherent dislike of work and will avoid it if possible.

- Because of this human characteristic of dislike of work, most people must be coerced, controlled, directed, and threatened

32. *Ibid.,* p. 132.

with punishment to get them to put forth adequate effort toward the achievement of organizational objectives.

- The average human being prefers to be directed, wishes to avoid responsibility, has relatively little ambition, and wants security above all.[33]

With this "working man's" insight, a manager naturally directs his efforts toward techniques of direction and control. There is, of course, a contrasting set of attitudes. A manager can have a relatively high opinion of the capacity and intelligence of the average worker. Such a manager may be aware that he has special qualifications, but he does not perceive himself as a member of an elite group. They see most workers as having a definite capacity for growth and development, for the acceptance of responsibility, and for creativity. Subordinates, in this situation, are considered genuine assets, and the manager works to create conditions whereby they will be fully realized. The manager does not believe workers are stupid, lazy, irresponsible, dishonest or antagonistic. This type of manager knows there are such people, but anticipates encountering them only occasionally. In sum, such a manager holds to Theory Y.

This theoretical orientation requires the manager to be primarily concerned with the quality of relationships. Maximum effort is directed toward creating an environment that will encourage commitment to management objectives. The employee is provided with the opportunity to exercise initiative and self-direction.[34] The assumptions about human nature that portray the beginning of this new theory identified as *Theory Y* are as follows:

- The expenditure of physical and mental effort in work is as natural as play or rest.
- Man will exercise self-direction and self-control in the service of objectives to which there is personal commitment.
- Commitment to objectives is a function of the rewards associated with their achievement.
- The average human being learns, under proper conditions, not only to accept but to seek responsibility.
- The capacity to exercise a relatively high degree of imagination, ingenuity, and creativity in the solution of organizational problems is widely, not narrowly, distributed in the population.
- Under the conditions of modern industrial life, the intellectual potentialities of the average human being are only partially utilized.[35]

McGregor acknowledges that the assumptions of *Theory Y* are not fully validated, but he expressed the belief that they were far more

33. *Ibid.,* pp. 33–34.
34. *Ibid.,* pp. 132 and 140.
35. *Ibid.,* pp. 47–48.

consistent with existing social research than other methods. The creator of *Theory Y* perceived it as an invitation to innovation. Two researchers found that command personnel of the San Diego Police Department saw organizational personnel as truly functioning from a *Theory Y* posture. Employees were motivated, dedicated, and competent with a commitment to departmental goals. They pointed out, "the department does not take a concise position in regard to employee motivation, direction and control. Rather, the police department provides a communal working environment and attempts to facilitate self-motivation."[36]

Management Systems

Rensis Likert of the Institute for Social Research at the University of Michigan is a behavioral scientist who has developed a typology of management. In his approach, emphasis is based upon the necessity of considering human resources as an asset requiring proper management.[37] Management of human resources is a critical task and is viewed by Likert as a relative process. As a controlling influence to efficiency, Likert identified the following managerial features:

- Employee oriented.

- General supervision.

- Non-punitive.

- Communicative.[38]

Within the management system typology, Likert has utilized a number of variables central to his theory, such as leadership, motivation, communication, decisions, goals and control. The management style characterizing leadership in organization were arranged on a continuum from System One through System Four. Each of the systems portrays a management style ranging from authoritarian to participative.

System One. The management style at this point of continuum reflects absolutely no confidence in subordinates. Supervisors depicting this style do not create an environment where subordinates feel free to talk about the job, and workers ideas are sought on a very limited basis. Compliance to orders is usually obtained through fear, threats and punishment. Superiors know very little about subordinate's problems and formal decisions about those problems are made at the top. Organizational goals are based upon specific orders because strong resistance to the goals is present. Subordinates are not involved in decision-making so the process does not contribute to their motivation. Control functions are carried out entirely by top management; therefore the informal organization resists the formal structure.

36. Ayres, *op.cit.*

37. Hersey, *op. cit.*, p. 60.

38. Rensis Likert, *New Patterns of Management,* New York, McGraw–Hill, 1961, pp. 21–24.

System Two. Management is condescending toward subordinates and ideas are sometimes sought. Control data acquired by the management is used for either rewarding or punishing employees and control functions are concentrated in the higher echelons. Very little "communications" is aimed at achieving organizational goals and those that do exist are mostly downward and are generally accepted with some suspicion. Most of the policy decisions are made at the top and occasionally subordinates are consulted about decisions relating to their work. The informal organization usually resists the formal one and moderate resistance to organizational goal attainment occurs.

System Three. Management at this level demonstrates substantial confidence in subordinates and their ideas are usually sought and applied. Employee motivation is bolstered mostly by utilizing rewards, but occasionally by resorting to some punishment or by additional involvement. Communication flows both ways, however employees accept downward communications with some caution. Broad policy decisions are made at the top and delegation does occur. Generally, subordinates are consulted about decisions related to their work and there is an effort to have the decision-making process contribute to motivation. There is a moderate delegation of control functions to lower levels and control data is used primarily for rewarding subordinates and is occasionally utilized for self-guidance.

System Four. Management at this end of the continuum reflects complete confidence in subordinates to the point where their ideas are always sought and used. Motivational efforts are based upon reward and involvement, and are related to group-set goals. Information flow is down, up and sideways. Downward communications is accepted with an open mind and upward communications is considered accurate. Decisions are made at all levels of the organization and subordinates are fully involved in decisions related to their work. The informal organization does not resist the formal one, and control data is used for self-guidance and problem solving.

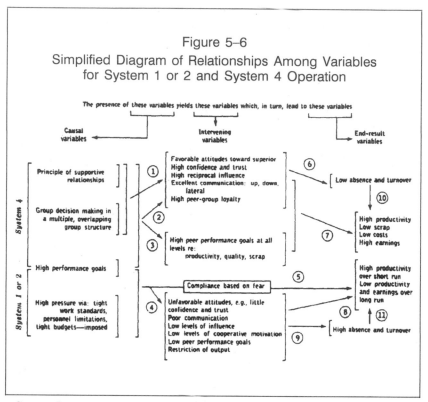

Figure 5–6
Simplified Diagram of Relationships Among Variables
for System 1 or 2 and System 4 Operation

Source: Rensis Likert, *The Human Organization: Its Management and Value,* New York, McGraw–Hill Book Company, 1967, p. 136. Reprinted with permission of the McGraw–Hill Companies, February 3, 1999.

In analyzing an organization's behavior, Likert has developed an instrument with twenty-two variables allowing organizational members to rate the perceived management system. Managers are asked to rate both the highest producing unit and the least-productive unit. With few exceptions, high-producing sections have been found to be using management systems more to the right (toward System Four), and low-producing units as more to the left (System One).[39]

The numerous dimensions of the human organization and its operation are illustrated in figure 5–6. Likert's variables are grouped into three broad categories labeled causal, intervening and end-result. In System Four, the principle of supportive relationships is stressed and group decision-making is utilized. These causal variables lead to the intervening ones such as favorable attitudes toward superiors, high confidence and trust, excellent communication and high peer-group loyalty.[40] The end-result variable then becomes high productivity based upon high performance goals. In Systems One and Two organizations, when supervisors establish high performance goals and tight work

39. Rensis Likert, *The Human Organization,* New York, McGraw–Hill Book Co., 1967, p. 11.

40. *Ibid.,* p. 138.

standards, there is usually high productivity over the short-run because of compliance by fear. The intervening result is a work atmosphere reflecting little confidence and trust, poor communications, low peer performance goals and a restriction of output. In the long-run production is low and is coupled with a high rate of employee absenteeism and turnover.[41] The Rensis Likert survey-feedback instrument can be utilized to determine the current management style being employed in an agency. The management style can be characterized by the following variables;

- Leadership.

- Motivation.

- Communication.

- Decisions.

- Goals.

- Interaction.

- Control.

The popular view is that police departments are automatically identified as *System One* organizations. The rigid bureaucracy expresses no confidence in subordinates. Compliance to orders is insured through fear, threats and punishment. Goal-setting and decision-making is accomplished by top management while the informal organization is ignored. Utilizing Likert's instrument, one study tested the characterization of police organizations by asking law enforcement officers to rate how their own organization functioned.[42] In addition to the initial rating each officer rated their organization 2 years later in order to determine if the climate had changed in any significant manner. One hundred seventy one officers who were attending the National Academy of the Federal Bureau of Investigation responded to the survey. Eighty-three percent of those officers had a college degree (associate, baccalaureate, or masters) or were working toward that goal.[43]

41. *Ibid.*

42. Gerald W. Shanahan, J. David Hunger, and Thomas L. Wheelen, "Organizational Profile of Police Agencies in the United States," *Journal of Police* *Science and Organization,* September 1979, Vol. 7, No. 3, p. 354.

43. *Ibid.,* p. 356.

Figure 5–7

Diagnose Your Management

		SYSTEM 1 Exploitive authoritative	SYSTEM 2 Benevolent authoritative	SYSTEM 3 Consultative	SYSTEM 4 Participative group
LEADERSHIP	How much confidence is shown in subordinates?	None	Condescending	Substantial	Complete
	How free do they feel to talk to superiors about job?	Not at all	Not very	Rather free	Fully free
	Are subordinates' ideas sought and used, if worthy?	Seldom	Sometimes	Usually	Always
MOTIVATION	Is predominant use made of 1 fear, 2 threats, 3 punishment, 4 rewards, 5 involvement?	1, 2, 3, occasionally 4	4, some 3	4, some 3 and 5	5, 4, based on group set goals
	Where is responsibility felt for achieving organization's goals?	Mostly at top	Top and middle	Fairly general	At all levels
COMMUNICATION	How much communication is aimed at achieving organization's objectives?	Very little	Little	Quite a bit	A great deal
	What is the direction of information flow?	Downward	Mostly downward	Down and up	Down, up, and sideways
	How is downward communication accepted?	With suspicion	Possibly with suspicion	With caution	With an open mind
	How accurate is upward communication?	Often wrong	Censored for the boss	Limited accuracy	Accurate
	How well do superiors know problems faced by subordinates?	Know little	Some knowledge	Quite well	Very well
DECISIONS	At what level are decisions formally made?	Mostly at top	Policy at top, some delegation	Broad policy at top, more delegation	Throughout but well integrated
	What is the origin of technical and professional knowledge used in decision making?	Top management	Upper and middle	To a certain extent, throughout	To a great extent, throughout
	Are subordinates involved in decisions related to their work?	Not at all	Occasionally consulted	Generally consulted	Fully involved
	What does decision-making process contribute to motivation?	Nothing, often weakens it	Relatively little	Some contribution	Substantial contribution
GOALS	How are organizational goals established?	Orders issued	Orders, some comment invited	After discussion, by orders	By group action (except in crisis)
	How much covert resistance to goals is present?	Strong resistance	Moderate resistance	Some resistance at times	Little or none
	How concentrated are review and control functions?	Highly at top	Relatively highly at top	Moderate delegation to lower levels	Quite widely shared
	Is there an informal organization resisting the formal one?	Yes	Usually	Sometimes	No—same goals as formal
	What are cost, productivity, and other control data used for?	Policing, punishment	Reward and punishment	Reward, some self-guidance	Self-guidance, problem solving

Source: Donnelly, Gibson, Ivancevich, *Fundamentals of Management: Selected Readings,* Dallas, Texas, Business Publications, Inc., 1975, p. 144, printed with permission of the publisher.

The data from the initial year of rating was in the upper part of *System Two* and two years later the officers placed their respective organizations close to the midpoint of *Systems Three*. Of the eight dimensions measured, three of the categories (communications, training, and decision-making) changed the most. This suggests that the organizations are becoming more open.[44]

Immaturity—Maturity Theory

As a critic of the policy of adjusting the individual to the organization, Chris Argyris clearly sets forth his position in a series of texts and articles. He studied the work environment in order to determine the effect management had on individual behavior. The healthy individual follows the directions and dimensions set forth in figure 5–8. Human beings in our culture move from left to right on the continua. Growth is a matter of degree—the development of any given human being can be plotted at a given time.

Figure 5–8

Immaturity—Maturity Continua

Immaturity	**Maturity**
● Passivity	Activity
● Dependence.	Independence
● Behaving in a few ways	Behaving in many different ways
● Erratic, casual, shallow interests	Deeper interests
● Short-time perspective	Longer time perspective
● Subordinate position.	Equal or superordinate position
● Lack of awareness of self	Awareness and control over self

---

Source: Chris Argyris, *Understanding Organizational Behavior,* Homewood, Illinois, The Dorsey Press, Inc., 1960, pp. 8–9. Adopted from the author's model.

Argyris views *man* as fundamentally an interpersonal organism and assumes that while *man* strives toward growth on the continua, he behaves in such a way as to permit others to grow.[45] This is in contrast to a formal organization that maximizes the principles management that places employees in work situations where they are:

- ● provided minimal control over their work-a-day world.

- ● expected to be passive, dependent, and subordinate.

- ● expected to have the frequent use of a few skin-surface shallow abilities.

- ● expected to produce under conditions leading to psychological failure.[46]

All of these characteristics are incongruent to what is desired by relatively mature individuals. While the tendency is to move toward *maturity* on the continua, organizational emphasis on the rationality of task specialization, chain of command, unity of direction, and span of

---

44. *Ibid.*

45. Chris Argyris, *Understanding Organizational Behavior,* Homewood, Illinois, The Dorsey Press, Inc., 1960, p. 9–10.

46. *Ibid.,* p. 14.

control work against such growth. In reality an excessive emphasis on organizational conformity limits the development of the individual. Argyris proposes that conflict and frustration will tend to be high when the formal organization, the leadership, and the controls require "maturity-directed" people to be guided toward infancy, and "infancy-directed" employees to be directed toward maturity. In either case the conflict will result in employee absenteeism, apathy and excessive turnover.[47]

He also suggests that conversely, conflict and frustration will be minimal when "maturity-directed" employees are required to behave maturely, and "infancy-directed" employees are required to behave immaturely.[48] Argyris has identified an effective organizational structure as one that approaches the "ideal" for employee mental health and creates an environment whereby they can:

- experience the wholeness of the organization;
- be required to be self-responsible, self-directed, and self-motivated;
- aspire toward excellence in problem-solving;
- strive to decrease compulsive behavior and organization defenses and to increase control of the work environment;
- utilize their abilities, especially their cognitive and interpersonal abilities; and
- increase their time perspective.[49]

He argues that motivation can be maximized when each employee pursues goals and experiences psychological growth and independence. On the other hand, very close supervision diminishes motivation, limits psychological growth, and hampers personal independence and freedom.[50] Police management theorists generally agree that the current typical law enforcement management style reflects a concern for organizational needs to the detriment of individual needs, thereby limiting the growth of the "maturity-directed" employee if one accepts this theory.

Theory Z

This management theory represents a synthesis of different theories and is predicated on the belief that organizations are social

47. *Ibid.*, p. 19.

48. *Ibid.* For additional studies see: Chris Argyris, *Personality and Organization,* New York, Harper and Rowe, Publisher, 1957; Chris Argyris, *Integrating the Individual and the Organization,* New York, John Wiley and Sons, Inc., 1964; Chris Argyris, *Interpersonal Competence and Organizational Effectiveness,* Homewood, Illinois, The Dorsey Press, 1962, and Chris Argyris, "Person-

ality vs. Organization," *Managerial Review,* October, 1974.

49. Chris Argyris, "The Integration of the Individual and the Organization," in *Social Science Approaches to Business Behavior,* ed. George B. Strother, Homewood, Illinois, Dorsey Press and Irwin, 1962, p. 76.

50. William G. Ouchi, Theory Z, New York, Avon Books, 1981, p. 69.

organisms and like other social units, are shaped and reshaped by the social environment in which they exist.[51] Theory Z postulates that employee behavior can be influenced by changing the culture. It is acknowledged that culture changes slowly because its values permeate the organization. The advantage of theory Z is that it takes the spotlight off of the individual and places the individual in the context of the group, the organization and the culture.[52] Figure 5–9 shows the relationship of previously discussed management theories. For the most part, the classical bureaucratic management model espoused by Max Weber is rejected, with the exception that Theory Z maintains that the ultimate decision-maker is the manager,[53] not the employee. The Z organization utilizes hierarchical control methods and does not rely upon employee goal congruence.[54]

The true Z organization uses symbolic means to promote an attitude of egalitarianism and mutual trust. In fact, a wholistic relationship between employees is strongly encouraged. Every effort is made to replace hierarchical direction with self-direction as a means of enhancing commitment, loyalty and motivation. A wholistic management orientation requires every employee to deal with one another as a complete human being. Thus the organizational environment creates a condition eliminating depersonalization, autocracy is exceedingly unlikely and the most significant organizational features are egalitarianism, trust, open communications and commitment.

51. *Ibid.,* p. 74.

52. Terry D. Anderson, Ron Ford, and Marilyn Hamilton, *Transforming Leadership: Equipping Yourself and Coaching Others to Build the Leadership Organization,* Boca Raton, FL, CRC Press LLC, 1998, p. 267.

53. William G. Archambeault and Charles L. Weirman, "Critically Assessing the Utility of Police Bureaucracies in the 1980's: Implications of Management Theory Z," *Journal of Police Science and Administration,* Winter 1983, Vol. 11, No. 4, p. 425.

54. *Ibid.,* p. 70.

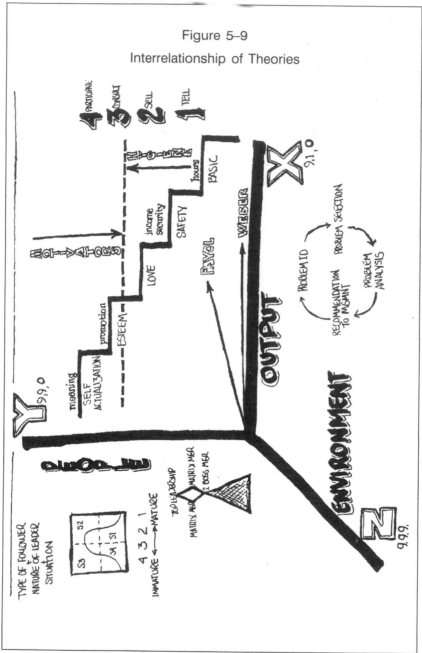

Figure 5–9

Interrelationship of Theories

Source: Robert Wong developed this figure in a graduate management class at San Jose State University.

Theory of Sensitivity

Steven Reiss and Susan M. Havercamp suggest that sensitivity theory can be used to identify individual differences in motivational needs that are key to predicting human behavior. It is a genetics-behavior-cognitive model of axiomatic motivation. These psychologists divide human motivation into two categories based on the purposes of the behavior:

- **Means**. This is indicated when someone performs an act for useful purposes.
- **End.** This occurs when a individual performs a behavior for no evident reason other than its own purpose.

When *means* arc important an individual may pursue higher education for the sole purpose of making themselves eligible for a significant increase in salary. Or an individual who saves money to purchase a home. This is in sharp contrast to an individual who pursues an *end*. An individual who hikes for enjoyment or an individual who exercises to lose weight illustrates working toward an *end*. The researchers postulate that human desire stem from 15 absolute motives. They range from extremes such as vengeance to social contact, and from bodily wants like food or sex, and more intellectual elements like order or curiosity. Everyone is concerned with the 15 motives, but the intensity and priority will vary from individual to individual. When compared to other motivational theories the list is long and exhibits great diversity. It is clear that this research goes well beyond maximizing pleasure and minimizing pain.[55]

Figure 5-10

Fundamental Motives
- Social contact.
- Honor.
- Social prestige.
- Curiosity.
- Independence.
- Order.
- Citizenship.
- Physical exercise.
- Sex.
- Power.
- Aversive sensations.
- Food.
- Family.
- Vengeance.
- Rejection.

Source: Steven Reiss and Susan m. Havercamp, "Toward a Comprehensive Assessment of Fundamental Motivation: Factor Structure of the Reiss Profiles," *Psychological Assessment,* 1998, Vol. 10, No. 2, pp. 97–106. Copyright (1998) by the American Psychological Association. Adapted with Permission.

Theory of Values

Clare Graves has postulated that individuals evolve through numerous *levels of existence,* viewed as a hierarchical system both infinite and relatively independent on intelligence. As people grow psychologi-

55. Steven Reiss and Susan M. Havercamp, "Toward a Comprehensive Assessment of Fundamental Motivation: Factor Structure of the Reiss Profiles," *Psychological Assessment,* 1998, Vol. 10, No. 2, PP. 97–106.

cally, they move from a limited value system to higher ones that are contributive to better conditions of life. Old values are subordinated and the new are developed appropriate to an elevated level of existence (see figure 5–11).[56]

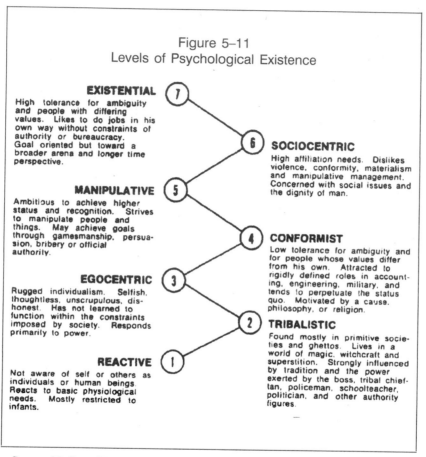

Figure 5–11
Levels of Psychological Existence

EXISTENTIAL ⑦
High tolerance for ambiguity and people with differing values. Likes to do jobs in his own way without constraints of authority or bureaucracy. Goal oriented but toward a broader arena and longer time perspective.

⑥ **SOCIOCENTRIC**
High affiliation needs. Dislikes violence, conformity, materialism and manipulative management. Concerned with social issues and the dignity of man.

MANIPULATIVE ⑤
Ambitious to achieve higher status and recognition. Strives to manipulate people and things. May achieve goals through gamesmanship, persuasion, bribery or official authority.

④ **CONFORMIST**
Low tolerance for ambiguity and for people whose values differ from his own. Attracted to rigidly defined roles in accounting, engineering, military, and tends to perpetuate the status quo. Motivated by a cause, philosophy, or religion.

EGOCENTRIC ③
Rugged individualism. Selfish, thoughtless, unscrupulous, dishonest. Has not learned to function within the constraints imposed by society. Responds primarily to power.

② **TRIBALISTIC**
Found mostly in primitive societies and ghettos. Lives in a world of magic, witchcraft and superstition. Strongly influenced by tradition and the power exerted by the boss, tribal chieftan, policeman, schoolteacher, politician, and other authority figures.

REACTIVE ①
Not aware of self or others as individuals or human beings. Reacts to basic physiological needs. Mostly restricted to infants.

Source: M. Scott Myers and Susan S. Myers, "Toward Understanding the Changing Work Ethic." Copyright (1974), by the Regents of the University of California. Reprinted from the *California Management Review*, Vol. 16, No. 3, p. 9. By permission of the Regents.

- **Level One.** The *reactive* level emphasizes physiological existence. *Man* has an imperative need-based concept of time and space, and no concept of cause or effect. Physiological needs dominate and the individual is child-like. According to Graves, few people stay at this stage.

- **Level Two.** This is the first established way of life and is identified as the *tribalistic* stage. It is characterized by a domi-

56. Clare W. Graves, "Levels of Existence: An Open System Theory of Values," *Journal of Humanistic Psychology*, Fall 1970, Vol. 10, No. 2, p. 143.

nant concern for safety and the principal value is tradition. Tribal values are considered to be absolutely non-violable. When discontent occurs, *man* searches for another value level.[57]

- **Level Three.** At the *egocentric* level, rugged self-assertive individualism becomes prevalent. This level is best described as "Machiavellian". Rights become absolute and are perceived as the prerogatives of management. Power becomes an inalienable right of those who have achieved.[58]

- **Level Four.** The *conformist* stage typifies an individual accepting his position in life and inequality as a fact of life. The prime value is self-sacrifice and the task is to strive for perfection in one's assigned role. Rigid ordering is desirable and absolute moral laws are acceptable. Rules are *black* and *white* and *man* is the absolute authority.[59]

- **Level Five.** This level is best described as *manipulative* or materialistic. Pragmatic, scientific, utilitarianism is the dominant mode of existence at this stage. The end value is materialism and problems are viewed as resolvable based on a mechanistic, quantitative approach. Individuals at this stage utilize gamesmanship, favor competition, and are willing to take a calculated risk. Efficiency is considered important, goal orientation is paramount and work simplification is stressed.[60]

- **Level Six.** In the *Sociocentric State* of being, "getting along with" is valued more than "getting ahead." Emphasis is placed on communication, committeeism and majority rule. Respectability is more important than power. Here *man* values commonality over differential classification and sensitivity takes preference to objectivity.[61] Two researchers have suggested that persons at this level (who do not ultimately capitulate by regressing to the organizationally accepted modes of manipulation and conformity, or adapt by evolving to the next level) may become organizational problems and resort to alcoholism, drug abuse or other disfunctional behavior.[62]

- **Level Seven.** This stage is the *existential* level in which one focuses on the prime value—existence. The individual values spontaneity over conventionality and "continuing to develop" is perceived as very important. Universality is valued over provinciality—These people want to bring good to themselves and the entire universe.[63] This individual is intolerant of closed systems, overtly restrictive policy and arbitrary use of authority. This

57. *Ibid.,* pp. 143–145.

58. *Ibid.,* pp. 141 and 146.

59. *Ibid.,* pp. 148–149.

60. *Ibid.,* p. 150.

61. *Ibid.,* p. 151.

62. M. Scott Myers and Susan S. Myers, "Toward Understanding the Changing Work Ethic," *California Management Review,* 1981, Vol. 16, No. 3, p. 10.

63. Graves, *op. cit.,* pp. 153-154.

person may be eliminated from the organization for failure to conform to rules and regulations.[64]

Research by the Myers' suggests that with increasing frequency, managers are finding themselves out of step with employees. Conformity can no longer be accepted as an organizational norm. Management systems reflect the values of their creators; hence people in the organization have an increasing tendency to oppose organizational goals. Value conflict exists within the organization when a manager is at a level of existence different from subordinates.[65] It is suggested a manager must operate from a new source of influence—one considering the competence of employees at all levels of the organization.

Graves suggests the participative approach to management may be based upon an oversimplified belief of human behavior. Although research is limited, it indicates many people do not fit the "Theory Y" stereotype. The levels of existence portray distinct personality types and Graves believes that most adults remain at one level for most of their life or at best, move up one level.[66] Robert C. Albrook, in reviewing the theory of values, points out that persons in all the levels of existence up to manipulative, are not candidates for participative management. The higher levels of existence are motivated by a need for "belonging," for "information," and for an "understanding" of the complete work environment. For each of these levels some form of participative management will maximize the relationship of the individual to the organization.[67] Collaboration will prove to be successful when officers are viewed as partners who think. It means listening to them and using their ideas. Letting them share in the feeling of accomplishment and giving credit where credit is due. Real motivation is intrinsic to the individual and can never be imposed by executive fiat, but motivational train is an essential ingredient of employee development.[68] When an organization is truly collaborative positive things happen within an organization.[69] What management wants is a goal-oriented individual who at the same time is highly individualistic. Theories reviewed in this chapter should be real food for thought and whatever theory seems appropriate to you the thing to do is to keep and open mind and search for what seems to be best for each individual and for the organization.

64. Myers and Myers, *op. cit.,* pp. 10–11.

65. *Ibid.,* pp. 15–19.

66. Robert C. Albrook, "Participative Management: Time for a Second Look," *Fortune,* May 1967 cited in James H. Donnelly Jr., Editor, et al., *Fundamentals of Management,* Dallas, Texas, Business Publications, 1975, p. 149.

67. *Ibid.*

68. Edward S. Brown, "Police Motivational Training: The New Frontier," *Law and Order,* May 1998, Vol. 46, No. 5. pp. 63–66.

69. Charles Higgins Kepner, and Hirotsugu Iikubo, *Managing Beyond the Ordinary: Using Collaboration to Solve Problems, Make Decisions, and Achieve Extraordinary Results,* New York, AMACOM, 1996, pp. 199–205.

Case Study

Chief Roberta Farr

Chief Farr has just assumed this position after a nation-wide search. The city of Spruce has a population of 23,000 and is a wealthy suburban community. There are 29 sworn officers and 11 civilians in the department. The department had its own communications center having never opted to join the county communications department. It is the only department out of nine in the county that operates in this manner. The department has the latest equipment and on the surface appears to be a well functioning department. The chief executive officer that Roberta Farr replaced ran the department with a managerial style that is best described as System One. The former chief has always performed in a manner that clearly demonstrated that he did not have a lot of confidence in subordinates. Officer ideas were never sought and rules and regulations prevailed. Organizational goals were based on specific orders and the formal chain of command dominated the decision-making process. The Chief knew little about subordinate problems and operated in isolation from line personnel. The former Chief retired after 27 years of service and had a strong political base in the community.

Chief Farr knew that she was going to have a great deal of difficulty and the honey-moon period would be for a limited time. Prior to accepting the appointment she talked with many of the officers and found that:

- Moral was very low.

- Officer performance left a great deal to be desired.

- Sick leave was being abused.

- A number of officers just worked hard enough to get by.

- The older officers avoided situations that could create waves.

- Many officers were just biding their time pending retirement.

Overall she felt that most of the officers were dissatisfied with working conditions. Younger officers were leaving for greener pastures, and there was a general feeling of despair. Chief Farr had previously worked in a department where participative management dominated the working environment and she was confident the department could be turned around.

What would be the first thing to be done in this department? Why? What specific motivational strategies should Chief Farr consider using? Why? How would you go about involving personnel in the decision-making process?.Why?

For Further Reading

Edward S. Brown, "Police Motivational Training: The New Frontier," *Law and Order, May* 1998, Vol. 46, No. 5, pp. 63–65.

> If there is a contemporary challenge to law enforcement management it is that of the need to motivate officers. The challenge is to create a working environment that is conducive to officer enrichment. Reviews contingency theory as a means of addressing a myriad of motivational factors including benefits and career development. Suggests that police agencies with high morale makes for a win-win situation. Recommends continuous motivational training.

Charles Higgins Kepner and Hirotsugu Iikubo, *Managing Beyond The Ordinary: Using Collaboration to Solve Problems, Make* Decisions, *and Achieve Extraordinary Results,* New York, AMACOM, 1996, pp. 23–204.

> Reviews findings that in evolutionary psychology humans have a strong predisposition to cooperate and work together to accomplish a common purpose. Suggests motivating people to want to work together to solve problems. Recommends determining what specific things motivate employees and using these to improve participation. Indicates that self-interest is a great motivator of people. If valued conditions are created collaboration will follow.

Tony L. Jones, "Autocratic vs. People–Minded Supervisors," *Law and Order,* May 1998, Vol. 46, No. 5, pp. 32–36.

> The author points out that the autocratic philosophy will follow the traditional absolute power concept while the people-minded philosophy will emphasize respect, competence, and fairness. Recommends the evaluation of officers by their actual performance utilizing clear cut departmental standards. Suggests creating a working environment wherein people are dealt with truthfully, and are informed about things that affect them. Suggests leading by example and dealing with employees fairly.

Steven Reiss and Susan M. Havercamp, "Toward A Comprehensive Assessment of Fundamental Motivation: Factor Structure of the Reiss Profiles, "*Psychological Assessment ,1998,* Vol.10, No. *2, pp. 97–106.*

> Describes the development of two instruments to provide a comprehensive assessment of the strength of a person's fundamental end goals and motivational sensitivities. One instrument was a self-reporting inventory and the other an informant rating-scale. Each instrument had a 15–factor solution. The authors suggest a genetics–behavior–cognitive model of fundamental motivation.

Chapter 6

HUMAN FACTORS: Responding
to the Organization

Learning Objectives

1. List eight informal work reinforcers.
2. Write a short essay describing what is a good place to work.
3. Compare the v-shaped trend to the straight-lined trend of job satisfaction.
4. Describe the nature of job satisfaction that results from being involved in a team effort.
5. List six elements of job satisfaction that are generally found in most studies.
6. List five factors influencing job commitment.
7. Write a short essay describing some of the sources of stress in law enforcement.
8. List ten signs that could mean too much stress.
9. Describe the organizational impact that can be caused by stress.
10. Identify five troubles at work characterized by the New Social Adjustment Rating Scale.
11. List the four events with the highest values for the Law Enforcement Critical Life Events Scale.
12. Write a short essay describing the characteristics of participative management.
13. Describe the importance to managers of the informal organization.

The quality of organizational working life is *central* to the success of any police agency. A resonant and viable working environment proves to be a pleasurable place in which to work, and management should create such an atmosphere. The efforts of individuals and groups to motivate people are needed in order to attain organizational goals hence why not strive to create such a viable entity. Goals cannot be gained, for any sustained period of time, by executive fiat, coercion or threat. Most individuals or groups voluntarily adjust very positively to the organization for varying reasons. An adaptive organizational climate accepts conflict of values and attitudes by individuals and groups as a normal consequence of the collective pursuits of organizational goals. Conflict therefore must be "managed" if the organization is to be vibrant and alive. As a minimum requirement, conflict manage ment must at least address the following factors:

- Employees concept of work.
- Job satisfaction.
- Stress.
- Participation.
- Informal organization.

The police manager who ignores the ecology of the organization will seldom be successful. Job satisfaction is a product of the interaction of the employee with the organization and the attitudes generated. It is inevitable, conflict will occur because of differing interpretations of what constitutes *participation* by employees and management. As conflict takes place it must be properly directed in an environment including the stress that is created. Every effort must be made to maximize each employee's control over job activities (while increasing their output), as long as the total process requires the individual to adjust to organizational goals.

Work

A very fundamental, human and natural aspect of every person's daily living is his or her work. It plays a powerful role in the economic, social and psychological part of our lives. Numerous experts have described it as central institution.[1] In this capacity it is affected by and influences other basic institutions of society.[2] Work can be defined as "an activity that produces something of value for other people." This definition places it within a social context implying there is a purpose to work.[3] A person's sense of identity is often obtained from their work as evidenced by most people describing themselves in terms of work *groups* or organizations.[4] At the same time it must be realized, although work is central to most of our lives, there is a small minority for whom a job is strictly a means of existence.[5]

In all societies, the necessity of work stems from the fact that human survival demands disciplined productive effort. But its importance to human well being is more than the essential role of providing the basic necessities of life. Work performance also provides a sense of personal identity and accomplishment not otherwise achieved. And, it often challenges the skills and ingenuity of the worker. For some workers, self-fulfillment through achievement of work-related goals is as important as material rewards of useful work. Historically, labor has

1. Task force to the Secretary of Health, Education and Welfare, *Work in America,* Cambridge, Massachusetts, MIT Press, January 1973, p. 2.

2. *Ibid.*

3. *Ibid.,* p. 3.

4. *Ibid.,* p. 6, and Robert L. Kahn, *Work and Health,* New York, John Wiley and Sons, 1981, p. 11.

5. *Ibid.,* p. 10.

been regarded as a regrettable necessity rather than a means of self-fulfillment. For most people, the daily tasks required for simple survival could only be seen as unpleasant, inescapable servitude. Yet, we know that the work place, whether field or factory, has always been a center of life and physical exertion. Through the ages the social interaction accompanying most work provided a sense of community, a sharing of duties and a social bond that could not otherwise be experienced.[6] Today identification mechanisms continue to be present in the workforce coupled with the pervasive human drive to identify with the social system that surrounds them.[7]

Experts suggest management must create a working environment employees can perceive as the place where they really want to work. The culture of the organization creates "work reinforcers" that are either formal or informal. The significant point is that reinforcers maintain work behavior. They are, in fact, the rewards motivating an officer to function effectively.[8] Formal work reinforcers are traditional including such things as pay, sick leave, annual leave, retirement, and other benefits. In most instances, these are delineated by union or employee association work agreements. In recent years other formal reinforcers have proved to be significant, such as, officer rights, promotional policies, and working conditions. There is also a strong movement suggesting that employers need to modify their cultures to assure that employees can perform at a high level of effectiveness while remaining strongly committed to their families. This suggests that a viable employee must of necessity be committed to both their occupation and their family. [9]

Informal reinforcers are less tangible. If one needs freedom and the job is one requiring close supervision, then that factor is not a reinforcer. One's needs define the particular informal work reinforcer. Figure 6–1 lists a range of typical informal work reinforcers. The line officer position calls for a number of informal work reinforcers. Of special interest is the positional authority possessed by line officers. There are few entry positions in the public work world having the degree of freedom and discretion found in the position of police officer.[10]

6. Bureau of the Census, *Social Indicators III,* Washington, U.S. Government Printing Office, December 1980, p. 305.

7. Denise M. Rousseau, "Why Workers Still Identify with Organizations," *Journal of Organizational Behavior,* May 1998, Vol. 19, No. 3, pp. 217–234.

8. Donald A. Laird, Eleanor C. Laird, and T. Fruehling, *Psychology: Human Relations and Work Adjustment,* Seventh Edition, New York, McGraw–Hill, 1989, pp. 282–283.

9. Saroj Parasuraman and Jeffrey H. Greenhaus, *Integrating Work and Family: Challenges and Choices for a Changing World,* Westport, CT, Greenwood, 1997, pp. 1–240.

10. Laird, Laird, and Fruehling, *op. cit.,* p. 284.

```
Figure 6–1

Typical Informal Work Reinforcers

Working to capacity.
Fulfillment.
Work Diversity.
Action.
Creativity.
Positional authority.
Discretion.
Responsibility.
Independence.
Service.
Status.
Advancement.
Ethical values.
```

Line officers have considerable responsibility and the potential for achieving tasks with minimal supervision. In many agencies there is a power vacuum at the operational level. This allows task-oriented individuals to assume power clearly exceeding the position description for a patrol officer. Each employee has different needs that define the most important reinforcers that are an integral part of a positive work environment.

Management has a responsibility to develop strategies fostering a positive working environment. It is clearly a mandate. When defining the values of a law enforcement agency it is common to include a statement acknowledging the importance of the work place. For example, the Houston Police Department has a value statement addressing the need to improve the quality of work-life by stating, "We are dedicated to improving the quality of work life in our department through interaction and concern for each other."[11]

Studies show a good place to work is one where employees view it as one that fostering freedom and fair treatment occurs. An organization emphasizing mutual trust between the agency and the employee describes a good place to work. Other good organizational characteristics are found in departments fostering price, and most importantly employees can make mistakes.[12]

In one study of the workplace, employees described it as good when it had certain characteristics. First, a good working environment is one where there is a constant feeling the organization is friendly. The best description, it is, "A friendly place." Interaction between all members of the organization, without regard to rank, occurs continuously. Such interaction is fostered and employees do not stand on ceremony. Additionally, it is positive and spontaneous. Figure 6–2 lists characteristics of a good working environment. Another common phrase is,

11. Richard M. Ayers, *Preventing Law Enforcement Stress: The Organizational Role,* Alexandria, VA, The National Sheriffs' Association, 1990, p. 47.

12. *Ibid.,* p. 23.

"There isn't much politicking around here." Using "juice" to get ahead or to obtain favorable assignments does not occur. Backstabbing is non-existent and officers do not need a Rabbi to get ahead. Jockeying for position among co-workers or trying to show others up is not a criterion for assuring advancement. Politicking creates a truly negative atmosphere. It destroys any sense of cohesiveness and teamwork.[13] Politicking either detracts or destroys one's feeling of belongingness and the desire to work toward the joint achievement of goals.

Figure 6-2

Phrases Describing What is a "Good Place to Work"

A friendly place
There isn't much politicking around here.
You get a fair shake.
More than a job.
It's just like a family.

Adopted from: Robert Levering, *A Great Place to Work,* New York, Random House, 1988, cited in Richard Ayres, *Preventing Law Enforcement Stress: The Organization's Role,* Alexandria, VA. The National Sheriffs' Association, 1990, pp. 23–24.

An additional descriptive phrase concerning the organization is, "You get a fair shake." Employees believe fair treatment guides the organization. They sense that acts of favoritism, bias, inequity, and abuse do not occur. The organization focuses on equal treatment. If something occurs resulting in discipline, the employee is given a fair and impartial hearing. If discipline is applied unfairly, it is rectified immediately. Capricious and excessive discipline is not allowed and punishment is appropriate to the violation.

"More than a job."—this phrase occurred frequently when employees described their workplace. The job is viewed as making a contribution to the organization and the community. Work performed has meaning and importance. The good workplace gives the employee a high degree of control over the tasks performed. The officer is allowed to determine priorities and can express opinions without fear of retribution or retaliation. Another description of a good organization is, "It's just like family." This phrase is especially important because it conveys commitment to the organization in an atmosphere emphasizing a feeling of harmony and well being. Officers are important individuals not just another employee. Personal needs are acknowledged and dealt with positively. A familylike atmosphere permeates the total organization and serves as a foundation for interpersonal relationships.[14] Commitment to the organization is more than transient it is for a lifetime. In such an organization, employees feel they are an integral part and not just an appendage.

13. *Ibid.,* pp. 23–24.   **14.** *Ibid.*

Job Satisfaction

When a police officer's work environment needs are met that individual is said to be satisfied. Researchers in this area have found there are two types of feelings about jobs. One is global in nature and is indicative of an employee's feelings toward the job. The other is facet—the worker expresses feelings about a specific aspect of the job.[15] An officer, for example, might feel a supervising sergeant is authoritarian and concerned about minute and irrelevant details. Concurrently, the officer expresses satisfaction with other aspects of the job, such as, peer support, pay and general working conditions.[16] An employee's job satisfaction can change over time. It can occur as a V–shaped trend over a career or a straight–line trend (see figure 6–3). In a V–shaped trend of job satisfaction an officer may start out all starry eyed, resolving to confront the evils of the world, and to render the community safe. Each day presents new issues and challenges. Initially new situations cause some trepidation, but over time the officer adjusts successfully to varying challenges. As self-confidence increases, job satisfaction becomes a positive by-product.

This stage can last for a number of years, but generally after seven years service an officer begins to feel the job is less satisfying. The officer also can be faced with the reality of neither promotions nor special assignments forthcoming. These and other factors can result in an officer hitting a low point in job satisfaction. During the latter part of the career an officer finds the interest in the job has returned. Promotions may have occurred and work skills honed to such an extent that greater job satisfaction occurs. In other instances, special assignments enhance job satisfaction.

15. Robin Fincham and Peter S. Rhodes, *The Individual, Work, and Organizational Behavior, Studied for Business and Management*, London, Oxford University Press, 1995, pp. 54–102.

16. Robin Fincham and Peter S. Rhodes, *The Individual, Work and Organization* London, Weidenfeld and Nicolson, 1988, p. 90.

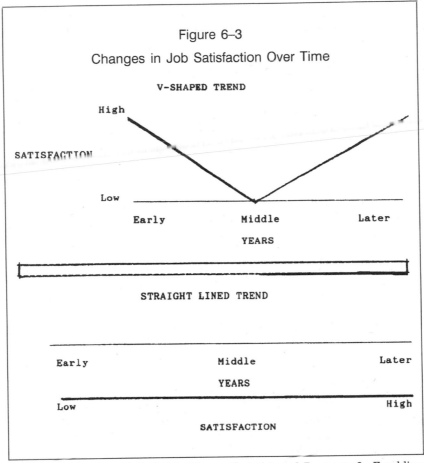

Figure 6-3

Changes in Job Satisfaction Over Time

V-SHAPED TREND

Adopted from: Donald A. Laird, Eleanor C. Laird, and Rosemary L. Fruchling, *Psychology: Human Relations and Work Adjustment*, Seventh Edition, New York, McGraw-Hill, 1989, pp. 291-292.

The straight-line trend holds that job satisfaction improves over the lifetime of one's career. New members of the organization either adapt to the organization, during the beginning years, or find the job does not meet their needs. Consequently, employment is sought elsewhere (for some, the grass is always greener on the other side of the road). Others slowly become aware the job is not fulfilling them and engage in other activities. In this instance, the individual performs minimally and obtains satisfactions from their family, sports, or other activities. Some become organizational renegades and openly confront the organization. Union leadership provides these individuals with satisfactions they cannot obtain from the job.

Eventually, a "weeding out" process occurs and the dissatisfied, recalcitrant or disenchanted officers leave the organization. Those who stay find ways to obtain satisfaction from the job. Ultimately, the dissatisfied leave and the satisfied remain. This results in a straight-lined trend of satisfaction over the careers of remaining officers. In actuality, both trends exist in an organization. Some officers react to the V-shaped trend and others to the straight–line trend.[17] Assessing the nature and significance of work in our society requires a definitive consideration of the degree of satisfaction felt by workers with their jobs and working conditions. In a government study, close examination of job characteristics affecting overall job satisfaction revealed the perceived meaning of the job, i.e., belief that the work is important and yields a feeling of accomplishment remains the most important characteristic. Half the respondents ranked it as most important and two-thirds ranked it first or second. In a recent study, only about one-fifth of the respondents ranked "chance for advancement" as most important, but over half ranked it first or second. A high income also ranked first for about one-fifth of the respondents, but fewer than half ranked it either first or second. Neither job security nor short working hours are considered now to be of comparable importance in the overall quality of a job (see table 6–1).[18]

What constitutes job satisfaction for police officers also proves to be somewhat elusive. One study reported assignments, conditions and management as producing moderate satisfaction while another refuted this position.[19]

Table 6–1

Relative Importance of Selected Job Characteristics

Job Characteristic	Most Important (Percent)	Second in Importance (Percent)
Work Important and Gives a Feeling of Accomplishment	48.7	18.2
Chances for Advancement	18.8	35.4
High Income	20.5	23.5
No Danger of Being Fired	7.8	14.4
Working Hours are Short, Lots of Free Time	4.2	8.5

A study of eight municipal law enforcement agencies measured the level of satisfaction regarding ten elements of policing. These were: salaries, fringe benefits, promotional opportunities, facilities, equipment, policies and procedures, supervision, internal communications, training, and executive leadership.[20] Three dimensions of satisfaction emerged from the officers' response:

17. Laird, *op. cit.*, pp. 291–292.

18. *Ibid.*, p. 306.

19. Paul M. Whisenand, "Work Values and Job Satisfaction: Anyone Interested," *Public Personnel Review*, 1971, Vol. 32, No.1., and J.W. Sterling,

Changes in Role Concepts of Police Officers, Washington: I.A.C.P., 1972, 1–85.

20. Jeffrey S. Slovak, "Work Satisfaction and Municipal Police Officers," *Journal of Police Science and Administration*, December 1978, Vol. 6, No. 4, p. 464.

- Hardware/preparation dimension—facilities equipment training
- Compensation/advancement dimension—salaries fringe benefits promotion opportunities
- Management/organization dimension—leadership supervision communications policies and procedures.[21]

Slovak's study determined that police officers' work satisfaction is highly structured and composed of independent components. On interesting aspect of the study was that the greater number of "best friends" that an officer had in the department the greater the satisfaction with the job. Two studies of the police found no clear relationship between rank and attitudes. One study involved the comparison of sergeants to those of lesser rank, and the other study found no difference between patrol officers and detectives.[22] One researcher in looking at community policing found that such programs could have an impact on job satisfaction because the job of the officer was redesigned. One other study found that job satisfaction was higher when managers allowed task variability and rejected the military style of leadership.[23] In organizations that use teams it has been found that the teams organizational culture ties people together and creates different standards to live and work by. When problems and opportunities are shared there is a greater sense of belongingness. In a team effort employees have a greater opportunity to perform a variety of task, and learn new skills. Other employee satisfaction from being involved in a team effort include:

- Greater feeling of contribution.
- More self-control.
- Sense of pride in the work performed.
- Freedom to be creative.[24]

Finite conclusions must await further research; however, Herzberg's contention that job satisfaction is separable into "extrinsic" and "intrinsic" factors may not adequately describe these perceptions. Neither is Maslow's theory of hierarchical needs supported by this research. Until further evidence either supports or rejects current research, police administrators should develop programs intended to improve job satisfaction—preferably by tailoring to individual dimensions. Notably, the key elements of job satisfaction vary from study to study, but the following list seems to be reasonably comprehensive:

- Accountability.
- Comfort.

21. *Ibid.,* p. 467.

22. Anne M. O'Leary–Kelly, and Ricky W. Griffin, "Job Satisfaction and Organizational Commitment," in Neil Brewed and Carlene Wilson, Editors, *Psychology and Policing,* Hillsdale, NJ, Lawrence Erlbaum Associates, 1995, pp. 367–383.

23. *Ibid,* p. 383.

24. David I. Cleland, *Strategic Management of Teams,* New York, John Wiley & Sons, 1996, pp. 278–279.

- Challenge.
- Compensation.
- Advancement.
- Work load.
- Supervision.
- Management.
- Relationships.
- Accomplishment.
- Resources.[25]

Employee reaction to each of the above factors will vary. Nevertheless, the idea is for the individual and the manager to work toward identifying a load factor optimizing worker performance without producing undesirable side effects.[26] The eleven job variables do not account for every possible element of job satisfaction but they do provide an assessment format for examining various police jobs.

Organizational Commitment

There are a number of variables that make up one's commitment to an organization. It can be seen from the listing in figure 6–4 that there are wide ranges of determinants that impact on the degree to which individuals are committed to the working environment. Historically a strong work ethic has been looked upon as an important component of commitment. While some content that the protestant work ethic is waning, it does not seem to hold true for those who have a resolution that strongly identifies with their involvement in an organization. The committed individual has no difficulty in identifying with the organization and striving energetically to attain established goals. The advantage of this type of response is that the individual finds job-satisfaction because their behavior results in the job becoming all-important.[27]

Another important element of commitment is autonomy and when one is given a reasonably free rein it can serve as a mechanism that reduces work tension and allows the individual to respond in a professional manner. The factor of functional independence cannot be under estimated. Job involvement generates feelings of importance that in turn gives an individual a feeling of being a contributor to the organization. Expectations having been meant and an awareness that the organization is dependable, and is looking out for the employee interests reinforce this concept. It would seem that the stronger the com-

25. Modified from: Karl Albrecht, *Stress and the Manager,* Englewood Cliffs, New Jersey, Prentice–Hall, Inc., 1979, p. 139, Slovak, *op. cit.,* p. 464, and Bureau of the Census, *op. cit.,* p. 305.

26. *Ibid.,* p. 140.

27. Anne M. O'Leary–Kelly and Ricky W. Griffin, "Job Satisfaction and Organizational Commitment," in Neil Brewster and Carlene Wilson, *Psychology and Policing,* Hillsdale, NJ, 1995, pp. 367–383.

mitment to a departmental culture that rewards individuals for work performance the greater the possibilities that the individual will respond by becoming increasingly committed. There are of course modifiers to the commitment process and each individual will normally strive to respond based on their own perception of organizational and individual needs. It is a balance that is difficult to achieve and it can change over time as events modify the relationship of the individual to the organization.

Figure 0–4

Elements of Organizational Commitment
Strong personal work ethic
Autonomy
Lack of tension
Functional independence
Concept of professionalism
Feeling of contribution
Enjoyment of work
Outlet for creativity

Adapted from: Anne M. O'Leary–Kelly, and Ricky W. Griffin, "Job Satisfaction and Organizational Commitment," in Neil Brewer and Carlene Wilson, Editors, *Psychology and Policing,* Hillsdale, NJ, 1995, pp. 367–384.

Assuming the validity of the importance of commitment, it would seem realistic for an enlightened manager to vary managerial style based on employee commitment toward work. Top levels of management, because of their personal work ethic orientation are readily responsive to different determinants. This assumption is not true at the lowest level of management. The first line supervisor must, therefore, attempt participative techniques with caution. This application of the human skill process has to be based on a realistic understanding of subordinate motivators in a particular situation. There is no *one* style of management. The effective type, however, is based on adaptive management principles emphasizing the individuality of each employee.

One employee will respond to a control approach while another will react to a participative process. It is essential that managers discern that there are differing degrees of commitment to work. It should also be recognized that every employee has the capacity to change from a low to a higher level of commitment. As a consequence managers must learn to deal with every individual and not group officers into ill-defined categories.

Stress

Stress is an inherent part of life and something affecting everyone. In recent years, administrators have become increasingly aware of job conditions producing psychological, physiological and behavioral reaction possibly detrimental to the individual and the organization.

Through the years, stress experts have found workload to be a stressful feature of occupations. For example, early studies associated coronary heart disease with working excessive hours, or holding down more than one job (see figure 6–5). More recent studies show the amount of work is not as critical to health as the control the worker has over the actual work rate and related work processes.[28]

Shift work, which is very common in police work, is an additional job demand affecting the health of workers. There is evidence that night and rotating shifts can lead to such things as sleep disorders, gastrointestinal disorders, emotional disturbances, and increased risk of occupational injury. A disruption of biological rhythms seems to occur, resulting in biochemical and physiological disturbances. Additionally, shift work can change the behavior of the worker. There can be an increased use of alcohol and tobacco, and eating habits are altered.[29]

Other stressors in law enforcement, related to job/task demands, range across a wide spectrum. Officers occasionally confront extraordinarily stressful and traumatic events. These can range from disaster or accidents to public disorder.[30] Needless to say facing a suspect with a gun in their hand, seeing a badly burned child or the body of a victim of a drive-by shooting is an emotionally traumatizing event.[31] Other incidents are of a less tragic nature, such as constantly confronting life's miseries and brutalities. This included drunkenness, injuries, drug abuse, beatings, knifings, and accidents. Life can be sordid—police officers deal with it repeatedly. The Critical Incident Stress Debriefing (CISD) is specifically designed to prevent or mitigate the development of post-traumatic stress among emergency personnel who have been involved in a critical incident.[32]

28. Lawrence R. Murphy and Theodore F. Schoenborn, Editors, *Stress Management in Work Settings,* National Institute for Occupational Safety and Health, Washington, D.C., U.S. Government Printing Office, 1987, pp. 33–34.

29. *Ibid.*

30. Jennifer M. Brown, and Elizabeth A. Campbell, *Stress and Policing: Sources and Strategies,* New York, John Wiley & Sons, 1994, p. 58.

31. Arthur W. Kureczka, "Critical Incident Stress in Law Enforcement," *FBI Law Enforcement Bulletin, February/March 1996,* Vol. 65, No. 2/3, pp. 4–7.

32. ICISF, International Critical Incident Stress Foundation, Inc., November 12, 1998. http://www.icisf.org//

Figure 6–5

Sources of Stress in Law Enforcement

Lack of adequate training or supervision
Lack of career development opportunities
Shift work (with some shifts perhaps more stressful than others).
Lack or reward or recognition.
Fear and danger of the work
Equipment deficiencies and shortages
Second guessing of officers' action an lack of administrative support.
Antagonistic subcultures within the department (e.g., between different squads, unite, shifts).
Unfair workload distribution
Unproductive management style.
Paramilitary structure.
Perceived excessive or unnecessary paperwork.
Perceived favoritism.
Inconsistent or arbitrary internal disciplinary procedures.
Police culture (e.g., machoism, code of silence regarding corruption).
The police grapevine (e.g., gossip, lack of privacy, feeling that a few officers are not trustworthy).

Adapted from: Ellen Kirschman, "Organizational Stress—Looking For Love in all the Wrong Places," *The Police Chief, October 1998,* Vol. LXV, No. 10, p. 127, and Peter Finn, and Julie Esselman Tomz, *Developing a Law Enforcement Stress Program for Officers and Their Families, Washington, DC, Office of Justice Programs, March 1997. pp. 6–7.*

Boredom is another stressor found in law enforcement. An officer can patrol a beat for many hours and do very little. In other instances the inactivity will be interrupted occasionally, but then a call can occur causing the officer's adrenaline to flow. The event, usually prompted by a call from a dispatcher, causes the officer to shift gears. Alertness occurs and energy is mobilized to deal with unknown aspects of an emergency. The event might prove to be dangerous—this is borne out by statistics. In 1997 there were 65 officers killed in the line of duty. Firearms killed sixty-two of the 65. Arrest or exceptional means have cleared 64 of the killings, and one suspect remains at large. Nineteen officers were slain during arrest situations: eight were attempting to prevent robberies or apprehend robbery suspects; five were investigating burglaries and/or attempting to apprehend burglary suspects; five were serving arrest warrants; and one was investigating a drug-related situation. Fourteen officers were slain while answering disturbance calls, and 11 died in ambush situation. Additionally, 60 officers were killed accidentally while on official duty. Line of duty assaults totaling 49,151. Eighty-three percent of these assaults were committed with personal weapons (hands, fist, and feet), with 27 percent resulting in injuries to the officer. [33]

33. Federal Bureau of Investigation, *Law Enforcement Officers Killed and As-* *saulted,* 1997, Uniform Crime Reports,

Organizational factors are another area where the psychological and physical effects of roles have been examined. Role ambiguity is a critical factor in law enforcement. Studies suggest this duality involve a lack of clarity about objectives associated with the work role. It also involves different expectations about the work role and job responsibilities. Employees who experience role conflict have reported more job tension and less job satisfaction. Physiologically, workers have reacted with an increased heart rate and higher blood pressure.[34] Functioning as an enforcer of the law and one who monitors human behavior in society requires skills differing from those needed to serve the public. In many communities, the service function occurs more frequently than the law enforcement function and an officer must shift back and forth from one to the other. The skills to perform each role effectively differ, but an officer needs to shift between the two. Thus frustration occurs because of the competing demands.

Individual factors, studied extensively, have emphasized what is known as the coronary prone Type A. This person is one who is an intense striver for achievement, highly competitive, controlled by a time urgency, and excessively committed to work. Research associates coronary heart disease with the Type A pattern. This person shows more severe and widespread coronary arteriosclerosis.[35] From this, researchers conclude the interaction between job stressors may produce reactions leading to heart disease. In fact, in several states, the courts have found heart disease is job related for police officers, and it leads to disability retirement. There are many symptoms indicating when an individual is under too much stress (see figure 6–6). Stress is a natural reaction to a demand made by something either pleasant or unpleasant. Currently, concern is expressed for the psychological demands placed on police officers. Experts agree job stress can affect one's health, personality, and job performance.[36] Not everyone reacts to stressors the same way. The hardy personality mediates the relationship between stressors and symptoms. These individuals seem to possess various beliefs and tendencies are useful in coping with stressors. The hardy personality appraises events optimistically, and takes decisive action when coping with stress. These individuals report less illness in the face of stressors.[37]

Washington DC, USGPO, 1999, pp. 2–32.

34. Murphy and Schoenborn, *op. cit.,* p. 34.

35. *Ibid.,* p. 36.

36. Hope Heart Institute, *Adapting to Stress,* Seattle, WA, Hope Heart Institute, 1998, p. 5.

37. Murphy and Schoenborn, *op. cit.,* p. 36.

Figure 6–6

Signs That Can Mean Too Much Stress

Dry mouth	Headache
Sighing	Overeating/undereating
Chain smoking	Skin problems
Diarrhea/Constipation/Nausea	Fatigue
Feeling "faint"	Stroking beard/mustache
Hair twirling/pulling/tossing	Clammy hands
Nervous cough	Mouth noises (e.g., tongue cluck-ing)
Talking too much/too fast	Inability to talk
Nightmares	Indigestion
Ready tears	Fingernail biting
Leg wagging	Hypochondria
Depression	Anger/Irritability/Resentment
Excessive giggling	Desire to "run away"
Muscle spasms/tightness	Fatigue/Weariness
Continual boredom	Heart palpitations
Impatience	
Chest pain	Irritability
Proneness to errors	Decreased productivity
Confusion	Alcoholism/Drug dependence

Adapted from: The Hope Heart Institute, *Stress—Simple Steps to end Distress,* Seattle, WA, The Hope Heart Institute, Distributed by: Internal Health Awareness Center, Kalamazoo, MI., 1998, p. 5. Reprinted with permission, Hope Heart Institute.

First-line supervisors and managers can intentionally or unintentionally develop stressful situations to which subordinates respond. For example, a Theory "X" manager in dealing with Theory "Y" line personnel can create tensions and pressures inimical to their well being. Compliance to orders is demanded and any type of participation is rejected. In time, employees respond to exploitive authoritarianism in one of several ways. Some officers will repress the conflict and appear to be calm and passive. The repression of tension and hostility can result in higher blood pressure over a period of time.[38]

Another response can be spontaneous outbursts resulting in conflict and aggression in the workplace. This causes a stressful work environment and will lead to the development or reinforcement of the informal organization.[39] Overall, the officers' response to organizational stress can be personally devastating, resulting in one or more significant behavioral changes identified in figure 6–7. The impact of individual distress reflects directly on the organization causing poor performance. Officers who constantly experience a level of stress that is too high will, in all probability, become less effective and eventually

38. James C. Quick and Jonathan D. Quick, *Organizational Stress and Preventive Management,* New York, McGraw–Hill Book Company, 1984, p. 38.

39. *Ibid.*

will not be able to constructively contribute to the organization.[40] As one becomes aware of occupational stress, they can instinctively identify the pressure impact and determine the best tolerated stress level.[41]

Figure 6–7

Officers Stress Response and Organizational Impact

Individual	Organization
Family problems	Turnover
Depression	Absenteeism
Suicide	Late to work
Sleeping problems	Grievances
Heart disease	Accidents
Backache	Strikes
Ulcers	
Cancer	Quality of work
Diabetes	Lack of motivation

Adopted from: James C. Quick and Jonathan D. Quick, *Organizational Stress and Preventive Medicine,* New York, McGraw–Hill Book Company, 1984, pp. 4–51.

Dr. Hans Selye suggests the antidote to the stresses of life is to:

- Identify your own stress level.

- Establish your own life goals.

- Look out for yourself by becoming necessary to others.[42]

An organization cannot achieve its goals unless employees strive to be useful. This is easily accomplished if each employee acquires the skills to function positively on the job. Managers must take the view that attitude is central to a synergistic organization emphasizing attainment of goals. Attitudes determine whether an experience is pleasant or unpleasant. Viewing things positively can convert a negative stress into a positive one.[43] Inimical stressors then convert to eustress (positive stress). Stress is not only inevitable, but also a function of living in a complex society. Each employee will have there own combination of life and job stress, as well as relief skills combining to establish a reactive posture to the organization.[44] The task of management then becomes one of integrating the skills of the individual into the organization.

Occupational stress can and should contribute to individual health and well being. An assessment tool receiving increasing attention in recent years is the New Social Adjustment Rating Scale. It is based on the examination of a large number of medical case histories in an effort

---

40. *Ibid.,* p. 90.

41. Hans Selye, "On the Real Benefits of Eustress," *Psychology Today,* March 1978, p. 63.

42. *Ibid.,* p. 70.

43. *Ibid.,* p. 63.

44. Albrecht, *op. cit.,* p. 150.

to identify life experiences and their correlation with major health problems.[45]

The inventory assigns a number reflecting the relative severity of change and adaptation to that change. Some of the events measured are positive while others are negative, such as, "death of spouse"—119 points or "marriage"—50 points. The developers of the inventory identified fifty-four life events. Of that number, seven were occupational incidents:

Item	Points
Change to a different type of work	51
Changes in working hours or conditions	35
Loss of job	
laid off from work	68
fired from work	79
Retirement	52
Troubles at work	
with your boss	29
with co-workers	35
with persons under your supervision	35
other work troubles	28
Major readjustment such as: reorganization	60
Change in responsibilities at work:	
more responsibilities	29
fewer responsibilities	21
promotion	31
demotion	42
transfer	32[46]

These variables clearly transcend all aspects of an employee's relationship to the organization. A manager *must* deal with them in order to allow for the creation of an organizational environment optimizing worker performance without creating undesirable side effects.[47] Modeled after the Holmes–Rahe life-stress inventory, a law enforcement critical life event scale was developed by James D. Sewell (see figure 6–8). This inventory in its final form included 144 life events with a high rating of 88 for the most stressful situation, "violent death of a partner in the line of duty," to a low grade of 13 for the least stressful, "completion of a routine report."

45. Karl Albrecht, *op. cit.* p. 50.

46. Hope, *Adapting to Stress,* Seattle, WA, Hope Heart Institute, 1998, p.

5. Reprinted with permission of the Hope Heart Institute.

47. Albrecht, *op. cit.,* p. 140.

Figure 6–8

Law Enforcement Critical Life Events Scale

Event	Value
1. Violent death of a partner in the line of duty	88
2. Dismissal	85
3. Taking a life in the line of duty	84
4. Shooting someone in the line of duty	81
5. Suicide of an officer who is a close friend	80
6. Violent death of another officer in the line of duty	79
7. Murder committed by a police officer	78
8. Duty-related violent injury (shooting)	76
9. Violent job-related injury to another officer	75
10. Suspension	72
11. Passed over for promotion	71
12. Pursuit of an armed suspect	71
13. Answering a call to a scene involving violent non-accidental death of a child	70
14. Assignment away from family for a long period of time	70
15. Personal involvement in a shooting incident	70
16. Reduction in pay	70
17. Observing an act of police corruption	69
18. Accepting a bribe	69
19. Participating in an act of police corruption	68
20. Hostage situation resulting from aborted criminal action	68

Event	Value
21. Response to a scene involving the accidental death of a child	68
22. Promotion of inexperienced/incompetent officer over you	68
23. Internal affairs investigation against self	66
24. Barricaded suspect	66
25. Hostage situation resulting from a domestic disturbance	65
26. Response to "officer needs assistance" call	65
27. Duty under a poor supervisor	64
28. Duty-related violent injury (non-shooting)	63
29. Observing an act of police brutality	62
30. Response to "person with a gun" call	62
31. Unsatisfactory personnel evaluation	62
32. Police-related civil suit	61
33. Riot/crowd control situation	61
34. Failure on a promotional examination	60
35. Suicide of an officer	60
36. Criminal indictment of a fellow officer	60
37. Improperly conducted corruption investigation of another officer	60
38. Shooting incident involving another officer	59
39. Failing grade in police training program	59
40. Response to a "felony-in-progress" call	58

Event	Value	Event	Value
41. Answering a call to a sexual battery/abuse scene involving a child victim	58	51. Departmental misconduct hearing	55
42. Oral promotional review	57	52. Wrecking a departmental vehicle	55
43. Conflict with a supervisor	57	53. Personal use of illicit drugs	54
44. Change in departments	56	54. Use of drugs by another officer	54
45. Personal criticism by the press	56	55. Participating in a police strike	53
46. Investigation of a political/highly publicized case	56	56. Undercover assignment	53
47. Taking severe disciplinary action against another officer	56	57. Physical assault on an officer	52
		58. Disciplinary action against partner	52
48. Assignment to conduct an internal affairs investigation on another officer	56	59. Death notification	51
		60. Press criticism of an officer's actions	51
49. Interference by political officials in a case	55	61. Polygraph examination	51
50. Written promotional examination	55	62. Sexual advancement toward you by another officer	51
		63. Duty-related accidental injury	51
		64. Changing work shifts	50

Source: The author, Dr. James D. Sewell, provided the critical life event list.

This life event scale has a number of implications for police managers. Stress can be analyzed and corrective steps taken. In addition, the agency can develop and implement stress management training programs. Emphasis must be placed on effectively and productively helping the *majority* of employees seek and cope within their acceptable stress level. If an employee is found to be in an overstressed mode, the manager should attempt to provide support and manage conflict — but the overlying element must be an acceptable level of job performance. It is a function that cannot be ignored or brushed aside—an acceptable performance level is the "sin qua non" of the organization.

The cumulative negative effects of stress can create numerous problems for management to included:

- Impaired officer performance and reduced departmental productivity.
- Reduced morale.
- Public relations problems (e.g., after a suicide or case of police brutality).
- Labor-management friction.
- Civil suits because of stress-related failures in personnel performance.
- Tardiness and absenteeism.

- Increase turnover due to leaves of absence, early retirement as a consequence of stress-related problems and disabilities, and the resulting expense of training and hiring new recruits.

- The added expense of paying overtime when the agency is left short of staff.[48]

From this list it can easily be seen that negative effects of stress can be highly detrimental to a department and its employees. Addressing stress will hopefully help officer to steer clear of some types of stress and to help them deal with the stress they cannot avoid.[49]

Participation

Management by participation is viewed by many as the primary vehicle for solving all problems. It is perceived as the mode superior to all others. Exponents of the participative approach view it as omnipotent, if not omniscient and are widely quoted as exemplified by the works of Blake and Mouton, McGregor, and Likert (see chapter 5). Management Style 9.9, Theory Y, and System Four have achieved preeminence in managerial parlance. This does not presuppose that participation is totally inimical to attaining organizational goals, but that there are clear-cut limitations to its application. McGregor acknowledges there are times when a supervisor must issue a direct order, perhaps disciplinary action becomes necessary, or employees must be terminated.[50]

Grid Management studies show many people lack the competence to deal independently with complex work situations and consequently require high degrees of planning, directing, and controlling of their efforts by others.[51] Blake and Mouton further postulate that if a specific problem is the supervisors' alone, according to common understanding, the subordinates should not want to be involved.[52] Likert states the orientation of approximately 17 percent of employees is toward dependent rather than participative behavior. He further suggests it is virtually impossible for the manager to be supportive of a subordinate if organizational objectives are in conflict with the desires and needs of that individual.[53] Subordinates, in many situations, are apathetic and do not seek participation in decision-making that may affect them. This is notable in several ways—the selective interests of

48. Peter Finn and Julie Esselman Tomz, *Developing a law Enforcement Stress Program for Officers and Their Families,* Washington, DC, Office of Justice Programs, March 1997, p. 16.

49. *Ibid,* p. 17.

50. William M. Fox, "Limits to the Use of Consultative–Participative Management" *California Management Review,* Winter 1997, Vol. XX, No. 2, p. 17 citing D. McGregor, *The Human Side of*

Enterprise, New York, McGraw–Hill, 1960, pp. 18, 25–26, and 29.

51. *Ibid.,* citing R.R. Blake and J.S. Mouton, *The Managerial Grid,* Houston, Gulf Publishing Company, 1964, pp. 45, and 155–156.

52. *Ibid.*

53. *Ibid.,* citing R. Likert, *New Patterns of Management,* McGraw–Hill, 1961, pp. 92–95, and 115.

employees, inability of leaders to deliver, differential leader expertise, and apathy.[54]

A fundamental assumption of humanism is that there will be greater production and employee satisfaction when participation prevails.[55] However, in one study, Hugh Clegg found participation through representation did not, by itself, appreciably increase worker satisfaction and productivity was not related to participation.[56] In another study, Arnold Tannenbaum similarly found little relationship between participation and work satisfaction.[57] The conflicting views of what constitutes job satisfaction are evident. Some findings support the position that officers are satisfied while others refute this position.[58]

Participation is only part of the rhetoric of the organizational humanists. Kaplan and Tausky point out the unmistakable ideological air of humanism that has led to the distortion of facts concerning employee motivators.[59] An excessive emphasis on participatory democracy has led to an orientation that all workers can be placed under a single motivational scheme. Employees differing orientation to work must be recognized—not ignored.[60] Divergence between some individuals' egoistic interests and organizational goals is inevitable. Participation is not a panacea for creating congruence between individual and organizational goals. In some situations and with certain employees, participatory management techniques can be stressed, but in other situations it is definitely not appropriate.[61]

Police leadership (desirous of dealing with people-oriented problems found in bureaucratic organizations) can turn to a truly participative style of management.[62] For the majority of officers in progressive agencies, the characteristics of participative management, as set forth in figure 6–9, are clearly a means of enhancing employee satisfaction and improving performance. It is a sharing of power threatening to those entrenched in the control-oriented approach to work force management.[63]

54. *Ibid.*, pp. 18–19.

55. H. Roy Kaplan and Curt Tausky, "Humanism in Organizations: A Critical Appraisal," *Public Administration Review*, March–April 1977, Vol. 37, No. 2, p. 173.

56. *Ibid.*

57. *Ibid.*

58. Whisenand, *op. cit.* and Joel Lefkowitz, "Job Attitudes of Police: Overall Description and Demographic Correlates," *Journal of Vocational Behavior*, 1974, Vol. 5, No. 2, pp. 32–39.

59. Kaplan, *op. cit.*, p. 177.

60. *Ibid.*

61. Dennis P. Slevin, "Observations on the Invalid Scoring Algorithm of 'NASA' and Similar Consensus Tasks," *Group and Organizational Studies*, December 1978, Vol. 3, No. 4, p. 506.

62. Martin N. Nowak, "Participative Management: An Approach for Improving Employee Relations," *Law and Order*, February 1983, Vol. 34, No. 2, p. 41.

63. Richard E. Walton, "From Control to Commitment in the Workplace," *Harvard Business Review*, March–April 1985, Vol. 63, No. 2, p. 77.

Figure 6–9

Characteristics of Participative Management

- Participation leads to an acceptance of managerial decisions with a corresponding reduction of anxiety associated with change.
- Creates personal commitment to the implementation of managerial decisions.
- Leads to a greater understanding of managerial decisions and the plan to achieve departmental objectives.
- Better under standing of the intrinsic and extrinsic reward system.
- Allows participants to achieve, gain self-identity, to grow personally, and an opportunity to self-actualize.
- Group decision-making allows the group to pressure individuals into accepting decisions.
- Collaborative-problem-solving tends to increase teamwork and facilitate continued cooperation.
- Enhances resolving difference by mutual concessions.
- Results in better decision-making.

Harry W. More, and W. Fred Wegener, *Behavioral Police Management,* New York, Macmillan, 1992, pp. 399–400; and Gary A. Yukl, *Leadership in Organizations,* Englewood Cliffs, NJ Prentice–Hall; 1981, pp. 41–129. Reprinted with permission of the publisher.

The real difference is a managerial style based on totally imposed control in contrast to one eliciting commitment.[64] Successful implementation demands support from the top executive based on a philosophy of management truly concerned with employees well being. Support limited to "lip service" rather than concrete and emphatic action will lead to negative rather than the positive characteristics of participative management. Effective participation requires employees to think and act as if they are truly an integral part of the organization. Acceptance of this calls for the creation of a real partnership. Employees shift their focus from being a passive, dependent subordinate to a proactive member of the team. Managers and employees work jointly to solve problems. The primary focus is on achieving agency objectives and goals. Members of the organization readily accept individual differences, and utilize different employee skills.[65]

Acceptance of disagreement is inevitable and an essential element of problem solving. Participation requires each employee to accept others imperfection. Being tolerant of others, their weaknesses and strengths, is essential if a partnership is to be functional. A basic assumption is that the individual performing line duties has the expertise and is the one who knows best how to solve problems.[66]

---

64. *Ibid.*

65. Allan R. Cohen and David L. Bradford, *Influence Without Authority,* New York, John Wiley & Sons, 1990, pp. 251–252.

66. Charles A. Aubrey, II and Patricia K. Felkins, *Teamwork: Involving People in Quality and Productivity Improvement,* White Plains, New York, American Society for Quality Control, 1988, p. 1.

Management acknowledges the importance of the individual when decision-making involves employees. Employees possess valuable ideas and knowledge needed to solve problems. It is a process where officers express work-related concerns, strive to improve their jobs, and contribute to the attainment of departmental goals.[67]

Central to the involvement of employees in the decision-making process is the need to learn new skills and techniques for solving problems. This can vary from participation in quality circles to the development of statistical and measurement skills. Sometimes, employee involvement means monitoring and evaluating tasks performed. It also includes continuous feedback. This requires a refocusing of efforts by managers and line personnel. Adjustment is essential. Some managers will be reluctant to give up power, and some employees will not want to assume additional responsibilities. A real partnership requires the acceptance of new ground rules for superior/subordinate relationships. When both sides accept the new focus, a powerful combination evolves. This allows participants to reinforce and complement each other's strengths.[68] It is normal for individuals to resist change. The status quo is appealing to many. Also there are some who are so comfortable with doing things a certain way that they feel little need to become involved in any participation effort. When the general attitude is, don't rock the boat—leave things alone, participative efforts can be in jeopardy.[69]

Joint participation dilutes resistance to change. Employee anxiety can be reduced as commitment evolves. True participation requires a high degree of give and take between members at every level. One department has dealt with this problem by setting forth a value statement that transcends some of the problems inherent in the participative process. These are set forth in figure 6–10. It should be noted that emphasis is on the importance of the individual and the contribution to be made to the organization and the community. This type of value statement by a police department serves as a philosophical underpinning. It allows the agency and personnel to focus on goal achievement.

67. *Ibid.*

68. Cohen and Bradford, *op. cit.*, p. 253.

69. Jerry L. Gray, *Supervision: An Applied Behavioral Science Approach to Managing People*, Belmont, CA., Kent Publishing, 1984, pp. 497–498.

Figure 6–10

Commitment to the Quality of Organizational Life that Emphasizes Participation

- We respect, care about, trust, and support each other.
- We enjoy our work and take pride in our accomplishments.
- We are disciplined and reliable.
- We keep our perspective and sense of humor.
- We balance our professional and personal lives.
- We consult the people who will be affected by our decisions.
- We have a positive, "can do" attitude.
- We cultivate our best characteristics: initiative, enthusiasm, creativity, patience, competence, and judgment.

Source: Correspondence from Chief Charles E. Samarra, City of Alexandria, VA, dated December 16, 1998.

Adaptive management responds to the dilemma of participation by sharing managerial functions to the fullest extent possible using the concept that attainment of organizational objectives is primary and individuals goals are subordinate.

Informal Organization

Adaptive management accepts the informal organization as a consequence of the nature of bureaucracy itself. The informal organization is superimposed on the formal organization and constantly modifies the relationship of the individual to the organization. The informal organization cannot be ignored—indeed, it must receive a response with an integrative management style. The importance of the informal organization is a "given," but the objectives of the formal organization must take precedence. Individual needs become subordinate. Consequently, conflict is perceived as inevitable as the values and needs of the individual compete with organizational goals. This divergence becomes a positive organizational characteristic acknowledging the uniqueness of each employee and the different orientations to work.

Many practitioners, acknowledging the presence of informal organization, view it as irrational; however it does exist and arises spontaneously from the sentiments, sympathies, traditions and belief stereotypes of employees.[70] The manifestations of informal organization are subtle and usually are not subject to orderly prescription. The social organization reflects such factors as ethnic or language differences, economic status, value systems, educational attainment, and personal likes and dislikes. The table of organization reflecting the structural interrelationships of positions within a department becomes, in reality, a very rough approximation. The social organization conditions and reconditions the formal organization. The ingredients of the informal

---

70. John M. Pfiffner, *The Supervision of Personnel,* Second Edition, Prentice Hall, Inc., Englewood Cliffs, New Jersey, 1958, p. 4.

organization are the result of certain universal phenomena prevailing wherever people work together:

- People band into informal groups that may or may not correspond to hierarchical groupings.
- Growing out of this tendency is the informal or indigenous leader.
- An informal status system assigns roles to individuals.
- An underground communication system is rapid and subtle.
- A belief system exists that often runs counter to management logic and seems irrational to the management mind, but is nevertheless very real.
- The formal theory of hierarchy is often modified in practice by a pattern of internal conflict characterized by personal antagonism, factionalism and struggle for power.[71]

In police departments the social characteristics of the informal organization are evident in: rivalry between deputy chiefs; the conflict between specialized units such as patrol and investigations. One can also find the tension produced by conflicting goals of officers working in internal affairs or community relations. There are also officers who form cliques or the secretary who exercises administrative authority. Cliques are commonly depicted as falling into three categories:

- vertical.
- horizontal.
- random.

A vertical clique usually occurs in one of the major units of the police department such as patrol or investigation. This working relationship generally occurs at the lower levels of an organization. This occurs because of the general isolation of line units from administrative entities. Probably the most common relationship is between a first line supervisors and employees under their command. The supervisor in this type of clique does everything possible to assist and protect underlings, and those supervised reciprocate. If problems occur they are worked out informally. When it is necessary to demand something from an officer, the request is temporized. When errors are made, they are disregarded or everything possible is done to minimize the problem. Generally, this type clique serves to humanize the organization and reduce friction.

The horizontal clique differs from the vertical inasmuch as it cuts across departmental lines and can include officers of varying ranks. This clique will function either defensively or offensively depending upon the situation and the nature of the threat. If the threat is imminent, the clique will take an aggressive posture, but prefers to work defensively because of the bureaucratic nature of most police

71. *Ibid.*, p. 138.

departments. The horizontal clique functions effectively under most circumstances because of the experience its members have acquired from working within the bureaucracy. The horizontal clique generally assumes a defensive posture and only functions when the situation dictates that it must respond to ensure the status quo. It is generally more powerful than the vertical clique is and it can be utilized effectively by a manager when the issue is of general interest. This is especially true when it involves such issues as a reduction in authority, an expansion of review procedures, a significant reorganization or a reduction in force.

The random clique bears no semblance to the other two types of cliques. Rank, role and unit assignment have no bearing in terms of its membership. Officers become members for the primary purpose of exchanging information. There is no effort by its members to strive for a change in working conditions, just a basic desire to associate with other members of the department. The random clique proves to be important to a manager because it is usually the primary source of rumors. It can be utilized to pass on information or as an information source. It serves a highly important function by intensifying social relationships within the department. The officers who get together at the end of the shift for a beer or a meal are an excellent illustration of a random clique.[72]

Groups are of vital importance to a police organization—of special interest are the informal groups. These exist in every organization as members strive to fulfil social needs. Informal groups have an acute and enduring influence on members of an organization. They help to form attitudes, opinions, and basic values such as social and disciplinary controls. Understanding group behavior presents management with a sincere challenge. Interestingly enough, seldom can one understand a group by studying individual members. Interaction between group members makes a group as something exceeding the sum of its parts.[73] In many instances the informal organization comes into existence because the formal organization fails to meet individual needs. As groups evolve, they can either support or not support the formal organization. Such groups have informal leaders and if management can gain the support of these leaders, then work assignments can be carried out more effectively. Informal leaders bring judgment, interpretations, needs, skills, attitudes, and common sense to bear on work situations.

The positive aspects of the informal organization are numerous and include the indispensable function of communication. The "grapevine" is commonplace in most organizations and while in some instances it serves as a vehicle for rumors, it can also serve in the facilitation

72. John Gastil, *Democracy in Small Groups: Participation, Decision Making, and Communications,* Philadelphia, PA, New Society Publishers, 1993, pp. 23–104.

73. Program Development Center, *Human Behavior,* Washington, D.C., USGPO, 1984, p. 7–1.

of official communications. A second function is cohesive maintenance of the formal organization, accomplished by regulating the employees' willingness to produce. An additional function is the maintenance of the individual's integrity, self-respect and independence of choice. There is evidence that formal organizations create informal organization. It remains the responsibility of a department's manager to acknowledge its existence and channel social efforts in order for employees to maintain their identity and the department to attain its objectives.

Case Study

Deputy Chief Charles Stone

Charles Stone has been the deputy chief of police for three years in the City of Tramway. There are 231 sworn officers and 33 civilians in the patrol division that he commands. Personnel are divided between four platoons, and a support section that handles communications and detention. The division is also responsible for traffic enforcement. The city is in a metropolitan area and has considerable commercial and light industrial areas within the city limits. The crime rate is still high (compared to similar sized cities) even though it has dropped during the last two years.

A state-of-the-art dispatching system has been discussed for two years and a major study has recommended the purchase of a new system but no action has been taken. Currently calls for service are backlogged during the hours from 800 PM to 200 AM and the patrol division has difficulty in

responding to urgent calls. With life threatening calls taking priority other calls stack-up sometimes with up to a one-hour delay. Efforts to improve current dispatching by creating categories of seriousness have done little to alleviate the problem. Officers of the patrol division feel that all they do is to a report as quickly as possible and move on to the next call for service. Completing paperwork seems to be more important than serving the public. During the last three months errors in prioritizing calls have been made that has resulted in adverse publicity. The media has been having a hay day and hardly a week will go by without revelations of poorly handled calls for service. The police department and the city council are under extreme pressure to change the situation.

Morale of line officers is at an all time low. It seems to them that no what matter what they do they are wrong. The "bitch" syndrome has always been high, but it has been accepted as a normal way of blowing off steam. As the criticism of the department has escalated all of the locker room discussion has focused on the dispatching problem. Officers feel that management has, in reality, done little to resolve the problem, and let them down. In recent days more and more officers have been taking sick leave, arrived late for roll call, and performing duties in a slip-shod manner. All of is compounding the dispatcher problem, and many line officers seem to be stressed out.

Chief Stone has consulted with his operational managers and decided upon a two pronged attack as a means of dealing with the problem. He has with the approval of the chief of police scheduled a meeting with the city manager to discuss what can be done to deal with the serious need for a new dispatching system. The second consideration is to deal with the stress that the line officers have been put under. If you were Stone what would you do first? Why? How would you involve the officers in solving the dispatcher problem? Why?

For Further Reading

Edward C. Byrne, "Putting Police Work Back on the Street," *Law and Order,* May 1997, Vol. 45, No. 5., pp. 43–45.

> Describes the reorganization of a police department that included the elimination of ranks, the reduction of administrative staff by 21%. These human resources were reinvested in field police services, and the decentralization of the department. The elimination of supervisory and management ranks allowed the officers to become problem-solvers. An important byproduct of the reorganization was that officers were given the latitude to become responsible risk takers.

Peter Finn and Julie Esselman Tomz, *Developing a Law Enforcement Stress Program for and Their Families,* Washington, DC, Office of Justice Programs, March 1997, pp. 1–223.

> This report provides a comprehensive and up-to-date look at a number of law enforcement stress programs that have made serious efforts to help departments, individual officers, civilian employees, and officers' families cope with the stresses of a law enforcement career. The publication is based on nearly 100 interviews with mental health practitioners, police administrators, union and association officials, and lie officers and their family members. It provides pragmatic suggestions for reducing debilitating stress.

Sam Hishmeh, "Total Quality Management," *Law and Order,* April 1998, Vol. 46, No. 4, pp. 92–95.

> The author describes Total Quality Management as a management process and set of disciplines that are coordinated to ensure that the organization consistently meets and exceeds customer requirements.

> TQM is best viewed as a philosophy that must be continuously measured by the community. Benefits include reduced costs, improved morale and increased employee participation. Additional

TQM generates stronger employee loyalty from team productivity and rewards.

Jeffrey Pfeffer, "Seven Practices of Successful Organization," *California Management Review,* Winter 1998, Vol. 40, No. 2, pp. 96–123.

Suggests that it is important to have some overall philosophy or strategic vision of profits through people, because an overall framework increases the likelihood of taking a systematic, as contrasted to a piecemeal, Approach to implementing high-commitment organizational arrangements. Lists seven practices that indicate success that range from selective hiring to reducing status distinctions and barriers. Recommends thinking about high-performance management practices in terms of the effect on the time horizon that characterizes organizational decisions.

Chapter 7

STRUCTURING THE ORGANIZATION:
Form and Substance

Learning Objectives

1. List five modifiers of line numerical strength.

2. Write a short essay describing the span of executive control.

3. Describe four factors that modify the span of control.

4. Illustrate the importance of unity of command.

5. Distinguish between line and staff.

6. Compare organizing by major purpose to organizing by clientele.

7. Distinguish between organization by time an area.

8. Write a short essay describing functional distribution.

9. Compare the organization of the executive office of the San Jose Police Department and the Metropolitan Police Department.

10. Contrast the duties performed by the chief of staff to inspectional services.

11. Describe how civilians can be utilized in law enforcement agencies.

12. Illustrate the relationship between an internal investigation unit and an independent auditor.

13. Write a short essay describing the use of police reserves.

14. Describe contract law enforcement.

15. List six support services that can be consolidated.

Society has organized itself on many fronts for the protection and the promotion of human welfare. Through the years various approaches have been used to accomplish this task. Initial efforts used to insure order and security involved the use of night watches. Individuals selected for these functions were conscripted and the results were far less than desirable. Consequently, it proved necessary to turn to the cities as a means of stabilizing society. As government was looked to for solving numerous ills of our society it has grown to be big business. Government itself represents the greatest single organization within

182

the geographical limits of the country. In fact, one-third of the working force of this Nation is employed in governmental positions. How well it is organized and the extent to which performance meets the needs of the society it serves, are matters of overwhelming importance. The structuring of the organization long neglected has been receiving increased attention. This is especially true of the American police system. The number of employees providing police protection at every level of government exceeds 865,000 at a cost exceeding five billion dollars annually.[1] This is a staggering cost hence everything possible must be done to structuring organizations in such a way as to maximize their effectiveness.

Numerical Strength and Line Capability

Conscientious police executives know that the mere addition of manpower does not enhance, to any appreciable degree, the over-all effectiveness of the department as a whole. Mere numbers do not make a strong organization capable of dealing with the problems that it must thwart. The number of officers on the payroll of a police department is among the least of several factors determining the efficiency of the organization. The line capability of a police organization is the measure of ability and thrust toward the achievement of objectives. It may be concerned in one situation with the prompt solution of a murder case through laboratory examination and identification of evidence materials. In another instance, it may be exerted toward the threat of an upward trend in the traffic accident rate, or to an epidemic of automobile thefts or service station hold-ups. Or it may be the resources needed to resolve as problem and improve the quality of life. It may be further reflected in the amount and quality of police leadership needed in the community to prevent crime. On the other hand it may be a disorderly crowd, disasters, parades or athletic events may be the occasion for bringing the line resources of the department into play.

Within a brief space of time during the night or day it may find expression throughout the whole range of human relationships. It may be a show of force and even gunfire in bringing an armed robbery to a socially acceptable conclusion, or in quelling civil disorder. It may symbolize the scientist in the extent to which the arts and sciences are brought into play in crime control and prevention. It may express the language and technique of the statesman in the application of supreme tact and judgment to the case of a neighborhood or family dispute, or in an officer's contact with a youngster.

1. Kathleen Maguire and Ann L. Pastore, *Sourcebook of Criminal Justice* *Statistics–1997*, Washington, DC, Bureau of Justice Statistics, 1998, p. 18.

Figure 7–1

Modifiers of Line Numerical Strength
Time required taking reports.
Prioritization of investigations.
Utilization of one person patrol units.
Limiting accident investigation to injury only.
Use of motorcycles/scooters in congested areas.
Use of dogs and horses.
Number of staff personnel.
Reserves employed.
Volunteers utilized.
Number of civilian personnel.
Degree and extent of specialization.
Directed patrol.
Prioritization of dispatching.
Problem-solving.

Table 7–1

Full Time Law Enforcement Officers—
Rate per 1,000 Inhabitants

Size of Cities	Average Number
Cities 250,000 and over in population	4.0
Cities 100,000 to 249,000	2.5
Cities 50,000 to 99,999	22.3
Cities 25,000 to 49,999	2.3
Cities 10,000 to 24,999	2.4
Cities under 10,000	3.7

Source: Federal Bureau of Investigation, *Crime in the United States–1997,* Uniform Crime Reports, Washington, D.C., Government Printing Office, 1998, p. 239.

Success, mediocrity or failure may describe the end result, depending upon the degree and quality of manpower that can be put into play. In a modern society, the line capability of a police force is directed toward complex objectives. As if these were not enough, the growing complexity of the social and economic order has increased the burden of the police by giving them additional duties and responsibilities of a regulatory nature. Some of these have had the effect of greatly reducing the line effectiveness of the organization for handling problems which only the police can deal with effectively in its effort to serve the public.

All of the modifiers listed in figure 7–1 either limit or enhance the allocation of line personnel. Most police budgets allocate from 80 to 95 percent of their funds to personnel costs. Consequently it is a place where personnel resources can be allocated to deal with crime and other social problems confronting the police. Ignoring the importance of line power a detachment from reality is readily apparent when a recent study showed that one major police department assigned only 16 percent of its officers to street patrol, and even those officers were ill equipped for the emergencies they might encounter. Additionally, 68 percent of patrol time was spent responding to 911 emergency calls, and less than ten percent of officers were assigned to scout cars for preventive reconnoitering.[2] Thus, in police operations, the numerical strength of a police department is not a true measure of the line capability of the organization it is what one does with manpower. Management has an obligation to maximize its resources by the judicious distribution of personnel to address the critical problems confronting the community.

The Nature of Organization

Federal and state laws, the City Charter and the rules and regulations of a police department impose multitudinous and very important duties upon the Chief of Police. In order that the executive may accomplish the ultimate delivery of police service, there must be a systematic arrangement of a wide variety of functions and functional tools. Such arrangement has for its main purpose the extension in reach of the executive in order to facilitate the accomplishment of tasks assigned. This is the simple fact of organization, too often ignored. Organization on any scale is, in fact, organization of the executive. It is a fundamental premise that organization must be geared directly to goals and objectives. In order to carry out these important functions and objectives, the police enterprise requires organization on a sound and effective basis. Experience tends to confirm the view that a chief of police with superior qualifications would be handicapped with structural defects in the organizational pattern, and those high caliber personnel would be thwarted in their best efforts by faulty organization. Such being the case, all structural aids to good management should be carefully examined. *Organization* stated simply, is the assignment of work to people who are placed in a structure of authority so the total operation may be coordinated by orders of superiors to subordinates, reaching from the top to the bottom of the enterprise. *Work* may be looked upon as the carrying out of assigned responsibilities for the achievement of results, goals and progress toward objectives.

The ultimate unit of organization is a group of operations performed directly by one individual, constituting a personal satisfactory workload. This is called "a position." In a small community with a population of from one to two thousand inhabitants, the basic police functions may be performed successfully by one person. The workload in this instance would not exceed the capacity of a single individual. However, all of the major functions of police service to be found in the more complex organization of a large city are represented on a small scale in the one-person department, and even here, organization is necessary. The town marshal, as the sole representative of law and

2. Office of Justice Programs, *The Challenge of Crime in a Free Society: Looking Forward Looking Backward,* Washington, DC, US Department of Justice, May 1998, p. 86.

order, must organize personal time, energies and the available facilities if work is to be effective.

As the size of a community increases, expanded workloads create a need for the services of more individuals. The executive is unable to do everything alone, hence, the necessity of extending personal reach and capacity for achieving goals by delegation of functions to a subordinate or subordinates. An extension in the organization of the executive is thus indicated. This is accompanied by creation of lines of authority and responsibility through which executive guidance may find expression in the coordination of work by orders. In a metropolitan police department, the organization of the executive tends to become complex. This may include five or more administrative levels between top management and the individual police officer. It calls for a high degree of coordination from the top to the bottom. The far-flung operations of such an organization require coordination of a very superior order.

In the evolution from a one-man department to a large-scale organization, functional specialization appears. As the complexity and volume of operations increase, the need for specialists to handle certain functions becomes evident. One by one these functions are differentiated from the original functions, and specialized units are created for their execution. In the process of organizational growth and development, for example, the time arrives when the investigative workload of the department may justify the establishment of the post of detective. This enables one or more individuals to concentrate their energies and time exclusively on the investigation of criminal cases. Subsequent increases in this phase of departmental operations leads to the assignment of additional detectives to this work and the establishment of a detective division as a major administrative unit.

At a later stage in the evolution of police organization, crime volume in the various offense classifications may expand to the point where the need is recognized for functional decentralization of the detective division. This is accomplished by the creation of special details or squads who give their undivided attention to investigation of crimes in a single category, such as homicide, robbery, burglary or computer crimes. At this juncture, it may become economical for the department to provide itself with laboratory facilities and a laboratory technologist. This provides for the scientific examination and identification of questioned materials involved as evidence in criminal cases. The presence of patrol, traffic, records and crime prevention divisions, (as well as other administrative units such as human resources, communications, transportation and property control), in a police department provide additional examples of functional specialization. It should be noted here that specialization has made serious inroads upon the line strength of American police forces. Admittedly, as a department grows, some degree of specialization is necessary and desirable. However, heavy emphasis must be placed upon eliminating as far as possible, the sacrifice of personnel, (usually from the patrol force) in order to strengthen any shift toward specialization.

Span of Executive Control

The executive of any enterprise can personally direct the activities of only a few persons. As a result, this chief executive must depend upon these to direct others, and upon them in turn to direct still others, until the last person in the organization is reached. There is some difference of opinion concerning the number of subordinates who can be effectively supervised by any one supervisor, but all agree there is a limit to the span of managerial contacts that can be accommodated by a single individual. It has long been known that one of the surest sources of delay and confusion is to allow any superior to be directly responsible for too many subordinates. Based upon what is known to psychologists as "the span of attention," the number of separate items to which the human brain can pay attention at the same time is strictly limited. Just as the hand of man can span only a limited number of notes on the piano, so the mind and will of an administrator can span but a limited number of managerial contacts.

This limitation on supervisory capability is further accentuated by cross-relationships involving the supervisor and the supervised. If A supervises B, C and D, there is much more involved than the direct relationship between A and each subordinate. The cross-relationships between B and C, between C and D and between B and D, with all that this can mean, must be accommodated by the supervisor's span of attention. It is generally accepted that as one moves upward through the levels of organization to the top of the enterprise, the number of subordinates supervised should be progressively reduced. Congestion results when decisions are too highly centralized. In attempting to keep up with routine demands, the executive may neglect planning and policy matters of much greater importance, simply because the detail has to be settled while the planning can wait. These decisions made at long range, may overlook or wrongly evaluate important considerations whose importance would have been appreciated at once by a line officer. Excessive centralization of decision wastes the resources of the organization.

It is impossible to lay down any fixed rule as to the number of subordinates who should report directly to the chief of police. But it is clearly preferable for the executive load to be kept within the range where this official can give proper attention to the duties of the position. Experience indicates the number of such subordinates should not be less than three nor more than seven. The evidence seems to show that when the chief of police attempts to supervise directly the activities of more than nine individuals, it is possible for this office to become a bottleneck and impede the work of the entire organization. Factors influencing span of control include:

- **Manager's ability.** Individuals who can effectively delegate authority and practice a "good" leadership style are capable of supervising more subordinates.

- **Communication.** Effective communications can increase a manager's span, because they can spend less time discussing trivia and clarifying distortions.

- **Employees.** Managers can supervise a larger number of employees if they are well trained and self-motivated.

- **Job**. Executives can supervise more subordinates who are performing stable operations than subordinates managing unstable situations.[3]

The general structure of a police organization lends itself easily to the observance of reasonable limits in the span of executive control. In recent years capable observers in the American police field have reached the conclusion that even the largest police structure can be set up so its head exercises direct supervision over only six or seven divisional commanders. The same general principle will apply to supervisory and command personnel generally, such as assistant chiefs and captains, since the size of any office unit or field force should not be greater than can be adequately supervised. As one moves from the subordinate to the top level of management, since ordinarily the complexity of the matters to be settled between supervisor and subordinate, and hence the amount of time to be spent in conference, increases at the higher levels. A reduced distribution of responsibility for the supervision of subordinates and one found in many departments are graphically shown in figure 7–2.

3. Adapted from Gerald H. Graham, *Management, The Individual, The Organization, The Process,* 1st edition, by © 1975. Reprinted with permission of South–Western College Publishing, a division of International Thompson Publishing. Fax 800–730–2215, p. 125.

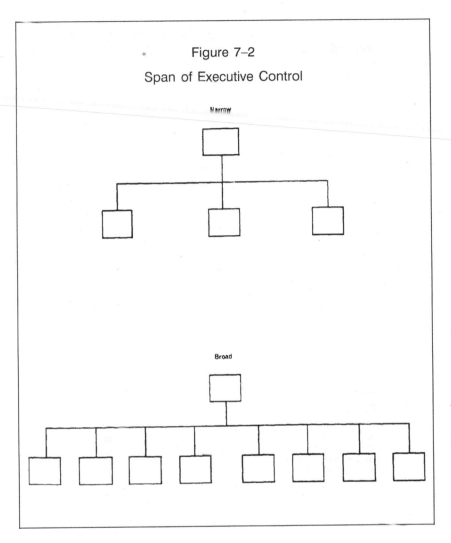

Figure 7–2

Span of Executive Control

Narrow

Broad

Unity of Command

Foremost among the indispensable prerequisites to successful organization is unity of command. Subordinates there must be, but command is singular, whole and indivisible. At the top level of management the police chief executive should be responsible to one superior and only one. The same principle should find expression from the top all the way down through organization to the bottom of the enterprise. A police officer subject to orders from several superiors will be confused, inefficient, and irresponsible, while an officer subject to orders from but one superior may be methodical, efficient and responsible. The significance of this principle in the process of coordination and organization must not be lost from sight. In building an organization structure it is often tempting to set up more than one boss for a person who is doing work which has more than one relationship. The rigid adherence to the principle of unity of command may have its absurdities; these are, however, unimportant in comparison with the certainty of confusion, inefficiency and irresponsibility that arise from the violation of the principle.

Line and Staff

The concept of staff and line is a critical distinction that must be made in a police organization. The difference between support and operations is a fundamental one and possesses many implications.[4] It necessarily follows that the two major administrative areas of activity in a police organization are line operations and staff services.[5] Recognition of the concept of line and staff is the first step toward the arrangement of related functions under unified supervision and command. The chief value of this distinction is that it gives proper location and status to the two major functions of police organization—preparation for the delivery of police service, and the delivery of police service. Within this frame of reference, the staff services the line, supplying it with qualified trained personnel. Among other services provided are records, data, communication facilities, vehicle maintenance and supplies, so it may operate efficiently in the discharge of its functions. The terms "housekeeping functions" and "auxiliary services" have been applied by some observers to staff activities in what would seem to be inadequate recognition of the importance of the staff function. The line translates plans and policies into action in the field; it is the point at which the discharge of police service is made. The ultimate delivery of police protection and the provision of services to the community are the responsibility of the line.

The accepted classification of staff functions and line operations in police organization follows:

- Systems development.   )
- Inspection.   )
- Personnel administration.   )
- Information resources.   )
- Statistical operations.   )
- Audits.
- Identification services.   )
- Property.   )
- Communication system.   )
- Fiscal operations.   )　　Staff Functions
- Purchasing.   )
- Motor transport.   )
- Jail administration.   )
- Supply.   )
- Scientific investigation.   )
- Public affairs.   )
- Intelligence.   )
- Internal affairs.   )
- Community relations.   )

4. Mark H. Moore and Darrel W. Stephens, *Beyond Command and Control: The Strategic Management of Police Departments*, Washington, DC, Police Executive Research Forum, 1991, p. 73.

5. Phil Herman, "Moving Away From Top–Down Management," *Community Police Exchange*, November/December 1998,Phase VI, No. 23, p. 4.

- Plant operations.
- Crime analysis.
- Media relations.
- Training.
- Behavioral sciences.
- Employee relations.

- Patrol.   )
- Criminal investigation.   )   Line
- Vice investigation.   )
- Traffic regulation and control.   )
- Crime prevention.   )   Operations
- Youth development.   )
- Drug Abuse Resistance Education   )

The foregoing elements lend themselves to orderly arrangement in the structure of a police organization. Although administrative separation of these two broad phases of police organization and management is essential, examination of the organizational structure of American police departments reveals a frequent lack of a clear distinction between line and staff functions. Staff services often are to be found under direct line supervision and in an organization where this situation prevails, it is also likely that one or more line functions are directly controlled and supervised by a staff agency. Under this faulty arrangement, coordination is frustrated through interruptions in the normal flow of authority and control and the effective line power of the organization is reduced.

Organization by Major Purpose

The purpose of an activity or operation is an important determining factor in organizational relationships. In municipal government, for example, organization by major purpose, such as water supply, crime control, or education, furnishes the basis for bringing together in a single large department all of those who are concerned with the rendering of a particular service. The divisionalization of a police department is largely the expression of the need for effective division of labor in the organization of the enterprise. Thus, because of its peculiar function and the comprehensive character of the patrol operation, patrol services are assembled in the police organizational structure under unified supervision. Other functions included under field operations include such functions as parking regulation, youth services, crime prevention, and community services.

The administrative functions are distinguished in major purpose from all other units by virtue of the specialized attention given to the numerous activities to including budgeting, personnel, training, psychological services and the issuance of permits. Unified control over personnel engaged in these specialized activities makes more certain the accomplishment of the purpose of bringing under a single command the departmental operations that lie within this frame of reference. It clarifies objectives for a large group of workers drawing upon their energies and loyalties to give focus and drive to an important police role. The same considerations apply to functions that can be categorized as technical in nature, where the major purpose or objective is directed toward supporting other police activities. This includes activities such as records and identification, warrants, information coordination, and communications. One of these areas that have received increasing attention in recent years is crime analysis. The major purpose in this area is to receive, assemble, digest and analyze the data concerning the police problems of crime, delinquency, vice and traffic, and thereby afford an intelligent point of departure in administrative planning for their solution.

Another range of activities is that of investigations. As departments increase in size specialization become inevitable. It is quite common to find a grouping of investigations into two areas: persons, and general crimes.

General crimes generally include narcotics juvenile, missing persons, burglary, fraud, and auto-theft. Investigative specialization for crimes against persons includes homicide, sexual assault, child exploitation, robbery, and violent crimes. More recently we have seem investigative units including court liaison as a means of improved coordination and the scheduling of personnel who have to appear in court. In most departments internal affairs and intelligence are functions performed in the chief's office. These hypercritical functions, in many instances, are sensitive enough that the chief must receive timely information as soon as possible.[6] If a chief works in a highly volatile political environment survival in office can be dependent upon the outcome of the internal and special investigation. Economy and efficiency in organization demand that all operations related to each of these major entities and located under single command and supervision as a basic principle of sound organization.

Organization by Clientele

Superimposed upon purpose and process as they condition the structure of organization is the influence of the type or class of persons dealt with or served. For example, the nature of police work brings organization and personnel into contact with a relatively large volume of potential and actual offenders at the juvenile level each year, in addition to those whose behavior patterns are much further advanced in the direction of delinquency and crime. The youngster represents a very special type of clientele, so in recent years the crime prevention unit has become a standard feature of police organization in this country. This development represents an attempt to gear organization to the needs of a specific clientele. Additionally, police departments have created special units to deal with child exploitation and abuse. Functional specialization within the detective division is to a considerable extent the expression of organization by clientele. The establish-

6. *Law Enforcement News,* "Police Intelligence Moves one Step Away From the Top Cop at NYPD," November, 1998, p. 9.

ment of homicide, robbery, burglary, bias and automobile theft details is in recognition of the gains to be made through the highly specialized study of the operational characteristics and modus operandi of a particular type or class of criminal offenders. Foreign language and racial clusters such as the Chinese in San Francisco, Italians in New Haven, Cubans in Miami, Vietnamese in San Jose, Mexicans, Koreans, and Filipinos in Los Angeles, and Blacks in Birmingham, may likewise warrant separate recognition in police organization.

Organization by Area

The line delivery of police service requires a territorial decentralization of operations. In no other way can the police organize to reach the people who are to be served or who are to be controlled. A universal feature of police organization and administration throughout the civilized world is the sub-division of the area policed, into small units known as patrol areas, police service areas (PSAs), service areas, regional operations districts, and finally patrol beats. This is the concept of "territorial I imperative" wherein personnel respond to and work diligently within an area they can call their own. The police patrol beat is the ultimate unit of organization in the police structure. It may be regarded as a geographical area of operation in which the demands for police service constitute a workload not exceeding the capacity of a single officer, or two officers where double-officer patrol is employed.

The selection of the beat as the basic unit in all police operations conforms to the fundamental principles involved in all police strategy— breaking the total problem into its smallest divisions and attacking each one singly. The existence of the beat is based upon the conviction that effective patrol service is the foundation of police organization. The individual patrolman is society's first line of defense against the criminal and in the best position to improve the quality of life on the beat. Under community policing the beat might become an apartment complex or a special problems area. In large cities, the overwhelming number of police beats and the extent of the problem of supervision has led to the grouping of these patrol areas into districts or precincts. Each precinct has a commanded officer who directs police operations in one prescribed area and who is directly responsible to a regional command or to headquarters.

Organization by Time

The police conduct an around-the-clock operation that creates the necessity for chronological distribution of the personnel resources of the department. Most police organizations operate with a three-shift or three-platoon basis. Distribution of the manpower of a police department on a three-shift basis is something more than dividing three into twenty-four, or dividing three into the number of personnel available. The amount and nature of the demands for police service are not the same on all three shifts. When this fact is combined with the basic principle that in a crime fighting organization, maximum manpower must be made available at the time and place of the greatest demand for police service. Thus it becomes apparent that chronological distribution of staff services and line power is a matter of considerable importance and difficulty. Studies of police organization and management reveal the caseload peak for a twenty-four hour period occurs as a rule between 9:30 P.M. and 11:30 P.M. The normal excess of manpower assigned to the 4:00 P.M. to 12:00 midnight shift in most jurisdictions is intended to accommodate this increase in the volume of police activity. Thus in thinking through the structure of police organization, when organization by major purpose, process, clientele, time and area are brought into play, the project is brought into sharper focus and the basis is strengthened for the delivery of effective police service to the community.

Functional Distribution

The competition for manpower occasionally becomes critical and the chief executive is hard-pressed to weigh the relative importance of the various requests. Will the addition of two officers to the traffic division secure better results in protecting life and property than the addition of two officers to the detective division, or to the patrol division, or to the records division? Or, would the addition of a crime analyst prove ultimately of greater value? Since the chief executive must work within well-defined fiscal limits, some sort of answer to these questions must be obtained.

What, for example, is the relative social significance of preventing one case of juvenile delinquency, one death due to a traffic accident, one adult case of robbery in which a citizen is brutally clubbed, one murder, or one ten–year old girl from being attacked? These are the subjective, qualitative determinations the chief executive must make in balancing the competing demands for manpower presented. The chief can, to be sure, take into account operational costs, caseload, and the frequency of various types of crime. Executive judgment will also be shaped by public sentiment prevailing at the moment. It is apparent the problems presented by functional distribution of the force will challenge the best executive talent available.

It will be noted that the organizational structure for the smaller department represents organization by time, although organization by area is also involved to the extent that provision is made for patrol beats (see figure 7–3). In this situation, the chief would probably provide the necessary supervision of personnel during the day shift—8:00 AM—4:00 PM. In the event two or more officers are on duty during Shifts 1 and 3, it would be necessary for a senior officer or Sergeant to act in a supervisory capacity on each shift.

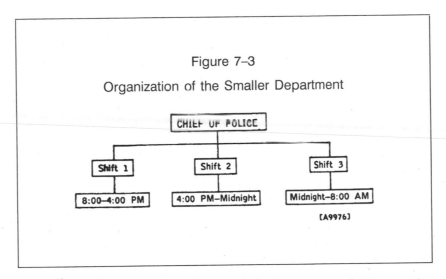

Figure 7–3

Organization of the Smaller Department

As previously indicated, all of the major functions of police service to be found in the larger, more complex police organization, are represented on a reduced scale in the smaller department. Here, staff services, including personnel management, the records system, communications system, property control, purchasing, and jail the chief would perform management. There may come a point where the personnel strength of the department indicates the delegation of one or more of these services to other officers. While the basic principles of police organization and management are applicable regardless of the size of the department, the chief of police in the smaller community (where a large segment of police service in this nation is delivered) is in the main, the "forgotten person".

Figure 7–4 illustrates the structure of the organization needed to provide police services in a medium sized department. There are two major units with the majority of personnel assigned to line operations. This is in sharp contrast the small sized police department and it can be easily seen that functional specialization has come into existence. In other departments of the same size one can find a greater division of function by creating four major divisions: operations, investigations, services, and staff. Each approach reflects differing attitudes to structuring an organization. As the cities increase in population the organizational structure becomes more complex. When one finds five major divisions reporting directly to the chief it does flatten the organization and theoretically makes for easier departmental communications. As a police department grows, specialized functions, initially supervised out of the chief's office, are placed else where. This occurs with such units as vice, intelligence, planning, and inspections. This is apparent in the organizational arrangement for the

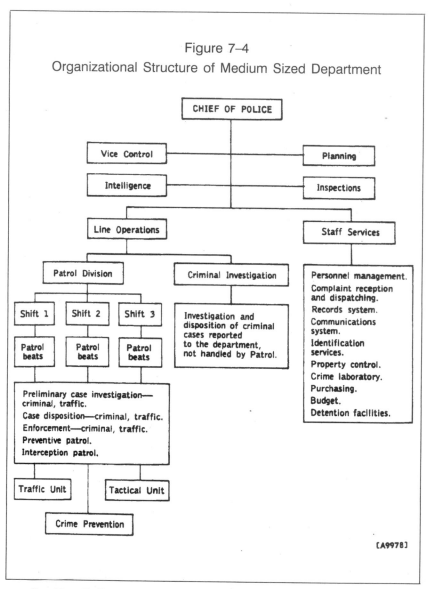

Figure 7-4

Organizational Structure of Medium Sized Department

CHIEF OF POLICE

Vice Control — Planning

Intelligence — Inspections

Line Operations   Staff Services

Patrol Division   Criminal Investigation

Shift 1   Shift 2   Shift 3

Patrol beats   Patrol beats   Patrol beats

Investigation and disposition of criminal cases reported to the department, not handled by Patrol.

Personnel management.
Complaint reception and dispatching.
Records system.
Communications system.
Identification services.
Property control.
Crime laboratory.
Purchasing.
Budget.
Detention facilities.

Preliminary case investigation—criminal, traffic.
Case disposition—criminal, traffic.
Enforcement—criminal, traffic.
Preventive patrol.
Interception patrol.

Traffic Unit   Tactical Unit

Crime Prevention

[A9978]

Reading Police Department as indicated in figure 7–5. The chief has retained the professional standards unit under his immediate supervision. The department has two major units: special services, and patrol each headed by an inspector. Additionally, patrol is organized into four platoons and a support section. This latter unit is responsible for communications and detention. The Special Services unit has two divisions: investigations, and community & support services. This latter division is responsible for community response, crime prevention, training, and records. Interestingly vice investigations is placed two levels below the chief of police.

Figure 7–5
Reading Police Department

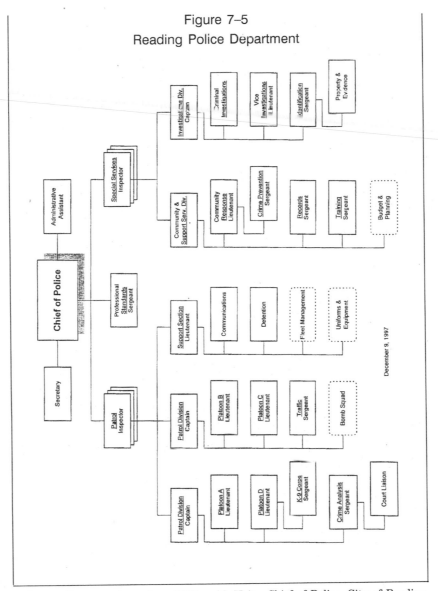

Source: Correspondence from William M. Heim, Chief of Police, City of Reading, Pennsylvania, dated January 13, 1999.

In Miami, FL., a somewhat different approach is taken. In this city with a population of approximately 363,000 there are three major units: field operations, administrative, and investigations (see figure 7–6). The department has 1012 sworn and 340 civilian positions.[7] Field Operations is divided into three districts and further divided into 12 specific service areas such as the Little Haiti and Coral Way.[8]

---

7. Brian A Reaves and Andrew L. Goldberg, *Census of State and Local Law Enforcement Agencies, 1996*, Washington, DC, Bureau of Justice Statistics, June 1998, p. 6.

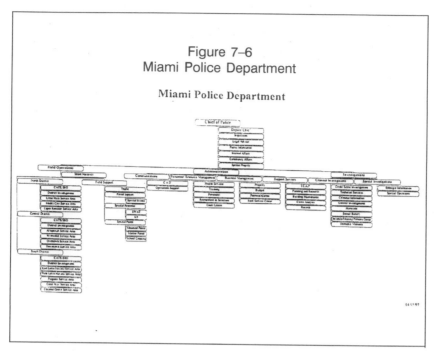

Figure 7–6
Miami Police Department

Source: Correspondence with Major P.M. Shepard, Commander, Field Support Section, Miami Police Department, Miami, FL, dated November 5 1998.

8. Miami Police Department, *1997 Annual Report, Unity, Teamwork and* *Professionalism,* Miami, FL., City of Miami, 1998, p. 10.

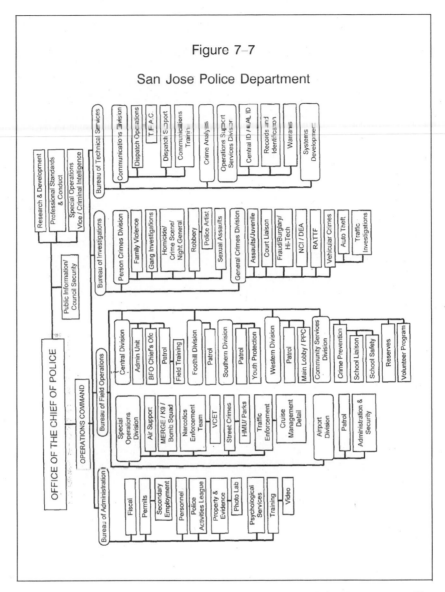

Figure 7–7

San Jose Police Department

Source: Correspondence with Lt. David Kiniller, San Jose Police Department, City of San Jose, San Jose CA., dated November 6, 1998.

The San Jose Police Department in 1996 had 1,300 sworn personnel that is an increase in the number of officers by more than five percent as compared to four years earlier.[9] The City of San Jose has a population of approximately 821,000. The department has organized in such a fashion as to place four major units under an operations command (see figure 7–7). These bureaus are field operations, investi-

9. Reaves and Goldberg, *op.cit.*

gations, technical services and administration. This arrangement places all operations, where they belong—under one individual. This way there is less friction between major units, and resources can be directed to goal attainment. A unique feature of the San Jose Police Department is the Mounted and Parks Enforcement Unit. Started in 1986, the unit presently has one Lieutenant, two Sergeants, ten Mounted Officers, one Civilian Trainer, four Park Officers, and 16 horses that are divided into two teams to cover the entire week. The purpose of this unit is to patrol the downtown area and the parks, enforcing laws and the municipal code. The unit also works at special events such as festivals and parades.[10]

10. San Jose Police Department *SJPD Mounted and Parks Enforcement* *Unit,* San Jose, CA., 11/10/1998, http://www.sjpd.org/mounted.html.

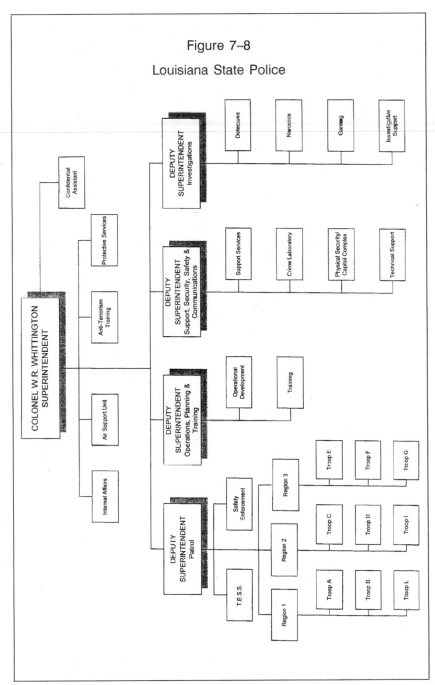

Figure 7–8

Louisiana State Police

Source: Correspondence with Genny May, Captain, Operational Development, Louisiana State Police, dated February 1, 1999.

State police organizations have special organizational characteristics. The prominent feature is the aspect of decentralization. Geography plays a very important part as indicated in the table of organization of the Louisiana State Police (see figure 7–8). The state has three regions—each with a major in command. Unique in the organization is the protective services unit that provides security for the governor. Additionally, the organization has a Chief of Staff who supervises a diversity of functions including operational development, training, the crime laboratory, and support services. As in many larger municipal agencies, this organization has an aviation section.

State police organizations have traditionally emphasized traffic enforcement and accident investigation. They also engage in patrol and first response activities. Other functions they perform include the keeping of computerized files on stolen property, stolen vehicles, vehicle registration, and warrants. Additional functions performed by state police organizations vary considerably. As new functions are added, it has an impact on the organizational structure. These newer units include: bias-related crimes, community crime prevention, and drunk drivers. It also includes units for environmental crimes, repeat offenders, and victim assistance. Twenty-eight of the departments have primary drug enforcement responsibility. In Texas the Department of Public Safety has 260 officers assigned to drug enforcement. At the other extreme the Nevada Highway Patrol has two officers assigned to its narcotics unit. Another unique feature is that ten-state police organizations operate emergency medical services.[11] It should be kept in mind that organizational structure is not static, but a reflection of the integration of internal goal achievement and external demands. Certain basic functions have to be accomplished and the structure should reflect that need for task achievement.

Organization of the Executive

Since the police chief executive cannot perform all the prescribed duties, it seems sensible to be confined to those matters of general management, presuming no one else can do as well. In order to do this in the larger organizations the chief will divide the major tasks into different organizational entities. Such organizational arrangements vary considerably, but the key is to separate function so as to allow for line command over assigned operations. Structural change is quite apparent in many agencies as a continuing effort is made to respond more effectively to community needs. Traditionally it has been quite common for departments to create three major administrative branches:

- Staff services.
- Line operations.
- Inspectional services.

11. Brian A. Reaves and Andrew L. Goldberg, *State and Local Police Departments, 1993,* Washington, D.C., Bureau of Justice Statistics, September 1995, p. 10.

The chief executive must then appoint a head for each of these major units. Duties should be defined, jurisdiction established and authority allocated. Additionally, physical support as may be required for the satisfactory performance of their respective duties should be allocated.

Staff services refer to personnel, material, planning, research, public relations and the maintenance of equipment and buildings. Staff services line operations so the latter may be more productive. Line operations constitute the field activities that are more immediately directed toward achieving the objectives for which the department is organized. The inspectional branch, as the word implies, is the division of the administrative unit that evaluates performance in the staff and line in the discharge of their responsibilities. It also inspects the members of the organization, facilities and equipment.

Because the economical and efficient administration of the police organization rests upon all three of these administrative branches, it is imperative the most competent men in the department are selected as the executive heads of these major units. The sole purpose is to distribute the executive load of the head of the department in a fair and equitable manner and according to accepted administrative principles. These branch chiefs are not intended to deprive the chief executive of either authority or powers because nothing that any one of them could do could be done without his implied approval. The addition of managerial aids to extend the reach of the executive does not contradict the principle of unity of command. They act only by and through the authority of the chief executive. In organization, the aids become just so much additional executive capacity for planning and for supervision.

In order for the authority of the chief to be properly established and recognized by subordinates, it is necessary to direct orders and directives through immediate subordinates—the assistant chief, the deputy chief and the chief inspector. This is also important in establishing the responsibility and authority of intermediate subordinates. A collateral purpose of this procedure is to prevent members of the department in positions below that of the administrative group from taking up the chief's valuable time unnecessarily with minor matters that should be settled by subordinates. A wise chief will learn how to insist on this as a general rule without cutting off communications from subordinates further down the line who have good reason to think their problems can be settled only by the chief executive.

Triple extension of the executive is thus achieved through subordinate command of the three major administrative units of organization—staff services, line operations and inspection. It must be kept constantly in mind that the end result sought is line power, intelligently controlled and directed toward police objectives, and service to the community. This is the essence of police organization and management. A police department may boast of an eminent crime laboratory, an excellent training school, a merit system, and superior communication facilities. It can also have a crime prevention program, a traffic division, a record system and all the other trappings of modern police service but all of these will be of no avail unless they can be and are translated into line power. Too often this basic principle is obscured and even forgotten in the confusion of activities characterizing the average police department. It is the measure of capability at the point where the line delivery of police service occurs that determines the extent to which a police organization is capable of achieving its objectives. Thus, organization of the executive through staff services, line operations and inspection has for its major purpose one end result, and only one—line power. The manner in which this result may best be achieved and applied constitutes the central thesis of the present work.

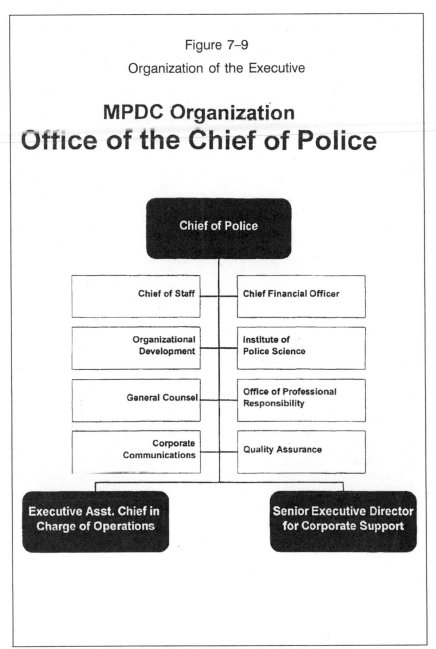

Figure 7–9

Organization of the Executive

MPDC Organization
Office of the Chief of Police

Source: Correspondence from Charles H. Ramsey, Chief of Police Metropolitan Police Department Washington, DC, Government of the District of Columbia, dated January 13, 1999.

There are of course alternatives to this structural relationship. This is evidenced by a recent effort set forth in the Metropolitan Police Department, Washington, D.C. The recent reorganization of the department has focused on moving from an incident driven agency to one focused on becoming a customer-driven service organization. Originally organized with four major bureaus patrol service, technical services, support services, and human resources the department created a "lateral" structure and moved away from the traditional "vertical" organization.[12] Geographical accountability is apparent in the utilization of a business model with 83 police service areas (PSAs). Figure 7–9 is a representation of the office of the office of the chief of police with eight immediate staff entities and two major units. The latter two are an executive Assistant Chief in Charge of Operations and a Senior Executive Director for Corporate Support. The Chief of Police, Charles H. Ramsey, stressed that he had focused a lot on the structure of the MPDC, because he firmly believed that structure drives almost everything that one does. The goal was to structure the organization to provide personnel with the tools, training, access to resources, and management support needed so tasks could be accomplished.[13]

Duties of the Chief of Staff Services

The Chief of Staff Services is charged with command of the administrative branch of the police department referred to as staff services. This Chief of Staff Services has the responsibility of managing police affairs having reference to personnel and materiel for the men engaged in field operations. Included are administrative duties associated with the selection, training, disciplining, and management of personnel; equipment, materiel and supplies; housing and maintenance. Directive control is also maintained over the records division, the communication system, the property custodian and the departmental accountant and the crime laboratory. The primary function of services is to implement operations and when these duties are well performed, line operations will receive the right type of personnel, materiel, communication facilities and the statistical data needed to plan and carry to a successful conclusion the general and special operations of the department. As departments grow in size a further division of labor appears as indicated by the approach used by the Los Angeles Police Department wherein the Chief Of Staff exercises line command over the operations of governmental liaison, administrative group, internal affairs group, and the office of ombudsperson. Additionally, the Chief of Staff performs and coordinates special administrative audits and investigations.[14]

Duties of Chief of Operations

Technological advances and a pronounced tendency toward specialization in police work have produced organizational hazards tending to violate this cardinal rule and dissipate efficiency. New activities and functions are accorded special recognition by the creation of new

12. *Law Enforcement News,* "Capital Ideas DC Chief Unveils Blueprint for Top-to Bottom Overhaul," October 15, 1998, pp. 1 and 9.

13. Charles H. Ramsey, "Rebuilding the MPDC: Next Steps," *The Link,* Washington, DC, Metropolitan Police Department, September 1998, Vol. 1, No. 3. p. 1.

14. Los Angeles Police Department, *Chief of Staff,* 1/30/99, http://www.lapdonline.org/organization/office_police/chief_of_s . . ./chief_of_staff_main.ht.

administrative units and details, accompanied by a disposition to treat each one as something separate and apart, with separate personnel acting under special supervision, and each moving in a semi-independent orbit. For example, the appearance of traffic regulation and control as a major police function brought about the establishment of the traffic unit in police departments throughout the country. Some police departments became "traffic-centered," resulting in a disproportionate percentage of personnel and equipment being assigned to this function. In such departments the extreme emphasis on traffic matters tends to obscure the approach to other major police problems of equal if not greater importance, and to throw the organization out of balance. The necessity for accommodating this emphasis by transfers of personnel to the traffic division has played a large part in the depletion of patrol strength in American police departments. More important, however, is the semi-independent status usually accorded the traffic division in its approach to a specialized problem. Overmanned as a rule and over-emphasized, it tends to hold itself aloof from contact with any police problem outside the restricted realm of traffic administration and seems surprised if called upon to assist in meeting other police problems.

Likewise, the divisional lines setting it apart in exclusive control of all operations dealing with traffic control and regulation tend to bar the invasion of the traffic function by any other individual or unit in the organization. Members of the patrol division come to ignore even the most flagrant traffic infractions on the theory these are the exclusive concern of the traffic division. Divisional competition for departmental budget funds and the position of the traffic unit generate interdivisional rivalry and are destructive of morale and coordination. In this manner, the total potential of the organization is disintegrated into a number of semi-independent parts.

Similarly, in many American police departments, the detective division has developed unwarranted power and in many instances, dominates the organization. The tyranny of detective domination leads to unhealthy rivalry among the various divisions of the department and weakens the strength of an organization.

Functional specialization increases the need for administrative controls and coordination. It is futile to expect a number of semi-independent divisions to function together as a unit unless they are placed under single, unified command. There is no alternative. Organizational efficiency depends upon consolidation of command at one point. Only in this manner can the effective personnel strength in the various divisions of the line be coordinated and directed intelligently in time and place toward the complex problems of crime, confronting the police. It is essential, therefore, for all operations of the following line units be placed under the single, direct command of the Chief of Operations:

- Operations.

- Investigations.

- Technical Services.

- Administration.

The commanding officer in charge of line operations will have immediate subordinates—the heads of all divisions of the line. These commanding officers report to the Chief of Operations and not to the Chief of Police. They are accountable to the Operations Chief for the honest and proper performance of their duties, and this manager, in turn, is responsible to the Chief of Police. Except in extreme emergencies, all orders by the Chief of Police are directed to the division heads through the office of Chief of Operations. The Chief of Operations plays an important role in the administration of police affairs. This person must possess very superior intelligence and be a competent, outstanding leader as demonstrated by a prior experience and performance record. The Chief of Police must use the utmost care in the selection of the officer for this position. The administrative abilities of the chief executive can be largely measured by the judgment exercised in making the appointment to this important post.

Merging the combined personnel strength of line divisions under one command makes possible definite lines of control and responsibility. It locates power and authority, and fixes the lines of responsibility. Reorganization of line operations under a single command paves the way for the elimination of much of the friction and petty jealousy generally characterizing the relationships between divisions, which are destructive of morale and efficiency. Equally important, it increases flexibility of management in concentrating various sections of the force at points and at hours where records data indicate the need is greatest. Furthermore, it implements the intelligent planning of operations because with control of personnel strength located at one point, the total line strength of the force can be maneuvered with precision and certainty of control when and where power is needed.

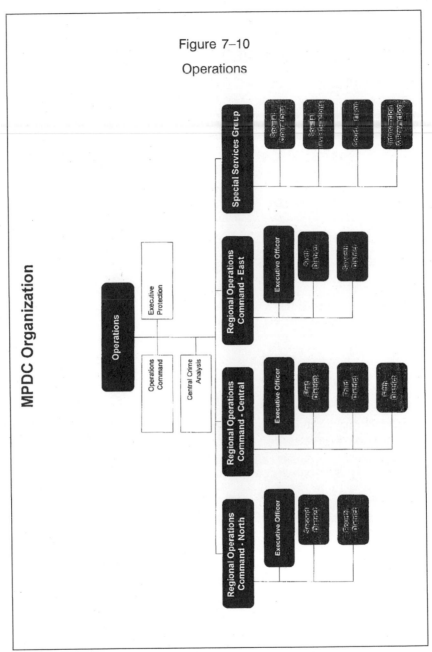

Figure 7–10

Operations

The Metropolitan Police Department has a unique approach when it created three regional operations commands with full service police districts. Figure 7–10 depicts the table of organization for operations. Each district headed by a commander was allocated focused mission teams, operations support team, youth investigations, and crime analysis personnel. Detectives that were previously centralized were placed in each district with two squads. One squad specializes in property crimes and the other violent crimes. With the restructuring of the organization new roles and responsibilities were created at the same time. It called for lieutenants to assume 24–hour accountability for addressing crime and disorder assisted by a team of Police Service Area sergeants.[15]

Duties of Chief of Inspectional Services

Executive control must provide itself with the means for evaluating the quality of work. It is the function of inspection to be sure the quality of performance is at all times in agreement with the standards of the department. Inspection does not create quality but it does control quality, by providing the means for measuring personnel, materiel and operational performance. It embraces preventive measures that may be invoked to prevent failure and raise the probability of success. Quality control is the function of insuring that personnel, materiel and performance conform to the prescribed standards. With the gradual but steady professionalization of the police, the public is becoming accustomed to a higher standard of quality in police service and this has imposed increased responsibility on the function of inspection. There must be provision for a measuring agency to prevent deviations from departmental standards, and to initiate, through the Chief of Police, the necessary action when these violations are observed. Inspection is the examination and evaluation of procedure, performance and the implements of performance measured by departmental standards. Independent periodic inspection of methods and performance is indispensable to a high degree of efficiency in both staff services and line operations. Supervision of men and department materiel must be consistent and according to a well-developed plan, so nothing will be overlooked.

Forms should be developed for this purpose so inspectors, on their tour of duty, will be sure to check every detail. The end-result sought in the inspectional function is the maximum development of the line strength of the department. All other considerations are tributary to this single purpose. It inspects staff services to determine whether staff functions are being discharged efficiently in providing the department with the implements of line power, including personnel, materiel and equipment. It inspects line operations to evaluate the extent to which these tools are being properly applied to the attainment of police objectives. It inspects itself to determine that the inspectional function is being efficiently exercised as a tool of executive control.

Use of Civilian Personnel

In recent years, there has been a marked increase in the use of civilians in police departments. Due to limited budgets, a shortage of police officers, and more complexity in communications, information and management systems, one expert observed, it is time to re-evaluate the use of civilian and sworn personnel. If police departments are to

15.   Ramsey, *op. cit.,* pp. 1–2.

maintain and improve their service capabilities police administrators are justified in giving greater attention to the use of civilian specialist personnel as a realistic and economical alternative. In police departments with a large budget it has been estimated that there are a reasonably large number administrative, supervisory, technical and clerical positions that could be filled with greater efficiency by trained civilians. Thus releasing a significant number of police officers to patrol and other strictly law enforcement duties. In smaller departments, a proportionate number of positions would be affected

There are 234,668 civilian employees of police agencies in the United States that constitute 28 percent of all the employees in law enforcement agencies. Less than half of this total are employed by local police departments. In sheriff's departments there are 152,922 civilian employees. Interestingly women occupy enough 62 percent of all civilian positions.[16] The larger departments have a great number of civilian employees. For example, in New York City with 36,813 employees, there are 7,401 civilians. Overall one will find a greater percentage of civilians employed in rural and suburban departments (237 and 38% respectively). The type of functions performed by civilians varies from agency to agency (see table 7–2). In large police departments, about 20 percent of the civilians are employed in field operations. Approximately fifty-seven percent of the non-sworn officers are employed in technical support areas.[17] The distribution of positions in the Sacramento, CA Police Department represents an exceptional use of civilians.

Table 7–2
State and Local Law Enforcement Agencies with 100 or More Officers

AVERAGE PERCENT OF CIVILIAN EMPLOYEES BY JOB FUNCTION CATEGORY

Function	County police	Municipal police	Sheriff	Special police	State police
Technical support	68%	68	38	37	78
Administration	14	10	11	32	14
Jail operations	1	4	38	0	0
Court operations	1	-	5	3	-
Other functions	4	6	2	14	-

Source: Brian A. Reeves, and Pheny Z. Smith, *Law Enforcement Management and Administrative Statistics, 1993: Data for Individual State and Local Agencies with 100 or More Officers*, Washington, DC, Bureau of Justice Statistics, September 1995, p. ix.

Out of a total of 1124 positions there are 371 permanent and 111 temporary civilian positions.[18]

16. Federal Bureau of Investigation, *op. cit.*, p. 290.

17. Bureau of Justice Statistics, *op. cit.*, pp. 2–3.

Internal Investigation

The chief executive of a police department is responsible for the discipline and control of the agency's members. Command responsibility can seldom be accomplished without some type of formal machinery for the investigation of complaints concerning police activity or employees. Corruption or police misconduct must be dealt with forcefully by each department, having a planned program insuring departmental integrity. In small departments, the chief, or a designated representative can perform internal investigations, but in medium-sized and larger police departments there is generally a sufficient caseload to warrant the creation of an internal investigation unit. Misconduct will occur in any law enforcement agency, however, it is imperative the departments establish machinery to respond adequately by insuring the agency's integrity and publicly demonstrating appropriate standards of fairness and impartiality. Police departments should handle every complaint from the community with concern and professionalism. Listening to citizen complaints shows the department what concerns exist within the community and also reveals how the community feels about their police service.[19]

Numerous departments have articulated rules & regulations and codes of conduct that encompass and describe expectations of behavior and conduct. Typical of these are some of the guidelines developed by the Whitewater Police Department:

- Police officers shall be aware of the extent and the limitation of their authority in the enforcement of the law.

- Police officers shall follow legal practices in such areas as interrogation, arrest or detention, searches, seizures, use of informants and the collection and preservation of evidence.

- Police officers shall not restrict the freedom of individuals, whether by detention or arrest, except to the extent necessary to legally or reasonably apply the law.

- Officers shall not knowingly make false accusations of any criminal, ordinance, traffic or other law violation.

- Officers shall not consider their badge of office as a license designed to provide them with special favor or consideration.[20]

It is clear that these types of rules and regulation set law enforcement apart from other professions, and that the police are granted a public

18. Sacramento Police Department, *Distribution of Positions in the Department, Fiscal Year 1996–97,* Sacramento, CA, 11/11/98. http://www.sacpd.org/strategic-goals.html.

19. Richard R. Johnson, "citizen Complaints What the Police Should

Know," *FBI Law Enforcement Bulletin,* December 1998, Vol. 67, No. 12, p. 5.

20. Correspondence from Lt. Thomas R. Guequierre, Whitewater Police Department, City of Whitewater, WI, dated November 3, 1998.

trust that requires that they consistently demonstrate the highest degree of integrity. A law enforcement agency must maintain high-level personal and official conduct if it is to command the respect and confidence of the public it serves. Within the police structure it is the internal affairs unit that addresses the problem of police deviance.

The placement of internal affairs within a police organization varies considerably. Under the "new" Los Angeles Police Department organization the commander of the internal affairs group reports directly to the chief of staff. Previously the unit had been under an office of special services. In New York City, after the Mollen Commission investigation of police corruption, internal affairs operations were placed in a bureau headed by a civilian deputy commissioner. Prior to the reorganization it had been located in the inspectional services bureau. In an effort to strengthen the capability of New York's internal affairs unit the department allocated over two million dollars for the purchase of investigative equipment and a new computerized case-tracking system.[21] In the Miami police department the internal affairs unit is located in the chief's office. A Major heads up the unit and reports directly to the deputy chief. Organizationally this places one police executive between the head of the unit and the chief of police.[22] In The Dallas Police Department there is an Internal Affairs Division that handles both the commendation of officers and complaints lodged by a citizen. Complainants are apprised of the results of the investigation and the action take. Citizens can appeal decisions to the Citizen/Police Review Board. Officers can follow established procedures when appealing the findings of an investigation.[23]

The internal affairs section of the Miami police department is responsible for accepting and investigating complaints regarding allegations of misconduct or unlawful activity of city employees. The section is divided into two components, international investigations, and anti-corruption. In a recent year the internal investigation personnel initiated and completed 277 investigations.[24]

In recent years there has been a trend toward external review of the police. One study of departments with 100 hundred or more officers found that 92 communities had a civilian review board.[25] Typical of these is the Office of Independent Police Auditor (IPA) found in San Jose, CA, and Tucson, AZ. In the latter city the Auditor position was established to audit the investigation of citizen complaints of misconduct by Tucson police officers. The Auditor determines if the investigation made by the Tucson Police Department's Office of Professional

21. Milton Mollen, *Commission Report, Commission to Investigate Allegations of Police Corruption and the Anticorruption Procedures of the Police Department*, New York, City of New York, July 7, 1994, p. 137.

22. *Op. cit.*, p. 17.

23. Dallas Police Department, *Internal Affairs Division F.A.Q. Commendation and Complaint* Information, Dallas, TX, 10/13/98, http://www.ci.dallas.tx.us/dpd/iad.faq.htm.

24. City of Miami, *op. cit.*, p. 17.

25. Reaves and Smith, *op. cit.*, pp. 253–263.

Standards was complete, through, objective, and fair.[26] In San Francisco, CA the Office of Citizen's Complaints was established more than a decade ago. In 1996 the voters of San Francisco passed a ballot measure that required the Office to have no less than one line investigator for every 150 police officers.[27]

The Reserve Force

Many conscientious police administrators recognize the tactical advantage of a reserve force to supplement the line strength of the department. Circumstances may arise where the available personnel strength of the department is inadequate to cope with community problems and the availability of a well organized and trained reserve force may provide the difference between success and failure. Known generally as reserve police units, these supplementary forces are recruited from among the reliable citizens in the local community. Their duty assignments may involve traffic regulation and control along parade routes, athletic events and other community functions. It can also include general crowd control, assisting in surveillance, civil disturbance control, service under disaster conditions, road-lock operations, routine patrol and other functions. In some instances, air squadron units, scuba diving units, marine units, mounted units, and rescue squads have been organized as a part of auxiliary police activities.

Auxiliary police units must be recruited, organized and trained under the supervision of regular officers in the department who possess the necessary capabilities for this important assignment. A reserve police officer is a non-regular, sworn member who has either all or specific police powers while functioning as the agency's representative and who participates in agency activities on a recurring basis. Generally a reserve officer is not compensated for services performed.

Reserve units function in two ways. The first type serves as a small manpower pool from which regular officers are hired. Reserve officers are employed, trained and evaluated for potentiality to eventually attain full-time employment. The second type of reserve unit is composed of members who have an interest in performing police duties. This ranges from individuals looking for an opportunity to provide a service, to those who want to be a police officer, but they are engaged full-time in other occupations. The reserve force should be considered a manpower alternative, not a substitute for full-time sworn officers. Reserves can and should be an integral part of the department. They must be carefully selected and trained, and their duties and responsibilities should be carefully delineated.

26. City of Tucson, *Office of the Independent Police Auditor,* Tucson, AZ, 10/12/98.   http://www.ci.tucson.az.us/ia.html.

27. Mary C. Dunlap, *Annual Report–1996,* San Francisco, CA, Office of Citizen Complaints, San Francisco, City and County of San Francisco, November 1996, p. 5.

In San Jose, CA reserve officers donate over 33, 000 hours per year. The department has over 140 reserve police officers, and they receive training in patrol operations, officer safety, department policy, tactics, and numerous other police procedures. The reserve unit has it's own rank structure, different divisions, and special units (e.g. background investigations, administration, training, professional standards, and bicycle).[28] In the City of Los Angeles reserve officers receive the same training as regular officers and work along side them in every aspect of departmental operations, and the Reserve Corp has over 900 active officers. There are two types of reserve officers in Los Angeles. The first is the Technical Reserve who are unarmed and perform various administrative functions within the department. The Technical Reserve officer receives 200 hours of professional classroom training, and an additional 26 hours of basic self-defense. They must serve a minimum of two eight-hour shifts per month and attend a monthly reserve officer meeting. Line Reserve officers perform the same duties as regular, full-timer police officers. They are armed and uniformed peace officers who work along with full-time officers. They receive 620 hours of classroom instruction.[29] Each police agency must determine its own needs for a reserve unit, its selection criteria, training curriculum, and type of duties that reserves can perform. Reserves can be an excellent supplement to the regular force. The entire concept is a unique method of increasing community involvement in the local police service.

Contract Law Enforcement

In recent years, several alternatives to the conventional police department have appeared on the scene, and they have proven of particular interest to the police and other officials in the smaller communities and cities of this country. Each one of them appears to serve the interests of both efficiency and economy, and with no sacrifice on the part of professional growth. In fact, the professional stature of the police is being enhanced by these developments. One of these has been the appearance of contract law enforcement. Under this arrangement, a municipality dissolves its local police force and enters into a contractual relationship with the county or state for the delivery of police service. In Los Angeles County the Sheriff's Department has had contracts with 39 incorporated cities within the county, to perform all of the law enforcement functions of a police organization.[30] Opinions differed somewhat on the question as to whether contract law enforcement is a temporary, transitional or the final development in the Los

28. San Jose Police Department, *San Jose Police Reserve Program,* San Jose, CA, City of San Jose, 2/1/99, pp. 1–2. http://www.org/reserves.html.

29. Los Angeles Police Department, *Reserve Police Officer Program (Volunteer Officers),* Los Angeles, City of Los Angeles, 1/30/99, pp. 1–5, http://www.lapdonline.org/get.involved/reserve_program/reserve_program_main.htm.

30. Correspondence from John E. Radeleff, Lieutenant, Contract Law Enforcement Bureau, Office of the Sheriff, County of Los Angeles, Los Angeles, CA., dated November 9,1998.

Angeles metropolitan area. Supporters of the plan feel it offers the following advantages:

- Economy—police service is delivered at a lower cost than would be the case where the city maintains its own police force.

- Professionally trained personnel are on the job.

- The immediate availability of emergency re-enforcements at no additional cost, permits a city to pay for only the minimum necessary level of protection, while having the advantages of necessary emergency strength being available.

- Vehicles are completely equipped.

- Unbiased, non-partisan service—people who might have sufficient political influence to obtain special favors from a local police agency is unable to obtain them from the Sheriff's personnel.

- There is complete freedom from local pressures and local ties.

- Availability of a crime laboratory and technically trained personnel in the investigation of criminal cases.

The Los Angeles County contract law enforcement program is the largest in the United States, and typifies a trend. Some smaller cities have eliminated the law enforcement function. Others have found the need to create special districts. Law enforcement is becoming increasingly expensive as noted in table 7–3. These rates include various direct and indirect costs for relief personnel, support staff, supervision, management and other related overhead expenses. For example a 40–hour unit manned for one-deputy costs $153,015 annually.

Table 7–3

Contract City Law Enforcement Rates— Los Angeles Sheriff's Department for Fiscal Year 1998–1999

Service Unit	Yearly/Hourly Rate
Deputy Sheriff Service Unit	
One deputy, no-relief	$136,447
One deputy, 40 hour	153,015
One deputy, 56 hour	214,221
One deputy, 84 hour	321,331
Two deputy, 40 hour	306,030
Two deputy, 56 hour	428,442
Deputy Sheriff Service Unit (Bonus level)	
One deputy, no. relief	144,887
One deputy, 40 hour	162,480
On deputy, 56 hour	227,473
One deputy, 84 hour	341,209
Sergeant (supplemental)	**114,528**

Supplemental Support Units

Watch deputy	92,980
Intermediate clerk	33,984
Station clerk II	42,427
Law enforcement technician	47,479
Data conversion equipment operator	36,344
Operations assistant I	46,430
Operations assistant II	57,496
Operations assistance III	65,748
Crime analyst	65,415
Custody assistant	55,573

Miscellaneous Units

Catalina Island deputy	131,440
S.A.N.E. (education)	84,081
Crossing guard (hourly)	9.58
License detail (hourly)	54.52

Community Service Officer

With vehicle	27,707
Without vehicle	23,478
Hourly, with vehicle	13.18
Hourly, without vehicle	11.15

Growth Deputy Unit   **89,121**
(Liability insurance costs are not included in
these rates.

Source: Correspondence from John E. Radeleff, Lieutenant, Contract Law Enforcement Bureau, Office of the Sheriff, County of Los Angeles, Los Angeles, CA., dated November 9, 1998.

In California approximately 21.3 percent of all cities contract with sheriff's departments for law enforcement services, and it has been estimated that a savings of more than 30 percent can be achieved by contracting for police services. The reasons for the lower costs are because of decentralized overhead and economies of scale. The Pima County Sheriff's Department (AZ) provides contract service and its cost basis is a Law Enforcement Unit that is defined as a deputy sheriff on patrol for an eight-hour shift, seven days per week, 52 weeks per year. The total annual unit cost was $131,124 for fiscal year 1996/1997. Unit costs services include supervision, criminal investigation, anti-gang enforcement, traffic enforcement, communications, SWAT, and K–9.[31]

Following a similar pattern, in at least one state, municipalities may contract with the State Police for the delivery of police service. Known as the Connecticut Resident Trooper System, the plan concerns small towns without full time police protection. Under this plan 94 state troopers are on duty in 59 towns, under contract with the Connecticut State Police to carry out all of the functions of police service. The towns pay approximately seventy percent of the cost of

31. Captain Brad Gagnepain, *Information Guide on Law Enforcement Services Provided to Contract Communities,* Tucson, AZ, Pima County Sheriff's Department, 10/12/98, http://biz.rtd.com/pcsd/contract.htm.

compensation, maintenance and other expenses. Observers of the Connecticut resident police system unanimously agree that it is working well. Townspeople involved are impressed with the fact that for a nominal sum, the services of the professionally trained and well-equipped Connecticut State Police are readily available.[32] Maryland has provided state troopers to communities since 1974 when there were ten Troopers under contract, although the field of contractual law enforcement was authorized six years earlier by State law. Currently, five contracts involving 59 positions are in place with the State providing police services to communities/counties. Initially state matching funds were authorized but currently the annual contacts are remitted at 100 percent by the county/municipality. [33]

Consolidation of Support Services

Many local governments can benefit from the consolidation of support services. Such consolidations take differing forms and in each instance the nature and type of consolidation must be predicated upon providing police services in the most effective and efficient organizational means available.

The combining of police support services should be provided through enabling legislation allowing local governments, with the concurrence of their governing bodies, to enter into interagency agreements that permit total or partial consolidation of specific services. In every instance the participation in any such agreement must provide for an organizational arrangement insuring reasonable local control and responsiveness to the needs of each jurisdiction.

The consolidation of support services should include major functional areas such as:

- Communications.
- Records and Identification.
- Information System.
- Intelligence.
- Purchasing.
- Laboratory Services.
- Recruitment and Selection.
- Training.
- Community Relations.
- Research and Planning.

32. Correspondence from Colonel John F. Bardelli, Deputy Commissioner, Division of State Police, Department of Public Safety, State of Connecticut, dated February 2, 1999.

33. Correspondence from Jesse N. Graybill, Lieutenant Colonel, Chief, Field Operations Bureau, Pikesville, MD, Maryland State Police, dated February 11, 1999.

During the last three decades all 50 states have POST (Police Officer Standards and Training), but too many states require fewer than 400 training hours for recruits. Laboratory services are currently available for a vast majority of police departments. Unfortunately the same has not occurred in many instances for communications and records. In fact, there is little political will to support such consolidation.[34] A welcome exception has been the Kearney Police Department and Buffalo County Sheriff's Department when they co-located to the Law Enforcement Center. This allows both departments to share information and work more efficiently. The 911 center is responsible for all requests for service from police, fire, and emergency medical services for the 900 square mile county.[35]

However, it must be noted here that partial or fractional merger of police operations is not the best answer to good government. Nothing less than total consolidation of police services on an area basis is likely to bring to an end this costly proliferation of small police departments, and an end to this needless duplication of effort and services that is draining the pockets of the taxpayer. This means one crime laboratory, one computer operation, one records system, one communications system, one recruiting operation, one police training academy and one intelligence system, in one consolidated area, for example, on through the entire gamut of the police enterprise. The key word is ONE. Furthermore, only in this manner can the police field reach out and make contact with the mechanisms of professionalization.

As a part of professional growth in the American police field, the consolidation or merger of police operations on an area basis can be expected to continue on an accelerated scale. All of the evidence points in that direction. The taxpayer and citizen representatives in local government are becoming more and more aware of the reduction in public expenditures resulting from curtailing the duplication of facilities and costs through merger and consolidation. In an era of high taxes and increasing governmental costs, eliminating the duplication of services at the local level invites close scrutiny. This chapter closes with the observation that personnel resources are the over-riding determinant in the performance of the Police Chief Executive and the performance level of the Department. It is the men and women who do the job, not the organization chart!

Case Study

Chief Roger Imhoff

The city of Tranvalley has a population of 229,000 and is located in the southeastern part of the United States. It is the hub of an agricultural area serving a large population. It has numerous foods processing plants and is the rail center for the area. In addition, it has

34. Office of Justice Programs, op. cit.,p. 10.

35. Buffalo County, *Law Enforcement Center,* Kearney, NE, 10/12/98, http://lec.Kearney.net/.

a regional airport, a major highway bisects the city, and a large river abuts the city on the East Side. On weekends and holidays the population explodes as people from the region come to the city to shop, attend sports events and concerts, and participate in other available recreational activities. The city has gown substantially during the last decade as communications companies have come to town because of the availability of relatively cheap labor. The city has a university with 22,000 students and has been responsible for attracting several major hi-tech companies.

The police department has 397 officers and 185 civilians. Organizationally, it has seven operation units reporting directly to the Chief of Police, and an Assistant Chief who manages three divisions and two other specialized units. The major line units are patrol, traffic, and investigations. The patrol division has eight precincts. The last three chiefs of police were strong supporters of traffic enforcement and through the years this division has received support at the expense of the other major divisions. The crime rate is equal to that of similar sized cities and over the last three years the violent crime rate has dropped 9 percent, and property crimes has decreased by 11 percent. The department has had a major corruption scandal and 12 officers, two supervisors and a captain were successfully prosecuted as the result of drug payoffs.

Chief Imhoff was formerly an assistant chief in a comparably sized city and is the first outsider hired after a nation wide search. He has a master's degree in criminology and has been in law enforcement for 19 years. He is very progressive and hired with the expectation that he would restructure the organization, and establish controls that will insure the integrity of the department.

If you were Chief Imhoff how would you reorganize the department? What would be the span of executive control? Why? How would you determine what activities are line and what are staff? Would you create an internal affairs unit? Where would you locate it with the structure? Why? What would you do the traffic unit? Why?

For Further Reading

Richard R. Johnson, "Citizen Complaints–What the Police Should Know," *FBI Law Enforcement Bulletin*, December 1998, Vol. 67, No. 12, pp. 1–5.

> Suggests that research on citizen complaints against the police highlights several areas of dysfunction between the police and the community. Points out that a misunderstanding exists between the police and young males from lower socioeconomic neighborhoods and also suggest a general lack of faith in the police by most ethnic minority groups. Recommends training in human relations, and

diversity training. The author also the taking of corrective action to reduce the causes of citizen complaints.

James G. Koltz, *The Los Angeles County Sheriff's Department Report,* Los Angeles, County of Los Angeles, July 1992, pp. 1–359.

> In the general background of this report there is a review of contract enforcement. The report states that the department should be reformed in the areas of force, complaint resolution, internal investigation, and community policing. Contains nine principal recommendations ranging from ending the discouraging of citizens to file a complaint to and the creation of an independent internal affairs bureau that should report directly to the sheriff. The reports covers other critical issues such as training, stress management, accountability and the culture of the department.

Milton Mollen, Commission Report–Commission to investigate allegations of Police Corruption and the Anti-corruption Procedures of the Police Department, New York, New York City, July 1974, pp. 1–158.

> This report is an anatomy of failure and a path for success. It is the report of a commission that spent 22 months investigation the nature, extent, and causes of police corruption in New York City. They found a multi-faced problem that extended beyond the corrupt individual cop. Points out that the principle of command accountability was abandoned.

> Recommends that the primary responsibility of combating police corruption is with the department, but acknowledges the need for external oversight. Discusses the flaws in the internal affairs investigations and the failure to employee pro-active investigative techniques.

Bernard C. Parks, *Achievements, Accomplishments and Future Initiatives—First Year in Office,* Los Angeles, Los Angeles Police Department, August 12, 1997/98, pp. 1–5.

> Describes the refocus of the department toward its primary mission, by reorganizing the department that resulted in a reduced layer of bureaucracy, institutionalized community policing, and established a visible. Identifies things done to increase the availability of training for all personnel, improving officer safety, and promoting employee wellness. The author also lists 23 issues that need future strategic action.

Chapter 8

CHANGE: A Reality of Organizational Life

Learning Objectives

1. Discuss the impact of managerial functions on the change processes.

2. Identify the conditions in a department that foster change.

3. Examine the differences between technical and organizational change.

4. Differentiate between planned and unplanned change.

5. List and discuss the values that need to be accepted if an OD effort is to be successful.

6. Define Organizational Development (OD).

7. Describe the objectives of Organizational Development (OD).

8. Identify five types of OD intervention techniques.

9. Assess the importance of the survey feedback process.

10. Compare System Two and System Three management styles.

11. Describe the features of a Quality Circle.

12. Discuss the hindrances to change.

13. Explain the dynamics of change management.

Change is endemic in our society. It can be thought of as a process that is seldom static and it can cause an organization to be in a state of perpetual unrest, turbulent, chaotic, confused, or ambiguous. Under the concept of rationality, few organizations make the choice to undergo substantial change unless there is a life threatening certainty form the external environment. Historically, this has been a tumultuous event or a political catastrophe. Generally, if change is to be made it is done on a marginal and incremental basis.[1] Another compounding factor is that change is unpredictable. It is everyone's wish to be able to forecast the future, but the actuality is that the future is basically unknown. Change is not just a current phenomenon it has been with us throughout history. Police managers have had to deal with change since the organizing of the first police departments. Change presents a

1. Jihong Zhao, *Why Police Organizations Change: A Study of Community-Oriented Policing* Washington, DC, Police Executive Research Forum, 1996, pp. 81–82.

constant challenge to management as the search goes on for an appropriate and enduring response. In fact, change presents an organization with an opportunity and should not be viewed as strictly a negative event. Change is not abnormal it is a recurring event and demands a positive response. One can not hide from change it is a part of everyday organizational life.[2] Goal attainment in law enforcement requires the fulfillment of a planned change activity and the continuous evaluation of current and impending change.

Managerial Functions

As previously noted, change does not just occur—it is the inevitable consequence of conflict and realistically dealing with that conflict. During the alteration process, a natural stimulation takes place, requiring the individual and the organization to adapt. Functional conflict must be utilized to further organizational objectives-indeed. It is an essential characteristic of adaptive management. If change is to be effective it is the application of the managerial processes of planning, organizing, directing, or controlling (see figure 8–1).

Organizing. Some type of logical plan must distribute workload with in an organization. This is done in law enforcement agencies by structuring the organization. Over the years as departments have added numerous functions the structure has become increasingly complex. Activities, which were sufficiently related, have been placed under unified command. In police agencies the grouping of related activities is usually predicated on a number of fundamental issues such as: major purpose, the process or method, the nature of the clientele, geographical distribution, and time. Each of these can operate simultaneously or they can be mutually exclusive. With more than 18,000 law enforcement agencies in this nation organizational structure varies from simplistic to extremely complex. As organizations grow in size there is a corresponding increase in the number of levels within the organization.

Planning. The process of change occurring in our society demands that police departments actively engage in planning. A laissez faire response to change can only result in ineffective management. Obsolescence in planing becomes an everyday reality. An effective pursuit policy for today can become totally ineffective because of technological or social changes. Police departments must have an ongoing process that continually evaluates policies and procedures in order to insure their efficacy. Planning in law enforcement agencies range across a relatively broad spectrum to include specific plans such as fiscal matters or operational.

The purposes of planning in a law enforcement agency varies from department to department, but commonly provides for organizational

2. William M. Boast, *Masters of Change: How Great Leaders in Every Age Thrived in Turbulent Times*, Provo, UT, Executive Excellence Publishing, 1997, pp. 26–27.

flexibility, easier attainment of objectives, improved decision making, and the identification of problems confronting the agency.[3]

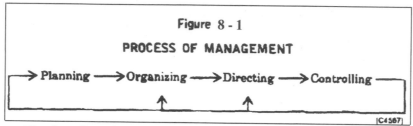

Figure 8 - 1

PROCESS OF MANAGEMENT

Planning → Organizing → Directing → Controlling

[C4587]

The benefits of planning vary but generally include an enhanced unity of purpose, improved coordination, and greater commitment of all of those dealing with the police problems confronting a community. Other benefits include the identification of need through the assessment of existing resources, the analysis of problems, and a frame of reference for defining organizational objectives.

Directing. A police agency is a static entity unless the energetic force of leadership becomes an actuality. When managers provide direction tasks can be accomplished and goals can be reached.

Truly energized directing provided by positive leaders can serve as a focal point for the integration of the individual into the organization, which is the essence of adaptive management. Over the years, traditional management styles in law enforcement, that were dominated by autocratic leadership, are totally unacceptable in contemporary police departments. Coercive techniques of directing, and the refusal to communicated with employees continually and constantly can result in the failure of an organization to achieve departmental goals. Directing that is emphatic in nature acknowledges the importance of working with and through individuals in order to achieve established goals. When a manager engages in directing activities there is an excellent opportunity to create a results-oriented working environment. Managing employees is not easy and it requires leaders to have a special awareness of how individuals respond to the managerial function of directing.

Controlling. As part of the planning process it is essential to create guidelines and procedures for determining whether or not agreed upon objectives are attained. Adequately prepared formats can provide for the periodic reporting of accomplishments based upon established milestones. This allows police managers to judge progress and provide information to others. If deviations from anticipated results occur the explicit deviations should be identified and measured against established standards.[4] Control techniques, which have been proven effective, include budgetary control, status reporting and peri-

3. Harry W. More and Michael O'Neil, *Contemporary Criminal Justice Planning,* Springfield, IL, Charles C. Thomas, 1984, pp.1–18.

4. James Lundy, *Lead, Follow, or Get Out of the Way,* San Diego, CA., Avant Books, 1986, p.71.

odic progress meetings (see figure 8–2). Additional effective control activities include the creation of policies, and rules and regulations.

The managerial processes discussed above are not mutually exclusive, but eminently interconnected. They do not necessarily occur successively, but can transpire at any time. Besides, these processes can be modified by a number of variables ranging from managerial to follower competence. Other prominent modifying factors include the level within the organization and the nature of the activity.

Figure 8–2

Managerial Functions

Organizing	**Directing**
Structuring	Leadership skills
Grouping related activities	Coaching
Purpose	Style
Process	Results orientation
Clientele	
Geographic	
Time	
Planning	**Controlling**
Types of plans	Standards
Operational	Corrective action
Procedural	Development of
Tactical	Procedures
Fiscal	Policies
Management	Rules
Program	Regulations
Setting of objectives and goals	Acquisition of data

Conditions Fostering Change

An alert student of the police managerial process will easily determine that everything pertinent to police operations is concerned with a reaction to or the implementation of change. Such things as the testing of police applicants for drug use is of recent origin and has required agencies to respond with an appropriate policy in this area. The key variable is to determine what can managerial intervention do to insure that change is adequately dealt with and the new policy or procedure will be a positive response acceptable to line officers, police managers, and members of the community. In some instances managers easily resolve the impact of change, and in other instances the complexity of the change requires a more careful and detailed response.

The identification and analysis of some problems is relatively easy. The solution is apparent and implementation is almost automatic. In other instances, a problem can be exceedingly complex and require department wide efforts if a preferred choice is to be made. In most instances substantive change cannot be ignored because it can result in a failure of the organization to successfully complete milestones of accomplishment. The complexity of this process is compounded when one realizes that a police manager is confronted with the paradox of providing for change and organizational stability at the same time.

Successful managers balance these competing demands by diagnosing situations and creating viable change responses. A healthy police agency will be in equilibrium when:

- There is enough organizational stability that goals are attained.

- Prevailing continuity allows for systematic change.

- Organizational adaptability is such that there is a positive response to internal and external conditions.

- When circumstances warrant the organization can respond proactively.[5]

Effective police managers respond to change with differential skills by being fully aware of the human process involved in change and utilize a variety of techniques when introducing change.[6] The management of transition must be predicated on the importance of conflict for individuals and organizational growth. Planned change provides for organizational goal attainment. It acknowledges that people will be affected and that the response to alterations can impact positively or negatively on goal attainment.

Organizations respond to two primary sources of pressure to change. These sources are labeled as either organizational or external. There are other approaches to the process of change but these two categories provide a frame of reference for the analysis of the forces of change.

External Forces. There is a wide range of external forces that that serve as inputs to a police organization. It includes economic conditions, the size and nature of the labor force, social norms and values, and the community. One of the most important is the community, which because of its diversity can express varying concerns. In most instances the community will be issue oriented and aimed at a particular level within the organization. Other external sources include elected representatives, administrators of other governmental entities, community organizations, members of the media, and staff and line personnel of other criminal justice agencies. Managers who are aware of the importance of external forces place themselves in a better position to adapt and learn from their influence.

Organizational Forces. These forces range over a wide spectrum of change factors such as conflict, administrative variables, technology, and members of the agency.[7] Conflict is not necessarily harmful. It has

5. Fremont E. Kast and James E. Rosenzweig, *Organization and Management: A Systems and Contingency Approach,* Fourth Edition, New York, McGraw–Hill, 1985, p. 232.

6. Dan L. Costley and Ralph Todd, *Human Relations in Organizations,* St. Paul, MN, West Publishing, 1978, p.336.

7. Harold J. Leavitt, "Applied Organizational Change in Industry: Structural, Technical and Human Approaches,"

to be accepted an inevitable and an actually provide a basis for a healthy and productive agency. Conflict, when acknowledged, and used can provide for creative problem solving, and a viable organization. Administrative changes run the gamut from the restructuring of the organization to the issuance of detailed rules and regulations. The creation of new polices and procedures can have a profound impact on an agency and it's personnel. Technological changes in the last two decades have altered the way that departments operated. This includes such thing as computer aided dispatching, innovative laboratory techniques, and equipment such as protective vests. Current members of police departments have differing values, attitudes, and beliefs. This creates different on-the-job behavior and when coupled with other internal factors the change is both synergistic and cumulative. These influencing forces present a challenge to police managers as change confronts them with greater force and intensity.

Technological Change. In recent years this type of change has impacted American law enforcement so forcefully that it has changed it forever. There has been an explosion of knowledge unequaled in the history of this nation. Developments in police departments have paralleled the increasingly complexity of society. Technology has permeated every aspect of police work from the streets to planning unite. Common place are such things as voice mail, e-mail, satellite-linked computers, Global Positioning Systems (GPS), computerized mapping, personal computer PC) databases, mobile data terminals (MDT), and computer-aided dispatch (CAD). Others include automated fingerprint identification systems (AFIS), laptops, hand-held digital computers, infrared surveillance, drug testing, voice print analysis, forensic odontology, electronic eavesdropping, accident reconstruction, and digital imaging. With the technological revolution the line officer is in a position to obtain information that allows for an improvement of service and officer safety. With a personal computer the patrol officer can not only record offenses but it also allows for the analysis of crimes that have occurred on their beat. [8]Unfortunately, technology that is current today will be obsolete tomorrow, which requires police managers to maintain the skills necessary to keep up with the rapidly changing technology.

Sociocultural Changes. Another factor of concern to police managers is sociocultural changes. A decisive manager will not only contemplate changes in the American society, but also actually welcome the change.[9] In the past police managers have reacted to sociocultural change rather than attempting deal with it. Our values in this nation are shifting rapidly concerning, life, human existence, social

cited in W. W, Cooper, H. J. Leavitt, and M.W. Shelly, Editors, *New Perspectives in Organizational Research*, 1964, p. 141.

8. J.J. Campbell, "Computer Support for Community–Oriented Policing," FBI Law Enforcement Bulletin, *February 1994, Vol. 62, No.2, pp. 16–18.*

9. Bil and Cher Holton, *The Manager's Short Course,* New York, John Wiley, 1992, p.70.

equality, productive work, ethics, morality, and the role of the police department in a changing community. As a consequence of shifting immigration policies we have become an increasingly diverse nation. Cities throughout the nation have become ethnically disparate and police managers have responded by striving to hire employees who are more representative of the diverse population.

In addition, our population is aging which creates a different need to which law enforcement agencies must respond. Social change in law enforcement agencies is most evident. Women are entering police work in increasing numbers. Bilingual proficiency is increasingly important. Promotions, in some instances, are made to obtain racial diversity. Urban police departments openly recruit homosexuals, which would have been unheard of a few years ago. Gay police organizations are present in the following cities: Los Angeles, San Francisco, Denver, Seattle, and Springfield, MA.[10] The promotion of nontraditional employees to managerial positions has become increasingly common. Women and minorities have been elevated to executive positions in many agencies and their number will increase in the years ahead. Police managers must monitor sociocultural changes and adjust accordingly.[11] Organizational factors are powerful forces that impact every aspect of the organization. One must be concerned that when a change is made in one area it will have a cross ripple functional effect and impact other areas. The mastering of change requires managers to create an atmosphere that provides for competitive differentiation and success. Officers cannot be viewed as mere cogs in a wheel (see figure 8–3). There is a need to provide employees with information that will enable them to do their job.[12] It can be seen from the above discussion that change is intrinsic and a central part of police organizational life. Consequently, there is a need for police executives to actually plan change.

10. Stephen Leinen, *Gay Cops*, New Brunswick, Rutgers University Press, 1993, pp. 194–201.

11. Harry W. More and W. Fred Wegener, *Behavioral Police Management,* New York, Macmillan Publishing, 1992, pp. 413–415.

12. Douglas K. Smith, *Taking Charge of Change: 10 Principles for Managing People and Performance,* Reading, MA, Addison–Wesley, 1996, p. 22.

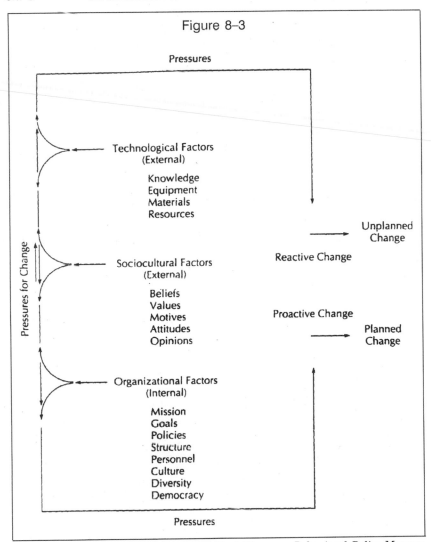

Figure 8-3

Pressures

Technological Factors (External) — Knowledge, Equipment, Materials, Resources

Sociocultural Factors (External) — Beliefs, Values, Motives, Attitudes, Opinions

Organizational Factors (Internal) — Mission, Goals, Policies, Structure, Personnel, Culture, Diversity, Democracy

Pressures for Change

Reactive Change → Unplanned Change

Proactive Change → Planned Change

Pressures

Adopted from Harry W. More, and W. Fred Wegener, *Behavioral Police Management, New York,* Macmillan, 1992, p. 416. Reprinted with permission of Simon & Schuster/Prentice-Hall.

Organizational Development (OD)

The importance of the individual to the organization cannot be overlooked—therefore *organization development* must be answerable to that requirement. The underlying value is *choice*.[13] Emphasis is placed on the collection and feedback of relevant data, consequently choices are enhanced and positive decisions can be rendered. Organization development *(OD)* is the process of planned change with the goal of improving the organization through the application of the behavioral sciences.[14] Organization development is a goal oriented process, with

13. Warren G. Bennis, *Organization Development: It's Nature, Origins, and Prospects,* Reading, MA, Addison-Wesley, *1969, p.17.*

14. Ricky W. Griffin and Gregory Moorhead, *Organizational Behavior,* Boston, Houghton Mifflin, 1986, p. 6.

the concluding intent of improving organizational effectiveness. It is no permissive leadership. It does not prescribe a specific style of leadership other than to suggest that the style must be open and confronting.[15] It does not require group consensus as a prerequisite to application. It is an educational strategy directed toward evaluating and implementing organizational choices.[16]

The success of an OD effort depends upon the acceptance of a number of values that include:

- Trust and openness.

- Feedback.

- Confronting conflict.

- Risk-taking. [17]

A continuing objective of an OD effort is to create a climate of *openness* and *trust*. Some advocates of OD identify it as the cornerstone of a process that reorients *man's* thinking and behavior toward the work environment. To do this means that the manager has a humanistic view of employees and employees a managerial method in support of that doctrine. Open communications cannot occur without trust in interpersonal and intergroup relationships.[18]

All efforts must be directed toward effectively solving issues confronting the organization. Trust does not just happen—it has to be created and become the central feature binding all other contingencies together. Trust is based on an acceptance of conflict as the by-product of the interaction between the individual, the group, and the organization. When trust is not a property of the relationship between managers and officers it can result in a negative working environment. Trust acknowledges that employees are not manipulators, but that they have the capacity to contribute to the organization and have the capacity to make independent decisions. It is unfortunate that over the years a number of police managers have operated in such a manner that trust had never been a part of the managerial equation.

The communications skill of *feedback* is a process by which assumptions are verified or corrected. When positive *feedback* occurs in organizations an operational climate exists where information can be shared freely and without restraint. Accurate data is essential as it contributes to a definitive decision-making process. Employees should feel free to express their impressions about work issues. A truly corrective feedback climate is styled to be non-accusatory. When rela-

15. *Ibid.*

16. *Ibid.*

17. Lyman K. Randall, "Common Questions and Tentative Answers Re-garding Organization Development," *California Management Review,* 1984, Vol. LXIII, No. 3, pp. 45–52.

18. *Ibid.*

tionships are based on trust and openness, the work process can be understood and tasks accomplished more effectively. [19]

Managers can use a number of techniques to determine whether they function effectively when requesting feedback from officers. The techniques vary to include interviewing officers and other managers, preparing written inquiries, or holding group meetings. An increasingly popular technique is to circulating questionnaires that allow for an anonymous response. In most instances it is best to use more than one technique so employees can feel free to express their true feelings and beliefs about work related issues.[20]

Another value of OD is the aspiration and potential to confront conflict. Within organizations conflict is inevitable. It is as sure as death and taxes. It has always been present when an organization reacts to pressures within and outside of the organization. For years conflict has been ignored or rejected, but it can be beneficial both for individuals and the organization. Conflict can be positive when it is directed constructively, but it can be destructive when it is allowed to run rampant and not controlled by management. For example, in some agencies the traffic function dominates the organization while in other departments the detective's view himself or herself as superior and regard the patrol function as an necessary evil and not equal to the duties performed by investigators. In other instances, juvenile officers are *kiddie cops,* community relation's officers are *plastic cops and community policing officers are* social workers. The lowest level, in the pecking order, as viewed by some are the officers who serve in internal affairs units, and they are identified as *head hunters.* When one unit is viewed as superior or specific assignments reflect negatively it is an excellent opportunity for an OD effort to work to resolve the discrepancies. It is essential that discord should be managed—not avoided or denied.

The concluding value of consequence to OD is *risk taking.* If organizational growth is to occur management must take a risk. When a manager engages in *risk tasking* ambiguity is more than likely to happen. As things are worked out this must become an acceptable element if the organization is to respond to change. Occasionally an unpopular stand must be taken, such as implementing a procedure that is opposed by a number of organizational members. Sometimes a popular officer or manager must be disciplined which can create discontent. *Risk-taking* creates a stressful situation that can place incredible pressure on an individual or the organization.[21] *Risk-taking* will generate errors or mistakes and these must become an acceptable part of the process. It is essential that mistakes are turned into learning situations and those who commit errors are not blamed or become someone who is scapegoated. In essence, this means that the

19. *Ibid.*

20. William G. Dyer, *Contemporary Issues in Management and Organiza-* *tional Development,* Reading, MA, Addison–Wesley, 1991, p. 34.

21. Randall, *op. cit.*

organization must create an atmosphere of blameless error.[22] The values of OD create an ongoing process that will maximize organizational effectiveness by actualizing the potential of individuals and the work group.[23]

Managers in police organizations who are fully aware of OD potentials can utilize it for solving current problems and creating an organizational climate that maximizes the effective and efficient use of resources. The objectives of organization development vary, but generally are to:

- Create an open department culture concentrating on problem-solving.

- Build trust between individuals and groups.

- Move decision-making responsibilities to the lowest possible location in the organization.

- Maximize individual self-control and self-direction.

- Help managers achieve organizational objectives.

- Foster an organizational climate stressing a commitment to organizational objectives and growth of people.

- Develop authority of knowledge and competence.

- Maximize collaborative goals.[24]

It is readily apparent that this list of objectives focuses on the individual as well as the group. Values, trust, openness, attitudes, relationships and the organizational culture are clearly the central issues of organization development. There is not a simple formula that can be utilized to change an organization. However, there are multitudes of approaches that can be used separately or in combination. These include such techniques as barrier analysis, survey feedback, and force field analysis. Change approaches to be effective focus on the members of the organization. To date OD has proven to be highly effective in bringing innovation to law enforcement agencies.

The OD process is especially useful in modifying the managerial perception of the way to achieve change. Change for change sake is objectionable and serves no purpose. What is needed is to predicate change in police department by:

- Making only useful, necessary changes and timing them carefully to diminish employee anxiety that the organization is overwhelming them with change.

22. Gary A. Bielous, "Create an Atmosphere of Blameless Error," *Supervision, May 1995,* Vol. 56, No. 5., pp. 3–5

23. *Ibid.*

24. Warren Bennis, "Using our Knowledge of Organizational Behavior:

The Improbable Task," in Jay W. Lorsch, Editor, *Handbook of Organizational Behavior,* Englewood Cliffs, NJ,Prentice–Hall, 1987, pp. 41–42.

- Studying the possible effects of change in advance, and introducing a new program with adequate attention to human relations. More employee consensus toward change and less tell and sell approaches to change may involve delays in initiating a program, but the delays are worthwhile if it results in increased employee acceptance.

- Diagnosing the problems when change is introduced and treating the problems will improve the possibility of employees accepting change. Participation in change, at all levels, must be a continuing effort, not just a preliminary task.[25]

Expectations

Adaptive management views OD as a process of focusing human energy toward specific output—namely the attainment of organizational objectives. An OD effort that is fully implemented and supported from the top to the bottom of the organization can result in one or more of the following:

- Increased productivity.

- Improved utilization of human resources.

- Greater motivation.

- Problem solving improvement.

- Improvement in individual performance.

- More effective planning.

- Greater acceptance of change.

- Reduction in dissatisfaction.

- Improved union-management relations.

- Improvement of inter-personal relations.[26]

Organization Development (OD) is a means of dealing with the environmental conditions of the organization. This is best done by implementation of an OD technique–a number of which are identified in figure 8–4. Interventions are specific activities in which agency personnel and consultants participate during the implementation of an organizational development program. It is the responsibility of those involved in such a program to select OD activities that will encourage departmental improvement by creating a greater awareness of team and organizational culture. This is not an easy task it requires a careful examination of the environmental ambient factors of the agency.[27]

25. James Datzman, "The Impact of Rapid Change on Organizations: Middle Management," unpublished, 1984, pp. 1–10.

26. Adopted from the lecture notes of Paul O'Rourke, Management, Consultant, San Francisco, CA, 1983, pp. 1–9.

27. Wendell L. French and Cecil H. Bell, Jr. *Organization Development*, Englewood Cliffs, NJ, Prentice–Hall, 1974, p. 97.

Figure 8–4

OD Intervention Techniques

- Diagnostic
    interviews
    questionnaires
    surveys
    meetings
- Team Building
    task issues
    skills
    resource allocation
    relationships
- Intergroup
    joint activities
- Survey–feedback
    acquisition of data
    action plans based on data
- Education and Training
    improvement of skills
    decision–making
    problem solving
- Planning and Goal Setting
    theory of planning
    problem solving models

Adopted from Wendell L. French and Cecil H. Bell, Jr., *Organization Development,* Englewood Cliffs, NJ, Prentice–Hall, 1974, pp. 103–104.

Survey Feedback Process

A technique that is increasingly being use in law enforcement is an internal questionnaire that is an integral part of a survey feedback process. To be effective it must be designed in such a way as to be totally factual and task oriented. Above all there has to be commitment from every level within the organization, especially top management. It is an excellent way to test the pulse of the organization, in a neutral manner, which is not threatening to those who participate in the survey. Attitudes, beliefs, perceptions and opinions can be determined through surveys that cannot be obtained through any other process.[28] Questionnaires can focus on a wide range of employee attitudes to include:

- Communications.
- Motivational factors.
- Coordination.
- Control.

28. Bureau of Justice Assistance, *A Police Guide to Surveying Citizens and Their Environment,* Monograph, Washington, DC, National Institute of Justice, 1993, p. 8.

- Planning.

- Directing.

- Satisfaction.

When there is a recognition that a planned change should be considered it should be based on accurate diagnosis of the real problem confronting the organization. If the police manager believes that the information needed is best obtained from a number of employees distributed throughout the organization it will in all probability be best to utilize a questionnaire. The type of questions will be predicated on the identifiable organization problem. If it is a question of general satisfaction the following questionnaire may provide the needed information (see figure 8–5).

Figure 8–5
Employee Attitude Questionnaire

To the employee:

Please answer the following questions as thoughtfully and accurately as possible. This information will help to create a picture of working conditions and social climate in our organization that will be useful to managers at all levels.

Classification Factors:
1. What is your age range?
   1) 20–29.
   2) 30–39.
   3) 40–49.
   4) 50–59.
   5) 60 and over.
2. What is your sex?
   1) Male.
   2) Female

3. What is your educational background?
   1) Less than a high school diploma.
   2) High school diploma.
   3) 1–2 years of college
   4) 2–4 years of college
   5) 4 years or more of college
4. How long have you worked for the organization?
   1) Less than 1 year.
   2) 1–4 years.
   3) 5–9 years.
   4) 10–19 years.
   5) 20 or more years.

Job Factors:

5. What is your overall level of satisfaction with your day-to-day work on the basis of factors such as difficulty, challenge, variety, interest, workload, sense of accomplishment, and so on?
   1) I hate my job
   2) My job is generally unpleasant
   3) It's just a job to me.
   4) I enjoy my job.
   5) I find my job very satisfying.
6. To what extent do you consider your pay and other benefits to be fair and equitable for the work you are doing?
   1) Not at all fair.
   2) Somewhat fair
   3) Adequate.
   4) Better than average.
   5) Very favorable,
7. How effective do you consider your immediate supervisor?
   1) Very poor.
   2) Poor.
   3) So-so.
   4) Fairly effective.
   5) Very effective.
8. How well do you get along with your co-workers?
   1) Very poorly.
   2) Poorly.
   3) So-so.
   4) Well.
   5) Very Well.
9. To what extent do you feel "in" on the important aspects on the important aspects of your unit's operation?
   1) Not at all.
   2) Mostly left out.
   3) Moderately involved and included.
   4) Usually feel a part of things.
   5) Very involved; I feel I'm an important member of the group.
10. To what extent do you feel your work and contributions are generally appreciated by your supervisor?
   1) Not at all.
   2) Not very much.
   3) To some extent.
   4) Mostly.
   5) Very much.

11. What is you opinion about opportunities for advancement in the organization?

    1) Nonexistent.
    2) Poor.
    3) Fair.
    4) Good.
    5) Excellent.

12. To what extent do you consider upper management loyal to you and your co-worker?

    1) Not at all.
    2) Not very.
    3) Moderately.
    4) Usually loyal to us.
    5) Very loyal to us.

Source: Reprinted with the permission of Simon & Schuster from STRESS AND THE MANAGER by Karl Albrecht. Copyright © 1979 by Prentice-Hall, Inc., Englewood Cliffs, NJ, pp. 415–417.

Information obtained from the questionnaire can be very valuable to management. It can reflect the level of job satisfaction within the organization, and the data can be analyzed based upon classification variable such as age, sex, level of education and how long the officers and civilian employees have worked in the organization. Information can be utilized as the basis for group discussions that are focused on problem solving.

It is important that during such discussions that an agenda is followed that considers only issues and not personalities. Under no circumstances should the discussion be allowed to become contentious. A task orientation prior to discussion should, in most instances, keep the discussion focused and responsive. A survey feedback approach can prove to most useful in surfacing problems and clarifying issues. It is imperative that the groups are small enough to allow input from every member and when it is possible the group should include team members or every one assigned to a particular squad or unit. Each entity should be allowed enough time to adequately discuss the issues and provide input for possible action.

At the very least, each unit should be given the opportunity to recommend changes. The best thing to do is to establish ground rules before distributing questionnaires. This way everyone involved knows what to expect. Above all management should never allow a situation to develop wherein the process is viewed by employees as manipulative.[29]

Reaction to the acquired information by the group problem-solving process should be reported to everyone involved in the survey process. This is especially true for supervisors and managers. Management studies show that managers view their impact differently than do those being supervised. The key is to tell it like it is. Success of the program depends upon a firm commitment of the organization starting with top managers. For those who have tried it the survey feedback method works because it addresses the critical issues through the processes of involvement, communications, and commitment. It works because it involves, managers, supervisors and front line employees in a job context. Its efficacy is predicated upon making a sincere effort at meeting personnel needs and achieving organizational objectives.

Determining Your Managerial Style

The late Rensis Likert was a strong advocate of participatory management. He believed that management styles ranged on a continuum from autocratic to participatory. He developed an instrument based on the survey feedback concept to determine the current management style employed within an agency. The instrument was designed in such a way as to measure specific element of managerial style. Each of these attributes is a requisite feature of a specific style. Each of the styles included variables ranging from leadership to interaction. He believed that managers performed certain functions and he used a scale to measure attitudes, and values of managers. These organizational attributes are discussed extensively in chapter 5. He identified four fundamental management styles, or leadership modes include: exploitive authoritative, benevolent authoritative, consultative, and participative group.

There is a general belief is that most police organizations should be categorized as expletive authoritative. Such entities are rigid bureaucracies that exhibit neutrality, conformity, and obedience.[30] Deviation from the norm is looked upon as intolerable, and management expressed limited confidence in line personnel. Top management set the tone for the organization and the executives retained all the power needed to make decisions and support organizational objectives. The informal organization was considered to be non-existence and every aspect of working life. There is evidence that change is occurring in our police system, but it is painfully slow so far. This is especially true when the police strive to redefine the mission of the agency in a

---

29. *Ibid.*   **30.** Zhao, *op. cit., p. 6.*

changing society. Effective change dictates the need to change the internal operations of the departments and the capacity to respond to external utilitarian change.[31]

Planning and Goal Setting

Numerous police agencies throughout the nation have utilized the expertise of management experts as the process of implementing planned change. In one instance a police department employed an OD consultant to examine organizational concerns with an emphasis on improving the organization by enhancing the interaction between divisions and units. The consultant initiated a team building effort that involved all of the organizations supervisors and managers. Meetings were held to discuss such topics as organizational goals and participative decision-making. This was followed by a team-building workshop that was held in a retreat environment where a serious effort was made to heighten interpersonal skills. Next a questionnaire containing sixty-nine items was administered do all of those involved in the team building effort as a means of identifying organizational concerns. The categories of for the questionnaire included:

- Leadership/management.
- Administration.
- Personnel.
- Crime control.
- Operations.
- Training.
- Traffic.[32]

The chief then met with each individual utilizing the results obtained from the questionnaire to discuss, in depth the results. The outcome was that problems needing attention were identified as: improved cooperation between units and divisions, enhanced crime control techniques, and an improved traffic management system. The next step was to create problem-solving teams. One of the teams dealt with interagency cooperation. A lieutenant headed it and the other members were sergeants from each unit/division. All of the team held periodic and structured meeting with input from all level of the organization.

Recommendations from each team were presented to at meeting attended by managers and supervisors. Typical of the conclusions were the final recommendations for improving communications:

- More frequent attendance of managers at patrol briefings.

31. Zhao, *op. cit., p. 84.*

32. Ronald E. Lowenberg, "Problem–Solving Teams: Building a Healthier Organization," *The Police Chief,* September 1985, Vol. LII, No. 9, p. 56.

- Implementation of a program wherein patrol personnel would be assigned to the detective division for a ninety day period on a rotation basis.

- Require patrol supervisors to utilize the case disposition log as a training tool.

- Emphasize the importance of improving human relations' skills.

Initial feedback indicated that the problem-solving team approach had a positive impact on the organization. The long-range impact is unknown, but at this point the department made the decision to use this method when addressing future problems.[33]

OD intervention techniques are not a panacea for all managerial problems, but they will lead to the creation of a department that can successfully cope with the changes that are occurring in society. The focus is on people with the goal of improved performance. This is something that is not a one shot operation. It must be long term and not just a response to a crisis. Management must be judged by one criterion–results. [34]

Quality Circles

Quality circles are becoming increasingly common in law enforcement agencies. In a survey of 300 departments 16 percent reported having used quality circles in the previous three years. A quality circle is typically composed of non-supervisory employees and a circle leader, who is usually the first-line supervisor for the involved work unit (for example, a patrol supervisor or the team leader). However, some other person, such as another member of the work unit, can be the leader. In order to be effective, circle members receive considerable training, particularly in techniques for group interaction and problem solving. A quality circle facilitator, chosen by the department from outside the work unit, provides the training, helps the circle get underway, and provides continuing help and guidance to the circle on problems that are encountered.

The facilitator helps the group remain focused on the problems at hand and develop feasible solutions. The facilitator also acts as a liaison between the circle and other units when the circle needs information, assistance, or cooperation from organizational units external to its own problems for study. Although there is no consensus on the purposes of quality circles, objectives usually include the improvement of services provided by the members of the unit, working conditions, worker morale and/or communication within the organization, and the personal development of circle members.[35] Officers must not

33. *Ibid, pp. 57–58.*

34. Harold Geneen and Alvin Moscow, *Managing,* Garden City, NY, Doubleday, 1984, p. 57.

35. Harry P. Hatry and John M. Greiner, *Improving the Use of Quality Circles in Police Departments,* National Institute of Justice, Washington, DC, 1986, pp. 1–10.

only be trained, but also systematically developed in the workplace. Enlightened leadership is an essential ingredient of the process and employees must be viewed as a vital organizational resource.[36]

Quality circle programs create a parallel organizational structure that is superimposed on the formal organization. It emphasizes different group processes, assigns members a new role and takes members outside of their normal day-to-day work activities. The circles report results back to the formal organization which is the object of the change.[37] Figure 8–6 graphically depicts the steps utilized by quality circles. Each of the indicated steps is vitally important, and must be completed successively. Based on analysis the police can identify problems that are of concern to themselves and the community. Once a number of problems are identified they can be prioritized and addressed accordingly. Numerous variables can modify problem selection such as its extent and nature of the specific problem, its seriousness, and the resources needed to deal with it. With systematic analysis a problem can be attacked from a pro-active problem-solving posture, rather than an incident driven response.[38]

36. Richard J. DeParis, "Situational Leadership: Problem–Solving Leadership for Problem–Solving Police," *The Police Chief,* October 1997, Vol. LXIV, No. 10, pp. 74–86.

37. Edward E. Lawler III, and Susan A. Mohrman, "Quality Circles After the Fad," *Harvard Business Review,* January–February, 1985, p. 66.

38. Herman Goldstein, *Problem-Oriented Policing, New York, McGraw–Hill, 1990, pp. 35–42.*

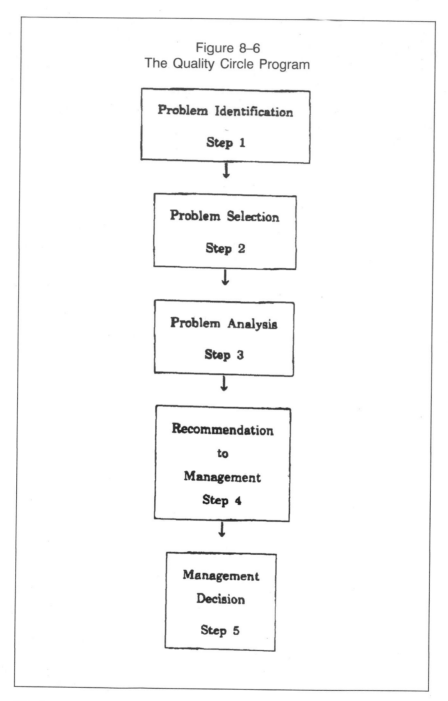

Figure 8–6
The Quality Circle Program

Hindrances to Change

The resistance to change is common place in organizations. It is not unidimensional and can occur throughout the organization. It can emanate from individuals or from work groups. It can occur in one division or cut across functional lines.[42] Resistance to change presents management with a challenge that must be acknowledged and confronted. People cannot be forced to change so they normally react, by accepting the change, resisting it, or trying their best to ignore it. [43] Even when change is accepted it can be complied with grudgingly because of fear, anxiety or perceived ambiguity. An initial reaction when confronted with change is to deny it, or dodge the issue. Members of an organization have a great facility to ignore or minimize indicators that change is necessary. If the change is threatening it will be reacted to more vigorously than if the change is perceived as having little consequence. It should be noted that resistance could be either active or passive. [44]Even when partial agreement occurs hindrances might be strong enough to thwart change. To arrive at consensus demand a great deal of effort on the part of management. Sometimes even the best-laid plans never come to fruition.

Resistance can manifest itself in differing ways ranging from generalized negativity to actual sabotage. Resistance can be rational or even highly emotional. One author identified thirty-three reasons why individuals are resistance to change ranging from homeostasis to human mindlessness.[45] Generally, the reasons for hindering the implementation of change varies from individual to individual but occurs because of one of the following reasons:

- **Self-Interest.** When the potential rewards from the change are out weighed by loses that can occur.

- **Misunderstanding/Lack of Trust.** When officers have a differing knowledge base or management is looked upon as *we vs. they* it is a basis for resistance to occur. Trust is vitally important. Management cannot be viewed as opponents. Officers must feel that there is total commitment to a change, and must feel that they have a vested interest in the change.

- **Different Assessments.** Quite often managers will have a completely different viewpoint of why a proposed change is being considered or implemented. Officers may actually feel that the change will be detrimental in contrast to a managerial viewpoint.

- **Low Tolerance for Change.** Resistance to change is primarily an effort to maintain the status quo. Change threatens organizational and individual norms. In many instances norms are woven into the fabric of established power relationships.[46] Many offi-

42. Nicholas S. Rashford and David Coghlan, *The Dynamics of Organizational Levels: A Change Framework for Managers and Consultants,* Reading, MA, Addison–Wesley, 1994, pp. 84–90.

43. Jeanenne LaMarsh, *Changing the Way we Change: Gaining Control of Major Operational Change,* Reading, MA, Addison–Wesley, 1995, pp. 6–18.

44. Kenneth P. De Meuse and Kevin K. McDaris, "An Exercise in Managing Change," *Training & Development,* 1994, Vol. 48, No. 2, pp. 55–57.

45. James O'Toole, *Leading Change–Overcoming the Ideology of Comfort and the Tyranny of Custom,* San Francisco, Jossey–Boss, 1995, pp. 10–85.

46. David K. Carr, Kelvin J. Hard, and William J. Trahant, *Managing the Change Process: A Field book for Change Agents, Consultants, Team Leaders, and*

cers are comfortable in doing things the way they have always done them. They operate at a comfort level, which leads to inertia, and a high resistance level. The view is that we have always done it this way and there is no need to tamper with current procedures or policies.[47]

Change Management

Resistance should be expected in organizations and management must distinguish between rational and emotional hindrances. Resistance is natural and should be expected. In some instances, the providing of information will resolve a problem, while in other situations it will be necessary to deal with individuals or team in an effort to determine the reason for the resistance. What is needed is to create an organizational attitude that is best described as change-readiness. This calls for the creation of an organizational environment that can only be described as open and receptive to new ideas. This is a far cry from the traditional bureaucratic police organization. A really open agency is excited about change rather than being anxious about it. Change should be accepted as a challenge rather than being threatened. Additionally, openness requires a definite commitment to change as an on going process. Change-readiness is a predisposition provides for the taking of actions that actually anticipates change.[48] Fundamentally it is a process that challenges the status quo and creates change. A truly healthy organization is one where individuals generate change from a pro-active posture.

Organizational change is seldom spontaneous. In many instances it can be an excruciatingly slow process.[49] Significant change requires an understanding of the difficulty involved in the change process and an awareness of potential resistance. The conflict created by change should be worked through and as new issues arise they must be dealt with and discussed openly. With adequate planning and preparation potentially damaging conflict can be prevented. Creative management of conflict can reveal and clarify problems, improve the analysis or problems and the implementation of solutions. [50]Positive change in an organization requires more than tinkering or widow dressing. If it to be effective it must call for substantial and positive organizational response. It must be planned and coordinated. Above all it requires

Reengineering Managers. New York, McGraw–Hill, 1996, pp. 72–77.

47. Robert Albanese, *Managing Toward Accountability for Performance,* Homewood, IL, Richard D. Irwin, 1981, pp. 32–56. Reprinted with permission of the publisher.

48. Robert Kriegel, and David Brandt, *Sacred Cows Make the Best Burgers: Paradigm–Busting Strategies for Developing Change-ready People and Organizations*, New York, Warner Books, 1996, pp. 8–10.

49. Zhao, *op. cit.*, p. 83.

50. Harry W. More, W. Fred Wegener, and Larry Miller, *Effective Police Supervision,* Third Edition, Cincinnati, OH, Anderson, 1999, pp. 233–254.

managers to take the time needed to make the changes as well as being diligent throughout the process, and learning from experience.[51]

Case Study

Captain Roger Schlitz

Roger Schlitz is an administrative captain in a police department that has 972 sworn personnel and 101 civilians. The population of the city is 952,000 and is in a major metropolitan area.

The city is cosmopolitan in nature and has a large Mexican American population. The city is located in the center of the state and is a major transportation center. The remainder of the state is rural in nature and has only two cities with populations in excess of 120,000.

During the last decade the city's population has increased dramatically as it has become a communications center and has considerable hi-tech industry. The department has not kept up with the population explosion and has had difficulty in meeting the demands for police service. Calls for service are backlogged on the swing shift, and only the most serious calls are given a priority one response.

There is a critical need for increased manpower. The department has received funding for 90 new officers to be hired over three years. New officers will be trained in the regional academy and on probation for one year. During the probationary period the officers will be supervised by Field Training Officers (FTO's). During the last decade several major cities that hired a large number of new officers found that a number of the officers were found to be less than qualified as recruitment standards were lowered. In fact, a number of new hires committed crimes while on duty. In order to avoid this problem the administrative captain has been asked to develop a position paper describing how this large number of candidates would be recruited, trained, and supervised during their probationary period. There was an additional concern for the impact that would be caused by the integration of so many new officers into the department. The labor market is very tight and recruitment is expected to be a problem.

If you were Captain Schlitz what changes would you propose to accommodate the influx of so many new officers? Would you make changes in the recruitment process? Why? What would you do in order to adequately plan for the changes that will occur because of adding so many new officers?

---

51. Herman Goldstein, *The New Policing: Confronting Complexity*, Research in Brief, Washington, DC, 1993, pp. 1–4.

For Further Reading

William M. Boast, *Masters of Change: How Great Leaders in Every Age Thrived in Turbulent Times*. Provo, UT, Executive Excellence Publishing, 1997, pp. 19–35.

> This author takes the position that change is unpredictable and at the same time a very normal process. Change is described as something that has to be dealt with since the beginning of time, and not just a current phenomena. Change is presented as an opportunity and at the same time it involves risk. The author reviews the importance of positive thing and identifies variable that leaders have used when dealing with change.

David K. Carr, *Managing the Change Process: A Field Book for Change Agents, Consultants, Team Leaders, and Reengineering Managers*, New York, McGraw–Hill, 1996, pp. 25–76.

> Reviews a range of topics involving change from the understanding of the human change process to how one becomes an effective change leader. Additionally, the author presents a comprehensive management approach for dealing with change. Presents an excellent section on the resistance to change and strategies for dealing with resistance. The author also press a three step process for ensuring that empowerment works and is practical for an organization.

Florence M. Stone, *The Manager's Balancing Act*, New York, AMA-COM, 1997, pp. 91–132.

> Presents a rule of thumb process to encourage employees to support change efforts that stresses: communicate, communicate, communicate. Suggests doing it such a way as to show employees what is in it for them, allowing employees to vent, and asking employees for suggestions. Discusses how to plan for change and how one can manage the change effort. Additionally, the author discusses how to overcome resistance.

Jihong Zhao, *Why Police Organizations Change: A Study of Community–Oriented Policing*, Washington, DC, Police Executive Research Forum, 1997, pp. 1–123.

> This book examines contemporary organizational change in policing as exemplified by community-oriented policing. The author discusses prominent organizational values, external influences and presents data identifying both key inhibitors and facilitators of organizational change. Includes an excellent discussion of theoretical models of organizational change.

Chapter 9

LEADERSHIP: Nature and Style

Learning Objectives

1. Write a short essay describing the types of qualifications that a police chief should possess.

2. Contrast the leadership of a candidate who has bad-character and one who has self controlled character.

3. List five conceptual skills that a chief should possess.

4. Contrast human and knowledge skills.

5. Write a short essay discussing the elements listed in the announcement for the Chief of Police for the City of Los Angeles.

6. List eight traits of an effective police executive.

7. Identify the two measure components of the leadership quadrant.

8. Compare an impoverished to a middle of the road leader.

9. Describe the least referred co-worker scale.

10. Identify the way subordinates relate to a leader under the path-goal leadership theory.

11. Write a short essay describing the concept of tenure.

12. Contrast how five of the largest cities in the U.S. can appoint and remove a Chief of Police.

13. List eight possible components of an executive contract.

14. Describe the advantages of the examination process.

15. Write a short essay describing the assessment center.

Leadership is the catalyst in organization and management of a police department. The significance of this statement becomes apparent on considering the observation by some that in a democracy, "A city gets the kind of police service that it deserves, because it can get any kind that it wants." The statement is misleading because it assumes the people know what to want, which is not the case in the United States today. There has been a general failure in America to recognize the basic principle that formulation of the means and method is not a responsibility of the people. They can approve or disapprove. But the average citizen has no time for an intensive study of police science and administration. One must rely upon administrative talent in this

professional field to initiate and put in motion personnel and procedures that will produce results.

It may be stated, then, that the quality of American police service
is a direct responsibility of police administration and is not predetermined, as is generally assumed, by public opinion. The responsibility
rests squarely upon the shoulders of police administration. Too often,
either through incapacity or indifference, it has failed to interpret its
problems to the people, and has failed to formulate and present to
them for their approval an organization and program equal to the
demands of a modern social order. A virile administration is called for,
capable of presenting to the people the specifications of modern police
service. Until the people know what to want, until they can visualize
the possibilities of a scientific police administration in terms of lowered
crime and delinquency rates and lowered unit costs, they never will get
the kind of police service they deserve. Those who believe in democracy
are convinced that once the people are in possession of the facts, they
can be depended upon to support the kind of administration to which
they are entitled. In those few American cities where administration
has performed this missionary work, the people are enjoying an experience in modern police service altogether unknown to other sections of
the country. In every corner of the country police administration
operates in an atmosphere of mutual confidence and respect, proving
that it can be done.

The critical importance of the executive as an organizational
determinant of line performance suggests a more detailed treatment of
the qualifications for the top administrative position and the mechanics
of selection by which individuals are brought into this office. No
greater responsibility confronts the appointing power in American
cities than the choice of the individual who is to be given control of
police administration. Leadership is the most important single factor in
the success or failure of police operations. Invariably in observing a
successful police organization one finds a strong executive who has
been the driving force in elevating the level of performance. Conversely, where mediocrity or failure characterizes the work of a police
organization, it generally can be traced to incompetence in management. The fundamental basis for the success of a police enterprise is to
be found in the ideas and efforts of the police chief executive.

Too frequently, patrol vehicles, laboratories, traffic investigation
units and other observable expressions of performance are looked upon
as the beginning and the end of police service. True, they are component parts of great importance, but back of all these is the intricate job
of management performed by the executive. It is the manager who
guides and controls the far-flung operations of a metropolitan police
organization, or those of a smaller department, and without whom the
enterprise would become shapeless and inoperative. The leader is a
dynamic force in the actual work of organization and operation. The
value of this person's service cannot be expressed in dollars and cents
on the balance sheet, but executive effort or lack of it is clearly

reflected in the success or failure of the police in the community they serve. As one goes up the scale of supervisory and command personnel in a police department from the sergeant through the chief executive position emphasis is placed increasingly on judgment, self-reliance and resourcefulness. The scope of duties gradually broadens and planning in advance expands in importance until one comes to the chief executive who is the chief strategist and the one who is responsible for the operation of the entire enterprise. At one time the sin qua non—was "promotion from within" and it was adhered to religiously. For many years the chief's position has been advertised nationwide in many departments, and a trend is emerging that opens up other key management positions to outsiders [1]

Qualifications

Generally speaking, top management in the police field is entering a new era as an increasing number of highly qualified individuals have assumed the position of police chief executive. Unusual strides have been made in procedures for the selection of personnel and excellent managerial training programs exist throughout the Nation. These gains are apparent, as progress has been made in the techniques of management. Technology has revolutionized police departments from the bottom of the enterprise to the top. Extensive efforts have been devoted to the improvement of the position of the patrol officer and the investigator, and increasing attention has been given to the development of competent police executives.

Throughout the early history of law enforcement it was assumed, the person who has the longest service (or if several are approximately equal on this point, then the one with the best record as a patrol officer) may confidently be expected to be successful in the management of the department. The fallacy of this procedure is demonstrated by its failure. The administration of a police department is a monumental undertaking, requiring not only successful experience as an officer, but also special talent and a number of skills not acquired in the course of routine police experience.

Among the indispensable qualifications of the executive is an extended and successful police experience characterized preferably by service at various ranks in the department. The knowledge gained first hand concerning the problems at diverse levels can add immeasurably to the capacity for management of the police enterprise. If experience includes periods of service in each of the major operational divisions the chief will be even better prepared to assume the responsibilities of the new position. Armed with a technical knowledge of the functions and problems of these various staff and line units of police organization, the Chief is in a position to weigh their relative importance in the equation of, public service, crime control, and to exercise intelligent

1. Gregory P. Rothaus, "From the Outside–In Making a Successful leadership Transition," *Law and Order*, September 1998, Vol. 46, No. 9, 82–86.

budget management. This allows the chief to integrate their joint effort toward the immediate and long-term objectives of police organization.

City officials seem to be looking for a wide range of attributes when advertising for the position of chief of police. In a survey of announcements for the position of chief of police representing differing regions of the United States a number of common denominators are readily apparent. These range from length of service to educational requirements and are set forth in table 9–1. Announcements for specific position can be quite restrictive. In one city the selected candidate had to be POST certified within one year after appointment. In another each candidate had to have seven years experience in a large city. In yet another city the announcement was even more restrictive stating that the candidate had to have experience in a city with a population greater than 250,000. In the announcements scrutinized only one referred to age and stated that the applicant must be not more than 60 years of age. This is a violation of the Age Discrimination Employment Act and is not a *bona fide occupational qualification (BFOQ)*, that is, a valid, job–related requirement reasonably necessary to the normal operation of a police agency. The age discrimination act makes it illegal to discriminate against person's 40 years of age or older and advertising that tends to discourage people over that age from applying for a position might be deemed discriminatory.[2]

Every-time a qualifier enters an announcement it reduces the base of eligible candidates. Hence great care must be taken to insure that every adjective in an announcement describes an actual position requirement. For example, the issue of experience raises a critical issue. The question is how much experience is need? In the announcements studied the experience requirement varies from five to ten years. There must be some cut off point but is it really ten years? As indicated in figure 9–1 there are qualifiers to even the length of service when such descriptors as service in a large department, experience with progressive responsibility, or experience including serve in patrol. In one agency eight modifiers of experience appear that would in all probability restrict the applicant pool. Obviously the thing to look for is not only depth of experience, but breath. The thing to avoid is experience that is redundant, such as, ten years experience in which the applicant failed to grow or acquire the skills needed to be a strong leader. Another example, is the requirement that candidates must have had experience as a chief or deputy chief. This immediately eliminates many progressive and highly competent individuals at lower ranks. Consequently great care must be taken when one decides what experience is relevant.

The greatest subjective in announcements for the position of chief of police revolved around the specific skills needed to ensure that the best qualified candidate is selected. With human skills it includes

2. Harry W. More, *Special Topics in Policing*, Second Edition, Cincinnati, Anderson Publishing, 1998, pp. 227–228.

things such as interpersonal, written, and public speaking skills. These things can be assessed during the review of the applicants resume and/the interview. Conceptual skills are more easily measured by the use of an assessment center. This evaluative process can include problem-solving skills, and the competencies in special areas, such as, technology or working in a diverse community. An often-overlooked technique in evaluating candidates is to have them submit a position paper. This is especially valuable when one is trying to assess the values that a candidate holds or the *vision* they have as to what the department should become in the future, and how that *vision* could be implemented.

Knowledge-based skills can be measured quite effectively during oral interviews as the applicant is asked to respond to specific entries in the statement of qualifications/application, and the resume. This can include such thing as questions about personnel evaluation, grantsmanship, budgeting, records management, and/or knowledge of community policing. Personal attributes bear careful scrutiny, as do all aspects of a candidate's background. A detailed background investigation can cover most of these issues to include verifying previous employment and education. Too often this is one of the weakest points of the employment process. Every aspect of a candidate's job application and a resume should be checked. If there is any disparity it should be resolved in favor of the department not the candidate. During the background investigation and the interview of the candidate questions should be directed toward issues of moral character and integrity.[3]

Special efforts should be made to determine leadership qualities to include measuring the character of the candidate:

- **Bad Character.**
    - a. Seeks opportunity to profit by victimizing others.
    - b. Feels no shame.
    - c. Must be weeded out.

- **Uncontrolled character.**
    - a. Weak willed, vulnerable to temptation.
    - b. They have a price.
    - c. Maybe teachable, but not worthy of a position of trust.

- **Self-controlled character.**
    - a. Self-disciplined.
    - b. But, envy others getting away with illegality.
    - c. Leaders must foster admirable behavior in face of temptation and discouragement.

3. Neal C. Griffin, "The Five I's of Police Professionalism: A Model for Frontline Leadership," *The Police Chief,* November 1998, Vol. LXV, No. 11, p. 24.

- **Excellent character.**
  - a.   Habits of trustworthiness integral in lives.
  - b.   Loves honesty; it has become second nature.
  - c.   Truly incorruptible.
  - d.   Fit to bear the public trust.[4]

Each of the items discussed above are elusive, but no one can dispute the necessity of striving to select a candidate who exhibits the qualities of good character. As abstract as these items may seem every effort must be made to select a candidate who has deep reservoirs of temperance and courage. Integrity becomes a quality that cannot be sacrificed. Every candidate should have demonstrated a high degree of honor, honesty, judgment and common sense.

Figure 9–1

Various Attributes and Abilities That City
Officials are Looking for When Recruiting for
the Position of Police Chief*

Education (Ten different department).
- Bachelor's degree in political science, police administration, law enforcement, criminal justice, public administration, business administration, or a related field.
- Master's degree highly desirable.
- Master's degree in public administration, business administration or related field.
- Master's degree or additional training and experience working in a racially and culturally diverse community.
- Baccalaureate degree.

Experience
- Five years of supervisory/managerial experience with at least three in the capacity of chief or deputy chief.
- Five years executive experience in a governmental police agency.
- Seven years as an administrator in a large department.
- Nine years as a police officer and attained the rank of lieutenant for at least one year.
- Ten years with some administrative experience as chief or deputy chief.
- Ten years of experience with increasing responsibility.
- Ten years of progressively responsible law enforcement experience.
- Ten years law enforcement experience including patrol, investigative techniques, traffic, crime prevention and control, communications systems, public relations, case preparation and prosecution, and computers.

Human Skills
- Outstanding written and oral communication skills.
- Interpersonal.

---

4. Walt H. Sirene, James M. Kelly, and Marita V. Malone, *Leadership in Developing the Organizational ethics:*   *Ethics in Policing.* Quantico, VA, FBI Academy, June 1997, p. 21.

- Foster team environment.
- Public speaking.
- Experience working with diverse communities.
- Team player.

Conceptual Skills
- Strong leadership.
- Vision.
- Strong citizen service values.
- Problem-solving skills.
- Managerial.

Knowledge Skills
- Effective labor-management collaboration.
- Background in media and community relations.
- Knowledge of community policing.
- Knowledge of public safety services.
- Competencies in working with technological advances.
- Knowledge of record keeping.
- Budgeting preparation.
- Personnel evaluation and supervision.
- Preparing grant requests and administering grants to augment city funding.

Personal Attributes
- Good moral character.
- No convictions for criminal offenses other than minor traffic violations.
- Unquestioned integrity.

Every state or local jurisdiction should require the new police chief executive to have a baccalaureate prior to appointment and preference should be given to candidates with a master's degree or higher. In fact it is becoming quite common to find police chiefs with a JD. or Ph.D. This is a far cry from only thirty years ago when it was proposed that Chiefs should have 60 semester units at an accredited college or university. While higher education for police officials is not a panacea it is clearly a step forward in the professionalization of law enforcement.[5] In terms of the college major it would seem to be clear that an administrative degree would be better preparation for a potential police executive than a degree in education or the social sciences.[6] Additionally, individuals who have acquired degrees from non-accredited institutions of higher education should be dismissed from the pool of candidates. While some of these institutions might well obtain accreditation at some point reviewers should reject them out of hand until such time as the institution has received full accreditation. They are just too many diploma mills that sell a degree for a price–it is a thriving business.

There is a need for a new generation of educated police executives. Future leaders must deal with responsibilities that are becoming in-

5. International Association of Chiefs of Police, "Police Leadership for the 21st Century," *The Police Chief,* March 1999, Vol. LXV., No. 3, pp. 57–60.

6. Harvey Rachlin, "The Hiring Process," *Law and Order,* March 1995, Vol. 43, No. 3, p.23.

creasingly complex. Poorly trained and educated managers will not have the tools that are needed to deal with a rapidly changing and complex society. Police chiefs are truly managers—not police officers who have attained the top position because of longevity. Progressive police executives should be capable of approaching their job, and working within a milieu, unknown a few years ago. Urban communities with a multi-ethic constituency, a complex governmental entity, a constantly changing social system, and a dynamic environment require leadership that is both innovative and creative.[7] The skills needed that can only be obtained from the benefits offered by graduate education. Generally speaking, it is clear the educational level of the police has risen significantly, but actual professionalism has not been fully attained, but tremendous strides have been made in this area.

7. Michael D. Breen, "Today's Leadership Challenge for Police Executives," *The Police Chief,* March 1999, Vol. LXVI, No. 3, pp. 61–67.

Figure 9–2
Position Announcement

City of Los Angeles
CHIEF OF POLICE

The City of Los Angeles is seeking a high impact leader and manager with vision to guide its police department into the 21st Century. The position offers a salary in the range of $143K to $215K. The Chief of Police reports to a five-member civilian Police Commission. The candidate is appointed to a five-year term by the Mayor and confirmed by the City Council. He/She may be appointed to a second five-year term by the Police Commission. The Los Angeles Police Department (LAPD) serves a multi-ethnic population of 3.6 million residents residing in 485.9 square miles. The current budget of the LAPD is $758.2 million. A total of 12,183 positions are authorized, of which 9,262 are sworn officers.

The successful candidate will have a minimum of 10 years of progressively responsible police service experience. At least five years should have been in a senior executive role. The position requires a minimum of a Bachelor's degree from an accredited college or university. A Master's degree in Business Administration, Public Administration, criminal justice or a related discipline is preferred. Leadership of a community-based preventive policing program is highly desirable. Prior experience should have been gained with a police agency serving at least 250,000 people, with a minimum of 1,500 full time employees. Previous fiscal responsibilities should have been for a budget in excess of $50 million. Past employment in a diverse urban metropolitan area is highly desirable. State of California Peace Officer Standards and Training (POST) Commission certification at the executive level will be mandatory within one year of appointment.

Interested and qualified candidates should submit a resume and a two-page statement of interest postmarked no later than midnight PDT on June 12, 1997. The statement of interest should include the candidate's vision of the future of the Los Angeles Police Department, including how he/she will develop a strategic process to implement and achieve that vision. Application information and materials should be sent to:

THE OLDANI GROUP

The City of Los Angeles is an Equal
Employment Opportunity Employer M/F/H

MR. JERROLD OLDANI or MR. DAVID K. WASSON
THE OLDANI GROUP, INC.
188-106TH AVE NE, STE 420
BELLEVUE, WA 98004
PH (206/425) 451-3938 FAX (206/425) 453-6786

E-MAIL jerryo@theoldanigroup.com • http://www.theoldanigroup.com

Source: Correspondence from Jerrold Oldani, *City of Los Angeles, Chief of Police*, Bellevue, WA, The Oldani Group, December 15, 1998. http://www.theolandigroup.com.

While this statement may not be as true as when it was initially written it does give one a great deal of food for thought. In addition to all other credentials, the police administrator of today must qualify as a criminal justice professional who can meet the new pressures and stress coming from performing a job in a complex interactive society.

There is another need for a police chief candidate and that is to have the capacity to interpret and become accomplished in the language and politics of the scientific and technical community. As more and more police efforts are evaluated it becomes very important for a chief to have the capability of evaluating the research effort, and determine its applicability to the department and the community. These types of questions must be answered. Do the results of recent research undermine the concept of directed patrol? Is community policing the best way to police a city? Does D.A.R.E. really work? Will the investment in lap top computers for patrol officers been a good expenditure of public funds? What is called for is a police administrator, a criminal justice professional, who can assess problems and recommendation solutions.

In addition, candidates should have demonstrated the ability to provide effective leadership, identify and define problems, and most importantly, obtain desired results through skilled management efforts. Other significant qualities include the candidate's ability to motivate personnel, develop subordinates, relate to the community, effectively organize personnel and functions, administer internal discipline, and establish and communicate objectives and priorities. But the foregoing qualifications—experience and training—are of little avail unless the individual possesses administrative capabilities and the attributes of executive leadership. Above all other considerations, the police executive must be a leader of men and women. The selection of traits that a police chief executive should possess remains elusive, but the search goes on.[8] Figure 9–3 lists selective traits of effective police administrators

The Anatomy of Leadership

Organization alone is an inert, inanimate thing until it fuses with leadership to become a dynamic force with a compelling thrust toward the achievement of objectives. There is much more to police service than storefront stations, patrol cars, radio communications, police records and all the other material elements of a modern police system. There must be *leadership* present to control, plan and direct the involved activities of a police organization. The fire of inspired leadership is a contagious thing. It usurps the role of command and leads subordinates to go on beyond the call of duty to new levels of performance.[9] Many books have been written on the psychology of leadership. They are to be found in every library and await their use by those interested in improving their capabilities in this important area of the profession. What is an executive? What is leadership? Why do some fail miserably in positions involving the supervision and command of personnel while others seem to meet such responsibilities with confidence and comparative ease? The answer is not simple; the formula of

8. Terry D. Anderson, Ron Ford, and Marilyn Hamilton, *Transforming Leadership: Equipping Yourself and Coaching Others to Build the Leadership Organization,* Boca Raton, FL, CRC Press LLC, 1998, p. 271.

9. James M. Kouzes and Barry Z. Posner, *The Leadership Challenge: How to Keep Getting Extraordinary Things Done in Organizations,* Second Edition, Jossey–Bass, Inc., Publishers, 1995, pp. 10–11.

successful leadership is yet to be derived. No satisfactory set of rules has ever been developed insuring success as an executive.

Whatever the diagnosis of leadership may be, the executive must be an acknowledged *leader*, capable of inspiring officers to accomplish assigned tasks. This type of leadership leads instead of drives, in contrast with the approach that depends upon fear or intimidation. An intelligent group of followers will not respond when driven, whereas, there is almost no limit to the sacrifices they'll make under inspired leadership. The complexity of relationships between the executive and personnel requires a peculiar insight into human nature with all of its strength and all of its weaknesses. A high order of intelligence and good judgment is called for, with a measure of common sense (that will permit discrimination and decision as to the relative importance of things) and the selection from among several possibles lines of action the one that will yield the most favorable return. Strength or power of personality intangible and indefinable though it may be is a common denominator of successful leadership and will always be found transmitting its impulses to the staff in an effective organization.[10] Another quality that appears strongly essential is a scientific turn of mind. The technical problems involved in coordinating the work of a group of officers, materials, and equipment in such a way as to achieve maximum amplification of the line power of an organization are often exceedingly complex.

The primary functions of the executive are directing, planning, organizing, and controlling the activities of people in the undertaking of official responsibilities of the office. It is uniformly characteristic of the police day that situations are constantly changing. A local management-labor dispute holding potentialities for a strike or disturbance, the unexpected death of a prisoner in a jail cell, or a sudden upsurge in the volume of automobile thefts or other crimes, an increase in gang activities need a responded. The same is true for a change in the density distribution of police problems, the development of new business district, or the activities of pressure groups represent but a few of the new situations that may confront the police executive from day to day. Most assuredly, a possession of the intelligence and originality to relate one's previous background and experience to planning of operations and the solution of new problems is very essential.

Figure 9–3

Selected Traits of Effective Police Executives

- Inspirational.
- Intelligent.
- Good judgment.
- Common sense.

---

10. Keith D. Bushey, "The Unproductive Executive," *The Police Chief,* March 1999, Vol. LXVI, No. 3, pp. 69–71.

- Positive personality.
- Scientific turn of mind.
- Responder to change.
- Originality.
- Audacity.
- Fine judgment.
- Results orientation.
- Mental courage.
- Interest in people.
- Professional attitude.

Audacity tempered with fine judgment and discrimination characterizes most successful executives. Much of their work is concerned with planning for unforeseen emergencies and the removal of interference with the execution of those plans. There are times when a great deal of mental courage is required to initiate action in situations where there is a possibility of failure. The line of least resistance is to play safe, as for example, when there is opposition within the department itself to plans whose adoption the executive believes are sound and necessary. The executive is responsible for accomplishing results, and the temptation to yield to the pressure of others will not relieve executive responsibility in the event of failure. A considerable degree of mental courage is needed, together with the strength of character and ability to follow through with plans in the face of opposition.

The true executive possesses an innate interest in and affection for people. Executives are molders of human stuff. They know the possibilities and capabilities of those associated with them and endeavor to build them into better instruments for the accomplishment of the objectives of the enterprise. They also know that increased professional stature of their people increases the quality of departmental performance and that this in turn reflects credit upon the head of the organization. This trait was among those that contributed to the successful leadership of August Vollmer during the years he was Chief of Police in Berkeley, California. Chief Vollmer encouraged the individual to reach for the highest rungs on the ladder of achievement in their chosen profession. As a matter of fact, under his expert supervision, the Berkeley Police Department became the nation's training school for police chiefs and more than twenty of his officers subsequently became police chief executives in other American cities. It must be noted that the analysis of leadership, based upon traits, has proven an elusive task. The utilization of leadership traits is appealing because it reduces the manager's characteristics to easily understood and common sense propositions. It has also been used extensively in describing qualities for specific jobs.[11] Leadership traits currently have a number of weaknesses inasmuch as there is little agreement on the best traits fitting

11. W.J. Reddin, *Managerial Effectiveness*, McGraw–Hill Book Company, New York, 1970, p. 20.

all situations, that managerial effectiveness cannot be related to a group of traits, and there are just too many traits. The use of traits is limited until such time as there is a single sound theory to provide for a conceptual frame of reference allowing for the identification of traits perceived as important in particular management situations.

Many social scientists have conducted extensive formal leadership studies during the last quarter of a century identifying numerous leadership styles. One researcher suggests that there are three basic types of leadership that have been identified as autocratic,[12] democratic, and laissez-faire [13] Another list is somewhat similar, dividing managerial approaches into five styles including authoritarian, democratic, laissez-faire, bureaucratic, and charismatic.[14] On the other hand the Michigan Style Continuum perceives leadership behavior that ranges from a style that is employee-centered to one that is production-centered. The application of the continuum suggests that when a manager responds by becoming more employee-centered there will be a reduction in production-centered behavior. In other words, too much of a good thing can have negative results.

Leadership Quadrants

The Ohio State studies have questioned the validity of viewing leadership behavior on a single continuum and have developed a two-dimensional independent factor approach that describes the behavior of a leader. These two factors are identified as Initiating Structure and Consideration and are viewed as the two most important dimensions of leadership.[15] Initiating Structure is defined as "the leader's behavior in delineating the relationship between himself and members of the work group and in endeavoring to establish well-defined patterns of organization, channels of communication, and methods or procedures." Consideration is defined as "behavior indicative of friendship, mutual trust, respect, and warmth in the relationship between the leader and staff members".[16]

These studies determined leadership styles vary considerably from individual to individual. Some leaders are characterized as task oriented and rigidly structure the activities of subordinates, while others exhibit behavior emphasizing building and maintaining good personal relationships. Other leaders exhibit leadership style characteristics

12. Susan Smith Kuezmarski, and Thomas D. Kuezmarski, *Values-based Leadership: Rebuilding Employee Commitment,* Englewood Cliffs, NJ, 1995, p. 240.

13. Anthony G. Athos and Robert E. Coffey, *Behavior in Organizations: A Multi–Dimensional View,* Prentice–Hall, Englewood Cliffs, NJ, 1968, p. 163.

14. Philip B. Applewhite, *Organizational Behavior,* Prentice–Hall, Englewood Cliffs, NJ, 1965, p. 131.

15. Paul Hershey and Kenneth H. Blanchard, "Life Cycle Theory of Leadership," *Training and Development Journal,* May 1969, p. 26.

16. Roger M. Stogdill and Alvin E. Coons, editors, *Leader Behavior: Its Description and Measurement,* Research Monograph No. 88, Bureau of Business Research, Ohio State University, 1957, pp. 10–31 . .

having a mixture of task and relationships. Needless to say the study of leader behavior has not resulted in the identification of one dominant style.[17] This pattern of leadership behavior result in a model of four quadrants plotted on two separate axes. The axes illustrate leadership styles in terms of Initiating Structure and Consideration as indicated in the following figure 9–4.

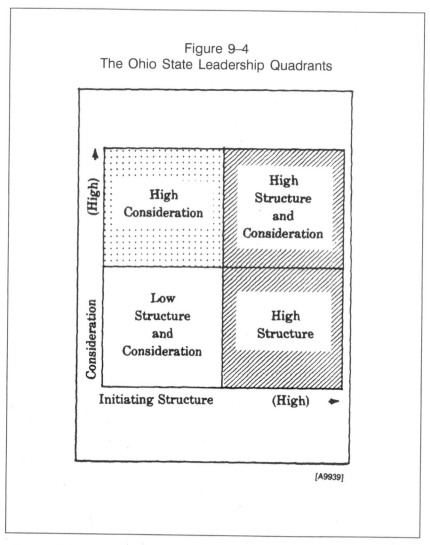

Figure 9–4
The Ohio State Leadership Quadrants

[A9939]

Source: Adapted from Robert M. Fulmer, *The New Management,* New York, Macmillan, 1983, and R.M. Stogdill and A. E. Coons, *Leader Behavior: A Description and Measurement,* Research Monogram 88, Bureau of Business Research, Columbus, OH, The Ohio State University 1957, pp. 15–32.

17. Hershey, *op. cit.*

The Grid

A humanistic theory of leadership the managerial grid provides an operational blueprint of change and development for both the individual and the organization. It identifies five different styles of leadership based on the relationship of concern for production and the concern for people. As illustrated in figure 9–5, the horizontal axis shows the concern for production with ratings from low to high. A leadership style rating of 9 reflects maximum concern for production. The vertical axis illustrates a regard for people—the higher the rating the greater the concern. With a rating of 0 on this axis the style of leadership depicts maximum concern for people. The managerial grid analysis of leadership styles views (1,1) management as:

- **Impoverished** (1,1).
- **Task** (1,9).
- **Country Club** (9,1).
- **Middle of the Road** (5,5).
- **Team Management** (9,9).[18]

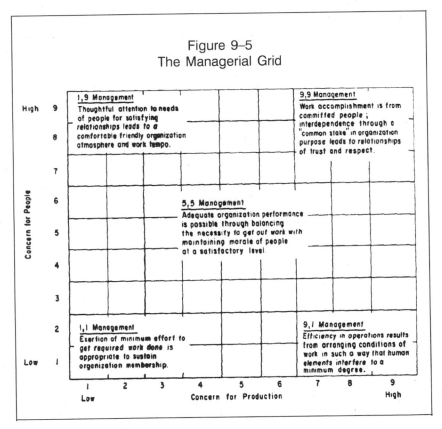

Figure 9–5
The Managerial Grid

18. Robert R. Blake and Anne Adams McCanse, *Leadership Dilemmas– Grid Solutions,* Gulf Publishing Company, Houston, TX, 1991, p. 29.

Source: Robert R. Blake and Anne Adams McCanse, *Leadership Dilemmas–Grid Solutions,* Gulf Publishing Co., Houston, Texas, 1991 p. 29. Used with permission. All rights reserved January 25, 1999.

The five leadership styles are clearly different approaches to management situations and present a definite set of tentative assumptions about people:

Impoverished Management. This approach places people in jobs and then goes to the extreme of leaving them alone. As a consequence the manager experiences little conflict between production and people because this type of leader is "out of it." With non-existing expectations this type of manager responds by functioning as a non-entity. This type of manager is viewed as a 1,1 manager—"lost among" rather than managing people. Just collect a check and forget it.

Task Management. A manager operating at this level is generally classified as a head honcho concerned only with immediate results. "Human elements" become meaningless and are ignored. Above all they are never allowed to interfere with efficiency and output. If any person has the audacity to impede the attainment of a goal they are relegated to obscurity or pawned off on another manager. One thought monopolizes the 9,1 manager—results at all costs–achieve--achieve is the motto.

Country Club Management. This style gives very low attention to the amount of work accomplished, but on the other hand has a high concern for people. The attitudes and feelings of people are of real concern. People come first and the 1,9 manager arranges conditions so personnel, social and welfare needs are paramount. This type of manager does just enough to get by but never does anything that will upset employees. Employees can come in late or spend too much time on coffee breaks but such actions are viewed as acceptable behavior–keep them happy. Above all be a nice person and don't rock the boat.

Middle of the Road Management. This approach reflects intermediate concern for production and moderate concern for people. There is an assumption there will be conflict between production goals and needs of people. The 5,5 manager assumes people are practical and they will put forth some effort. Since conflict is inevitable let it happen and deal with it. [19]

Team Management. The upper right hand corner of the Grid is 9,9 where there is high concern for both production and people. It is assumed there is no conflict between organizational goals and people. Effective integration of the two is obtained by involving people in determining working conditions and developing strategies of work. This is true participative management at its zenith. If there is a most ideal style of management it is Team 9,9.

19. *Ibid.,* p. 110.

There has been limited application of the Grid system to the police field, but two studies have focused on police managers. One study of seventy-six police managers indicated approximately 70 percent had a primary style of Team Management, 9,9 and the back-up styles (stress) were dominated by Middle of the Road Management, 5,5 and Country Club Management, 1,9.[20] The primary and back-up management styles are conditioned by variables in the managerial process such as philosophy, planning and goal setting, implementation, and evaluation. Leadership is a complex issue, however research is being conducted, slowly but surely, providing greater insight into this process. As Hershey and Blanchard have pointed out, the Grid has a great deal of similarity to the Ohio State studies excepting the fundamental approach to each study. The Grid is an attitudinal model that attempts to measure the predisposition of a manager, while the Ohio State study is a behavioral model examining how leader actions are perceived by others.[21]

Contingency

The contingency model of leadership has been given extensive consideration in leadership literature.[22] It moves away from the "one best way" model of leadership to one that is best described as situational. It holds that actual effectiveness in an organization depends upon two interacting factors. The first is the personality of the leader that is fundamental to leadership style. The second factor is the control provided to leaders (according to the situation) over the group's behavior, the task and the outcome. This latter factor is usually called "situational control"[23] Fiedler suggests the underlying goals in the leadership situation can be identified by the Least Preferred Co-worker (LPC) Scale which is presented in figure 9-6. One must think of all the people with whom you have worked and then think of one person with whom you could work *least well*. This person is then identified on the Scale for each variable by placing an "X" in the appropriate space. The scale consists of a pair of words that have an opposite meaning. The score obtained by adding the responses is a measure of your leadership style.[24]

20. Jay Hall, Jerry B. Harvey, and Martha Williams, *Styles of Management and Interpretive Score Sheet*, Conroe, Texas, Teleo–Metrics International, no date.

21. Paul Hershey and Kenneth H. Blanchard, *Management of Organizational Behavior*, Second Edition, Englewood Cliffs, New Jersey, 1972, p. 76.

22. Anderson, Ford, and Hamilton, op. cit., 278.

23. Fred E. Fiedler, Martin M. Chemers with Linda Mahar, *Improving Leadership Effectiveness: The Leader Match Concept*, New York, John Wiley & Sons, Inc., 1976, p. 3.

24. *Ibid.*, p. 9.

Figure 9–6

Least Preferred Co–Worker (LPC) Scale

		Scoring
Pleasant	_ _ _ _ _ _ _ _ Unpleasant 8 7 6 5 4 3 2 1	_____
Friendly	_ _ _ _ _ _ _ _ Unfriendly 8 7 6 5 4 3 2 1	_____
Rejecting	_ _ _ _ _ _ _ _ Accepting 1 2 3 4 5 6 7 8	_____
Tense	_ _ _ _ _ _ _ _ Relaxed 1 2 3 4 5 6 7 8	_____
Distant	_ _ _ _ _ _ _ _ Close 1 2 3 4 5 6 7 8	_____
Cold	_ _ _ _ _ _ _ _ Warm 1 2 3 4 5 6 7 8	_____
Supportive	_ _ _ _ _ _ _ _ Hostile 8 7 6 5 4 3 2 1	_____
Boring	_ _ _ _ _ _ _ _ Interesting 1 2 3 4 5 6 7 8	_____
Quarrelsome	_ _ _ _ _ _ _ _ Harmonious 1 2 3 4 5 6 7 8	_____
Gloomy	_ _ _ _ _ _ _ _ Cheerful 1 2 3 4 5 6 7 8	_____
Open	_ _ _ _ _ _ _ _ Guarded 8 7 6 5 4 3 2 1	_____
Backbiting	_ _ _ _ _ _ _ _ Loyal 1 2 3 4 5 6 7 8	_____
Untrustworthy	_ _ _ _ _ _ _ _ Trustworthy 1 2 3 4 5 6 7 8	_____
Considerate	_ _ _ _ _ _ _ _ Inconsiderate 8 7 6 5 4 3 2 1	_____
Nasty	_ _ _ _ _ _ _ _ Nice 1 2 3 4 5 6 7 8	_____
Agreeable	_ _ _ _ _ _ _ _ Disagreeable 8 7 6 5 4 3 2 1	_____
Insincere	_ _ _ _ _ _ _ _ Sincere 1 2 3 4 5 6 7 8	_____
Kind	_ _ _ _ _ _ _ _ Unkind 8 7 6 5 4 3 2 1	_____
	Total	_____

Source: Fred E. Fiedler, Martin M. Chemers with Linda Mahar, *Improving Leadership Effectiveness: The Leader Match Concept,* New York, John Wiley & Sons, Inc., 1976, p. 8. Reprinted by permission of John Wiley & Sons, Inc.

First, there are two different kinds of leadership styles that are measured by the Least Preferred Co-worker (LPC) Scale:

- **Relationship-motivated** (high LPC, score of 64 or above). Leaders tend to be most concerned with maintaining good interpersonal relations, sometimes even to the point of letting the task suffer and work going undone. In peaceful and well-controlled situations, this type of person has a inclination to reverse behavior and become more task aware.

- **Task-motivated** (low LPC, score of 57 or below). Leaders place primary emphasis on accomplishing assigned tasks. These leaders are the no-nonsense people who tend to work best from guidelines and specific directions. In other words going by the book. If guidelines are lacking, this type of leader prioritizes work and develops guidelines. Then the identifiable duties are assigned to subordinates. However, when taking it easy in a controlled situation, task-motivated leaders can turn the other check and become pleasant. Additionally, they pay more attention to the esprit de corps of their employees.

Leaders whose score falls between 58 and 63 will have to determine for themselves which category they most nearly resemble.

Second, there are three kinds of leadership situations:

- **High control** situations allow the leader a great deal of control and influence that allows for a predictable environment in which to direct the work of others.

- **Moderate control** situations present the leader with mixed problems—either good relations with subordinates but an unstructured task and low position power, or the reverse, poor relations with group members but a structured task and high position power.

- **Low control** situations offer the leader relatively low control and influence, that is, where the group does support the leader, and neither the task nor the position power gives the leader much influence. Stress or high group conflict may also contribute to low control.

Third, there are three dimensions determining the situational control of a job. These are:

- Leader-member relation's measures how well the group and the leader get along.

- Task structure measures how clearly the procedures, goals, and evaluation of the job are defined.

- Position power measures how much authority the leader has to hire, fire and discipline.

Fourth, in matching leadership styles to appropriate situations it is found that:

- Relationship-motivated leaders perform best in moderate control situations.

- Task-motivated leaders perform best in either high or low control situations.

Finally, it is possible to change or modify your leadership situation if you find that your leadership style does not match the situation in which you are working. You can engineer your job by adjusting the three dimensions of situational control and making it higher or lower, thereby matching your leadership style. Transfer and rotation, selection and placement, are management tools to improve the performance of your subordinate leaders, thereby increasing organizational effectiveness.[25]

While the studies discussed above present added dimensions to the concept of leadership, there is still a great deal of research to be conducted before a number of ideal leadership styles, appropriate to all situations, will be identified. This is particularly true of police organizations geared to respond to a crisis at any time, while the majority of efforts are being directed toward routine activities and providing community services.[26]

25. *Ibid.*, pp. 213–214.

26. For additional works referring to leadership, see: Don Dinkmeyer and

Path–Goal

Robert House developed a situational theory of leadership called Path–Goal Theory. This model does not provide the "best" way to lead, but is concerned with situations where leader behavior can be most effective.[27] A leader must engage in activities leading to a clarification of paths and allowing subordinates to achieve goals. The goals might be an improved working environment, a promotion or a feeling of accomplishment. It is anticipated, the creation of a situation providing the opportunity to achieve goals will promote job satisfaction.[28] In actual practice the leader enhances the psychological state of subordinates resulting in the desire to perform a task. How this is accomplished varies but includes task clarification, elimination of the barrier precluding the completion of a task and providing opportunities allowing subordinates to obtain personal satisfactions.[29]

The key to Path–Goal leadership theory is that the truly *effective* leader creates a connection between subordinate goals and organizational goals.[30] The style of leader behavior is conditioned by two situational variables characteristics of the subordinates and task structure. Subordinates perceive leadership behavior as acceptable when it is an immediate source of satisfaction or when it will lead to future satisfaction. This theory holds that subordinates respond differently to various types of leadership. For example:

- Supportive leader behavior may serve as an immediate source of satisfaction when subordinates have a need for esteem and affiliation.

- Directive leader behavior is more likely to motivate subordinates who have a need for autonomy, responsibility and self-actualization.

- Subordinates who like to control their own behavior prefer leaders who are supportive.[31]

The leadership behavior to which subordinates respond includes:

- Directive behavior, characterized by activities letting subordinates know what is expected of them. Work is scheduled and standards of performance are established.

Danile Eckstein, *Leadership by Encouragement, Delray Beach, FL, St. Lucie Press, 1996, pp. 1–25,* and Frances Hesselbein, Marshall Goldsmith, and Richard Beckhard, *Editors,* The Leader of the Future: New Visions, Strategies, and Practices for the Next Era, Jossey–Bass, SF, 1996, pp. 280–289.

27. Robert House, "A Path–Goal Theory of Leader Effectiveness," *Administrative Science Quarterly,* 1971, p. 321.

28. Gary Johns, *Organizational Behavior* Dallas, TX, Scott, Foresman and Company, 1983, p. 316.

29. Don Hellriegel and John W. Slocum, Jr., *Organizational Behavior Contingency Views,* St. Paul, West Publishing Co., 1976, p. 310.

30. Johns, *op. cit.*

31. Hellriegel and Slocum, *op. cit.,* p. 311.

- Supportive behavior is that which is friendly and where the needs of subordinates is taken into consideration. The style is employee-centered.[32]

Task structure is a major variable in path-goal leadership. When the task is of a routine type, leadership efforts to clarify path-goal relationships are perceived by subordinates as unnecessary control. This will in all probability result in decreasing job satisfaction. When dealing with a routine task structure a supportive leader is more likely to have satisfied employees than one who is directive. Mundane tasks do little to create a situation where subordinates can derive any degree of internal satisfaction such as esteem or self-actualization. A directive leadership style is more appropriate when tasks are varied or complex. Subordinates can be helped by clarification of paths leading to highly valued goals. Goal achievement as practiced under directive leadership is not perceived as excessive, but a style more likely to lead to job satisfaction.[33]

Tenure

Continuity of administration is an essential condition to the effective expression of the qualities of leadership. It represents a principle not yet invading the American public services to any marked extent. The law enforcement enterprise needs stability in leadership. The tenure of the police executive is, on the average, alarmingly short. A considerable number of chiefs never complete their initial year in office, When one becomes aware of the fact that fewer than half of the chiefs have headed their agency for four years. It is little wonder, many police departments have difficulty in implementing and sustaining positive management programs when turnover is so frequent. The chief of police in American cities is too often appointed on the basis of political considerations. Further, since the American chief of police rises universally from the ranks, prevailing entrance requirements for patrol officer and limited training facilities still serve to limit seriously the area of selection, but this is changing rapidly. Police executive talent in this country is becoming increasingly impressive. The American police department continues as a center of political attack and a shift in the balance of political power in the community or a change in the complexion of the city council often results in replacement of the chief. Some of America's foremost police administrators have passed through this disheartening experience. The police executive is subjected to various pressures from those wielding political influence in the community and from miscellaneous interest groups. These have produced an instability of tenure endangering administrative efficiency by frequently changing the Chief of a police department; there can be no continuity of policy. More important, demoralization usually follows a change in leadership (this is especially true in police organization). Individuals who are friendly to one administration are penalized when

---

32. *Ibid.*   **33.** *Ibid.,* p. 312.

a new administration gains control. Thus there become a number of cliques in the department, functioning for their own welfare and individual interests rather than for those of the department and the community. No executive (however strong) can command the absolute obedience and cooperation of subordinates as long as they know their leader to be a political puppet that will pass out of office at the next election.

The greatest single factor contributing to the short tenure of American police chiefs is the concept that the terms of department heads should be the same as the political chief executive, a heritage of the Jacksonian administration. Under this arrangement, the terms of department heads end with that of the mayor or other appointing authority, and the new head of city government replaces them with new department executives. It is held by those who continue to support this procedure that a newly elected mayor, for example, should have the whole—hearted support of principal subordinates at the outset, and that they should be individuals who are in sympathy with this mayor's outlook and aims.

Insulating the position of police chief with civil service protection might be sound public policy in one jurisdiction, whereas, in another, the results would be disastrous. The question pivots largely on the character of personnel administration in the city concerned. If it is based upon the merit principle, there is some justification for placing the position of chief of police in the competitive classified service. On the other hand, if, as in many jurisdictions, civil service were merely a beautiful theory, no useful end would be served by applying the dead letter to a high administrative position.

The controversy over the Rodney King beating by Los Angeles police officers led to the appointment of an independent commission (Christopher Commission) by the mayor. Charged with the investigation of the Los Angeles Police Department, one of the things considered was the civil service status of the chief of police. Historically, after the selection the chief was protected by civil service constraints, thus there was limited control of the Chief. In Los Angeles the consequence of civil service status for the chief excluded outside competitors. The commission felt however, there was no reason to bar (from the pool of candidates) qualified officers from other jurisdictions. The Commission also pointed out that any organization having the same chief executive for an extended period of time can become stagnate, insensitive, and insular. Additionally, younger leaders would move on because of the lack of opportunity. The conclusion was a balance was needed whereby the Chief could be made accountable to the Police Commission and to the public. At the same time the Chief should be able to defend the department against corrupting pressures.[34]

34. City of Los Angeles, *Report of the Independent Commission on the Los Angeles Police Department*, Los Angeles, CA., City of Los Angeles, 1991, pp. 215–217.

The final recommendations of the Christopher Commission regarding the position of Chief of police addressed the appointment process and included a term limitation:

- The Chief of Police should be charged with direct accountability for managing the operations of the Los Angeles Police Department, setting goals and policies consistent with the directions of the Police Commission.

- The Chief should be protected from improper political influences.

- The position should be exempt, held in open competition, and the Commission should select and submit names to the Mayor for final appointment.

- The Chief should serve a five-year term renewable for an additional term at the discretion of the Commission.

These recommendations were implemented through a Charter amendment, adopted in 1992, and through the process of the non-renewal of the former Chief of Police and the selection of the current Chief for a five-year term renewable at the discretion of the Police Commission for one additional five-year term.[35]

Table 9–1

Governance Structures–Twenty One Largest Cities in U.S. Appointment and Removal of Police Chiefs

	APPOINTMENT[1]					REMOVAL[2]			
	Mayor	City Manager/ Public Safety Director	Police Commission	W/City Council Confirmation	Term (years)	Mayor	City Manager/ Public Safety Director	Police Commission	W/City Council Confirmation
Baltimore, MD	X			yes	6	cause			no
Boston, MA	X			no	5	cause without			no
Chicago, IL	X			yes	no	cause			no
Cincinnati, OH [3]		X		no	no		cause		no
Columbus, OH		X		no	no		cause without		no
Dallas, TX		X		no	1		cause without		no
Detroit, MI	X			no	no	cause without			no
Houston, TX	X			yes	no	cause without			no
Indianapolis, IN		X		no	no	cause			no
Jacksonville, FL	(elected	office)		no	4	(by	voters)		no
Los Angeles, CA			X	no	no		without	cause	no
Memphis, TN	X			yes	no	cause			no
Milwaukee, WI			X	no	7			cause	no

35. Police Commission, *Independent (Christopher) Commission Revised Recommendations for Organizational Change,* Los Angeles, Los Angeles, Police Commission, August 1998, p. 4.

City					Removal		
New York, NY	X		no	5	without cause[4]		no
Philadelphia, PA	X		no	no	without cause		no
Phoenix, AZ		X	no	no	without cause		no
San Antonio, TX		X	no	no	without cause		no
San Diego, CA		X	yes	no	without cause		no
San Francisco, CA			X	no	no	without cause	no
San Jose, CA		X	yes	no	without cause		no
Washington, D.C.	X		yes	no	without cause		no

1 Based on 1990 Census data.

2 The information reflected in this table was received via phone calls to the respective cities and verified against municipal, and in some cases state statutory authority.

3 Cincinnati has both a Safety Director and a City Manager, with each having a role in the appointment and removal process. The Safety Director makes a recommendation to the City Manager for the appointment of a Chief, whose appointment is not subject to City Council confirmation. The Chief reports directly to and is removable for cause only by the Safety Director whose decision is subject to the approval of the City Manager. The Safety Director is selected by the City Manager who in turn is selected by the City Council).

4 Under the New York City Charter, the police commissioner (chief) serves for a term of five years and is removable by the mayor or the governor whenever in the judgment of the mayor or the governor the public interests shall so require. Chap. 18, § 431, New York City Charter.

Table 9–2

Governance Structure—Twenty One Largest Cities In U.S. Appointment, Removal and Powers of Police Commissions

	Appointment Process [1]	Removal Process [2]	Principal Powers
Baltimore, MD	no commission		
Boston, MA	no commission		
Chicago, IL	all appointed by mayor for staggered 5–year terms; city council approval required	by mayor [3]	makes policies/rules; conducts hearings where chief recommends significant disciplinary actions
Cincinnati, OH	no commission		
Columbus, OH	no commission		
Dallas, TX	no commission		
Detroit, MI	all appointed by mayor for staggered 5–year terms; city council approval required	by mayor without cause or council approval	makes policies/rules with mayoral approval; typically investigates minor complaints only, has subpoena power
Houston, TX	no commission		
Indianapolis, IN	4 appointed by mayor and 2 elected by officers; 2–year terms; city council approval not required	by safety dir. without cause or council approval	may overrule significant disciplinary action of chief; separate complaint review process
Jacksonville, FL	no commission		
Los Angeles, CA	all appointed by mayor for staggered 3–year terms; city council approval required	by mayor with city council approval [4]	broad rule-making power, decisions subject to voidance by city council; no significant disciplinary role
Madison, WI	all appointed by mayor for staggered 5–year terms; city council approval required	by mayor [5]	acts as civil service board; conducts disciplinary hearing upon initial citizen complaint or appeal by citizen of departmental decision; no real managerial or administrative responsibilities
Memphis, TN	no commission		
Milwaukee, WI	all appointed by mayor for staggered 5–year terms; city council approval required	by mayor [6]	broad rule-making power, decisions subject to voidance by common council; conducts hearings where chief recommends significant disciplinary action or upon filing of a complaint by a citizen
New York, NY	no commission		
Philadelphia, PA	no commission		
Phoenix, AZ	no commission		
San Antonio, TX	no commission		
San Diego, CA	no commission		
San Francisco, CA	all appointed by mayor for 4–year terms; board of supervisors approval not required [7]	by mayor without cause or board of supervisors approval	sets policy in consultation with chief; oversight of citizen complaint review body; conducts hearings where chief recommends significant disciplinary action or upon appeal
San Jose, CA	no commission		
Washington, D.C.	no commission		

1 Based on 1990 Census data. This table also includes Madison, Wisconsin.

2 The information reflected in this table was received via phone calls to the respective cities and verified against municipal, and in some cases state statutory authority.

3 The Chicago Municipal Code states that members of the Police Board are removable by the mayor "as provided by Law." (Chicago Municipal Code § 2–84–620). The city's legal affairs office was unable to provide Commission staff with statutory provisions setting forth a

removal process for Police Board members, indicating that the mayor's power to remove has not recently been challenged. The legal affairs office's unofficial view on this question, pending the results of research that had not been completed by the drafting of this report, was that the mayor may remove members of the Police Board without cause and without approval by the City Council.

4 Sections 73 and 73.1 of the Los Angeles City Charter on removal of commissioners do not specify whether removal may only be had for cause.

5 Section 62.13 of Wisconsin Statutes authorizing police and fire commissions for cities in Madison's class does not provide for removal of commissioners. Legal counsel to the Madison Police and Fire Commission stated that the removal process has never been addressed. He further offered his view that the ambiguities created by the absence of statutory provision for removal may likely only be resolved by litigation.

6 Section 62.50 of Wisconsin Statutes authorizing the fire and police commission does not provide for removal of commissioners. The Executive Director of the Milwaukee Fire and Police Commission offered his view that in the absence of such provision and as this question has not been addressed, the general assumption is that the mayor may remove for cause only, with the approval of the Common Council required.

7 The functional equivalent to a city council for the City and County of San Francisco is the San Francisco Board of Supervisors.

Source. City of Los Angeles, *Report of the Independent Commission on the Los Angeles Police Department*, Los Angeles, CA, City of Los Angeles, 1991.

Tables 9–1 and 9–2 set forth the structure in twenty-one large cities for the appointment and removal of a chief. In nine cities the mayor appoints the chief and in eight the city manager or public safety director make the appointment. The person who can remove a chief varies considerably. In ten cities it is the mayor. However in the case of Jacksonville, FL, the chief holds an elected office. In five cities the city manager or director of public safety does not have to show cause to remove the chief. In six cities the chief serves a specified term ranging from one year to seven.

The protection of tenure is one thing; the protection of incompetence in office is another. Unless the character of personnel administration is such that it will bring people into office with a high grade of administrative ability, a spoils system may be preferred. Before giving the position of police chief executive protected status, the officials of the city should retain the services of an unbiased personnel expert from the outside to inventory local personnel methods and measure their worth against the standards of modern public personnel administration. Failure to take this precaution is almost certain to invite disaster. Assuming the presence of a sound personnel system, the fact still remains that expert opinion in the police field is not unanimously in favor of protected status for the position of chief. It has been demonstrated that continuity of administration and high quality administration can be achieved without legally permanent tenure. During his thirty-two years as chief of police in Berkeley, California, August Vollmer was able to develop a sound system of police administration without tenure protection for himself or for his officers.

Salary

Compensation plans for police chief executives must be implemented to attract and retain persons who have the type of leadership and administrative abilities urgently needed in law enforcement. Every American has the right to expect and receive efficient, equitable, courteous, and lawful police service. That right is as deeply rooted in the most remote, sparsely populated corners of the nation as it is in its most populated cities. Whatever the size of the agency or of the population it serves, its constituent should be assured the security and protection of proper police service. Indeed, all police agencies do not provide the same level or quality of police service. Management authorities agree, the quality of a police agency is predicated upon the quality of its leadership. It should be an imperative in each State to assure all police service within that State meets or exceeds established quality standards. Police chief executives and superiors agree, the place to start is with the top management positions, particularly the police chief executive positions.

Good leadership is the most important and least expensive administrative factor in a police agency. In a major agency, an incompetent police chief executive can create millions of dollars of unnecessary expenses with one bad decision. On the other hand, just one efficient policy can save millions of dollars. In many jurisdictions, for example, enormous annual savings have accrued from civilianizing such tasks as traffic direction, clerical work, and custodial positions. Substantial savings caused by good leadership can also be realized by small police agencies. The process of conceptualizing and implementing cost-effective procedures is similar in large and small agencies. In every size agency, the additional compensation necessary to provide effective leadership, is miniscule in comparison with the probable return on the investment.

Comparable Compensation. Many governing bodies have agreed, the salaries of police officers, including the chief executives, will be equal to police salaries in other specified jurisdictions (such as within a particular geographic boundary, usually within the State). Such compensation agreements might be equitable if all the police agencies were within the same economic environment, and had identical duties and needs. Agencies within a given geographic boundary are not identical, however. As the agencies vary, so do the demands of the police chief executive position. The compensation for a police chief executive should be based on the demands of the particular position. Individual agency needs are ignored when this system is used to determine salaries. The flaw in this system becomes more pronounced as more jurisdictions adopt the same agreement. Even when only one or two agencies use it within a geographic area, it tends to involve the government and police personnel of one jurisdiction in the fiscal affairs of other jurisdictions. As wage issues are decided in the one, they are mandated in the others.

Compensation Relative to Other Department Heads. Another commonly used compensation formula maintains the police chief executive's salary at a fixed position in relation to other jurisdictional department heads such as the general managers of public works departments, departments of sanitation, departments of water and power, and fire departments. No argument is offered here to realign the juxtapositions of those department heads. The compensation of none should be predicated upon that of the others. The compensation of each should be predicated upon the specific demands of the positions.

Compensation Based on Evaluation of the Position. Compensation ranges for police chief executives should be based on the requirements of the positions rather than on the persons who occupy or might occupy the positions. Therefore, each position needs to be clearly defined and thoroughly understood. Such knowledge can best be acquired by dissecting the position and carefully analyzing each of its components. A value, determined by analysis, needs to be placed upon each position component. A primary factor in establishing compensation rates is then the total of the values of the position's components. Objective persons must perform this position analysis and value determination with professional expertise in the field of job evaluation. The evaluators must have the ability to weigh each of the many requirements of a chief's position against a valid base.

Executive Contract

Issuance of an executive contract to a law enforcement executive is of very recent origin. It is something that has been done in private enterprise for a number of years and has proven successful. In the public arena, city managers and chief administrative officers were the first ones to work under an individualized contract. Traditionally solely the appointing authority has determined the tenure of chiefs of police. A contract modifies this and disallows the age-old concept of "serving at the pleasure" of the appointing authority.

One useful purpose of a contract is to clarify the relationship between the employee and the employer. It also can define the employee's authority. On the other hand a contract can structure accountability and usually sets forth-specific responsibilities. Normally a contract specifies the length of appointment, and a variety of other features are set forth in Figure 9–6. A key feature in any contract is the spelling out of how conflict will be resolved as well as a commitment to due process prior to termination. It also should include a clear acknowledgment of the administrative appeal procedures. The contract can be beneficial not only to a chief but to the city or county appointing authority because the nature of the working relationship can be spelled out. Thus, misunderstandings and misperceptions can be dealt with at the time of appointment rather than later. The specifics of each contract will vary from agency to agency unless the jurisdiction has contracting experience. Local considerations can modify contract content such as civil service regulations and wage and benefit packages in the region or state.[36]

36. Sheldon F. Greenberg, *On the Dotted Line: Police Executive Contracts,* Washington, D.C., Police Executive Research Forum, 1992, pp. 7–10 and 88–89.

Figure 9–7

Typical Features Included in a Police Executive Contract

- Duties.
- Length of appointment.
- Termination.
- Salary.
- Standard benefits.
- Retirement.
- Moving expenses.
- Residency.
- Automobile.
- Professional development.
- Performance evaluation.
- Indemnification.
- Death benefits to family.
- General provisions.

Source: Sheldon F. Greenberg, *On the Dotted Line: Police Executive Contracts,* Washington, D.C., Police Executive Research Forum, 1992, pp. E–1 to E–5. Reprinted with permission of the Police Executive Research Forum, December 12, 1998.

Method of Selection

Municipal authorities may well ponder the relative yields on the investment to be gained by attaching to the position of chief police administrator a salary sufficient to attract the best person available. In a scheme of social accounting there must eventually be a scientific determination of the relative importance of the various municipal activities if there is to be an intelligent distribution of budgets and creation of an adequate salary structure it must be predicated on a serious consideration of many factors. It seems clear that the role of police administration as an agency of social control is being increasingly revealed in the light of its true importance and this branch of the public service will be accorded fiscal recognition on a rational basis.

The cornerstone of public personnel administration, or any personnel program for that matter, is the process of selection. It is precisely at this point that the course of events is determined (for years to come) concerning the caliber, quality, and effectiveness of police service. As will be noted, new trends are observable in the development of a screening process through which the necessary talent and capability can be brought to bear to fill the top command post. The appointing authority in municipal government is the Mayor, the Mayor and the Police Commission or in the City Manager form of local government, the City Manager. In some jurisdictions under the Mayor–Council plan, the appointment of the Chief of Police requires the confirmation of the City Council. This is unwise, since it opens the way for Council interference and the exercise of political influence in the affairs of police administration. One of the major attributes of the City Manager system is that it gives (to this professional administrator) exclusive power to appoint the department heads, including the Chief of Police.

The method employed in selecting a new Chief of Police is usually provided for in the City Charter. Conventional procedure (until recent years) has been to base the selection on rank, performance record and personal standing among the members of the department. Appointments have been made generally from the rank at the next level below the Chief of Police, usually from the rank of Captain in the average department. This method, essentially empirical in nature, is unsound since it amounts to little more than "sizing up the individual" on the basis of experience and observation. It has little predictive value in terms of later performance on the job. Performance is obviously important; the rank of Captain would indicate under a merit system that the individual had qualified for promotion on one or more occasions. To be held in high esteem generally by members of the department, would give the picture of an affable, socially adjusted person who gets along well with people. None of these, however, establish the presence of executive and administrative ability for the job of top management, and appointments made on this basis court mediocrity and failure at a vulnerable point in organization where nothing should be left to chance. The rank of an officer may have pivoted on considerations altogether foreign to the requirements of this high position. Performance records can (on occasion) be misleading; moreover, there is no assurance that a good criminal investigator is blessed with any great amount of executive capability. Getting along well with people is an acceptable personal attribute, but a popularity contest is hardly the arena in which to make such a critical appointment. The American police services must turn to modern personnel administration for a more valid method of selecting the Police Chief Executive. All the evidence points convincingly to a competitive selection procedure meriting, as far as possible, the stamp of scientific sanction.

Examination Procedure

It is standard practice in the American police field to fill the positions through the use of the competitive examination. The opinion is unanimous that it functions with a high degree of success .. It is a process wherein candidates can be selected for promotion to supervisory and command positions. That being true, it is equally applicable to the position of Chief of Police. The competitive examination for the selection of the Police Chief offers the following advantages:

- It is a democratic method.
- It is based upon the merit principal.
- It rewards merit.
- It fosters morale.
- It opens up the channels of promotion on a strictly competitive basis to the highest position in the organization.
- It fosters the elimination of politics, favoritism and prejudice in the selection process.

- It is an honest and valid attempt to select the best man available for one of the most important posts in the field of public management.

A competitive examination for the position of Chief of Police may be restricted to departmental personnel or opened to candidates on a state or national basis, with no residence requirement. A search for candidates on a nation-wide basis is recommended and the trend is in that direction. In preparation for an open competitive examination for this position, it is necessary to prepare and distribute a printed announcement, for national distribution. Appropriate application forms accompany the announcement. The next step is to audit applications and eliminating those candidates who obviously do not possess the necessary qualifications. In many instances applications can be rejected on their face because they do not meet the standards set forth in the announcement. Cover letter and resumes should be gone over item by item.[37] The next step is to administer some type of test. The proficiency tests include those designed to measure administrative judgment. They evaluate the candidate's ability to get the right answers to questions involving hypothetical supervisory situations. Work fluency and verbal manipulation ability characterize most leaders and these qualities, among others, are measured in the aptitude test. Another type of test is a general written test that involves formulating solutions to an extended series of problem-solving situations at the level of top management. The caliber of this test should be such that it proves to be an exacting experience for the candidate. The oral interview is a typical component of the selection process and Can be either a non-stress or stress. It is generally followed by a medical examination, and a comprehensive a background investigation.

The final element of the process occurs when the Examining Board receives the names of the three candidates (or more) making the highest combined score based on the following weight system (or another weighted system). The following weights may be assigned to the foregoing phases of the examination:

a. Aptitude—20.

b. Proficiency—20.

c. General Written Examination—30.

d. Oral Interview—20.

e. Medical Report—5.

f. Background Investigation—5.

The examining board usually consists of five persons, three in the department and two from outside the Department (the number varies from agency to agency), most of whom exercise supervisory or com-

37. Harvey Rachlin, "Cover Letters and Resumes: *Law and Order*", March 1995, Vol. 43, No. 3, pp. 31–33.

mand responsibility. In recent years a member of the community has served on boards. In addition, the services of an experienced psychologist should be retained for the oral interview.

The Assessment Center

A selection technique gaining increasing popularity is the Assessment Center. This procedure was developed by the armed forces of Great Britain and the United States during World War II. It is used extensively in private enterprise and in more recent years it has found widespread acceptance in the public sector.[38] The assessment process differs from traditional examinations and the International Congress on the Assessment Center Method has established a number of criterions that includes[39]:

- The technique is situational based and the process is custom-designed. Job analysis and terminal performance objectives are fundamental to the preparation of exercises.

- The process is more time consuming than the normal civil service examination.

- The training of multiple assessors.

- This type of testing is multi-phasic inasmuch as a variety of methods and instruments are utilized to measure job-related skills, knowledge and abilities.

- The process encourages self-discovery because every candidate is provided with feedback on actual performance.

- There is an enhancement of reliability and validity in identifying and measuring human traits.[40]

The components of an Assessment Center vary, but typically it consists of a series of exercises in which final applicants participate.[41] A number of assessors rank each candidate's performance on the basis of previously identified traits. Assessment centers have been found to comply with affirmative action requirements and are less discriminating than other selection procedures. If there is a draw back, it is that the process is time consuming and rather expensive. It also is somewhat sophisticated and assessment evaluators have to be adequately trained.[42] Hence the hiring authority must take these factors into

38. Deborah A. Kent, Charles R. Wall and Raymond L. Bailey, "Assessment Centers: A New Approach to Police Personnel Decisions," *The Police Chief*, June 1974, Vol. XLI, No. 6, p. 73.

39. Harvey Rachlin, "Assessment Centers, *Law and Order*", March 1995, Vol. 43, No. 3., pp. 29–31.

40. Don Driggs and Paul M. Whisenand, "Assessment Centers: Situational Evaluation," *California Law Enforcement, April 1976, Vol. 10, No. 4, pp. 132–133.

41. Kenneth Garner, "assessment Center Testing–A Survivors Guide to Coming Out on Top and Living to Tell About It," *Law and Order*, November 1998, Vol. 42, No. 11, pp. 77–82.

42. Jeff Bernstein, "Preparing for Promotion," *Law and Order*, February 1998, Vol. 46, No. 2, pp. 67–68.

consideration when determining whether to use it or not.[43]

Figure 9–8

In–Basket Exercise

Specific Instructions

Write down what you decide to do with each item in the in-basket. Draft form is acceptable, however, it must be *legible*. Write whatever instructions you want to leave or any memos or letters you want sent. If you plan to call any meetings, outline a plan for the meeting. Use extra sheets of paper if needed. Write your name at the top of any extra pieces. As you work on the items, briefly indicate the action taken and the reason on the enclosed *in-basket summary form.*

Organization charts, calendars, duty schedules and extra paper are provided for your use. The materials are *not* always in the proper Department format. Deal only with the content, and ignore the form it is presented on.

Please do not write on any of the documents in the IN–BASKET envelope provided you. Use the sheet of paper and identify each, with your name, followed by the subject, *i.e.,* JONES—Vacation Schedule Project. Then, place this sheet(s) immediately behind the original In-Basket item, as you proceed. Keep control of all the documents, as they will be reviewed later. Thank you. You are in competition with others and you are also being assessed for your personal development, so please proceed on that basis. Your entire efforts for the day will be accumulated and ranked by the assessors. You will receive cumulative feedback on your performance and your areas of strengths and weaknesses.

On completion of the exercises the center's staff ranks each candidate and presents a detailed evaluation of strengths and weaknesses.[44]

Situation

You have just been appointed acting lieutenant on the day shift. You have been out of town on vacation for the last 4½ days and were notified of your appointment by telephone by the Chief Tuesday evening. Your predecessor resigned suddenly to take another job, and you were asked to report back as soon as possible.

It is now 1540 hours, May 2nd. You will not be in your office next week since you have been scheduled for some time to attend a middle

---

43. Harry W. More, W. Fred Wegener, and Larry S. Miller, *Effective Police Supervision,* Third Edition, Cincinnati, OH, Anderson Publishing Co., 1998, p. 394.

44. Michael J. Kelly, *Police Chief Selection, A Handbook for Local Govern-* *ment,* Washington, Police Foundation, 1975, pp. 43–44. For a discussion of Assessment Centers see: Harry W. More and Peter C. Unsinger, The Police Assessment Center, Springfield, IL, Charles C. Thomas, 1989, pp. 1–15.

manager's training school beginning tomorrow morning and continuing through May 7. In fact, the Chief mentioned in the phone call that he expected you to attend this training.

The Captain has been tied up all day, but has indicated he will be able to get together with you for about 15 minutes to discuss your decisions on the materials in your in-basket. These materials have been accumulating and you must decide what to do with them.

The exercises in the Center for the International Association of Chiefs of Police consists of the following:

1. *In-basket exercise.* The candidates deal with a series of complaints, appointments, crises, political problems, internal discipline cases and other similar situations, all of which are contained in telephone messages, or letter. The candidate is evaluated based on the priorities established, authority delegated and the nature of the appointments. Each of the candidates is questioned as to the reasons for each in-basket decision.

2. *Creative planning exercise.* An essay presents the general challenges facing the department and each candidate. Resolution and oral presentation are evaluated by each assessor.

3. *City Council leaderless group discussion.* Each candidate represents a city department in a group discussion concerning how to allocate revenue-sharing funds. Candidates are assessed on the basis of their representation of departmental interests, impact on the group's decisions, and how each candidate dealt with fellow "council members."

4. *Management cases leadership group discussion.* Candidates conduct themselves as executive board members who must reach decisions on police problems such as labor-management conflict, women in policing or internal investigations. The group discussion is evaluated by assessors.

Figure 9–9

Assessor's Rating Sheet for Group Discussion

CANDIDATE _____

Using the scale of 1–9, please rate each worker characteristic by placing the appropriate number in the space to the right of the characteristic. It is important that the full range of the rating scale be used.

WORKER CHARACTERISTICS TO BE RATED FOR   Rank 1–9
GROUP DISCUSSION

1. **Oral Communication**—ability to communicate orally in a clear and concise manner

2. **Sensitivity**—the ability to perceive the point of view and sensitivities of others and respond with understanding to promote cooperation and amicable relations.

3. **Adaptability/flexibility**—ability to maintain an open mind or receive and consider new ideas and ways of doing things. Is open minded and able to separate personal feelings from issues at hand.

4. **Leadership**—skill in getting ideas accepted and leading a group to accomplish an objective; to inspire confidence and stimulate others to optimum performance. Able to control and influence individuals so as to focus on a particular issue or arrive at a solution to a problem.

5. **Initiative/independence/tenacity**—tendency to take action based on own convictions rather than through a desire to please others; tendency to initiate actions and influence events and go beyond what is normally called for; tendency to stay with a problem or line of thought until the matter is settled.[45]

6. **Analytical Ability**—effectiveness in seeking out pertinent data and determining the source of a problem by taking all relevant considerations into account. Able to identify problem and its causes.

7. **Organizing and Planning**—effective organization of presentation.

8. **Decisiveness**—ability to identify and choose appropriate solutions from a variety of alternate choices.

Leadership is the critical catalyst in this nation's police departments. At this point even the challenges of the future are unknown or received limited clarification, hence the leaders in the years ahead cannot rest on their laurels or rely upon the successes of the past. Future police leaders must deal with hazards, perils, and ambiguity. The path to be taken is not clear. Our nation is undergoing unprecedented rapid change, and it will take inspired leadership of the police enterprise if police departments are to provide the safety and security needed in our communities.[46]

Case Study

Sergeant Robert Rolland

Robert Rolland is the president of the Fraternal Order of Police for the City of Rockford and he has been chosen by the city manager to serve on a selection board that will be responsible for drafting the criteria for the position of chief of police. The FOP represents and negotiates wages and benefits for sworn officers and sergeants. The city intends to conduct a nation-wide search as a means of finding the best possible candidate. It is the first time that the city has opened up the selection process to outsiders. The city has a population of 92,300 and is racially and culturally diverse. It has diverse recreational facilities and an outstanding school system. The Chief will be appointed by and report to the city manager under a council/manager form of government.

45. Laurie L. Bergner, "Developing Leaders at the Beginning," *The Police Chief,* November 1998, Vol. LXV, No. 10, pp. 13–18.

46. Mark H. Moore and Darrel W. Stephens, *Beyond Command and Control: The Strategic Management of Police Departments,* Washington, D.C., Police Executive Research Forum, 1991, pp. 105–115.

Currently the salary for the chief's position is $92,382 annually.

The department has 171 commissioned officers and 103 civilian personnel. The annual budget is approximately $16 million, and the city has just contracted for a state-of the-art communications system. The department has three major bureaus: field operations, investigations, and administrative. The city manager has recommended that the new chief should have the capacity to implement a community-policing program. Additionally, the city manager wants the department to pursuing national accreditation from the Commission on Accreditation for Law Enforcement Agencies (CALEA).

If you were Sergeant Rolland what position would you take regarding such things as: level of education, administrative experience, knowledge of community policing, and experience with CALEA. Why? What interpersonal skills would you want the new chief to have? Why? What other expertise should each candidate have in order to insure that the best-qualified individual becomes the new chief?

For Further Reading

Bart Barthelemy, *The Sky is not the Limit—Breakthrough Leadership,* Boca Raton, FL, St. Lucie Press, 1997, pp. 1–201.

> Presents the process of breakthrough leadership that occurs when someone or some team really gets captivated with a vision or challenge. It requires as leader to become focused and open to innovation, creativity, and change. Suggests that if failures or disappointments occur they are overcome by personal and team commitment. What is important is determination and persistence. Suggests the need to keep spirits high and the fact that excitement should characterize the leadership process.

Philip B. Crosby, *The Absolutes of Leadership,* San Diego, CA, Pfeiffer & Company, 1996, 1–74.

> The author postulates that true leaders have absorbed and understand the absolutes of leadership. These include: a clear agenda, a personal philosophy, enduring relationships, and worldliness. He also suggests that leaders come in five versions. Their titles are destructor, procrastinator, caretaker, preparer, and accomplisher. The five types of leaders are identified by their personalities and their work patterns. Needless to say the accomplisher exemplifies the absolutes of leadership.

Don Dinkmeyer and Danile Eckstein, *Leadership by Encouragement,* Delray Beach, FL, St. Lucie Press, 1996, pp. 1–82.

> Supports the concept of focusing on the individual's assets as a means of building one's self-esteem, self-confidence, and feeling of worthiness. It is a process of removing self-imposed roadblocks and

viewing life in a positive manner. Recommends being energy directed, flexible, responsible, and significantly different by focussing on an encouraging philosophy of life.

James M. Kouzes, and Barry Z. Posner, *The Leadership Challenge: How to Keep Getting Extraordinary Things Done in Organizations,* San Francisco, CA, Jossey–Bass Inc., Publishers, 1995, pp. 1–35.

The authors identify five fundamental practices of exemplary leadership. It is a process wherein leaders get extraordinary things done. The best leaders are those who are able to challenge the process, inspire a shared vision, enable others to act, model the way, and encourage the heart. Leaders are viewed as pioneers who are will to step out and challenge the unknown. Suggests it is important for leaders to show employees that they can win. Points out that traditional management prevents people from becoming leaders. It is necessary to challenge the process and work for change.

Chapter 10

GROUPS: Dynamics of Team Behavior

Learning Objectives

1. Analyze the importance of groups to law enforcement.

2. Discuss group dynamics.

3. Identify how group and individual interests can prove to be a viable relationship.

4. Distinguish between formal and informal groups.

5. List the various types of cliques.

6. Describe the stages of group development.

7. Discuss why affiliation is important to the group phenomenon.

8. Why is power important to the group process.

9. What makes one's self-concept important to a group.

10. What part does economic needs play in the group process.

11. List the types of groups.

12. Discuss the characteristics of a fully functioning team.

13. Identify the key elements when managing a group.

14. Assess the role of groupthink when managing a group.

As we move into the next century groups will become increasingly important in law enforcement agencies. Groups/teams will serve as a vehicle for delivering police services, and participate more actively in organizational matters. Within our society and organizations individuals have banded together for reasons that vary from person to person. Officers belong to various groups that are strictly social and to others that are professional. An individual can belong to numerous groups including the church, the family, school, clubs, service organizations or the military. Some individuals become a member of a group by virtue of birth such as the family while membership in other groups is imposed such as military service or jury duty.[1] In addition, an officer can belong to an informal group like gathering with other officers in a bar after hours or a highly organized group such as a police association or union.

1. Harry W. More and W. Fred Wegener, *Behavioral Police Management,* Macmillan, New York, 1992, p. 222.

Every group provides a means for social interaction, which is very important to the development of each of us. This is especially true of special police groups such as tactical teams, and task forces. Typical of a task force is the Auto Theft Task Force (ATTF) consisting of seven officers created in Atlanta, GA. Created in 1996 in its first year of operation it made 2,5000 arrests.[2] A close examination will show that just about everything one does is done within the sphere or influence of a group, and such forces have proven to be very strong and lasting. Ones attitudes, values, and behaviors evolve through a lifetime as a result of interchange with others in varying situations.[3]

Man is a social animal and groups serve a predominate role in the growth of individuals. Some experts view groups as the basic unit of social organization that perform a number of singular and discrete functions. Groups provide their members with a human infrastructure. Officers react to how roll call is conducted, who in the organization is informed of changes, and how they are informed.[4] Additionally, groups concern themselves with a wide range of things including issues of working conditions and policy changes that impact operational procedures. Another significant feature of groups is their impact on organizational rumors. Groups are a meaningful component of the informal organization that occurs in agencies. This is especially true of police departments who actively engage in community policing and problem solving. If teams are empowered and become involved in the decision making process it alters the working relationships within the organization. It must be kept in mind that it is next to impossible to impose a team approach on a traditional bureaucratic organization. Success dictates the need to change the culture of the agency. Such a paradigm shift requires changes in key areas such as selection, training, rewards, and performance evaluation.[5] During the last few decades groups/teams, in police agencies, have evolved from being a discouraged entity to an increasingly important part of organizational reality.

Group Dynamics

Organizational effectiveness demands that police managers become knowledgeable about the nature of groups. Their significance cannot be discounted and as an integral part of the organization they must be of concern to managers at every level in the organization. Groups vary considerably in term of their magnitude, influence, and function. Some are unidimensional, and others perform a variety of significant activi-

2. Calvin W. Moss, "An Auto Theft Task Force," *Law and Order*, September 1998, Vol. 46, No. 9, pp. 107–109.

3. Herbert J. Chruden, and Arthur W. Sherman, Jr., *Personnel Management*, Chicago, South–Western, 1976, pp. 8–21.

4. Darrel Ray and Howard Bronstein, *Teaming Up: Making the Transi-tion to a Self–Directed, Team–Based Organization,* New York, McGraw–Hill, 1995, p.80.

5. Richard S. Wellins, William C. Byham, and George R. Dixon, *Inside Teams: How 20 World Class Organizations Winning Through Teamwork,* San Francisco, 1994, pp. 320–323.

ties. Groups can focus on the need to redefine and adjust the responsibilities and work relationship within the organization.[6] Some groups carry out a number of functions simultaneously in a highly effective manner. Groups take on their own personality. Some carry on activities with a great deal of enthusiasm; others are the essence of delay and procrastination and still some are a mixture of both extremes. Groups also vary in size, composition, and complexity, all of which modify the interaction between members and interpersonal transactions. Some groups have considerable influence on members and others are close to being insignificant. The importance and significance of groups cannot be underestimated if a manager is to function effectively.

It is generally accepted that a group can be defined as consisting of two or more people who interact with and influence each other for a common purpose. The critical elements of this definition are 1) interaction and 2) influence. When members of a group interact its attributes can vary considerably. It can be a close interrelationship between two officers that can best be described as close, personal and intimate or it can be distant and infrequent. What is important is whether the interaction is meaning or not. Influence is the second component of the definition and can range from minimal to extensive. The extent and nature of the influence can depend upon such variables as position power, rank, experience, reputation or expertise. As a result of the nature of police work most officers respond to the previously mentioned factors. Rank and position power is of importance because of the fundamental bureaucratic nature of many police[7] organization. Additionally, the socialization process gives a great deal of prominence to reputation and expertise. In some instance experience can be most meaningful but not if it is one year's experience replicated numerous times. Between the two variables the group becomes a viable entity and experience shows that individuals seldom exhibit behavior that is not influenced by one or more groups. It should also be kept in mind that in many instances success is clearly dependent upon one's ability to get along within the group. Loners seldom achieve a position of power or influence within an organization, and if it is done it is usually for a short period of time.

Working in a Group

Collective behavior occurs within the context of the day-to-day work environment for a police officer. Traditionally officers worked alone except in dangerous areas. However, this is not the case today as more departments operated with teams, quality circles, task forces, and increasingly expand into community policing. Without question a department is a social organization and officers can be accepted or

6. Thomas A. Kayser, *Mining Group Gold: How to Cash in on the Collaborative Brain Power of a Group*, El Segundo, CA, Serif Publishing, 1995, p.1.

7. Tony L. Jones, "Autocratic vs. People Minded Supervisors," *Law and Order*, May 1997, Vol. 46, No. 5, pp. 32–36.

rejected by organizational groups. Groups that are healthy satisfy an officers need for affiliation, affection, recognition and self-esteem.

They have the capacity of promoting altruism, loyalty, and a genuine sense of belonging. Feeling that one belongs to an organization can be especially important to an individual because it provides for a sense of stability. Cooperative interaction is a by-product of the group process and provides a framework for achieving departmental goals. Some who take an extreme position propose that groups should decide everything, but this is an untenable position. There are numerous situations in law enforcement where one in a command position, such as a raid or a rapidly moving critical incident, should make the decision not a group. Clearly numerous situations occur where group decision making could be detrimental to the successful completion of a critical task.

Groups and individual interest, within an organization, do not have to be diametrically opposed. They can be supportive of each other and contribute to the common good for individuals and the organization. The viability of this relationship is event form the fact that:

- Groups, formal and informal, exist in organizations. It has been confirmed that the group decision-making process has produced substantive changes in the behavior of individuals exceeding that that has occurred when efforts have been made to modify isolated individual behavior.

- Groups are both inescapable and universal because human beings have an axiomatic need to interact with others. Supportive interpersonal relationships enhance communications between individuals and create the opportunity for the formation of groups acknowledging and rewarding participants.

Synergism occurs as a result of several individuals working together. It produces greater results because of the cumulative effect than the efforts of a single person. Members can affect the behavior of others and the way they feel about themselves. Group membership can be something that is coveted. Once attained it can be a rewarding and positive experience. On the other hand exclusion from a group can have negative results for the rejected individual.

Groups are eclectic and as such can make decisions that can result in differing consequences ranging from desirable to destructive. As multifaceted as they are it must be kept in mind that groups respond to situations and their effectiveness varies in direct response to the reality of the situation. Groups should never be classified as organizational entities that are solely worthy or evil.

There is a basic presumption that the desirable outcome of group interaction can be deliberately enhanced. Managers, who are knowledgeable, about the group process, can support groups in such a way that they will be more effective and productive.[8] As groups/teams become more prevalent in law enforcement police executives will have to learn how to work through and with groups. They will not go away and they are a vital and integral part of a viable organization. Groups' have a profound influence on people and are a powerful organizational force. An aware manager can excel in the attainment of objectives by working through others. This type of interaction can lay a foundation that allows for the attainment of positive results.[9] In this necessary circumstance each individual and the group are viewed as positive elements of the organization and commitment can be realized that allows for positive input by all involved. Work groups shape attitudes, and modify opinions creating a commitment to the team. Group members develop skills within a team that allow them to be more productive, and the shared values of the group develop standards for measuring performance. Management can articulate standards for the group but the interactive process between members is the medium that makes them a practicable part of the working group. The socialization process serves as a unifying media shaping and reinforcing values, norms and moral orientation. The accentuation on the group rather than the individual refines the convictions of its members and reinforces conformity to group standards. Not all friction is bad and it is to be expected. When controlled it can aid in the refinement of procedures and techniques. It serves as a catalyst for questioning the status quo, dictates the need for clarifying issues, and determining better ways of doing things. The tension created by a diversity of opinions, in the long run, allows the manager to remove roadblocks that restrain officer achievement and improvement. The concept of adaptive management, discussed earlier, accepts conflict as inevitable and a normal consequence of the collective pursuit of organizational objectives.

The Attributes of Groups

Normally an organizational decision creates a working entity consisting of two or more individuals and charges such a team with the achieving aspects of departmental goals or objectives that are compatible with the mission of the organization. The creation of a formal work group expresses an agency's desire to respond to community needs and once this decision the new group usually becomes a part of the formal organization. This decision is generally reflected in the group becoming a formal entity in the structure of the organization. As a permanent work group it attains status and power depending upon its location on the organizational chart. Work groups are normally permanent or temporary, depending upon organizational needs. Over the years departments have created permanent groups such as tactical units, bomb

8. Dorwin Cartwright and Ronald Lippit, "Group Dynamics and the Individual," in Robert A. Sutermeister, Editor, *People and Productivity*, New York McGraw–Hill, 1976, pp. 215–217.

9. Richard S. Wellins, William C. Byham, and Jeanne M. Wilson, Empowering Teams: Creating Self-directed Workgroups That Improve Quality, Productivity, and Participation, San Francisco, Jossey–Bass, 1991, pp. 132–167.

squads, and narcotics taskforces. Even more recently we have seen the creation of asset forfeiture units and community policing divisions. On a temporary basis groups have been created to revise police pursuit policies, perform periodical roadblocks, and develop mission and value statements. In one department a temporary taskforce reviewed the requirement for officers to wear hats when in uniform. Another temporary group reviewed grooming policies.

It is increasingly common to see the generation of taskforces that are cooperative in nature and involve agencies from different levels of government. This is especially true in the area of narcotics and serial murder investigations. Recently a regional narcotics unit was created, with federal funding, in the Southwest. The Chief of Police of Tucson, AZ resigned to head this new cooperative organizational entity. In some instance a temporary task force becomes permanent and in other cases it is dissolved after a specified period or the accomplishment of a task and personnel return to other duties.

Formal groups have specified leaders. It is normal for each individual to have attained the position by being appointed through a civil service personnel process. Such an appointment carries the rank, position power, and vestiges of the position to perform circumscribed duties through the efforts of others. In most groups there are leaders other than those formally designed. Informal leaders may assume leadership when they have the needed expertise and skills to accomplish a task and as a consequence exert influence over other members of the group. In fact different members of the team may assuming the leadership position as the situation demands.

Formal groups are easy to identify in an organization. They have a prominent position on the table of organization. This is not true of informal groups. Informal groups are not formally recognized and function as a shadow organization. Their nonconformity to the organization is clearly illustrated by the fact that they can cut across the structural relationship of the traditional bureaucracy. For the most part rank and position power are viewed as not important. What counts is a common interest. Members are not assigned to these groups. Membership is voluntary and dependent on the mutual attraction the individual and the group have for each other. Informal groups create intricate patterns of influence over the formal organization depicted by the structural relationship found on a formal table of organization. Typical of such an informal group would be a number of individuals who join the group because of a common interest. For example, officers became active in a group that participated in sky diving because they found it to be very enjoyable. A number of other officers served as umpires and coaches for a little league. Their department sanctioned neither of these groups.

Based on personal preference informal groups come into existence naturally and as a part of the organizational socialization process. As officers search for a means of fulfilling their needs they establish a number of personal relationships within the organization. Informal groups help to satisfy needs for companionship, security, and self–esteem. These groups are not created by the formal organization but they can be exceptionally influential in the organization.[10] In most instances the formal organization is not in a position to meet the varying needs of individuals. Organizations exist that deny or thwart the needs of organizational members, and the informal organization step in and fulfills the demand for psychosocial needs such as camaraderie, and security.[11]

Some informal groups work to actually support organizational efforts, others function neutrally, and some are antagonistic in nature. Officers become members of informal groups for numerous reasons such as improved working conditions to include salaries, fringe benefits, differential shift pay or a better retirement system. In other instances, officers have gathering together to obtain improved equipment, or to oppose civilian review boards. Historically, a number of police unions have evolved from informal groups that emphasized social functions.

Informal groups provide a frame of reference for individuals to meet their social needs by interacting with others. Friendship and interchange between individuals can lead to a cultural ambience wherein officers feel that they belong. This type of culture can support the attainment of tasks, decrease absenteeism and heighten job satisfaction. This is in contrast to some social interaction that can prove to be inimical such as when officers gather in parking lots to socialize even though it is necessary for some of the officers to leave their beat assignment in violation of departmental policy. It is always distracting to a member of the public to see four or five marked police vehicles parked at a fast food establishment. In another instance, members of a tactical unit, while on duty, went to a movie.

Informal groups can be supportive of an organization as illustrated by officers helping each other to perform tasks or when they show a fellow officer a better way to do something. This occurs when an officer illustrates a better way of performing a car search, or helps a fellow officer to interpret the law and its application to a specific situation. These types of activities bolster the formal organization and serve to make it more effective.[12] Informal groups create loyalty and a feeling of being. They develop trust between officers and commitment to fellow officers. Members who become a viable part of the group become the recipient of information and develop faster through the internal working of the group because of the empathy of fellow team members. Slowly but surely an informal work group develops a singular philoso-

10. David H. Holt, *Management: Principles and Practices,* Englewood Cliffs, NJ, Prentice–Hall, 1987, p. 69.

11. Richard W. Plunkett, *Supervision: The Direction of People at Work,* Dubuque, IA, 1983, pp. 321–333.

12. More, Wegener, and Miller, *op. cit.,* p. 211.

phy. Members stick together, mutual approval exists, and interdependence dominates. As one become committed to the group it plays an increasingly important role in the culture of the organization.[13]

An antagonistic informal group can serve as the monitor for productive rates of the organization. Norms are set and officers become fully aware of how may car stops they should make each shift, the number of traffic tickets to be issued, or how many field interrogations should be conducted. When a *hot dog* joins a group and immediately begins to exceed the norms pressure builds up to insure conformity. The group reacts by letting such an officer know that their behavior is not acceptable. To be competitive is one thing, but it is not acceptable for one officer to make others look bad. The group code of behavior demands acquiescence and when this does not transpire the offending officer can be ostracized, and excluded from group activities and social events.[14]

In some organizations informal groups take on an entirely different aura and evolve into cliques.[15] This is a normal occurrence and occurs in most organizations. When cliques dominant it can, in some instances, lead to disagreement even antagonism between the clique and the organization.[16] Cliques generally fall into three categories: vertical, horizontal and random.[17]

Figure 10–1

Types of Cliques

Vertical
Horizontal
Random

Vertical Cliques. This type of clique consists of two or more officers from the same unit within the police department who function at different levels. For example, it could involve officers of varying ranks within an unformed division and include line personnel, supervisors, and command officers. This type of clique generally comes into existence as the result of socializing together, and because of mutual interests and common needs. In one department officers were interested in flying and created a club to fulfill that purpose. Another group of

13. Ray, and Bronstein, *op. cit.,* p. 81.

14. Allan R. Cohen, Stephen L. Fink, Herman Gadon, Robin D. Willits, and Natasha Josefowitz, *Effective Behavior in Organizations,* Fifth Edition, Homewood, IL, Richard D. Irwin, 1992, p. 291.

15. Lee A. Peck, *Coping With Cliques,* New York, Rosen Publishing Group, 1992, pp. 32–41.

16. John Gastil, *Democracy in Small Groups: Participation, Decision Making, and Communications,* Philadelphia, New Society Publishers, 1993, pp. 222–231.

17. Dalton Mevlille, *Men Who Manage: Fusions of Feeling and Theory in Administration,* New York, Wiley, 1959, pp. 3–12.

officers who had an interest in computers gathered periodically to share information and software. Many officers can belong to a vertical clique, and in some instance they can belong to more than one such clique. These cliques will, in many instances, help each other on the job when the situation demands. The clique humanizes the organization and reduces friction between departmental members. In-formation is readily exchanged in an informal setting where position and rank are ignored. If a mistake in judgment or an oversight occurs the clique will temporize the situation and do every thing possible to minimize the problem. If it appears that a member of the clique appears to be in trouble forces are gathered to minimize the occurrence. This is especially true if the type of occurrence is political in nature or something that will embarrass the individual or the department.

Horizontal Cliques. A distinguishing characteristic of this type of clique is that it cuts across departmental lines. Its membership can include operational personnel, supervisors and managers. The clique members share work, interests, and results as well as rewards. There is usually a high degree of interaction amongst its members, and it can function from a defensive posture or go on the offensive depending upon the situation. Normally, the horizontal clique has considerable power because its membership can include numerous individuals from major elements of the organization. Generally, it will operate from a defensive posture because of the bureaucratic nature of the organization. If it is going to rock the boat it must be done with finesse and care. It can prove to be successful because its members have worked within the bureaucracy and are fully aware of the techniques that can be used to manipulate the system. It is most effective when it works to maintain the status quo and is more effective that the vertical clique. When the department is proposing changes that appear to be inimical to clique members such as a reduction of discretion, changing policies to more carefully circumscribe behavior, or an expansion of review procedures the clique can exert a great deal of influence within the organization.

Random Cliques. This clique can come from anywhere in the department, and bears no similarity to the other types of cliques. Members enjoy the convenience of working together and sharing information. They work together to achieve an objective, and operate effectively when fighting organizational red tape. They are comfortable in working together and thrive on the interdependence. Association with others dominates their operation and it is seldom that they will work for improved working conditions or strive to change policies. In some instance membership is fostered by membership in other entities such as service clubs, religious groups, ethnic organizations, or graduates of law enforcement training academies. The random clique serves an important function by providing a forum for social interaction and the participation in a meaningful activity. A major function of this clique is when it serves in its capacity as an information resource. It is not uncommon to find that it is the source of rumors and managers who acknowledge this can use its communications channels to pass on information. In most instances members of the random clique are not members of the vertical or horizontal cliques, and are completely satisfied with active membership in the clique.[18]

Effective police managers will be fully aware of the nature and types of cliques present in the organization. At some point and time they will have to work with the varying cliques. They must learn to identify clique leaders and will find it profitable to work with them in order to achieve departmental goals. At the same time they should reciprocate by helping the cliques to attain personal objectives and objectives that are consistent with the departmental mission and values. To ignore cliques is to court disaster. Informal clique leaders do not have explicit authority, but procure power from the constituents of the group. Informal leaders influence members of the clique by virtue of their personality, knowledge, skills and overall abilities. They assume their position because of their voluntary submission and willing tractability conferred upon them by clique members. Even though this type of informal leadership comes into existence spontaneously and is not sanctioned by the formal organization it is clearly just as forceful and situational as formally designated leadership positions.

Developmental Process of Groups

Groups evolve through a maturation process over a period of time before they become truly functional. It is an evolutionary procedure wherein members adjust to each other as they learn more about each member and increasingly accept each other. Working in a team environment requires a different set of skills and motivations than those required in the traditional organization that has a bureaucratic perspective.[19] Group interaction serves as the medium for converting input to output. The group develops a set of norms and values that regulate membership behavior in matters of mutual interest. The group process harnesses energies and the resultant variable is a dynamic force that impacts task achievement and job contentedness. As managers become increasingly aware of the prominence of groups they must respond by including them in the managerial equation.[20]

18. More, Wegener, and Miller, *op. cit.* pp. 211–212.

19. Richard S. Wellins, *Inside Teams: How 20 World–Class Organizations are Winning Through Teamwork,* San Francisco, Jossey–Bass, 1994, p. 322.

20. Marshall Sashkin, and Molly G. Sashkin, *The New Teamwork: Developing and Using Cross–Functional Teams,* Teams, New York, AMACO, 1994, pp. 3–18.

Figure 10–2

Stages of Group Development

Number	Stage
1	Orientation
2	Conflict and Challenge
3	Cohesion
4	Delusion
5	Disillusion
6	Acceptance

Source: L. N. Jewell and H. J. Reitz, *Group Effectiveness in Organizations,* Glenview, IL, Scott Foresman, 1981, pp. 198–201. Reprinted with permission of the publisher.

It is generally accepted that groups develop in six recognizable and easily distinguished stages: orientation, conflict and challenge, cohesion, delusion, disillusion, and acceptance.[21] In some instances the group developmental process can occur rapidly and in other instances the evolutionary process from one stage to another will never occur. Contingencies that that can cause this variability include such things as group maturity, the size of the group, its composition, the difficulty of the tasks to be performed, and the extent and nature of available resources.

Orientation stage. This stage is especially critical to the success of any group. Neglect at this point can hamper or eventually destroy the effectiveness of a group. Initially members will tentatively identify with the group and interact with other members. Initial acceptance and embracing of other members in a positive relationship is usually a given during the formative period. Members of a new group recognize the importance of common interests, the mutual acceptance of tasks to be performed, and the acceptance of the group's existence. Immediate identify occurs as a result of the status of the group within the organization. Additionally, members become aware of how the group can satisfy their psychosocial needs. When a group leader establishes ground rules for behavior, identifies reasons for group reality, and creates procedures group coalescence begins and can serve as a foundation for entry into additional stages of the developmental process. Members of a group want to know what is going on and what is expected of them. During this initial stage much of the knowledge about the group obtained by each member is impressionistic in nature. It is a subjective process as one evaluates the input, characteristics, and behavior of each member and the leader. The initial meeting of a new group that is properly conducted and where information sharing is a positive experience and ground rules are readily apparent can go a long

21. L. N. Jewell and H.J. Reitz, *Group Effectiveness in Organizations,* Glenview, IL, Scott Foreman, 1981, pp. 198–201.

way in insuring the prospects of a viable and organizationally responsive group.

Conflict and Challenge. The second stage is generally one of conflict and challenge. There is a certain amount of noise entropy as members react to each other and the leader. Formal and informal leaders can be challenged as members respond to the composition of the team. This is especially critical as some members strive to determine how they will satisfy their own personal needs and respond to potential conflict with organizational needs. A process of exchange can occur as work strategies are established and members respond from their own personal perspective. Coalitions within the group will, in some instance, arise as job priorities are established and members become aware of their relationship to the team. Today's officers, for the most part, are trained to be assertive, taught to control situations and are skilled in expressing themselves. This can result in immediate conflict as well as competition. It can be healthy, if acknowledged by the leader, but if ignored it can be destructive. Roles relationships, and responsibilities must be adjusted and actually negotiation.[22] The leader must assume responsibility for fostering needed change and creating a new culture that focuses on goal attainment and the importance of each member of the group.[23] During conflict the real role of the group leader is to reject the control paradigm and to evoke commitment to the group and the department. The inability of a leader to shift gears from control to commitment can prove to be detrimental to the positive growth and cultural change within a group.[24]

Cohesion. When members work together they become aware of the values and assumptions of others. Strengthens and weaknesses of team members become apparent as the team evolves from a gathering of individuals into an increasingly cohesive unit. This awareness process does not occur over night, but becomes apparent as officers' work together over a period of time. As members become more focused as part of a problem solving process and engage in-group decision-making the team becomes more and more important to each team member. Positive participation tends to reinforce relationships and focused leadership that emphasizes common goals enhances efficiency and effectiveness. When members are given authority, information, and adequate resources they are more apt to invest their skills and expertise into group activities. The by-product is psychological commitment to the group process and the social satisfaction of interacting with committed team members. The potential for attaining cohesiveness starts with the selection of team members. Polarization of members must be rejected from the outset, and care should be taken to insure that working relationships are such that members feel that they are contributors to the attainment of team objectives. It is also important

22. Kayser, *op. cit.,* p. 181.
23. Patrick J. Solar, "Changing Organizational Culture," *Law and Order,* May 1998, Vol. 46, No. 5, p. 22.
24. Kimball Fisher, *Leading Self-directed Work Teams,* New York, McGraw–Hill, 1993, p. 256.

that initial problems to be considered by the team are not controversial. It takes time for members to assimilate, and see the value and rewards that can be obtained from group dynamics.

Delusion. Rocks in the roadway occur in every group. It should be anticipated, by every group leader, that uncertainty may dominate at some point. Efforts to alleviate problems prove to be less than effective and the focus on purpose becomes nonexistent. Vision and values seem remote and not connected to reality. Even tenaciousness can have limited effect on team members. When problem solving appears to be inept interpersonal issues can arise that disrupt and impede relationships. In some instances, team members will go along with things as a means of avoiding conflict, even though they disagree with the direction that things are going or how thing are done. Others will perceive that their position within the group is such that they have no influence so why fight it because it will not change things.[25]

Disillusion. This stage concerns itself with members rejecting the group processes, and takes the position that the situation is fundamentally intolerable. The assumption is that they are on a road to nowhere and just treading water. Team members are polarized with some confronting every issue and others are totally passive and refuse to take sides or express opinions. Agitation and conflict rule and there is a refusal to work amiably and arrive at a consensus. If positive leadership is to occur it must happen as soon as disillusion becomes apparent. Ground rules must be reiterated and the group should be managed by principle not by policy. Values should be emphasized, and coaching and facilitation must dominate. This is a difficult task but the team leader should do every thing possible to pass through this stage with as little agitation as possible.

Acceptance. This is the point where the group interact positively and each member works toward goal attainment. As the team matures the group process strives for greater stability and reinforcement of common values. Standards for the group are set jointly by members and control is internal rather than external. As members become part of the whole values, norms and ethical principles direct behavior and ensure congruity. Conformity to rule and regulations is a product of individual adjustment to the team as the disparity between personal goals and unit goals narrows. Over time the group becomes a self-directed work team.[26] The reality of maturity results in the work group directing its efforts toward achievement as the result of self-direction and the motivation needed by the team to attain identifiable goals. Additional characteristics of the mature team include responsiveness, flexibility, rejection of groupthink, and a truly visionary approach to problem solving.

The life cycle of a group and the length of time spent in each of the stages vary considerably. Some teams achieve a sense of maturity in a

25. More, Wegener, and Miller, *op. cit., p.* 213.   **26.** Fisher, op. cit., p. 257.

short period of time and others seem to be a continuous state of flux. Maturity can be elusive as a group strives for a sense of dynamic balancing of internal forces. As membership within the group varies the degree of solidity can falter until internal dynamics are refocused. On the other hand, some teams can reach an impasse as change is ignored, and at the extreme the group can become extinct by default or a meaningless entity within the organization. Team leaders must work constantly to rejuvenate and energize teams as a means of increasing their effectiveness and efficiency. Work groups have many positive aspects serving as a vehicle for disseminating knowledge and job skills

Additionally, the group provides members with behavioral guidelines, and group pressures insure compliance. The interaction between members reinforces the importance of the team, provides task assistance to new members, and feedback addresses critical areas of job performance. The beliefs and predisposition about work can be altered by the influence of the group. Influence on production standards can be either positive or negative. In highly cohesive groups tolerance levels are immediately apparent and productivity levels become standards to be followed by every member.[27] Finally, it should be noted that groups provide a sense of identity and an involvement in a satisfying endeavor.

Maximizing Positive Group Behavior

Groups are an inevitable consequence of human behavior and police managers can find these phenomena will provide them with an edge when dealing with agency personnel as well as formal and informal groups. Numerous studies distinctly reflect that when employees work together rather than competing the results are positive. The work group's cohering becomes immediately apparent creating a positive work environment. At the same time employees find that working with others fulfills personal needs. Cohesiveness and cooperative efforts have a positive effect on productivity. Group dynamics serve as a vehicle for developing commitment. With commitment the group enhances personal relations, satisfies needs, and provides a base for the creation of a closely-knit entity. As loyalty to the group develops identity to the group allows for the acceptance of group decisions and conformity to team norms. The importance of group cohesiveness cannot be under estimated. It has the power of creating a workplace that is friendly and pleasant. Officers want to come to work and participate in group activities and problem solving. Cohesiveness becomes apparent when communications flow freely, norms are acquiesced to, and each member of the group is allowed to utilize and develop skills needed for goal attainment. Managers should work with groups and strive to make the group as cohesive as possible. When a manager's positive attitude toward a group is apparent it is contagious and exceptional performance can occur. When group resources are

27.   Cohen, Fink, Gadon, Willits, and Josefowitz, *op. cit.*, pp. 145–176.

utilized effectively and officers become motivated emphasis is placed on activities that are important to the organization

The Group Phenomenon

A group consists of a number of people acting together as a functional component. The key is that the group consists of officers who are capable of a congruous, concomitant that results in the performance of activities directed toward a common objective with the anticipation of some type of fulfillment.[28] Operationally individual membership in the group process is less important than actually taking part in an aggregated activity. Individual behavior that contributes to a collective activity is what is important. Independently motivated conduct by team members directed toward the accomplishment of shared goals is what every team works for and results in collective results that can not be achieved by an individual. Viewing a group in this way it is readily acknowledged that there is an interdependence, mutual influence and interplay that clearly results in team members striving to achieve a mutual purpose.[29]

A truly functional group is one that is best described as synergistic. With the interchange between team members the resultant becomes greater than each individual. Synergism is looked upon as the process of the totality of interaction of officers working together as group members produces a greater total effect than when individuals independently.[30] It means that the totality is generally greater than the sum of the parts.[31] Individuals join formal or informal groups for varying reasons, and one of the most important is the fact that homo sapiens are social animals with a need for interaction. When officers join a department they find that they are assigned to a specific unit and many time a specific shift consequently they find that these are the working individuals with whom they interact the most. Consequently the group becomes an important part of their working life. It is looked upon as a resource for positive feedback and it becomes more important as the intensity of interaction increases. The greater the positive feedback the greater the commitment to the group. Members expect to be involved in working relationships that will be of benefit and when this occurs it intensifies their relationship to the team. Based on one's relationship to groups prior to joining a police force there is reason to see why commitment is anticipated and that initially attitudes and responsiveness are positive. Officers join formal and informal groups in police departments because they benefit from the rewards offered as a consequence of group participation. With the absence of benefits group

28. Tamotsu, Shibutani, *Society and Personality: An Interactionist Approach to Social Psychology,* Englewood Cliffs, NJ, Prentice–Hall, 1961, p. 126.

29. Robert Albanese, *Managing: Toward Accountability for Performance,* Homewood, IL, 1981, p. 49.

30. More and Wegener, *op. cit.* p.228.

31. Robert M. Fulmer, *The New Management,* New York, Macmillan, 1983, pp. 23–29.

participation is reduced, and in most instances an officer will looks for rewards elsewhere.

In non-responsive bureaucratic organizations officers are more apt to look to informal groups for rewards of some kind. This is especially true of team leaders who rule the roost by subjecting team members to the control paradigm. When and if this occurs it inevitably leads to a rejection of the team by its members and eventually to team failure. If a team leader views officers as lazy and incompetent these values and assumptions are immediately apparent and the creation of a self-directed work team becomes the figment of the imagination.

Psychosocial Needs

These needs of individual officers are very strong and prove to be exceptionally influential. Officers join groups in order to interact with others engaged in the same activities. This type of bonding starts with entry into the academy and is reinforced by the initial assignment to field operations. There are many positive outcomes associated with group membership that cannot be obtained any other way. Positive reinforcement from a group can prove to be a most meaningful. It is something that is coveted and looked forward to as part of the group process. When one belongs it makes one feel a part of the whole and worthy as an individual. Positive reinforcements are cumulative and serve to reinforce one's attitudes about alliance with a group.

Affiliation. In the police service each officer has something in common with other officers–the work. It provides a companionship that starts in the agency and extends to social activities. They learn to not only socialize with officers, but depend upon them when working. Even over a short period of time this process can develop an intense group allegiance. It is fostered by shared experiences, and reliance upon each other during a crisis—all of which creates a loyalty that is pervasive, and can become a predominant ethic of the police culture.[32] With in the department officers can join more than one subgroup and pursue mutual interests. All of this meets the affiliation needs of officers.

Security. As noted previously officers, as theorizes by Maslow, have a basic need for safety and security. As the result of media exposure to police work, war stories set forth by fellow officers, and recruit training programs recruits perform early police service with a definitive concern for real or imagined external threats. Thus, it is natural for young officers to look for support from other officers. This is especially true for probationary officers who normally have some anxiety because of their status and their working relationship with a Field Training Officer, (FTO) consequently they find support from other officers who have survived what they are going through. Additionally, by relating to other officers they learn the ropes faster and

---

32. Milton Mollen, *Commission Report: Commission to Investigate Allegations of Police Corruption and the Anti-* *Corruption Procedures of the Police Department*, New York, New York City, 1992, p.53.

became an integral part of the group grapevine. This provides them with information that reduces anxiety and allows them to survive the scrutiny of, senior officers, FTO'S and supervisors. Groups, formal and informal, serve as a vehicle to indoctrinate new officers into the desired routine of the system, and reinforce the socialization process. The ability to foster the inculcation of new members, with few restraints, provides groups with a great deal of power.

Power. Group membership serves as a source of power for several reasons. It is seldom that individuals can exert the powers that emanate from a group. The cumulative power of more than one individual exceeds that can be exercised by a lesser number. Officers soon learn that the individual is powerless and that the power of the group can exceed all expectations. One officer, who exhibits a reasonable degree of expertise exercises, within the group, more power than a single person can ever anticipate. Group power is exponential and when it is reinforced by recognition and praise it can be overwhelming. A secondary aspect of power is that the group environment provides an opportunity for individuals to assume as position of leadership. Through expertise and knowledge one can exercise power over other members of the group even thought they do not have a bureaucratic power of position. One advantage of position power in a group is that responsibilities are avoided that is a normal accruement of a formal bureaucratic position. The closeness of a group and the drive for acceptance confers power that is seldom found in a structured position.

Self-esteem. Group membership confers numerous things on each individual, but one of the most important is that of self-esteem. Members soon develop a sense of worth and importance that is conferred upon them because of their inclusion in a group. This is particularly true when an officer becomes a member of an elite group within the department such as the tactical unit, a high-tech investigative unit, swat team, K9 unit or the bomb squad. Praise for these units comes from throughout the department and these positions are sought after. In fact these assignments are both intrinsically and extrinsically rewarding. The interpersonal relations that emanate from a close affiliation can transcend external rewards because the officer finds that the praise and recognition is something that is meaningful and only bestowed upon members of the group. In addition this type of praise is noteworthy because the average formal organization restricts its praise. Overall groups provide aid, acceptance, and standing that becomes a voice of reality and a protective environment. Self-esteem is elevated through this process and a notable byproduct of affiliation.

Self-Concept. Membership is groups provide individuals with an opportunity to deal with the introspective question of "Who am I?" Officers have a need to be completely aware of their personal identity in the culture in which they work. There is of course more than one culture in a police department and in many instances there is a true dichotomy between operational personnel and police managers.[33] The belief of peers is especially important and it has been said that individuals perceive themselves as others see them.[34] This suggests that in most instances peer assessment is a most powerful force and it can shape the mindset of each officer as they respond to police sub-culture. One's self-concept is a reflection of the interaction between officers, and as teams become more prevalent in police work it is anticipated that it will be an increasingly powerful influence on the sub-culture of operational personnel. Members of groups interact continuously with fellow officers and it is seldom that they are not candid in their feedback. Overtime this type of interaction provides an officer with a concise evaluation of their behavior as viewed by the group and an indication of their self-concept.[35] Officers' have a real need to be perceived as a "real cop" by their peers and this can prove to be more important than how they are viewed by management.

Accomplishment. It is normal for group to evolve because more than one person is needed if a task is to be accomplished. Cooperative effort can accomplish what a single person cannot do. This is especially true for the formal organization that puts individuals into specialized entities to accomplish tasks. This is especially true in investigative units where tasks are grouped by type. For example, homicide, high-tech, forgery, fraud or crimes against a person. The informal organization approaches the task differently. As a consequence of the need to interact with others officers work together as in order to achieve individual and organizational goals. Officers join many sub-groups as a means of pursuing mutual interests generated by a desire to engage in numerous specialized activities such a self-defense, an interest in personal computers or athletics. Whatever the activity officers are prone to pool their wisdom, dynamism, aptitude, aptitude and skills to accomplish collective tasks. This is done because when officers engage in such tasks it proves to be satisfying and there is a sense of fulfillment that cannot be attained in any other way.

Economic Needs

Since the early part of the twentieth century officers have joined groups in order to pursue economic needs. This includes a wide range of groups ranging from promotional study groups to police unions. Historically police have been members in fraternal and social organizations and professional associations. Initially many of these groups fulfilled social needs and over time many of the groups became focal points for unionization and eventually bargaining units. Membership of this nature generally expects some improvement in their economic

33. William A. Geller and Michael Scott, *Deadly Force: What We Know,* Washington, DC, Police Executive Research Forum, 1992, p. 407.

34. Ronald W. Smith and Frederick W. Preston, *Sociology: An Introduction,* New York, St. Martin's Press, 1982, p. 210.

35. More and Wegener, *op. cit.,* p. 229.

welfare. Economic welfare was missing from the police scene for many years, but such is not the case in many areas of the United States. The rapid growth of police unions and their increasing power has lead to a significant improvement in all aspects of compensation in the police service. As the power of the unions increased it has become quite common to see officers compensated for things such as weapon proficiency, seniority, training certification, and hazardous duty. In fact, unions in some cities exert power that exceeds that of the chief executive officer and they have filled a void left by management.

The Functionality of Groups

Groups whether they are formal or informal usually prevail when they are successful in meeting the needs of members and the organization. Success begets success and the perpetuation of the group occurs when it creates a balancing of forces within the organization allowing for the attainment of individual and organizational goals. Within organizations groups can overlap and met differing needs. Within this context officers can belong to a wide range of groups to include those that are strictly social and those that are formally structured entities. Groups can be categorized in a number of different ways ranging from ideal types to theoretical. A very practical way to view groups is to group them by functionality. The most dominant functional groups include (1) command, (2) task, (3) interest, and (4) friendship.

Figure 10–3

Types of Groups

Command
Task
Interest
Friendship

Command Groups. As a police departments grows in size in response to the complexity of operations it responds by creating additional levels within the organization and provides for specialization. The chain of command provides for organizational stability and the formal table of organization defines the division of power. The span of control, and unity of command define the working relationship between organizational entities Line and staff become important as related functions are grouped under unified command. Rank is important within the organization and defines the relationship between operational and managerial positions. The command group is viewed as a vertical group within the organization through which orders are given. It is usually composed of a specified police manager and those within the chain of command. Rules and regulations emanate from the top and compliance is expected. Rank means power and privileges and tends to foster the status quo.

Task Groups. These groups are usually temporary in nature and are creatures of the authority held by the organization. Normally they are created to address a specific problem or issue. In some instances, they come into existence as a managerial maneuver and a delaying tactic or to diffuse an issue and let time heal wounds or dissipate dissension. Task groups provide managers with a vehicle that can respond rapidly, because it is not encumbered with trappings of the bureaucratic and authoritarian organization. Smaller in size than most command groups the task force usually transcends the formal organization and can include members from various units. This allows for the gathering of expertise that can focus on issues that need to be resolved. Task groups are significant because of their ability to solve problems in such a way that all levels of the organization more readily accept them. A significant element of this process is due to that fact that communications and coordination are improved.

Interest Groups. This type of group places emphasis on problem resolution, dealing directly with issues of mutual interest or pursuing specific objectives. At time officers gather together to attend city council meeting to support improved benefits. Officers have been especially effective in gaining support for improvement of working conditions, wages, overtime pay, and health benefits. Other will picket governmental meetings or gather together and march in protest of action being taken by a governing body that is perceived as being inimical. On some occasions officers will march in support of an officer who has been involved in a shooting incident. This type of support is perceived as critical, because each officer envisions himself or herself as possibly being in such a situation. In other instances officers have launched a campaign to oppose the creation of civilian review boards that has been successful in prohibiting its implementation. In one city officer gathered to protest opposition to the chief of police and demonstrate their support. Another common interest stems from affiliation with a professional organization. This includes such groups as those interested in training, the functioning of a SWAT team, tactical operations, or the future of law enforcement. Other interests include organizations with a gender base, sexual orientation or ethnic alliance. Interests groups bear some similarity to formal organizational entities, but most of them tend to be less structured and rely upon voluntary support. For the most part the issue is what is important and its resolution generally leads to the demise of the group.

Friendship Groups. This type of group is apt to arise spontaneously because of the desire of officers to be together. The key is that the officers get along together, enjoy each others company, and an opportunity arise for the friendship to be extended to other activities that allow for a continuation of the friendship. Members generally have one or more attributes in common that draws them together. To start with just being a police officer sets one apart from other community members. The job and all of its folklore solidifies personal relationships and over time the concept of "we vs. they" becomes a reality. The association usually starts because of the proximity of officers to each other. This is especially true for officers working in field operation working on the same shift or on adjoining beats or in contiguous areas. Additionally, it is quite common for the personal relationships to evolve from social gathers such as getting together after a shift to hoist a beer. This extension beyond the workplace reinforces the solidarity of officers and internalizes their relationship with members of the department. Many officers have limited socialization with non-police groups. When socialization occurs between officers it generally involves activities such as sports, hobbies, or other special interest. It other instances a friendship group is based on a common interest in religion, previous military affiliation or a fraternal association.

Each of the groups discussed above are not mutually exclusive. They overlap and intertwine as officers join or leave a specific group. When officers belong to a large number of groups it can dissipate their influence on any single group as the time that can be devoted to an effort becomes an important variable. Some groups support each other while others prove to be antagonistic. Whatever the case groups clearly modify the formal organization Leadership with an organization must acknowledge the existence of groups that stratify the organization. Beyond acknowledging their existence it is essential for managers to work with and through groups and never underestimates the importance to the effective functioning of the organization. Every organization has numerous formal and informal groups that serve to define how things are accomplished and serve to distinguish the organization from all other organizations. Overtime each agency develop its own culture.

Developing Operation Effectiveness

The effectiveness of an operational group is predicated on the necessity for managers to view the group differently. There is a need for the implementation of a distinct type of management that is aware of the importance of shifting from controlling groups to developing committed groups. Today's employees need guidance not detailed directions, they need to be coached not ignored, they need to be trained not left to fend for themselves, and they need to be lead not supervised to the point of distraction. Research suggests that employees are more effective when the work environment is such that they feel they belong to the organization and what they do makes a difference.[36] Managers must have a well thought out vision of how groups/teams fit into the scheme of the total organization. In many organizations managers covet power and care taking is the by word of the day. Successful management of groups requires managers to rethink how the do things. There must be a rethinking or transformation of the organization if the future is to be confronted, and groups are to be allowed to be

---

36. Ray, and Bronstein, *op. cit.* p. 80.

a vital element of the department. Simple, single-focused fix-it schemes must be relegated to the past and one shot panaceas rejected.[37]

Group/team building is a complex process that does not just transpire it takes a great deal of leadership and the utilization of numerous skills before they can become contributing units. Scrutiny of research indicates that effective group leaders exhibit the following types of behavior:

- Capacity to focus constantly on an objective.
- Function as a detached leader by observing the activities of the group and participating at the same time.
- Aware of the need to assume primary responsibility for controlling the relationship between the group and other units and individuals.
- Facilitates group members in the assumption of leadership the situation dictates, as a consequence of changing team needs.[38]
- Positive team leadership allows members to have a significant influence on their work environment.

Once officers feel that they belong and realize that they can make a difference, when growth opportunities are apparent, the maturity of the team will reach a point where team members feel that they have been empowered. Unfortunately many team do not reach this level because they have not been given the means, shared power, and responsibility to accomplish assigned objectives. When team members are allowed to influence the work environment magical things can happen. There is a realization that they are no longer just a cog in the wheel. When they are given this chance the committed officer will accept the challenge of the newly created working environment. Members of a team once they become committed to a work unit will respond by exercising self-management and self-direction.[39]

A fully functioning team will normally have a number of characteristics that set it aside from other working units. For one thing authority emanates from knowledge rather than rank or position. Decision-making and participation that are localized and based on the enhanced knowledge and skill of team members provide for a working environment that is results oriented. Loyalty and commitment to the team is apparent and trust serve as the essential ingredient of a winning team. Team vitality is readily apparent when each officer is given the opportunity to achieve, grow, and advance within the team. Contributions are acknowledged and rewards extended for teamwork and collaboration. Overall the effective team is one where there is a

37. John C. Cotter, *The 20% Solution: Using Rapid Redesign To Create Tomorrow's Organizations Today,* New York, John Wiley & Sons, 1995, pp.4–5.

38. Don Hellriegel, John W. Solcum, Jr., and Richard W. Woodman, *Organi-zational Behavior,* Third Edition, St. Paul, MN, 1983, pp.89–130.

39. Ray and Bronstein, op. cit. pp. 80–81.

focus on organizational excellence wherein the team works to achieve distinguished results not just fulfill a minimal obligation. A focus on performance allows the team members to commit to each other and the result is a continuous team development process.[40]

Managing Groups

Groups can only succeed when management realizes the importance of dealing with the tensions and conflict that occur within a team. Before team performance can be maximized conflict must be confronted. It cannot be ignored or just swept under the rug. Involvement in a team is a learning process, and as a team evolves the leader has to work objectively and deal directly with problems.[41] There are a number of guidelines that can be followed if a team is to flourish within an organization. The effective management of teams will produce high commitment, involvement, and performance. A truly self-managed team is one that meets the challenge of making decisions about tasks and objectives and demonstrates the capacity of managing their own internal affairs.[42]

Fundamental to the success of a self-directed work team is a well-thought out understanding of how it fits into the design of the entire department. Skillful managing requires imparting the vision to every member of the team. A truly impacting vision is based on the value system of the organization and the identifiable mission. It cannot be just words supported by rhetoric, but an actual commitment as to the real reason the organization exists. When values are translated into goals the team must accept them. It is also essential for the goals to be realistic, demanding and as precise as possible. As goals are developed they must be held in common and support the organizational vision. It is essential that everyone in the organization is functional within the purview of the vision and when necessary the organizational culture should be changed so as to support the positive development of group dynamics.[43] Figure 10–4 sets forth the key elements needed to insure managerial success when working with teams.

40. John R. Katzenbach and Douglas K. Smith, *The Wisdom of Teams: Creating the High Performance Organization,* Boston, Harvard Business School Press, 1993, pp. 16–18.

41. Harvey Robbins and Michael Finley, *Why Teams Don't Work: What Went Wrong and How To Make It Right,* Princeton, NJ, Peterson's/Pacesetter Books, 1995, pp. 41–42.

42. Steve Alper, Dean Tjosvold, and Kenneth S. Law, "Interdependence and Controversy In–Group Decision–Making: Antecedents to Effective Self–Managing Teams," *Organizational Behavior and Human Decision Processes*, April 1998, Vol. 74, No. 1, pp. 33–52.

43. Thomas Capozzoli, "How To Succeed With Self–Directed Work Teams," *Supervision*, August 1995, Vol. 56, No. 8, pp. 18–19.

Figure 10–1

Managing Work Groups

Vision
Facilitation
Development
Resources
Cooperation and Collaboration
Non-competitive Goals
Groupthink

It is essential that team leaders perform as facilitators and function as a coach rather than a controller. This attitude of a coach should permeate every action taken by the leader. Emphasis should be place on developing the camaraderie that is an essential byproduct of the group. The leader should be firm, fair, and demand that each member of the team perform within the same value structure as the team. Meaningful participation should be solicited that allows each member to enhance his or her self-esteem.[44] The reality of coaching comes into fruition when what you do is more important than what you say. Leading by example allows the team to focus on purpose rather than being bogged down in trivia.[45] The true coach reduces the anxiety that comes with the adventure into new and unexplored activities. Roles have to be clarified and changed when needed as competencies in leadership are developed within a helping atmosphere.

Development of the team and each member is essential and is a challenge that management must accept. Members must be trained in the skills need to function effectively. This includes such things as conflict management, communications, problem-solving and decision-making. Each team member should become self-reliant and perform within the parameters of the team concept. Upon completion of training the team should be allowed to develop its newfound skills. Managers must be patience during the growing period and allow for mistakes and errors and allow for the maturation of the team. Interpersonal need to be developed tested and corrected. Some teams will develop rapidly and others will take more time. It is essential for each team to be involved in an ongoing developmental process. As the teams mature less attention can be given to the developmental process as the training is reinforced in the actual workplace.[46]

Change to team management necessitates the allocation of adequate resources to insure success. When time, fiscal support, and an appropriate number of people are not committed the probability of success is limited. If resource allocation is based on faulty thinking or a

44. W. Richard Plunkett, *Supervision: The Direction of People at Work,* Dubuque, IA, William C. Brown, 1983, pp. 201–233.

45. Fisher, *op. cit.,* p. 257.

46. Capozzoli, *op. cit.,* p 19.

lack of resolution the needed changes will not occur. Commitment must be sincere and the time frames for the implementation generous enough to result in the development of competencies that allow for the elimination of barriers.[47] Normally an agency will have in-house personnel who can provide for the initial training and continuing development of personnel.

Team leaders should strive to develop an attitude of cooperation and collaboration. Members should be required to work through issues and problems and develop an interdependence within the group. Though coaching and appropriate facilitation a team will soon see the importance of developing competent team member. Collaboration can and should be spontaneous and members will see the value of active team membership. As cooperation becomes an ongoing process the interaction between members becomes an important part of the team's work. This results in a synergy that sets a team apart from a collection of individuals. In time, controversy and disagreements will be accepted as part of the team process as it confronts new challenges. Truly self-managed teams create an atmosphere of trust and loyalty.[48]

Non-competitive goals interfere with constructive contention and can inhibit the creation of an really effective entity. Research suggests that when a team has a highly cooperative goal it is able to discuss opposing views open-mindedly and constructively. This leads to an interactive process that results in effective team performance. When teams grapple with problems candidly and with out fear of requital it allows them to gain confidence in their ability to work effectively. Consequently teams that are self-managed are most effective when they work within a framework of structured cooperative goals and constructive controversy.[49]

More than a quarter of a century ago Irving Janis coined the term groupthink. Since that time it has received increasing attention from supporter and distracters of the theory.[50] Groupthink is something that a good team leader is fully aware of especially the potential for a cohesive in-group working toward unanimity and ignoring the need to realistically appraise alternative courses of action.[51] Additionally, an extensive amount of time can be spent justifying the decision. Groupthink is more apt to occur when a group becomes increasingly isolated from the organization, develops a highly cohesive characteristics and ignores input from external sources. A group leader can confront

47. Fisher, *op. cit.*

48. Ray and Bronstein, *op. cit.* p. 80.

49. Alper, Tjosvold, and Law, *op. cit.*, p. 33.

50. Marlene E. Turner, and Anthony R. Pratkanis, "Twenty–Five Years of Groupthink Theory and Research: Lessons from the Evaluation of a Theory," *Organizational Behavior and Human Decision Processes*, Processes, February/March, 1998, Vol. 73, Nos. 2/3, pp. 105–115.

51. Gregory Moorhead, Christopher P. Neck, and Mindy S. West, "The Tendency toward Defective Decision Making within Self-Managing Teams: The Relevance of Groupthink for the 21st Century," *Organizational Behavior and Human Decision Processes*, February/March 1998, Vol. 73, Nos. 2/3, pp. 327–351.

groupthink by selecting someone who is a member of the team to be the devil's advocate, to sincerely question the proposed explanation. When this technique is used it should be rotated within the membership so as not to stigmatize any one person. Identifiable weaknesses of a proposed solution should be addresses one by one and when necessary experts should be brought in to present an opposing opinion. With imagination and ingenuity, a group leader can maximize to positive aspects of group decision-making and negate its questionable aspects. Consensus decision-making can elicit member commitment to the implementation process.[52]

Case Study

James Ralston

James Ralston is training officer in the Stanton Police Department. The city has a population of 115,500 and the police department has 118 sworn personnel and 19 civilians. The city is primarily a bed room community in a large urban area. It has three major shopping centers and a light industrial area. The city is racially mixed with Caucasians, Mexican–Americans, and Blacks. During the last decade there has been an influx of Asians, primarily from Hong Kong and Cambodia. Ralston is a lieutenant and has been in training after spending nine years in the uniformed division, three years in the detective division, and in his current position for two years. He is a graduate in educational leadership from a private university and is currently in masters degree program. He is married and has two children. He lives in the city and his children attend a private religious school. His wife is a registered nurse in one of the local hospitals. As the training officer he teaches in the recruit and supervisory courses at the regional training academy. In house he supervises the Filed Training Officer (FTO) program, supervises roll call training and prepares training bulletins. Additionally, he is responsible for maintaining the training records for each member of the department. The chief has asked Lt. Ralston to develop a pilot program for team policing and implement it on the swing shift in the uniformed division. The test period will run for one year after which it will be evaluated. The team will consist of nine officers and supervised by a sergeant. If the project proves to be successful it is anticipated that it might be the forerunner of a community-policing program. The chief has recommended that Sergeant Frank Oates head up the team and suggested that Lt. Ralston work with Sgt. Oates in selecting the team members.

In fulfilling this assignment if you were Lt. Ralston what would be the first thing you would do? Why? What type of training would you provide for the team leader and its members? How would you monitor the developmental process of the team? What criteria would you use for the selection of team members?

---

52. Robbins, and Finley, *op. cit.*, p. 42.

For Further Reading

Steve Alper, Dean Tjosvold, and Kenneth S. Law, "Interdependence and Controversy in Group Decision Making: Antecedents to Effective Self–Managing Teams," *Organizational Behavior and Human Decision Processes,* April 1998, Vol. 74, No. 1, pp. 33–52.

> Based on a review of a number of studies the authors summarize the importance of self-managed team meeting the challenge of decision making and managing their internal affairs. The authors determined that teams with highly cooperative goals were found to discuss their opposing views open-mindedly and constructively which in turn developed confidence in team dynamics that contributed to effective team performance.

Thomas Capozzoli, "How to Succeed With Self–Directed Work Teams," *Supervision,* August 1995, Vol. 56, No. 8, pp. 18–19.

> Presents a number of guidelines that will help to develop a successful self-directed work team. Stresses the importance of having a vision that changes the organizational culture. Explores the importance of allocating adequate resources, and training members of a team in a range of key functions ranging from conflict management to communications skills. Discusses the importance of feedback, and boundaries within which teams will operate.

Darrel Ray and Howard Bronstein, *Teaming Up: Making the Transition to a Self–Directed, Team–Based Organization,* New York, McGraw–Hill, Inc., 1995, pp. 80–103.

> Describes in detail how to realign an organization's human infrastructure in a way that supports employee empowerment and a team structure. Emphasizes the importance of top management supporting such a dramatic transition. Discusses in detail the characteristics of an effective team and the process of continuous team development. Additionally, the authors review the importance of the culture of the organization.

Harvey Robbins and Michael Finley, *Why Teams Don't Work: What Went Wrong and How to Make it Right,* Princeton, NJ, Peterson's/Pacesetter Book, 1995, pp. 52–56, and 188–200.

> Discusses how a leader might deal with four different types of personalities that the authors identify as: analytical, driver, amiable, and expressive and the impact of each on a team.
>
> Describes the stages of team development that are specified as: forming, storming, performing, and norming. Every team passes through each stage and each is discussed in term of their importance to actual teamwork and eventual success.

Chapter 11

FIELD OPERATIONS: Providing Services to the Community

Learning Objectives

1. Discuss the importance of having all other police units collateral to the patrol division.
2. List eight specialized units operated by large police departments.
3. Distinguish between geographical and functional distribution.
4. Define the concept—consumed time.
5. Describe the use of geographical information systems (GIS).
6. List the four elements of performance expectations.
7. Describe chronological distribution of police resources.
8. Identify the key elements of patrol beat responsibility.
9. Write a short essay comparing single and two-officer patrol.
10. List five advantages for a program of take-home police vehicles.
11. Describe how dogs can be used to supplement police patrol.
12. Write a short essay describing team policing.
13. Compare fluid and directed patrol.
14. Illustrate the use of women in the police service.
15. Compare the mental health and domestic violence response teams.

In the control and suppression of crime and other police problems, patrol service is the most important responsibility of police management. The patrol/field operations division is the basic element of line power. Patrol carries out in police service the functions that are unique to local and state government. It represents the front line where policies and plans are translated into action, including the prevention and suppression of crime, preservation of law and order, and the protection of life and property. Since the strength of a police organization is almost entirely a measure of the available power of the patrol force, all the tools of management and managerial procedures should be directed toward maximum accretion of patrol. Any organizational function, which does not serve this end, represents lost motion and wasted resources and should be abandoned forthwith + as a matter of sound administrative policy.

Since the work of the uniformed force includes the primary police functions, the more effective the patrol division, the less need there is for more special operating units. Although it is impossible for the patrol force to be one hundred percent effective in the discharge of police functions, the other operating line divisions are necessary only to the extent that the patrol division falls short of this ideal. A balanced organization is one in which the various units have been developed in accordance with the relative importance of their contributions to the total line power of patrol service. All other line units including investigations traffic, and support, are secondary and collateral to the patrol division and are only extensions of that division. Failure to recognize this relationship results in an unbalanced organization.

Size and Distribution

Amplification of patrol line power by every means possible should be a managerial objective of the commanding officer in charge of line operations, and a major concern of the chief executive. Determination of the amount of patrol power required and its distribution are among the gravest administrative problems confronting police management. The problems involved in determining the size of the force are complex. Obviously, with unlimited funds, it would be possible to provide police officers in sufficient numbers to deal promptly and effectively with virtually every public emergency within the jurisdiction of the police. No community would be willing to make expenditures on this lavish scale.

On the hypothesis that other operating divisions are necessary only to the extent of the patrol division failing to achieve its objectives, it follows that the size of the patrol force determines the size of its supporting elements, including staff services and other operating line units. Application of this principle delimits the problem to a determination of the amount and quality of patrol line power required, which in turn resolves itself into an analysis of the requirements and specifications of the individual patrol service area or beat. As stated earlier, the ultimate unit of organization is a group of operations that can be performed directly by one individual, constituting a satisfactory single workload. It is safe to say that not only the size of the force but the development of a scientific police administration in all of its aspects depends upon the derivation of a valid formula for beat construction, with all it implies. The effective distribution of the personnel resources of a police organization occurs simultaneously in three directions—by function, by area and by time.

Functional Distribution

The distribution of the available personnel strength by function involves a determination of the number of individuals to be assigned to the administration, patrol, investigation, support services, technical services, and other administrative units in the department. It is here that organization by major purpose, by major process, and by clientele enter the picture to influence the divisional assignment of manpower. In may municipal departments one can find a wide range of specialized units performing numerous activities. Whenever a specialized unit is created, it is usually detrimental to patrol because resources are usually drawn from there. Specialization ranges from those operated a special unit for crime prevention to those dealing with child abuse.

The percentage of officers assigned to patrol varies considerably in the largest cities in the United States. New York City has 25 percent of its sworn personnel on patrol. Houston and Chicago follow this with 21 and 16 percent respectively. Detroit is next with 12 percent of their officers on patrol and Los Angeles had 19. percent on patrol. In the six largest U.S. cities Houston has the largest percentage of officers assigned as detectives (17.2), and Chicago had the smallest percentage with 8.9. Between two and five percent of the sworn officers are assigned to traffic in Chicago, Detroit, New York City, and Philadelphia. This is in sharp contrast with Los Angeles having 11.7 percent, and Houston that has eliminated its traffic unit. The degree of specialization is especially notable in Philadelphia with 32 percent of the sworn personnel in units other than patrol, traffic, and investigations.[1] It is a responsibility of the Chief of Operations to maintain a continuous inventory of the relative requirements of the several line units. Special details of every type and kind should be given careful scrutiny and any doubt should be resolved in favor of maintaining the patrol division at full strength.

Geographical Distribution

The basis for geographical distribution of the patrol force is the individual patrol area or beat. It may be described as a circumscribed area to which one or two officers are assigned, and within which the officer is held responsible for the prevention of crime. The officer(s)is also held responsible for performing traffic duties, preservation of law and order, the protection of life and property, and the improvement of quality of life on the beat. All the line functions of police service are discharged largely within this frame of reference. The selection of the beat as the point of attack in all police operations conforms to the fundamental principle of decentralizing the total problem into small units.

How to distribute the patrol force equitably and strategically on the basis of sound beat construction has given conscientious police executives concern for many years. This must be accomplished if every officer is to carry their share of the total load and if each section of the community is to receive its share of police protection. Executives have recognized first, that if the patrol officer is overloaded with work, the person becomes dissatisfied and inefficient, and if not given enough to do, the officer becomes lazy and dodges responsibilities. Second if the

1. Antony Pate and Edwin E. Hamilton. *The Big Six: Policing America's*   *Largest Cities,* Washington, D.C., 1991, pp. 5 and 59–60.

distribution is uneven the lawless element quickly discovers the weakness and plan their depredations accordingly; and finally, that an ill-balanced plan ultimately draws complaints from political leaders and members of the community.

The individual beat must be constructed on sound principles, or the entire organization will be structurally weak and will cease to function effectively as an agency for the safety of the public, and the improvement of the quality of life. In the beginning it was the custom to take a map of the city and divide it into a number of patrol areas of equal size, the number corresponding to the number of patrolmen available. Later, patrol officers were distributed according to population density, the ratio being one officer to approximately one thousand inhabitants. The method of patrol in American cities today is based more or less on the principle that patrol officers should be distributed by areas in proportion to the amount of work to be done. In recognition of this principle, the size of the beat in most cities gradually increases from the center of the city outward toward the perimeter, due to the ecological pattern of decreasing density of offenses and other work-generating factors.

Selected intervals must be set forth when revision of beat boundaries becomes a continuing policy of intelligent management and control. There are many instances where beats, once star contributors to the city's crime total, take on the air of a peaceful and respectable neighborhood. Social life and organization are in a constant state of flux. Changing population density and nationality, shifting business areas, changes in the character of suburban residential districts, appearance of new motels, banks, theaters, jewelry stores, and other mercantile establishments render existing beat distribution obsolete. Beat boundaries often are maintained long beyond the time when the conditions first determining their limits ceased to exist.

Proportional distribution of the patrol force was conceived as early as 1909, when Chief August Vollmer assigned the force (which then was bicycle-mounted and in 1911 became auto-borne) to two 12-hour shifts. In this instance beats were laid out in accordance with the number of calls for the police anticipated in each part of the city. Some officers worked very large beats and some patrolled areas far smaller, where calls were more highly concentrated. Generally, in the distribution of the patrol force by beats and in the determination of the size and boundaries of patrol beats, case load patterns, inspectional services and the distribution of police hazards are the major factors to be considered. The sociological characteristics of the area are not to be ignored; however, where they are of unusual police significance, they find expression as police hazards in one form or another and are, therefore, automatically taken into account. It is thus necessary as a first step, to tabulate by hour of day and by existing beat boundaries, the number of Part I and Part II offenses, miscellaneous reports, accidents and number of arrests for the preceding six months period.

But this is not enough. It is necessary to translate work into time units or man hours in order to have a common denominator with which to compute existing work load distribution and to project necessary changes in work load distribution. The average time spent in case investigation varies from one crime classification to another. In terms of personnel hours, the investigation of a traffic accident and a worthless check investigation may present two entirely different situations. The staff/labor time picture will vary from one department to another, depending upon recruiting and training standards, departmental policy with respect to assignment of the investigative function, quality of the investigation, morale and a number of other factors. Hence, it would be impractical at this juncture to establish norms that would be applicable to every department. Each department must take its own measure.

The conversion of work into time units or worker hours is not a difficult operation. It is merely a matter of each investigating officer making a systematic and accurate record over a reasonable period of time, of the amount of time spent. Averages are then obtained from the reports of all investigating officers and a time factor is thus established for each category. In this manner, each work unit is *weighted*. It is then an easy matter to compute the percentage distribution of workload by existing beat layout and by platoon shifts. At this point, solutions suggest themselves. Patrol beat boundaries may be adjusted, on a rational and sound basis, thus effecting an equitable distribution of workload by patrol beat. Since the number and size of patrol beats vary from one platoon shift to another, the foregoing procedure also offers an effective basis for the organization and distribution of patrol beats by platoon shifts.

In the past some jurisdictions employ the *consumed time* concept in the geographical distribution of the patrol force by beats. In addition to the conversion of work into time units, these units are then weighted. All types of police service, including the various crime classifications, are placed in four categories—those requiring more than one hour, those requiring forty-five minutes to one hour, those requiring thirty to forty-five minutes, and those requiring less than thirty minutes. Weights were then given to the various types of police activity:

- More than one hour Weight 4.
- Forty-five minutes to one hour Weight 3.
- Thirty minutes to forty-five minutes Weight 2.
- Less than thirty minutes Weight 1.

The weighted data is then tabulated for each sub-census and the percentage of the total patrol workload computed for each sub-census area. The weighted workload and the percentage of the total patrol work load is then calculated for each beat. In this manner, through the shifting of reporting districts or sub-census areas, the size and boundaries of patrol beats were effectively adjusted to permit an equitable adjustment of workload for each beat. In the smaller department, even with strength of only a few, patrol officers can be advantageously allocated on a need-for-service basis. In this manner, the power of a relatively small force can be amplified up to a point equivalent to the addition of more human resources. It only remains to have available an efficient police records unit where the tabulation of the necessary information can be produced as a basis for the effective deployment of patrol personnel.

Departments with computer capability have inaugurated a continuous statistical assessment of patrol workloads and deployment. Through the use of geographic information systems (GIS) police managers have a puissant tool to view information that is map-based. GIS provides a range of information to include a depiction of incidents by types of crime, date and time. Additionally, a beat or other designated geographical area can display incidents by location such as Part II crimes within 1,000 feet of a school. Advanced GIS capabilities can generate incident density maps that can be used to predict the probability of crime activity in certain locations. As futuristic as GIS may sound it is a viable process that can greatly enhance the capability of line power. [2]Another sophisticated product that has a specific application to law enforcement is the BeatBuilder created by Corona Software, Inc. Using proprietary algorithms the BeatBuilder aggregates small areas to optimize police beats on variables of the user's choosing, providing for optimal placement of line power.[3]

Performance Expectations for Patrol Officers

Problem solving, teamwork and technical skills are essential elements of good patrol work. When these things are accomplished it is apparent that patrol is the backbone of a department. Performance expectations that support problem solving shift away from the traditional approach of measuring statistics, such as arrests, citations issued, and field interrogations (FIs). As the Seattle Police Department moves toward a restructuring of many of the operational and administrative functions in an effort to better support problem solving it has identified four major performance expectations:

Teamwork. Each of us has individual skills and talents that we bring to the squad. As team members we need to recognize these attributes and use them in a cooperative fashion to build our team. Teamwork will require us to speak directly and honestly with each other and look for solutions to problems rather than place fault with individual team members. Teamwork requires officers to ensure each other's safety. Esprit de corps results from quality team work.

2. ESRI, *GIS for Law Enforcement,* 11/30/98, http://www.esri.com/partners/developers/pubsafety.html.

3. Corona Software, Inc., *Public Safety/Emergency Management,* 11/30/98, e-mail: dale_harris@corona-soft.com.

- **The Beat.** We must be committed to work with the communities in their geographic area of responsibility to address crime and crime related problems. This will require officers to know the people in their community, the businesses, the schools, the parks, the streets, the crime trends, and historical perspective of the community as it relates to police related issues. Officers will communicate respectfully and effectively with the community members she/he deals with on a daily basis. Finally, we need to continually work towards improving the level of trust between the community and ourselves.

- **Technical Skills.** These skills are a combination of both mental and physical: strong written and verbal communication ability; knowledge and updating of relevant laws; officer safety techniques; and proficiency at skills that support proper patrol procedures. We should possess these skills and should continually be looking for ways to enhance them as well as build new ones in order to grow as a police officer.

- **Problem Solving/Decision Making.** We need to be able to perceive and reason through the most complex patrol situations, making reasonable conclusions and proper decisions. We need to be able to recognize when a situation is a one-time event, or may be a symptom of some underlying condition. This analysis may require the officer to engage community members, a variety of social services and enforcement agencies as well as departmental units in the identification and responses to the this problem. Key elements of problem solving include creativity, reasonable risk taking, time management (including being available to assist other officers), officer safety and good old-fashioned police work.[4]

The Seattle Police Department uses the above expectations as a foundation for both supervisors and line officers to develop a mutual understanding of standards of behavior. The next step is to create a process through which sergeants can coach officers in problem solving, troubleshooting and helping with project management. Finally documentation of these activities will feed into a revised annual evaluation, that, rather than counting statistics. Will look at both qualitative and meaningful quantitative information, and appraise an officer's performance accordingly.[5] The Portland Police Bureau has made tremendous strides in providing officers with time needed for problem solving. The average time available for problem solving and self-initiated calls for service per patrol unit of 37 percent that equates to 21.9 minutes per

4. Correspondence from Barbara Raymond, Program Coordinator, *Seattle Police Department Performance Expectations for Patrol Officers, Seattle, WA,* *Seattle Police Department,* dated *August 7, 1997.*

5. *Ibid.*

hour. This means that the average patrol officer can devote just short of three hours to problem solving during a typical shift.[6]

Chronological Distribution

Since the police conduct an around-the-clock operation, the force must be efficiently distributed by hour of day in accordance with the crime, delinquency, vice and traffic accident experience, as shown by the records. The need for police service is the determining favor in the chronological distribution of the force. Many American police departments follow a plan, known as the three-platoon shift, in which the line power of the department, particularly the patrol force, is divided into three shifts of eight hours each, as follows:

First Platoon—8:00 A.M. to 4:00 P.M.

Second Platoon—4:00 P.M. to 12:00 Midnight

Third Platoon—12:00 Midnight to 8:00 A.M.

The exact time for platoon relief or change may vary slightly from one department to another, but the general schematic arrangement is now an almost universal characteristic of American police service. But the question cannot be disposed of quite so simply. On what basis can it be said that platoons should change at 8:00 A.M., 4:00 P.M., and 12:00 Midnight, respectively? Would 9:00 A.M., 5:00 P.M. and 1:00 A.M., or some other variation more appropriately meet the operating demands placed upon a police department? Furthermore, what should be the exact distribution of the available patrol strength among the three platoons? The answers to these questions cannot be provided by rule-of-thumb methods or speculation but depend upon painstaking analyses of data that should be made available by the record division of the department concerning the distribution of the need for police services by hour of day. It is obvious here in the approach to an important administrative problem that a good police records system is indispensable.

The variation in need for police service from hour to hour throughout the day follows a fairly consistent pattern. So the distribution of the force by hour of day presents no serious statistical difficulties where a police records system is properly maintained and the necessary statistical reports and analyses are provided and used. Since the police caseload for a twenty-four hour day does not arrange itself categorically by eight-hour periods; special deployment is needed. Patrol power superimposed over the regular shifts is being accepted by an increasing number of police administrators as the answer to caseload peaks that occur within an hour to a three-hour interval. Where this procedure is based upon careful analysis of caseload as indicated by available data, it

6. Portland Police Bureau, *Summary of Performance Measurements,* Portland, OR, Portland Police Bureau, 11/6/98, http://www.teleport. com/(police/index.html.

represents a desirable refinement in the selective distribution of manpower.

Patrol Beat Responsibility

Police service, simply speaking, is patrol service. Specialization has made serious inroads upon the line power of the patrol force. The compelling requirement or prerequisite for the elimination or modification of this special deployment of patrol personnel resources is a determination of policy by police management with respect to *patrol beat responsibility*. Everything pivots on this determination. Once the amount and the most effective distribution of patrol power have been determined, it still is necessary to locate the individual patrolman in the organizational structure where operating with maximum efficiency is possible. Under accepted administrative practice, the individual patrol officer is assigned to a given patrol beat and is held directly responsible for handling police problems in that circumscribed area. This serves to focus responsibility upon a given individual for the accomplishment of a given unit of work. Upon the successful application of this principle rests the fate of the police department and its administrators.

But the problem is not so simple. The important question arises immediately—where does the work and responsibility of the patrol-officer end and where does the detective's begin? This basic question and its answer should be high on the administrative agenda of every police department. If it is not the most important, it is among the most important of all administrative problems. Police administrators will do well to ponder its significance in the attainment of police objectives and re-examine their patterns of operation in the line. Policy in regard to this important matter, which is among the most important of all problems presented to police management, will vary from one department to another. At one end of the administrative spectrum, detectives are charged with total investigative responsibility. The officer merely responds to the radio call, makes an arrest, if perchance this is possible, and protects the scene until the detectives arrive to launch the investigation. Under this ill-advised policy, the detective division usually finds itself overloaded with uncleared cases in every category, with the result that major crime fails to receive the attention it deserves, and the officer has relatively little to do. It is difficult to escape the observation that under this arrangement, the department experiences a tragic waste of manpower because of the unused resources of the patrol division—this despite the sobering fact that patrol salaries represent the largest single item in the police budget.

There follows in succession those departments where the officer is held responsible for the preliminary investigation of cases originating on the assigned beat and the filing of a report covering all investigative activities on the case. The follow-up investigation and final clearance are a responsibility of the detective, except perhaps in minor cases. In an increasing number of other departments, the investigative responsibilities of the officer are even greater. At the other end of the spectrum is the department operating under a policy where virtually total case investigation and case clearance responsibility are assigned to the officer on the beat. Under this concept, the officer is responsible for the investigation and clearance of all cases originating on the beat, regardless of classification.

The officer is geared to the total delivery of police service. This means being held responsible for the robbery rate, the burglary rate, the automobile rate, the amount of grand and petty larceny, the extent of juvenile delinquency, the number of traffic accidents, traffic congestion, and all other police problems originating within the limits of the assigned patrol area. All uncleared cases represent a direct charge against the efficiency of the individual patrolman concerned, and provide a fair index to the person general performance record. Not only that, as pointed out above, the officer is responsible for the case investigation and its final disposition in all of these categories. The following significant paragraph appears in the General Information Bulletin for Applicants furnished by one police department to potential candidates for the position of patrolman, before an application form is issued:

> A patrol-officer is responsible for all crimes or reports arising on the assigned beat. The officer reports off the beat after completing a tour of duty, and is then required to write reports on all cases personally handled. This may take only a few minutes, or it may take several hours, depending upon the nature of the reports handled and the ability of the individual. Patrol-officers are held responsible for the investigation of all complaints regardless of seriousness and regardless of the fact that detectives or supervisory officers may assist and counsel in the investigation.

Obviously, the individual officer cannot discharge these manifold duties and responsibilities without considerable assistance; hence, there are at their disposal the entire resources of the department. The facilities of the detective division or in any jurisdiction where the position of detective has been abolished—experienced patrol-officers in plain clothes fulfill this function. They are available to give the necessary aid in the investigation of felony investigations, and in other instances where the case investigation would take the officer beyond the beat boundaries. Experts in the traffic unit are at their disposal in meeting the various situations and problems associated with the regulation and control of traffic in their area. Members of the crime prevention unit likewise come to the officer's assistance in the solution of problems connected with the prevalence of juvenile delinquency in the officer's assigned area. Similarly, the facilities of the crime laboratory, crime analysis, and all other support units in the organization assist the individual patrol-officer in keeping the beat clean. But regardless of the type or volume of assistance officers may bring into play, they cannot "pass the buck;" the responsibility for the delivery of police service in the area to which they are assigned belongs to them.

In Edmonton, Canada the principle of ownership is practiced. Twenty-two officers are assigned to villages where patrol on foot and have their own store-front offices manned by volunteer citizens. These officers take care of, as much of the daily policing needs as possible and request specialists as needed.[7] A system of beat responsibility requires a superior officer in police uniform, superior recruiting standards, and a superior training program, together with a salary structure attracting this type of personnel. Today, this is the caliber of officer being recruited on an increasing scale into the American police services.

Single vs. Two–Officer Patrol

In the past, patrol has been carried on in American police departments largely with two officers in each car. Early in his career, Vollmer came to the conclusion that in the interests of both economy and efficiency, this costly practice should be discontinued. For more than forty-five years, the city of Berkeley, California, was policed by single-officer patrols. The record speaks for itself. It has now been demonstrated that one officer in the patrol car is more efficient than two officers. As a general rule, when two officers are placed in a car, both become lazy and indifferent; experience shows one individual in a car must, of necessity, keep on the alert. The use of one individual in a car makes possible a much broader and more intensive patrol of the city by releasing officers for additional patrol. Twice as much patrol service is thus provided; a police car gives twice the attention to the area; a given police problem is inspected during a tour of duty twice as many times as it would be if there were only half as many units. Further, the factor of safety of the individual officer is increased by the availability of a larger number of patrol units. Not only does the use of the one-person car extend the range of patrol coverage, but it also discourages the inattention to police duty that often is the result of two officers fraternizing together or engaging in non-police activities.

The adoption of computer aided dispatching has eliminated the last substantial argument against the single-officer motor patrol. Thus, any one beat becomes the nucleus of a large patrol unit; the patrol cars on adjacent beats constitute a reserve force instantly available and capable of being massed or concentrated in the affected area at a moment's notice. In an emergency situation, as many officers as are available can be moved quickly into the scene of operations. In a controlled experiment and study of single v. double officer motor patrol it was determined that one-man patrol cars are safer, more efficient, and cheaper. Savings from the use of one-person cars are significant. Eighteen one-person cars can be deployed for the same cost as ten two-person cars. The study involved the use of 44 patrol units, half one-officer and the other half two-officer. The design included a number of comparisons between the two groups. The underlying assumption was

7. Chris R. Braiden, "Enriching Traditional Roles," in Larry T. Hoover, Editor, *Police Management–Issues &* *Perspectives,* Washington, DC, Police Executive Research Forum, 1992, p. 103.

that "the substantial extra cost of two-officer units would not be justified for a given situation unless there were favorable and important differences between one-and two-officer units in one or more of several areas." [8]

In the six largest cities, the current staffing of patrol units varies considerably. Officer safety seems to be playing a larger part when deciding whether one or two officers should staff cars. In New York City two officers man the patrol units. Chicago and Detroit use two officer patrols during the evening and night shifts, but during the day shift, 10 percent of the Chicago units and 33.1 percent of the Detroit units have two officers. In Houston an emphasis is placed on the use of one-officer vehicles although on the evening and night shifts a number of two-officer units are used. Los Angeles has mostly two-officer units during the evening and night shift but during the day almost one-half of the units are manned by one officer.[9] Table 11–1 reflects the average percent of all patrol units on shifts of seven hours or longer during designated 24–hour periods that were comprised of one-officer and two-officer patrol units. County police departments had the highest percentage of patrol units with one-officer followed by sheriff's departments and state police agencies. More Special police agencies (airport, transit, and school) used more two-officer patrol units (23 %) than any other type of law enforcement department.

Table 11–1

One–Officer and Two–Officer Patrol Units
by Type of Agency

Type of Agency	County	Municipal	Sheriff	Special	State
One-officer Units	97%	89%	95%	77%	94%
Two-officer Units	3	11	5	23	6

Source: Brian A. Reaves and Andrew L. Goldberg, *Law Enforcement Management and Administrative Statistics, 1997: Data for Individual State and Local Agencies with 100 or more Officers,* Washington, DC, Bureau of Justice Statistics, April 1999 p. xv.

Take–Home Police Vehicles

Known variously as the take-home car plan, car saturation program and the police fleet program, an increasing number of police

8. Clyde L. Cronkrite, "Facing Increasing Crime with Decreasing Resources," *FBI Law Enforcement Bulletin,* April 1983, Vol. 52, No. 4, p. 4.

9. Pate and Hamilton, *op. cit.,* pp. 8–9.

departments now permanently assign a patrol car to a particular officer, thereby enabling its use on-duty as well as off-duty. The advantages claimed include:[10]

- During shift changes there are two shifts on the road.
- Increased enforcement.
- Decreased call-out time for emergencies.
- Reduced maintenance expenses.
- Longer life of patrol vehicles.
- Improved officer morale.
- Citizens feel more secure.

In a recent survey it was found that 35 percent of municipal police officers were allowed to take marked vehicles home. In about a fifth of these departments, off-duty officers were allowed to use the cars for private errands (see table 11–2).[11] Sheriffs are more liberal in this area. Seventy Three percent of the departments permit sworn officers to take marked cars home. Special police allowed fewer officers to commute in marked vehicles (18%) and never allowed officers to run off-duty errands.[12]

Table 11–2					
Agencies Allowing Officers to Drive Marked Vehicles For Commuting Purposes and Off–Duty Private Errands					
Type of Agency	County	Municipal	Sheriff	Special	State
Commuting	58%	35%	73%	18%	90
Off-duty private Errands	30	15	27	0	14

Source: Brian A. Reaves, and Pheny Z. Smith, *Law Enforcement Management and Administrative Statistics, 1993: Data for Individual State and Local Agencies with 100 or more Officers,* Washington, Dc, Bureau of Justice Statistics, September 1995, p. xii.

The Indianapolis Police Department was the first to apply the program to municipal police service when they inaugurated a plan under which police officers assigned to patrol cars take them home at the end of their tour of duty for their own personal use. The only requirement is that whenever they are in their car, they must keep the radio turned on and respond to police calls. The Centralia Police Department purchased used vehicles from the Washington State Pa-

10. Tom Yates, "Take Home Cars: After the First Shock There are Benefits," *Law and Order,* May 1992, Vol. 40, No. 5, p. 88.

11. Reaves, and Smith, *op. cit.,* p. xii.

12. *Ibid.*

trol. These vehicles are (at a maximum) five years old and with less than 100,000 miles. The WSP assigns personal vehicles to each trooper, consequently these automobiles are "one owner" vehicles and generally are in better condition than "pool" vehicles. Dollar cost comparisons indicate that the acquisition costs for 14 used state patrol vehicles as compared to four new patrol vehicles there was a projected savings of $17,350. The advantages to the officers in the program include the savings in gas, convenience, and the availability of departmental transportation to training activities and for other support details.

Benefits to the department, apart from the financial savings, include the immediate availability of officers to respond to major crime alerts. It also makes for better utilization of officer time, an extra 15 to 30 minutes of service time daily due to officers being in service and on the air from the time they leave their residences until they arrive at their station. It also has more police units on the street at any given time, and the increased availability of units for rapid response to emergencies.[13] The Jacksonville, FL, Police Department has found their take-home vehicle policy has proven highly successful. In one-month off-duty officers driving marked vehicles made 210 drunk driving arrests, and handled 210 accidents. During the month, there were 12,000 off-duty incidents taken care of by these officers. Consequently, on-duty officers had more time to handle other events.[14]

Foot Patrol

During recent years, the use of foot patrols has increased somewhat, and at the present time a large number of municipal police departments utilize _____ foot patrol along with other means of patrol such as, horse, boat, bicycle, motorcycle, and automobile.

Table 11–3

Agencies That Deploy Various Types of Patrol Units
on a Routine Basis

Type of Agency	County	Municipal	Sheriff	State
Foot	43%	55%	14%	10%
Automobile	100	100	100	100
Motorcycle	63	68	40	2
Bicycle	57	76	28	16
Horse	17	21	7	2
Marine	27	14	49	16

Note: Percent of agencies with patrol that deploy each type of patrol unit on shifts of seven hours or longer during designated 24 hour periods.

13. Robert Berg, "The Personal Car Program in a Small Police Department," *The Police Chief,* May 1984, Vol. LI, No. 5, pp. 64–65.

14. Yates, *op. cit.*

Source: Brian A. Reaves, and Andrew L. Goldberg, *Law Enforcement Management and Administrative Statistics, 1997, Data for Individual State and Local Agencies with 100 or more Officers*. Washington, D.C., Bureau of Justice Statistics, 1999, p. xv.

With the motorization of the force, the use of foot patrols declined and until recently was viewed by many departments as uneconomical and inefficient. Its resurgence is attributable in part to a perceived need to establish a closer relationship between the police and the people they serve. The evaluation of a neighborhood foot patrol in Flint, Michigan showed it was successful. Crime was reduced by 9 percent and calls for service reduced crime by 42 percent. The residents in the experimental area felt safer and police community relations improved. Interestingly enough, more than one third of the residents knew the name of the foot patrol officer. The program was widely accepted and residents voted to increase property taxes so the entire city would have officers on foot patrol. Currently there are 64–foot beats in the city.[15] One expert has concluded foot-patrol is neither a panacea nor a replacement for motorized patrol. Without question, it is an effective method of improving face-to-face communications between officers and residents.[16] In Flint, MI, and Newark, NJ, evaluations of the effectiveness of foot patrol concluded that:

- Residents were well aware of the program.

- There was a perceived reduction in the level of crime problems.

- The perceived level of neighborhood safety increased significantly.

Unfortunately there were study limitations. Foot patrol occurred only in commercial areas. The sample was too small, thus limiting the value of the study. One researcher concluded that the Flint study was, in reality, an analysis of the effectiveness of patrol officers initiating citizen contacts not foot patrol.[17] Opponents of foot patrol claim that its use restricts the police officer's mobility and lengthens the amount of time needed to cover his patrol area without providing proportionate benefits. The officer's efficiency can be curtailed further by inclement weather, the inability to carry certain equipment (report forms, specialized firearms, flares, first-aid kits, etc.), and limited capacity for pursuit. Furthermore a motorized police officer in the regular course of his duties, covers almost as much ground on foot as an officer assigned to foot patrol. Under the concept of community policing it has been recommended that it not only be a department-wide commitment, but

15. Robert C. Trojanowicz, "Foot Patrol: Some Problem Areas," *The Police Chief,* June 1984, Vol. LI, No. 6, p. 47.

16. *Ibid.,* p. 49.

17. Dennis Jay Kenney, *Police and Policing: Contemporary Issues,* New York, Praeger Publishers, 1989, pp. 117–117.

that all motor patrol officers should be required to leave their automobiles and interact face-to-face with citizens.[18]

Use of Dogs

The use of dogs in police service to supplement patrol activities has gained increasing acceptance throughout the police field. Just after the middle of the last century police departments in 120 cities were making use of the dog in patrol service, in addition to their expanding use in the Armed Forces.[19] Typical of K9 programs is the San Jose Police Department that created a canine unit in 1962. Originally all of the dogs were donated, and currently purchased by the individual officer. Every dog in this specialized unit is an imported German shepherd. The unit is located in the bureau of field operations and commanded by a lieutenant. The unit consists of two sergeants and twelve officers that are split into 2 six-officer-dog teams. The initial training is a 160–hour police/handler class, and then the team must pass a rigorous qualification course to be accepted into the canine unit. The training includes tracking, obedience, and protection work. Officer/dog teams also participate in a minimum of 20 hours per month of maintenance training.[20]

Generally, dogs used in police work fall primarily into two distinct categories: First is the dog trained to attack on command and capable of searching for a suspect hiding inside a building. This animal is also useful in stopping the use of deadly force.[21] The second category of dog has the added ability to track a suspect and locate either explosives or drugs.[22] Police departments have found dogs of particular value with officers patrolling the waterfront, railroad yards, transportation terminals, factory, warehouse and industrial areas, back alleys, parks, business districts, deteriorated areas and other high hazard locations, particularly during the night. Their usefulness appears to be well demonstrated in the following situations:[23]

- Psychological advantage and reduction of risk to the officer in hazard and potential hazard situations.
- Protecting an officer under attack.
- Preventing and curbing crimes of stealth and violence.

18. Robert Trojanowicz, and Bonnie Bucqueroux, *Community Policing—How to Get Started,* Second Edition, Cincinnati, OH, Anderson Publishing, 1998, p. 3.

19. Samuel G. Chapman, "Dogs Versus Crowds," *Journal of Police Science and Administration,* December 1980, Vol. 17, No. 1, p. 316.

20. San Jose Police Department, *San Jose PD Canine Unit,* San Jose, CA, 10/10/98, http://www.sjpd.org/K9.html.

21. Phyllis Raybin and Howard Schroeder, *Police Dogs,* New York, Crestwood House, 1985, pp. 1–24.

22. John R. Kidwell, "Dogs and Dollars," *The Police Chief,* February 1979, Vol. LV, No. 2, p. 45.

23. Samuel G. Chapman, *Dogs in Police Service,* Public Administration Service, Chicago, 1960. A Summary of Experience in Great Britain and the United States. This publication also contains an excellent bibliography of the rather extensive literature now available on the use of dogs in police service.

- Searching for and holding criminal suspects.

- Searching a building.

- Indicating to the officer the presence of a suspicious person.

- Crowd control.

- Guarding police vehicles.

- Deployment to those areas in the city where the records indicate crime is most prevalent.

- Open country searches, where the dog is trained for tracking.

Police departments planning to initiate canine corps programs should confer in advance with departments where the use of dogs has extended over a substantial period of time. It is advisable to study carefully the need, the cost, and impact on the officer's work patterns, to ascertain the details of program administration. Since the police throughout the country are now accepting the use of dogs, police departments will do well to explore their value and usefulness in the patrol services. In addition to routine patrol, they would seem to be particularly well adapted in certain types of situations for use with the SWAT team.

Team Policing

Closely related to apprehension capability and somewhat similar to the fluid patrol system and the tactical unit operation, which is treated in this Chapter, is a concept, now attracting the attention of American police departments—*team policing or interception patrol*. Unlike the fluid patrol system, it operates within the existing beat. It has for its central thesis the principle that the patrol force is a body of police manpower who are mobile and have available large blocks of time to devote to the prevention of crime by their presence on the streets. It can also intercept crime while it is in progress, and apprehend criminals during the commission of a crime or immediately after it has been committed.

Team policing or interception patrol is designed to accomplish three functions:

- It acts as a deterrent to criminal activity.

- It detects and/or intercepts criminal attacks.

- It is a reaction force to criminal attack (criminal investigation).

A term unit consisting of eight to ten officers headed by a Team Leader and a Deputy Leader, operates within the confines of a single patrol beat selected on the basis of its crime experience, as indicated by the records. The team unit operation uses random area patrol or search. Patrolling in a random manner means there is no fixed sequence or pattern by which the patrol visits each point in the area, yet all points in the area are visited within some average time limit such as a ten-minute interval. The theory of random area patrol pivots on the probability of detecting a crime-taking place within a given area by a patrol officer moving continuously in the area in a random manner. From a prevention point of view, the objective is to give the impression that the police are everywhere.

Team policing is based on the use of one-office patrol cars. It is held that unless one-office patrol units are used, the fielding of an effective interception patrol becomes an economic impossibility. But with the use of one man patrol cars, team policing can be implemented on one or two or more beats without appropriating more money for additional manpower. In other words, team policing can become operational with the presently available personnel strength in most police departments. However, this is contingent upon several factors. There must be a drastic reduction in the non-criminal activities of patrol services, so it can devote itself almost exclusively to crime prevention and control. This means patrol service must divest itself of the responsibility for traffic accident investigation, family disputes, public intoxication, and other non-criminal incidents and services to the public.

The enforcement section of the Traffic Unit must assume the responsibility for traffic accident investigation. The patrol wagon must be out on the streets patrolling and is delegated the responsibility for handling all drunks and disorderly calls. It is recommended that special two-officer units be set up to handle family arguments. Furthermore, criminal investigation itself must be reduced to the lowest possible minimum. Team policing is an offensive strategy and it means prevention and/or interception and arrest, not criminal investigation that is considered a defensive strategy or after-the-fact action by the police. As a matter of fact, some advocates of team policing hold that—*If a crime is not cleared after devoting one man-hour of investigation effort to the matter, close the case and forget it.*

They point out, however, that the one man-hour figure is to be regarded as arbitrary and should serve only as a point of departure. It can be decreased or increased as experience dictates and should be applied primarily to crimes against property. The central idea of team policing is to reduce the need for criminal investigation. Obviously, the more it can be reduced the greater the time that can be devoted to prevention, interception patrol and arrest. Team policing or interception patrol is deployed during the hours of darkness and on those days of the week when the records indicate the need for this special type of police operation. During daylight hours, when people are in circulation, they act as a deterrent to criminal activity.

One of the most serious problems confronting police agencies today is isolation from the community. Several factors, including police organizational inflexibility and the attitudes of both the police and the public, have caused this isolation. Team policing places the police officer in an environment encouraging cooperation with the public and thus reduces isolation. Team policing brings the police organization down to the community level. This enables individual officers to cultivate community support and build personal relationships essential to the goal of police-community partnership. Effective police-community cooperation is critical to the success of a policing project. The public must be informed of the team-policing concept; its objectives and goals; public assistance and participation must be solicited actively. Successful community involvement programs depend on direct participation of citizens in the planning stages. Ongoing public commitment is encouraged by continually seeking the opinions, ideas, and assistance of citizens in resolving problems of mutual concern. In the 1970's the Los Angeles Police Department implemented team policing and was successful in reducing major crimes. Starting in 1977, the department was confronted with a loss of over 10 percent of its personnel over a five-year period and team policing was eliminated.[24]

Fluid Patrol

A unique method for the deployment of the patrol force has now made its appearance, under which the conventional beat system is abandoned. Known as the *Fluid Patrol System,* it completely replaces the patrol beat concept and provides for the shifting of patrol personnel hour by hour into sections of the community where and when current records data indicate the greatest demand for police service is most likely to occur. One city is divided into small grids or reporting districts of approximately one-quarter mile in area. Crime data and data concerning other demands for police service are tabulated by grids, from which special reports are prepared by the police records division and made available to the patrol commander at the beginning of each tour of duty. The platoon is divided into squads, each under the command of a field sergeant.

The city is separated into four sub-sectors, with a sergeant and squad assigned to each sub-sector. The supervisor may require a number of officers to report for duty in plain clothes for a stakeout. Or two or more officers may be assigned to patrol the entire sub-sector. Another alternative may be to assign officers to saturation patrol of two or more "hot" grids—all depending on the flow of reports and information from the police records division and what they have to say about the current situation.

Under certain circumstances, the radio dispatcher may direct all broadcasts to the sergeant who in turn assigns officers accordingly. This arrangement represents a special type of situation in which, for

24. Cronkhite, *op. cit.,* p. 2.

the duration of the emergency, radio control is temporarily vested in the field, subject, of course, to the receipt of additional instructions and information from headquarters. From the standpoint of police records administration and investigative responsibility, when a member of a squad becomes involved in a case, that person carries it through to final disposition. As an alternative, one or more officers may be assigned exclusively to follow-up case investigation. The police records unit or division is the life-blood of the Fluid Patrol System. The mainstay of the system is the computer and the machine tabulation of statistical data based upon the grid or reporting area.

It is strongly recommended that departments, even those with a personnel strength of from one to seventy-five officers, make a conversion to the grid system of tabulating criminal offenses, traffic accidents and other calls for police service. Whether the department moves toward the fluid system of patrol deployment or remains with the conventional patrol beat concept, the grid system will expedite a sound determination of patrol areas based upon the crime and traffic accident experience.

Directed and Preventive Patrol

Preventive patrol experiments like that instituted in a number of cities calls into question two widely held hypotheses about patrol:

- A visible patrol presence prevents crime by deterring potential offenders, and

- Public fear of crime is diminished by police presence.

In other words "free patrol time" should be directed rather than waiting for something to occur and then responding.[25] Traditionally, patrol operations have occurred as a result of calls for service. Beyond that type of duty officers engaged in administrative duties, self-initiated tasks, and preventive patrol. It has been estimated that up to 40 or 50 percent of an officer's tour of duty could be spent on routine patrol, with little direction given to them as to how to use the time. Research on the effectiveness of preventive patrol is mixed. For example, the Kansas City Preventive Patrol Experiment reported no observable difference in the level of crime in areas of high, regular, and low patrol intensity. Similar conclusions were found in studies in Nashville, and Albuquerque. On the other hand, some departments have experienced a reduction in reported crime when they increased patrols. In Wilmington, DE, during their Split–Force Experiment, patrol officers were assigned to either a basic (call for service) or a structured (preventive patrol) unit. There was a decline in reported crime and an increase in the number of arrests.

25. *Ibid.*, p. 3.

Even though the research on the effectiveness of preventive patrol has been inconclusive, many departments have sought ways to better manage uncommitted patrol time. One approach has been the use of directed patrol assignments. That is, preplanned, crime-and location-specific activities are substituted for some portion of the time normally spent on random patrol. The directed patrol assignment address beat problems, and can be measured against specified goals. As part of its Integrated Criminal Apprehension Program a department conducted a directed patrol project in one division. Manpower deployment and workload demands were matched. Dispatch alternatives were developed and a call prioritization policy was established. This freed up patrol time for directed patrol assignments. Manpower utilization forecasts, based on an analysis of dispatch data, provided the percentage of time and the number of officers likely to be available. With this information, 10 percent of all patrol time was devoted to directed patrol assignments without adding more officers. Even though it is only one of the factors that should be considered in developing a department's patrol plan, it is import to define the average amount of time officers should devote to calls for service, administrative duties, personal relief time, routine preventive patrol and proactive directed patrol.[26]

Differential Response

Recent studies indicate that immediate response to all requests for service is not cost-effective. Consequently, a number of police agencies are now providing immediate response only to requests involving serious crimes in progress or where there is a present threat of death or serious injury. Other responses to calls for service are delayed and scheduled when sufficient radio units are available. In some cases, low priority requests are made on an appointment basis during non-peak work hours (see Figure 11–1).

In Los Angeles, under a program called System to Optimize Radio Car Manpower (STORM), a specifically deployed small percentage of radio units handle, on a scheduled basis, a large percentage of non-critical, low priority calls for service, *e.g.*, barking dogs, loud radios, etc. Other radio units, therefore, remain available for immediate response to critical calls. Additionally, on all calls where a delay in dispatching occurs, a callback is made to determine if the citizen still requests a police unit when one becomes available. This has reduced dispatching radio units when they are no longer needed. STORM provides the equivalent of approximately 56 officers in additional field time.

26. Margaret J. Levin and J. Thomas McEwen, *Patrol Deployment*, Washington, D.C., National Institute of Justice, 1985, pp. 5–6.

Figure 11–1

Differential Incident Classification

Major Personal Injury—Denotes that the victim has been injured in such a manner that medical attention is needed immediately, or that the victim is dead. Examples of calls for service that might be classified in this fashion are aggravated assaults, serious traffic accidents, robberies, homicides, and serious domestic disturbances.

Major Property Damage/Loss—Denotes the theft of items (or damage of items) whose value is over $500. Some of the calls for service that might fall into this classification include motor vehicle theft, extensive vandalism, burglaries, larcenies, robberies, and traffic accidents.

Potential Personal Injury—Describes incidents where there is a possibility that a citizen will be injured. Incidents that might be classified in this manner include domestic and neighborhood disturbances, disorderly persons, suspicious persons, mental disturbances, hazardous road conditions, and any incident involving an armed suspect at the scene.

Potential Property Damage/Loss—Denotes a possibility that theft of property, or damage to property, will occur. Incidents that might fall into this category include prowler, suspicious person and suspicious vehicle.

Minor Personal Injury—Refers to incidents where the victim has been injured but not to the extent that medical attention is warranted. Some incidents that might be included in this category are traffic accidents, simple assaults, fights or brawls, domestic disturbances, and purse snatches.

Minor Property Damage/Loss—Refers to the theft of, or damage to, property whose value is less than $500. Included in this classification might be the following types of incidents: Burglaries, larcenies, traffic accidents, and vandalism.

Other Minor Crime—Refers to incidents of a criminal nature when there are no personal injuries and no property damage or loss. Some incidents that might be classified as such are malicious mischief, neighborhood disturbances, and public drunks.

Other Minor Non-Crime—Includes calls of mainly a service nature where no crime has occurred. Examples of such calls are most animal complaints, non-violent mental disturbances, and citizens' requests for assistance.

Source: Michael T. Farmer, Editor, *Differential Police Response Strategies,* Washington D.C., Police Executive Research Forum, 1991, p. 43.

Some agencies, including the San Diego Police Department (SDPD), have worked with their city council to establish a prioritized list of activities performed by radio units. By forming an agreement between the city council and the police department as to the desired activities to be performed, appropriate response times, how long each activity should take, and how much available patrol time should exist, they have established the basis for manpower requirements. If requests for service from the public increase, then the city council must provide funding for additional personnel or recognize that response time will increase and lower priority activities will not be handled. By this method, the council directly shares in the responsibility for proper service to the community. Other agencies have strict control over the number of units responding to a dispatched call. Units other than those assigned are not allowed to respond. Additionally, units may not go "out to the station" unless approval is received from the dispatcher. To facilitate this procedure, field sergeants must announce their location by radio periodically so nearby units can meet them for crime report approval in the field. Also, approval for booking is often given by telephone when jail facilities are located some distance from the approving watch commander.[27]

Use of Computers

Computer models have gained increasing popularity among police departments. Models applied most frequently include:

- Patrol Car Allocation Model (PCAM).
- Hypercube Model.
- PATROL/PLAN Model.
- BEAT/PLAN Model.

These models were specifically designed to assist in resolving patrol resource allocation issues. Their advantage is they can handle multiple objectives easily. Thus, for example, if there are objectives on travel time, unit utilization, and delayed calls, the models can determine the minimum number of patrol units needed to satisfy all objectives simultaneously. Some of this performance measures—particularly the queuing measures—are difficult to calculate and the necessary formulas require mathematical training to understand. By employing models, the analyst can concentrate on the development of performance objectives and not have to spend time calculating.

Using these models also helps the analyst and police managers to focus on the issues in terms of objectives and supporting data. They require managers to be specific on what is to be achieved in the patrol allocation plan. In this regard, the models are beneficial in getting managers to focus on exactly what the department desires. A police department requires careful thought before it decides to use a computer model. A key consideration is whether the department has the technically qualified staff, or can hire the staff, to run the model. In addition to a solid understanding of police operations, the staff needs to have a good background in computers and mathematics.[28]

27. Cronkhite, *op. cit.*, pp. 2–3.   **28.** Levin and McEwen, *op. cit.*, pp. 47 and 55.

At the operational level exciting things are impacting line officers. The Los Angles Police Department is presently engaging in a Field Data Capture (FDC) project. If this pilot testing proves successful it will revolutionize the traditional methods of gathering data in preliminary and traffic investigations. Data is transmitted digitally by officers from lap top computers back to community police stations via wireless transmission using radio frequencies. This eliminates the need for officers to return to their stations for report approval. It saves significant officer time.[29]

Women in Police Service

Traditionally, policewomen were widely used for secretarial, switchboard, and clerical duties. In other police departments, women usually were assigned to specialized divisions handling juvenile offenders or dealing with community relations, and many departments select women on the basis of their knowledge and experience in these areas. However, policewomen also participated in special investigative assignments, such as in cases of rape, obscenity calls, or voyeurism. They were also utilized as jail matrons. There is a strong trend to integrate women into other areas of law enforcement, such as radio dispatching, criminalistics, and broader criminal investigative duties. Many policewomen hold professional positions in police administration and teaching positions in police academies. Among the most controversial is assignment of policewomen to patrol operations. In 1968, the Indianapolis Police Department assigned policewomen to full patrol functions. New York City and Washington, D.C. followed, as did other departments throughout the United States. By 1971 one survey found that 15 different departments assigned women to field operations and that there were approximately 3,700 police women employed full-time by law enforcement agencies. By 1996 a survey showed there were 206,629 female sworn officers. This is a 24.9 percent of all full-time sworn officers. Table 11–4 identifies the characteristics of sworn personnel by gender. Statistics showed the larger the department the higher the percentage of female officers. In cities with populations greater than 250,000, the percentage of female sworn officers was 15.2. On the other hand, in towns with populations under 10,000 only 6.7 percent of the officers were female.[30] Part of the increased use of women in law enforcement has come about because of class action law suits and court decisions. This has occurred in Tallahassee, FL, Syracuse, NY, and the Ohio State Police. In one study, 11 percent of the respondents stated they hired women because of governmental pressure.[31] The number of women in departments varies considerably.

29. Bernard C. Parks, *Achievements, Accomplishments, and Future initiatives,—First Year in Office,* Los Angeles, CA, Los Angeles Police Department, August 12, 1997/98, p. 31.

30. Kathleen Maguire and Ann L. Pastore, Editors, *Sourcebook of Criminal Justice Statistics–1997,* Washington, DC, Bureau of Justice Statistics, 1998, p. 46.

31. Arthur R. Sharp, "Recruiting (& Retaining) Women Officers," *Law and*

For example, in Miami Beach, FL sworn female officers constitute 28 percent of the department, and 26 percent of the officers in Madison, WI. There are 22 percent in Pittsburgh, PA, and 19 percent in Birmingham, AL.[32] In a 1998 national police survey the International Association of Chiefs of Police found that large departments were more apt to recruit women than smaller ones. In larger departments slightly more that one-third of the departments found it very difficult to retain women police officers, while approximately one-fourth pointed out it was difficult to retain male officers.[33] Two experts point out masculine with their own feminine identities, while some respond to male resistance by leaving law enforcement.[34] In the Albuquerque Police Department that the "new policewoman" acts as a professional by balancing work defined as as study by the Institute for Women in Trades, Technology & Science (IWITTS) found that many of the problems confronting women police officers was caused by the failure to integrate women into the male workplace. Some of the problems identified included the inability of supervisors to apply the light duty police to pregnancy; ill fitting uniforms and equipment; limited help with childcare and physical education instructors not pacing women.[35]

Table 11–4

Full–Time Sworn Personnel in Local Police Departments, by Sex and Population Group

Police Officers (sworn)

Population group	Total	Percent male	Percent female
Total cities: 9,907 Group 1	390,590	89.9%	10.1%
65 cities, 250,00 and over Group 11	145,312	84.8	15.2

Order, May 1993, Vol. 41. No. 5, pp. 89–92.

32. Bureau of Justice Statistics, *Law Enforcement Management and Administrative Statistics*, Washington, DC, Department of Justice, 1995, pp. 1–9.

33. International Association of Chiefs of Police, "Women Policing—IACP, Gallup Assess Recruitment, Promotion, Retention Issues," *The Police Chief*, October 1998, Vol. LXV, No. 10, pp. 36–40.

34. Susan Ehrlich Martin, and Nancy C. Jurik, *Doing Justice, Doing Gender: Women in Law Enforcement and Criminal Justice Occupations*, Thousand Oaks, CA, 1996, pp. 1–84.

35. Joseph Polisar and Donna Milgram, "Recruiting Integrating and Retaining Women Police Officers," *The Police Chief*, October 1998, Vol. LXV, No. 10, pp. 42–52.

144 cities: 100,000 to 249,999	40,790	90.1	9.9
Group 111			
359 cities, 50,000 to 99,999	43,744	92.4	7.6
Group 1V			
682 cities, 25,000 to 49,999	42,278	93.5	6.5
Group V			
1,699 cities: 10,000 to 24,999	50,616	94.4	5.6
Group VI			
6958 cities under 10,000	67,850	93.3	6.7

Source: Kathleen Maguire and Ann L. Pastore, Editors, *Sourcebook of Criminal Justice Statistics 1997*, Washington, DC, Bureau of Justice Statistics, 1998, p. 46.

Susan E. Martin, in her definitive study, found that while there are more women in local law enforcement today, functioning as sworn officers, there has not been any great inroad to administrative positions, but things are changing. In view of the late entry of women into police work this is not surprising because it takes time to make oneself eligible for promotion. Seniority is still a common requirement as part of promotional criteria. It has also been suggested that the promotional process screen out women when the process is subjective.[36] In recent years, one study showed that more women are working at every rank in police departments. Female officers (3.7 percent) worked as first line supervisors (sergeant). The percentage dropped as they moved up the promotional ladder. Two and one-half percent held the rank of lieutenant and 1.4 percent held a higher rank.[37] A few women have become "top cops." This has occurred over the years in several larger cities such as Atlanta, GA, Houston, TX, Portland, OR, and Tucson, AZ. Others have become chief executive officers in smaller departments and one study estimated there were 123 occupying this auspicious position.[38]

The road to equality for female police officers has not been an easy one to travel. Many obstacles have impeded their progress as is best illustrated by the case of Mark Fuhrman who when interviewed by an aspiring screenwriter described systematic misconduct. During the investigation of Fuhrman, the Internal Affairs Division (IAD) found that four officers of the West Los Angeles division created an association known as Men Against Women (MAW). This group set out to create a hostile work environment for female officers. Investigators

36. S. Grennan and R. Munoz, "Women as Police Supervisors in the Twenty-first Century: A Decade of Promotional Practices by Gender in Three Major Police Agencies," in R. Muraskin and A.R. Roberts, Editors, Saddle River, NJ, Prentice Hall, 1996, pp. 34—354.

37. Susan E. Martin, *On the Move : The Status of Women in Policing*, Washington, DC, Police Foundation, 1990, pp. 30–31.

38. *Ibid.*

determined that the conduct of MAW inhibited some policewomen from safely and effectively performing their duties and created the fear that they would not be backed up by male officers. It was also found that MAW officers would ostracize male officers who did not support their boycott of female officers.[39] As the result of the Fuhrman the LAPD recognized the need to take more initiative in handling issues related to sexual harassment and discrimination. As a result, policies and procedures were changed and training provided. With the reorganization of the LAPD in 1998 there is now an Office of the Ombudsperson (reporting to the Chief of Staff) and reporting to that office is a Women's Coordinator. The latter office is available to all departmental employees as counselor and advisor for assisting sworn and civilian female employees regarding promotional and assignment opportunities. The Women's Coordinator acts as spokesperson for female officers in the resolution of problems unique to women, assists and monitors the efforts to recruit and retain female officers. It also advise in matters involving affirmative actions as relates to women; and counsels and advises on personnel, equipment and uniform problems involving female sworn employees.[40]

The National Center for Women and Policing serves as a resource for women police, law enforcement agencies, community leaders and public officials seeking to increase the numbers of women police. The center works to:

- conduct educational campaigns to raise awareness among decision-makers and the general public about the benefits of increasing the numbers of women in policing.

- promote innovative action strategies to increase the numbers of women in policing and women's representation in policy-making positions.

- conduct training programs for community and women leaders seeking reform.

- Promote specialized Family Violence Units within law enforcement agencies as a strategy for more effective police response to family violence crimes.

- Develop a *pro bono* attorney network for women on law enforcement agencies experiencing sexual harassment and discrimination.

- Publish and disseminate research and educational materials on women in policing.[41]

39. Los Angeles Police Department, *Mark Fuhrman Task Force, Executive Summary,* Los Angeles, CA, Los Angeles Police Department, 1997, pp. 1—69.

40. Los Angeles Police Department, *Women's Coordinator,* 2/9/99, *http://www.lapdonline.org/index.htm.*

41. National Center for Women in Policing, *Prospectus,* Los Angeles, CA, A Project of the Feminist Majority Foundation, 1995, p. 1.

In the future, more and more women will enter law enforcement and agencies must work diligently to integrate them into the organization. There are still personnel in some departments who feel police work should remain a male-dominated occupation. This and other obstacles must be overcome so law enforcement can benefit from the skills the females can bring to law enforcement.[42]

Domestic Violence Response Team

Domestic violence calls are usually responded to with reluctance. One of the reason is the danger involved. For example, in 1907 fourteen officers died after responding to disturbance calls, and 11 of which involved family disputes. It also equaled the 10–year average.[43] Domestic disturbances are especially difficult to handle and are usually time consuming. Unfortunately, it can be a repetitive call unless certain measures can be taken to alleviate the problem. In the past, patrol officers have coordinated their findings with social agencies that are experts in the field of child abuse, domestic violence, or elder abuse. Some departments have seen fit to put together a domestic violence response team. This team consists of both law enforcement and social service personnel. It includes a wide range of people, starting with the dispatcher. It also can include hotline volunteers. Follow-up personnel are numerous including officers and social workers. Investigators conduct criminal investigations and social workers provide preventive services.

In 1993, fifty-three percent of the municipal police departments had units specializing in domestic violence.[44] Crisis interventionists are team members in some communities and usually include shelter personnel. The actual team composition varies and depends upon the resources in each community. In small communities regional or state resources may be needed to accomplish desired results. The key to success in this area is to develop a program to protect the victim and helps them deal with the current situation. If prosecution occurs, the victim is helped to cope with the justice system. Experts point out that the Domestic Violence Response Team, adequately staffed and trained, can reduce non-stranger violence.[45] Such a team is a valuable resource for line officers.

Mental Health Response Team

When the police perspective, combines with sound psychological consultation a team can be created that is invaluable to the police in

42. International Association Chiefs of Police, "The Future of Women in Policing: Mandates for Action," *The Police Chief,* March 1999, Vol. LXVI, No. 3, pp, 53–56.

43. Federal Bureau of Investigation, 1997, *Law Enforcement Officers Killed and Assaulted,* Uniformed Crime Reports, Washington, D.C., U.S. Government Printing Officer, 1999, p. 3

44. Reaves and Smith, *op. cit. p xiv.*

45. Neil R.M. Stratton, "The Domestic Violence Response Team," in John A. Brown, Peter C. Unsinger, and Harry W. More, Editors, *Law Enforcement and Social Welfare, The Emergency Response,* Springfield, IL, Charles C. Thomas, 1990, pp. 47–48.

helping them attain departmental goals. To be effective, members of the team should have an understanding of police techniques and procedures and be especially adept at identifying and categorizing human behavior. The number of people on such a team varies from two to ten. The combination of backgrounds can be psychology, psychiatry, clinical social work, or mental health. Whatever the composition of the team, they should be trained as a group and prepared to respond to police emergencies. The team is especially helpful to police in a hostage situation or with a barricaded individual(s). The duties include:

- **Relationship assessment.** The team observes the negotiation, and provides feedback regarding the nature of the responsiveness. They suggest conversation that should be emphasized and which to avoid.

- **Negotiation support.** Based on negotiation conversations, they provide information on the hostage-takers personality.

- **Diagnosis of the hostage-taker.** Place the subject into a diagnostic category, e.g., schizophrenic, personality disorder. Such categorization can lead to predicting an outcome of the negotiation and suggesting potential approaches.

- **Gather information about the hostage-taker.** Constructing a personal history of the subject does this. It can include gathering information from relatives, friends, co-workers, and others.

- **Hostage analysis.** Team members gather information about the hostage(s) in order to identify unique problems.

- **Debriefing.** Provide assistance by analyzing the strengths and weaknesses of the negotiation process.

In providing further assistance, mental health response team members can train police officers in negotiation techniques, and assist in the creation of operation instructions. This team can enhance the ability of the police department to respond to special situations that they encounter daily.[46] This team provides valuable support to line officers when the situation dictates. In St. Petersburg, FL everyone of its 550 officers receive training in police contact with the mentally ill. It is an eight hour program developed in partnership with mental health professionals.[47]

Crisis Intervention Team

Mentally ill members of a community come into constant with the police. On occasion headlines will describe encounters by the police with those who are allegedly mentally ill. In some instance these

46. Bruce W. Ebert, "The Mental Health Response Team," in John A. Brown, Peter C. Unsinger and Harry W. More, Editors, *Law Enforcement and Social Work, The Emergency Response,* Springfield, IL, Charles C. Thomas, 1990, pp. 10–20.

47. Ronald J. Getz, "Reaching Out to the Mentally Ill," *Law and Order,* Vol. 47, No. 5, pp. 51–54.

encounters have resulted in the death when an ill person has stopped taking their medication. Advocates of the mental health community have developed a Crisis Intervention Team (CIT) training program. This 40–hour of training prepared selected patrol officers to deal with calls relating to "mental disturbances." Officers who work in the community on a daily basis respond to these calls throughout their jurisdiction. In Memphis, TN, five percent of the line personnel (30) were initially trained to handle these special calls and now there are 160 officers who have completed CIT programs. Beyond helping someone in need trained personnel performing this function are usually back on patrol within 15 minutes as contrasted to two to six hours dealing with mental health facilities.[48]

Case Study

Lieutenant Richard "Rich" Greigs

Rich Greigs is a lieutenant in the Grangerville Police Department where he has most recently been assigned to the management section. He has nine years experience and most recently supervised a team of officers utilizing the problem solving process of community policing. His team was very successful in dealing with problems and fostering a team environment and he provided strong leadership and vision. He is a graduate of the local university with a degree in human resources management. The community has a population of 104,981 and is best described as a racially and culturally diverse community. It has an excellent tax base because of several light industrial plants and three major shopping centers. The city has been plagued by residential burglaries, but has a below average crime rate in other categories for cities its size. The department has 160 sworn officers and 140 part-time or civilian personnel. It has a budget of $15 million and has a state of the art communications system.

The department has strived to employee women in the department other than clerical positions, but has not been successful in this effort. Over the last four years the department has recruited 23 women, but only seven have remained with the department. Six of the women were unable to complete the physical training part of the academy program and the others left the department for varying reasons. The department has received a lot of pressure from women's groups to hire and retain more women. Additionally, there is a class action suit pending against the department filed by three former members under city affirmative action policies charging discrimination. Women who have left claimed they were evaluated by a different standard and that they were constantly harassed and told that police work was a "man's job". The city manager has told the chief of police that she wanted the

48. Donald G. Turnbaugh, "Crisis Intervention Teams: Curing Police Problems with the Mentally Ill," *The Police Chief,* February 1999, Vol. LXVI, No. 2, pp. 52–54.

"mess" cleaned up as soon as possible and mandated that the department create a viable recruitment and retention plan.

Lt. Greigs has been asked to pinpoint the cause or causes of the problem an recommend managerial strategies designed to remedy the situation. He has been given two months to complete his report and submit a plan to eliminate the dysfunctional behavior.

If you were Lt. Greigs what would be the first thing you would do? Why? What would you do about the physical training part of the academy program? What training would you recommend to deal with the police culture? Why? What would you do to improve the retention of women police officers?

For Further Reading

Bernard C. Parks, *Achievements, Accomplishments, and Future Initiatives-First Year in Office,* Los Angeles, CA., Los Angeles Police Department, August 12, 1997/98, pp. 1–45.

> Presents the myriad of accomplishment by the Los Angeles Police Department under the guidance of Chief of Police Bernard C. Parks, Describes the reorganization of the department, the quest for accountability, and the enhancement of communications between the rank and file of the department. Reviews data for sworn personnel by rank, gender and ethnicity. Lists 1998 departmental initiatives that range from reducing crime and the fear of crime to promoting healthy working and interpersonal relationships amongst employees.

Timothy N. Oettmeier, "Matching Structure to Objectives," in Larry T. Hoover, *Police Management–Issues & Perspectives,* Washington, DC, Police Executive Research forum, 1992, pp. 31–60.

> The author describes the patrol function in transition starting with the traditional method and ending with the emergence of a new perspective. Reviews the research initiatives ranging from the studies in the 1970s. To include preventative patrol and response time studies. Presents ten conclusions from these studies ranging from the need to eliminate preventive patrol to the need to have stronger tie with the community. Recommends the need to "proactively" initiate patrol strategies that can interdict criminal activity, and the necessity of a coactive relationship with members of the community.

Joseph Polisar, "Recruiting, Integrating and Retaining Women Police Officers–Strategies That Work," *The Police Chief,* October 1998, Vol. LXV, No. 10, pp. 42–52.

> The author describes the participation of the Albuquerque Police Department in a national demonstration project designed to create

technologies and strategies for helping employers to recruit and integrate women into male-dominated occupations. Describes women-specific strategies that addresses sexual harassment and pregnancy policies. Recommends training for line officers and their supervisors. Points out the necessity of determining the special needs of women in law enforcement.

Donald G. Turnbaugh, "Crisis Intervention Teams: Curing Police Problems with the Mentally Ill," *The Police Chief,* February 1999, Vol. LXVI, No. 2, pp. 52–54.

Describes the unique partnership that mental health providers and the police can engage in that will change how society deals with mental illness. Crisis Intervention Teams (CIT) can prevent a tragic event from occurring and reduces the number and severity of incidents and injuries to officers and citizens. Training is 40 hours in length and the instructors are mental health professionals and provides officers with the skills to calm and contain a situation rather than exacerbate it.

Chapter 12

INVESTIGATION: Process and Management

Learning Objectives

1. List the three types organizational structure for criminal investigation.

2. Identify the components of a generalist model of investigation.

3. Describe the benefits of decentralized criminal investigation.

4. Write a short essay describing the benefits of Coordinated Team Patrol.

5. List the disadvantages of having a specialized investigation division.

6. Compare the two major approaches to case screening.

7. Contrast the burglary and robbery decision models.

8. List three objectives of a managed investigative process.

9. Describe how the computer can help the investigative process.

10. Discuss the measurement of performance in an investigative unit.

11. Describe the relationship between the police and prosecutors.

12. Write a short essay describing the case information that prosecutors need.

13. List the four stages of a targeted investigation.

14. Define behaviorally anchored.

15. Describe the selection process for the position of detective.

Since the work of the patrol force includes the majority of police functions, the more effective the patrol division, the less need there is for the more specialized operating divisions and units. It has been shown that, although it is impossible for the patrol services alone to be one hundred percent effective in the discharge of all police functions, the other operating line divisions are necessary only to the extent that the patrol division falls short of this objective. It follows, as a corollary, that all other line divisions or units in police organization, including investigation, traffic, crime prevention, and vice, are to be regarded fundamentally as secondary, supporting elements of patrol power, although not subordinate to it in the organization structure.

The Investigations Division

The primary function of the detective is to apprehend those offenders who escape arrest at the hands of the patrol division and the recovery of stolen property. In the growth of a department, the necessity may arise for a specialized investigational unit of one or more investigators when the uncleared case load of the patrol force reaches a point where departmental efficiency demands specialized assistance. Numerous offenses come to the attention of the police that require extensive investigation both in time and place for their solution. The number of these offenses and the grave character of many of them may make necessary the organization of a separate division in the police department manned by persons assigned exclusively to criminal investigation. The duties of the detectives supplement those of the patrol division, and the coordination of the work of these two units is among the most important of all problems confronting the police chief executive.

The number of officers assigned to investigative units varies considerably. It should be noted that even those percentages might not indicate the number of investigators in an organization. For example, in one city, the internal affairs unit, staffed by sworn officers, works out of the chief's office and not the investigative bureau. Consequently the percentages can change. The same is true if vice and intelligence functions are placed organizationally outside the major investigative unit. Out of seven large cities, detectives accounted for between 8.9 and 17.2 percent of sworn personnel. The city, with the smallest percentage of detectives, was Chicago. Houston had the largest percentage, with 17.2. Additional modifiers of the percentage of personnel assigned to an investigative bureau depends upon other specialized assignments such as narcotics, and anti-terrorism units.[1] In a nationwide survey it was found that in state and local law enforcement agencies 13 to 16 percent of sworn personnel were assigned to investigative positions (see table 12–1).

Table 12–1

Sworn Personnel Assigned to Investigations in
State and Local Law Enforcement Agencies

Type of Agency	Percent Assigned to Investigations
Municipal	16
Sheriff	13
Special	15
State	15

---

1. Anthony Pate and Edwin E. Hamilton, *The Big Six—Policing America's Largest Cities*, Washington, D.C., Police Foundation, 1991, p. 59.

Source: Brian A. Reaves and Andrew L. Goldberg, *Census of State and Local Law Enforcement Agencies, 1996,* Washington, DC, Bureau of Justice Statistics, June 1998, pp. 11–15.

Agencies throughout the nation have different organizational structures for criminal investigation, with substantially different characteristics. The Virginia Beach Police Department conducted a survey of 50 responding agencies serving cities with populations ranging from 6,000 to 681,000. Ninety percent had a centralized detective division.[2] Essentially, however, there are three common types:

- Detective Specialist/Centralized Model.

- Detective Specialist/Centralized and Decentralized Model.

- Detective Specialist/Centralized and Detective Generalist/Decentralized and Patrol Division (Team Policing) Model (see figures 12–1 and 12–2).

In addition, a few departments in the nation have a "generalist" model in which the primary responsibility for the investigation of crimes rests with the patrol officer. In these agencies, detectives, if there are any, function essentially as consultants and advisors to the uniformed officer. One police department in California, employs such a model. The responsibility for investigation of crime is assigned as follows:

2. D.G. McCloud, et al., "Investigative Practices Survey," *The Police Chief,* September 1985, Vol. LX, No. 9, p. 44.

Figure 12–1

Typical Organizational Structure: Detective
Specialist/Centralized Model

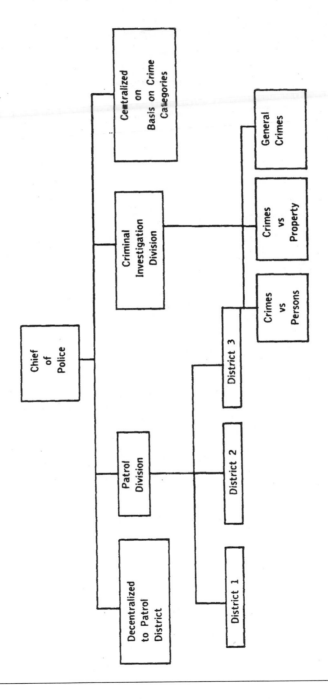

Figure 12–2

Typical Organizational Structure: Detective Specialist/Centralized and Decentralized Model

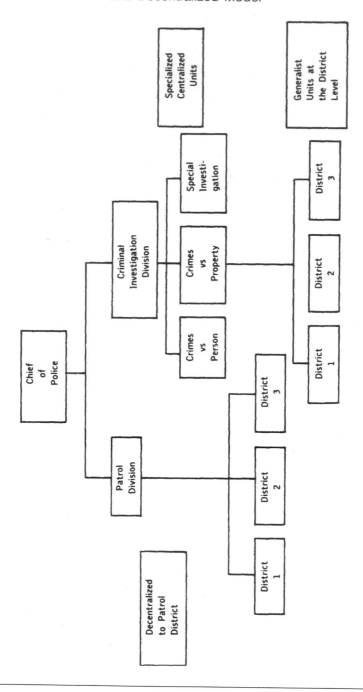

The investigation of crime is considered to be an essential police function for which each officer in the department is responsible. To a great extent, the investigation section serves the field officers. Much of the investigative load is handled by patrol officers. An investigator is called to assist a patrol officer on a case only if a Patrol Section supervisor or Operations Officer determines the need for one according to the following criteria:

- Special knowledge or expertise of the investigator that would materially enhance the investigation.

- If a suspect is known but not in custody, and there is a need for an immediate follow-up and apprehension.

- The nature of the investigation precludes sector officers from completing it, due to unusual constraints, *e.g.,* investigation out of the city, need to respond to other calls for service.

- A suspect is known and in custody and is providing information that would be valuable in clearing other serious offenses.

- Other unusual situations as approved by Operations Officers, the Investigative Commander, Division Commander, or Chief of Police.

This model is generally most useful in smaller cities where the size of the agency and the crime problem do not warrant investments in specialized units. In the centralized investigative model responsibility for investigating crime is assigned to a specialized criminal investigative unit. Members of the patrol division play a perfunctory and minimal role of collecting basic information when they respond to the scene of a crime.[3] Since the ultimate measure of effectiveness is whether the organization is producing the desired results and outcomes, the assessment of current levels of performance must be directed toward evaluating that end. Whatever the outcome of the final determination, there is a need to critically challenge the worth of the existing arrangement in each police agency. Even if the determination is that the existing organization is efficient, effective, and productive, the police administrator will at least feel more comfortable as a result of the reaffirmation of prior judgments. On the other hand, this administrator may find there are better ways to maximize the results of the criminal investigation effort.

In many agencies, where hard critical assessment has been made, changes have, in fact, been made and experimentation with different organizational models has begun. In these agencies, at least, there was dissatisfaction with performance and productivity levels in the criminal investigation system. One variation of the traditional model features a decentralization of some investigators to the district or precinct level. Essentially, however, this model retains the same basic characteristics of the purely centralized model. That is, the assignment of investiga-

3. Donald F. Cawley, et al., *Managing Criminal Investigations Manual,* Washington, D.C., University Research Corporation, 1976, pp. 166–167.

tive responsibility remains in the Investigations Division. There is a distinct organizational reporting relationship to the chief, specialized crime units by category remain at the centralized level, and the uniformed officer's role is still perfunctory and minimal.

The placement of some portion of the criminal investigators at the decentralized level (or "street" level) appears to be designed to accomplish several benefits. They are:

- Assigning the investigators closer to the community they serve.

- Fostering a better communication with patrol officers.

- Making possible a more timely response to reported crimes.

- Facilitating the cultivation of sources of information.

- Increasing the generalist's knowledge about generalist criminals in the particular community.[4]

Still another modification to the traditional organization is the Team Policing Model (see figure 12–3). This model features a specialized centralized detective unit with the decentralized generalist investigator assigned to the Patrol Division Commander. In this arrangement uniformed officer and investigator work together in a "team" which is assigned to a particular community or segment of the jurisdiction to be policed. In essence, this represents a return to the generalist model mentioned earlier. The operations of the "team" policing unit has been found to promote, among other benefits, a good relationship between uniformed and investigative officers, a more rapid response by the investigator to the scene of a crime and the development of community identification with "its" police. Numerous departments throughout the country have adopted this model or have begun experimenting with a team-policing concept.

One department experimented with a Coordinated Team Patrol (CTP) to determine whether improved activities in investigation and apprehension could be effected. Over the period of the experiment, evaluations and adjustments were made. The results of assigning teams of patrol officers and investigators to work together in fixed geographical areas (sectors) were as follows:

- Teams made arrests in a higher percentage of burglary, robbery, and larceny cases than did non-team personnel in other sectors.

- Teams cleared a higher percentage of burglaries, robberies, and larcenies than did non-team personnel.

- Teams made on-scene arrests in robbery and larceny cases more often. However, there was no apparent difference in burglary cases.

4. William J. Smith, "Investigation at the Local Level: How Decentralization of a Big Department is Working in Philadelphia," *Law and Order,* September 1994, Vol. 42, No. 9, pp. 63–65.

Figure 12–3
Team Policing Model

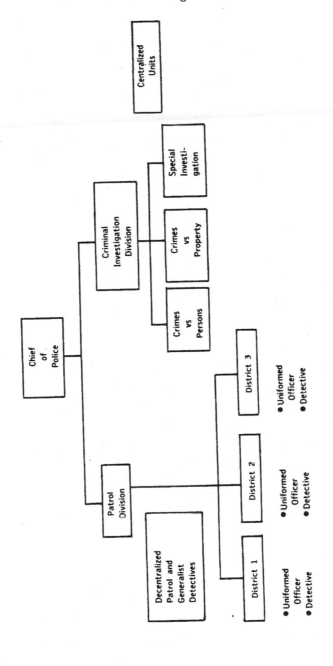

- Team on-scene arrests for burglary, larceny, and robbery were more likely to result in prosecutions than those made by non-team personnel.

- No significant differences were found in the quantity of information contained in the preliminary investigation reports of team and non-team personnel.

- Burglary and robbery arrests resulting from follow-up investigations were made in a larger percentage of cases by team personnel than by non-team personnel.

- Prosecutions resulting from follow-up investigation did not vary between team and non-team cases.

- Both team and non-team personnel felt the CTP method was more effective in dealing with crime.

- Both team and non-team personnel felt the CTP model helped to improve the relationship between patrol and detective personnel.

- Team patrol officers reported a much higher level of cooperation with team investigators than with non-team investigators.

While these results may not necessarily be typical, the outcomes produced by the criminal investigation process were improved upon in that city by altering the organizational structure and changing the allocation mix of investigative resources.[5]

Alternative Roles of Patrol

The matrix on the following pages shows the role of the patrol officer in an initial investigation from the perspective of:

- The patrol responsibility.

- The process by which patrol assists in referring cases for continued investigation.

- Some consequences of patrol activities on policies regarding investigation.

- Suggested organizational policy initiatives that can be taken by management.

Applying these perspectives to the many roles that a patrol officer could perform in an investigation, the matrix describes and displays several alternative models. Local constraints may legitimately inhibit the exact adoption of any of the models. However, the value of the matrix is that it does highlight a sequential enhancement—with each new model—of the uniformed officer's role in the investigative process, beginning with the typical role of the patrol officer in conducting the initial investigation.[6]

5. *Ibid.*, pp. 168–172.   6. *Ibid.*, p. 10.

Figure 12–4
Matrix of Model Roles of Patrol Officers in
Conducting Criminal Investigations

(Each Model Builds Upon and Includes Activities Outlined in Preceding Model)

MODELS	PATROL RESPONSIBILITY	CASE REFERRAL PROCEDURE	CONSEQUENCES	MANAGEMENT POLICIES
A. TYPICAL	• Prepare and complete basic report form.	• Refer all cases, including preliminary investigations, to detectives.	• Redundancy • Insufficient data collected • Low level of productivity • Low morale in patrol	
B. BETTER INFORMATION COLLECTION	• Conduct a complete initial investigation and fill out revised initial investigation report for selected categories of crime.	• Refer the reports of the initial investigations for selected categories of crime to detectives for follow-up investigation. (In these types of cases, detectives do not conduct preliminary investigations.)	• Elimination of redundancy. • More complete data collected. • Productivity increased. • Improved case load for detectives. • Better morale.	• Define crime categories to be investigated by patrol. • Define exceptions. • Design new initial investigation form. • Train patrol and detectives in use of new forms. • Train supervisors.
C. PATROL RECOMMENDATION	• Conduct initial investigation and complete detailed investigation report. • Decide whether to call for forensic or evidence specialists. • Recommend closing or continuing case based on presence or absence of solvability factors.	• Supervisor reviews patrol recommendation. • Case screening criteria are used to close cases when initial investigation reveals lack of solvability factors. OR • Case screening criteria are used to refer cases for follow-up investigation by detectives.	• Recommendation and screening, after initial investigation by patrol, focuses resources only on probably solvable cases. • Increases productivity. • Promotes interdependency between detectives and patrol.	• Establish policy and procedures for case screening. • Establish policy and procedures detailing the role of patrol and follow-up role of detectives. • Provide additional training for patrol and supervisors.
D. LIMITED INVESTIGATIVE ROLE OF PATROL	• Investigate crimes in selected categories beyond initial investigation phase. • Patrol continues and completes investigation of certain categories of crime which do not require the service of detective specialists.	• Crime cases in selected categories are not referred. • Other cases are referred to detectives for follow-up investigation.	• Reduces detective workload. • Permits detective to increase specialty or to adopt new roles.	• Establish policy and procedures delineating investigative roles of patrol in selected categories of criminal investigation and of detectives in other categories of crime. • Provide additional training for patrol.
E. ENHANCED INVESTIGATIVE ROLE OF PATROL	• Investigate crimes in increased number of categories. • Closure can occur on scene after initial investigation.	• Refer only those cases which require high level of skill or which are of an exceptional nature.	• Maximal use of detectives by assigning them to follow up only those cases with high probability of solution and/or those which require specialized skills. • Maximal use of patrol resources in all investigations. • Improved relationships between public and police. • New roles and opportunities available for detectives.	• Establish policies detailing the differing authority and relationships between patrol and detectives. • Adopt case screening system which incorporates early, on-scene, case-closure criteria.

Source: Donald F. Cawley, et al., *Managing Criminal Investigations Manual,* Washington, D.C., University Research Corporation, 1976, pp. 11–12.

Both experience of police managers and recent studies have identified most important or dominant information elements—solvability factors—which can effectively be used in developing an expanded role for the patrol officer in conducting a more comprehensive initial investigation. Solvability factors have been shown to have such a direct relationship to case clearances that several police agencies applied these factors in the development of management strategies for the improvement of the criminal investigation process. Incorporating these findings into an enhanced role for patrol may enable police managers to develop a management framework within which local policies and procedures can be developed with a view to improving the entire investigative process. Considered from this angle, one can define the preliminary investigation process as the initial fact-finding phase of the investigation of a reported crime by which the responding patrol officer identifies factors resulting in one or more of the following:

- The reported case is founded or unfounded and investigation continues or the case is suspended.

- An arrest is made because solvability factors are demonstrably present and known to the patrol officer.

- The reported case is continued and/or referred to others because dominant solvability factors are present.

- The reported case is continued and/or referred to others for investigation because there are exceptional reasons for continuation even though solvability factors are not present.

- The reported case is not continued or referred for investigation because solvability factors are not present and because there are no exceptional reasons for continuing the investigation and/or referring the reported case.

This definition overcomes some of the limitations in other descriptions and theories about the investigative role of patrol. It states clearly that the preliminary investigation has a definite investigative goal: to get the facts enabling the patrol officer to make a determination about continuation. It also states the manner in which that goal is to be achieved—by the "hunt" for solvability factors that local policy has determined are the most important and predictable elements regarding the probability of solving the crime. The task for police managers is to organize the resources of local departments in such a manner that the patrol officer receives guidance, support, and direction in conducting the "search for solvability".

It is important to remember what the definition does and does not state about the role of the patrol in the investigative process. It does not state patrol officers will be responsible for conducting and completing all the investigation of all reported felony or misdemeanor crimes. It does state patrol officers will follow agency policy and procedures regarding the search for solvability and apply them in making an initial determination about continuing, referring, or suspending cases. It does not state patrol officers will do anything beyond the scope of their authority. It does state the patrol officer will do everything possible to collect facts indicating the presence of solvability factors and to use these facts to make an initial determination about referring the case or closing it. It does not state patrol officers will act unilaterally in making decisions or determinations. It does state they can make certain determinations based on local police policies and procedures. Procedures regarding the supervisory review of field decisions or determinations are also included. It does not state the agency organizational structure or the patrol units and the detective units must be reorganized, or that police personnel must be deployed in a different way. The definition is silent on this issue. It does not state the patrol officer cannot perform services within the investigatory process not included in the definition. It does, however, set forth the essential *investigative* elements of preliminary investigation.

Finally, it seems obvious the roles of patrol and detectives cannot be viewed as completely separate and distinct functions. Patrol fulfills not only a crime suppressant role but also performs an investigative function. How effectively the patrol officer documents the events of a crime responded to has a definite impact on the case outcome when investigators attempt to pursue the case. Whatever new roles are assigned to the patrol officer (and we have delineated only the best known to date) will have an effect not only on the case outcome but also on the effective management of the entire process of criminal investigation.[7]

Specialization

While there are a number of advantages to having a specialized detective division, there are an equal number of disadvantages. Both sides of the issue can be briefly outlined as follows:

Advantages

- Definite, fixed investigative responsibility.
- Enhanced development of higher skill levels.
- Facilitation of training in latest investigative technologies.
- Development of higher morale and pride in accomplishment.
- Stronger sense of identification with goal and investigative performance levels.
- Development of public interest and support.

7. *Ibid.*, pp. 18–20.

- More time for uniformed officers to patrol their areas.

Disadvantages

- Internal communication of information is stymied and ineffective.

- Negative impact on the morale of the uniformed officer.

- Timely response and, thus, the effectiveness of investigation suffers.

- Increase in administrative and clerical workloads.

- Negative impact on public relations because of time delays in the investigation.

This listing can be expanded upon in support of either position, it is sufficient to make the point that the plusses and minuses should be weighed and considered.[8]

Case Screening

One of the latest tools to be introduced into the management of criminal investigations is case screening. Based upon experience and research efforts, an increasing number of police executives are looking at case screening as a means by which they can maximize the effectiveness of their investigative and uniformed personnel, a critical need in the light of the fiscal constraints most municipalities face. What is case screening? Simply stated, it is a mechanism to facilitate making a decision concerning the continuation of an investigation based upon the existence of sufficient solvability factors obtained at the initial investigation.

Solvability factors are those elements of information regarding a crime having proven, in the past, to be important in determining the likelihood of solving a crime. Case screening is designed to provide sufficient information about a case at the earliest possible time in the investigative process to permit a decision with respect to the desirability of continuing to provide investigative resources in the case. The outcome will be either early suspension of unpromising cases or a follow-up investigation of the reported crime. The proper use of the screening procedure enables the police executive to exercise control over the expenditure and kind of investigative effort to be made. Is case screening a new concept? The answer is an absolute NO! Police agencies have always screened cases in one manner or another. However, the screening process in the past has usually occurred as a result of individual detective's action on an informal basis. Each detective has traditionally taken the cases assigned to him or her and sorted them into two categories. Those which are worth pursuing because informa-

8. *Ibid.*, pp. 167–168.

tion and leads are alive and likely to lead to solution ,and those which will never be solved on the basis of information available (and on the basis of experience gained in attempting to track down similar cases in the past).

The establishment of a formal case screening system can bring about a major and critical improvement over an informal system. It takes the decision-making authority for investigation of reported crimes out of the hands of individual detectives and places it in the hands of management—where it properly belongs. The police executive cannot manage and control the investigative process workload unless actively monitoring the commitment of investigative resources and then making critical determinations concerning allocation of resources.[9]

There are two major approaches to case screening criteria. The first approach involves the development of a listing of unweighted criteria for the screening of cases, and the second establishes a listing of weighted criteria. Both these methods work best when a task force, representative of personnel who will eventually utilize the case screening criteria and who have a real input into the design of the program, is created to establish the criteria. The task force should include managers as well as investigative and line personnel. The acceptance of another agency's system without internal review by the staff who will be expected to carry it out is likely to lead to strong resistance within the organization and may lead to the development of a system unresponsive to the needs of the particular agency.

Unweighted Case Screening Approach

Inherent in the "unweighted screening" approach are two basic methods for establishing the criteria. They can be established by a unilateral determination by a police executive or by the task force of experienced investigative personnel without the benefit of an in-depth statistical analysis of how cases have been solved in the past. In Rochester, a departmental task force designed and field-tested a case screening system using experimental solvability factors. After considerable testing, the department became convinced the most productive initial investigation by the uniformed officer involved a search for solvability factors that could lead to an early decision to suspend a case. A new form was developed permitting the patrol officers to search for solvability factors and decide whether early suspension was appropriate.

Consequently, patrol officers were reoriented from viewing the initial investigation as an exercise in miscellaneous data collection to viewing it as an integral part of the investigative process. A review of

9. *Ibid.*, pp. 37–38.

the patrol officer's decision is conducted by a supervisor before the decision on continuation or suspension is finalized. In order to respond to special and community demands for a follow-through investigation, the supervisor who reviews the early closure recommendation is accorded some flexibility to continue an investigation, even if the solvability factors suggest an early suspension. The new form asked the field officer to answer the following solvability questions:

- Was there a witness to the crime?

- Can a suspect be named?

- Can a suspect be located?

- Can a suspect be described?

- Can a suspect be identified?

- Can the suspect vehicle be identified?

- Is the stolen property traceable?

- Is there a significant MO present?

- Is there significant physical evidence present?

- Has an evidence technician been called? Is the evidence technician's report positive?

- Is there a significant reason to believe the crime may be solved with a reasonable amount of investigative effort?

- Was there a definite limited opportunity for anyone except the suspect to commit the crime?

Other departments throughout the country have developed similar programs to use solvability factors in determining the outcome of initial investigations. They have derived case-screening rules, in part, from an analysis of cases that have been successfully solved. In effect, the agencies have learned from their successes and failures. These agencies have also established representative task forces consisting of patrol and detective personnel to evaluate the results of successful case investigations to design a case screening plan incorporating those informative items leading to successful case outcomes.

To select cases with the highest probability of solution, the factors most often leading to a successful investigation are isolated so they may be incorporated into the screening procedure. A named suspect has proven to be he strongest solvability factor. To determine whether a case should be continued as an active investigation, the answers to the following questions are often critical:

- Can complainant or witness identify the offender?

- Is the offender known to the complainant or witness?

- Does the complainant or witness know where the offender is located?

- Is there physical evidence at the scene which would aid in the solution of the case (fingerprints, other physical evidence)?

- Is the complainant or witness willing to view photographs to aid in identifying the offender?

- Can the complainant or witness provide a meaningful description of the offender e.g. home address, auto driven?

- Scars or other distinctive features?

- If the offender is apprehended is the complainant willing to press the complaint in court?

In order to evaluate whether the case should be further investigated, the initial investigation should provide information concerning the following so supervisory review is more meaningful and on target:

- Estimate of the reaction of the community to the crime, based on the opinion of the reporting officer.

- Does the crime involve a sensitive or unusual place or person (abortion clinic, church, temple, school; child, or disadvantaged)?

- Is there a pattern of such crimes in the area pointing to a single individual or gang operating in the area?

- Does the number of similar type crimes in the area raise questions concerning the department's image concerning performance and efficiency?

The process should require that cases identified as not solvable because of insufficient success criteria be suspended as soon as possible.

Weighted Case–Screening Approach

The weighted case-screening methodologies vary from the non-statistically derived system to the statistically derived system. The department's team-policing task force attempted to list types of cases in their order of priority. This step was believed to be a critical part of the department's "de-specialization program." The resulting system is viewed as flexible enough for field officers to be able to establish case priorities after conducting preliminary investigations. In this approach to establishing investigative priorities, officers consider the seriousness of the crime, the amount of readily available information about suspects, the availability of agency resources, and community attitudes. The officers consider four major aspects of the crime and rate it accordingly.(see table 12–2).

Table 12–2

Factors Amenable to Prioritization

Type of offense.
1. Felonies are serious crimes for which the offender can be sentenced to state prison.
2. Misdemeanor are less serious crimes for which the offender can be sentenced to various combinations of probation, county jail, and fines.
3. Status offenses deal with under age offenders.
4. Infractions are the least serious crimes and are generally punishable by a fine.

Solvability Factors.
1. Suspect known, described or located.
2. Witnesses know the location of the offender or can identify them.
3. Physical evidence is available that will aid in the investigation.
4. Potential leads developed.

Seriousness of the Offense.
1. A potential danger to others.
2. One of a series of crimes of the same nature.

Community Reaction.
1. Political implications.
2. Quality of life issues.
3. Media response.

Managerial Considerations.
1. Departmental policy.
2. Sensitivity of the crime.
3. Nature and extent of investigative caseload.

Weighting
1. Each of the above factors are given a weight that is statistically derived based on the analysis of similar offenses creating. Based on the weights given to each factor the case is followed up or suspended.

Source: Lee P. Brown, "Team Policing: Management of Criminal Investigation," The Police Chief, September 1976., Vol. L11, No. 9, p. 57; Bernard Greenberg, et. al. Felony Investigation Decision Model, Washington, DC, USGPO, p. xxvi and 2–31, and John P. Kenney and Harry W. More, Principles of Investigation, Minneapolis/St. Paul, West Publishing, 1992, pp. 346–376.

In a major research study, a case follow-up decision model was developed for a West Coast police department. In this study, the researchers developed a checklist of activities to guide patrol officers and detectives in the investigation of burglary cases. A case follow-up decision model was statistically derived through an examination of past cases. A set of weighted variables emerged predicting case outcome with a high degree of certainty. Table 12–3 depicts the burglary case disposition decision rule. The Police Executive Research Forum utilizing 26 departments replicated another study. This was an effort to determine the performance of the burglary investigation decision model and whether it could predict case outcomes accurately by comparing the model's productive qualities with actual cases.

Table 12–3

Burglary Case Disposition Decision Rule

Information Element	Weighting Factor
Estimated time lapse between crime and the initial investigation:	
Less than 1 hour	5
1 to 12 hours	1
12 to 24 hours	0.3
More than 24 hours	0
Witness's report of offense	7
On-view report of offense	1
Usable fingerprints	7
Suspect information developed—description or name	9
Vehicle description	0.1
Other	0
TOTAL SCORE:	

INSTRUCTIONS

(1) Circle the weighting factor for each information element that is present in the incident report.
(2) Add the circled factors.
(3) If the sum is less than or equal to 10, suspend the case; otherwise, follow up the case.

This research proved to be very accurate inasmuch as the model was correct in 85 percent of the 12,000 burglary cases examined. Presently the characteristics of burglary cases, not follow-up investigations, determine the success or failure rate of burglary investigations. The decision model can and does make investigators more productive.[10] The same study, resulted in the development of a robbery decision model usable in identifying cases having sufficient probability of clearance to warrant follow-up investigation. Then the research team sought to minimize the police investigator's intuitive judgment on case handling by statistically analyzing factors having significantly contributed in the past to case clearance. The study results suggested that "unless offender identification was made by the responding officer, case solution at the detective level was minimal." Table 12–4 lists the dominant case-solution factors related to the victim's knowledge of the offender.

10. John E. Eck, *Managing Case Assignments: The Burglary Investigation Decision Model Replication,* Washington, D.C., Police Executive Research Forum, 1979, pp. 3–4.

Table 12–4

Robbery Investigation Decision Model

Information Element	Weighting Factor
Suspect named	10*
Suspect known	10*
Suspect previously seen	10*
Evidence technician used	10
Places suspect frequently named	10*
Physical evidence each item matched	6.1
Vehicle registration	
Query information available	1.5
Vehicle stolen	3.0
Useful information returned	4.5
Vehicle registered to suspect	6.0
Offender movement description	
On foot	0
Vehicle (not car)	0.6
Car	1.2
Car color given	1.8
Car description given	2.4
Car license given	3.0
Weapon used	1.6

    These values as calculated actually exceed the threshold of
10. The values provided here are conceptually simpler and make no difference in the classification of groups.

(1) Circle the weighting factor for each information element that is present in the incident report.

(2) Add the circled factors.

(3) If the sum is less than 10, suspend the case; otherwise, follow up the case.

(4) Weighting factors do not accumulate; *i.e.,* if both the auto license and color are given, the total is 3.0, not 4.8.

An analysis of the two decision models shows there is a similarity between variables and their relative weights in contributing to case clearance. In both models, a witness or victim provides the most useful information leading to case clearance. One difference notable between the two models is the dominance of vehicle information in the robbery decision model as the next-most-important information element. It appears clear, regardless of the method used, there are certain critical pieces of information needed if a case is to be solved through investigative activities.

The components of a case-screening system include the accurate and complete collection of crime information by the patrol officer, and an on-scene determination of the sufficiency of crime information collected. This is followed by a process wherein the patrol officer is permitted to make decisions concerning follow-up investigation. Then the decision is reviewed by a supervisor. The incorporation of case-screening created the need to develop a monitoring or management information system providing police administrators sufficient feedback on the system's effectiveness.[11]

Case Management

While it may not be clear how much improvement can be achieved by establishing a management system in the continuing investigation process, it seems reasonable to assume some improvement is likely in comparison with the non-managed process. And even if there is little or no improvement, the manager will at least be able to make intelligent decisions about resource allocations and alternative courses of action. In establishing the management system for continuing investigations, the overall goal should be to increase the number of case investigations of serious crimes cleared by prosecutable arrests of the criminals responsible for these crimes. Objectives of a managed investigation process could include:

- Assigning case investigations more effectively.
- Improving on the quality of case investigation and preparation.
- Monitoring the progress of case investigation and making decisions about continuation.
- Evaluating results on the basis of investigative outcomes.

The supervisor of the investigative unit, as is the case for all managers, should be held accountable for achieving stated goals and objectives through their team's effort. The supervisor must:

- Organize the unit.
- Establish work schedules and deploy resources.
- Determine effective and economical assignment policies.
- Organize workloads.
- Assign cases on an equitable and skills basis.
- Make decisions about "exceptional" investments of time to certain
- Coordinate and direct the unit's investigative efforts.
- Develop required records to facilitate direction, monitoring, and evaluation of efforts.
- Supervise personnel on a continuous basis.
- Evaluate performance.
- Train and develop investigators.
- Promote a rapport with internal and external units affecting the ability of the unit to meet its goal.

Other management activities may also be called for. However, the above listing should be a good starting point. In organizing the unit,

11. *Ibid.,* pp. 40–47.

the supervisor must make decisions about hours of operation, deployment of investigative personnel based on workload needs, and whether investigators will work alone, in pairs, or as part of a team. Many agencies emphasize the economic advantages of having investigators work alone and reject the "luxury" of a partner approach. However, the mix of resource use is limited only by the imagination of the supervisor or the requirements of a fixed policy mandating a particular assignment pattern.

One of the most important decisions to be made is the assignment of a referred case. Not only must the manager consider current caseloads, but must also assess who has the skills required to bring the case to a successful conclusion. If the case is of low-level priority or the investigative abilities and skills of each member are reasonably equal, this assessment need not involve more than a quick judgment. On the other hand, if the case is very serious or will require special skills or expertise, a reasoned judgment must be made as to who is best qualified to conduct the investigation. If putting the right investigator on the case requires a re-shuffling of workloads, the manager must make this decision.

Such a judgment obviously assumes the supervisor knows the investigative backgrounds, strengths, and weaknesses of all their personnel. In units with many investigators, it may be necessary to develop a skills profile of each investigator for the supervisor's reference. Case assignment records should be maintained by the supervisor to ensure adequate and timely information concerning case assignments and ensure proper review of the investigative progress. Such records would indicate the date the case was assigned, the category of crime, a list of review decision dates, and close or continuation information. The supervisor should also maintain a record of the distribution throughout the unit of case assignments. Assignment of unequal caseloads, unless done deliberately for good reasons, can be self-defeating for efficient and effective performance.

Clearly, the supervisor should also be knowledgeable about the activities undertaken by criminal investigators. The list is by no means exhaustive and can be expanded or shortened depending on local agency requirements. This listing of activities might later be developed into a report providing needed information concerning the amount of time spent by the investigator in developing the investigative plan, interviews, office activities, records searches, and field investigative efforts. If every investigator were required to prepare a Daily Activity Plan/Results Report, supervisors would have a way of monitoring their activities and of eliminating duplication of effort by investigators. It would be possible to use one investigator to do the work of two or three who are all in the same locale to do the same thing.

Another very important responsibility of the supervisor in monitoring case investigations is to review progress on a regular basis with each of the investigators so decisions can be made as to whether various investigations should be continued. The investigator should be required to make a recommendation. If recommending to continue, the investigator should be required to show reasons to believe the case can be solved. Upon receipt of the preliminary investigation report, the investigator should carefully analyze the amount and quality of information supplied. An experienced investigator will look for the solvability factors as well as the unusual aspects in the case. It should be clear that a well-constructed preliminary investigation form will provide the bulk of the information needed and will substantially reduce the amount of time needed to conduct a case analysis.

Once the analysis has been made and a decision reached for further investigating the case, the investigator should develop an investigative plan. A plan should be discussed with the supervisor. There should be agreement as to the decision to continue, the appropriateness of the plan, and the first review date to further decide on continuation. The supervisor, not the investigator, controls the access to the information. Other investigators seeking information on the case, or access to the folder, should seek approval from the supervisor. This rule not only maintains the integrity of the information but facilitates the supervisor's task of coordinating the unit's entire investigative effort. Another critical responsibility of the supervisor is to measure the efficiency and effectiveness of the unit's, as well as the individual's performance. While not perfect, one common measuring stick is the number of cases cleared by arrest.

In many agencies use is made of detective case management with the aid of a computer program. It allows for the assemblage, handling, and use of information essential to the investigative process. This software allows for a variety of tasks to include time management, and case tracking. Evidence can be more easily tracked and custody for legal purposes is much easier because of the documentation. Witnesses names and history entered into the system allows for easier monitoring of the case. Supervisor can generate input into solvability factors, and investigators can share information.[12] In Los Angeles case management uses software developed by the city's information technology agency (ITA) that allows detectives to track cases on a citywide basis. A detective on one side of the city is able to set a computer terminal and determine whether if any other detective in the city is pursuing a similar cases against a suspect and review the investigative data gathered by other detectives. All pertinent investigative data will be part of the database and accessible city-wide. The system will automate many of the reporting functions that detectives have traditionally completed by the use of hand tallies. It also has a Field Data Capture (FDC) system is being tested and it is anticipated that it will revolu-

12. John P. Boyle and Liz Clapp, "Detective Case Management–How to Make it Work for Your Department," *The Police Chief,* April 1997, Vol. LXIV, No. 4, pp. 171–175.

tionize the traditional methods of gathering data in preliminary investigations and traffic accident. In this instance officers will use lap top computers to gather investigative data, then transmit that data back to community police stations via wireless transmission using radio frequencies. This will eliminate the need for officers to return to their stations for report approval.[13]

Reports provide basic information on the performance of the individual investigator, the overall performance of the unit, and the relative performance of each investigator as well as an indication of the quality of the investigative effort as viewed by the prosecutor. Many other reports could be developed to measure performance. It is also recognized that there are other factors impacting upon the performance of the individual investigator as well as the unit, and the manager must carefully consider all those factors before arriving at a decision concerning the effectiveness of an individual investigator. In summary, continuing to do business as usual, with the investigator making personal management decisions, will only perpetuate the very dismal record of cases cleared by arrest. While it is not a certainty that substantive improvements in investigative performance will occur once management assumes control of the investigative process, it is reasonable to assume improvements are likely. If improvements do not occur, managers would at least be able to make more responsible decisions about allocation of resources and alternative courses of action to deal with the continually escalating crime problem. Indeed, the police administrator may find the present investigative process is an exercise in wishful thinking.[14]

Measurement of performance in an investigative division is essential. Division heads and those in charge of specialized units should be fully aware of how effective their units are operating. Table 12–5 lists the key measures of performance for the Investigative Service Bureau of the Tucson Police Department. It should be noted that crimes are grouped under eight headings ranging from neighborhood to burglaries. The mission statement, in part, for the Bureau indicates that it will conduct follow-up investigations and ensure that violent and habitual criminals are arrested and prosecuted to the fullest extent. The statement also includes directing programs to reduce youth violence and increase the safety of the community, and combat the illegal drug trade through various interdiction and activities to reduce the financial incentive.

13. Bernard C. Parks, *First Year in Office–Achievements, Accomplishments, and Future Initiatives,* Los Angeles, CA, Los Angles Police Department, August 12, 1997/98, pp. 31–32.

14. *Ibid.,* pp. 78–83.

Table 12–5

Key Measurement for the Investigative Service Bureau

Benefit the community through the resolution of cases that are potentially solvable and result in an assignment to a detective	**Adopted for Fiscal Year 98–99**
Neighborhood Crimes	
Total number of cases received	48,000
Number of cases assigned to a detective	5,208
Percent of assigned cases resolved	40%
Homicides	
Total number of cases received	45
Number of cases assigned to a detective	45
Percent of assigned cases resolved	75%
Robberies	
Total number of cases received	650
Number of cases assigned to a detective	566
Percent of assigned cases resolved	30%
Misdemeanor sex crimes	
Total number of cases received	460
Number of cases assigned to a detective	127
Percent of assigned cases resolved	25%
Forcible and attempted rapes	
Total number of cases received	220
Number of cases assigned to a detective	172
Percent of assigned cases resolved	30%
Other felony sex cases	
Total number of cases received	80
Number of cases assigned to a detective	51
Percent of assigned cases resolved	25%
Aggravated assaults	
Total number of cases received	1,600
Number of cases assigned to a detective	539
Percent of assigned cases resolved	40%
Burglaries	
Total number of cases received	6,500
Number of cases assigned to a detective	458
Percent of assigned cases resolved	10%

Source: City of Tucson, *Tucson–Adopted Budget Operating Detail, Fiscal Year 1998–99,* Tucson, AZ, City of Tucson, 1999, Volume II, p. 163.

Police–Prosecutor Relations

Most of the elements of new approaches to managing criminal investigations are concerned with internal police agency operations. In any effort to improve the management of criminal investigations, however, consideration must be given to the element of a two-way police/prosecutor relationship since this relationship provides the necessary external linkage between the police and the next stage of the criminal justice process—prosecution. The inputs generated by a meaningful police/prosecutor relationship will facilitate the assessment of internal police policies and procedures affecting the impact of the initial investigation, case screening, follow-up, case management, monitoring, and reorganization. One of the most important questions to ask in the development of a case disposition feedback system is: "What does a chief or manager need to know in order to improve the investigative efforts?" The police administrator at least needs to know the disposition of cases, why a case was rejected for prosecution, and why a case submitted by the prosecutor resulted in a dismissal.

The American Bar Association, has underscored the importance of a case disposition feedback system. The development of such a system is a needed and appropriate project to encourage the police and prosecutor to work together toward improving the outcome of the judicial process. For example, the Chief of Police may want only major case summaries and broad comparative data. On the other hand, the heads of other units may want more detail. In short, as the information descends through the departmental layers its form and scope will change. Another factor to consider is how often various managers need information. he data needed may be the number of cases in various crime categories that are:

- Presented for prosecutorial screening.

- Rejected by prosecutor (with reasons).

- Accepted for prosecution.

- Returned for investigation.

Throughout the agency, this information will be needed in different forms. The Chief of Detectives may want this information in a form allowing its identification by investigative unit or section. Within the detective division, commanders of units will have slightly different needs for information. A unit commander may require data keyed to individual investigators to identify performance. In addition, this management information system may need to be designed to provide feedback to the manager on individual detective caseload, status of case, and age of cases.

The results of an information needs analysis will facilitate the development of feedback forms and procedures. Serious efforts must be made to resist developing unneeded forms and data. It is all too common for managers to figuratively drown in data generated for data's sake particularly when a computer is available. While the tendency to create and use unnecessary forms and data is a very real and counterproductive threat to be guarded against, a method should be developed to provide a current update on each case under investigation.

Essentially, the informational needs of police managers may be met by collecting data from two primary forms, a *case feedback form* and a *case workload report*. The data may be compiled by any unit within the agency. It must be summarized for managers. Data from the caseload reports should be transferred to a master form and routed to the chief of detectives who will summarize the data for the chief. A listing of all data summaries from case feedback forms should follow a similar route. A simple summary with a line graph to show trends over time could be sufficient to keep most police chief executives informed of the information they require to raise appropriate questions concerning performance.

Prosecutor's Needs for Information

The police investigator must carefully gather all the available evidence, evaluate the available facts, make arrests where warranted, and present the evidence upon which the charge is justified. Video filing is being pilot tested in Los Angeles at two of the 18 community policing stations. It will allow detectives to use video teleconferencing to file their cases. Necessary filing information can be sent via facsimile to the district attorney's office and eliminates the traditional face-to-face conferencing. Needless to say it is anticipated that it will realize a significant time saving for the investigators.[15]

The prosecutor must then evaluate the evidence, and accept or reject the case on the basis of the facts presented. If the choice is made to accept the case for prosecution, the case must be prepared for trial and the defendant formally charged in the manner prescribed by the court having primary jurisdiction over the offense within the geographical area where the crime was committed. When the case is called for trial, the prosecutor must then present the case and prove beyond a reasonable doubt that a crime did in fact take place and the defendant committed it. Through the experience gained in court, the prosecutor is in the best position to identify the elements of information needed to present and substantiate the charges in court.

The following list of questions were developed jointly between a police agency and a prosecutor—each serving the same jurisdiction. It is but one example of the type of joint efforts producing a checklist for both police and the office of the prosecutor, for use by police in developing and preparing criminal cases (see figure 12–5).

15.   Bernard C. Parks, *op. cit.*

Figure 12–5

Case Information Desirable for Prosecution

1.   What INTERVIEWS were conducted?

OFFENSE

2.   Is there a verbatim report of the instant OFFENSE?
3.   Is there a verbatim report of the FORCE USED?
4.   What was the PHYSICAL HARM to the victim?
5.   Is there a detailed description of the PROPERTY TAKEN?
6.   What was the method of SUSPECT's ESCAPE?
7.   What type of VEHICLE was used by S?
8.   What type of WEAPON was used by S?
9.   If a gun was used, was it LOADED?
10. If a gun was used, when was it ACQUIRED?
11. Where is the LOCATION of the weapon now?

SUSPECT

12. Was S UNDER THE INFLUENCE of alcohol or drugs?
13. What are the details of S's DEFENSE?
14. What is S's ECONOMIC STATUS?
15. Was S advised of CONSTITUTIONAL RIGHTS?
16. If multiple suspects, what is their RELATIONSHIP?
17. Is there evidence of PRIOR OFFENSES by S?
18. Is there evidence of S's MOTIVES?
19. Is there evidence of past PSYCHIATRIC TREATMENT of S?
20. What is S's PAROLE OR PROBATION status?
21. Does S have an alcohol or drug ABUSE HISTORY?
22. Where is S EMPLOYED?
23. What is the RELATIONSHIP between S and V?
24. What is the CREDIBILITY of the W?
25. Can the W make a CONTRIBUTION to the case prosecution?
26. Have or will MUG SHOTS be shown to V or W?
27. If shown, are the PROCEDURES and RESULTS adequately described?
28. Was a LINE–UP conducted?
29. If conducted, are the PROCEDURES and RESULTS adequately described?
30. Was an effort made to LIFT FINGERPRINTS at the scene?
31. If made, were USABLE FINGERPRINTS OBTAINED?
32. Were PHOTOS TAKEN at the crime scene?
33. Is the EXACT LOCATION where the photos and prints were taken given?
34. Did V VERIFY statements in the crime report?
35. Did V have IMPROPER MOTIVES in reporting the offense?

ARREST

36. What was the legal BASIS FOR SEARCH AND SEIZURE?
37. How was the LOCATION OF EVIDENCE learned?
38. How was the LOCATION OF S learned?
39. How was the ARREST OF S made?

Mutual Priorities of Police and Prosecutors

Major developmental effort should be devoted to setting forth joint investigatory and prosecutorial priorities. Since all offenses committed cannot be investigated by police, there is a need for each law enforcement agency to establish priorities of enforcement reflective of the best interests of the community. If managers fail to set enforcement priorities, the determination will be made by each officer at the street level. Therefore, the police executive should establish priorities as agency guides in day-to-day general operations. Ideally, those priorities will represent the thinking of the prosecutor as well as the police executive.

Enforcement priorities are set to address major community concerns. Emphasis may also be placed on those crimes generating other crimes, such as those related to narcotics and organized drug distribution systems or high-stakes gambling operations. A clear understanding of, and agreement with, the enforcement priorities will help the prosecutor's office gear-up for more effective prosecution of these crimes. Mutual priorities are clearly preferred in order to increase the combined impact of the police/prosecutor relationship. But, at least an understanding of the priorities of both prosecutors and police should be seen as a necessity. A prosecutor's commitment to the priority of prosecution of recidivists, and the knowledge of that priority by police officers, will affect the style of their investigation and the speed at which an arrested recidivist will be presented for charging.

Mutual priorities would be seen as preferable because of the progress being made by both police and prosecutors toward achieving their goals. Interactive goal orientation will tend to bind the two elements into a more professional, cohesive, and unified organization in the interests of justice in the community. Agreeing on and clearly stating mutual priorities also will aid in the development of more effective approaches to dealing with crime. Examples of such approaches run the gamut from special diversionary programs i.e. detoxification centers, drug rehabilitation programs, and juvenile management projects to high-impact crime units such as multi-agency narcotics units.[16]

Targeted Investigations

Citizens' reports of offenses dominate the detective's work-load. Investigation occurs after the fact and therefore the response is reactive rather than pro-active. Under such circumstances investigative planning becomes extremely difficult if not impossible. Managers cannot focus on the sources of the problems. Another approach receiving increased attention, is identifying problems confronting the police and targeting them for investigation. Herman Goldstein in proposing this problem-solving approach defines problems as:

16. Cawley, *op. cit.,* pp. 109–114.

the incredibly broad range of troublesome situations that prompt citizens to turn to the police, such as street robberies, residential burglaries, battered wives, vandalism, speeding cars, runaway children, accidents, acts of terrorism, even fear.[17]

The most notable and successful type of target investigations has been the career criminal program. Forty-one percent of municipal police department, with more than 100 sworn officers, have a specialized unit for these investigations.[18] But as indicated by the definition listed above, such investigations should deal with community problems such as armed robberies or juvenile burglaries. Targeted investigations are easily divided into four stages:

- Identify the problem.

- Examine the problem.

- Decide on a solution.[19]

- Monitor the solution to see if it's working and adjust accordingly.

There must be a clear definition of the problem and careful analysis so appropriate planning may occur. All these factors dictate the nature and type of investigation to conduct. Finally the total process should be evaluated in order to determine whether the investigation was successful.[20] Targeted investigation approaches have several distinct advantages, among which are the following:

- They direct police resources to high priority problems instead of waiting for the problems to dictate the use of police resources. By removing targeted individuals or groups responsible for large numbers of crimes, it should be possible to reduce the number of offenses reported, thereby reducing caseloads.

- Investigations are currently restricted by the availability of witnesses and the knowledge of victims. With a targeted investigation strategy, evidence and leads from several cases can be combined and information from informants, surveillance, and records can be used to combat the problem.

- Investigators have an opportunity to develop new skills and use skills they did not have a chance to use previously.

- Innovative investigations may lead to the arrest of criminals not typically arrested by traditional reactive investigations.

17. Herman Goldstein, *Problem Oriented Policing,* New York, McGraw–Hill, 1990, pp.–38.

18. Brian A. Reaves and Pheny Z. Smith, *Law Enforcement Management and Administrative Statistics, 1993: Data for Individual State and Local Agencies with 100 or More Officers,* Washington, DC, Bureau of Justice Statistics, September 1995, p. xiv.

19. Chris Braiden, *Community Policing: Nothing New Under the Sun,* in Daniel L. Lungren, COPPS–Community Oriented Policing & Problem Solving, Sacramento, CA, California Department of Justice, November 1992, p. 22.

20. John E. Eck, *Solving Crimes: The Investigation of Burglary and Robbery,* Washington, D.C., Police Executive Research Forum, 1983, pp. 318–325.

- Finally, this approach uses existing resources on an as-needed basis. If no problems are identified, no targeted investigations are launched. This avoids the problem of specialized units that exist regardless of the existence of the problem they were created to address.

These facts notwithstanding, this approach has several drawbacks reducing the effectiveness of targeted investigations if special care is not taken to avoid them.

- Defining a problem precisely is not easy. Unfortunately, it is easy to identify a target in a nebulous way and to define success as being whatever is needed to look good in the eyes of one's supervisors or critics.

- Lack of initial success may create pressure to extend the period of time allotted for conducting targeted activities. Such extensions can be granted indefinitely if one is not judicious in their allocation.

- The opposite may occur when the original plan is overly ambitious for the time allowed for the investigation. Lack of initial success might cause the investigation to be called off when an extended investigation might be successful.

- Targeting individuals and groups for investigations gives rise to the potential for violations of citizens' constitutional rights.

- In addition to the civil rights issue, such investigations also open up avenues of police corruption.

Although these drawbacks must be carefully considered, they can be minimized or eliminated by careful management of the investigators conducting targeted investigations. In fact, they are not problems with the approach but rather problems arising from a failure to implement the approach properly. Indeed, such problems pervade almost all facets of policing and, consequently, methods for avoiding these pitfalls have been developed. Overall, the threat of such problems does not seem to outweigh the potential benefits of such an approach to investigations.[21]

The compelling requirement for the elimination of this special deployment of patrol personnel resources to a separate administrative section is a determination of policy by police management with respect to *patrol beat responsibility*. Everything pivots on this determination. Policy in regard to this critical decision will vary from one department to another. At one end of the administrative spectrum, the detective is charged with total investigative responsibility. At the other end, with variations in between, the individual officer is charged with the total delivery of police service, including the investigation and disposition of cases in all categories originating on that beat.

It is fundamental for tasks ordinarily assumed by specialized divisions that *can* be satisfactorily performed by the patrol division to

21. *Ibid.*, pp. 325–327.

actually be reserved for patrol in order that its manpower may be increased and the force of the special unit decreased. This basic principle of police management is not widely followed. Too frequently, detective divisions are observed handling a large volume of petty cases that should be carried through to final disposition by the patrol officer. Thus, departmental policy with respect to patrol responsibility is a highly important factor in determining the personnel strength of the detective division.

When because of case-load, the patrol force cannot discharge this responsibility with maximum efficiency, it must have the specialized assistance of the detective. But this does not diminish the responsibility of the patrol officer. An uncleared case originating on the patrol's beat remains as a direct charge against personal operations. The detective division should be regarded only as a supporting element available to the patrol officer in meeting responsibilities as the person charged with the delivery of all the line functions of police service on the beat. Adherence to this form of patrol policy results in maximum employment of manpower in the largest administrative unit in the organization. Wherever this patrol policy has been applied, it has reduced the volume of uncleared cases that must be referred to the detective division for investigation and clearance.

As a result of the yield from specialization in criminal investigation, detective divisions, particularly in the larger cities, are decentralized functionally into special details, such as the homicide, robbery, burglary, automobile theft, worthless check, bunco, and other squads. Case-load will determine the necessity for the creation of a special squad. Such units should be created only in response to a real need and liquidated or consolidated with another unit when the need has passed or ceased to be acute or continuous.

Selection of Detectives

Extraordinary care must be used in recruiting detectives. They may possess the qualities necessary to patrol beats or supervise patrol officers, but they must have other personal qualifications characteristically fitting them for specialized investigative services. A deep interest by the investigator is essential for this phase of police work. This interest must be supplemented by an intimate knowledge of the arts and sciences applicable to a particular field of investigation, plus an acquaintance with and personal knowledge of criminals who specialize in particular types of offenses.

Like the patrol officer, the detective must have energy, persistence, courage, resourcefulness, initiative, intelligence, imagination, alertness, discriminating observation, memory, and judgment—only to a greater degree. Contrary to popular impression, a criminal case—whether it be murder, robbery, burglary, or automobile theft—is seldom solved by miraculous sleuthing powers or by the methods exploited in detective mystery thrillers, but by persistent, intelligent hard work. The selection of competent criminal investigators for assignment to detective work presents a difficult problem. Some police authorities hold that competitive written examinations, as a prerequisite to assignment to detective duty, fail to accomplish their purpose; they point out that experience generally has proved formal tests cannot finally determine detective aptitude or capacity. Nevertheless, in the selection of officers for transfer to the detective division, some criteria must be applied. No measuring device, whether written examination or other forms of tests, should be overlooked in the effort to select officers who are best qualified for this type of work.

Traditionally, police departments have used a wide range of methods when selecting investigators. Many of these methods were clearly subjective in nature. More recently, some departments have used concrete behaviors when selecting candidates. This is a process of breading down general judgmental concepts into specific measurable behaviors. This standardization of general traits is known as behaviorally anchored scales (BAS). An example of this is the measurement of the trait "teamwork." Figure 12–6 sets forth the framework that a rater should use when rating candidates on the trait of "teamwork." The rating of candidates is on their actual behavior, that in this instance is: poor, average, and superior. Each of these is explained in detail and allows the rater to evaluate specific behavior. This is in sharp contrast to abstract rating scales.

For example, if the candidate's actual behavior showed the person to be a loner (one who rarely shares significant crime information), always tried to take credit for a team arrest, and was disruptive and uncooperative with other officers—the individual would be rated as "poor" for "teamwork." This anchored behavior is clearly unique and distinctive, based on the definition of "teamwork." Departments using a behaviorally anchored scale have found them to be more reliable and valid than other rating systems.[22]

22. Bernard Cohen and Jan Chaiken, *Investigators Who Perform Well,* Washington, D.C., National Institute of Justice, 1987, pp. 21–22.

Figure 12–6

Behaviorally Anchored Scale

Teamwork: The capacity to work and cooperate with fellow officers; accepts and gives constructive criticism; shares knowledge and crime information with peers.

Poor	Average	Superior
* Is a loner.	* Is friendly and supportive of officers.	* Encourages other officers to participate in police work.
* Rarely shares significant crime information with peers.	* Is willing to be a team player.	* Always shares significant crime information with others.
* Always tries to take credit for a team arrest.	* Periodically shares some crime information.	* Is cooperative and supportive.

A detective selection system should be designed so the best possible candidates are selected. An effective selection system has the following elements:

- Equal access to the system.

- Equal opportunity.

- Valid.

- Job related.

- Useable.

- Efficient.

- Training.

- Evaluation.

When these elements are present, selection results are positive. Figure 12–7 describes the selection process. The first step is to create a job description for the position. It establishes minimum qualifications and carefully spells out the deadline for filing an application. A maximum effort allows all personnel to find out when a position is open. This is done by publicizing the position opening at lineups, posting announcements on bulletin boards and announcing the position in the departmental newsletter.

Figure 12–7

Selection Process for the Position of Detective

Eligibility
     Three years a patrol officer.
Announcement
     Job description.
     Minimum qualifications.
     Deadlines.
Posting
     Bulletin boards.
     Newsletter.
     Lineups.
Master application list
     Eligible applicants.
     Ineligible applicants.
Examination procedures
Interview—35 points.
Presentation—40 points.
Personnel file review—25 points.
(Sick leave—5 points).
(Performance evaluations—15 points).
(Sustained internal affairs investigations—5 points).
Training and evaluation procedures five weeks.
     Multiple trainers.

The goal of this effort is to ensure that each qualified officer has an equal opportunity to apply for the position. Upon receipt of application forms, a master list is drawn up, and ineligible candidates notified of the reasons. The review panel consists of one detective and two officers who hold the rank of sergeant or higher. The panel presides over the oral interview of each candidate. This covers such topics as previous training, experience, general knowledge of criminal statutes, and other job related factors. This panel also presides over the presentation made by each candidate on an assigned investigative topic.

The head of the investigative unit is responsible for reviewing personnel files. This part of the selection process includes an assessment of sick leave measured by standard deviations. Another part is the review of the last two behaviorally anchored supervisory ratings. These ratings include ten items: investigative skills, report writing, interviewing, punctuality, street sense, criminal law, knowledge of referral agencies, ability to follow instructions, cooperation, and observance of work hours. Finally, serious and non-serious sustained internal affairs investigations are reviewed. In the absence of complaints, the candidate receives a total of 5 points. Points are lost for each sustained investigation. For example, a candidate with one serious complaint loses five points, whereas a candidate with one non-serious complaint loses 2.5 points. Furthermore, a candidate with one serious and one non-serious complaint loses 7.5 points resulting in a negative score for this element. The final element is the training and evaluation phase.

Each detective trainee receives training and supervision over a five-week period. Significantly, each trainee is supervised by more than one trainer.[23]

Case Study

Chief Ralph Ammerman

Chief Ammerman has just been in office for three months as the head of a police department in Santa Novata, a community of 55,320 population, with 91 sworn officers and 29 civilians. The city is situated in valley separated by a major river from a neighboring metropolitan area. The city is essentially a bedroom community, but is does have one major shopping center and considerable light industry. The City is racially mixed and whites constitute 59 percent of the population and Mexican–Americans are the second largest group. Chief Ammerman came from a major metropolitan city where his last assignment was as head of the unformed division serving a city with a population of 392,000.

The present organizational chart has 16 assigned to the investigation section, and 72 sworn personnel assigned the patrol section. The remainder of the personnel are assigned to community services, records, and traffic. The new chief, during his short tenure, has found that bureaucratic specialization

Dominates the organization. Uniformed officers respond to calls for service and conduct preliminary investigations of minor crimes and spend the rest of their time on preventative patrol. All other investigations are conducted by patrol officers assigned to the investigative section. There is not a designated rank of detective. Patrol officers are not allowed to deviate from their job description and there is considerable friction between patrol and the investigation section. Line officers feel that they are excluded from becoming real contributing members of the organization.

There is a real problem within the patrol section:

1. Morale is low.
2. The crime rate is higher than it should be.
3. Response time is less than desirable.
4. Citizen complaints are up.
5. Sick call is higher than desirable.
6. The job is viewed as dissatisfying.

Chief Ammerman after discussion with command personnel and several sergeants and line officers feel that the division of labor between patrol and investigations is the crux of the problem. If the department is to move ahead and properly serve the community this problem must be resolved as soon as possible. The Chief feels that a

23. *Ibid.*, pp. 36–38.

new division of labor between the two major units is essential. He wants the patrol section to assume more investigative responsibilities, and he would like to reduce the size of the investigative section and have only enough personnel assigned to conduct complex investigations. Additionally, officers remaining in investigations should serve as coordinators and assist line officers as needed.

If you were Chief Ammerman what is the first thing you would do? Why? Would you create a task force? Is so, who would serve on the task force? Would you considering implementing the team policing model? Why? What crimes would you have the investigative unit handle? Why?

For Further Reading

John P. Boyle, "Detective Case Management–How to Make it Work for Your Department," *The Police Chief,* April 1997, Vol. LXIV, No. 4, pp. 172–175.

> The author describes the Detective Case Management (DCM) computerized network and data management system that was designed to help law enforcement agencies effectively gather, manipulate and use information in criminal investigation. Discusses time management, case tracking and information sharing among detectives. Reviews the implementation challenge to include data input and retrieval, ongoing costs. Discussed management efforts need to insure the successful implementation of the system.

Lois Pilant, "Computerized Criminal Investigations," *The Police Chief,* January 1993, Vol. LX, No. 1, pp. 29–38.

> Describes the advantages of developing one's own system rather than using a commercial vendor to develop a computerized criminal investigation system. Reviews the advantages of a centralized computer system wherein each law enforcement agency acts as a user with access to all of the information in it. Briefly describes programs such as STOPS (standard Tactical Online Public Safety System), CANE, (Computer-Assisted Narcotics Enforcement) and LEAPS that tracks evidence, vehicle information, and stolen and recovered property.

William J. Smith, "Investigation at the Local Level–How Decentralization of a Big Department is Working in Philadelphia," *Law and Order,* September 1994, Vol. 42, No. 9, pp. 63–65.

> Describes the shift to community policy and the decentralization of investigative services. It's implementation is guided by a 5–year plan wherein detectives and juvenile aid were moved from headquarters into seven field divisions. The only functions still performed from a centralized location include special investigation, intelligence. Under the new system investigators are involved and accountable to local communities.

Tony Lesce, "Developing Special Investigations Units," *Law and Order,* October 1998, Vol. 46, No. 10, pp. 175–178.

The author describes the functions performed by a Special Investigation Section. This unit is charged with gathering criminal information, coordinating investigations, serves as a clearing house, and enforces administrative law pertaining to liquor and gaming. The unit has assigned personnel to work with a drug enforcement task force, and has developed a domestic terrorism task force to share information with other agencies. The unit also liaisons with national and international law enforcement entities to include INTERPOL and the National White Collar Crime Center.

Chapter 13

HUMAN RESOURCES: Selection, Training and Career Development

Learning Objectives

1. Compare the per capita expenditures for sworn officers in four population groups.

2. List eight different selection criteria generally found in police departments.

3. Describe the importance of intelligence as a selection criteria.

4. Discuss the importance of good physical and mental condition.

5. Write a short essay supporting the induction minimum age of 25 years.

6. Discuss the need for eliminating residency requirements.

7. Compare content and construct methods of validation.

8. Write an essay supporting the use of a probationary period.

9. Describe what can be done to recruit minority candidates.

10. Discuss the importance of career development.

11. List ten subjects taught in a basis peace officers course.

12. Describe why there is a need for a field-training officer (FTO).

13. List eight subjects generally taught in supervisory courses.

14. Discuss the subject content of the Command College.

15. Describe Internet training.

The caliber of police service is almost completely determined by personnel policy, and very largely at the intake by recruiting standards. From the point of view of the taxpayer, personnel policy in the American police field invites close scrutiny of costs and quality of service rendered. Furthermore, the increasing tendency to measure police administration against the standards of modern social service marks personnel policy as a problem of the first magnitude. In terms of the total municipal budget, the cost of police protection generally is second only to appropriations for public works. Of this amount, between EIGHTY and NINETY percent is accounted for by the single budget item of police salaries! This percentage is in agreement with the distribution of the police budget in most American police departments.

If for no other reason, the mere fact that the major share of the cost of law enforcement is to be found in the monthly payroll, merits inquiry into the soundness of the principles upon which these expenditures are made. In the ten largest police departments the number of full-time sworn officers range from 36,813 in New York City that is approximately 51 percent of all of the officers in New York State. In the State of Illinois the Chicago Police Department has 35 percent of all of the sworn officers employed in that State. At the State level the California Highway patrol is the largest agency with 6,219 officers and Los Angeles County is the largest sheriff's department with 8,014 sworn officers. These figures are staggering when one realizes there are 18,769 local and state law enforcement agencies and the majority of police departments are relatively small.[1]

One way to look at police costs is to compare police expenditures to total city expenditures. This varies considerably from community to community. In Chicago, one-fifth of the budget goes to the police department and in Tucson 23 percent goes to public safety. Another way to illustrate that police work is big business is to look at total police expenditures. In three cities with more than 1 million population the police mean expenditures were just short of 28 million dollars and the per capita expenditure was 26.6. This is in sharp contrast to communities with less than 25, 000 population where the per capita cost averaged 104.4. As noted in table 13–1 the largest per capita expenditure for sworn personnel is 146.3 for cities in the population group ranging from 250,000 up to half a million. Additionally, central cities had the largest per capita expenditure followed by suburban communities and then independent cities. Regionally, the West South Central part of the United States had the smallest expenditure per capita (89.7) and the South Atlantic has the largest (126.0).

Police department budgets are awesome and in some instances dwarf municipal costs in other areas of government. One major department spends 35 percent more for each sworn police officer than another large department. In municipal police department with more than 100 sworn officers the expenditure per officer was $70.670 and during the same year state police agencies spent $82,562 per sworn officer.[2]

Table 13–1

Mean and Per Capita Police Department
Personnel Expenditures
in Cities of 10,000 Persons and Over

---

1. Kathleen Maguire and Ann L. Pastore, *Sourcebook of Criminal Justice Statistics–1997*, Washington, DC, Bureau of Justice Statistics, 1998, pp. 38–39.

2. Brian A. Reaves and Andrew L. Goldberg, *Law Enforcement Management and Administrative Statistics, 1997: Data for Individual State and Local Agencies with 100 or More Officers*, Washington, DC, Bureau of Justice Statistics, September 1999, p. xiv.

Expenditure for Department Personnel

	Number of Cities reporting	Mean expenditure	Per Capita expenditure
Total, all cities	1,381	$ 5,056,805	$106.95
Population Group			
Over 1,000,000	3	27,999,246	26.6
500,000 to 1,000,000	7	67,062,057	91.5
250,000 to 499,999	24	53,788,219	146.3
100,000 to 249,999	67	17,020,381	121.9
50,000 to 99,999	183	7,686,759	112.2
25,000 to 49,999	343	3,693,341	105.2
10,000 to 24,999	754	1,677,639	104.4
Metro System			
Central	270	14,447,616	117.3
Suburban	814	3,070,143	107.3
Independent	297	1,964,626	95.5

Source: Kathleen Maguire, Ann L. Pastore Editors, *Sourcebook of Criminal Justice Statistics–1997,* Washington, DC, Bureau of Justice Statistics, 1998, p. 43 citing Evelina R. Moulder, "Police and Fire Personnel, Salaries and Expenditures for 1997," *The Municipal Year Book 1998,* Washington, DC, International City/County Management Association, 1998, table 3/13. Reprinted with permission of the International/City County Management Association, 777 North Capitol Street, NE, Suite 500, Washington, DC 20002. All Rights Reserved.

The personnel resources of a police department are its greatest asset. All the way, from the top to the bottom of the enterprise, the caliber of personnel sets the stage for standards of performance in the delivery of police service. The degree of intelligence, zeal, determination and devotion to duty that a police officer brings to roll call in preparing for the tour of duty, is determined in advance by police personnel policy with respect to recruiting standards.

Fundamental to successful police service is the individual police officer, selected with care and well trained for the job. The officer of today is the Sergeant, the Lieutenant, the Captain, the Chief of Police of tomorrow. Thus, the character of police service is almost completely determined by personnel policy and very largely at the intake by recruiting standards. Police Chiefs and other officials of local government are recognizing this basic principle and as a result, recruiting standards are moving upward in order to attract to the police service, the career-minded young men and women.

But there are other factors suggesting the propriety of an inventory of police personnel resources in the United States. Technological advances and the application of scientific disciplines to the police field have created major personnel problems. Today, most of the arts and sciences find important expression in this branch of the public service with a progressive multiplication in the tools and procedures that must be employed for the delivery of police service. Personnel standards of yesterday fail to meet the test of an emerging profession that almost overnight has become an exceedingly technical and complex undertaking. Effective line power in a modern police organization is dependent upon an array of qualifications in the individual officer that would have seemed strange indeed, fifty years ago.

Conscientious police executives know that the quality and quantity of police service are not exclusively a function of numerical strength, and recognition of that fact is bringing the problems of police recruitment and training into sharp focus. Management in the police field is becoming personnel conscious. The measurement of personnel resources relates not merely to numerical strength, but also to the intelligence, ability, skill and "know-how" available in the organization for the execution of plans and operations. Recruiting standards must be adjusted to attract a higher type of individual, and training facilities are an essential part of the administrative program.

Entrance Criteria

A satisfactory personnel program in any enterprise requires the establishment of entrance standards that will bring into the service young men and women equipped to meet successfully the tasks they will be called upon to perform. The most critical stage in police personnel administration is recruitment, for it is at that point the caliber of the police force is determined. Entry requirements into law enforcement agencies generally include some of the following selection criteria:

- Age.
- Proportionate height and weight.
- Education.
- Vision.
- Background investigation.
- Medical examination.
- Oral interview.
- Written examination.
- Psychological examination.
- Physical agility test.
- Polygraph examination.
- Non-smoker.
- Type of drug use.
- Recent drug use.
- Residency requirement.
- Arrest record.
- Citizenship.

- Physical condition.

The above requirements will vary somewhat from one department to another but may be regarded as a cross-section or average of entrance qualifications in the American police services today. Some departments are less exacting in this respect than others, and wherever this is true, the people of the communities they serve suffer a corresponding reduction in the quality of police protection. The Dallas Police Department requirements are typical of many departments and qualifications for employment include:

- Forty-five (45) semester hours from an accredited college or university with a "C" average or better.
- Twenty-one years of age at the time of application or 19 ½ years of age with at least 60 semester hours with a "C" average or better.
- United States citizenship.
- If applicable, military serve with an honorable discharge as stipulated on a DD–214.
- Valid driver's license.
- No felony convictions.[3]

As an equal opportunity employer the Dallas Police Department attempts to reach a broad base for recruiting as indicated by the fact that a recruiter can be reached at 1–800–527–2948.

On the average, law enforcement agencies screen about ten candidates before making a single hiring decision. A rigorous screening process is time-consuming and expensive, but essential if strides are to be made in the professionalization of the police. The officer of the 21st century should be an individual who can function as a true professional. If this is to be done, it will require the flattening of the organization. Power will have to be diffused throughout the organization and one's expertise should be the determining criteria for its allocation, not rank. Additionally, discretion will have to be increased at the operational level and, needless to say, the pay of line personnel increased substantially. The line officer of the future should be a true "white collar" worker. Such an officer should be a manager and a problem solver, not just a taker of reports.[4] True community-policing has the capacity to alter the way that law enforcement deals with crime and strives to improve the quality of life in neighborhoods. As more and more departments move toward a community policing mode officers at the operational level will have to perform a variety of skills that were unknown a few years ago.[5] This means that the quality of the police

3. Dallas Police Department, *Recruiting,* Dallas, TX, City of Dallas, 3/7/99, http://www.ci.dallas.tx.us/dpd/rrcrt.htm.

4. Mark H. Moore and Darrel W. Stephens, *Beyond Command and Control: The Strategic Management of Police Departments,* Washington, D.C., Police Executive Research Forum, 1991, p. 84.

5. Robert Trojanowicz and Bonnie Bucqueroux, *Community Policing: How to Get Started, Second Edition,* Cincin-

recruit must be enhanced. Based upon the complex tasks the police must perform, it would seem the following minimum requirements should be required for induction into the American police services.

Intelligence. Admittedly, the person possessing an absorbing interest in the police service may be able to overcome intellectual defects; advocates of interest tests assert that a consuming interest in any field cannot fail to bring success to its possessor. It is extremely doubtful, however, that there ever was a *successful* officer who was not unusually intelligent. In some positions a person with limited mental equipment who is greatly interested will make a good showing, but in the police service there appears to be a level beyond which an officer cannot go without superior mental equipment. Interest, initiative, and dynamic personality may carry some persons up the promotional ladder, but it does not follow that they have the capacity to fill their positions adequately after they have reached the higher levels.

The misinterpretation of these and similar qualities as intelligence has greatly retarded the progress of police service. The highest degree of intelligence available is none too good for the trying tasks daily confronting every police officer. The organizational chain is no stronger than its weakest link, and the stupid, blundering individual, who by certain acts can bring discredit upon an entire organization, becomes the public's measuring stick for the whole department. One inferior officer who fails to rise to an emergency can ruin the reputation of an otherwise excellent police force.

Rapid and accurate thinking is an essential quality of the police officer. The officer must decide instantaneously matters possibly affecting one or several persons lives. The officer must reach decisions concerning the application of the law without delay, and must make no errors in arriving at this decision because the public is always the "second guesser." A police officer made a decision, on one occasion, and it later took the State Supreme Court six months to decide whether it was right or wrong. The officer's perceptive powers, imagination, ability to concentrate attention upon the tasks, memory—visual and auditory—reasoning and judgment must all be the best, otherwise, the individual will fail when confronted with some of the crucial tests that are the lot of every police officer. Furthermore, a high order of intelligence is necessary if the new recruit is to absorb readily the material submitted in the training programs, (preliminary, intermediate and advanced).

Police entrance standards must provide for the selection of officers possessing a superior degree of intelligence in order to assure satisfactory performance in positions to which the candidate may later advance. A minimum intelligence quotient from 110 to 112 is recognized by leaders in the field for entry into police service. With the trend toward a minimum educational standard of two years preparation at the university and college level, the minimum IQ is virtually set

nati, OH, Anderson Publishing, 1998,
pp. 1–123.

automatically. An individual with less than this rating would experience difficulty in completing course work at the university level if the faculty has maintained reasonable achievement standards.

The intelligent use of tests and examinations will go far toward reducing the element of chance in the selection of police personnel. In the case of smaller police departments, contact with the police personnel officer in nearby cities and the State Police will prove very fruitful in connection with the content of the written examination. Normally the intelligence test is part of the written test that can be administered by the personnel department, the civil service commission or an independent testing firm.

Education. Educational requirements in American police departments vary from the ability to read and write, to high school graduation with a slight trend toward a university degree in the criminal justice major. Accidental infiltration of individuals with university training into the police services has escaped the attention of most observers. As early as the middle of the last century in one metropolitan police department with a total personnel of 628 men and women, there were 84 individuals possessing from two to eight years of university training. The head of one division in this department held the Phi Beta Kappa key. This may be attributed in part to the rise in average educational levels among the total population but it is undoubtedly true that the complex nature of modern police service and the trend toward professionalization have operated as factors in challenging the interest of college trained men and women. The presence of candidates with a university background is no doubt largely responsible for an ascending average intelligence level among the personnel of American police forces today.

It can now be said that an increasing percentage of the total personnel in metropolitan police departments of the United States possess from one to four years or more of university training! This infiltration, although proceeding for the most part unnoticed, marks a significant turning point in American police history. The performance record of these officers is paving the way for formal elevation of educational standards in the police service and has directed attention to the need for the establishment of professional curricula in universities and colleges affording specific training of men and women for entry into this branch of the public service.

In terms of the sworn police officers a survey of police operational and administrative practices twenty years ago showed that one department had slightly more than one-half of it's sworn personnel had a baccalaureate degree and in one northwest city 85 percent had acquired a four-year degree.[6] In another survey during the same period

6. Police Executive Research Forum, *Survey of Police Operational and Administrative Practices—1981,* Washington, D.C., Police Foundation, 1981, pp. 102–106.

only three of the 1,087 departments responding required a four-year college degree at the entry level.[7]

A study by the Police Executive Research Forum during the same period that included 347 municipal police departments, 94 sheriff's departments, 38 state police agencies and 23 consolidated departments found that almost three fourths of the sworn officers had some college education. Just under 20 percent had two years of college, and 55.1 percent of the officers had more than two years of college.[8]

In a more recent national study it was determined that nearly all (88 percent) local police departments have a formal educational requirement for new officer recruits (see table 13-2). The minimum educational requirement for 9 in 10 departments was completion of high school. About 12 percent of the departments require education beyond high school, usually completion of college courses or a 2-year college degree. Less than one-half of one percent of all surveyed departments in 1990 required new officers to have a 4-year degree and that is still true at the end of the twentieth century. Clearly the trend toward a more educated police is a positive step toward the ultimate professionalism sought by many in the police field, but it is something that one can hope for but it is still an elusive attainment.

Table 13–2

Percent of Agencies with Educational Requirements for New Officers

Type of Agency				
	County	Municipal	Sheriff	State
4–year college degree	3%	2%	1%	4%
2–year college degree	13	7	5	16
Non degree college	10	16	5	16
High school diploma	73	75	89	61

Brian A. Reaves and Andrew L. Goldberg, *Law Enforcement Management and Administrative Statistics, 1997: Data for Individual State and Local Agencies with 100 or More Officers,* Washington, DC, Bureau of Justice Statistics, September 1999, p. xiv.

A true exception is the City of Portland, OR, that has an open and continuous recruitment for community police officer. The qualifications for applicants for the position are set forth in figure 13–1. The examination for the position consists of five phases:

● Phase I. An objective multiple choice written test weighted 50%.

7. James F. Fyfe, *Police Personnel Practices, Baseline Data Reports, Vol. 15, No. 1,* Washington, D.C., I.C.M.A., January 1983, p. 4.

8. David L. Carter, Allen D. Sapp, and Darrel W. Stephens, *The State of Police Education: Policy Direction for the 21st Century,* Washington, D.C., Police Executive Research, 1989, p. 44.

- Phase II. An oral performance test weighted 50%.

- Phase III. Once proof of degree has been submitted, an in depth background history investigation by the Portland Police Bureau. Upon successful completion and acceptance of a conditional offer of employment, candidates must pass Phases IV and V.

- Phase IV. A qualifying psychological evaluation to determine the candidate's personal suitability for police work.

- Phase V. A qualifying medical evaluation to determine the candidate's physical capability to do police work.

Figure 13-1

Announcement for the City of Portland, Oregon for the Position of Community Police Officer

This is an entry level law enforcement position with an emphasis on Community Policing. The City of Portland Community Police Officer works with all citizens to preserve life, maintain human rights, protect property and promote individual responsibility and community commitment.

Applicant to Qualify must:

- Possess a BACCALAUREATE DEGREE from an accredited college or university no later than six months following date of application.
- Be 21 years of age by date of employment.
- Be a US citizen within one year of date of employment.
- Meet all applicable medical requirements.
- Possess or be able to obtain a valid Driver's License at date of employment and not have excessive traffic violations.
- Not have been convicted of a crime, the punishment for which could have been imprisonment for at least one (1) year or a crime involving domestic violence (applicants with lesser criminal records will be evaluated on an individual basis).
- Not have a dishonorable discharge from any branch of the military.
- Meet the requirements listed in the Supplemental Application.

City of Portland, *Community Police Officer*, Portland, OR, Portland Police Bureau, 1/30/99. http://www.ci.portland.or.us/jobs/job98072.htm.

Selected individuals attend a State sponsored seven week "basis" academy after which they must attend an "advanced" academy conducted by the Portland Police Bureau. Officers appointed to the Portland Police bureau are on probation for 18 months, during which time they work under the supervision of a coach who teaches fundamentals of police work.

Character. The character and reputation of a police officer must be unassailable. Examination procedure includes taking fingerprints from the candidate and submitting them to local, state and national fingerprint files. This is a highly important phase of the recruiting process, as police departments, first of all, should assure themselves they are not employing persons with criminal records. It is a sad commentary on the American police services that there are instances where known felons have worn a police uniform.

In addition, inquiry is made of persons mentioned as references in the candidate's application form. It should be noted and emphasized that references, as such, given by the applicant constitute the weakest source of information concerning character and that the greatest reliance should be placed upon other methods of investigation. A detailed report should be secured from the police department in the applicant's home town in case of recent residence elsewhere. These measures will uncover important information concerning the candidate's relations with friends and previous employers, credit standing, and reputation with persons qualified to judge honesty and reliability. When ever possible unnamed reference should be interviewed regarding the applicant. These individuals can be identified when interviewing reference and friends. Although back ground investigations are costly and time consuming, the background investigation should be conducted before appointing an individual to probationary status. Investigators should use every bit of data available on a candidate to include a home visit with the candidate and his or her family and interviews with neighbors. Additionally qualifying credentials should be verified. [9]All inquiries should be conducted by capable investigators and every effort expended to obtain all the information possible concerning the applicant's life history and habits. This stage of the screening process should be considered as qualifying only, and there should be no hesitation in rejecting applicants whose previous reputation for character is not of the highest type. All border-line cases should be resolved against the applicant.

Height. An examination of many qualification schedules in American police departments reveals a height range from 5 feet to 6 feet 5 inches. In the past it was believed that the small officer was invaluable at times in the police service, but there was a psychology that goes with the taller officer in the control of people, singly or in groups, that is generally not overlooked. Twenty years ago it was common to find height requirements ranging between 5 feet 8 inches and 6 feet 5 inches. Most departments recruited candidates who were a minimum of 5 feet 10 inches. This requirement prevailed because police managers felt the taller individual could perform police duties better. One study a quarter of a century ago found there was a relationship between the height of officers and the number of assaults on those officers. Shorter officers had a greater probability of being injured and involved in more vehicle accidents. They also had more complaints filed against them than taller officers. While this study supported the practice of hiring taller officers, it clearly excluded certain members of ethnic groups and women. There were other studies that contradicted these findings. A survey of selection criteria in 1983 for entry level full-time sworn

9. Commission on Accreditation for Law Enforcement Agencies, *Standards*   *for Law Enforcement Agencies*, Fairfax, VA, January 1999, pp. 32–2 and 32–3.

personnel showed that 41.8 percent of the respondents (1,240 departments) had height requirements.[10]

In 1991, out of the six largest police departments, only Los Angeles had a height requirement. This was a minimum of 60 inches and a maximum of 80 inches. The other large cities (Chicago, Detroit, Houston, New York, and Philadelphia) do not have any written guidelines addressing a height requirement. Today height requirements have been virtually eliminated from recruitment announcements as departments strive to create a diverse force, and there has been little negative impact on performance of officers of varying heights.[11]

Weight Where formerly 200 pounds of brawn constituted the primary requirement for service in a police uniform, the weight factor now represents only a nominal significance. The requirement today will vary somewhat from one department to another, but most departments agree upon a minimum of 106 pounds. Variation of as much as 30 pounds either way, however, is noted in some instances. A reasonable and safe procedure is to consider weight in proportion to height. There is an observable and justifiable tendency among American police departments to place greater emphasis upon physical and mental health than upon height and weight. In the past, it was also common for departments to exclude persons considered to be *underweight* from the force by setting a minimum weight requirement at the hiring stage. These requirements have been challenged as being discriminatory on the basis of sex. Although the Supreme Court has not spoken on the issue, the U.S. Court of Appeals decision in *Smith v. Troyan*, 520 F.2d 492 (6th Cir.1975), struck down one such provision. In that case, a woman applicant demonstrated that the weight requirement disqualified 80 percent of the women applicants, whereas only 26 percent of the men applicants were thereby excluded. The court concluded there was no rational support for the weight requirement and that based upon the testimony of even the police department's expert witness, the weight requirement is neither rationally related to physical strength nor to psychological advantage.

Physical and Mental Condition. The candidate must have robust physical health in every respect, as determined by a competent doctor of medicine, aided by the facilities of a medical laboratory and laboratory technicians. Equally important, accurate determinations must be made with respect to mental health, personality, emotional stability, glandular functioning, temperament, social intellect, habits and ideals. These evaluations can be made only by a competent and qualified psychiatrist, neurologist, endocrinologist and psychologist.

The time and cost involved in appraising physical condition may seem out of proportion to their importance. But experience has proved otherwise in those few departments where the exercise of rigid precau-

10. Fyfe, *op. cit.*

11. Antony Pate and Edwin E. Hamilton, *The Big Six, Policing America's Largest Cities,* Washington, DC, Police Foundation, 1991, p.76.

tions in this respect has lowered personnel turnover and brought about other economies in administration offsetting this additional expense. On the credit side of the ledger also is the enhanced personnel performance on the job of candidates who can meet these standards. The same considerations dictating a rigid physical examination for all candidates suggest the necessity for annual physical examinations of all departmental personnel. In addition to personal incentives evoked by this procedure, it offers a definite advantage to each officer. From the standpoint of preventive medicine, incipient difficulties may be discovered and proper remedial measures taken at a time when they can produce the best results. Such examinations serve the interests of both the officer and the department in connection with retirement procedures. If for no other reason, annual physical examinations are justified on the ground that management needs information concerning the health and physical condition of its personnel.

Recruits in doubtful health should be rejected. In addition to the liability of sub-standard performance, the officer may become a pensioner in a short time with the necessity of being replaced, and with the result that two officers are carried on the payroll for the rest of their lives rather than one. Days lost on account of sickness in American police departments continue to seriously drain effective personnel strength and add tremendously to the cost of police protection in this country.

Equally disastrous is the individual who becomes irritable and whose actions bring the department into disrepute and who is frequently the subject of disciplinary action. The mentally unstable person may take a life unnecessarily, become brutal and commit other abnormal acts subjecting the department and the city to damage suits and other forms of embarrassment. The incompetent officer might have the intelligence, but generally sees nothing, hears nothing, and does nothing. This officer may be found asleep on duty and loses much time (off duty) as a result of factors traceable to physical conditions. The temperamental individual makes trouble in the ranks and among the citizens. This type of person is destructive of both morale and public relations, and must eventually be replaced.

The emotional stability to withstand the stresses of police work must of necessity, be a primary requirement of police personnel. Officers must be prepared to cope rationally with violence, verbal abuse, resentment and emergency situations. The emotionally unfit cannot meet these stress situations. One incompetent officer can trigger a riot, permanently damage the reputation Police service operates within a context of danger and emergency, and the emotionally unstable person is no match for the exacting demands police duty will impose upon an officer.

Although a comprehensive character and background investigation may eliminate some socially maladjusted individuals, personality defects in some of the applicants will be latent and not easily discernible.

Hence, the necessity for psychological screening in order to protect the department against the danger of moving an acute personality problem into the ranks. Its extreme usefulness as a screening tool in exposing those personal traits that are incompatible with service in a police uniform, has been amply demonstrated.

In the six largest cities in the United States applicants are required to be interviewed by a psychologist or a psychiatrist. Additionally, each department administers a test to screen for psychological problems. Figure 13–2 lists each city and name or type of test applicants take. The most widely used test is the Minnesota Multiphasic Personality Inventory (MMPI).[12]

Figure 13–2

Written Psychological Test Requirements for Applicants to Sworn Positions

Lines City	**Requirement**	**Name/Type Test(s)**
Chicago	Yes	Inwald Personality Inventory & Minnesota Multiphasic Personality (MMPI)
Detroit	Yes	MMPI & Rorschach
Houston	Yes	MMPI & Clinical Analysis Questionnaire
Los Angeles	Yes	MMPI & 16 Personality Factor Questionnaire
New York	Yes	MMPI, California Personality Inventory, Cornell, House–Tree–Person New York City Police Questionnaire
Philadelphia	Yes	MMPI

Source: Antony Pate and Edwin E. Hamilton, *The Big Six, Policing America's Largest Cities,* Washington, D.C., Police Foundation, 1991, p. 76.

Physical Strength and Agility. The courts have imposed upon employers this specific responsibility, so in reaction to this requirement a number of law enforcement agencies have been involved in the validation of agility tests. The methodology utilized by the Los Angeles County Sheriff's Department encompassed three phases: (1) questionnaire design, application, cross validation, and evaluation; (2) design and construction of the physical agility test site, and (3) establishing of time parameters through testing.

In terms of skills deemed essential for the position of deputy sheriff, they are listed in rank order from most often used to the least used: climbing, running, jumping, lifting, balancing, pulling, pushing, carrying, wrestling, crawling, dragging, and hitting or kicking. During

12. *Ibid.,* pp. 76–77.

the evaluation phase of this validation study it was decided the skills of wrestling, hitting and kicking could not be tested so were not included. The other skills were incorporated into specific activities and a test site was constructed resembling (as closely as possible) actual conditions that would be encountered.[13]

Age. The prevailing age limits for induction into police service were for many years from 23 to 35. There has been a discernible trend during the past few years toward a reduction in both limits. A large number of jurisdictions have reduced the minimum to 21, and the maximum to 31. AS early as 1929 one city raised the age limit from 21 to 23 on the grounds that the young candidate does not reach the age of reason until he is 23. It was further felt that at the age level of 21, a candidate is something of an adventurer and, therefore, not as reliable as the older candidate. In addition it has been argued that police service demands officers of more mature years in order to assure the exercise of discretion and settled habits. This concept has eroded because of court decisions and enforcement patterns of regulatory agencies. Recently the City of Chicago raised its age requirement to 22 for recruits and surprised its critics when there was no adverse impact on minority applicants. In Philadelphia applicants must be at least 19 years old.[14]

Appropriate habits and discretion can be acquired and directed under discipline in the police school and the service. Young candidates are more flexible and, therefore, more easy to mold to the aims, ideals and accepted practices of the department. They learn easier in the police school. They possess more vigor, energy and alertness than the older men and are not likely to have had their initiative stifled by some previous job failure. From the standpoint of personnel turnover, if the officer has not already been firmly established in some trade, there is less likelihood of leaving the department when industrial production is at its peak and jobs are plentiful. Insistence upon youth in recruiting police officers is generally found wherever effective police departments are maintained.

The age of 21 is not considered as the absolute minimum limit for induction into police service on the questionable basis that this used to be the age at which the candidate first attained, legally, the status of adulthood. So far as police objectives and the means for achieving them are concerned, mental age is of far greater importance than chronological age, and it offers a more scientific basis than minimum age requirements. It is not at all unlikely that this concept ultimately will prevail.

13. Gary D. Osborn, "Validating Physical Agility Tests," *The Police Chief,* January 1976, Vol. XLIII, No. 1, p. 43.

14. Committee of 70, *Philadelphia Police Department Governance Study,* Philadelphia, PA, 09/09/98, p. 2. http://www.libertynet.org/seventy/cops3.htm.

There is strong testimony for fixing the maximum age limit no higher than 25. There is strong evidence indicating candidates between 21 and 25 make the best material for officers. They learn quicker and make better records in the Academy than do officers who are past 25. It is the belief also, that the younger person, after a few years of experience, is a far better police officer than an older officer with the same amount of experience. Young officers are more readily trained than are men of 30 or over. Furthermore, failure to take police action has been found to be due not so much to lack of maturity as to lack of experience in similar situations. It is experience in the exercise of the type of judgment required of police officers that counts the most, and not the general maturity attached to age. In addition, it is of the greatest importance to observe that as the applicants approach 30, the more likely it is they have failed at everything else tried. Concurrently the U.S. Equal Employment Opportunity Commission has sued one city for refusing to hire candidates older than 35 and prevailed. It is based on the concept of age discrimination that requires equal opportunities for people from 40 to 70.

Residence Requirements. An important obstacle to career service in the police field is the "home talent" tradition in American cities. This expresses itself in the local residence requirement for appointment to the force. Much public education will be required in order to overcome this pernicious requirement and to replace it by a broader and more enlightened public policy. Any gain will be worth the effort. In a recently completed survey (see table 13–3) it was found that 50 percent of responding departments municipal police departments (n=454) require some or all of the sworn personnel to reside within the State, the city limits or other specified area. In sheriff's departments 42 percent required applicants to live in the county, and state police agencies limited it's application pool (45 percent) to residents of the State. Special police (e.g. school, transit) had the least restrictions in terms of residency, with 68 percent having no requirements.[15]

	Table 13–3				
	Percent of Agencies with Residency Requirements for New Officers				
	Type of Agency				
	County	Municipal	Sheriff	Special	State
Within State	18%	5%	6%	9%	45%
Within city or county	12	26	42	5	10
Within other specified area	6	19	7	18	35
No requirement	40	36	38	8	

Source: Brian A. Reaves and Andrew L. Goldberg, *Law Enforcement Management and Administrative Statistics, 1997: Data for Individual State and Local Agencies with 100 or More Officers,* Washington, DC, Bureau of Justice Statistics, 1999, p. xiv.

15. Reaves and Smith, *op. cit., p. ix.*

The local residence requirement denies the police and the community they serve the opportunity to recruit promising candidates who may, in some instances, provide a superior grade of qualifications possibly lacking among local applicants. The police and local officials in the community should take steps to abolish the local residence requirement and should also encourage the removal of state residency requirements, if they exist. Every effort should be made to overcome the pernicious requirement of local residence and replace it with a more enlightened policy more nearly fitting the public interest. It is noteworthy that in recent years, an increasing number of cities and communities have abandoned the residence qualification and only require the candidate to be a citizen of the United States.

There are, of course, exceptions to the trend of eliminating residency requirements. Philadelphia requires applicants to have been bona fide residents living in the city for one year before applying for a job. This requirement originated as a deliberate policy decision to ensure that city jobs go only to city dwellers. One elected official who supports the pre-employment residency requirement explained "it is unfair to Philadelphians to make them compete with the rest of the world." Another supporting rationale applied to the Police Department is that Philadelphians make better police officers. "People could theoretically be flying in from all around the world to take the [police] exam and our entire department could be filled with cops who wouldn't even know their way around the town," another official said. Supporters of this requirement expressed satisfaction with the status quo. Another individual said, "Police officer is one of the most sought after jobs in the city, and we have more than enough qualified people to take the test."

In a study of the Philadelphia Police Department some individuals familiar with the pre-employment residency pointed out that the elimination of the requirement had specific racial and political overtones. City jobs have historically offered some of the best available opportunities to minorities in Philadelphia and some fear that any change would be perceived as attempt to fill the Police Department with suburban white men instead. The requirement has also historically become a powerful tool for elected officials, allowing them to promise voters an advantage (in applying for city jobs) over those who cannot vote for them. Thus, any elected official supporting a change could be portrayed by opponents as supporting suburbanites over his or her own constituents.[16]

The specific requirements for entry into the police service have changed over the years and for the most part, the changes have provided for the selection of higher quality personnel. Recruitment is still the key to success in the police business and everything possible must be done to insure the best candidates are selected for the police

16.   Committee of 70, *op. cit., p. 1.*

service. August Vollmer, the father of modern police administration, stated with a great deal of accuracy, what the average citizen expects of a police officer (see figure 13–3).

Figure 13–3

Attributes the Police Officer Needs

The police officer should have the wisdom of Solomon, the courage of David, the strength of Samson, the patience of Job, the leadership of Moses, the kindness of the Good Samaritan, the strategy of Alexander, the faith of Daniel, the diplomacy of Lincoln, the tolerance of the carpenter of Nazareth, and finally, an intimate knowledge of every branch of the natural, biological and social sciences. If one has all these attributes, they might be a good officer.

Source: August Vollmer, *The Police and Modern Society,* Berkeley, CA, University of California Press, 1936, p. 222.

Court Decisions and Regulatory Requirements

Legal decisions and regulatory mandates at the federal level have altered the police selection process. There is little resembling the occurrences in some agencies at the turn of the last century. A new officer received a gun and a badge, and was put on the street. Today there are fundamental principles guiding the total selection process. The selection of a new recruit must be not only efficient but effective. Most importantly, it must be "fair." An analysis of each stage of the selection process insures satisfaction of professional and legal requirement. To use a specific procedure, or test, or to cite a selection requirement, it must be valid. In other words it must be job-related. There are three acceptable methods for determining the validity of a part or the total selection process. These validations are:

- Criterion-related.

- Construct.

- Content.[17]

Through careful study criteria, selection identifies characteristics of successful job performance. Then one establishes a performance rating for the criteria. When there is a high correlation between the two, there is a useful predictor of job performance. Another method is construct validity. This involves identifying traits or characteristics needed to perform successfully as a police officer. Once a trait identification occurs, a test has to be found to measure whether the candidate for the position has that trait. The last method, is content validity. In this instance, a specific part of the task to be performed by a police officer is measured. This can be the analysis of what a police officer

---

17. John Gales Sauls, "Establishing the Validity of Employment Standards," *FBI Law Enforcement Bulletin,* August 1995, Vol. 64, No. 8, pp. 27–32.

does, such as, tools, equipment, and work aids needed to perform certain police tasks. Whatever method, it must meet legal requirements and have predictive validity. If criteria are not job-related they must be eliminated.[18]

Figure 13–4

Position of the U.S. Commission on Civil Rights on the Burden of Proof in Disparate Impact Cases

In cases using the disparate impact theory, the plaintiff makes a prima facie case of discrimination by demonstrating that an employment practice(s) of the defendant has an adverse impact. This is usually done by comparing the composition of the employer's work force with the composition of the qualified applicant pool or, in some cases, with the composition of the qualified population in the relevant labor market. If the plaintiff succeeds in persuading the court that an employment practice has a disparate impact, then the burden of proof shifts to the defendant to prove the practice is justified by business necessity. If the defendant proves business necessity, the plaintiff can still prevail by showing there exists an alternative employment practice with less of an adverse impact, meeting the defendants business needs equally well.

Source: United States Commission on Civil Rights, *Report of the U.S. Commission on Civil Rights on the Civil Rights Act of 1990,* Washington, DC, USGPO, July 1990, pp. 2–3.

When evaluating the legality of test that have a disparate impact, courts speak of job-relatedness and business necessity. In evaluating whether an employment standard has a disparate impact, a statistical assessment must be made of a particular group's success rate in regard to the standard, as compared to the success rate of other groups. Where the standard creates no disparity, no demonstration of business necessity is required.[19]

If a selection process is to meet acceptable standards it must be useful, job-related, and non-discriminating. This means the impact of the testing procedure is the same for all applicants. An essential part of the selection process is the institution of administrative practices and procedures meeting legal standards. Candidates should be informed, at the time of formal application of every element of the selection process. They should be notified in a timely fashion, at every critical point in the selection process. These features should be set forth in written directives. The goal is to select individuals who have the skills, knowledge and abilities (SKA) to perform effectively as a law enforcement officer.[20]

---

18. Commission on Accreditation for Law Enforcement Agencies, *op. cit.,* p. 31–1.

19. Sauls, *op. cit.,* p. 29.

20. *Ibid,* 32–1.

Consideration also should be given to adverse impact. This occurs when there is a different rate of selection, less than 80 percent, effectively working to the disadvantage of individuals of a race, sex, or ethnic group. In other words, if specific criteria such as a height requirement excludes 80 percent of females or members of a specific minority group there is, in all probability, an adverse impact. A test of statistical significance should be calculated, if there is large enough number of cases, to determine whether there is an adverse impact. Detailed records should be kept of the selection process in the event of litigation or appeals alleging discrimination. Figure 13-3 describes the position of the U.S. Commission on Civil Rights regarding adverse impact.[21]

Police managers should be cognizant of and follow the guidelines for pre-employment evaluation services. These have been developed by the International Association of Chiefs of Police and provides a frame of reference for keeping current on psychological standards for pre-employment screening. The standard includes such things as testing, interviewing evaluation, and follow-up. These revised guidelines takes into consideration the impact of the Americans with Disability Act (ADA) and the Equal Employment Opportunity Commission (EEOC).[22]

Mechanics of Selection

Following the establishment of adequate entrance standards, the next and perhaps the most essential step of the whole recruitment process is an active search for qualified candidates. The best selection procedure that can be devised will be ineffective if not applied to as outstanding a group of people as can be attracted to the examination. A thorough canvass should be made of all possible sources of likely candidates. Appropriate publicity concerning forthcoming police entrance examinations can be planned and executed with telling effect.

The Search for Candidates. There is a certain fascination in police work, characteristic of no other profession and which can prove useful in attracting candidates. Individuals in all walks of life are intrigued by the detective mystery thriller, the crime buster radio programs and front page stories of major crimes, despite the fact that all of these present, for the most part, an inadequate image of police service. Any police officer will certify that these presentations, dramatized against a backdrop of murder and graft for the benefit of the gullible reader or listener, are seldom in agreement with the facts and fail to portray the challenging dimensions of police work in modern society. Police service is infinitely more interesting than the year's best mystery thriller. Nevertheless, this widespread popular interest has not yet been properly exploited in the recruiting process.

21. Commission on Accreditation for Law Enforcement Agencies, Inc., *Ibid.*, pp. 32–1 through 32–4.

22. Stephen F. Curran, "Pre-employment Psychological Evaluation of Law Enforcement Applicants," *The Police Chief*, October 1998, Vol. LXV, No. 10, pp. 88–95.

The search for candidates should not be confined to persons who happen to be unemployed at the time the examination is announced. An effort should be made to attract the most able young candidates obtainable, which means the police service enters a highly competitive market in the search for talent and ability. Different methods can be used to attract potential candidates. This includes recruiting at educational institutions, obtaining referrals from community groups, and posting announcements. Other methods include advertising in the news media, mobile recruitment programs, and referrals from public employment services. Some departments obtain referrals from police employees, and recruit at military separation centers. Another widely used technique is to have a continuous examination period. Additionally, Los Angeles, Detroit, and Philadelphia obtain referrals from labor organizations.[23] More recently police departments have used a Web site to recruit candidates.

Coordinated Recruiting. Police departments and police associations in each state should take the initiative and pool their resources in the establishment of a coordinated state-wide recruiting program. This would be especially helpful to the smaller and medium-sized departments, where the field of potential candidates is limited. A coordinated state-wide recruiting program offers the following advantages:

- It makes possible a more widespread recruiting effort.
- More sophisticated advertising of openings is justified.
- It provides the opportunity to conduct recruiting and selection programs under the leadership of professional personnel officers.
- The applicant has the opportunity of taking a single examination for openings in several jurisdictions.
- Potential candidates would be informed of all vacancies in police departments throughout the state.
- More extensive budgets could be appropriated for recruiting at substantially less cost than would necessarily have to be incurred by individual departments acting alone.
- Uniform procedures in applying for positions in all departments could be formulated.

In those states where Commissions on Police Selection and Training Standards have been established, the Commission is in an excellent position to organize and administer a coordinated state-wide recruiting program.

Competitive Examination. All applicants who apparently meet the minimum standards set up by the department, as indicated by oral interview and their application forms, are admitted to the examinations. This is a crucial point in the selection process. The means for improving selective methods in police personnel procedure are now ready at hand. With the employment of carefully validated and stan-

23. Pate and Hamilton, *op. cit.,* p. 69.

dardized tests, there is as much difference between selection on the basis of their results and haphazard selection as between the purchase of an automobile "sight unseen" and its purchase after careful trial. Where such tests are not a part of the screening process at the intake, selection and replacement are necessarily uncertain matters. The myth of the individual who can correctly judge character or ability at a glance has been exploded by an extended array of psychological experiments. The intelligent use of tests and examinations, now accepted as a part of standard procedure in the best American police departments, will go far toward reducing the element of chance in the process of selection, placement and promotion.

Collateral Elements of the Examination Process

The oral interview is the final stage in the initial recruitment process. The interview should be conducted in such a manner as to appraise the traits of personal appearance, ability to meet others, social intelligence, ability of the candidate for self-expression and ability to fit into the departmental organization.

Qualifying Oral Interview. Generally speaking this interview may aid in determining appearance, likeableness, affability, attitude toward work, outside interests, forcefulness, conversational ability and disagreeable mannerisms. The total score is computed for qualifying candidates and they are ranked on an eligibility list in the order of their final grades.[24]

The foregoing selection procedure will produce the best possible police recruits, but no recruiting process is so perfect as to not occasionally pass candidates who will fail when tested by the actual performance of police duties. There are many persons of intelligence, character and ability who never, under any circumstances, can become good police officers; they may work hard, long, loyally and faithfully and yet prove incompetent. In the interest of the service as well as for their own good, they should be eliminated at an early date.

Probation. A probationary period is thus an indispensable part of the examination process. A probationary period of not less than one year, preferably two, is recommended during which superior officers may give close attention to the candidate's actual ability to do police work before the tenure protection becomes absolute. There are many undesirable traits controllable by the new recruit for short periods.

---

24. *Veteran's Preference* may influence favorably the final score of the individual candidate, although it must be conceded that the allowance of extra grade points on this basis is in conflict with the merit principle. *Veterans' Preference* is obviously a question of politics and outside the pale of sound personnel administration. In approaching this problem, governmental agencies must decide how far they are willing to go in compromising the merit concept. It should be emphasized at this point that military experience is definitely an asset to a career police officer; however, if credit is given, it should be variable and based upon an evaluation of the extent and character of military experience rather than mere status as a veteran. *Veterans' Preference* as presently understood and applied in most jurisdictions is basically unsound.

Even a periodic drunk might not be discovered, or an epileptic might escape notice. The lazy person would naturally speed up while without tenure protection and the temperamental person would be able to exert self control for short periods. However, it would be rare indeed, if competent supervision were provided, adequate training courses were established, frequent ratings were taken and carefully scrutinized, and work performance studied monthly over a two-year period, that the potentially unsatisfactory employees (whom the examinations failed to detect) would remain in the organization.

This check on performance is concerned with the probationer's capacity to understand and execute directions, and upon alertness and the rapidity with which the person learns the techniques of a patrol officer's job. Also considered is the ability to fit into the organization harmoniously, loyalty to the force and to the municipal government, aptitude in comprehending the fundamentals of criminal law and procedure and skill in performing police duties. The candidate can be dismissed without the filing of charges and without hearing at any time during probation. It is quite natural for probationers to put their best foot forward and to cooperate in every way with the educational program, which should be more or less continuous during this period. The probationer will, in the majority of cases, attempt to conform to the rules for conduct, matters of policy, standards of practice, and standards of quantity and quality of work performed. If the period is sufficiently long, the probationer will form habits in agreement with departmental standards and are unlikely to be abandoned in the future.

No probationer should be given the rank of patrol officer until the end of the probationary period and only then, upon the specific recommendation of superiors. It is too often the case that rank and tenure are acquired by default. The only safe practice is to drop summarily all probationers who do not demonstrate something above the minimum ability, for once given rank, it is more difficult to eliminate incompetents. The Department should be given the benefit of the doubt in all borderline cases as long as this does not violate the rights of the individual.

Minority Recruitment

Increasing emphasis must be placed on recruiting qualified blacks, to serve as police officers in communities with black residents. In communities with Mexican–American residents, there is a need to recruit qualified Mexican–Americans. This standard, however, is not limited to any one ethnic minority group. Whenever there is a substantial ethnic minority population in any jurisdiction, no matter what the ethnic group may be, the police service can be improved by employing qualified members of that minority group. Every police agency should adhere to the principle that the police are the people and the people are the police.

Although the need to employ minorities as police officers may be obvious, their employment in many instances has not been appreciable despite the best intentions and diligent efforts of many police administrators. But in view of the need for minority police officers to create better community relations and increase police effectiveness, police administrators not only should recruit minorities, but also should insure that unwarranted cultural bias is eliminated from the total selection process.

Any reluctance by police administrators to employ minority police officers is being overcome by Federal courts, establishing a definitive record of eliminating cultural bias in the selection process and demanding preferential minority employment to rectify the effects of past discrimination. In most cases, preferential recruiting and hiring is directed toward approximating the minority composition of the community within the employee ranks.

Numerous recruitment techniques and programs have been particularly effective in attracting minorities. Police agencies seeking to recruit minorities should consider techniques described below and should develop techniques appropriate for the particular needs in their community. Special programs used to recruit disadvantaged and minority groups varies considerably across the nation. The vast majority advertise in the minority news media. In the large departments pre-examination counseling and training is available. Other departments operate "storefront" centers within the inner city as a means of providing information about employment. The majority of major cities teams visit colleges and universities. One problem exacerbating the minority recruitment process is the relatively poor retention rate once they complete the academy and assume full-time duties. [25]

However, the employment of persons from all ethnic groups within the community should be a recruitment goal, not a personnel policy governing the hiring of police personnel. *Primary consideration should be given to employing the very best qualified candidates available, regardless of ethnic background. The ethnic makeup of a community should be viewed as a guide for recruitment policies and procedures, not as a basis for quota hiring nor a mandate.* If recruitment procedures fail to attract minority candidates from whom qualified applicants can be selected, there may be a need for new recruitment techniques, but selection standards and procedures should remain the same.

Although the employment of minorities in jurisdictions with minority communities is essential, the employment of minority group police officers without regard to their qualifications weakens a department. *Standards for the selection of police officers should be applied across the board without regard to race or ethnic origin.* The number of minority applicants will not increase much if discrimination continues

---

25. Arthur G. Sharp, "Recruiting Minority Officers," *Law and Order,* May 1996, Vol. 44, No. 5, pp. 68–72.

in the assignment and promotion of personnel within the agency. It is the total police image that will influence minority interest in police careers, not just selection.

Minority officers are not second-class police officers; they should be selected by the same basic standards as all other officers and should therefore compete on an equal basis for every assignment. They should be deployed in minority neighborhoods but not restricted to working there; they should be allowed to work with all officers and not be forbidden to work with other minority officers. If minorities are hindered from advancing to supervision, management, and administration, they are less likely to respond to initial recruitment. As with employment qualifications, it may well be that minority officers are discriminated against by invalid promotion standards. Therefore, police administrators should identify the attributes of supervisors, managers, and administrators, and develop valid and reliable standards for the selection of personnel for promotion.

While there is no room for bias or prejudice in police recruiting policy, in terms of race, color or creed, there is also no room for a compromise in police entrance standards jeopardizing the professional gains made by the police. To manipulate these standards arbitrarily would be equivalent to watering down the state bar examination or the state board examination that must be hurdled in order to enter medical practice. The demands and the challenges confronting the police in a complex social order call for the best human material available.

Lateral Mobility

The horizontal movement of personnel, particularly at the supervisory and command levels, among police departments has not yet been widely accepted in the United States. However, in business and industry, lateral mobility or lateral entry is commonplace and has been for many years. Furthermore, in the professions generally, it has been accepted for years as an effective managerial practice. It is to be noted that lateral entry is designed to allow a police officer with prior experience to move to another organization without being compelled to start with the rank of a beginning patrol officer. Instead, there may be acceptance without complying with some of the usual entrance requirements, at a higher salary level, with prior service counting toward promotional eligibility, and with transfer of retirement funds.

Promotional opportunities in the small and medium-sized police departments, and even in the larger departments, are somewhat limited. The number of supervisory and command positions is relatively small when compared to the total personnel strength of the department. This circumstance tends to freeze personnel in the lower ranks for extended periods of time, resulting in the exposure of the department to possible loss of morale and incentive. With the increasing emphasis on the police field as a career service and the growing influx of college trained personnel into the police uniform, this problem is now pressing forward for attention. The risk of frustration because of the lack of movement upward through the channels of promotion has important implications for police management.

The trend toward lateral mobility or lateral entry of police personnel is one bright light on the horizon. For some years now, an increasing number of cities and communities have been selecting their Chiefs of Police through open competitive examination. Additionally, it is increasingly the case where supervisory and command positions are being filled on an open competitive basis. Several police departments recently held open competitive examinations for the rank of Captain, which were open to any law enforcement officer with the proper qualifications. These qualifications included five years experience as a police officer plus three years as a Police Lieutenant, or a Police Sergeant with at least one year of college level training in police science or related subjects. One school of thought is that good officer material in some of the smaller forces is often wasted because of the lack of opportunity for promotion in those forces, where the number of higher ranks in the organization is small and vacancies in them are few and far between. It is felt appointments in the higher ranks of all police forces should be made on an open competitive basis for selected applicants recruited from forces in all parts of the country. Some of the apparent advantages of lateral mobility or lateral entry are:

- It opens up the channels of promotion.
- It fosters initiative and enthusiasm for the job with the knowledge that the opportunities for advancement are greater than before.
- It enhances police morale.
- It encourages a career service.
- It widens the field of candidates for supervisory, command and administrative positions in the police service.
- Police service becomes more attractive to the police candidate and the new recruit, when knowing the channels of promotion are open and the chances for promotion are amplified.

It has been estimated that one-third of the departments permitted officers to enter at advanced levels ranging from sergeant to chief. The level at which this was most dominant was for the position of chief. At the entry level, specific figures are not currently available. Many agencies allow lateral entry because a trained officer can be recruited at no expense to the recruiting agency. It becomes a truly cost-savings device. Why hire someone and loose their services while they are attending recruit school?

Career Development

What has been said concerning lateral mobility, in terms of opening up the channels of promotion, speaks for itself. Promotion is one of the most important mechanisms in the entire field of personnel management. It serves two major purposes in organization. First, the promotion, of supervisory and command personnel officers. Secondly, it gives expression to the opportunity for personal achievement and success, with all this can mean in terms of morale and initiative.

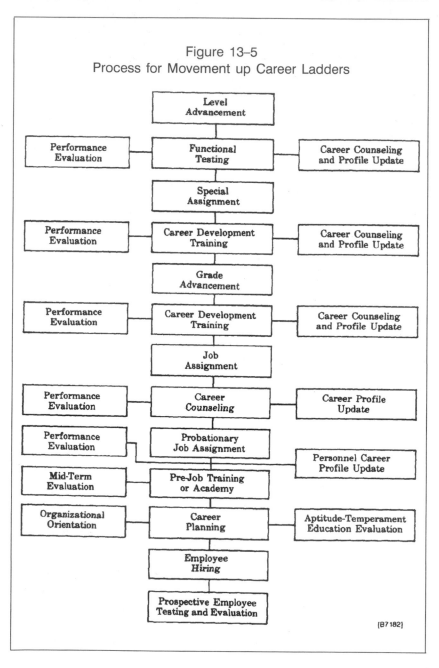

Figure 13–5
Process for Movement up Career Ladders

Figure 13–6
Career Ladder

COMPARABLE EXISTING RANKS:	FUNCTIONAL LEVELS:				
COLONEL	VI		CHIEF		4 CHIEF EXECUTIVE
					3 CHIEF EXECUTIVE
					2 EXECUTIVE ASSISTANT
LT. COLONEL			DEPUTY CHIEF	EX-MANAGEMENT	1 EXECUTIVE ASSISTANT
					4 MANAGER (SENIOR ADVISORY LEVEL)
MAJOR	V		INSPECTOR		3 MANAGER (SENIOR ADVISORY LEVEL)
					2 MANAGER (DIVISION LEVEL)
CAPTAIN		COMMANDER	MANAGEMENT		1 MANAGER (DIVISION LEVEL)
					4 COORDINATIVE (SECTION LEVEL)
LIEUTENANT	IV	COORDINATOR			3 COORDINATIVE (SECTION LEVEL)
					2 SUPERVISORY-COORDINATIVE (SECTION LEVEL)
	SERGEANT II	COORDINATION			1 SUPERVISORY-COORDINATIVE (SECTION LEVEL)
					4 GENERALIST (GENERAL INVES., PROGRAMS) (SUPERVISORY-UNIT LEVEL)
SERGEANT	III	SERGEANT I			3 GENERALIST (GENERAL INVES., PROGRAMS) (SUPERVISORY-UNIT LEVEL)
		SUPERVISORY/ GENERALIST			2 FIELD GENERALIST (FIELD TRAINER, SECTOR LEADER, SPECIAL INVES.)
	AGENT				1 FIELD GENERALIST (FIELD INVESTIGATIONS)
					4 FIELD SPECIALIST (CRIME SCENE PROCESSING, HELICOPTER, TRAFFIC INVES., EVIDENCE ANALYSIS, K-9)
	II	SPECIALIST			3 SECTOR SPECIALIST (RANGE, BREATHALYZER, BOMB)
					2 SECTOR OFFICER
		BASIC			1 SECTOR OFFICERS
					4 PROBATION (ASSIGNED TO SECTOR)
	I				3 PROBATION (ASSIGNED TO TRAINING OFFICER)
					2 ACADEMY (MID-TERM)
OFFICER	SUPPORT				1 ACADEMY (ENTRY)

(R7409)

Career development has recently been manifested on the police scene and provides management with the means of systematically developing organizational manpower. In a recent study, a proposal was made to a municipal police agency to implement a career ladder plan providing for both grade and level differentiation. A positive career plan provides for annual salary increments based upon an employee's achievement, job performance, and greater value to the organization.[26] This contrasts with the normal personnel process providing annual increments to all individuals in an organization unless they demonstrate extreme negative organizational input that management cannot ignore. The career development plan illustrated in figure 13–6 provides for development based upon demonstrated achievement. Performance evaluations are accomplished at successive levels as the individual is assigned greater responsibility. If regression occurs at any level, it should be met with immediate counseling and remedial training. The key to a positive career ladder is not longevity, but demonstrated ability, and performance evaluation.

Career development, if properly implemented can breathe life into an organization. Coupled with other aspects of a personnel manage-

26. Valdis Lubans and Richard F. Dart, *A Career Ladder Study for the Portsmouth Police Department*, Hartford, Connecticut, Social Development Corporation, 1976, p. 29.

ment system it can become an effective method for developing an organization's human resources. The Los Angeles Police Department has an excellent career program. Part of this program is set forth in figure 13–7. The program provides classes for persons in the rank of police officer, detective, sergeant and lieutenant. For example, upon successful completion of probation, Police Officer I is appointed to Police Officer II. There are seven steps within each class allowing for salary progression rather than the typical five step program found in more traditional personnel systems. These are base salaries and do not include such things as longevity pay, and marksmanship bonuses. In this program, a detective at the highest level earns more money than a rated sergeant at the top of the schedule.[27] Career development prepares officers for the future and it preserves an agency's proficiency to meet current needs.

Figure 13–7

Class and Schedule for Police Officer, Detective Sergeant and Lieutenants with the Los Angeles Police Department

Class	Schedule
Police Officer I	1
Police Officer II	2
Police Officer III	3
Police Detective I	5
Police Detective II	6
Police Detective III	8
Police Sergeant I	6
Police Sergeant II	7
Police Lieutenant I	9
Police Lieutenant II	10

Source: Los Angeles Police Department, *Memorandum of Understanding No. 24 Jointly Submitted to the City Council Regarding the Police Officers, Lieutenants and Below Representation Unit*, Los Angeles, City of Los Angeles, 1996–2000, Appendix E–1.

Taking the time and putting forth the energy necessary to be committed to career development benefits both the agency and every individual.[28]

In–Service Training

In-service training has found expression in the American police services in a wide variety of forms. Until about 1915, the old American

---

27. Los Angeles Police Department, *Memorandum of Understanding No. 24 Jointly Submitted to the City Council Regarding the Police Officers, Lieutenant and Below Representation Unit*, Los Angeles, City of Los Angeles, January 1, 2000, Appendix E–1.

28. Paul J. Mendofik, "Career Development," *Law and Order*, May 1995, Vol. 43, No. 5, pp. 41–45.

concept of there being "more law in the end of a nightstick than in all the law books," was the operating criterion of the police officer. Any idea that a police officer should "go to school" would have been received with both astonishment and skepticism. However, the police began to feel the impact of new and unexpected forces. Preparation for police service, as in other professional fields, had its beginnings in a form of apprenticeship. Without previous training of any kind whatsoever, the new recruit was instructed to don a uniform and a gun and go to work. The formalities were quite simple and elementary. As a freshman in the school of experience, new officers began to learn what they could at public expense through a process of trial and error, with the errors predominating. Personal instruction began when it became the practice to send the recruit out with an experienced officer. In an increasing number of departments the new officer was detailed for duty with a veteran as a type of conditioning process. This procedure adapted itself nicely to the almost universal system of double officer patrol. The length of this apprenticeship varied from a few days to several months, and the recruit was then considered a trained officer.

Fewer American police officers today are the product of this type of training program. Let no one underestimate the value of experience. Regardless of training, it has no substitute. Some police officials in this country today are graduates of on-the-job training. On their own initiative, these officers of superior talent and ability supplemented their meager training by intensive study and application to the job, rising to the top of their profession through a natural process of selection.

Recruit Training

It is important for all new appointees to the department to be put through the recruit training program. The beginning phase is a period of indoctrination. It includes instruction in the origin and nature of police work, general police responsibilities under the federal and state constitutions, federal and state laws, and the city charter. Attention is directed during this period to the history of the police and the elements of police organization and administration. The ideals of police service and the ethics of the profession should be given strong emphasis. The new recruit learns the importance of public relations in this branch of the public service. The line power concept of police operations and the patrol system are analyzed, and careful instruction is given in the techniques of patrol, as well as in patrol strategy and tactics. The new officer must know what to do and how to do it in all types of situations. Tested procedures in the approach to an armed criminal under a great variety of circumstances, transportation of criminals, handling crowds, gatherings, parades, disorderly crowds and mobs, disaster operations, raids, surveillance and other related subjects are presented in detail.

The recruit becomes acquainted with the art and science of criminal investigation and comes to understand something of the potential evidence resources of every crime scene. The services of the laboratory and the expert are explained so rookies will know how, when, and where to request the assistance of these technicians in the solution of cases assigned for investigation. It is essential for all new appointees to the department to be exposed to the recruit training program. The course content of this program is a matter of the greatest importance. It is now widely accepted that the following types of subjects should be included in the recruit training school and these are listed in figure 13–8. These topical areas were created by the Texas Commission on Law Enforcement Officer Standards and Education and are considered to be minimal

---

Figure 13–8

560–Hour Basic Peace Officer Course

Subject

Fitness and wellness
History of policing.
Professionalism and ethics
U.S. & State Constitution and Bill of Rights
Criminal justice system.
Code of criminal procedure.
Arrest, search and seizure.
Penal code.
Traffic
Civil process and liability
Alcoholic beverage code.
Drugs.
Juvenile issues.
Stress management.
Field note-taking.
Interpersonal communications/report writing.
Use of force–law.
Use of force concepts.
Strategies of defense–mechanics of arrest.
Strategies of defense–firearms.
Emergency medical assistance.
Problem solving and critical thinking.
Professional police driving.
Multiculturalism and human relations.
Professional policing approaches.
Patrol.
Victims of crime.
Family violence and related assaultive offenses.
Recognizing & interacting with persons with mental illness and mental retardation.
Crowd management.
Hazardous materials awareness.
Criminal investigation.

Source: Texas Commission on Law Enforcement Officer Standards and Education, *560–Hour Basic Peace Officers Course,* Austin, TX, 10/15/98, pp. 1–3. http://www/geocities.com/CapitolHill/Lobby/5715/97index.html.

Table 13–4 delineates the training requirements for recruits in different types of agencies and it should be noted that the classroom training hours range from 640 to 800 hours. Additionally, the field training hours vary considerably depending upon the type of law enforcement agency. [29]

Table 13–4
Median Number of Training Hours Required for New Officers

| | Type of Agency | | | | |
	County	Municipal	Sheriff	Special	State
Classroom training hours	704	640	480	725	800
Field training hours	400	480	400	240	320

Source: Brian A. Reaves and Andrew L. Goldberg, *Law Enforcement Management and Administrative Statistics, 1993: Data for Individual State and Local Agencies with 100 or More Officers*, Washington, D.C., Bureau of Justice Statistics, September 1999, p. xiv.

The recruit training program through the beginning phase requires at least three months full time, eight hours per day and five days per week. At the end of this period each recruit should be assigned to an experienced officer under the immediate supervision of a field training officer(FTO) and should accompany the officer on their regular tour of duty for a period of three months, during which time the rookie should begin attending classes in the intermediate phase of the recruit training program.

A competent field-training officer is an essential ingredient of this phase of a new officer's professional experience. A field training officer (FTO) should have the demonstrated ability of conveying essential job elements. Above all, the FTO should be strongly interested and desirous of instructing new personnel. An incompetent or disinterested field training officer can completely negate a formal training program. A successful method of insuring a cadre of excellent field training officers is to provide adequate incentives to officers who participate in such a program.

An FTO has a very important role to play. It is at a minimum triple in nature. This means operating as a trainer, counselor, and evaluator. As a trainer this officer should be sensitive to the needs of a recruit. One must be aware of the stress a new officer sustains when helping that individual solve their problems. The goal is to coach, train, and evaluate each recruit producing an officer who can perform effectively. Approximately one year after conditional appointment, new

29. Reaves, *op. cit.,* p. 6.

recruits may be candidates for divisional assignment if they have survived the rigorous training program and have received satisfactory ratings by superior officers. It should be remembered, the recruit training period is a part of the entrance examination process. Recruits are on probation during this time and may be "screened out" if they fail to meet the standards of the department in any way. The recruit-training period provides an excellent opportunity to discover disqualifying characteristics escaping detection during previous stages of the examination.

The new officer should enter the assignment to a division with a comprehensive grasp of the department and its program as a whole. In addition to formal training of rigorous proportions, the opportunity has been presented to become familiar with the functions, procedures and problems of all the organizational units in the department. Having passed all these tests, the recruit is in a position to become a member of a winning team. Immediately following divisional assignment, the rookie is automatically enrolled in the "refresher" phase of the department's training program, which provides for review and amplification of subjects previously studied, as well as the presentation of new developments in police procedure. Since the new officer can never hope to master completely even a fractional part of the field and its procedures in an in-service training program, the recruit's enrollment in the refresher school is continuous until retirement from the service. The refresher schedule of instruction can be presented on a less intensive schedule than in the case of the recruit training program.

Divisional assignment involves the necessity for specialized training beyond that provided in the recruit training period; it is concerned with the facilities, functions, procedures and techniques peculiar to a particular division. The necessity for divisional instruction can be appreciated when the functions and procedures of a particular division are analyzed. Thus, workers in the Police Records Unit are confronted with tasks altogether different in nature from those of any other division in the organization. They require distinctly specialized training if any degree of competence is to be attained. The ordinary qualifications of a skilled clerk or typist fail completely when measured by the nature of the work to be performed in this important division.

The necessity for specialized training is equally apparent upon assignment to the Patrol Division. A recruit training program limited to one year could not possibly prepare a person for competent service in this division. It therefore becomes necessary to superimpose upon this preliminary period of instruction, thorough specialized training covering the skills and information peculiar to this important branch of the service, and to it alone.

Supervisory Training

It is necessary to provide for these officers a specialized program of instruction dealing with the principles and techniques of command and supervision. Instruction of supervisory and command personnel should be conducted by the conference technique as distinguished from the classroom method employed in recruit training, and the class size should be limited.

The content of the training curriculum and the amount of time required for training should be predicated on a detailed analysis of the tasks to be performed by a first line supervisor. Topical areas widely accepted in supervisory training programs include:

- Supervisory techniques.
- Disciplinary process.
- Counseling
- Performance evaluation
- Motivational strategies.
- Management of employees.
- Handling grievances.
- Diversity programs.
- Harassment cases.
- Community or problem oriented policing.
- Problem solving.
- Liability.
- Measures of effectiveness.
- Coaching.
- Progressive discipline.
- Dealing with a problem employee.
- Managing change.[30]

General Pershing when asked to identify the most important rank in army organization replied without hesitation the Sergeant! The same can be said with reference to police organization. No administration can achieve its objectives without effective supervision of officers and their performance. Intelligent supervision activates the constructive drives in the individual; there is no known substitute for it. The rank of Sergeant is the point at which direct supervision of the officer occurs, and the grade of supervision delivered, exercises an important influence upon the efficiency of the department. Hence, it is necessary for a large part of the supervisory training to be focused upon the preparation of Sergeants for dealing with subordinates.

30. L.D. Armstrong and C.O. Longenecker, "Police Management Training: A National Survey," *FBI Law Enforcement Bulletin,* January 1992, Vol. 61, No. 1, pp. 7–10, and Robert DelCore, *Training Catalog–1999,* Alexandria, VA, International Association of Chiefs of Police, 1999, pp. 1–60.

Command Training

The operation of the law of the span of control makes it mandatory upon the chief executive to delegate responsibility and power to subordinates in a hierarchy of several levels of authority. In police organization, the arrangement provides in a descending scale for Captains, Lieutenants and Sergeants. The size of the work load in the larger departments and the need for another level of administration calls for a further division of the executive at higher levels by the introduction of one or more ranks above that of Captain. The top administrative ranks immediately below the chief executive are referred to variously as Assistant Chief of Police, Deputy Chief of Police, or Commander.

Training is no less important for the highest administrative officers in the department than for the first line supervisors. There is no human effort more complex and technical than organization and administration, whatever the enterprise may be. The chief executive of a police department is met with a technical job of management requiring a very high order of intelligence and administrative ability. But to this must be added a high order of administrative training. It is absurd to assume that, given leadership qualities and an extended experience in the department, a Captain suddenly elevated to the position of chief will meet new responsibilities with any degree of success. The expenditure of every dollar in a police budget where it will yield the greatest social return requires not only intelligence but executive training as well. There is a wide gap between mere leadership ability and administrative "know how" that must be bridged. The best authorities are not in complete agreement concerning the techniques of successful administration. It is hardly possible for the police chief executive to expect to measure up to a chief's responsibilities without some mastery of the known principles developed and tested in the field of organization and administration.

As in the case of supervisory training, this phase of the in-service training program is presented by the conference method or on a consultation basis. Departmental officers should participate personally in the training of command personnel. They should be supplemented by lay experts in other fields who can be invited in as instructors. Emulating the methods developed by the Army War College, tactical field problems and their solution should occupy an important position in the supervisory and command curriculum.

One of the optional training programs offered by the Commission on Peace Officer Standards and Training (POST) for the State of California is the Command College. It is a one year program designed to develop a future perspective of issues affecting law enforcement. It is designed to assist students in identifying emerging trends, create alternative scenarios, prepare for change, develop strategies that impact the issues, and develop an evaluative approach for monitoring forecasts. Two classes are scheduled annually consisting of 25 students each. Officers attending the course are required to reside at the course site. There are six sessions scheduled approximately eight weeks apart. Each student must complete a future-oriented case study that is publishable as an article in a professional journal. [31]

Figure 13–9

Command College

Session One–Defining the Future

A conceptual road map for studying the future and the role of a leader will be introduced during the first session of the program. Using the STEEP futures forecasting model (Social, Technological, Environmental, Economic, and Political), the students will learn techniques to identify faint signals and emerging issues that may be important to the future of California law enforcement.

Session Two–Enhanced Leadership

This session will focus on the various leadership theories and how they relate to the students personally as leaders. Self-assessment instruments, facets of self-mastery, and creative decision making will be instrumental in identifying their roles as leaders today and in the future.

Session Three–Futures Forecasting and Social Issues

Forecasting methods and the importance of scenario writing will be covered in this workshop. Today's faint signals and emerging trends as they relate to social issues, the first element of STEEP, will be discussed. The potential impact of these social issues on the student's agency and his/her role as a leader will be explored.

Session Four–Technological and Political Issues

This session will include discussions on broad-based technological and environmental issues. Students will be required to research cutting edge technology and environmental issues, share information, and assess the impact on law enforcement leadership.

Session Five–Economic and Political Issues

This session will explore multiple forecasts of economic and political issues. In-depth discussions will be conducted concerning the impact of these issues on law enforcement. Students will create alternative scenarios and define probable futures.

Session Six–Futures Planning Tools

This session will provide a "tool box" that includes strategic planning skills, transition management systems and evaluation components. Emphasis is placed on expanding the student's knowledge of resources that enhance leadership roles and strategies for mitigating the impact of change on the agency.

Source: Correspondence from Ed Pecinovsky, Senior Consultant, POST, State of California, dated November 6, 1998.

31. Correspondence from Ed Pecinovsky, Senior Consultant, POST, State of California, November 6, 1998.

Regional In–Service Training Schools

Occasionally, metropolitan police departments have extended their training facilities to members of the smaller police forces in suburban areas as a measure of improving police services and enhancing cooperative efforts. Police administrators were fully aware that crime did not stop at the city limits. The mobility of the criminal population with the advent of freeways suggests the desirability of a common training program. It also serves the purpose of promoting coordination during emergency situations and other operations involving large-scale cooperation over an extended area in emergencies and disasters.

More police agencies should consider pooling their resources to create a cooperative facility. In California, the community college system has helped considerably in this effort. Police agencies in some areas of the Nation have joined forces with other local agencies and the area's community colleges to develop training centers generally exceeding the requirements of state police training commissions. In Placer County, CA, after the death of an officer the Placer Law Enforcement Combined Agency Training Program was created. After class room sessions on case law and the use of force officers were exposed to such scenarios as high-risk traffic stops, building searches, critical incident response, defensive tactics, and confrontational simulation.[32]

The Southern Arizona Law Enforcement Training Center is regional in nature serving the city, county and law enforcement agencies of Southern Arizona. It is housed in a multi-discipline fire and police training facility located on 115 acres. The facilities include an amphitheater and standard classroom configurations, weight-training room, defensive tactics room, driving track, shooting ranges, and a situational village with specially designed buildings to add realism to scenario based practical training.[33] The mission statement of the center is set forth in figure 13–10.

Figure 13–10

Mission Statement
    The Southern Arizona Law Enforcement Training Center will provide fair, impartial, job-related instruction. The training provided will be demanding, as is the job of law enforcement. The academy staff will provide a positive, professional environment for recruits so that they may acquire needed knowledge, physical skills and become confident in their ability to become successful peace officers. The basic training program will be emotionally, academically and physically challenging to recruits while emphasizing individual responsibility. In order to assure the best possible chance of future success, autonomy and teamwork will be stressed and required. The overall training experience will be one that emphasizes dignity, respect, and discipline.

---

32. Dave Rose and Rocky Warren, "Combined Agency Training: Success in Collaboration," *Law and Order,* May 1999, Vol. 47, No. 5., pp. 48–50.

33. City of Tucson, *Southern Arizona Law Enforcement Training Center,* Tucson, AZ, 1/5/99, http://www.ci.tucson.az.us/police/aleta.

Source: City of Tucson, *Southern Arizona Law Enforcement Training Center,* Tucson, AZ, 1/5/99, http:/www.ci.tuscon.az.us/police/aleta/.

Some cooperative ventures provide training free of charge, others accept only what the state may reimburse the employing agency, and some charge tuition. Some afford participating agencies a voice in program operation and development; others do not. But all cooperatives have one thing in common: they exceed the individual resources of their participating agencies.

The Federal Bureau of Investigation also has conducted a series of regional law enforcement conferences in all the states, which are in the nature of short training schools for police personnel. Such conferences usually are scheduled at central points and officers attend them from the surrounding area. These sessions usually require three days in addition to the officer's travel time. Some state police organizations have also made their training facilities available to local law enforcement officers through the organization of regional training schools.

Internet Training

Through the auspices of the Department of Public Service at Rio Hondo College in California students can enroll on online courses and participate in a variety of learning modes to include: e-mail, class discussion, web-site exploration, and traditional textbook reading and written assignments. Through asynchronous conferencing instructors can make assignments and post discussion prompts allowing students to respond and interact with other students. The web is used for various activities to include attending online lectures, obtaining assignments, conduct research, participate in online "field trips" and obtain the latest class news and information. These courses are designed for peace officers or persons anticipating work in the field of law enforcement. Currently a wide range of classes are offered to include crime scene investigation, domestic violence, and investigative report writing.[34] Distance learning and training (DLT) has evolved rapidly in recent years with the advances in technology, and it is anticipated that the law enforcement field will respond positively to this type of training. Clearly the advantages out-weight the disadvantages. It provides for a significant reduction in travel expenses and scheduling becomes much easier. As computers become less expensive law enforcement will make greater use of web-supported courses, but it should be kept in mind that officers who participate in this type of training must be highly motivated and task oriented.[35]

34. Rio Hondo College, *Professionalism Through Training–On the Internet Your Future is Now!* Rio Hondo College, CA, 11/12/98, http://www.rh.cc.ca.us/departments/academic/pubserv/leo/whatare.htm.

35. Bernard H. Levin, "Training and Learning at Distance," *The Police Chief,* January 1999, Vol. LXVI, No. 1, p. 12.

Case Study

Chief Cliff Walters

Newly appointed as Chief of Grapeline Police Department Cliff Walters had only been in office for three months when a Federal court ruled that the department discriminated against minorities in hiring police officers. In this instance the court based its findings on the department's use of a written cognitive test on which the pass rate for minorities was significantly lower for minorities than the pass rate for non-minorities. The department has 169 sworn officers and minority members constitute six percent of the sworn positions. In the community Blacks and Hispanics make up 29 percent of the population. It is this disparity that must be address in terms of a job analysis for the position of police officer that will allow those appointed to perform effectively.

In the decision the court talked about job-relatedness and business necessity and the City Manager, Ed Hernandez, has asked the chief to review the knowledge, skills, and abilities needed for the position of police officer. Then the chief has been asked to work with a qualified psychologist and select a test that will meet legal scrutiny. It has also been recommended that the test be evaluated to determine its usefulness utilizing criterion-related validation. Of special concern is the use of supervisory performance appraisals wherein the vast majority of officers receive the same rating. The court decision has received considerable coverage in the local press and members of minority pressure groups have expressed a strong interest in the issue.

You have been instructed to hold a press conference as soon as possible. What would you say? Why? What type of report would you have the psychologist prepare? Beyond selecting a new test what would you do to enhance minority recruitment? Why?

For Further Reading

Committee of Seventy, *70 Philadelphia Police Department Governance Study,* Philadelphia, PA, Committee of Seventy, 1998, pp. 1–22.

This publication presents an excellent analysis of the governance of the Philadelphia Police Department, including an overview of the current system, a review of its history and the views of experts. Discusses recruitment procedures, pre-employment residency, entry-level hiring requirements, judicial consent decrees, collective bargaining agreement, and residency requirements. Includes a consideration of other major cities and how they address problems in the above areas.

Paul J. Mendofik, "Career Development" *Law and Order,* May 1995, Vol. 43, No. 5, pp. 41–45.

> Takes the position that a progressive tool in law enforcement is to provide guidance to departmental personnel and creating a system that allows for the selection of the best qualified candidate for each position. Recommends a career development program that provides a path for achievement by preparing officers for the future as a means of preserving the agency's proficiency to meet current needs. Recommends the development of a career development plan that includes defining needs, developing qualified candidates, and monitoring personnel.

John Gales Sauls, "Establishing the Validity of Employment Standards," *FBI Law Enforcement Bulletin,* August 1996, Vol., 64, No. 8, pp. 27–32.

> Suggests that the validation process should not be looked upon as merely a legal obligation. It provides an opportunity to examine critically the selection procedures to enhance effectiveness. Selection systems that can be scientifically shown to produce highly qualified candidates in a fair manner are most likely to withstand legal scrutiny. Such systems also produce candidates most likely to effectively serve and protect the community. Includes a discussion of criterion-related, content and construct validation.

Arthur G. Sharp, "Recruiting Minority Officers–Attracting Minority Candidates for Policing is More Easily Said Than Done," *Law and Order,* May 1996, Vol. 44. No. 5, pp. 68–72.

> Written in a journalistic style the author reviews some of the problems in recruiting and retaining minority officers. When interviewing officers in different departments he found that respondents rejected the idea of lowering standards, and felt that quotas would not benefit police departments. Discussed in detail the hiring standards for the Hartford, CT Police Department. Describes the police union opposition to the standards. Pointed out that the chief drafted guidelines that were less stringent and left some lee way for discretionary application of the guidelines.

Chapter 14

TECHNICAL SERVICES: Communications, Records, and Crime Analysis¢

Learning Objectives

Describe the major features of the mobile digital system.

1. List the main advantages of computer-aided dispatching (CAD).

2. Write a short essay describing the enhanced 911 system.

3. List eight purposes of a police records system.

4. Identify the primary classes of information on an offense report form.

5. Write a short essay describing the index classification used in a modus operation system.

6. Describe the documentation needed when entering a report in the NCIC.

7. List three of the files in the national crime information data base.

8. Describe the value of the Interstate Identification Index (III).

9. List five activities included in the fingerprint matching subsystem.

10. Write a short essay describing the decisions and events that rely upon the use of criminal history record information.

11. Identify some of the functions that municipal and state agencies use the computer for.

12. Describe the value of the Internet to law enforcement.

13. List five uses of mapping in law enforcement.

14. Describe the national clearinghouse for criminal justice information.

The whole complexion of technical services has undergone significant change and moved into a new configuration involving the advances that have occurred in modern engineering and technology. New and sophisticated equipment has become a standard on the police scene. Just consider the police communications system, that is often viewed as the central hub of control and coordination of police resources since it is the initial point of contact for most citizens, and agencies requesting assistance and/or information. With current technology police managers can monitor all departmental vehicles, automatically determine the location of vehicles and, immediately determine whether in service or out of service by viewing a map display at dispatch positions. Computer controlled and assisted dispatching are quite common as is computerized deployment of the patrol force. Additionally, vastly improved hand-held transceivers for out-of-the-car reception and transmission have enhanced the ability to communicate with officers, and scramblers protect the confidential nature and security of police communications traffic.

Communicating with the Field

Since the introduction of police radio communications, the apparatus has been greatly refined. Transmitters have been reduced in size and weight, and their operation so improved that portable equipment can be operated successfully in the field. As a matter of engineering, two and three-way radio patrol communication presents no difficulty at present, and manufacturers now have available portable transmitting equipment specifically designed for police-patrol communications. These improvements presage a new era in patrol technique and operation. As a tactical instrument, it represents a radical increase in the available channels of communication between headquarters and the dispersed patrol force, with a corresponding increase in availability of police field strength.[1] Speed of action, flexibility, and mobility of the force are increased through accelerated interchange of information and instructions in emergencies.

Through the ability of the patrol car to acknowledge immediately the receipt of a message, the control-station dispatcher is assured the broadcast has been properly received, and that the car or cars assigned are on their way to the scene of the emergency. Furthermore, while proceeding to the scene of action, including actual contact with the emergency, an officer may report progress to the central station and to other patrol units in the area. Thus, the officer may directly solicit, in many instances through dispatch, the assistance of other patrol units in the vicinity thus saving valuable time by relaying the request for help through the central-station transmitter. Radio communication makes mobilization almost instantaneous by increasing the speed with which patrol strength may be concentrated at crucial points.

Conditions change very rapidly in emergencies. A situation originally reported as a minor disturbance, may suddenly assume the proportions of a felony and require a speedy exchange of information and orders with headquarters and with all mobile patrol units in the area. An officer dispatched to a vacant lot on a report of an intoxicated man lying there, may arrive to find a man brutally clubbed and left to die. Or, officers arriving at the scene of a reported murder may

1. Lois Pilant, "Communications Trends," *The Police Chief,* October 1998, Vol. LXV, No. 10, pp. 58–75.

discover the blood-stained body of a woman lying on the bathroom floor, a victim of a fatal lung hemorrhage. Within the space of a few moments, a simple traffic-accident report may involve the entire patrol force in the search for a hit-and-run driver, wanted for manslaughter. A patrol vehicle detailed to the investigation of three suspicious characters loitering in the vicinity, finds a bank robbery under way. On another occasion "It is murder, not suicide!" and the hunt begins.

Examples are innumerable. The actual facts and circumstances often fail to coincide with the original report of information given the department in a hurried call over the telephone for police assistance. A patrol officer arriving at the scene of trouble may discover additional manpower is needed to handle the situation. Through direct conversation, immediate assistance can be mobilized, and later, if necessary, the flow of help can be diverted to highway control points, at the same time directing the central station to get outside departments into action. Thus the patrol operating time interval is drastically reduced, and in a most flexible manner the motor patrol force, either as individuals or as a unit, functions with a minimum loss of time. This arrangement represents a special type of decentralization in which, for the duration of the emergency, radio control is temporarily vested in the field commanding officer. This authority, of course, is subject to the receipt of additional instructions and information from central dispatch. Traditional voice transmission in the police services has rapidly become secondary in importance to a new development—the mobile computerized digital communications system. With this equipment, an officer in a patrol car can command information almost instantaneously without going through the dispatcher.

The key instrument in this new system is the computer terminal mounted alongside the officer on the front seat of the patrol car. The instrument is equipped with a keyboard (similar to a standard electric typewriter) and a video display screen for sending and receiving. It resembles a typewriter with a plasma television screen mounted above the keyboard. The screen size varies but generally is 3.4 inches high, 9.1 inches, wide and 1.3 inches thick. High voltage and implosion dangers are eliminated because of the plasma screen display. No high voltage supplies are necessary and the current drain on the car battery is only 3.5 amps. Messages are displayed on the screen and the patrol officer makes inquiries by typing on the keyboard (the message is displayed for the purpose of double-checking). Replies are displayed on the screen. The seventeen-pound unit is portable and may be moved easily from one car to another, depending on shift needs.

To get computer-stored information, even from the computerized National Crime Information Center in Washington, DC, the officer types a request and waits six to nine seconds for the reply. Under ordinary voice communications, the dispatcher would be asked to query the computer by teletype and would then wait about ninety seconds for the reply. The major features of the mobile digital system are:

- The system allows for direct linkage between the officer in the field and the computer based terminals right up to the National Crime Information Center.

- The terminal is mobile, lightweight, safe and small enough to fit easily into patrol cars.

- The system uses the normal radio channels.

- The system is designed to maintain the voice contact between the patrol cars and the dispatcher.

- It reduces substantially the work-load of the dispatcher.

- Because of the speed of digital communications, the congested voice channel frequencies are given important relief.

- The entire system is designed to provide automatic functions with minimum entry technique.

- Digital communications, unlike voice communications, *cannot be monitored.*

In the latest data from a survey of larger municipal police agencies it was found that 59% of the departments had car-mounted digital terminals and 14% had hand-held digital terminals. Additionally, 59% of the municipal agencies had laptop computers.[2] Another innovation currently being tested is the placement of in-car video units (ICV) in departmental vehicles. In Los Angeles 100 units are being tested as a means of enhancing communications. It allows managers to communicate directly with officers and it is anticipated that the system will prove to be advantageous to everyone in the department. A complete review of this system is being made over a five-year period.[3]

The rapid development of communications systems and other technology applicable to law enforcement has revolutionized the way that police departments use advanced technology. Wireless communications is a key component in providing officers with real-time access to local, state, and federal data bases from the patrol vehicle.[4] Additionally, with appropriate tools and software officers can file incident reports directly from the field. Also it is anticipated that with the emergence of cellular digital packet data (CDPD) the police will have an alternative method of transmitting voice, data, and images.[5]

2. Brian A. Reaves and Andrew L. Goldberg, *Law Enforcement Management and Administrative Statistics, 1997: Data for Individual State and Local Agencies with 100 or More Officers,* Washington, DC, Bureau of Justice Statistics, September 1999, p. xvii.

3. Los Angeles Police Department, *In the Course of Change: The Los Angeles Police Department Five Years After the Christopher Commission,* Los Angeles, Police Commission, August 1998, p. 12.

4. Richard Porth and David Kimball, "Wireless Technology Makes Regional Computer System Possible in Connecticut," *The Police Chief,* January 1999, Vol. LXVI, No. 1, pp. 25–29.

5. SEARCH, *Wireless Communications,* Sacramento, CA, The Consortium for Justice Information and Statistics, 4/16/99, pp. 1–3, http://www.mobile.search.org/wireless.htm.

Computer Aided Dispatching (CAD).

The computer terminal at police headquarters logs all transmissions between a car and another computer terminal for record purposes. This data may be used by the dispatcher to transmit messages to an individual patrol car, to a group of cars or to all cars, depending upon the nature of the situation or emergency. One has only to examine the figures on the murder of police officers each year in order to recognize the importance of ten second or less reply. Thus, for example, doing a license check before stopping a car increases the percentage in favor of the officer because of this knowledge when about to deal with a dangerous person.

The significance of these portentous developments stirs the imagination, bringing as it does to the individual police officer out on the street the total resources of a national criminal data bank—*and in a matter of seconds!* Thus it is, the march of time in the American police services is the march toward professionalization as police administration recognizes the dimension of its problems and moves forward in a scientific approach to their solution.

One purpose of computer assisted police dispatching is to tie the address given by a citizen requesting police service to a particular beat and identify the patrol car or cars on that beat, available to answer the call. The main advantages of a computer-aided police dispatching (CAD) system extend beyond decreasing response time to include:

- In most situations, the system can respond in an average of ten or fewer seconds to basic information entered into the computer file by the telephone clerk. The patrol car is selected and the information relayed to the dispatcher in those few seconds.

- Because less time is spent on each call dispatchers are able to handle more calls.

- The online system makes it possible to inquire and receive accurate information.

- Immediate accessibility of information increases the efficiency of patrol officers.

- The system makes the best use of personnel and reduces operating costs.

- Valuable statistical reports based on information entered into the system during the dispatching process are generated by the computer, including current crime statistics that can be used in deploying the patrol force.

Additionally information is readily available from the national level. An NCIC offline search can be made with only one search parameter. Searches may be made on non-unique personal descriptors, such as sex, height, weight, estimated age, and hair coloring, to identify a wanted, missing, or deceased person or on a partial vehicle identification number to identify a car. Gun make, article type, securities descriptors, date of theft, and date of warrant may also be used as offline search parameters. Inquiries on a large number of securities believed to be stolen may be handled quickly via the offline search rather than a time-consuming individual operator online inquiry. Data retrieved as a result of an offline search can be provided on a printout or magnetic tape. The ideal CAD system is comprised of a series of software and hardware components that include access to a variety of local, state, and federal databases, and are integrated into an E–911 system with computers in each patrol vehicle. The system is particularly effective operating alongside geographical information and automatic vehicle location systems (AVL).[6]

The Enhanced 911 System. Another development in recent years has been the expansion of the enhanced 911 system to police departments of varying sizes. Among law enforcement departments participating in the system, the proportion with an enhanced or expanded system, that electronically locates the caller, make up 83 percent of participating department. The next largest group (15 percent) have a basic system.[7] Unfortunately, approximately two percent of the communities do not available themselves of the 911 service. The tasks performed by communications sections are monumental as indicated by the statistics of the Miami Police Department that show that in one year they answered a total of 805,614 calls for assistance and the E911 call-takers answered 94 percent of these calls within ten seconds. This public safety answering point (PSAP) is the third busiest in the southeastern part of the United States.

In this E911 system an automatic call distribution feature ensures that all calls are promptly handled. Calls coming into the system are routed to a call-taker serving as a screener. The screener first determines if the call is a life-threatening emergency, or a serious crime in progress. If the call is determined to be less serious it is classified as a priority or non-priority, and is routed to the appropriate language queue of either English, Spanish, or Creole. In the event all of the screeners are occupied, the call is automatically routed to the first available agent who then functions as a screener. Each person in the Communications Section has been designated a language skill, and a system log-in ID. This log-in ID tells the system what type of calls they can handle. The system also knows the next best place to rout a call if no one in that language is available. Once the appropriate information is entered in the computer aided dispatch (CAD) system the call is automatically routed to the dispatcher for that geographic area.

In Miami the dispatcher is responsible for dispatching officers to the calls generated by the E911 call-takers. They must make sure that the correct officer is sent according to his/her prospective zone, and

6. SEARCH, *Computer-Aided Dispatch* , Sacramento, CA, The National Consortium for Justice Information and Statistics, 4/16/99, http://www.mobile.search.org/cad.htm.

7. Reaves and Goldberg, *op. cit.,* p. xv.

according to current policies and procedures. Officer safety is always on top of the list. Dispatchers keep track of up to as many as 50 officers at any given time. For example, they must be able to talk to the officers, type, depress the transmission pedal, receive updates from call-takers, and respond to bridge supervisors' requests–all at the same time–and free of error.[8]

In the Dallas Police Department the Communications Division answers 911 calls and dispatches patrol officers based on a four level priority system. Foe example, under Priority I officers respond immediately to possible life threatening situations such as felony in progress, shootings, cuttings, and emergency blood transfer. On the other hand Priority IV involves disturbances, minor accident, animal complaint and parking violations. Table 14–1 lists the types of calls, frequency and percentage of each classification. Of special interest is the placement of 911 Hang-up as Priority II and 41,420 of these were responded to for the last year for which data was available.[9] Recently, Buffalo, NY, and other cities have taken steps to stem the flow of non-emergency calls to their 911 systems by providing an alternative telephone number. Baltimore, Chicago, and Dallas have established 311 numbers and Buffalo has set up a 853–2222 as an option for such calls. In Buffalo citizens are asked to call the non-emergency number when they need advise or assistance that does not require an immediate response.[10]

---

8. Donald H. Warshaw, *Miami Police Department Annual Report*, Miami, FL, The City of Miami, 1999, pp. 20–21.

9. Dallas Police Department, *Information–Communications Division*, Dallas, City of Dallas, 3/7/99, pp. 1–2, http://www.ci.dallas.tx.us/dpd/om.htm.

10. Gerald W. Schoenle, Jr., "Buffalo's Alternative to 911," *FBI Enforcement Bulletin*, May 1999, Vol. 68, No. 5., pp. 18–21.

Table 14-1

Communications Division–Calls for Police Service

Priority I		
Cutting	1,576	0.2%
Assist Officer	461	0.0%
Shooting	1,423	0.2%
Emergency Blood Transfer	4	0.0%
Felony in Progress	13,367	1.4%
Pursuit	556	0.1%
Priority II		
911 Hangup	41,420	4.4%
Major Disturbance	165,170	17.5%
Random Gunfire	10,193	1.1%
Major Accident	24,668	2.6%
Prowler	4,995	0.5%
Fire Alarm	1,174	0.1%
Robbery	5,162	0.5%
Holdup Alarm	9,951	1.1%
Criminal Assault	1,361	0.1%
Poisoning	5	0.0%
Suicide	2,707	0.3%
Priority III		
Drunk	3,569	0.4%
Burglary	45,522	4.8%
Burglar Alarm	90,791	9.6%
Injured Person	13,494	1.4%
Missing Person	12,790	1.4%
Dead Person	794	0.1%
Sick Person	5	0.0%

Open Building	2,499	0.3%
Prisoner	10,838	1.1%
Suspicious Person	27,338	2.9%
Abandoned Child	1,974	0.2%
Other	99,214	10.5%
Priority IV		
Disturbance	44,682	4.7%
Minor Accident	46,533	4.9%
Theft	51,173	6.1%
Animal Complaint	489	0.1%
Parking Violation	6,024	0.6%
Abandoned Property	23,157	2.5%
Criminal Mischief	15,391	1.6%
Street Blockage	13,638	1.4%
Meet Complainant	9,690	1.0%
Racing	3,528	0.4%
911 HangUp(Not Dispatched)	124,136	13.2%
TOTALS	943,114	100.0%

Source: Dallas Police Department, *Information–Communications Division,* Dallas, TX, City of Dallas, 3/7/99. pp. 1–2, http://www/ci.dallas.tx.us/dpd/com.htm

Organizational Arrangement

Within police departments a communications section can be found in varying organizational entities within the department. In the San Jose Police Department Communications is a sub-unit under the Technical Services Bureau. This contrasts with the Miami Police Department that house communications under the Administration Division. In the Tucson Police Department communications is part of the Support Services Bureau, and this latter entity consumes 23 percent of the total departmental budget. In the Los Angeles Police Department there is an Information and Communications Services Bureau that has as a sub-unit the Communications Division. This latter Divisions mission statement conveys the intent and purpose of the unit--"To provide quality service to the community and the police officers we support by demonstrating compassion, a desire to serve, professional conduct, and comprehensive knowledge and ability."[11] It is readily noted that placement of communications varies from department to department, but what really counts is not the location in the structure of the organization, but how effective it operates as a vital link between the department and the community.

Records and Identification

The intelligent planning and execution of police operations must of necessity be predicated upon critical estimates of the situation, involving expert statistical interpretation of records data. It has been previously emphasized that in complex undertakings performed by police officers, precision and certainty in action and control over far-flung operations can be achieved only with the assistance of scientific record controls. In the detection and analysis of emerging situations and in the identification of the points where the preventive work of the department may be focused, the strategic position of the police record system again becomes apparent. Functioning in an area of social control where short-term and long-term planning could be productive of far-reaching results, police management must make use of basic intelligence procedures founded on its own information and records as one of the basic devices of administration.

All authoritative works place a strong emphasis upon the importance of an adequate system of records and reporting as a basis for the planning and execution of operations. Further, there is no lack of agreement concerning the principles to be applied in providing management with these professional tools of control. A competent administrator appreciates the indispensability of the police record system in the intelligent control of operations, services and inspections, and makes use of this important facility in the diagnostic approach to the manifold problems presented to the department for solution. This type of administrator must know the facts concerning the character, extent and distribution of crime, delinquency, and other police problems in the community before operations can be intelligently planned and executed. The administrator discovers that adequate records data constitute an accounting system for the police business—a prerequisite to successful management and the measurement of departmental performance.

The Records Unit is more than a mere depository for routine records. A police record system is not a question of bookkeeping but is rather a form of accounting for the police business. It is not concerned with the mere recording of events as an historical record so much as with the intelligent planning and control of operations, with measuring the result of those operations and with the study of the problems facing the police. Just as the records and accounting office in any corporation is the tool upon which the management must rely in deciding questions

11. Los Angeles Police Department, *Communications Division–Mission Statement,* Los Angeles, CA, City of Los Angeles, 3/6/99, p. 1. http://www.lapdonline.org/organization/info.comm.__bureau/comm.__division/comm.mission.htm.

of policy in distributing its personnel, and in eliminating wasteful operations. So too, the police records system may provide the police chief executive with one of the major tools of administrative control. The most successful police departments have been those which have based their administrative actions upon facts in the form of reports and analyses prepared from basic data covering the nature and distribution of police problems referred to the Department for investigation.

The Records unit serves in the first instance as a control over the police business. It is the mainspring of police administration and unless the records are correct and the information concerning offenses and complaints is properly filed, tabulated, and chartered, the head of the police department is helpless. Without knowing the—who, where, when, what, why, and how of police work, it is impossible for the chief or assistants to cope with the situation.

Among the important purposes served by a police record system is the:

- Determination of the nature, extent and distribution of the police problems of crime, delinquency, vice and traffic.
- Access to data that indicates the distribution of the force by beat zone, area or precinct.
- Control over crimes committed and their investigation.
- Apprehending criminal offenders through a study of their Modus Operandi or method of operation.
- The analysis of traffic accidents with a view toward prevention and selective enforcement.
- Control over arrests and their disposition.
- Making administrative predictions in terms of what, how much, when and where with respect to crime, vice, traffic accidents and other demands upon police service, in order to maximize deployment of the force.
- Revealing unusual problems and the detection of emerging situations.
- Selecting the best officers for particular assignment and for promotion.
- As a management tool for criminal investigation and as a source of investigative leads.
- Determining the amount, nature and distribution of police equipment.

Specifications of a Police Record System

The minimum standards for a police record system have been made available to the profession from reputable sources, including a number of American police executives whose achievements in the police field have been accorded national recognition. This includes the consolidation of all record functions into one division, the Technical Services Division, under one head responsible to the Chief of Staff Services, affording a centralization of responsibility and control. Additionally, police managers have integrated police operations through the inauguration of a standard police complaint record system and reporting procedure.

The location of the records function in a police organization is a matter of prime importance. A crime records system can never attain its greatest effectiveness so long as it is operated by a line agency. The maintenance of records is a staff function, and the current audit of police operations, which they facilitate, can be effectively conducted only by a staff unit. Operating the Records Unit is not a routine clerical duty but an administrative task of the highest order. It is the focal point of all police administrative controls.

The Police Complaint Record System

The proper organization of the police record system is contingent upon the establishment of approved record and reporting procedure. All complaints and reports received by the Department for investigation, involving violations of city ordinances, state, and federal laws, should be typewritten on standard complaint record forms. Each complaint should be given a consecutive serial number in the order of its receipt, regardless of classification so there will be no question concerning the integrity of the records or the accuracy of the total number of complaints received. The reports should be recorded immediately after receipt of the original information. Failure to record properly any matter referred to the Department for investigation should constitute a violation of departmental rules and regulations. After being so recorded, each item is entered on the Daily Bulletin in numerical sequence. At the end of the tour of duty, copies should be furnished to the various departmental units so the entire force may be kept informed concerning criminal happenings, stolen, lost and found property and persons wanted.

With a desk top computer or work station, the preparation of the Daily Bulletin occurs with greater ease than ever before. Each bulletin can be readied with the aid of sophisticated word processor programs. They also can be enhanced with graphics for which several software programs are available. Record retention is also facilitated by using floppy disks.

In earlier days the police complaint records system was maintained manually. With computers, the situation has changed immeasurably. With a computerized complaint system complete information regarding each complaint can be stored. Furthermore, entries can be made identifying the type of complaint, when reported, name of the officer(s) the report, and disposition.

Complaint Record Forms

Separate record forms must provide for two distinct steps in recording and compiling offenses. There must be:

- Records for the original entry showing a crime has been committed (offense report forms).

- Reports of investigations and results secured (supplementary reports of the investigating officer).

The offense report is for the original entry of facts about a crime when brought to the department's attention. It serves as the first formal record of the offense and as the fundamental basis for headquarters' control of the investigation. It is important that all "on view" arrests be transferred to offense reports, otherwise the offense record will be grossly incomplete (see figure 14–1). The following legend explanation covers the primary classes of information that can be provided on the offense report form. Many of these items can be presented in the narrative section of the form:

Where Committed: Location where offense was committed, or where incident occurred.

Date and Time Committed: Day of month plus year, and time of day that offense was committed, or when incident occurred.

Persons Attacked: The number of victims should be shown, their sex, whether adults or juveniles, race and, insofar as possible, their occupations. This is important because some criminals operate against a certain sex, grown persons or juveniles, certain races, certain types of professional people, etc.

Property Attacked: The type of premises in which the offense was committed should be stated. If a bank was held up, the property attacked would be *a bank*. Stores are described as to type of business, and whether independent or chain. Where a building is used for a number of purposes, specify first the purpose for which the particular room entered is used, followed by the general use of the building. For instance, a grocery store under apartment; dentist's office in front of residence; or conversely, sleeping quarters in rear of grocery. Buildings are described as to the number of families living therein, and the type of building, such as bungalow, apartment, or single house.

Figure 14–1
Offense Report

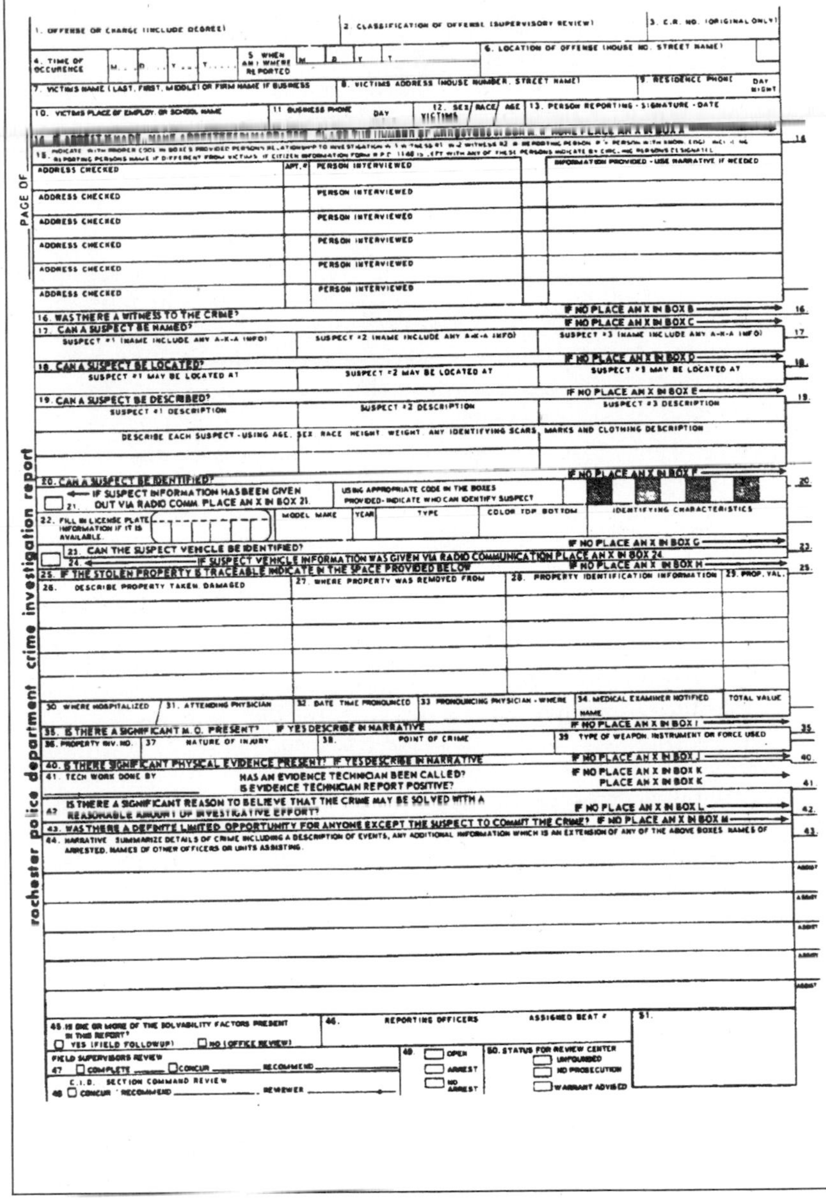
1. OFFENSE OR CHARGE (INCLUDE DEGREE) | 2. CLASSIFICATION OF OFFENSE (SUPERVISORY REVIEW) | 3. C.R. NO. (ORIGINAL ONLY)
4. TIME OF OCCURENCE M D Y T | 5. WHEN AND WHERE REPORTED M D Y T | 6. LOCATION OF OFFENSE (HOUSE NO. STREET NAME)
7. VICTIMS NAME (LAST, FIRST, MIDDLE) OR FIRM NAME IF BUSINESS | 8. VICTIMS ADDRESS (HOUSE NUMBER, STREET NAME) | 9. RESIDENCE PHONE DAY NIGHT
10. VICTIMS PLACE OF EMPLOY. OR SCHOOL NAME | 11. BUSINESS PHONE DAY | 12. SEX/RACE/AGE VICTIMS | 13. PERSON REPORTING - SIGNATURE - DATE
14. [illegible] PLACE AN X IN BOX A
15. [illegible]
ADDRESS CHECKED | APT. # | PERSON INTERVIEWED | INFORMATION PROVIDED - USE NARRATIVE IF NEEDED
16. WAS THERE A WITNESS TO THE CRIME? IF NO PLACE AN X IN BOX B
17. CAN A SUSPECT BE NAMED? IF NO PLACE AN X IN BOX C
SUSPECT #1 (NAME INCLUDE ANY A-K-A INFO) | SUSPECT #2 (NAME INCLUDE ANY A-K-A INFO) | SUSPECT #3 (NAME INCLUDE ANY A-K-A INFO)
18. CAN A SUSPECT BE LOCATED? IF NO PLACE AN X IN BOX D
SUSPECT #1 MAY BE LOCATED AT | SUSPECT #2 MAY BE LOCATED AT | SUSPECT #3 MAY BE LOCATED AT
19. CAN A SUSPECT BE DESCRIBED? IF NO PLACE AN X IN BOX E
SUSPECT #1 DESCRIPTION | SUSPECT #2 DESCRIPTION | SUSPECT #3 DESCRIPTION
DESCRIBE EACH SUSPECT - USING AGE, SEX, RACE, HEIGHT, WEIGHT, ANY IDENTIFYING SCARS, MARKS AND CLOTHING DESCRIPTION
20. CAN A SUSPECT BE IDENTIFIED? IF NO PLACE AN X IN BOX F
21. ← IF SUSPECT INFORMATION HAS BEEN GIVEN OUT VIA RADIO COMM. PLACE AN X IN BOX 21. | USING APPROPRIATE CODE IN THE BOXES PROVIDED - INDICATE WHO CAN IDENTIFY SUSPECT
22. FILL IN LICENSE PLATE INFORMATION IF IT IS AVAILABLE. | MODEL MAKE | YEAR | TYPE | COLOR TOP BOTTOM | IDENTIFYING CHARACTERISTICS
23. CAN THE SUSPECT VEHICLE BE IDENTIFIED? IF NO PLACE AN X IN BOX G
24. ← IF SUSPECT VEHICLE INFORMATION WAS GIVEN VIA RADIO COMMUNICATION PLACE AN X IN BOX 24.
25. IF THE STOLEN PROPERTY IS TRACEABLE INDICATE IN THE SPACE PROVIDED BELOW. IF NO PLACE AN X IN BOX H
26. DESCRIBE PROPERTY TAKEN DAMAGED | 27. WHERE PROPERTY WAS REMOVED FROM | 28. PROPERTY IDENTIFICATION INFORMATION | 29. PROP. VAL.
30. WHERE HOSPITALIZED | 31. ATTENDING PHYSICIAN | 32. DATE TIME PRONOUNCED | 33. PRONOUNCING PHYSICIAN - WHERE | 34. MEDICAL EXAMINER NOTIFIED NAME | TOTAL VALUE
35. IS THERE A SIGNIFICANT M. O. PRESENT? IF YES DESCRIBE IN NARRATIVE. IF NO PLACE AN X IN BOX I
36. PROPERTY INV. NO. | 37. NATURE OF INJURY | 38. POINT OF CRIME | 39. TYPE OF WEAPON, INSTRUMENT OR FORCE USED
40. IS THERE SIGNIFICANT PHYSICAL EVIDENCE PRESENT? IF YES DESCRIBE IN NARRATIVE. IF NO PLACE AN X IN BOX J
41. TECH WORK DONE BY | HAS AN EVIDENCE TECHNICIAN BEEN CALLED? IF NO PLACE AN X IN BOX K | IS EVIDENCE TECHNICIAN REPORT POSITIVE? PLACE AN X IN BOX K
42. IS THERE A SIGNIFICANT REASON TO BELIEVE THAT THE CRIME MAY BE SOLVED WITH A REASONABLE AMOUNT OF INVESTIGATIVE EFFORT? IF NO PLACE AN X IN BOX L
43. WAS THERE A DEFINITE LIMITED OPPORTUNITY FOR ANYONE EXCEPT THE SUSPECT TO COMMIT THE CRIME? IF NO PLACE AN X IN BOX M
44. NARRATIVE SUMMARIZE DETAILS OF CRIME INCLUDING A DESCRIPTION OF EVENTS, ANY ADDITIONAL INFORMATION WHICH IS AN EXTENSION OF ANY OF THE ABOVE BOXES, NAMES OF ARRESTED, NAMES OF OTHER OFFICERS OR UNITS ASSISTING.
45. IS ONE OR MORE OF THE SOLVABILITY FACTORS PRESENT IN THIS REPORT? ☐ YES (FIELD FOLLOWUP) ☐ NO (OFFICE REVIEW)
46. REPORTING OFFICERS ASSIGNED BEAT #
47. FIELD SUPERVISORS REVIEW ☐ COMPLETE ☐ CONCUR RECOMMEND
48. C.I.D. SECTION COMMAND REVIEW ☐ CONCUR RECOMMEND REVIEWER
49. ☐ OPEN ☐ ARREST ☐ NO ARREST
50. STATUS FOR REVIEW CENTER ☐ UNFOUNDED ☐ NO PROSECUTION ☐ WARRANT ADVISED
51.
PAGE OF
rochester police department crime investigation report

How Attacked: Refers to the way in which the person or property was attacked. In burglary, property is attacked by breaking in. The point of entry, as rear door, first floor, side window, first floor transom, should be given. In case of robbery, state whether victim was strong-armed, slugged, threatened, choked, or beaten. In worthless checks, drafts, notes, forgeries, etc., state if by passing, forging, or raising, or if fictitious or fraudulent checks, drafts, or notes. In larceny, specify the place from where the property was stolen, e.g., cash register, clothesline, desk, and kitchen.

Means of Attack: Refers to the instrument, tool, device, trick or method by which the person or property was attacked. In burglary all tools should be described briefly but specifically. In the case of robbery, give the best possible description of weapon used. In larceny, the means may be merely by carrying away, or climbing adjoining premises, fence, fire escape, ladder, porch, rope, driving away, shoplifting, or with any instrument.

Object of Attack: It is not necessary at this point to give details of the articles taken but rather the general class to which they belong. The objects of attack of one criminal may be money, overlooking other articles of real value. Others will take money and jewelry or certain types of clothing, or silverware, etc. In crimes against the person, not involving property, the object of attack will be the motive rather than a material thing, e.g., illicit love affair, or insurance plot.

Trade Mark: List the personal idiosyncrasies or peculiar methods of operation which may serve to distinguish the crime from other crimes committed in much the same fashion. Some criminals commit a robbery with no fuss and very little conversation, while others make a great deal of noise, commotion and conversation. Some turn on house lights in a burglary, while others burn matches or use flashlights. Some invariably raid the ice box, whereas others will take food into the premises. A person who gains entrance to a house by impersonating an inspector from a gas or electric company is an old type. Incidents committed during a funeral, parade, party, an assaulted occupant bathing, malicious damage to premises, poisoned dog, cut telephone wires, pretending to be blind, a sarcastic note, or re-arranged furniture, are all examples of the trademark. The more unusual, the more queer, strange, or peculiar the trademark is, the greater its value in identifying the perpetrator of future crimes, or of connecting a suspect with past crimes. Trademark is usually an act committed by the offender at the crime scene which has no relationship whatsoever to the commission of the offense such as, for example, the writing of an obscene note with a cake of soap on a mirror in the bathroom.

Vehicle Used: A brief but complete description of vehicle, if used in the commission of the crime is entered here.

The design and format of the master complaint form will vary from one department to another. Any letter, telegram or other communication requiring investigation by the Department should be transferred to an offense report immediately upon receipt, the classification being usually determined by the content of the communication. Where such communication originates with another law enforcement agency, the word "OUTSIDE" should be typed above the serial number. If in written form, it should be attached to the original offense report copy and routed to the R and I. Unit. Copies of such communications may be typed for the investigating officer on request, but no original communications or any part of the master complaint record should be removed from the R and I. In rare situations where the circumstances so indicate, and in such cases authority for removal of the record should be obtained from the head of the Records Unit.

Supplementary Reports of Investigation

The offense or complaint report provides for the original entry of facts about a crime when brought to the attention of the department, but if record procedure should terminate at that point, the means for control would still be missing. Through the requirement that the investigating officer assigned to a case must promptly file a written report covering the investigation results, the means for control is established. The supplementary offense report is used for recording the results of the investigation. It is prepared by the officer assigned to the case. It may also be used by other officers who have occasion to enter certain facts in addition to those appearing on the offense report.

It follows from this that there may be several supplementary offense reports concerning a single offense, falling under one or more of the following categories:

- Statements by investigating officers on the progress of the case. These should be submitted at regular intervals while the case is under investigation; when special developments occur; or upon request of the supervising officer.

- Statement by investigating officers that the report of the offense appears to be unfounded. A case should not be declared unfounded until this conclusion is approved by the commanding officer.

- When the investigating officer has not been able to make substantial progress and recommends the case be declared "inactive" (not cleared). In such event, the recommendation should carry the approval of the commanding officer. A case, therefore, remains open until the commanding officer countersigns the officer's recommendation for it to be declared inactive or until the case is closed by an actual final disposition, such as arrest of offender, recovery of property, etc. In this manner, active investigation is not discontinued without a review of the case by the commanding officer in charge. The investigating officer should be required to fully state reasons for dropping the case. A large proportion of cases declared inactive would not be a desirable feature of the performance and personnel record of an individual officer.

- When additional facts concerning the case come to the attention of the investigating officer or any other member of the department.

If the complaint or incident is not fully disposed of as a result of the first investigation and the submission by the investigating officer of the preliminary report, this person is required to make subsequent reports on follow-up report form blanks provided for that purpose. It should be an inviolable rule that follow-up reports be submitted in all open cases within three days following the date of the preliminary report and weekly thereafter until the case is closed. This follow-up report is used by the officer to report progress on the case, additional details, descriptions of new suspects, persons apprehended, property recovered, proposed changes in the classification of the offense report, and other action taken. The report may also be used by the officer to indicate no substantial progress appears possible and that the case should be declared inactive (not cleared). Since it has already been suggested that "on view" arrests are to be transferred to offense report forms, the arresting officer is required to submit such supplementary and follow-up report forms on them also, as may be indicated by he nature of the case.

If the investigating officer has not submitted the reports indicated above, the Records Unit will automatically, through its follow-up system note this failure and report the matter to the commanding officer. The case is kept open until the necessary reports are submitted. The other divisional commanders need to give full cooperation to the Records Unit in this matter. A considerable amount of supervision is required upon the inauguration of this procedure, if the officers have not been accustomed to the preparation of such reports.

Processing Reports in the Records Unit

It is fundamental to sound police record procedure for an accurate index and cross-index system to be established. This reduced to its simplest terms means that ALL offense reports should be indexed by:

- Name of complainant or injured party.
- Name of person arrested or suspected.
- Name of investigating officer.
- Names of all witnesses and other persons mentioned in either the offense report, supplementary report or follow-up reports.
- Crime classification.

In addition to the above general cross-index required for all types of offense reports, certain crime categories require additional entries in an expanded cross-index system. This distinction applies particularly to all forms of theft, including robbery, burglary, automobile theft, worthless checks, crimes committed by fraud, false pretense, or imposture. These additional cross-index facilities include the modus operandi system and property indices.

In the modus operandi system the method of operation, through index classification, is broken down and factored into its component parts as an investigative aid in the identification of a crime series, and as an aid in the identification of the offender. These index divisions include in part:

- Crime classification.
- Where committed i.e. location index; spot maps.
- Time of attack.
- Person or property attacked.
- How attacked.
- Means of attack.
- Object of attack.
- Trade–Mark.

The necessity for consolidation of property control in the Department has already been mentioned. The property index is one of the most important of all files in the Records Unit. This file should include cross-index facilities for all property reported stolen, lost, or found. The serial number of all articles bearing serial numbers serves as the first classification under that particular type of article. In case such serial numbers are not obtainable from complainants, the cards are filed by the make or maker's name or by other identifying marks. Musical instruments, watches, cameras, tools, typewriters, bicycles, and most mechanical contrivances bear serial numbers. Initials, monograms, and other special marks serve as additional index divisions.

Diamond-set articles, except rings (if unmarked) are filed according to the number of diamonds and next according to design. Other stone-set pieces are filed first according to type (for example, an emerald ring, or diamond ring), next by design, as i.e. Tiffany, Belcher, or Gypsy, and lastly, by size of stone. Clothing is classified as male or female, then by type of article; next by color; then by maker's name. Even though articles may carry serial numbers, they should also be indexed by other distinguishing features, such as monograms, make, or design. This file properly maintained and checked against local pawn shop activities leads to a considerable increase in property recovered and case clearances.

The Follow–Up Control System

Supplementary offense reports are connected to the master offense report by serial number in the Records Unit, and all cases not cleared are held in a pending file under the supervision of the follow-up person. Simply stated the follow-up system is a plan whereby every complaint report or other matter reported to the Department for investigation is inspected by the Records Unit to determine whether proper and timely action is being taken. Until a case is properly closed and finally filed away the progress is constantly checked by the follow-up individual. Upon the follow-up officer rests the responsibility for checking, approving or rejecting and questioning all the reports submitted to the division. The job is not to interfere with the actual work on the case, only to take up with the officer or commanding officer if necessary, instances of incomplete reports, and failures to follow prescribed rules in handling various types of cases. No case should be permitted to be permanently filed until every investigation is complete and until every effort has been made to clear the case.

The follow-up officer is concerned primarily with knowing the required work has been performed by the officer assigned to the case. Deviations from the departmental standards of procedure are to be recognized at once with steps taken to rectify them and prevent their repetition. The evidence of this performance appears in the officer's written supplementary and follow-up reports, through which the follow-up system maintains its check on cases under investigation by the department.

In many states, the statutory authorization for public access to police blotter information is in the state's freedom of information statute. Freedom of information statutes customarily require all government-held records to be made available, upon request, to any person for any purpose. These statutes customarily include a long list of exceptions identifying types of records to be withheld in certain circumstances. Criminal history record information is usually exempt. In some states the freedom of information statute declares that police blotter data is not exempt from the commands of the freedom of information statute, and must be made available.[12]

The need for compiling and analyzing offense reports and persons charged by means of computers increases with the size of the city. In the large department it is the only practical method of analyzing the facts of crime as embodied in the offense report and of analyzing the social characteristics and dispositions of the thousands of arrests made by the police. If full advantage is to be taken of the record system, the information on all offense and arrest records must be tabulated. Even though master sheets may serve as temporary makeshifts, many of the desirable analyses are either very difficult or too complex to make without data processing equipment. Except in crude form, modus operandi analysis is almost impossible. Further, it is a difficult matter to analyze the various social facts and dispositions of persons charged unless computers are employed.

Administrative Reports and Analyses

Since the Chief of Police or other commanding officers cannot personally supervise every act of every member of the force or visualize the sum total of departmental operations, they must utilize systematic controls and administrative reports. The mere recording of information on record forms is not enough. The records must be tabulated and analyzed so informative summaries of crime conditions, and the work of the department may be submitted daily, weekly, monthly, and annually. Only in this way can the department realize the objectives of

12. US Department of Justice, *op. cit.*, p. 21.

police administration. These summaries should include complete information on crime conditions, results obtained from investigations, persons arrested and their disposition, distribution of personnel, and of police problems in general. In preparing statistical reports, the standards set forth by the Committee on Uniform Crime Records of the International Association of Chiefs of Police in *Uniform Crime Reporting* and the *Guide for Preparing Annual Police Reports* should be adhered to.

The Daily Report

Figure 14–2
Daily Report

24 HOURS ENDING AT 5 A. M.

NUMBER OF OFFENSES KNOWN TO POLICE				UNIFORM CLASSIFICATION OF OFFENSES	ARRESTS - EXCLUDING TRAFFIC			
Past 24 Hours	Month to Date	Year to Date	Last Year to Date	A. MAJOR OFFENSES - Part I Classes	Past 24 Hours	Month to Date	Year to Date	Last Year to Date
				1. Criminal Homicide: a. Murder and Non-negligent Manslaughter... b. Manslaughter by Negligence........				
				2. Rape............... a. Attempt Rape (220 PC)...........				
				3. Robbery.................				
				4. Aggravated Assault (Felony)...........				
				5. Burglary				
				6. Auto Burglary				
				7. Larceny-Theft........ a. $200 and over....... b. Under $200				
				8. Auto Theft				
				9. Arson				
				TOTAL PART I OFFENSES				
				% DIFFERENCE vs LAST YEAR				

Classifications contained in this report are tentative. For an accurate tabulation of offenses consult departmental statistician.

* Not to be counted in the total as a Part I offense per the Bureau of Criminal Statistics Handbook.

ARRESTS SINCE PREPARATION OF PREVIOUS DAILY REPORT

Name	Race, Sex, & Age	Charge	Officer

BPD 316-901 (12-74)   Prisoners in custody at 5 A. M.   Males _____   Females _____   (C4228)

The function of the Daily Report is obvious from its content—to give the Chief and the Commanding Officers an accurate picture of *major crime for the Past 24 Hours, This Month to Date, This Year to Date and Last Year to Date,* together with the number of Arrests for the same time intervals. The Daily Report serves as the basis for crime data compiled for the Monthly and Annual Report (see figure 14–2).

The Monthly Report

The most important record from the standpoint of general police administration is the monthly consolidated report. This report shows crime tendencies and conditions and the effectiveness of the department in coping with them. It is an up-to-the-minute appraisal of the police work and police problems, including personnel, results of investigations, accidents and miscellaneous services with sufficient comparisons to point out trends. The monthly report serves as a very valuable aid to the Chief in administering the force. For example, a large decrease in the number of burglaries cleared by arrest may indicate faulty distribution of the force, lack of training, improper discipline, or inadequate personnel. The figures may indicate the need for special analyses. In fact, this is the major function of these administrative reports. The monthly report is as significant to police administrators as the monthly operating financial statement is to a large industrial corporation. Many of the tables in the monthly report find their counterpart in the *Guide for Preparing Annual Police Reports.* Thus, the monthly reports build up the materials for the annual report, making its preparation a relatively simple matter.

Figure 14–3
Monthly Return of Offenses Known to the Police

DO-65a (Rev. 2-18-83)
Form Approved
OMB No. 11

CLASSIFICATION OF OFFENSES	Code Entry	OFFENSES REPORTED OR KNOWN TO POLICE (INCLUDE "UNFOUNDED" AND ATTEMPTS)	UNFOUNDED, I.E., FALSE OR BASELESS COMPLAINTS	NUMBER OF ACTUAL OFFENSES (COLUMN 2 MINUS COLUMN 3) (INCLUDE ATTEMPTS)	TOTAL OFFENSES CLEARED BY ARREST OR EXCEPTIONAL MEANS	NUMBER OF CLEARANCES INVOLVING ONLY PERSONS UNDER 18
1. CRIMINAL HOMICIDE						
a. MURDER AND NONNEGLIGENT HOMICIDE (score attempts as aggravated assault if homicide reported, submit Supplementary Homicide Report						
b. MANSLAUGHTER BY NEGLIGENCE						
2. FORCIBLE RAPE TOTAL						
a. Rape by Force						
b. Attempts to commit Forcible Rape						
3. ROBBERY TOTAL						
a. Firearm						
b. Knife or Cutting Instrument						
c. Other Dangerous Weapon						
d. Strong Arm (Hands, Fists, Feet, Etc.)						
4. ASSAULT TOTAL						
a. Firearm						
b. Knife or Cutting Instrument						
c. Other Dangerous Weapon						
d. Hands, Fists, Feet, Etc. - Aggravated Injury						
e. Other Assaults Simple, Not Aggravated						
5. BURGLARY TOTAL						
a. Forcible Entry						
b. Unlawful Entry - No Force						
c. Attempted Forcible Entry						
6. LARCENY-THEFT TOTAL (Except Motor Vehicle Theft)						
7. MOTOR VEHICLE THEFT TOTAL						
a. Autos						
b. Trucks and Buses						
c. Other Vehicles						
GRAND TOTAL						

CHECKING ANY OF THE APPROPRIATE BLOCKS BELOW WILL ELIMINATE YOUR NEED TO SUBMIT REPORTS WHEN THE VALUES ARE ZERO. THIS WILL ALSO AID THE NATIONAL PROGRAM IN ITS QUALITY CONTROL EFFORTS.

☐ NO SUPPLEMENTARY HOMICIDE REPORT SUBMITTED SINCE NO MURDERS, JUSTIFIABLE HOMICIDES, OR MANSLAUGHTERS BY NEGLIGENCE OCCURRED IN THIS JURISDICTION DURING THE MONTH.

☐ NO SUPPLEMENT TO RETURN A REPORT SINCE NO CRIME OFFENSES OR RECOVERY OF PROPERTY REPORTED DURING THE MONTH.

☐ NO LAW ENFORCEMENT OFFICERS KILLED OR ASSAULTED REPORT SINCE NONE OF THE OFFICERS WERE ASSAULTED OR KILLED DURING THE MONTH.

☐ NO AGE, SEX, RACE, AND ETHNIC ORIGIN OF PERSONS ARRESTED UNDER 18 YEARS OF AGE REPORT SINCE NO ARRESTS OF PERSONS WITHIN THIS AGE GROUP.

☐ NO AGE, SEX, RACE, AND ETHNIC ORIGIN OF PERSONS ARRESTED 18 YEARS OF AGE AND OVER REPORT SINCE NO ARRESTS OF PERSONS WITHIN THIS AGE GROUP.

☐ NO MONTHLY RETURN OF ARSON OFFENSES KNOWN TO LAW ENFORCEMENT REPORT SINCE NO ARSONS OCCURRED.

DO NOT USE THIS SPACE	INITIALS
RECORDED	
EDITED	
ENTERED	
ADJUSTED	
CORRES	

Month and Year of Report   Agency Identifier   Population

Date

Prepared By   Title

Agency and State   Chief, Commissioner, Sheriff, or Superintendent

Special Studies and Analyses

The consolidated morning report, the monthly and annual reports need to be supplemented by intensive, specialized studies of records data bearing upon specific police problems. Such studies facilitate effective planning and lead to economic use of departmental resources in a professional approach to problems and situations pressing forward continuously for attention and solution. These problems may be operational or administrative in nature. A high traffic accident or burglary rate may command at the moment. Competent traffic administration is predicated almost completely upon the application of statistical analysis to factors involved in traffic accidents, congestion, retarded traffic flow and other problems.

Crime in all its categories can be attacked successfully only upon the basis of painstaking records analysis. Personnel problems, organizational changes, budget requests, design of a new headquarters building, distribution of the force by function, time, and area are representative of an almost endless succession of problem situations requiring analytical attention if they are to be met effectively. Consolidated morning reports, with monthly and annual reports, merely reveal problems; they do not furnish solutions. The method of attack or the procedure to be employed can only be determined through special study and analysis of raw data to be found available in a well administered police records system. The strategic role of records administration in amplifying the striking power of a police organization becomes more evident as record systems become more sophisticated.

The National Crime Information Center

A new and powerful weapon was conceived for law and order when, the Federal Bureau of Investigation embarked on the development of a national electronic information system to be known as the National Crime Information Center in 1967. One of NCIC's first successes occurred in May of the same year–A New York City police officer, suspicious of a parked car, radioed in a request for a NCIC search of the license plate. Within a minute and one half, the patrolman was notified that the car had indeed been stolen a month earlier in Boston. It's been said that the last words of the patrolman over his radio were, "It works! It works!" About one year after the center was opened it had handled a total of two million transactions. Some 30 years later it was handling almost two million transactions–this time in one day. Success comes to NCIC through the close cooperation of local, state, and federal criminal justice agencies with the FBI. BY 1971, all 50 states, and the District of Columbia, had access to the NCIC files. Currently more than 80 thousand law enforcement and criminal justice agencies belong to the system. When NCIC first went on-line, it contained about 95,000 records in five data-bases, or files: Stolen Autos, Stole License Plates, Stole or Missing Guns, Other Identifiable Stolen Articles, and Wanted Persons. Over the year, existing NCIC files have been expanded and new ones added. Currently, there are some 17 files containing more than 10 million records, plus 24 million criminal history records contained in the Interstate Identification Index.

NCIC can furnish computerized data almost immediately to any agency participating in the centralized state system. A dispatcher can respond quickly to inquiries received from the officer on the street. Mobile terminals are becoming more common as a useful instrument to police officers. These vehicle-mounted terminals enable officers to communicate with computers from their units. A NCIC user accesses the computer through a regional or state computer system, or with a direct tie-in to the computer (see figure 14–4). To simplify the prompt return of responses to users, NCIC has established standards providing the most effective communications for all criminal justice agencies. One of these standards require responses to be returned within seconds.

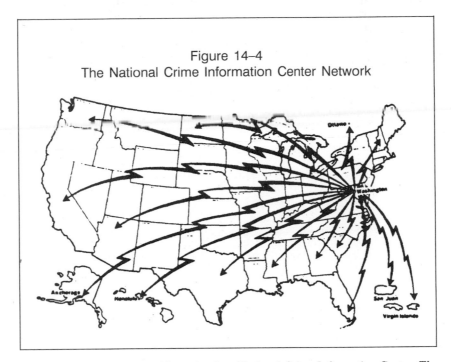

Figure 14–4
The National Crime Information Center Network

Source: Federal Bureau of Investigation, *National Crime Information Center, The Investigative Tool,* Washington, D.C., USGPO, no date.

Any entered record for NCIC must be documented. The following documentation is required:

- A theft report for items of stolen property.

- A warrant for the arrest of a wanted person.

- A missing person report for an individual filed with a law enforcement agency. This can be done by a parent, legal guardian, or next of kin. Another method is by a written statement from a physician or other authoritative source substantiating the missing person's physical or mental disability.

- Case documentation for an unidentified body.

- An arrest fingerprint card(s) for a criminal history.

Figure 14–5

Notable Files in the National Crime Information Data Base
- Missing Persons File, added in 1975. It was created to provide a centralized computerized system to help law enforcement agencies locate individuals–including juveniles–who are not "wanted" on any criminal charges but who are simply "missing."
- The Unidentified Persons File, established in 1983. It provides a way to cross-reference unidentified bodies against records in the Missing Persons File.
- The Interstate Identification Index, added in 1983. It gives law enforcement quick access to criminal justice history.
- The US Secret Service Protective File, also added in 1983. It maintains names and other information on individuals who are believed to pose a threat to the President.
- The Foreign Fugitive File was added in 1987. It was in response to the increasing international nature of crime and of law enforcement.
- The Violent Gang/Terrorist File became operational in 1995. It was established to help identify criminal gangs and their members to local, state and Federal law enforcement.

Source: Federal Bureau of Investigation, *National Crime Information Center: 30 Years on the Beat,* Washington, DC, US Department of Justice, 4/14/99, pp. 1–4, http://www.fbi.gov/2000/ncicnv.htm.

NCIC users access the computer through state computer systems known as "control terminal agencies." For example a police officer on a beat who stops a car that's been weaving in and out of traffic erratically, can radio back to the dispatcher and have an NCIC check run on the driver. If the officer is fortunate to have a mobile terminal mounted in the squad vehicle the officer can conduct the search without the assistance of the dispatcher. The initial request is sent to the state computer and if there's no "hit" then the search goes to the main NCIC terminal. Almost instantly, NCIC will respond with either a "hit" or a "miss." This gives the police officer a pretty good idea of who he or she is dealing with–whether the individual should be considered dangerous, or just a bad driver!

NCIC handles about 20 inquiries a second and it can be used for virtually any type of investigation. During a recent one year period 81,750 "wanted" persons were found, 113,293 individuals were arrested, 39,268 missing juveniles and 8,549 missing adults were located, and 110,681 vehicles recovered. One of the most recent notable cases was the Oklahoma City bombing. Federal investigators entered Timothy McVeigh's name through NCIC and discovered that an Oklahoma state trooper had stopped and run a search on McVeigh a little more than an hour after and some 88 miles away from the site of the explosion. He was still in custody and held for questioning.[13]

The use of mobile terminals has been increasing in recent years. The mobile terminal is a vehicle-mounted computer terminal. It gives a police officer access to state data banks and the NCIC without relaying the information to and from a dispatcher. The mobile terminal allows the officer to ask and receive a response quicker than relaying the information through a dispatcher. Saved time enables the officer to check more suspects and property. An example of a "hit" using a mobile terminal occurred when two Chicago police officers on a routine patrol observed a suspicious-looking vehicle in an alley. The officers entered its Louisiana license plate number into their mobile terminal. Within ten seconds, they received a response confirming their initial suspicion. The license plate was stolen. After verifying this information with the agency record, the driver was arrested. Subsequent investigation revealed the vehicle was stolen in California.

Article File. This file allows for storing information about stolen property not meeting the entry criteria for any other NCIC property files. Records in this file include:

- Automotive accessories.
- Bicycles.
- Camera equipment.
- Household appliances.
- Musical instruments.
- Office equipment.
- Radios.
- Televisions.
- Sound equipment devices.
- Sports equipment.
- Viewing equipment.
- Equipment not otherwise categorized e.g., measuring devises and tools.

Agencies can enter an item of stolen property if the item is worth at least $500 or more or if the item (regardless of value) is one of many items stolen in one theft and the value of all items taken exceeds $5000; finally an item can be entered if the circumstances indicate there is a probability of interstate movement, or the seriousness of the crime dictates the need to make an entry.

Many law enforcement agencies throughout the country have established programs for the unique personal identification of valuable property. These programs provide further aids in the protection and

13. Federal Bureau of Investigation, *National Crime Information Center: 30 Years on the Beat,* Washington, DC, US Department of Justice, 4/14/99, pp. 1–4, http://www.fbi.gov/2000/ncicinv.htm.

recovery of a stolen item. Personal identifying numbers are *owner applied* numbers and may be included as part of the record. An example of its use occurred when a mans partially decomposed body was found in a heavily wooded area near Broken Bow, OK. Since the victim was a resident of Dallas, TX, the FBI entered the investigation, because of a possible kidnapping. A search of the victim's residence by FBI agents revealed a receipt for a 19-inch color TV, showing the serial number and the model number of the TV. The TV was missing from the house so a report was made to the Dallas Police Department. The serial number of the stolen item was entered into NCIC. Several days later, the pawnshop detail, while checking pawned items, made an inquiry and received a *hit* on the TV. This information led to the identification and arrest of two suspects on federal kidnapping charges. Later, a first-degree murder charge was filed in Oklahoma. After a trial, both subjects were convicted. They are both serving a twelve-year sentence.

Boat File: For NCIC purposes, a boat is a vehicle for transport by water, constructed to provide buoyancy by excluding water, and shaped to give stability and permit propulsion. A record may be entered for any stolen boat having a registration or documented number affixed, and/or a permanently attached hull serial number. A loaned, rented, or leased boat, unreturned may be entered if a theft report is made or if a complaint results in the issuance of a warrant charging embezzlement, theft, etc. Additionally, supplemental records may be appended to a stolen boat record for any boat trailer and/or boat part stolen with the boat.

Canadian Warrant File. The data base for this file is maintained by Canada. Entries are for extraditable offenses. An agency making and inquiry and receiving a *hit* on a Canadian entry cannot make an arrest in the U.S. based on the Canadian warrant. The inquiring agency must contact the Royal Canadian Mounted Police to initiate the process of obtaining a U.S. extradition warrant. If the subject is not a U.S. citizen, the inquiring agency should contact U.S. Immigration and Naturalization.

Gun File. A gun is any weapon (including a starter pistol) designed to, or readily converted to expel a projectile by air, carbon dioxide, or the action of an explosive. Included are:

- Antique guns.
- Cannons.
- Machine guns.
- Pistols.
- Rifles.
- Shotguns.
- The frame or receiver of any such weapon.
- Any firearm muffler or silencer.

- Destructive devices such as grenades, mines, missiles, and rockets.

- Disguised guns such as knife guns, pen guns, belt buckles, and cane guns.

This file contains information on stolen weapons and recovered (abandoned, seized, or found) weapons for which no stolen report occurred. A recovered weapon must remain in the custody of the entering agency or be readily available for examination.

Interstate Identification Index (III). This file has an index containing identifying data on persons with criminal records. Each index record contains the location(s) of data base(s) storing a criminal history record. These data bases maintaining complete records, include the FBI and state central repositories. This file can be beneficial to agencies in several different ways. It can provide prior criminal history for:

- Criminal investigations.

- Bail/bond decisions.

- Pre-trial decision-making.

- Pre-sentence investigations.

- Parole/probation determinations.

Also a check of this file can provide additional information about the subject such as aliases, scars, tattoos, date of birth, and the social security number. Many agencies have adopted the policy of routinely checking every person arrested or taken into custody. Such inquiries can result in knowledge about previous arrests otherwise unknown.

Under a Federal/State compact States can exchange criminal history data about State offenders. This eliminates the need for the FBI to maintain duplicate data about State offenders. The compact also provides for the sharing of information on criminal histories in response to non-criminal justice requests from another State.[14] Figure 14–6 lists the participants in the III program as well as those states that are a National Fingerprint File (NFF) state.

14. Bureau of Justice Statistics, *Survey of State History Information Systems, 1995,* Washington, DC, Office of Justice Programs, May 1997, p. viii.

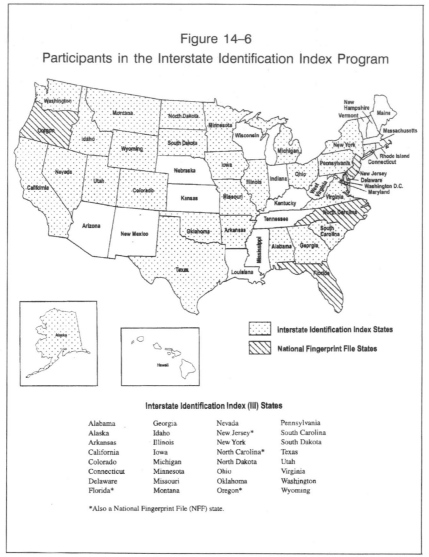

Figure 14-6
Participants in the Interstate Identification Index Program

Interstate Identification Index States

National Fingerprint File States

Interstate Identification Index (III) States

Alabama	Georgia	Nevada	Pennsylvania
Alaska	Idaho	New Jersey*	South Carolina
Arkansas	Illinois	New York	South Dakota
California	Iowa	North Carolina*	Texas
Colorado	Michigan	North Dakota	Utah
Connecticut	Minnesota	Ohio	Virginia
Delaware	Missouri	Oklahoma	Washington
Florida*	Montana	Oregon*	Wyoming

*Also a National Fingerprint File (NFF) state.

Source: Bureau of Justice Statistics, *Survey of State Criminal History Information Systems, 1995*, Washington, DC, Office of Justice Programs, May 1997, pp. 1–57.

License Plate File. An entry may be made into this file for an unrecovered stolen license plate(s), providing there is a theft report entry. When an agency enters, modifies, locates, or removes a record for a license plate registered in another state, the NCIC computer automatically notifies the state of registry.

Missing Persons File. This is a locator-type file used almost exclusively by state and local criminal justice agencies to locate missing juveniles. Although many missing juveniles (i.e., runaways) return home, a small but important percentage of those who do not must be found. Some police departments delay the entry of a missing person entry for a specified period of time, anticipating the return of the person. It should be noted that timely notification increases the utility of the file. Approximately 70 percent of the entries are for juveniles. A record may be entered for a person of any age who is missing and:

- Is under proven physical/mental disability or is senile, subjecting that person or others to personal or immediate danger.
- Is in the company of another person, under such circumstances that the person's personal safety is in danger.
- The disappearance is not voluntary.
- Is a possible catastrophe victim.

When filing a report for a missing person, it is important to gather all their personal data. This includes a description of the person, their clothing, jewelry, dental information, corrective vision prescription, and blood type. Most importantly it should include X-rays and information on other medical treatment. It also is helpful to include information on any vehicle associated with the disappearance.

Securities File. For NCIC purposes, a security is:

- Currency.
- Documents or certificates considered to be evidence of debt, such as, treasury issued bills, bonds, and notes. It also includes municipal and corporate bonds, and debentures. Lastly, it includes common or preferred stock.
- Documents representing subscription rights, including stock warrants and rights.
- Other types traded by security exchanges except for commodities futures.
- Postal and other types of money orders.
- Traveler's checks.
- Warehouse receipts.
- Savings certificates.
- Interest coupons on stocks and bonds.

Items not meeting the criteria for entry into the file include personal notes, U.S. Treasury checks and other types of government checks. Other items include lost or stolen credit cards and bank passbooks.

US Secret Service Protective File. This file aids the Secret Service in protecting the President and other protectees. It can provide investigative leads on: 1) the whereabouts of those individuals who may pose a threat to a protectee, and 2) the individual's criminal activity that may be related to a protectee. An agency making an inquiry should not arrest or detain an individual based solely on the information furnished in a "hit." Further, this information is not to be used for other than criminal justice purposes and cannot be disseminated outside the inquiring agency.

Unidentified Person File. The intent of this file is to help the investigator in the identification of unknown bodies. Besides the entry regarding a body, a record can be made of body parts. Descriptive data includes blood type, estimated year of birth, approximate height and weight, jewelry worn, and dental characteristics. This file operates jointly with the Missing Person File. Upon the entry of a record for an unidentified body, the computer automatically checks both files. A score is assigned to each candidate record found. The two highest scoring records are returned on-line followed by the NCIC numbers for up to 18 additional records.

Vehicle File. A vehicle is any motor-driven conveyance designed to carry its operator, including aircraft. However, trailers may also be entered. An entry includes stolen vehicles or those loaned, rented or leased (providing there is a theft report). An entry also can be for a vehicle used in the commission of a felony and its whereabouts is unknown. Finally stolen vehicle parts can be entered for the following items: certificate of origin, vehicle identification number plate, transmission, backhoe, rear axle, and other major parts.

Wanted Person File. A record for an individual, including parole and probation violators, for whom a federal, felony, or serious misdemeanor warrant is outstanding, may be entered. An agency must determine that the individual can be extradited. Any limitation concerning the extradition must be set forth in the record. Currently all of the NCIC 2000 hardware and software is located at the FBI facility in Clarksburg, West Virginia.[15] In the future this system will provide for the electronic transmission of photographs, mug-shots, photographs of stolen property, and fingerprint data. It will have an automated fingerprint matching system that will identify someone based on a right index fingerprint when the subject presents no identification or is suspected of presenting a false I.D. Another feature of the new system is that a mobile imagining unit will be installed in squad cars and this unit will include a personal computer, a hand-held fingerprint scanner, a had-held digital camera, and a small printer. Finally, it is anticipated that the new system will improve name search techniques, link all records relating to the same crime. It will also improve security through encryption, network management, and intrusion detection.[16]

The Fingerprint Identification System

Near the turn of the century, Sir E.R. Henry of Scotland Yard made a study of fingerprints as a possible means of criminal identification. As a result of his study of fingerprint patterns, he developed a rather simple system by which the ten fingerprints on the human hands could be classified into a formula. In 1898, a committee was appointed by the English Parliament to consider the possible adoption

15. Federal Bureau of Investigation, "Project Status Update," NCIC 2000, December 1998–January 1999, Vol. 2, No. II, p.1.

16. Federal Bureau of Investigation, *op. cit.*, p. 4.

of the fingerprint identification system by the police. The committee turned in a favorable report and in 1900, the new system went into operation in Scotland Yard, replacing the Bertillon system.

It proved so efficient and successful, its use soon spread to other English cities. The fingerprint system of criminal identification is now employed by the police everywhere throughout the civilized world. Today, even the smallest police departments use this method for the identification of criminal offenders. There are very sound reasons for the rapid adoption of the fingerprint system. If all the millions of people on earth were fingerprinted, it is safe to say that no two fingerprints would ever be found alike. Galton working with the theory of probabilities, found that by using the patterns of all ten fingers, the chances were 64,000,000,000 to 1 that no two human beings would ever possess fingerprints exactly alike. Additionally, fingerprints lend themselves to a very simple system of classification by which a fingerprint formula is derived. Since the fingerprints of an individual do not change throughout life, the fingerprint formula of each person remains the same from birth to death.

The fingerprint identification system or file is today a characteristic feature of virtually every police department. Even the smallest police department have the capacity for utilizing the services of state and federal fingerprint systems. As is well known to police officers, it is usually the case that not more than one or two latent fingerprints (most likely the thumb, index, or middle fingers) are recovered in a single criminal case. Since the presence of all ten fingerprints is necessary for a search in the conventional fingerprint file, the search of a single latent fingerprint found at the scene would be out of the question unless a single fingerprint classification system is maintained. Police departments employing this system report a high yield in terms of the number of identifications or "raps" made, particularly in juvenile burglaries. In 1996 at the feral level a test and evaluation period

Was conducted for a Latent Fingerprint Processing Section (LFPS). This is a stand-alone latent search capability that provides latent specialists with a latent search capability against a single Special Latent Cognizant Features (SLCF) file of 200,000 subjects.[17]

When a person is arrested and fingerprinted by the police, at least three sets of fingerprints are taken. One set is classified, searched and filed in the local police fingerprint files. The second is sent to the State Bureau of Criminal Records and Identification. As a result, each State Bureau has on file many thousands of fingerprint records of known criminal offenders. In this manner, it functions as a state-wide clearing house for criminal records and information. The third set of fingerprints is sent to the Federal Bureau of Investigation in Washington, D.C. Here again, all law enforcement agencies throughout the United States and its territories, follow the same procedure.

17. Federal Bureau of Investigation, *IAFIS Incremental Builds,* Washington, DC, US Department of Justice, 4/14/99, pp. 1–2, http://www.fbi.gov/iafis.htm.

As in the State Bureau, fingerprint experts in the FBI classify the third set of fingerprints and search them by formula. In the event an identification is made, a complete copy of the criminal record is sent to the department which originally forwarded the prints to the Bureau, and a copy goes to the State Bureau in the state where the department is located. Where the criminal record of an offender shows an arrest or arrests by other departments, a copy of the criminal record is also sent to the department or departments involved.

There are more than 174,949,883 standard fingerprint cards on file in the Identification Division of the Federal Bureau of Investigation. The Bureau also maintains a special single fingerprint file on a selected group of notorious criminals. The prints in this file are classified under a special system making it possible to search for duplicates of a single finger impression. When, for example, a single latent fingerprint is developed at the scene of a crime, it is this file to which the fingerprint expert refers, in efforts to identify the source of the print.

The criminal identification system is society's answer to the mobility of the criminal population. Wherever the criminal offender may operate—California, Texas or Pennsylvania, or even across international boundary lines—the shadow faithfully follows immediately behind. There is no escape.

Integrated Automated Fingerprint Identification System. This latest system represents a quantum leap in communications, computing and data storage, and retrieval technologies. It is a rapid-response paperless system.[18] With the computer and electronic data processing now a standard feature of the American police system, the application of computer technology to the automation of fingerprint classification, search and identification or "rap" was a foregone conclusion. This development qualifies on a scale of importance for a position almost equal to the original introduction to police service of the fingerprint identification system, in lieu of the Bertillon technique.

The manual searching of a set of fingerprints even in a file of 100,000 fingerprint cards, was a laborious and time-consuming affair, especially in the primary 1/1 all loop classification. To complicate matters still further, a thorough job may require the additional search of one or more, occasionally five to ten, reference classifications, which are the product of questionable patterns, variations in individual judgment, eyesight, inking, pressure, width of rolled impressions, worn ridges, scars, and other personal variables.

Automation eliminates all this. The system handles questionable patterns on one or two fingers by automatically searching for numerous file segments. Any number of segments can be searched in the semi-automatic directed mode. Ridge count and inner-outer-meeting trace references within a major file segment are of no consequence to the system since the entire primary segment is searched and scored for

18. *Ibid.*, pp. 1–4.

a match. The automated system thus ensures complete classification and full, tireless, and accurate reference searching on every card. Not the least in significance in this connection is the promise of the automated search of latent prints developed at the crime scene. Since it is usually the case that a *latent* is a fragmentary section of the complete print, ridge detail assumes considerable importance. The location of a bifurcation or ridge ending in the geography of a pattern, for example, can become quite crucial as an identification factor.

A new minutiae-based approach has appeared involving the location and orientation of two familiar points of identification—the ridge ending and bifurcation. Through a scanning technique, the computerized equipment reads directly from card or paper input and accommodates both the ten fingerprint and latent single fingerprint classification, search and identification. The system requires only six seconds to "read" a typical ten print set of fingerprints. During the same six seconds, the system enhances and classifies the input prints and converts the most important characteristics of each print into information that is readily understood by most general purpose computers. Suspect cards are read and classified in the same manner, and are then matched against a control computer file. Results of the matching process are presented to the operator in hard-copy form for final verification.

Automation of the fingerprint identification system is now well on the way to being within the reach of police departments everywhere, regardless of size. Conversion to the automated system is preceded by a feasibility study, including a thorough requirements analysis. Factors in this analysis include equipment requirements, expected transaction volumes, master fingerprint file size, necessary interfaces to user data bases, interfaces to existing user computer hardware and systems, network requirements, data base conversion requirements, manpower estimates, response considerations and other elements affecting the design of the proposed system. This is followed by the selection of appropriate hardware, and the design and development of the necessary computer programs to support the operation—including the capability for data-base management, information storage/retrieval and file search equipment.

The Facsimile Transmission of a 10–Finger Fingerprint Card. Nowhere in police records procedure is the need for speed and accuracy more essential than in the prompt identification of an arrested suspect and the immediate availability of any criminal record. The base resources are there—State Bureaus of Criminal Records and Identification, and the enormous criminal records of the Federal Bureau of Investigation. In addition to the large central criminal records and information centers in metropolitan police departments.

The transmission by voice or otherwise, of a fingerprint formula, is, of course, far from enough. It is the fingerprint pattern with its ridge detail—the type, the core, the delta, the bifurcation and the ridge ending and their location in the geography of the pattern, for example, that make possible the identification with mathematical certainty and precision. The facsimile transmission of a complete set of fingerprints, within the space of a few minutes, is the answer; the distance, whether a few miles or across the continent, is of no consequence. Such transmission has long since become an accomplished fact in the field of communications engineering, both by wire and over the air waves. For example, the Criminal Justice Information Systems Wide Area Network (CJISWAN) was a pilot program that demonstrated the use of the Electronic Fingerprint System (EFIPS) that for the first time allowed for the electronic transmission of fingerprints to the FBI.

Use of the facsimile fingerprint transmission system is limited to law enforcement agencies and under the condition they restrict the use of the system to situations of an urgent nature involving a suspected fugitive, an unknown deceased person or an amnesia victim. The time of transmission of a fingerprint card involves only a few minutes, and when an identification is established, the FBI identification record is transmitted back to the requesting agency over the same system. Two cases out of the many available, illustrate the value of the system. The Rhode Island State Police transmitted a fingerprint card on behalf of the East Greenwich, RI, Police Department, of a suspicious character they had taken into custody after he was observed in the vicinity of a bank. He gave the name, Mitchell Robert Wilson. He was promptly identified as one Cameron David Bishop, who had been sought as a Top Ten Fugitive. Typical of the success experienced in cases involving unknown deceased persons, the St. Louis Police Department transmitted a set of fingerprints from a homicide victim. He was promptly identified by a US Navy enlistment fingerprint card and the information was transmitted immediately back to the St. Louis Police Department. It is probably safe to say, that facsimile transmission networks have spanned this country.

Fingerprint Matching Subsystem (FMS). As part of the implementation and testing of this program Texas, New Jersey, and Sun Prairie, WI, participating in a ranger of activities to include:

- Entering wanted persons with fingerprints, mug-shots, and identifying images.

- Identifying wanted persons using a fingerprint.

- Modifying a fingerprint entered into NCIC 2000 with a new fingerprint.

- Canceling a wanted person's fingerprint.

- Receiving ownership of a linked fingerprint when the original owner canceled their entry.[19]

19.   Federal Bureau of Investigation, *op. cit.,* p. 3.

Each of the participants successfully completed the activities that were part of the test demonstrating the viability of the software and hardware that makes up this outstanding system.

Criminal History Records

Improving the data quality of criminal justice history records stored in local, state, and federal systems is a priority undertaken by all levels of government. This priority gained the support of national leaders. During the last few years there has been steady progress and changes in the technologies, automation, and data utilization. To complicate matters, laws have changed, and needed information is different. Policy-makers and practitioners have become increasingly aware of the need for accurate, complete, and timely records in support of criminal justice activities, and non-criminal purposes. Particularly acute is the lack of disposition information. The level of disposition reporting varies considerably depending upon the age of the records. Out of 48% of the Nation's criminal history records only 70% have final dispositions recorded within the last five years.

The importance of improving criminal justice history records cannot be overstated. Acknowledging the utility of the records there are many new needs. There is an increased use of these records for identifying habitual criminals, for making bail, and for pretrial release decisions. An additional, use is for sentencing determinations, and for correctional supervision and release decisions. Availability of accurate and complete records is especially critical to the task of identifying felons who attempt to purchase firearms. Other uses by non-criminal justice government agencies include background checks for licensing, pre-employment screening, and security checks. Also, with increasing frequency, the public demands that childcare and transportation workers do not pose a criminal threat.[20]

In the past grants from the Federal government allocated a percentage of its total awards for the improvement of criminal records emphasizing the:

- Completion of criminal justice histories to include the final disposition of arrests for felony offenses.

- Full automation of all criminal justice histories and fingerprint records.

- Frequency and quality of criminal history reports submitted to the FBI.

One study group has identified 28 events or decisions in the criminal justice process where officials rely upon the use of criminal history record information as a significant basis for informed decisions. When information is inadequate it can jeopardize the appropriateness of the decision that can have serve consequences. [21]

---

20. *Ibid.,* p. iv.

21. Bureau of Justice Statistics, *Increasing the Utility of the Criminal His-*

Figure 14–7

Criminal Justice Decisions and Events That Rely Upon the Use of Criminal History Record Information

- Law enforcement investigation
- Law enforcement patrol activities
- Arrest
- Booking
- Prosecutor's charging/review decision
- Initial appearance, including setting bail
- Grand jury action
- Pretrial release decision, including alternatives to detention and conditions of release
- Arraignment
- Diversions
- Trial court disposition
- Court-bind over decisions
- Plea negotiations
- Sentencing (including decisions on conditional sentences, community service and mental health commitments)
- Probation
- Probation revocation
- Appeal
- Other appellate decisions (for example, post-conviction procedures or release pending appeal)
- Custody and custodial supervision, including the screening of visitors to correctional facilities
- Parole
- Parole revocation
- Modification to sentences
- Pardons and executive clemency
- Firearms purchase and/or possession eligibility
- Dignitary protection
- Threat analysis
- Hiring for criminal justice position
- Certification of juvenile tried as adult

Source: Bureau of Justice Statistics, *Increasing the Utility of the Criminal History Record: Report of the National Task Force,* Washington, DC, Office of Justice Programs, December 1995, p. 7.

In a study of the status of state criminal history reporting systems, this Nation's was found to be in fair shape. For example the study concluded that:

- Eighty-six percent of the criminal history records maintained by state repositories are already automated.

tory Record: Report of the National Task Force, Washington, DC, Office of Justice Programs, December 1995, p. 7.

- Forty-four states and Puerto Rico have fully automated master name indexes.

- Over 49.8 million criminal history files are in the of State repositories.

- Five States and three territories have fewer than 30% automated criminal history files.[22]

With the advent of the Brady Act a large grant was allocated to ensure immediate availability of complete and accurate State records by funding for the National Criminal History Improvement Program (NCHIP) Additional funding was provided by the National Child Protection Act and the Violence Against Women Act. Funding beyond the development or the improvement of criminal history records systems was for the establishment of an interface with the FBI's National Instant Criminal Background Check System (NICS). During a recent year about 2,671,000 background checks of potential handgun buyers prevented an estimated 69,000 purchases. Sixty-two percent of those rejected had been convicted of a felony or were under felony indictment. Domestic violence misdemeanors accounted for over 9% rejection and domestic violence restraining orders 2%. Since November 1998 presale background checks have been required for sales of all firearms not just handguns.[23] In time, we will see an improved criminal history record system. Unquestionably, these records are more important than ever before. With greater accuracy, the system will prove to be well worth the money and effort needed for its improvement.

The Computer

The police are now at the threshold of a new era in which professional gains are beginning to dwarf even the fantastic achievements of the past quarter century in this field, and these gains are having a major impact on the apprehension capability of the police. The appearance of the computer and its related technology is generating a new renaissance in police affairs of major proportions. Through the communication channels of the telephone, radio, the teletypewriter wireless, and the computer, it brings police departments, regardless of size, into virtually instantaneous contact with unlimited resources, in terms of information management on a state wide or national basis. Notably, in most instances, state and local police computer installations are police-based and police-oriented. In some cases, computer installations are designed on a more comprehensive scale to serve the entire field of criminal justice administration, including the police, prosecutor, courts, probation, corrections and parole. Two law enforcement sys-

22. Bureau of Justice Statistics, *Survey of State Criminal History Information Systems, 1995*, Washington, DC, Office of Justice Programs, May 1997, pp. 1–5.

23. Donald A. Manson and Darrell K. Gilliard, *Presale Handgun Checks, 1997*, Washington, DC, Bureau of Justice Statistics, June 1998, pp. 1–7.

tems are examples of how automation is used to communicate essential information and to reduce the time it takes detectives to conduct criminal investigations:

- Automated Field Interview Systems—These systems link the thousands of daily observations made by field officers with crimes investigated by detectives. The computer connects suspects by location, description, vehicle, and activity to reported crimes.

- Modus Operandi (MO) Correlation Systems—These computer programs process large volumes of data from crime and arrest reports and correlate incidents that may have been committed by the same suspect. By linking these reports MO patterns, a conglomerate of information can often be compiled, providing valuable assistance in identifying crime perpetrators.

Computers are following the trend of many mechanical and electronic devices proving helpful to mankind. Mass production is increasing their availability while decreasing their cost. Already the cost of computers is within the financial reach of most police agencies. Today's desk-top computers have the capabilities of larger computer systems of a decade ago.

Municipal police departments with 100 or more sworn officers have been using computers for a variety of tasks ranging from budgeting to research (see tables 14–2 and 14–3). Nearly two-thirds these departments reported using computers for record-keeping and manpower allocation. Other computer functions reported by at least a fifth of the municipal local police departments including criminal investigation (86%), crime analysis (90%), and dispatch (89%). Most of these departments also use computers for fleet management and manpower allocation. It should be noted that with the exception of jail management municipal departments use computer at a higher percentage than other type of agencies.

The majority of municipal police departments reported they maintain computer files containing the following types of information: arrests (93%), calls for service (94%), traffic citations (73%), stolen property (80%), warrants (75%), criminal histories (76%), and Uniformed Crime Reports (40%). In every one of these categories there has been a significant increase in the use of computers for every category. Most of these departments were also maintaining computer files on payroll, personnel, departmental inventory, and evidence.[24]

24. Reaves and Smith, *op. cit.*, p. xiii.

Table 14–2					
Percent of Agencies Using Computers for Specified Functions					
Function	**Type of Agency**				
	County	Municipal	Sheriff	Special	State
Budgeting	91%	80%	88%	73%	86%
Crime analysis	85	90	75	73	45
Crime investigation	88	86	84	50	00
Dispatch	76	89	76	27	67
Fleet management	73	53	60	55	88
Jail management	6	21	78	0	0
Manpower allocation	64	60	51	68	59
Record-keeping	91	94	97	91	92
Research	67	60	40	50	63

Source: Brian A. Reaves and Pheny Z. Smith, *Law Enforcement Management and Administrative Statistics, 1993: Data for Individual State* and Local Agencies with 110 or More Officers, Washington, D.C., Bureau of Justice Statistics, September 1995, p. xiii.

Table 14–3					
Percent of Agencies Maintaining Computer Files by Type of Record					
Item	**Type of Agency**				
	County	Municipal	Sheriff	Special	State
Arrests	85%	93%	93%	91%	65%
Calls for service	82	94	84	59	55
Criminal histories	83	75	86	53	
Driver's license	43	33	40	49	
Evidence	87	78	86	47	
Fingerprints digital	50	39	58	35	
Stolen property	80	74	75	39	
Stolen vehicles	83	76	70	51	
Summonses	53	35	55	18	
Traffic accidents	73	78	57	84	
Traffic citations	73	67	66	59	
Uniformed crime reports NIBRS	43	58	57	41	
Uniformed crime reports					
Vehicle registration	33	29	32	39	
Warrants	80	70	95	49	

Source: Brian A. Reaves and Andrew L. Goldberg, *Law Enforcement Management and Administrative Statistics, 1997: Data for Individual State and Local Agencies with 100 or More Officers,* Washington, D.C., Bureau of Justice Statistics, September 1999, p. xvii.

Using the Internet

The opportunities to enter, share, and transfer an information base offered by the Internet and the World Wide Web continue to unfold at an inordinate rate. Law enforcement agencies are just beginning to see the value in creating a web site and using the Internet as a means of communicating within the organization, with other agencies, and the community. It is a means of achieving wireless communications, tracking gangs, and providing crime analysis maps for particular neighborhoods. In addition, departments have used this media to post their most wanted and sex offender registries to the web.

The Internet clearly offers agencies a more efficient way to conduct business, but it also raises security questions when sensitive data is being transmitted.[25]

With a grant the Illinois Criminal Justice Information Authority developed a model Internet application to criminal justice agencies. As a result of the grant an electronic handbook was created that identified the types of data and information that should be made available on the Internet, modeling the way it should look and disseminating the models and standards to police agencies. It is their position that the best place to start is with a strategic plan that could include the following objectives:

- Improve confidence in the agency through the release of public information.

- Motivate citizens to participate in the process.

- Reduce paper work.

- Prevent crime.[26]

Initially the agency should decide what kind of information it wants to release. The agency should be as be open and candid and release information that demonstrates a real community partnership. Realistic public disclosure lets the public know that they are truly interested in serving the community. The release of information that makes for a better informed citizen builds public confidence. The existence of a Web site tell the public that the police department is technologically advanced and prepared to work with the public in an effort to deal with the crime problem. Almost every agency will have personnel who are capable of creating and maintaining a Web site. The rewards that can be reaped from a well prepared site will, without question, exceed the efforts to maintain it. This process suggests to the public that the agency is keeping pace with technological and social change.

25. SEARCH, *Justice Agencies Use the Internet,* Sacramento, CA, The National Consortium for Justice Information and Statistics, 4/16/99, http://www.taexchange.search.org/internet.htm.

26. Illinois Criminal Justice Information Authority, *CJ Web Handbook Strategy Objectives,* Springfield, IL, 4/16/99, pp. 1–3, http//www.acsp.uic.edu/handbook/0401001.html.

The current emphasis on community policing and problem solving has established a frame of reference that supports the need for officers to assume the role of motivators. Citizens have to be made aware of the need to participate in improving the quality of life in the neighborhood through participative crime prevention. If the police want the public to assist them in problem-solving they must have information that addresses the problems that confront them.

Like most bureaucracies the police have created a plethora of paperwork that clogs the system and threatens to bring everything to a standstill. Much of this effort fails to address the real problems confronting the agency and society, and in many instances it is of little real value because it is out of date by the time it is received. Some departments register bicycles on line and other provide citizen complaint and commendation forms on line. In an effort to reach the community other departments, via a Web site, provides copies of annual report, community assessment surveys, strategic goals and organizational charts.

The Internet is in the process of becoming a powerful instrument for preventing crime. It is an excellent vehicle for describing crime prevention techniques and service that can be useful in self-help crime fighting tools. It has been useful in increasing participation in neighborhood watch and other crime prevention efforts. One agency provides information on how protect their automobiles and what one has to do to "park smart." In selected areas the department identified parked vehicles at risk and identified the owner and sent them a warning notification slip indicating the type of risk such as a rolled down window, unlocked doors or valuables in clear view of sight.[27]

E-mail is just beginning to become of value to law enforcement agencies. It can improve internal and inter-departmental communications, enhance contact with citizens and vendors, and ultimately lead to improved services to the public. Education is an critical element of the e-mail process and constituents must be alerted how to use it. It can do a number of things to include providing civilians with easy access to police officers, reduce the time wasted trying to contact people, facilitate communications between field personnel and supervisors, and provide information to the media. Another use is to solicit information about services provided to citizens.[28]

A recent innovation on the Internet is its utilization to get information on fugitives to a broad audience quickly and inexpensively. In 1996 a fugitive wanted by the FBI was arrested in Guatemala after having been listed as a wanted person on an Internet site. A viewer of

27. Portland Police Bureau, *Community Policing News,* Portland, OR, Portland Police Bureau, October/November 1998, pp. 1–6, http://www.teleport.com/police/news1098.html.

28. Arthur G. Sharp, "E–Mail: A New Way of Getting the Message," *Law and Order,* Vol. 47, No. 5, pp. 79–83.

the Internet site recognized the photograph of a fugitive and contacted authorities. This was a first for someone on the FBI's Ten Most Wanted Fugitives. Since then numerous other departments have followed suit. Cincinnati places fugitives and difficult crimes on its home page. Phoenix presents unsolved crimes and photographs of suspects on its web site as part of Silent Witness Program. Other departments that use the Internet include the Tennessee Bureau of Investigation, Florida's Department of Law Enforcement and the Dallas County Sheriff's Office.[29]

Crime Analysis

Police departments have for many years made important use of index systems, spot maps and other manually operated procedures and methods for classifying information on a geographical basis, in order to have this type of information available for operational planning and to serve other administrative purposes. With the appearance of the computer, and the use of the Geographic Information System (GIS) the management of information has expanded all expectations. As this process has evolved the reduction in implementation costs has brought the system within the reach of even the smaller departments.

GIS has given law enforcement the capacity to immediately view crime by type, time and date, and location. Another feature is that spatial relationships can be established at a location within a specified distance. For example, a "crack house" can be located and everything within 1000 feet. This allows for response planning and real time management of an incident. When data is stored in a records management system (RMS) it is immediately available such as displaying the location by beat, reporting district or zone.

With mapping application pending and active events can be displayed and automatically updated as new events are created, or removed. The map display can be set to automatically resize to include all active and pending events. Additionally, the user can define geographies, crime density, and repeat call investigations as part of crime analysis. [30]One research firm has taken the traditional text and statistical information used in crime analysis and displayed it on a map. This allows one to see crime patterns and relationships amongst factors associated with criminal incidents. For example, an analyst can create sophisticated crime incident reports and maps, access known offender files, and combine these with other geographic databases.[31] A one study

29. James R. Wolf, "Internet Crime Busters," *Government Technology*, 4/16/99, *http://www.gov-tech.net/1997/gt/may/may/1997–gov@internet/may1997–gov@internet.shtm.*

30. ESRI, *ESRI Business Partners,* Gainesville, FL, 11/30/98, pp. 1–21.

http://www.esri.com/partners/developers/pubsafety.html.

31. ESRI, *How Can You use Technology to Fight Crime?,* Gainesville, FL, 11/30/98, pp 1–2, http://www.ersi.com/industries/public_safety/lawenforce.html.

departments reported that mapping improves information dissemination, evaluation, and administration. Specifically departments use mapping to:

- Inform officers and investigators of crime incident locations (94 percent).

- Make resource allocation decisions (56 percent).

- Evaluate interventions (49 percent).

- Inform residents about crime activity and changes in their community (47 percent).

- Identify repeat calls-for-service (44 percent).[32]

The city of New York set the pace for crime analysis when it instituted a management review process that it called COMPSTAT. This process required borough managers to utilize crime statistics in a crime reduction program. By tracking crime resources were deployed within the frame of reference of a total crime reduction strategy. The resources utilized included community policing, directed patrol, bike patrol, and narcotic suppression teams. The success of this program has been unprecedented with a sharp decline in all categories of crime. Crime analysis had arrived. This lead was followed by the implementation of similar programs in Los Angeles County and in the City of Los Angeles. Both of which have proven to be successful. All three programs have forced police managers to respond to crime trends and patterns.[33]

In crime analysis software can be used to analyze and discover patterns relationships, and series in large databases. This process is known as data mining. It is unique inasmuch as it discovers underlying patterns. It presents the user with new information that distinguishes it from the Online Analytical Process (OLAP) wherein the user hypothesized the problem and strives to identify data that supports the hypothesis. It is a process of asking a specific question and answering the question utilizing the OLAP techniques. It is clear that automated crime analysis has a great deal to offer to law enforcement.[34] Figure 14–8 lists some of the software and hardware products that will increasingly be applied to problems confronting police managers.

32. Cynthia A. Mamalian and Nancy G. LaVigne, *The Use of Computerized Mapping by Law Enforcement: Survey Results,* Research Preview, Washington, DC, National Institute of Justice, January 1999, pp. 1–3.

33. Mike Woods, "Crime Analysis: A Key Tool in Any Crime Reduction Strategy," *The Police Chief,* April 1999, Vol. LXVI, No. 4, pp. 17–30.

34. Christopher S. Gebhardt, "Crime Analysis: The Next Phase," *The Police Chief,* April 1999, Vol. LXVI, No. 4, pp. 33–39.

Figure 14–8

Software and Hardware Products for Law Enforcement

Computer-aided dispatching (CAD)
Advanced vehicle locator (AVL)
Records management systems (RMS)
Crime view
Photo imaging
Hand-held saber radios
Document imaging
Automated fingerprinting
Jail management
Map magic
Sex offender notification and registration (SONAR)
Map based interface
Survival crisis management system (SCMS)
Wireless field reporting
In-car mapping
HazTrans
Global positioning systems (GPS)
BeatBuilder
Traffic control device inventory (TCDI)
Teleminder
Crime analyst
Welfare fraud linkage analysis database system (WFLADS)
Consequential assessment tool set (CATS)
Vision mobile

Source: ESRI, *GIS For Law Enforcement, 11/30/98. http://ersi.com/industries/public_safety/lawenforce.html.*

On the horizon that all of us can look forward to is the results of a Federal study known as the Advanced Generation Interoperability for Law Enforcement (AGILE). This initiative will study the effect and integration of technology interoperability. It is a significant development that will have lasting impact on law enforcement. When this project is completed it will have developed minimum standards for the procurement of equipment, services, hardware and communications technology. The technology revolution is here and with this type of assistance law enforcement will move rapidly forward to deal with the crime problems of the future.

The National Clearinghouse for Criminal Justice Information Systems

This excellent Web site provides members of the criminal justice community with on-line access to a innumerable of information resources. It provides impartial information on available software solutions, offers a comprehensive, interactive database of justice agency requests for proposals. It also provides information on justice agency use of the Web, promotes the development and exchange of public domain and shareware justice information systems, and provides a national forum for sharing information among practitioners. Finally, it lists events and Web links of interest to justice practitioners. By having access to a centralized source for the collection and dissemination of a wide range of criminal justice information systems resources agencies can learn from the experience of their peers and avoid "reinventing the wheel."[35]

Case Study

Lieutenant James Perkins

Lt James Perkins has been a member of the Sparksville County Police Department for eleven years. There are 354 sworn officers and 72 civilians in the agency. The city has a population of 213,000 with a diverse constituency consisting of approximately 62 percent Caucasians, 21 percent Mexican–American, 11 percent Black, and the remainder are Indians, and Orientals. The city has a strong manufacturing base including an automobile assembly plant. Additionally, the city is in a major metropolitan area in an agricultural state located in the central part of the United States. While serving in the department Perkins was in patrol for seven years and investigations for three years. His current assignment is in the Technical Services Bureau where he works in the training unit. Currently the department has its own police academy that prepared recruits and trains first-line supervisors. Managerial training is conducted by a local University under Peace Officer Standards and Training (POST) guidelines.

Within a 75 mile radius there are currently three different basic police academies and there has been a recent push to consider the possibility of consolidating these training entities. The Sparksville county training county has never allowed other agencies to send personnel to its academy and the other two academies function on a part-time basis depending upon hiring practices. Sparksville has a new chief, Sara Stewart, and she has expressed an interest in a consolidated academy. The State training commission has long been an advocate of centralized training and has indicated its desire to support a feasibility study.

Chief Sara Stewart has assigned Lt. Perkins the responsibility of serving on a study committee to investigate the implications of consolidated training for recruits and supervisors. She has asked Perkins to prepare a position paper supporting a consolidation and describing the implications. The local community college has indicated an interest in locating the academy on campus and creating a board of directors to supervise its operation. In Addition, POST has volunteered to monitor and fund the feasibility study.

35. SEARCH, *The National Clearinghouse for Criminal Justice Information Systems,* Sacramento, CA, The National Consortium for Justice Information and Statistics, 3/13/99, p. 1, http://www.ch.search.org/default.asp.

If your were Lt. Perkins what would you consider when preparing the report? Within the department who would you interview? What outside members would you interview? Why? List advantages and disadvantages of consolidated training?

What position would you take regarding a possible affiliation with the community college?

For Further Reading

Bureau of Justice Statistics, *Survey of State Criminal History Information Systems,* A Criminal Justice Information Police Report, Washington, DC, Office of Justice Programs, May 1997, pp. 1–56.

> This report is based upon the results of a survey of the administrators of the State criminal history record repositories. Fifty-four jurisdictions were surveyed and only one, Rhode Island, did not complete a survey form. The report describes the level of automation of master name indexes and criminal history files. Describes the level of disposition reporting, level of felony flagging, and timeliness of trial court disposition data. Identifies participants in the Interstate Identification Index (III) and the States that have been identified as National Fingerprint File States.

Donald A. Manson, and Darrell K. Gilliard, *Presale Handgun Checks, 1997,* Washington, DC, Bureau of Justice Statistics, June 1998, pp. 1–7.

> The authors report on the estimated of inquiries and rejections for potential purchasers of handguns. Provides data by States indicating the number of law enforcement agencies responsible for records checks, and the data bases accessed, such as criminal histories, mental health, and domestic violence misdemeanors. Briefly describes the implications of the Brady provisions of the law and the National Criminal History Improvement Program (NCHIP).

Mary A. Taylor, Robert C. Epper, and Thomas K. Tolman, *Wireless Communications and Interoperability Among State and Local Law Enforcement Agencies,* Research in Brief, Washington, DC, National Institute of Justice, January 1998, pp. 1–11.

> This study found that the fragmentation of the public safety spectrum is a complex problem as agencies have shifted to the use of 800 MHz that can isolate smaller agencies who are not using 800 MHz. The authors suggest that interoperability problems may be more a State and/or Federal issue than a local issue. Presents data that can be used by policy makers at all level, by agencies of all sizes and types. Agencies indicated that the two largest obstacles to interoperability were funding and the use of different bands.

Mike Woods. "Crime Analysis: A Key Tool in Any Crime Reduction Program." *The Police Chief*, April 1999, Vol. LXVI, No. 4, pp. 17–30.

The author recommends that crime should be analyzed from a multi-jurisdictional or a regional perspective, with resources directed immediately to suppress it. Points out that crime analysis is taking on new importance in law enforcement. Briefly reviews the history of crime analysis and recommends a crime reduction strategy that focuses on clearly defined goals, allows for the marshalling of all resources to achieve the goals and provides for a measurement of employee's effort.

Chapter 15

SUPPORT SERVICES: Administration, Fiscal, and Operational

Learning Objectives

1. Assess the importance of research and development in law enforcement.

2. List the seven types of planning.

3. Compare long-range and strategic planning.

4. Describe a typical budget preparation calendar.

5. Write a short essay describing the use of tactical units.

6. Identify the types of functions performed by community crime prevention units.

7. List the goals of a juvenile division.

8. Describe the goals for a futuristic traffic law enforcement system.

9. Compare the point system and the enforcement index.

10. Describe the use of sobriety check points.

11. Write a short essay describing motor vehicle theft.

12. Identify the responsibilities of the police in managing hazardous materials.

Functions a police department has to perform dictate organizational structure. The larger the department, the greater the number of services provided, and the greater the number of specialized units. In smaller departments individuals will wear a number of hats and perform duties that are performed by units in larger agencies. In every agency a multitude of functions must be performed if the department is to respond to organizational and community needs. As indicated previously all efforts should be directed toward enhancing the response of field operations. These activities include:

- Fingerprint processing.

- Identification and records.

- Civil process serving.

466

- Training.

- Laboratory operations.

- Warrants.

- Jail operations.

- Permits/alarms.

- Budget preparation.

- Planning.

- Inspections.

- Facilities management.[1]

When 411 municipal agencies were surveyed (with 100 or more sworn officers) it was determined that these departments performed the following functions: operating a training academy (38 percent), fingerprint processing (87 percent) and laboratory testing of substances (16 percent). Additionally, these departments had primary responsibility for civil process serving (6 percent) jail operations (19 percent) and ballistic testing (13 percent). Other support services that were performed included dispatching calls for service (89 percent), traffic direction and control (94 percent) and every department enforced traffic regulations and laws. Additionally, 77 percent of the departments participated in an expanded/enhanced 911 system and 19 percent operated with a basic 911 system.[2]

With the advent of additional functions, many became part of Bureaus of Administration or Bureaus of Technical Services. When one analyses support service and there location in the organization a great deal of variance can be found. Typical of this is the location of planning and research units. In the Miami Police Department this function is under the Administration Division while in the San Jose Police Department it is in the Office of the Chief. In the Sacramento, CA Police Department the planning and research division is part of Administrative Services. It is interesting to note Miami has a planning and research unit that is separate from a budget unit. In fact this latter unit is under a business management section. Whatever the location of various special units, staffing requires a considerable number of full-time sworn and civilian personnel. In the State of California out of 90 agencies, with more than 100 sworn officers, one to 18 percent of the officers employees were assigned to administrative duties. This does not include the civilians who served in that area.[3]

1. Brian A. Reaves and Pheny Z. Smith, *Law Enforcement Management and Administrative Statistics, 1993: Data for Individual State and Local Agencies with 100 or More Officers,* Washington, DC Office of Justice Programs, September 1995, pp. 1–286.

2. *Ibid,* p. xi.

3. *Ibid.,* pp. 12–18.

Research and Development

From an administrative point of view, a plan of operations is a synthesis of various plans: annual, long-term, short-term, and special. The need for a plan of operations is recognized by all, but the practice of providing one is not yet commonplace. Planning is the working-out (in broad outline) of the things needing to be done and the methods for doing them in order to accomplish the purpose set for the enterprise. It involves a forecast of the future problem and a scheme for meeting it. Police problems involving crime, delinquency, vice and traffic, occur and reoccur in time and place with such a high degree of regularity that administrative predictions are possible. The curves of yesterday and today can be projected into tomorrow in terms of what and how much is going to happen, when and where. Accurate estimates of the situation can be prepared and from them short-term, long-term, and special plans can be formulated.

Where the data is properly administered and analyzed, exceedingly reliable predictions can be made in statistical terms concerning the number of persons who will be killed and injured in traffic accidents, and when and where they will be killed and injured. Burglary operations can similarly be forecast (in advance) in terms of hour-of-day, day-of-week, month-of-year and the geographic location throughout the city. Likewise, robbery, automobile theft, assaults, larceny and other crimes, as well as the demand upon police time and manpower by miscellaneous services are amenable to accurate prediction concerning amount, hourly, daily and seasonal variation, and the geographical distribution. With this type of information it becomes possible to deploy equipment and personnel resources with great economy and effectiveness. In this manner, administration moves into its problems on a scientific basis, supplanting guesswork and haphazard methods of management.

Perhaps one reason for the lack of planning in the field of police administration is the great effort required and the lack of managerial ability to sustain such effort; another is because the basic data necessary for estimates and planning may be inadequate or not available at all. The extent and quality of police intelligence or administrative data depend upon the character and administration of the police record system. Extensive planning, administrative as well as operational, is one of the most critical needs of the police today. There are not many police chief executives who disagree with this, but few have taken positive steps to encourage or implement such planning although the number is increasing. This failure puts the burden on individual subordinates who must plan for their own operations without administrative direction and support, usually on a crisis basis (see figure 15–1).

Figure 15–1

Types of Planning

- Operational.
- Strategic.
- Procedural.
- Tactical.
- Fiscal.
- Management.
- Program.

Understandably, the failure of the police chief executive to provide for planning indicates to subordinates that planning is considered to be unimportant or there is no interest in how they perform their work. The first tends to encourage the subordinate to adopt the same attitude toward planning; the second lowers morale and efficiency. Neither contributes positively to the effectiveness of police operations. When the police chief executive does take steps to establish a planning unit or to assign administrative planning responsibilities, problems can develop if a clear delineation is not drawn concerning the relationship between the planning unit and other agency personnel. Planning personnel may feel removed from operations personnel and operations personnel may feel they have been relieved of all planning duties. It should be clear that the police chief executive must provide proper direction and an atmosphere encouraging operational planning throughout the agency. The first step should be the formation and dissemination of a strong and unequivocal policy statement expressing commitment to planning and to positive change.

It should be equally clear that the chief has a responsibility to provide the organizational structure and the staffing necessary to generate a full spectrum of effective planning for the organization. When a product is primarily the result of personal effort, its quality usually corresponds to the qualifications, training, attitudes, and personality of those who contributed to the effort. Police planning is no exception.

The purposes of planning vary considerably but at the very least include:

- Improved organizational flexibility.
- Goal attainment.
- A frame of reference for decisions.
- Involvement of personnel.
- Creation of indicators for measurement of performance.
- Determination of needs.
- Problem identification.[4]

---

4. Harry W. More and Michael E. O'Neill, *Contemporary Criminal Justice* *Planning*, Springfield, IL, Charles C. Thomas, Publisher, 1984, p. 14.

Planning can be formal or informal, structured or haphazard, painstakingly thought-out or completed on the spur of the moment, whatever its form, planning takes place in every police agency. The planning needs of each police agency are different, and the needs are not static. Obviously the large agency serving a densely populated urban area has different needs than the small agency serving a sparsely populated rural area. The newly created agency in a jurisdiction of rapid growth will normally have needs different from those of a long-established agency of equal size in a relatively stable jurisdiction.

Both the large urban agency and the small rural agency will find their planning needs altered as a result of changed demography in land use and in the nature, type, or rate of crime. Planning requirements of the agency experiencing rapid growth will vary as the growth and expansion within the jurisdiction accelerate; and those of the older agency will change if its once-stable community begins to fluctuate. Whatever the specific planning needs of an agency, there are general goals and objectives. No police function can be justified when it is not intended to further the goals of the agency, and planning is no exception. Providing assistance to the police chief executive who determines and forms agency goals, and then develops plans to further them, is really what planning is all about. No police agency can afford to remain static while the community is changing. Yesterday's plan may have only historical value today; a continual, critical re-evaluation of all existing plans, and an updating as needed, is essential to the furthering of agency goals. Each plan, to be of the most value to agency personnel, must be suitably recorded and made available to those concerned with its implementation. This record should be constantly updated.

The success of any plan lies in the success of its implementation; a good plan poorly executed is as ineffective as a poor plan. A plan is similar to an insurance policy—although there might be one to cover every occasion, it can remain on a shelf for years, and no one will know how well it will serve until the time arrives to use it. Each plan should include preparation for implementation, and each should provide for continuous planning throughout implementation giving assistance in adapting the plan to existing conditions.

Planning cannot take place in a vacuum. To be useful, it must be based on current information. The agency planning function should include continual gathering of information, organization of this information into a usable format, and distribution of information to all agency personnel responsible for planning. A comprehensive plan should through the intelligent acquisition of information allow for a response strategy that takes into account contingencies.[5]

5. Gary A. Allgeyer, "Social Protest in the 1990s–Planning a Response," *Law Enforcement Bulletin,* January *1996,* Vol. 65, No. 1, pp. 2–8.

Agency policy on planning, in addition to establishing the goals and objectives of the effort, should emphasize that planning cannot be a one-time activity; it should be an ongoing activity contributing to the guidance of the agency toward its goals and objectives. No area of planning, administrative or operational, can be neglected without jeopardizing the police function. Adequate guidance cannot be given to agency personnel if any phase of administrative planning—long range, fiscal, or other management planning—is not kept current. Long-range planning is intended to provide aid in establishing the scope and focus of agency goals, and in devising the means of accomplishing major projects of long duration.

Long-range planning involves building upon past experience by gathering, organizing, and interpreting data; forecasting future needs by analyzing public attitudes and values; making predictions on the basis of current trends; and offering ideas and suggestions for improvement through change. Many of the bases for long-range decisions are subject to variations, most of which are beyond police control. An effective, continual, long-range planning program will permit detection of these changes and corresponding modification of agency scope or focus. If, for example, an agency embarked on a long-range plan to establish a vice unit, and the state enacted legislation legalizing gambling, some modification of the plan would be necessary. Whether the plan should be abandoned, or continued with an emphasis on regulation, can be determined only with additional planning. Lack of continual long-range planning can result in misdirected effort.

Strategic planning has become increasingly important, as there has been a strong movement toward improving service to the public. As this type of planning has become more prevalent police managers have seen fit to synthesize this process so it is compatible with related types of planning. The Los Angeles Police Department developed a five-year plan that contained 10 goals and 27 strategic priorities in order to improve service to the community, take into consideration personnel needs, and improve the organizational structure of the department. As part of this process it was determined that there was a need for a strategic planning and research unit to oversee and coordinate the Department's strategic planning efforts. This planning effort is being integrated into related systems such as budgeting and annual wok plans.[6]

Through fiscal planning the police chief executive can assure adequate financial support of agency functions. A continual fiscal planning program helps the police chief executive determine the necessity for fiscal readjustments to meet contingencies, reassess expenditure priorities throughout the fiscal year, and expedite budget preparation for the succeeding fiscal year. All other management planning

6. Los Angeles Police Department, *The Los Angeles Police Commission Reform Task Forces Draft Reports*, Los Angeles, Los Angeles Police Department, August 1998, p. 28.

must be continual as well. The need for evaluation or reevaluation, for discontinuing or modifying the old or for implementing the new, and for supplementary data upon which to make planning decisions, does not arise at regular intervals or at predictable or prearranged times. The relaxation of an entrance requirement by a civil service commission, the increase in the minimum hours for a course required by the state's standards and training commission, each be initiators of a need for planning in recruitment, training, and disciplinary procedures, respectively. Planning cannot satisfy those needs unless it is a continual program.

Operational planning is, in general, planning for action. For this reason, the individual officers should plan their own daily shift, the supervisor should plan the activities of the squad, and the watch commander should plan the activities of the particular watch. A police officer must realize the plans will be constantly subject to the changing pressures of new priorities as unforeseen circumstances develop; preparation should be made to plan continually to fulfill all responsibilities in a dynamic environment.

Specific operational plans are the work programs of line divisions and must be correlated with the nature and extent of the workload, and the availability of manpower and equipment. Nevertheless, workload and resource fluctuations exceeding those anticipated in contingency plans necessitate crisis planning, and in some cases, revision.

Procedural plans are those adopted as the standard method of action to be followed under given circumstances and are no less subject to the need for change. Few examples could illustrate more clearly how suddenly this need can arise and how pressing it can be than the United States Supreme Court decision in Miranda v. Arizona, 384 U.S. 436 (1966). This decision created the need for every police agency in the Nation to amend its standard operating procedures to include specific admonitions to subjects prior to in-custody interrogation. This decision, in fact, triggered not only operational planning, but administrative (training) and inter-discipline (police-prosecutor) planning as well.

Tactical plans are actions to be taken under specific conditions at specific locations and must be enlarged as similar conditions develop, or be modified as existing conditions change. If, for example, an agency maintains tactical plans for combating bank robberies at each of its banks, it would have to develop a new plan when a new bank opened for business, and it would have to modify the existing plan if a bank relocated its entrances or exits.

Every police agency, no matter how simple or complex its needs, should devise its planning program to include each of these types of planning. The program should include all administrative planning required to support the agency's operations, and it should include all operational planning required to insure adequate performance and the achievement of the agency's goals and objectives. Inasmuch as many police functions require action or assistance from persons or agencies outside the police agency or are affected by them, police planning must be coordinated with them. This, of course, injects a major variable into the planning process—one that is in large measure beyond the control of the police. The need for cooperative planning on a continual basis is apparent in jurisdictions with a large college campus, a large military installation, or a large convention or amusement center.

Police agencies are constantly in need of new administrative methods, new operational techniques, and new equipment to fulfill their responsibilities. Although many police agencies have neither the manpower nor the resources to undertake an in-depth research and development program, all agencies should encourage such programs by participating in them when possible and by taking advantage of the results. Only by firmly committing one's self to planning—by formulating and articulating policy, by implementing an adequate program, and by encouraging and supporting planning by personnel at all levels regardless of basic assignment—can the police executive be assured the agency will perform with increasing effectiveness in a changing environment.

Fiscal and Budgetary Service Units

The Administration Bureau in a police department is most apt to house a budget or fiscal unit. Figure 15–2 depicts the components of the Fiscal and Support Bureau (FSB) Bureau of the Los Angeles Police Department. This unit coordinates and manages the payroll, and facilities. It also provides fiscal service and information to the department. Additionally, the Bureau oversees fleet facilities, the crime laboratory, custody and control of evidence, and contract administration. It also coordinates and prepares the budget for the department. Finally, it assists in budget administration.[7] In the Miami Police Department a major commands Business Management that includes the budget unit, the property unit, permit/alarms, and the fleet service center.[8]

A police chief is not simply a crime fighter or a police officer of special and superior rank. The Chief is also a business manager who should accept full responsibility for fiscal management of the department. Moreover, there is the additional work as a fiscal planner, responsible for developing the future expenditure requirements for personnel, equipment, facilities, and programs necessary to accomplish agency missions, goals, and objectives. While there is an obligation to follow all prescribed procedures, where necessary, government officials should be urged to improve the jurisdiction's fiscal policies and prac-

7. Los Angeles Police Department, *Fiscal and Support Bureau,* Los Angeles, Los Angeles Police Department, 3/6/99, http://www.lapdonline.org/organization/fiscal_support_bureau/fiscal_support_ma-in.htm.

8. Correspondence from Major P.M. Shepard, Commander, Field Support Section, Miami Police Department, City of Miami, November 5, 1998.

tices, and the chief executive should seek to raise the level of fiscal management to achieve the mission, goals, and objectives established. The person in this role should not be passive, but proactive and progressive.

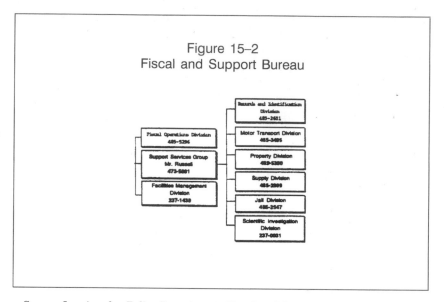

Figure 15–2
Fiscal and Support Bureau

Source: Los Angeles Police Department, *Fiscal and Support Bureau,* Los Angeles. Los Angeles Police Department, 3/6/99, http://www.lapdonline.org/organization/fiscal_support_bureau/fiscal_support_main.htm.

When the city administrator and the city council begin their task of allocating funds to all departments and units of government for the following fiscal year, the police chief will be in a highly competitive relationship with other municipal department heads. The council has difficult decisions to make and is concerned with effecting an appropriate allocation of limited resources according to public needs as expressed and demonstrated by various agency heads. Such decisions can never be precisely accurate or entirely acceptable to public constituencies, and the council is subject to many pressures.

Carefully developed budgets with adequate justification of all major items, especially on initial appearance in a budget document, are an important responsibility of the police chief executive. In view of typical limitations of revenue taking place in most local governments today, the police chief executive must be persuasive and objective with administrators and councilmen alike. It is imperative to demonstrate sound judgment in budget planning in order to gain acceptance of all recommendations. The budget document, as it leaves the office of the police chief, is the itemized monetary statement needed to initiate, maintain, or expand programs, functions, and activities of the police agency. Although the chief should not prepare the budget unassisted (except in very small police agencies), the responsibility for a sound fiscal document is a command function.

While the police chief may assign fiscal management tasks to subordinates, accountability for all aspects of the agency's fiscal policies, processes, and control remains with this officer. Within the framework of jurisdictional governmental structure, accountability is judged and its legislative body reviews practices by the jurisdiction's top executive and, ultimately, by its legislative body. Annually, before budget preparation begins, the chief executive of the city forwards a budget message to all agency heads. It is written in order to lay ground rules for budget preparation, establish time frames for the process (often in accordance with state law), explain the general financial condition of the city, detail how certain costs (such as personnel) are to be itemized, and set forth requirements for program justification. When properly prepared, it is of material assistance to the police chief in presenting the budget message to responsible police agency personnel.

Although budget preparation should be a matter of serious concern 12 months of the year, formal budget development usually is scheduled over a period of 6 to 8 months prior to the mandated budget adoption date. Certain budget review and presentation periods are established informally. The city council or the city executive may prescribe some, while state statutes or regulatory bodies require others. Table 15–1 illustrates a schedule of action periods and dates for a typical large city.

Table 15–1

Budget Preparation Calendar on Fiscal Year Basis

What Should Be Done	By Whom	On These Dates
Issue budget instructions and applicable forms	City Administrator	November 1
Prepare and issue budget message, with instructions and applicable forms, to unit commanders	Chief of Police	November 15
Develop unit budgets with appropriate justification and forward recommended budgets to planning and research unit	Unit Commanders	February 1
Review of unit budget	Planning and Research Staff with Unit Commanders	March 1
Consolidation of unit budgets for presentation to chief of police	Planning and Research Unit	March 15

Review of consolidated recommended budget	Chief of Police, Planning and Research Staff, and Unit Commanders	March 30
Department approval of budget	Chief of Police	April 15
Recommended budget forwarded to city administrator	Chief of Police	April 20
Administrative review of recommended budget	City Administrator and Chief of Police	April 30
Revised budget approval	City Administrator	May 5
Budget document forwarded to city council	City Administrator	May 10
Review of budget	Budget Officer of City Council	May 20
Presentation to council	City Administrator and Chief of Police	June 1
Reported back to city administrator	City Council	June 5
Review and resubmission to city council	City Administrator and Chief of Police	June 10
Final action on police budget	City Council	June 20

This schedule covers a span of eight months from inception to council approval. Ultimate responsibility for departmental budgets lies with the primary legislative body i.e. the city council. The mayor or manager, following extensive and prolonged preliminary discussions formally presents all department budgets. Finally, the budget is finalized, but even at this point certain modifications can be instituted. A very simple budget document is depicted in table 15–2 demonstrating a three year budgetary process.

By exercising the proper administration of fiscal controls, the police department fulfills its civic responsibility to provide prudent fiscal management of the taxpayers' money without neglecting the necessary level of police services expected by the community.

A system budgeting process, such as Planning Programming Budgeting System (PPBS), may offer advantages to large police departments. Such systems, however, are not universally applicable. Because of their cost and complexity, they must be studied carefully before complete or even partial adoption. Nevertheless, the police administrator should study and test all new budgetary methods. Occasionally a new procedure can be instituted to achieve departmental goals more effectively.

	Actual FY 96–97	Adopted FY 97–98	Estimated FY 97–98	Adopted FY 98–99
Table 15–2 Police Department Budget for Two Years				
POSITION RESOURCES				
PERMANENT				
Chief's Office—Administration	42.00	58.00	43.00	46.00
Police Grants	48.00	59.00	63.50	64.50
Field Services Bureau	595.00	552.00	553.00	583.00
Support Services Bureau	214.00	207.00	208.00	208.00
Investigative Services Bureau	240.00	278.00	278.00	290.00
Department Total	1,139.00	1,154.00	1,145.50	1,191.50
FINANCIAL RESOURCES				
Chief's Office—Administration	$ 2,062,825	$ 3,473,960	$ 2,478,399	$ 5,986,170
Police Grants	2,717,424	4,797,590	3,598,110	6,452,490
Forfeiture Funds Accounts	737,684	1,960,320	863,646	1,997,830
Field Services Bureau	29,001,911	28,676,060	28,147,812	30,824,230
Support Services Bureau	17,032,705	18,231,460	17,738,836	20,188,610
Investigative Services Bureau	13,431,071	14,726,980	15,479,448	15,882,470
Operating Total	64,983,620	71,866,370	68,306,251	81,331,800
Capital Improvements	515,707	7,601,700	7,283,993	5,616,700
Department Total	$65,499,327	$79,468,070	$75,590,244	$86,948,500

Source: City of Tucson, *Adopted Budget Operating Detail, Fiscal Year 1998–99,* Volume II, Tucson, City of Tucson, 1998, p. 149.

The concepts and practices of government budgeting have changed in the past few decades. Historically, budgeting has been control-oriented and this is the essence of the line item budget. Line item budgeting developed from an obvious need for expenditure accountability; its specific purpose was control. It remains the most common police budget system. In fact, it may be the only practical system in very small jurisdictions or in large ones when fiscal management talent is lacking. At the final hearing before the council, the mayor or manager may be supported by the police chief and, in large agencies annual budgets should be developed in cooperation with all major units within the department.

In police agencies large enough for functional organization (*i.e.,* requiring development of bureaus, divisions, or units), budget development should begin at the lowest, managerial level and should be a consolidation of all proposed unit budgets. Police managers and civilians of higher rank in large agencies should be involved and must assume responsibilities in budget development. Thus, in the staff of various administrative entities develop and justify unit budgets. In small agencies, watch or shift commanders should be involved in the budgetary process. Decisions are then made at each command level as the budget is processed. In very small agencies the chief may have sole responsibility for preparing the final budget. In larger ones with a planning unit, and perhaps even a fiscal officer, the unit or the officer should process recommendations and prepare the final document.

Police managers often complain about not receiving the necessary financial support to achieve their objectives and goals. However, those same managers seldom prepare budget requests with specific written justifications. Or if justifications are written, they are often poorly prepared. Detailed justifications for a budget item should include the reasons each item is needed. A police manager who recognizes a problem of needed financial support should prepare a written justification setting forth the need for the added expense. If possible, cost-effectiveness should be demonstrated. To identify problems, every police supervisor should inform an immediate superior of the need for additional personnel, equipment, or supplies if they are necessary. It is essential that every supervisor and every manager participate in determining budget needs. It may be helpful if participation extends to the lowest level in the hierarchy. Managers should prepare comprehensive justifications, but details such as projective costs of fringe benefits should be the responsibility of the fiscal affairs officer.

The police chief and top administrative staff should scrutinize division or bureau budget requests in order to assign priorities to items of the agency budget. The fiscal affairs officer should assist in the staff review by providing staff assistance to the police chief. Police agencies occasionally initiate new programs and then fail to evaluate them, especially on the basis of cost-effectiveness. A vigorous analysis of programs should be conducted periodically to evaluate program achievements and costs. As an exercise in determining priorities, police agencies should construct a budget at 80 percent of the current operating budget. To merely project a 20 percent across-the-board cut may not be the best way to cut costs and does nothing to establish priorities. Evaluation of programs for this exercise may suggest abandoning, reducing, or modifying activities within the hypothetical reduced budget. When the budget is reworked on a 100 percent basis, the new order of priorities may substantially influence it and provide essential support for top priority activities. It may result in a more efficient and effective police department.

Without adequate control over allocated funds, police agencies could run out of funds needed to carry out their programs. For this reason in addition to fiscal controls established by municipal controllers, police agencies should adopt well-designed fiscal controls to inform management of the status of the various salary, expense, and equipment accounts and take action, if necessary, to bring these accounts into balance.

One major department uses two important administrative tools for fiscal control—the Annual Work Program and the Expenditure Plan. The former reflects the planned production for the year, the total number of personnel performing the work, and relevant projected work units and statistics. The Expenditure Plan identifies the money allotted to each salary, expense, and equipment account for each of the thirteen 4-week periods of the fiscal year. At the completion of each allotment period actual expenditures are compared to the two model plans. This comparison reveals how closely the department is following projected fiscal planning. Unforeseen situations invariably arise where the need for additional police services cannot be anticipated by prior fiscal planning efforts; therefore, it is essential for interaccount transfers to be available to the police chief and major commanders. Examples of such situations range from additional funds needed to compensate for overtime expended during natural disasters or civil disturbances to funds needed to purchase material not authorized in the initial operating budget.

Line item budgeting is essentially cyclical budgeting. Its basic concern is with the next fiscal year and it is largely based on the current or previous year's budget. It provides great detail on the objects of expenditure and simplifies the comparison of one year's recommendations with the prior year's expenditures. Its use results in discrete additions to particular line items from year to year. It is neither performance nor program oriented. Its cyclical nature is both the key advantage and its key disadvantage. It does force—perhaps not too objectively—an annual review of expenditures with reasonable attention to functions, activities, and policies.

Line item budgeting also provides varying degrees of control over administrative products and work products, though it has a less effective control over the latter. It is usually effective in requiring budgeting on the basis of organizational units and specific items of expense. Because of its focus on particular aggregate expenditures to perform a service, line item budgeting is classed as one, which is input, oriented. On the other hand, there is a danger that it may tend to foreclose long-range planning. It may result in "getting by for another year" without consideration of, or action on, important expenditures and revenue needs of ensuing years.

Other problems confront the user of the line item budget, especially in charge jurisdictions. There is no provision, for example, for integrating planning, budgeting, and control. The item budgeting also makes it difficult to relate budgeting to objectives, and expenditures to accomplishments. Objective evaluation of alternative means of gaining prescribed objectives is impractical. It provides neither a sound basis for resource allocation nor a means of measuring the impact of current budget decisions on subsequent budgets. Finally, inherent in line item budgeting is a restriction on administrative flexibility with regard to on-going affairs; the police chief executive has little freedom to make even nominal changes in expenditure patterns and trends. While line item budgeting remains common practice particularly in small cities, it fails to support the concept of budgeting as an ongoing process.

In recent years increasing attention has been given to result-based budgeting. It involves the identification of indicators and specific performance measures. As simplistic as this may sound it is the intent of this approach is to improve performance. The intent of this accountability system is to improve the services that are provided by the agency. Historically emphasis in this area has been concerned with efficiency and effectiveness. More recently cost-benefit and return-on-investment measures have become increasingly important. Cost-benefit ratios compare the quantity of the benefit to the cost of the benefit (i.e. the cost to reduce response time by fifty percent).[9] Another area is the measurement of customer satisfaction. In Portland, Oregon, every two years the City of Portland has undertaken benchmark research to evaluate the community's perception of the work performed by the Portland Police Bureau. In conjunction with third-party researchers the 1994 survey results are used as a base line to track citizens' concerns regarding crime in their community, their level of involvement in public safety issues, and their attitudes toward the police.[10]

Tactical Units

Special operations are limited to the execution of temporary plans for the attack upon specific problems and emerging situations that arise at particular or irregular intervals. They are concerned with the execution of short-term plans designed to cope with critical situations of a temporary nature in order to permit an overwhelming concentration of striking power at a particular time and place to meet a specific problem. In a small department, such situations may develop only a few times during a month; their frequency increases with the increase in the population of a community. In an average city of from 100,000 to 200,000 populations, these operational crises may follow in comparatively rapid succession and require almost continuous provision for special deployment of manpower and equipment. Those departments where proper attention is given to special operational planning and execution can meet these crises as they arise without endangering the General Operations.

Routine duties occupy most of a police officer's time, and when these duties are carefully planned and the personnel properly supervised, they can be discharged with a considerable degree of success. There are times, however, when these daily activities must be interrupted, either briefly or for a long period, for the purpose of concentrating upon some problem demanding immediate action. Criminal emergencies, disasters, conflagrations, riots, mob situations, strike and

9. Mark Friedman, *A Guide to Developing and Using Performance Measures in Result–Based Budgeting,* Washington, DC, The Finance Project, May 1997, pp. 1–35.

10. City of Portland, *Portland Police Bureau On-line,* Portland, OR, 11/6/98, http://www.teleport.com/(police/index.html.

many other types of events occur when they are least expected. Accordingly, plans must be prepared in advance so the line resources of the department can be brought into play with dispatch at the time and the place where they are needed. A part of the force or the entire organization may be used to cope with the problem. The problems include such things as parades, meetings where there is a possibility of friction, visits by VIPs, athletic events, riots, strikes, fires, and disasters of any type. To this must be added any unusual or extensive criminal activity, unusual traffic or vice conditions. Increased criminal activities by one or more persons may lead to an emergency situation, which continues until they are apprehended. As a result of their activity, there is created during the hours and in the areas in which they operate a need for police service out of proportion to the year-around average.

These special situations require an orderly diversion of the uniformed force of the department in sufficient amount to bring about elimination of the problem. Members of the Tactical Unit are under normal conditions patrolling beats, or carrying out the routine work of their regular positions in the detective, traffic or other divisions, but subject to mobilization at a moment's notice for assignment on a special tactical operation. The number of officers actually engaged in a tactical operation at any one time will vary from one to a hundred or more, depending upon the nature of the problem. In the larger departments, the uninterrupted succession of emergencies may require the maintenance of one or more tactical units or mobile striking forces on a semi-permanent or permanent basis. The entire line strength of the organization may be involved, and in certain types of emergencies in the felony classification, police departments over a large area may be alerted into action where the perpetrator has escaped from the scene of the crime.

Strategy calls for audacity. Deployment of personnel on a tactical operation means a temporary reduction in the strength of beat patrol and other line units for the purpose of dynamic offensive tactics. A skeleton patrol will have to suffice until the objectives are achieved. Obviously, this is attended with some danger, but nevertheless it must be done in certain instances if the police are to fulfill their obligations. It is utterly impossible to assume the police can solve all the problems presented to them by merely placing the men on beats; therefore, they know a reasonable amount of ground may be lost while giving attention to one specific problem. By gradually clearing up one after another of these special situations they can, after a period of time, reduce the number of complaints received.

Tactical Unit personnel should be carefully selected on the basis of their personal qualities and performance records. The nature of the work may require moral courage, together with physical courage and endurance of a high order. Training is essential and there is a trend to cross-train members of a tactical unit.[11] This unit should be so organized and equipped that it can be moved rapidly from one point to another. Thus, its power may be felt at one place at one time, and then at a different place at another time, whenever this becomes necessary. The operational pattern of the tactical unit is seldom the same on any two assignments, and will depend entirely upon the nature and dimensions of the emergency problem or situation toward which its attention is directed at the moment. Police emergencies can be classified into two major categories and they are listed in figure 15–3.

Figure 15–3

Categories of Police Emergencies

- **Man-made emergencies.**
  - a. Criminal.
  - b. Traffic.
  - c. Vice.
  - d. Jail.
  - e. Riot.
  - f. Mob situations.
  - g. Disorderly crowds.
  - h. Labor disorders.
  - i. Gangs.
  - j. Other.
- **Natural.**
  - a. Earthquake.
  - b. Conflagration.
  - c. Flood.
  - d. Tornado.
  - e. Hurricanes.
  - f. Storms.
  - g. Other.

Criminal emergencies command the major share of the attention of the police in the conduct of tactical operations. The number and variety of situations in this category (calling for the emergency concentration of police striking power) cover the total range of the criminal spectrum. In the approach to criminal emergencies, the tactical commander must have the facts concerning the character, extent, location and time of occurrence of crimes and other incidents requiring police action. With this information available, the officer can identify police hazards, isolate the particular elements requiring attention, and personally direct the energies of the commanded force toward a solution of the problems at hand. Armed with pertinent data supplied by the crime analysis unit concerning the factors (character, extent, location, time) that the problem involves, the operations commander is in a position to launch programs to lower the crime rate. Effort may be directed at

---

11. Thomas Strentz, "Cross–Trained Versus Cross Qualified," *Law and Or- der,* October 1998, Vol. 46, No. 10, pp. 113–114.

resident burglaries in one section of the community, at car thefts in another, or at armed robberies during certain hours of the day. The particular groups or types of persons who are committing crimes are determined by analyses of the age, race, sex, residence and other characteristics.

In many cities, when the police emergency involves criminal activity cities have created SWAT Teams to handle such situations as hostage rescue or barricaded suspects. In other instances when SWAT officers are not engaged in a critical incident response they will sometimes work in two officer unmarked patrol vehicles. In this capacity they self-initiate felony arrests, stop and detain suspicious individuals and augment general and respond to calls for service. In the San Jose Police Department there is a Mobile Emergency Response Group and Equipment unit (M.E.R.G.E.) that is commanded by a lieutenant. Additionally, there are two sergeants who each supervise ten officers. When a critical incident or hazardous situation occur e.g. hostage situation, barricaded suspect, sniper or dangerous search warrant the unit responds and uses its highly trained personnel to handle the situation. The officers of this specialized unit engage in a rigorous training schedule that includes hazardous building searches, hostage rescue, crowd control, weapons training and sniper deployment. This unit also provides VIP protection when dignitaries visit the city.[12]

It has been estimated that there are approximately 1,714 departments with SWAT team in cities with 50,000 or more population. [13] There is a trend for smaller and medium-sized police departments to contract for SWAT service from larger departments because of the high cost of equipping and maintaining such teams.[14] An organization that is involved in the training of SWAT officers is the National Tactical Officers Association (NTOA). It has numerous training programs that are concerned with tactical operations, and high risk patrol officer response to critical incidents. Figure 15–4 lists some of the specialized courses taught that NTOA offers through its regional training program. One of the courses familiarizes students with the elements of high risk warrant service and another with explosive breaching capability. Another course deals with the use of noise flash diversionary devices.

12. San Jose Police Department, *The San Jose PD M.E.R.G.E. Unit,* San Jose, CA San Jose Police Department, 10/10/98, http:// www.sjpd.org/merge/html.

13. John Hoffmann, "Is There Too Much SWAT? Or is Criticism Unwar- ranted," *Law and Order,* September 1998, Vol. 46, N0. 9, pp. 75–80.

14. Robert L. Snow, *Swat Teams: Explosive Face-off with America's Deadliest Criminals,* New York, NY, 1996, p. 290.

Figure 15–4

Training Areas of the National Tactical Officers
Association (NTOA)

- Negotiations.
- Tactics.
- SWAT Management
- Tactical Firearms.
- Specialty Munitions.
- Explosives and Explosive Breaching.
- High Risk Patrol Operations.
- Specialty Courses

Source: Correspondence from Marsha J. Martello, National Tactical Officers Association, dated November 9, 1998.

Community Crime Prevention Units

Police departments are expending considerable effort on preventing crime. This involves a wide range of activities from the prevention of juvenile delinquency to neighborhood programs to preventing violence. Table 15–3 lists some of the specialized units the police have, to address juvenile and community problems. Ninety-eight percent of the departments responding to a survey have community crime prevention units. Also 95 percent of the agencies give drug prevention programs in schools, and there are 86 percent that have a specialized unit addressing delinquency. Additionally, 80 percent of the departments have child abuse units, and 74 percent have units dealing with missing children.[15]

Table 15–3

Types of Specialized Units
in Municipal Police Departments

Type of special unit	Percent of large departments
Community crime prevention	98%
Drug education in schools	95
Juvenile delinquency	86
Child abuse	80
Missing children	74
Drunk drivers	66
Gangs	76
Prosecutor relations	54
Domestic violence	53
Repeat offenders	41
Bias-related crimes	56
Victim assistance	46
Environmental crimes	20

---

15. *Op. cit.,* p. xiv.

Source: Brian A. Reaves and Pheny Z. Smith, *Law Enforcement Management and Administrative Statistics, 1993: Data for Individual State and Local Agencies with 100 or More Officers*, Washington, D.C., Bureau of Justice Statistics, September, 1995, p. xiv.

Departments have different ways of organizing crime prevention entities. In some departments there is a juvenile division under field operations. In others, juvenile units are under criminal investigation. In Miami, FL, the police department has domestic battery and domestic violence units in the Investigations Division. In the bureau of Investigations of the San Jose Police Department there are units for family violence, gang investigations, and assaults/juvenile. Additionally, in the Community Services Division one can find a crime prevention unit. In the Los Angeles Police Department there is a juvenile services group that is further broken down into a juvenile division and Drug Abuse Resistance Education (DARE).[16]

The prevention of crime is a fundamental responsibility of the patrol force. The preventive role of the individual patrol officer is a basic element of modern police service. The mere presence of a properly organized and efficiently operating patrol force is conceded to be one of the greatest crime deterrents thus far developed by organized society. The efficiency of the individual beat patrol officer is reflected in large measure by the amount of crime and delinquency reported in the assigned patrol area. A point is reached in the growth of a community and its police department when, due to increased juvenile caseload, the

16. Los Angeles Police Department, *Juvenile Services Group,* Los Angeles, CA, Los Angeles Police Department, 1/30/99, http://www.lapdonline.org/organization/operations_hq_bureau/ju /juvenile_services_group.htm.

preventive role of the patrol officer must be supplemented by specialized assistance. In recognition of this principle, the crime prevention or juvenile unit has become a standard feature of American police organization and practice.

The establishment of a new service unit for such a purpose in the department requires a determination of its personnel strength and involves drawing upon the personnel of an existing unit, usually the patrol division, or recruiting from the outside. Some departments allocate a minimum of five percent of the departmental strength to crime prevention work. This means the police administrator with a force of twenty officers should assign at least one to work primarily on juvenile cases. In smaller departments where such specialized assignment is unjustified, members of the patrol force must assume the responsibilities of the task.

Two general types of operations are observable in modern police practice. The distinction is determined largely by the procedural patterns employed in the disposition of juvenile cases. In the first type of operation the police function primarily as an agency of discovery and referral.[17] Juvenile cases are referred to the juvenile court, to the welfare department, or to some other social agency or agencies in the community and the disposition of the case rests with them.

Wherever this type of operation prevails, the police have very largely abdicated their obligations and responsibilities in the project of delinquency and crime prevention. In a more professional and enlightened approach, the police juvenile unit assumes responsibility for the disposition of a substantial number of juvenile offenders and beginning behavior deviation cases coming to the attention of the department. Here, the law enforcement function is augmented by a clinical approach to the adjustment of behavior difficulties. In the larger departments, the juvenile unit should be staffed with trained social workers who are graduates of an accredited Graduate School of Social Work, and who are schooled in the application of casework skills and techniques. In smaller departments where the caseload would justify the assignment one or two officers may be assigned to this type of work. Normally the agency will be able to arrange for technical assistance from others in the community, where this is indicated.

In one department the mission of a juvenile division is to provide information, training, evaluation, and auditing of juvenile policies and procedures. It also actively pursues eradication of the abuse and sexual exploitation of children. The mission also includes working to eliminate the sale, purchase, and use of narcotics. Toxic substances, and alcohol by juveniles. In fulfilling this mission the juvenile division identified a number of goals that are set forth in Figure 15–5. These goals ranged

17. Lawrence J. Szynkowski, "Preventive Patrol: Traditional vs. Specialized," *Journal of Police Science and Administration,* June 1981, Vol. LI, No 2. p. 167.

from auditing activities to increasing the issuance of juvenile truancy citations.

Figure 15–5

Goals for a Juvenile Division

- Ensure the backlog of child physical and sexual abuse investigations is no greater than five percent of all reports assigned to the Abused Child Unit (ACU), and ensure each investigation is completed within 60 days.
- Ensure that the clearance rate for those cases investigated by the ACU is at least 95 percent and the case filing rate is at least 85 percent.
- Increase detective-initiated arrests of juveniles involved in the trafficking and /or use of illegal drugs, narcotics, alcohol, or inhalants by 10 percent.
- Increase the issuance of juvenile truancy citations by eight percent.
- Meet with Area Community–Police Advisory Boards and area personnel to identify juvenile narcotics and related problems and to support the areas' problem-solving efforts.
- Increase by 25 percent the number of department-wide audits of juvenile operations.
- Develop and implement a computer database listing all active departmental explorers.
- Implement a 24–hour juvenile advisement desk.
- Provide coordination and direction to geographic bureaus and areas in order to provide safer parks for families and children.
- Facilitate the development of a Family Violence Detail (FVD) in each geographic area.

Los Angeles Police Department, *Juvenile Mission Statement and Goals,* Los Angeles, CA, Los Angeles Police Department, 1/30/99. http://www.lapdoline.org/orgainzxation/operations_hq_bureau/juvenile_s juvenile_mission.ht.

Since the early part of this decade police departments have given increasing attention to the enforcement of truancy laws. Many earlier efforts were sporadic and unsustained, unlike more recent programs proving successful.

In accordance with police and school policies, truant students can be:

- Released to parent.
- Returned to school.
- Returned home.
- Arrested.
- Cited.
- Placed in a shelter.
- Other.

In Los Angeles a city ordinance is the basis for truancy enforcement during the hours from 0830 to 1330. Fines for violating the ordinance range from $50. to $250., and a mandatory penalty assessment ranges from $85. to $425. Alternatives to the fines include performing 60 days of truancy free school attendance or performing 20 hours of community service under the supervision of the Juvenile Traffic Court. To ensure the success a collaborative task force was created that included the police department, the Juvenile Traffic Court, and the school district. Based on an evaluation of the program there was increased attendance of 2.62 percent at the middle school and 2.58 percent at the high school level. Although the increase in attendance was somewhat small it increased funding to the school district by $20 million based on average daily attendance. Additionally, there was a reduction of daytime crimes by 27.1 percent as compared to a similar period of time. The implementation of this truancy program clearly made to community safer.[18]

In San Jose, California the city has been operating a curfew law for four years and during three years of operation there has been a 24 percent drop in the number of juveniles victimized during the curfew hours. This program operates Thursdays to Sundays with a sergeant, 12 officers, a clerk, counselors and volunteers. The ordinance allows for nine reasonable curfew excuses. These include being on the sidewalk of their home or the residence next door to going on an errand for a parent or guardian without a detour. With a youth his stopped who does not have a valid excuse he or she are taken to one of three all-night community centers. There the youth is logged in, interviewed by a volunteer and a computer check is made to see if the youth has a juvenile record. Parents are notified and asked to come to the center and pick up the youth.[19]

In the Sheriff's Community Oriented Programs & Enforcement (S.C.O.P.E.) of the Santa Clara Sheriff's Office the team manages a comprehensive truancy enforcement program. Team members interact directly with the families of the truant referred by the school. The success rate of getting students to attend school is high. The team also manages a mentoring program, in which youth at risk are assigned to a Deputy Sheriff and the primary mission is to create a positive role model for the youth. The program stresses ethics, self worth and continued education. Another program addressing the problems of youths is the Sheriff's Teen Youth Leadership Education program (STYLE). It is a comprehensive combination of classroom instruction and community service, directed toward teenage youth at risk. The course is designed to develop leadership qualities, ethics, self worth, character, and help the youth to recognize the importance of preparing,

18. Bernard C. Park and Ben Gonzalez, "Truancy Citations and Crime Reduction," *The Police Chief,* August 1998, Vol. LXV, No. 8, pp. 41–46.

19. Dick Cox, "Curfews: Benefits or Bad News?" *Law and Order,* December 1998, Vol. 46, No. 12, pp. 87–90.

in positive ways, for the future. The team is also active in anti-gang initiatives and dealing with graffiti.[20]

There are many different community programs addressing particular community needs. Usually these programs are totally or in part functions performed by a police agency. They are aimed at reducing a particular problem or advising a segment of the population about a specified program. Community services can be in the form of informational activities, crime prevention seminars, or traffic safety education. Some examples of community services projects are:

- Neighborhood watch (burglary prevention).
- Operational identification (marking of personal property).
- Security surveys (business and residential).
- Robbery survival/prevention.
- Rape/assault prevention.
- Child molestation/abuse prevention (good-touch/bad-touch).
- Traffic safety education programs (occupant protection, STOP-D.W.I., pedestrian and bicycle safety).
- Halloween safety.
- Operation D.A.R.E. (drug abuse resistance program).[21]
- Police activities league.
- Child fingerprinting.
- Departmental appearances, tours, and presentations.
- Systematic community-based supervision.[22]

Projects such as these provide a law enforcement agency with two unique opportunities. First, to assist the department in reducing crime and traffic crashes and second, to enhance the agency's image and reputation. Both opportunities are compatible with police department objectives and part of a good public affairs program. The National Crime Prevention Council works to enable people to prevent crime and build safer, more caring communities. They suggest the police and sheriffs are where people generally look first for help in preventing crime. The Council points out that law enforcement focuses on helping neighborhoods solve problems interfering with security and well being, not just responding when trouble has already struck. The police have the facts about the crime situation and can help pick effective preven-

20. Santa Clara County Sheriff's Office, *Sheriff's Community Oriented Programs & Enforcement,* San Jose, CA, 10/12/98, http://claraweb.co.santa_clara.ca.us/sheriff/scope/htm.

21. Arthur G. Sharp, "Is DARE a Sacred Lamb?" *Law and Order,* April 1998, Vol. 46, No. 4, 42–47; and John W. Hough, "DARE: An Opponent's View," *Law and Order,* April 1998, Vol. 46, No.

4, pp. 48–50, and Charles A. Gruber, "A Positive Evaluation of DARE," *Law and Order,* April 1998, Vol. 46, No. 4, p 52.

22. George O'Rourke, "Coordinated Agency Network–Fighting Crime and Combating Juvenile Delinquency," *The Police Chief,* August 1998, Vol. LXV, No. 8, PP. 48–50.

tion strategies. The Council has posters, educational kits, and booklets to help people prevent crime and build a safer community. Community policing and its implications for both the community and the police are discussed in detail in Chapter 4.[23]

Traffic Enforcement and Control

The traffic problem is not limited to the larger cities. The officials of local government in towns, communities and the smaller cities have long since been met with the necessity of facing up to the problems of a smooth flowing traffic stream, the matter of life and safety, traffic accidents, parking and congestion. It would be extremely difficult to find a community, no matter how small, not presented with a traffic problem in some degree. Traffic regulation and control in small and medium-sized communities has now become big business. The problem has been compounded to the point where the application of the principles of sound traffic management is now mandatory.

In 1997 there were 43,200 motor-vehicle deaths and 2,300,000 injuries. This degree of human mayhem and suffering is beyond belief and because of its enormity it demand the attention of very progressive police manager.[24]

Organization. As suggested earlier, the function of traffic regulation and control is basically a responsibility of the patrol force. However, the necessity appears very early in the growth of a police organization, when the traffic caseload exceeds the capacity of the patrol force. Then provision must be made for specialized assistance and the assignment of one or more officers to full-time duty for studying traffic problems and creating plans for their solution. From such a beginning, the specialized traffic unit has become a conventional fixture in the average American police department.

Properly managed by individuals possessing the necessary skills and information, it can lead to the formation of a police traffic program approaching the problems associated with traffic accidents, traffic flow and congestion. Although located in the line, the traffic unit should be regarded primarily as a planning agency. It is an administrative error to give it large field strength and to clothe it with exclusive responsibility for carrying its plans into execution. Such administrative action is the function of the commanding officer in charge of field operations. With the total line resources of the department available, a traffic unit is then in a position to bring to bear upon the problem a degree of power altogether impossible where the traffic line function is exclusively a responsibility of one unit.

Typical of the current response to traffic enforcement is to accept an organizational response allowing for a moderate degree of specializa-

23. Correspondence from Susan Birrell, National Crime Prevention Council, Washington, D.C., dated July 27, 1992.

24. National Safety Council, *Accident Facts,* Chicago, IL, 12/30/98, http://www.nsc.org/gen/informa.htm.

tion. For example, the San Jose Police Department locates its specialized traffic enforcement unit within a special operations division (part of the bureau of field operations). Unique to this unit is a special detail for cruise management that has been a perennial problem in that city. The traffic investigations unit is located in the bureau of investigations and investigates fatal and hit-and-run accidents. It also prepares D.U.I. cases for court, and assists in unlicensed/suspended drivers license prosecution.

The traffic enforcement unit conducts traffic safety programs, provides traffic control, and investigates traffic accidents. The third unit is the parking regulation unit. Its responsibilities include the enforcement of parking meters/regulations. It also provides abandoned vehicle enforcement, and expired vehicle registration enforcement. Auto theft investigation is a unit under vehicular crimes and is located in the Bureau of Investigation.[25]

Police traffic units, in numerous cities, engage in a range of activities other than typical traffic education and enforcement activities. One of these is a city of 50,000 on the pacific coast, where during summer weekends its population can double. This unit performs the following functions:

- Regular patrol duty.

- Crime deterrence and prevention.

- Serves as backup units.

- Provides general assistance.

- Answers calls for service.

- Administers the school-crossing program.

- Schedules officers for special events such as parades, marches, and festivals.

Analysis of accidents and congestion, according to time, place, and nature, form the basis for selective enforcement procedures and makes possible the application of the line resources of the department when and where the need is greatest, and where they will accomplish the best results. In recent years a wide range of techniques, procedures and technology have been applied to improve law enforcement's response to the traffic problem. Increasingly available are such things as in-vehicle videos, mobile data terminal, and notebook and clipboard computer systems. Figure 15–6 lists four main goals for law enforcement to advance in delivering improved traffic services. Under each goal are several objectives essential for success.

25. Correspondence with Lt. Dave Kiniller, San Jose Police Department, San Jose, CA, dated November 6, 1998.

Figure 15–6

Goals for Traffic Law Enforcement for the 21st Century

- To improve quality of life issues for police traffic services through:
  - a. Crash reduction.
  - b. Criminal interdiction as a by-product of efficient enforcement.

- To improve the public and official perception of the advantages of police traffic services in crime control and crash and injury management through:
  - a. Police outreach.
  - b. Proactive approach to enforcement.
  - c. Traffic-related performance measures for enforcement personnel.
  - d. Improvement of public perception.
  - e. Better use of local data to measure quality-of-life issues and link them to crash and injury management issues.

- To use state-of-the-art management and training techniques, technology, research, innovation, information and evaluation to enhance the quality of police traffic services through:
  - a. Increased management and leadership training for law enforcement executives and mid-level managers.
  - b. Improved relationships between law enforcement and media.
  - c. Sharing information.
  - d. Exploring and securing alternative funding.

- To be proactive in identifying and adjusting to traffic safety issues and their relationship to other policing issues through:
  - a. Data management.
  - b. Community involvement.
  - c. Interagency cooperation and information sharing.
  - d. Internal and external education and training.

National Highway Traffic Safety Administration, *Police Traffic Services in the 21st Century,* Washington, DC, Department of Transportation, 3/11/99, pp. 1–4. http://www.nhtsa.dot.gov/people/outreach/safesobr/16qp/century.html.

Point System. Upon conviction for a traffic offense in a court of law, the state concerned records this event upon the record of the violator. With subsequent convictions on traffic offenses, the process is repeated until a point is reached where the driving record of the individual suggests suspension or revocation of the driving privilege. In this effective system for driver control, the state licensing authority maintains a central file of all resident drivers. When drivers lose their license in one state and move to another, the shadow continues to follow that person. A central national file contains the names of all licensees whose driver's license has been suspended or revoked. This information is available to all cooperating states. In California, the point system provides for the allocation of either one or two points for a violation and one point for an accident. Suspension or revocation of a driver's license to operate a motor vehicle is warranted when the total points accumulated are more than four, six or eight violations in one, two and three years respectively.[26]

Enforcement Index. Most authorities hold that an arrest index, which shows the ratio of traffic citations to injury accidents, is useful in maintaining a suitable level of enforcement and assuring its uniform application at the locations and during the hours as indicated by the

26. State of California, *Vehicle Code 1991,* Sacramento, CA, Department of Motor Vehicles, 1992, pp. 403–404.

records. The number of citations divided by the injury accidents gives the enforcement index.:

$$\text{EI} = \frac{\text{Number of convictions with penalties for hazardous offenses}}{\text{Number of fatal and personal injury accidents}}$$

An enforcement index of 20:1 is a balancing point and indicates some areas and their accident problems may warrant more activity and that in others slightly less than 20:1 may be satisfactory. The ideal EI for a specific jurisdiction is attained when an increase in enforcement actions does not reduce the accident rate, while less effort will result in a continued increase in accidents.

Driving Under the Influence. Driving Under the Influence. The most serious traffic violation, in most instances, is "driving under the influence," whether it is induced by alcohol or by drugs. In recent years, interest groups such as Mothers Against Drunk Drivers (MADD) and Students Against Drunk Drivers (SADD) have had a tremendous influence on state legislators. The results are laws allowing courts to incarcerate offenders for increasing lengths of time. Nearly one half of all fatal accidents involve one or more intoxicated individuals. DWI however, is no longer an acceptable way of life. With sustained enforcement efforts, it is anticipated there will be a significant reduction in the number of deaths caused by this type of driver. For the most part public opinion supports active law enforcement programs eliminating the intoxicated driver from the road. DWI arrests are becoming increasingly frequent as greater attention is given to this serious problem. During 1996 approximately 1,463,300 individuals were arrested in the United States for driving while intoxicated.[27] In fact drinking drivers have fostered a whole range of business from attorneys (who advertise on television) to companies preparing training films for DWI offender classes.

Officers should look for the following indicators of impairment during initial contact:

- Odor of alcoholic beverages or other drugs (i.e. marijuana, hashish, some inhalants).

- Bloodshot eyes.

- Alcohol containers or drug paraphernalia.

- Fumbling fingers.

- Slurred speech.

- Admission of drinking or drug user.

- Inconsistent responses.

27. Lawrence A. Greenfield, *Alcohol and Crime–An Analysis of National Data on the Prevalence of Alcohol In-* *volvement in Crime,* Washington, DC, Bureau of Justice Statistics, 1998, p. vi.

When an officer's suspicion is raised, further investigation should take place The officer should require the motorist to take a sobriety test. The number and nature of tests will vary from the time but it is recommended that the Standardized Field Sobriety Test (SFST) should be administered:

- Horizontal Gaze Nystagmus Test

- Walk–and–Turn Test

- One–Leg–Stand Test

After the completion of the SFST, the officer may use a portable breath-testing device (PBT), if permissible in that jurisdiction. The PBT device measures blood alcohol content for evidentiary purposes before an individual can be arrested for driving while intoxicated (DWI). The arrestee is required to exhale into a device, chemically analyzing the presence of alcohol in the breath. One device is designed so it does not use chemicals or gases and operates with a selected narrow-band infrared energy that is passed through a sample chamber alternately filled with ambient air and breath. The infrared energy is absorbed in proportion to the alcohol concentration. The analysis is then displayed digitally and a printout can be generated for a permanent record. In most jurisdictions the breath analysis test is utilized solely as a screening instrument. If a motorist refuses to take a breath analysis test, most jurisdictions empower the officer to arrest the driver on suspicion of intoxication. In several states the refusal to take a field test can result in the suspension of the driver's license.

After the arrest and transportation of the motorist to the police station or medical facility, medical personnel can take samples of the arrestee's blood or urine. Analysis of the sample by a laboratory determines the presence and degree of concentration of alcohol or drugs. In some agencies the motorist who is arrested for DWI is recorded on videotape, which many courts accept as evidence, and the tape has proven to be convincing court evidence.

Sobriety Check Points. The stopping of motorists at checkpoints is a police technique used for years although in many jurisdictions it has been limited to vehicle safety inspections. More recently it has been utilized throughout the nation for the purpose of identifying drivers who are "under the influence." Currently, 38 states and the District of Columbia conduct sobriety checkpoints. These checkpoints involve the stopping of every vehicle or a specified sequence of vehicles at a predetermined, fixed location to detect impaired drivers. Sobriety checkpoints allow officers to stop vehicles without any suspicion of wrongdoing. To be judiciously acceptable, sobriety checkpoints must satisfy two general goals:

- The checkpoint should be reasonably effective in detecting and preventing impaired drivers.

- The checkpoint should be minimally intrusive to the motorist.

Successful sobriety checkpoint strategists advocate that this type of enforcement activity be integrated aggressively with a continuous, systematic public information and education effort. This approach maximizes the perception that motorists who operate a vehicle while impaired by alcohol or other drugs are apprehended. Sobriety checkpoints meeting acceptable standards include the following similar components:

- An ongoing program and departmental policy for deterring impaired drivers.

- Judicial support.

- Site selection, appropriate warning devices, and visible police authority.

- Chemical testing capabilities.

- Contingency planning and operations briefing.

- Extensive training on the latest detection and investigative techniques, including Drug Recognition Expert training, if available.

- Comprehensive data collection and an evaluation plan.

A written sobriety checkpoint plan outlines procedures for the activity is required under current judicial guidelines (Stitz v. Michigan Department of Public Safety) to minimize intrusion and officer discretion, as well as establish site selection and publicity. A major issue for the courts is site selection for the checkpoints. Law enforcement officers must consider arrest rates and impaired driver crash rates for that area and time of day. A key element to site selection is safety to both law enforcement officers and motorists. Checkpoints are labor intensive, and place exceptional demands upon law enforcement agencies. Consequently, sobriety checkpoints may not be right for every jurisdiction or community, but they do play an important part in community awareness of the impaired driver program.

Motor Vehicle Theft. In a victimization study it was found that there were 1,980,280 completed thefts of motor vehicles and 555,540 attempted thefts in 1996. Of those stolen, recoveries occurred in 62 percent of the cases. Losses from these thefts were more than 50 billion before reimbursement by insurance companies. In 29.6 percent of the time the theft of the vehicle was from a garage or a parking lot. Automobile thefts, whether attempted or completed most often occurred at night. Ironically, they occurred most often near the victim's home (18.4%) or on the street near the home. About 88.8 percent of the completed and 45.8 percent of the attempted motor vehicle thefts were reported to the police. Reporting rates increased with the value of the stolen vehicle. The most likely victims of completed or attempted motor vehicle thefts were from Black households rather than whites or households or other races. Additionally, Hispanics were more likely than non-Hispanics households to be victims of motor vehicle theft.[28] The highest rate of auto thefts was from those who had an annual income of $75,000 or more.[29]

Table 15–4 lists the number of motor vehicle thefts, from 1990 through 1996. The numbers are staggering and indicate the seriousness of the problem. During this period the number of thefts has decreased per 100,000 registered vehicles. While this is an improvement it is still a major problem. Law enforcement agencies investigated 1,131,119 automobile thefts and 14 percent of these were cleared by arrest. The vast majority of the thefts were for automobiles, but the statistics include trucks, vans, and motorcycles.[30] The clearance rate for motor vehicle theft has always been low.

Table 15–4

Motor Vehicle Registrations and Thefts in the U.S.
from 1990 Through 1996

Year	Number	Thefts per 100,000 registrations
1990	1,635,900	841
1991	1,661,700	853
1992	1,563,100	831
1993	1,564,800	789
1994	1,539,300	763
1995	1,472,400	717
1996	1,395,200	664

Source: Kathleen Maguire and Ann L. Pastore, Editors, *Sourcebook of Criminal Justice Statistics–1997*, Washington, DC, Bureau of Justice Statistics, 1998, p. 304.

Under the Motor Vehicle Theft Prevention Act of 1994 the U. S. Department of Justice has sponsored a national Watch Your Car Program. It allows owners of motor vehicles to voluntary display a decal or device, such as State-issued, customized license plate, on their vehicles to alert police that their vehicles are not normally driven between the hours of 1 a.m. and 5 a.m. There are two program conditions. Under the first condition, the owner may consent to have the car stopped if it is being operated during the designated hours. Under the second condition, the owner may consent to have the car stopped if it comes within one mile of a U.S. land border or international port.[31]

28. Michael Rand, *Criminal Victimization—1997, Changes 1996–97 with Trends 1993–97.*, Washington, DC, Office of Justice Programs, 1998, pp. 1–11.

29. Kathleen Maguire and Ann L. Pastore, Editors, *Sourcebook of Criminal Justice Statistics*, Washington, DC, Bureau of Justice Statistics, 1998, p. 355.

30. *Ibid., pp. 193–199.*

31. Nancy E. Gist, *The Watch Your Car Program*, Fact Sheet, Washington,

Hazardous Material Enforcement. It was not too long ago that hazardous materials were not even acknowledged as a law enforcement problem. Today it is. Frequently one can read in the newspaper, hear on the radio, or see on television, a report of traffic diversion. This occurs because of an unknown substance spill on a street. The concern for hazardous material places an additional burden on law enforcement. The Research and Special Programs Administration (RSPA), a component of the Department of Transportation is responsible for protecting the Nation adequately against the risks to life and property that are inherent in the transportation of hazardous materials in commerce.

This unit has published a guidebook describing the emergency procedures that should be followed when handling hazardous materials. This guidebook was developed jointly by the United States, Mexico, and Canada for use by firefighters, police, and other emergency service personnel. The manual (revised every three years) is especially useful because it provides guides for handling explosives and explains the calling procedure for assistance when there is a chemical spill.[32]

Police officers who deal with hazardous materials should be capable of:

- Developing an awareness of hazardous materials and the risks in handling such substances.

- Understanding what can happen when a material is a component of an emergency.

- Quickly identifying the specific or generic classification of the material(s) involved in an accident.

- Protecting themselves and the general public during the initial response phase of the incident.

There are numerous regulations that help prevent accidents involving the transportation of hazardous materials and to lessen the severity of an accident. It is the task of RSPA to determine compliance with safety regulations by inspecting entities that offer hazardous materials for transportation.

Case Study

Captain Elizabeth Carter

In the City of Tuftville Captain Elizabeth Carter is the head of the Special Operations Division that is part of the Bureau of Line Operations. She has been in this position for two years and has been in the police department for 13 years. She has previous experience in patrol, community services, and training. She is married, has two children and

DC, Office of Justice Programs, February 1998, pp. 1–4.

32. Office of Hazardous Materials Safety, *The North American Emergency Response Guidebook, 1966,* Washington, DC, Department of Transportation, 3/11/99, http://hazmat.dot.gov/gydebook.htm.

lives in the northwest part of the city. She is a graduate of the local university and has a master's degree in business management. The police department has 329 sworn officers and 77 civilians. There are three major divisions: line operation, administration, and investigations. Specialized units include a SWAT team, crime prevention, youth services, and, vice. In addition, officers are detailed to an area wide narcotics enforcement team.

The city has grown considerably over the past eight years, as has the traffic problem. Additionally, the city has an automotive assembly plant and considerable light industry. There are two major centers than attract shoppers from a wide area. The city government has a weak mayor and a very progressive city manager. Part I offenses have leveled off for the previous two years with the exception of auto thefts that have increased by 12.8 percent. The city has become a central dropping point for stolen vehicles that have been taken from nearby communities. It seems that when an older stolen vehicle is taken it is left in the city and the thief's steal a newer vehicle. During the past two years a chop shop ring has been closed down and 11 defendants were successfully prosecuted.

The community is up in arms over the large number of auto thefts. It seems that if a citizen parks a vehicle that they will return to find it gone.

No section of the city seems to be safe. Community interest groups of every type have been pressuring the mayor and city manager to do something. The city manager has advised the chief to take care of the problem as fast as possible.

Traditionally Line Operations has handled traffic regulation and control as well as accident investigations. In a staff meeting it has been decided to assign Captain Carter the task of recommending how to deal with the problem.

If you were Captain Carter how would you go about resolving this problem?

Would you consider creating a separate traffic unit to handle all traffic matters? Why? Would you consider creating a task force to deal with the problem? Why? What might be a long-range solution for the problem?

For Further Reading

Cox, Dick, "Curfews: Benefits or Bad News," *Law and Order,* December 1998, Vol. 46, No. 12, pp. 87–90.

The author reviews the impact of curfew laws on selected California cities. Special attention is given to San Francisco and San Jose curfew programs. The San Jose ordinance is described to include a listing of nine excuses that can be used by those who come into conflict with the ordinance. The excuses range from going to or from and event to running an errand for a parent or guardian. The author briefly reviews the objections rained to the ordinance by the ACLU.

Office of Enforcement and Emergency Services, *The Use of Sobriety Checkpoints for Impaired Driving Enforcement,* DOT HS 807 656, Washington, DC, National Highway Traffic Safety Administration, 1996, pp. 1 124.

> These guidelines have been designed to provide law enforcement agencies with a uniform and successful method to plan, operate and evaluate sobriety checkpoints. Reviews 12 components of what is portrayed as an effective program. These include judicial support and contingency planning. Includes a sobriety checkpoint briefing guide and a model policy. Of special interest is the list of things to be considered when evaluating a sobriety checkpoint program.

Schneider, Jacqueline L., "Following the Leaders: Patterns of Arrests Among Gang Leaders," *The Police Chief,* April 1998, Vol. LXV, No. 12., pp. 40–50.

> This report focuses on findings of a research report derived from criminal histories of identified gang leaders. The author describes the arrest of gang leaders in Columbus, OH, in order to determine patterns of criminality among the gangs. It was found that arrest for weapons violations accounted for the least number of arrests. Suggests that programs must be developed to include the presence and use of weapons.

Sickmund, Melissa, "Offenders in Juvenile, 1995," *Juvenile Justice Bulletin,* Washington, DC, Office of Justice Programs, NCJ 167885, December 1997, pp. 1–12.

> Juvenile courts in the United States processed more than 1.7 million delinquency cases in 1995. This number represents a 7% increase over the previous year caseload and a 45% increase over the number of cases handled six years earlier. The author found that more than half of the delinquency cases were handled formally. Drug offenses were 145% greater than the number of cases four years earlier. It was found that law enforcement agencies were responsible for referring the majority of juveniles to the court system.

Chapter 16

ADMINISTRATIVE CONCERNS:
Managerial Imperatives

Learning Objectives

1. Describe the value of asset forfeiture to law enforcement agencies.
2. List the three objectives of the US attorney General uses as guidelines for seized and forfeited property.
3. Identify the primary purposes of equitable sharing under the concept of asset forfeiture.
4. Write a short essay describing a model forfeiture program.
5. Describe the opposition to forfeiture programs.
6. List the phases of police pursuit.
7. Discuss the research that has been done on police pursuit.
8. List the key components of a police pursuit policy.
9. Identify the three types of roadblocks.
10. Describe why the national data base on the use of force is important.
11. List the components of the use of force continuum.
12. Describe the part that body armor has played in the reduction of police murders.
13. Write a short essay describing alternatives to deadly force.
14. Describe the Houston Police Department deadly force policy.
15. Assess the importance of testing applicants for police work.

The law enforcement executive of today must be attuned to a variety of issues including competing and conflicting demands from the community, major changes in the law, diversity mandates, significant technological advances, the rise of the information age, and an increase in litigation.[1] Change is endemic and will continue to occur at an increasingly rapid pace. The police manager of the future must anticipate the nature and extent of changes.[2] A revolution is occurring in

1. International Association of Chiefs of Police, "Police Leadership for the 21st Century," *The Police Chief,* March 1999, Vol. LXVI, No. 3, pp. 57–60.

2. Jihong Zhao, *"The Nature of Community Policing Innovations: Do the*

police management generated by both internal and external forces. Probably, the single most significant incident, in the last decade, from an external stimulus, has been the Rodney King incident involving the Los Angeles Police Department. Millions of Americans viewed the 81–second videotape beating of an African–American man, by four police officers while seven other officers watched.[3] As a consequence of the beating the worst riot of the twentieth century occurred. As a result numerous cities across the nation tightened their review of police conduct and others have instituted police review boards. Unfortunately, it seems that periodically another alleged police abuse incident occurs.

Internally, progressive police executives are instituting and managing change. They are viewing crime reduction and all it implies, from a different perspective. Crime prevention is in favor. Community oriented policing is the go-go phrase of the day. Departments are engaged in proactive practices today, rather than reactive. Officers are performing functions clearly outside the traditional style of policing and *stranger policing* is slowly becoming a thing of the past.[4] Progressive administrators support working closely with the public to solve crime and improve the quality of life in the community. All this is distinctly different from historical police thinking.[5]

Police executives are dealing with many new problems and issues. The demographics of many communities have changed dramatically. Neighborhoods and communities have seen the creation of ethnic centers for varying groups. These subcultures demand a differing type of leadership and police response. The same is true, within police departments, where diversity programs have become increasingly common. Diversity and all of its implications has markedly altered the police personnel process. Another problem is corruption that rears its ugly head, almost every year—causing managers to create offices of professional compliance and review corruption control procedures. Every time an act of corruption occurs it lessens public support for law enforcement.[6] During the last decade significant acts of corruption occurred in Philadelphia, Chicago, Washington, DC, New Orleans, Newark and Atlanta.[7] Occasionally intelligence files, acquired by police

Ends Justify the Means," Washington, DC, Police Executive Research Forum, 1996, pp. 2–12.

3. Charles J. Ogletree, Jr., Mary Prosser, Abbe Smith, William Talley, Jr., *Beyond the Rodney King Story–An Investigation of Police Conduct in Minority Communities,* 1994, Boston, Northeastern University Press, pp. 1–132.

4. Raymond P. Manus, "Misconceptions and 'Urban Village Policing.'" *Law Enforcement News,* Vol. XX, No. 448, pp. 8 and 11.

5. William M. Oliver, *Community-Oriented Policing: A Systematic Approach to Policing,* 1998, Upper Saddle River, NJ, Prentice–Hall, pp. 3–41.

6. Larry Sabato and Glenn Simpson, *Dirty Little Secrets–The Persistence of Corruption in American Politics,* 1996, New York, Times Books, pp. 1–10.

7. Robert J. McCormick, "Police Perceptions and the Norming of Institutional Corruption," *Policing and Society,* 1996, Vol. 10, No. 3, pp. 239–246.

agencies, have been used for political purposes. Investigations ensue and additional controls are implemented and questions arise as to the efficacy of law enforcement agencies collecting data on citizens. As the drug problem has become endemic law enforcement agencies respond by testing employees for drug use. Because of the improper use of deadly force officers, managers, and cities are becoming increasingly involved in lawsuits. Liability awards in some cities have been exceptionally large. On the other hand, with the advent of asset forfeiture laws, police departments are receiving unprecedented monetary support from assets seized from law violators. Major issues such as these will continue to place excessive demands upon a police executive's time and skills.

Asset Forfeiture

Asset forfeiture is becoming so important in many police departments that special units have been created to handle related matters. In fact, it is difficult to imagine any sizable police department not having someone handling forfeitures. In some counties, the prosecutor's office has seen fit to create a racketeering forfeiture unit. Asset forfeiture places a new role upon the law enforcement community. Police officers now seize bank accounts, automobiles, and real property–all of which requires well-planned programs and procedures. The Chicago Police Department has an Asset Forfeiture Unit that performs five separate functions–local case management, vehicle forfeitures, real property forfeitures, Federal case management, and investigations. When monies are seized it is used for drug enforcement. The distribution of the money varies from state to state. A typical distribution of funds is that found in Illinois, where 65 percent of the money goes to the seizing law enforcement agency, 25 percent goes to the prosecutor, and ten percent goes to the State Police, who administer the program.[8]

In one city the police department used seized funds to purchase new police vehicles. In another city seized assets were used to purchase bulletproof vests, and computers. One county has used approximately $640,000 to construct a new building. Additionally, one community seized a sound system that was placed in the police department's pickup truck, and used in the Drug Abuse Resistance Education Program (DARE). Other communities have used the funds for safety and surveillance equipment.

As early as 1970 the federal government passed a law entitled Racketeering Influenced Corrupt Organizations (RICO), and soon after states created similar laws. An expansion of this type of law occurred in 1984 when the Comprehensive Drug Abuse Prevention and control Act increased federal forfeiture powers and the Department of Justice created an Asset Forfeiture Fund. This fund provided monies to law enforcement agencies. As of 1985, virtually all states authorized forfei-

8. Robert M. Lombardo, "Asset Forfeiture Units," *FBI Law Enforcement Bulletin,* March 1993, Vol. 62, No. 3., pp. 20–26.

ture in connection with drug trafficking and manufacturing. In 1984, the U.S. Congress amended search and forfeiture laws allowing federal agencies to share profits with local agencies when conducting joint investigations. These statutes give law enforcement an opportunity to take concrete action and utilize such laws as part of their effort to control crime. Agencies can seize property, cash, or anything purchased with proceeds from criminal activities such as gambling, fraud, drug trafficking, and prostitution. Some states have created statutes defining racketeering as any act committed for financial gain, chargeable or indictable under state laws, involving homicide, theft, bribery, prohibited drugs, organized crime, child pornography, and money laundering. In some states the seizure is limited to drug cases. In some instances, confiscated property goes to the state or local treasury. In other states, law enforcement agencies can keep the property for official use. Others use the funds for training law enforcement officers, restitution to victims, and prevention programs.

At the Federal level six department of justice components participate in the asset forfeiture program and the Treasury Department has its own program. The objectives of the program are set forth in the Attorney General's guidelines for seized and forfeited property and are:

- Law enforcement: to punish and deter criminal activity.

- Cooperation: to enhance law enforcement cooperation at all levels of government, both domestically and internationally.

- Revenue: as a by-product of the first two objectives, to produce funds to be reinvested into Federal, state, local, and international law enforcement.[9]

During the last decade forfeiture funds were provide to local and state government units to help combat the problem of inner-city violence and drug abuse. This included 9 million in cash and a total of 45 real properties were transferred to some 70 state and local communities to be used for drug abuse treatment, prevention, education, and job training. Civil forfeitures have become increasingly popular in recent years at the federal level, particularly in the war on drugs. In fiscal year 1996, as a result of justice activities, the government received 338.1 million in forfeited cash and properties. Table 16–1 lists the revenue received during one fiscal year and it can readily be seen that cash and the sale of properties were the most significant elements.

9. Department of Justice, *Asset Forfeiture Program Annual Financial Statement Fiscal Year 1996*, Audit Report 97–32A, (9/97), 3/19/99, Washington, DC, Office of the Inspector General, pp. 1–15. http://www.usdoj.gov/oig/au9732a/au9732tc.htm.

Table 16-1

Composition of Revenue During One Fiscal Year

Category	Amount (millions)	Percentage
Forfeited Cash	$185.7	54.9
Sales of Forfeited Property	73.5	21.7
Interest Income on Idle Funds	14.0	4.1
Refund of Prior Year Interest and Principal	28.7	8.5
Payments/Penalties	17.8	5.3
Other Miscellaneous Income	18.4	5.4
Total	$338.1	100.0

Source: Department of Justice, *Asset Forfeiture Program Annual financial Statement Fiscal Year 1996,* Audit Report 97–32A, (9/97). Washington, DC, Office of Inspector General, 3/19/99, p. 11.

Federal seizures are important because of equitable sharing programs providing for the transfer of forfeited property and proceeds from the sale of forfeited property to participating state and local law enforcement agencies. Nationally, in 1996, the U.S. Justice Department paid 150 million to state and local agencies. Since the inception of the equitable sharing over $1.8 billion in cash and property has been shared. Equitable sharing continues to serve its primary purposes:

- Removes impediments to state and local law enforcement efforts to strip criminal of their profits and tools by recompensing investigative and seizure efforts.

- Encourages enhanced cooperative among Federal, state and local law enforcement efforts.

- Supplements the resources of state and local law enforcement agencies without further taxing the public wealth.[10]

Typical of this cooperative working relationship is the forfeiture procedures used by the Drug Enforcement Agency (DEA). After a seizure in a joint case, the local or state agency may request a share of the property. DEA considers the following factors when determining the amount of equitable sharing in a joint case:

- The degree of direct participation of the state or local agency in the law enforcement effort, resulting in the forfeiture.

- If the agency originated the information leading to the seizure.

- If the agency provided unique or indispensable assistance.

- If the agency provided unique or indispensable seizure.

- If the agency initially identified the asset(s) for seizure.

10. *Ibid., p. 12.*

- If the agency seized other assets during the same investigation, that were forfeited pursuant to state or local law.[11]

In administrative forfeitures valued at less than 1 million, the DEA Asset Forfeiture Section determines the amount of the equitable share, based on the recommendation of the local DEA office. In judicial forfeiture cases valued at less than 1 million, the U.S. Attorney determines the amount based upon recommendation of the DEA. In all other cases, the Deputy Attorney General determines the amount. The Customs Service has expended significant resources in pursuit of joint operations throughout the United States, most notably in the southeast with the Blue Lightning Operations Center. This joint effort includes over 30 police and sheriffs' departments. There also are numerous cooperative investigative efforts along the southwest border. During one recent year the Customs Service transferred over 8 million in currency and assets to state and local police.

A Model Forfeiture Program. The Bureau of Justice Assistance has funded four model forfeiture projects. The intent of the program was to encourage state and local law enforcement agencies to make more effective use of state forfeiture laws. In Colorado Springs, CO., the model was designed to assist police operations. A Regional Asset–Forfeiture Team (RAFT) was created. This unit was housed in the metro vice, narcotics, and intelligence division. This division is a joint effort of two counties and the district attorney's office. A deputy district attorney directed RAFT. Besides clerical help, the unit had an investigative accountant. Since its inception, RAFT seized four residences, 36 vehicles, and $509,000 in cash.

One of the first cases undertaken by RAFT yielded more than twice as much money as the total sum of the original federal grant. The investigative accountant pointed out that the suspect had been dealing in narcotics for ten years. Financial records were gathered for a ten-year period so they could evaluate the person's net worth. It was shown that for at least eight years the suspect had no source of income other than from narcotics. With the net-worth analysis, the unit seized $225,000 in assets, an $18,000 truck and a jeep. In another case the investigative accountant examined the records in a drug case that already had been filed. It was discovered the suspect owned vehicles, boats, and cash missed during the initial investigation. The assets were seized. The investigative accountant now examines all financial documents found at the scene of drug arrests. Under Colorado law for instance, the investigator obtains state income tax and financial institution records that service as an investigative base. With the expiration of the federal grant the unit has continued to operate with financial support from agency and forfeited funds.[12]

11. Office of Chief Counsel, *Equitable Sharing of Federally Forfeited Assets,* Washington, D.C., Asset Forfeiture Section, Drug Enforcement Administration, October 1996, pp. 1–3.

12. BJA Asset Forfeiture Project, "Off and Running: Impressive Results

Management of Seized Property. The management of seized property is a relatively new activity for law enforcement agencies. Its importance is greater as local and state agencies become more actively involved in asset forfeitures. Successful property management units may take different forms. The components can be:

- An in-house professional property manager.

- One or more outside contractors capable of managing and disposing of real property, personal property, and vehicles.

- Access to asset location and the financial investigative group.

- Access to legal advice on management issues. This includes contract negotiation and compliance, foreclosures, bankruptcy, and general property law.

Seizure for forfeiture generally results in possession of valuable property that the seizing agency is responsible for safeguarding. Consequently, some preseizure planning must introduce every seizure for forfeiture, no matter how routine. Agency personnel must decide what property to target for seizure, when and where to execute the seizure, and how to approach the seizure in terms of agency roles and responsibilities. Both legal and practical considerations will affect decisions about what property to target for seizure. However, the practical concerns of the property manager should substantially limit the portion of legally permissible seizures the agency will actually make. Among the important considerations are the value of the item, its usefulness or marketability, the difficulty and expense of storing it, and any special management problems (Does it eat? Does its engine have to be carefully maintained?). Sometimes competing goals will weigh against one another. For example, taking possession of a rundown residential property may seem like an inappropriate use of resources—but if that property is a crack house in a residential neighborhood, the financial cost likely is a good investment of public funds.[13]

Asset forfeiture has declined somewhat in recent years and it is believed that it has been the result of adverse court decisions, especially as to the issue of double jeopardy. Since this issue was raised it has caused the government to evaluate its procedures for when bringing forfeiture actions. While some prosecutors backed off from some civil forfeiture actions the question of double jeopardy was raised by the Ninth Circuit Court of Appeals. In 1994 the case of U.S. v. $405,089.23 U.S. Currency found that the civil forfeiture action was a successful prosecution contrary to the double-jeopardy provisions of the Fifth Amendment and it reversed the order of forfeiture.[14] The circuit's

from Four Model Forfeiture Programs," *Asset Forfeiture Bulletin,* October 1990, pp. 1–2.

13. BJA Asset Forfeiture Project, "Preseizure Planning, Property Management and the Role of Seizure War-

rants," *Asset Forfeiture Bulletin,* Spring 1992, pp. 1–2.

14. Carol J. Moser, "Asset Forfeiture and Double–Jeopardy Issues," *The Police Chief,* September 1995, Vol. LXII, No. 9, pp. 12–14.

adverse ruling on the double jeopardy issue was reversed in 1996 by the Supreme Court when it decided in U.S. v. Ursery, and U.S. v. $405,089.23 when it held that civil forfeiture did not constitute punishment for purposes of the double jeopardy clause.

Opposition to Forfeiture Programs. While law enforcement has found forfeiture laws to be highly useful there are numerous individuals and organizations who are opposed to such programs and are demanding immediate reform. Recently the American Civil Liberties Union (ACLU) took out an large ad in the New York Times (12/11/98) informing readers of the abuses of asset forfeiture laws and asking for Congressional support for forfeiture reform. The ACLU points out that no criminal arrest of conviction is necessary to subject property to forfeiture. They indicate that 80 percent of the victims of forfeiture have never been indicted of a crime. It is suggested that all the police have to do is satisfy a requirement of probable cause that the property was used in an illicit activity or was purchased with funds from illicit activity. Figure 16–1 is the text of the ACLU ad.[15]

---

15. American Civil Liberties Union, *Features,* New York, NY, American Civil Liberties Union Freedom Network, 3/19/99, p. 1. *http://www.aclu.org/features/nytimessad121198.html.*

Figure 16–1

Let Me Ask You Something Did You Know There's a Three Out of Four Chance that the Money You're Carrying Could be Legally Confiscated?

Why? Because 75 percent of American Money is contaminated with cocaine.

What's more astonishing I that courts have ruled that cocaine residue is enough to warrant forfeiture of your cash! In 1984 Congress gave police the right to keep and spend any "drug-related assets" they seize.
Police have since taken cars, homes, restaurants, and cash in epidemic proportions.

And they can use these assets for anything from patrol cars to parties. Right now there is 2.7 billion in the federal government's "Asset Forfeiture Fund." And local police departments have filled their own coffers as well.

Most victims of forfeiture aren't criminals.
Like the 75–year-old grandmother who lost her home because her drug-dealer son once lived there. Or the landscaper whose $9,000 was seized at the airport because "only drug dealers carry that much cash."

These people were never arrested or even charged with a crime.
And they weren't entitled to a fair hearing, either.

It could happen to you.

One leading historian calls this nothing less than a government "license to steal."
The war on drugs has become a war on the Constitution.
What kind of country awards its police for shaking down its own citizens?

Think about it.

Source: ACLU, *Let me Ask You Something Did You Know there's a 3 out of 4 Chance the Money You're carrying could be Legally Seized.* New York, NY, ACLU, 12/11/98, p. 4. http://www.aclu.org/features/nytimessad121198.html. Reprinted with permission.

Although the ACLU and other advocates have mounted challenges to forfeiture laws in courts litigation in this area is limited. The U.S. Supreme Court has held, in a series of cases that civil forfeiture does not violate due process or any other constitutional right. Many are hoping that Congress will act upon the ACLU supported "Civil Asset Forfeiture Reform Act." This act has bi-partisan-support and is currently in committee.[16] Another organization leading the battle to change the forfeiture laws is the Forfeiture Endangers Americans Right (F.E.A.R.) foundation that has a web-site and a Forfeiture Forum where current news is discussed and the postings are automatically archived on the internet.[17] In addition F.E.A.R. has a 26 page position paper that includes a discussion recommending the abolishment of civil forfeiture to the restoring the principle of "innocent until proven guilty."[18]

From the law enforcement point of view asset forfeiture continues to be an extremely effective and powerful tool in the fight against organized crime, drug trafficking, and money laundering. The ability to remove the proceeds of crime from individuals and destroy the economic infrastructure of criminal organizations is an essential law enforcement tool. By seizing the assets of illicit organizations, the government can sharply curtail or eliminate their operations. Since large, established criminal enterprises replace individuals easily, asset forfeiture may represent the most significant tool avail for disruption of these enterprises.[19]

Police Pursuits

The most dangerous of all ordinary police activities is high-speed vehicle pursuit. Far more vehicle chases occur each year than police shootings. However, development of legally sound police pursuit policies lags behind the development of deadly force policies involving firearms although there has been considerable improvement in recent years. If there is reason to have an effective police pursuit policy, it is to protect life and property. Enough police pursuits result in serious property damage, personal injury, and death to make police pursuit a major public concern. In a recent Supreme Court case the family of Mr. Lewis (County of Sacrament v. Lewis, 118 S. Ct. 1708, 1998), brought a civil action under 42 U.S.C. § 1983 against the Sacramento County sheriff's deputies after Mr. Lewis was killed during a police pursuit.[20] The defendant's family argued that the decedent was denied substantive due process, guaranteed by the 14th Amendment to the Constitution. The Supreme Court held that in a high-speed chase, a police officer does not deprive an individual of substantive due process by causing death through actions that indicate a deliberate or a reckless disregard for the rights of others. Instead the standard to be applied in assessing officer culpability is higher. Only conduct that shows an

16. *Ibid,* p. 2.

17. F.E.A.R., *What's New at F.E.A.R.,* Washington, DC, Forfeiture Endangers America Rights Foundation, 3/14/99, pp. 1–4. http://www.fear.org/whatsnew.html.

18. F.E.A.R., *F.E.A.R.'s Proposal for Reform,* Washington, DC, Forfeiture Endangers American Rights Foundation.

12/1/98, pp. 1–26. http://www.fear.org/fposit.html.

19. Department of Justice, op. cit., p. 5.

20. Joseph E. Scuro, Jr., "Supreme Court Update–Greater Immunity for Officers Involved in Pursuits," *Law and Order,* January 1999, Vol. 47, No. 1., pp. 75–76.

intent on the part of the officer to cause harm unrelated to the legitimate object of making the arrest will meet the test of arbitrary and shocking conduct actionable as a deprivation of substantive due process.[21]

Pursuit Phases. The Pursuit Management Task Force was created to conduct a multidisciplinary effort to define police practices and the role of technology in high-speed police pursuits. As part of that effort the task force settled on the concept of "pursuit phases." It found that pursuits went through a series of predictable phases that are based upon the nature of pursuits in general rather than upon variables such as time, distance and geography. The four phases are:

- Pre-pursuit.
- Communications.
- Arrival of Resources.
- Post-pursuit.

The pre-pursuit phase can include a variety of considerations to include taking action to minimize the opportunity for flight to cooperative technologies such as anti-theft or vehicle recovery devices. Officers face a number of complicated variables as decision points occur during this phase. A decision may have to be made as to the location and manner of stop to be effectuated, determine whether the suspect is anticipating to flee or determine the known or suspected crime for which the suspect is wanted. Confronted by these and other decisions an officer may decide based on departmental policy to actually engage in a pursuit. The officer typically has about five to ten seconds to go through the complicated decision process and one must keep in mind that variables involved in the decision-making process vary from incident to incident. Within this phase an officer may have an opportunity to apply some type of technology before the suspect has an opportunity to flee in a vehicle. This includes the possible use of handheld tire deflators, tagging systems, tracking systems, or electronic disrupters to prevent vehicle mobility.[22]

The communications phase occurs immediately following the start of a pursuit and is usually characterized by a series of urgent radio communications between the pursuing officer and potentially assisting officers as well as dispatchers. It involves a range of decision points to include determining whether the pursuit should continue under departmental policy, the level of force that would be justified to terminate the pursuit, and tactical considerations. This phase may be short or

21. Lisa A. Regini, "Supreme Court Cases 1997–1998 Term," *"FBI Law Enforcement Bulletin,"* October 1998, Vol. 67, No. 12, pp. 25–32 and John C. Hall, "Due Process and Deadly Force–When Police Conduct Shocks the Conscience," *FBI Law Enforcement Bulletin*, February 1999, Vol. 68, No. 2, pp. 27–32.

22. Kenneth L. Bayless and Robert Osborne, *Pursuit Management Task Force Report, Rockville, MD, National Law Enforcement and Corrections Technology Center, September 1998*, pp. 11–12.

long in duration based upon a variety of factors–primarily the proximity of other officers and the availability of resources. Cooperative technologies might be useful during this phase if the officer could determine that the fleeing vehicle is equipped with a theft deterrent or vehicle recovery system through information gained by checking license numbers through computerized vehicle registration files.[23]

The resources phase begins when requested resources arrive. This gives officers increased options for bringing a pursuit to a successful conclusion. The options include letting a better-suited agency to continue the pursuit, allowing a helicopter to take over the pursuit, or employing a pursuit termination technology. This can include cooperative systems and mechanical, chemical, electronic, sensory and tactical interventions. Selection of appropriate options becomes an issue of policy, public safety and acceptance, timing and location, affordability, and availability.[24]

The last phase is post-pursuit. For the officers involved, the termination of a pursuit merely exchanges one tactical operation (the pursuit) for another (taking suspects into custody). If any type of technology is used to stop a fleeing vehicle must not unduly interfere with ensuing tactical operations. For instance, using a noxious gas to cause a driver to want to stop is not generally a viable option if pursuing officers would themselves likely be impacted as they attempt to make the arrest. Additionally, pursuit technologies must likewise have minimal impact upon the general public after conclusion of a pursuit. Mechanical devices must be able to target the pursued vehicle without unduly affecting other traffic, including pursuing officers. Currently there is no single technology on the horizon that affords a "universal" solution to pursuits.

Pursuit Duration and Collisions. It has been of interest to law enforcement if a correlation could be found between the duration of pursuits and any resulting collisions. From the data presented in table 16–1 it can be seen that a collision occurred in 26 percent of all pursuits. Over one-half of all pursuit-related collisions occurred in pursuits lasting one to two minutes; more than 73 percent occurred in pursuits lasting one to four minutes, and 83 percent of the collisions occurred in pursuits lasting 6 minutes or less. Pursuits lasting one to four minutes accounted for 68 percent of all pursuits and 73 percent of all pursuit-related collisions. This clearly presents a challenge for those seeking to develop pursuit termination technologies. To impact a substantial number of pursuits (47 percent) and pursuit-related collisions (52 percent) a technology would need to be deployed within the first two minutes of a pursuit.[25]

Research. In the study of three jurisdictions it was found that pursuit-related accidents occurred more frequently when pursuits were

23. *Ibid., pp. 12–13.*   25. *Ibid., pp. 15–16.*
24. *Ibid.* p. 13.

conducted for felonies than non-felonies These accidents were more apt to occur on surface streets rather than highways or freeways, and in urban and suburban areas rather than rural (see table 16–2). The prediction of personal injury resulting from a police pursuit depended primarily on four variables in Metro–Dade. The greater the number of police cars the greater the likelihood of injury; the involvement of other agencies also increased the likelihood of injury; high-speed chases resulted in more injuries than low-speed pursuits, and chases in residential areas resulted in more injuries than those conducted in non-residential areas.

In Omaha, pursuit related property damage occurred in 40 percent of pursuits. Also the pursuits least likely to end in an accident were those initiated because of vehicles being identified as "suspect." In Metro–Dade the likelihood of the suspect's escape was found to depend on the number of police vehicles and police departments involved in pursuit (increasing the number of vehicles decreased the likelihood of escape). Additionally, the location of the pursuit was important (fewer suspects escaped in business districts than in residential or rural areas), and the time of the day (fewer suspects escaped during daytime hours than at night).

Table 16–2
California Pursuit Statistics, 1994–1996

California Pursuit Statistics, 1994–1996

Pursuit Duration	1994		1995		1996		3 Year Totals		Percentage of:		
	Pursuits	Collisions	Pursuits	Collisions	Pursuits	Collisions	Pursuits	Collisions	Total Pursuits by Pursuit Duration	Pursuits Resulting in Collision	Collisions by Pursuit Duration
1–2 minutes	3,340	975	3,365	974	2,844	832	9,549	2,781	47%	14%	52%
3–4 minutes	1,635	431	1,487	375	1,174	303	4,296	1,109	21%	5%	21%
5–6 minutes	826	173	797	188	635	164	2,258	525	11%	3%	10%
7–8 minutes	412	90	266	88	318	76	996	254	5%	1%	5%
9–10 minutes	321	65	329	79	272	50	922	194	5%	1%	4%
11–15 minutes	367	89	376	87	302	65	1045	241	5%	1%	4%
16–20 minutes	179	41	163	19	135	19	477	79	2%	0%	1%
20+ minutes	314	73	294	57	227	48	835	178	4%	1%	3%
Total	7,394	1,937	7,077	1,867	5,907	1,557	20,378	5,361	100%	26%	100%

Source: Kenneth L. Bayless and Robert Osborne, *Pursuit Management Task Force Report,* Rockville, MD, National Law Enforcement and Corrections Technology Center, September 1998, p. 15.

Table 16–3
Number of, Reasons for, and Results of Police Pursuits

Number of, Reasons for, and Results of Police Pursuits

Reasons for Pursuit	Number (Percentage) of Incidents		
	Metro-Dade (Miami) Florida	Omaha, Nebraska	Aiken County, South Carolina
Traffic violations	448 (45%)	112 (51%)	5 (36%)
DUI/Reckless driving		8 (4%)	1 (7%)
"Suspect" vehicle		7 (3.5%)	2 (14%)
Driver known from previous incident		3 (1.5%)	
Felonies	344 (35%)	89 (40%)	6 (43%)
Armed robbery	117		2
Vehicular assault	67		
Aggravated assault	37		
Stolen vehicles	37	36	3
Burglary	24		
Other felonies	62	53	1
Accidents			
Personal injury	428 (41%)	31 (14%)	2 (12%)
Property damage	213 (20%)	91 (40%)	4 (24%)
Arrests	**784 (75%)**	**118 (52%)**	**14 (82%)**

Source: Geoffrey P. Alpert, *Police Pursuits: Policies and Training*, Washington, DC, Office of Justice Programs, May 1997. pp. 1–7.

In Omaha, the likelihood of escape was related to supervisory assistance (the lack of supervisory assistance increased the likelihood of escape). A positive supervisory role in pursuits has proven to be viable in other jurisdictions.[26] Also pursuits initiated for reckless driving or driving under the influence (DUI) were the most likely to end in an arrest (75 percent), while pursuits initiated because a vehicle was "suspect" resulted in the smallest proportion of arrests. Additionally, officers were most likely to terminate pursuit voluntarily when it was initiated for suspect vehicles (29 percent), and least likely in chases initiated for felonies.

Metro–Dade and Omaha show the strong effects of police changes. When Metro–Dade adopted a violent felony only pursuit police the number of pursuits decreased 82 percent the following year. When Omaha changed to a more permissive policy, permitting pursuits for offenses that had previously been prohibited, within a year the number of pursuits increased by more than 600 percent (see table 16–4).

26. Andre' Belotto, "Supervisors Govern Pursuits," *Law and Order*, January 1999, Vol. 47, No. 1, p. 88.

Table 16–4

Numbers of Police Pursuits Before and After Policy Changes

Numbers of Police Pursuits Before and After Policy Changes

Jurisdiction	Nature of Policy Change	Before Change	After Change
Metro-Dade, Florida	more restrictive	279	51
Omaha, Nebraska	more permissive	17	122

Source: Geoffrey P. Alpert, *Police Pursuit: Policies and Training,* Washington, DC, Office of Justice Programs, May 1997, p. 4.

Pursuit Policy. There can be little question that a police department should have an explicit pursuit policy.[27] The main question is what kind of policy will best serve the interests of the agency? It involves the balancing of conflicting interests. This includes the safety of police officers, of fleeing drivers and their passengers, and of innocent bystanders. Pursuits expose a department to a high risk of loss of life, serious personal injury, and property damage. If police officers are killed or injured, it is a serious loss to the agency. If private citizens are injured or killed the city may be liable for damages as the result of civil actions.[28] When the injured parties are innocent bystanders, liability is particularly difficult to avoid. If the department does not pursue suspects, its credibility with both law-abiding citizens and law violators will suffer. In the State of California a statute passed by the legislature contained four separate elements that were considered minimal if a policy was to enjoy immunity under the law.[29] A police pursuit policy should provide:

- Supervisory control (if available) of the pursuit.
- Procedures for designating the primary pursuit vehicle, and for determining the total number of vehicles to be involved in the pursuit.
- Procedures for coordinating operations with other law enforcement agencies.

27. Milton Thurman and Lorraine J. Feldman, "Departmental Guidelines May Avoid Officer and Municipal Liability for High–Speed Pursuits," *The Police Chief,* April 1997, Vol. LXIV, No. 4, p. 160.

28. Earl M. Sweeney, "Vehicular Pursuit: A Serious and Ongoing Problem," January 1997, Vol. LXIII, No. 1, pp. 16–21.

29. Rod Fick, "California's Police Pursuit Immunity Statute: Does it Work?" *The Police Chief,* February 1997, Vol. LXIV, No. 2., 37–43.

- Guidelines for determining when the interests of public safety and effective law enforcement justify a vehicular pursuit and when a vehicular pursuit should not be initiated or should be terminated.[30]

It would seem, at the very least, law enforcement agencies should develop a pursuit policy clearly limiting an officer's judgment while controlling their actions. There would seem to be little reason to allow pursuits when the suspect has committed a minor traffic infraction although this is still done in some jurisdictions. This is especially true when the officer has gotten the offender's license plate number and a description of the vehicle. It also seems valid to prohibit ramming, and boxing-in or blocking the road with police vehicles (fixed roadblock). This currently varies from agency to agency. The Nassau County Police, NY, have a definitive policy regarding ramming and roadblocks. In their policy they point out that roadblocks are "dangerous and difficult to establish." This is particularly true of fixed roadblocks.

Their policy identifies three kinds of roadblocks:

- Fixed roadblocks, which block the road to the extent that little or no outlet remains (rarely justified).

- Partial roadblocks, which consist of a series of barriers blocking the roadway in such a fashion that the pursued vehicle is diverted and forced to slow down.

- Moving roadblocks, which consist of two or more official vehicles in front of the pursued vehicle. They gradually slow down, forcing the pursued vehicle to slow down by allowing no outlet. This type is most effective on limited access highways.

If a roadblock is used, it can only be established after notifying the pursuing officer and the dispatcher. Significantly, Nassau County prohibits ramming a vehicle except in the instance where the pursued vehicle is already out of control and might collide with another occupied vehicle or a pedestrian. Figure 16–2 is the Phoenix, AZ Police Department pursuit policy. It includes a definition, a basis for pursuit and the role of the supervisor. Of special interest is the list of conditions delimiting when an officer should terminate pursuit.

Figure 16–2

Vehicle Pursuit Policy

Definition

A motor vehicle pursuit is an active attempt by a law enforcement officer, operating an emergency vehicle and utilizing simultaneously all emergency equipment, to apprehend one or more occupants of another moving vehicle when the driver of the fleeing vehicle is aware of that attempt and is resisting apprehension by maintaining or increasing his speed, disobeying traffic laws, ignoring the officer, or attempting to elude the officer.

---

30. State of California, *California Vehicle Code,* § 17004.7 (c).

Basis for Pursuit

Traffic violations, misdemeanors, non-violent felonies, violent felonies.

Participating Units

Only marked, fully equipped patrol cars. In pursuit of a suspected violent felon, one other marked patrol car may become backup car. All other units have support roles.

Radio Procedure

Prescribed in detail in policy.

Termination

An officer should terminate when any of the following occurs:

- Suspect is known to officer and offence is traffic infraction, misdemeanor, or nonviolent felony.
- Distance between officer and violator is such that continuing pursuit would require speeds endangering officer and public.
- Officer loses visual contact with suspect for extended time (approximately 15 seconds). Officer may continue to look for suspect, but at reduced speeds.
- There is clear and unreasonable hazard to officer, violator, or public. There is unreasonable hazard when speed dangerously exceeds normal flow of traffic, or when vehicular or pedestrian traffic necessitates erratic maneuvering exceeding performance capacities of vehicle or driver.
- Danger outweighs necessity for immediate apprehension.
- Environmental conditions such as rain, fog, or darkness substantially increase risk.
- Officer is unfamiliar with area and is unable to notify dispatcher of his location and direction of pursuit.
- Road conditions are congested by traffic or pedestrians.
- Violator goes wrong way down one-way street, freeway, freeway frontage road, or divided highway.

Boxing–In, Ramming, and Roadblocks

Ramming, boxing-in, and blocking the road with police vehicles are prohibited. The only exception is boxing in an unaware suspect to avoid a pursuit.

Firearms

No explicit policy on the use of firearms in high-speed pursuits.

Aircraft

When an aircraft is available and has suspect vehicle in view, guidelines give aircraft primary pursuit responsibility, vehicles on ground support responsibility.

Supervisory Role

Supervisors are to take control by monitoring a pursuit and taking whatever actions are necessary to ensure compliance with the department's pursuit policy. They are to terminate pursuit if apparent danger outweighs the necessity of apprehension.

Review Procedures

Formal review of all pursuits required. Supervisor of unit initiating pursuit submits written report outlining details of pursuit. Incident report is sent to Accident Analysis Committee within 15 days.

Source: Hugh Nugent, et. al., *Restrictive Policies for High–Speed Police Pursuits*, Washington, D.C., National Institute of Justice, 1990, pp. 29–30.

Every police pursuit policy should have a provision requiring the pursuing officer to submit a special report. An example of this section of a policy is the St. Petersburg, FL, Police Department. It requires not only the primary report, but if there is a second unit involved that officer must complete a supplementary report. The field supervisor also files a report in the case, if there are any unusual circumstances.[31] One police department, after a serious accident occurred during a pursuit, required all reports to be reviewed by a Deputy Chief. Within one year there was approximately a 51 percent reduction in the number of pursuits. Such a review forces each officer to weigh fully whether the pursuit should be initiated or not.

Police use of Force

The Rodney King beating, in Los Angeles, brought into sharp focus the alleged use of brutality by the police. The reduction of incidents of violence between the police and the citizens is of special concern to communities throughout the nation. Most studies have been confined to the use of firearms, but the problem extends beyond the ultimate use of force. While it is only one department, the report of the Independent Commission on the Los Angeles Police Department illustrates the complexity and the nature of the problem. Policy in this department specifies an officer may resort to force only where there is a credible threat, and then force should be limited to the minimum amount necessary to control the suspect. The Commission determined a relatively large number of officers consistently misused force and constantly ignored policies. This group was found to be poorly supervised and did not receive needed managerial guidance.[32]

Supervisors were not held accountable for the performance of officers under their command. There was no question that a number of officers used more force than they should have. "Problem officers" were well known in the area where they worked, and the controlling of excessive force was insufficient.

When personnel files were reviewed it was determined that 44 officers had 6 or more allegations of excessive force or improper tactics. Unfortunately, the complaint file did not reflect this information. It was at complete odds with coetaneous comments in the files. Overall, performance evaluation reports for the identified "problem officers" were quite positive. The files did not give an accurate picture of the officers' disciplinary histories. There was a failure to record "sustained" complaints or to discuss the significance as it related to overall performance. The Commission concluded the department had not made sufficient efforts to send a clear message to officers that excessive force would not be tolerated and officers and their supervisors will be evaluated by how well they abide by and advance use of force policy.[33]

31. *Ibid.*, p. 31.

32. City of Los Angeles, *Report of the Independent Commission on the Los An-* geles Police Department, Los Angeles, CA, City of Los Angeles, 1991, p. 3.

33. *Ibid.*, pp. 5–6.

Since the incident of using deadly force the department has revised its use of force methods, training and policies as well as its standards regarding the investigation of use of force incidents. Currently a supervisor is assigned to conduct an on-scene investigation for each use of force. The completed investigation is reviewed by the involved employee's commanding officer and bureau commanding officer. If an incident involves a serious injury (usually hospitalization), is classified as a Law Enforcement Related Injury Investigation (LERII), and the investigation is handled by detectives assigned to Detective Headquarters Division. In addition the Los Angeles Police Department has created specialized training to reinforce the use of verbal containment and control techniques. Another procedure incorporated in to the process is the review of use-of-force complaints by the Police Commission and the auditing of this process by the Inspector General. It is clear that the New Los Angeles Police Department has responded positively to the Report of the Independent Commission and has positioned itself to move forward to a more service-oriented agency.[34]

Within law enforcement it seem that an individual incident of the misuse of force by the police causes a marshalling of criticism of the police. In a recent incident in New York City a Haitian immigrant, Abner Louima, was allegedly tortured by uniformed officers in a police station. The suspect was hospitalized after severe internal injuries. The victim testified that he had been sodomized with a broom handle and beaten. Officer Justin Volpe became enraged when he thought the victim had punched him in disturbance outside of a Brooklyn nightclub. Five officers were arrested in this case and currently are on trial on charges of violating Louima's civil rights. Four officers have testified that they saw Volpe brandishing a stick on the night of the torture, August 9, 1997. During the trial officer Volpe changed his plea to guilty. Four of the officers were charged with beating the victim en route to the station and another officer was charged with covering up the incident.[35]

The American police have even received attention from an unusual source. In 1998 Amnesty International released a report recommending that within the United States authorities should take immediate action to halt human rights violations by police officers. Amnesty made 13 specific recommendations to include the need for police departments to establish early warning systems to identify and deal with officers involved in human rights violations. They want departments to keep detailed records of every officer's conduct, and perform regular audits of these records in order to identify, and take remedial action in respect

34. Los Angeles Police Department, *Status Report on Recommendations from the Independent Commission Revised Recommendations for Organizational Change,* Los Angeles, Los Angeles Police Department, August 1998, pp. 1–56.

35. *The Arizona Daily Star,* "Two More New York Cops Charged in Al-

leged Torture," Tucson, AZ, December 17, 1998, 3A and *The Arizona Daily Star,* "N.Y. Cop Accused of Torturing Prisoner Will Reverse Plea to Guilty, Lawyer Says," Tucson, AZ, May 25, 1999.

of, any patterns of abuse.[36] At the same time there is a growing source of anti-police brutality organizations on the world wide web. Some of these are listed in figure 16–3 ranging from national organizations to web pages sponsored by individuals.

Figure 16–3

Anti-Police Brutality Organizations and Links

The A.C.L.U. Organization.
The Amnesty International U.S.A. Home Page.
Criminal Justice Forum on Police Encounters.
Fighting Police Abuses–A community Action Manual (A.C.L.U.).
GloboCopWatch.
GloboCopWatch Directory.
Investigating the Police–A How-to Guide.
I've gotta Badge.
JusticeNet's Cops and Police Brutality.
Pepper Spray Victims.Org.
Police Brutality Must Stop.
Stop Police Brutality.
The Police Complaint Center Web Page.
United Voice Against Police Brutality Homepage.

Source: Links, *Anti-Police Brutality, Org.'s and Links,* 10/13/98. http://members.aol.com/turncopsin/index.html/newpage1.htm.

National Data. The Violent Crime Control and Law Enforcement Act mandated the collection of data by the U.S. Attorney General on the use of excessive force by law enforcement officers.[37] A report on the survey indicated that about 45 million residents, or about 21 percent of those age 12 or older, were estimated to have had at least one face-to-face contact with a law enforcement officer during 1996. Figure 16–4 lists the reasons for face-to-face contact with the police. The most common reasons given for having such contacts were that the respondents sought the assistance of or provided assistance to the police (15 million). The second greatest reason was because they were a victim of a crime or a witness to a crime (14 million). The third largest group were those who had received a traffic ticket from the police (11 million). Other reasons for contacts with the police included involved/witnessed a traffic accident, questioned as a possible suspect in a crime and seeing officers at a community meetings or because of a casual contact.

36. Amnesty International, *Recommendations to the United States Government to Address Human Rights violations in the USA,* London, England, 10/13,98, pp. 1–8. http://www.amnesty.org/ailib/1998/AMR/25104698.htm.

37. Bobby D. Moody, "National Police Use-of-Force Data base Project," *The Police Chief,* March 1998, Vol. LXV., No. 3., p. 6.

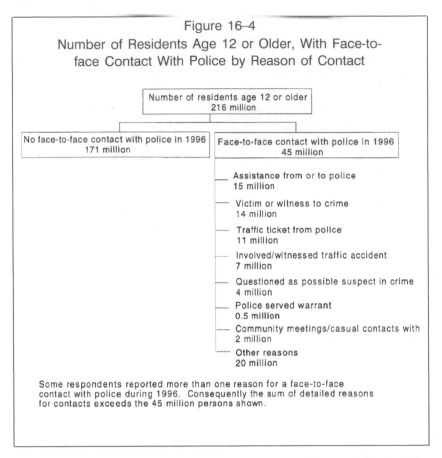

Figure 16–4

Number of Residents Age 12 or Older, With Face-to-face Contact With Police by Reason of Contact

Number of residents age 12 or older
216 million

No face-to-face contact with police in 1996
171 million

Face-to-face contact with police in 1996
45 million

Assistance from or to police
15 million

Victim or witness to crime
14 million

Traffic ticket from police
11 million

Involved/witnessed traffic accident
7 million

Questioned as possible suspect in crime
4 million

Police served warrant
0.5 million

Community meetings/casual contacts with
2 million

Other reasons
20 million

Some respondents reported more than one reason for a face-to-face contact with police during 1996. Consequently the sum of detailed reasons for contacts exceeds the 45 million persons shown.

Source: Lawrence A. Greenfeld, Patrick A. Langan, and Steven K. Smith, *Police Use of Force–Collection of National Data,* Washington, DC, Bureau of Justice Statistics, November 1997, p. 6.

Of those who received a traffic ticket (about 1.6 million) persons received more than one ticket during the year. Teenagers and persons in their twenties accounted for just over 60 percent of those with multiple traffic tickets, more than double their share of licensed drivers. Some of the respondents had repeated contact with the police. Among persons who reported a crime to the police, approximately one-fourth said they reported a crime on more than one occasion during the year. The repeat contact rate was also a fourth for certain other contact: ask police for help, offer help to police, and witness a crime. The repeat contact rate was highest among persons who had casual encounters with the police (60 percent) and those who attended community meeting (41 percent).

The survey included detailed questions about specific types of police force that might have bee used. Not one respondent alleged that they had been kicked, hit with a flashlight, attacked by a dog, or shot at by the police. The specific types of force that were alleged to have occurred were: hit, held, pushed, choked, threatened with a flashlight, restrained by a police dog, threatened or actually sprayed with chemical or pepper spray, threatened with a gun, or some other use of force used against them. The survey estimates that 500,000 persons had force actually used against them or the threat of force (see figure 16–5). An estimated 800,000 never had force used against them, but were handcuffed. When these two latter totals are combined it involved 1.3 million people or 0.6 percent of the population age 12 or older.[38]

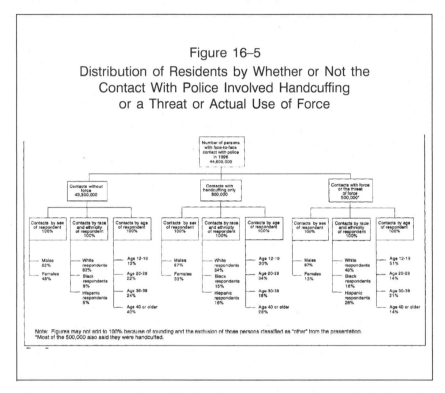

Figure 16–5

Distribution of Residents by Whether or Not the Contact With Police Involved Handcuffing or a Threat or Actual Use of Force

Source: Lawrence A. Greenfeld, Patrick A. Langan and Steven K. Smith, *Police Use of Force–Collection of National Data,* Washington, DC, Bureau of Justice Statistics, November 1997, p. 13.

38. Lawrence A. Greenfeld, Patrick A. Langan and Steven K. Smith, *Police Use of Force–Collection of National Data,* Washington, DC, Bureau of Justice Statistics, November 1997, PP. 11–12.

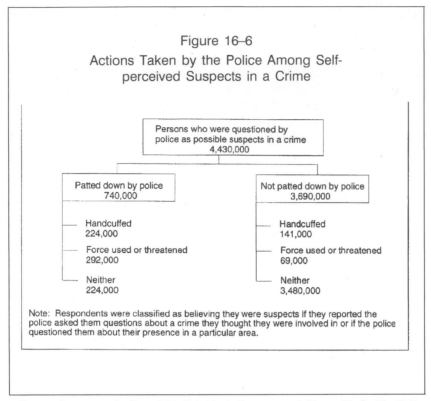

Figure 16–6

Actions Taken by the Police Among Self-perceived Suspects in a Crime

Persons who were questioned by police as possible suspects in a crime
4,430,000

Patted down by police
740,000

Handcuffed
224,000

Force used or threatened
292,000

Neither
224,000

Not patted down by police
3,690,000

Handcuffed
141,000

Force used or threatened
69,000

Neither
3,480,000

Note: Respondents were classified as believing they were suspects if they reported the police asked them questions about a crime they thought they were involved in or if the police questioned them about their presence in a particular area.

Source: Lawrence A. Greenfeld, Patrick A. Langan, and Steven K. Smith, *Police Use of Force–Collection of National Data,* Washington, DC, Bureau of Justice Statistics, November 1997, p. 14.

Based upon respondent descriptions of the reasons for a face-to-face contact with the police, an estimated 4.4 million persons age 12 or older were questioned either as possible suspects in a crime or because the police were suspicious about their presence in the area. About 17 percent or 740,000 persons, reported that during the contact they were "patted down" or searched by the police (see figure 16–6), and 224,00 were handcuffed. Among those patted down by police 70 percent said they were also handcuffed or force was threatened or used during the contact. For the five out of six respondents who attributed the contact to police suspicions about them and who were not patted down, less than six percent reported that they were handcuffed or threatened with force or had force used against them.

It cannot be determined from available data the order in which the police decisions occurred to pat down, handcuff, or invoke force or the threat of force or even whether the police considered them possible suspects prior to engaging in any of these actions. What is known is that about eight out of ten people who felt the police considered them possible suspects or who indicated they believed that the police were suspicious about them during the contact also reported they were not patted down, were not handcuffed, and were not threatened with force.

Among the estimated 500,000 persons who were threatened with force or against whom force was actually used, most self-reported that they had engaged in at least one of the following:

- Threatened the officer.
- Assaulted the officer.
- Argued with the officer.
- Interfered with the officer in the arrest of someone else.
- Possessed a weapon.
- Blocking an officer or interfering with his/her movement.
- Trying to escape or evade the officer.
- Resisted being handcuffed.
- Resisted being placed in a police vehicle.
- Inciting bystanders to become involved.
- Trying to protect someone else from an officer.
- Drinking or using drugs at the time of the contact.

While the data from the nationwide survey is not definitive, because of the small size of the sample, it does suggest that provocative behavior of a suspect may cause officers to react with some type of force.[39] In two of the most recent data years (1996–1997), additional findings show that suspects used chemicals against the police in 61 cases and that approximately two-thirds of reported cases involved situations where both suspects and officers used force during confrontations.[40]

Use of Force Continuum. The continuum is a guideline for field officers that provides for the selection of a level of force required to resolve a situation. It is a flexible sequence that can be tailored to a specific situation. It consists of a number of levels with each successive level representing an escalation from the previous level.[41] As technology has come to forefront the use of force continuum has changed to accommodate new tools.[42] The most prominent of these has been neutralizing agents. The goal is to use the lowest level of force possible in response to the level of force used by a suspect. In the national study it was found that there was a "street continuum" wherein officers during 1996–1997 used physical force first followed by chemical and finally firearms. Subjects used the same continuum except for replacing the use of firearms with impact weapons.[43] With the integration of neutralizing agents into the continuum it follows the following pattern:

39. *Ibid.,* p. 14.

40. International Association of Chief of Police, "IACP Report Shows Police Rarely Use Force," *The Police Chief,* June 1998, Vol.LXV, No. 6, pp. 18–22.

41. Tony L. Jones, "Tactical Use of Force," *Law and Order,* February 1997, Vol. 45, No. 2, pp. 84–86.

42. Lois Pilant, "Crime and War: An Analysis of Non-lethal Technologies and Weapons Development", *The Police Chief,* June 1998, Vol. LXV, No. 6, PP. 55–61.

43. Moody, *op. cit.*

- Physical presence.
- Verbalization.
- Neutralizing agents.
- Physical contact.
- Neutralizing agents.
- Hand-held impact weapons.
- Lethal force.

This expanded use of force continuum gives officers greater flexibility when dealing with suspects. Needless to say when force is used it must be appropriate to the situation. In a tense situation an officer must consider a wide range of factors from perceived physical prowess of the suspect to the availability of various non-lethal weapons. The current continuum stresses the use of neutralizing agents as key component, but one has to be aware of the fact that spraying an enraged intoxicated individual or a suspect under the influence of drugs will in all likelihood not prove to be effective. Consequently an officer should be prepared to use some other type of force.[44] When departments have employed a use of force continuum coupled with adequate training and supervision positive results have occurred. Fewer controversial shooting have occurred, and there have been fewer serious injuries to officers. In addition, there has been no reduction in the number of arrests or an increase in the crime rate.

The Use of Deadly Force. Of all the decisions a police officer makes the decision to use deadly force is the most serious. Such decisions normally occur when an officer is under a great deal of stress and a split-second decision must be made. Most would agree the use of force is justifiable in few situations. Circumstances must be extreme so most departments have created definitive policy in this important area. When extreme deadly force is used by a police officer(s), it usually makes headlines in local newspapers. In one large city a suspect was shot and killed after he struck an officer with his car and the officer fired his weapon three times shooting the subject twice in the arm and once in the chest. In another city a subject, an alleged bank robber, was shot eight times after he allegedly reached for a gun tucked in his waistband and ignored repeated requests to stop. In a medium sized city a suspect pointed a gun at officers and when he refused to lay the weapon down the suspect was fatally shot.

In Washington, DC an investigation by a newspaper found that the police fired their weapons at twice the rate that officers did in other large communities such as New York, Los Angeles and Chicago. Over a period of five years the DC police killed 85 people, and were involved in

---

44. Steve Ijames, "Tactics, Training and Technology for Unconventional Encounters, *The Police Chief,* March 1998, Vol. LXV, No. 3, pp. 31–37, and Steve Ijames, "Less Than Lethal,—Tactics, Training and Equipment for the Unconventional Encounter, *Law and Order,* December 1998, Vol. 46, No. 12, pp. 95–97.

640 shooting incidents.[45] In Los Angeles during 4 years 127 people died in officer-involved shooting. In reviewing 700 shooting reports the Los Angeles Police Department either disciplined or had officers retrained in three out of every four shooting incidents. In three of the incidents officers shoot out their own windshield while trying to stop a suspect. In another case an officer shot another officer in the back as they converged on a suspect during the hours of darkness.[46]

During an average year, the police in our nation shoot at about 3,600 individuals. Whether this is excessive or not is unknown. Ours is a violent society. In 19976 there were 1,634,773 violent crimes reported to the F.B.I. This includes such crimes as homicides, forcible rape, robberies, and aggravated assault. This is a decrease in the rate for several years that should be applauded it is still a whopping 169.1 percent increase over 1960. While these statistics do not tell the entire story it does, unfortunately, describe a violence prone society. Clearly too violent. Over the last four years numerous politicians, including the President have taken credit for the reduction in crime, but in reality no one really knows the reason for the decline. Is it incarceration of more individuals a reduction in the number of juveniles, better policing or more police on the street? But isn't it nice to take credit for something you cannot control and others may disagree with the conclusion but they cannot totally refute your claim. No one really knows what causes crime other than it is eclectic in origin. It is within this violent milieu that the police operate. It is one where citizens are shot by the police and officers are murdered while in the line of duty.

The Public Health Service is the only federal agency that collects data on justifiable homicides. This data is taken from the Standard Death Certificate completed by coroners and medical examiners. Review of this data shows that the number of civilians killed by legal intervention has decreased considerably. In 1971 the total deaths were 412 but in 1986 this had declined to 247. Table 16–5 identifies the number of civilian deaths for five-year periods starting in 1972 and for other selected years. Clearly the number of justifiable homicides has been reduced on a year to year basis, taking into consideration the increase in population. Race is another variable in this equation. More non-whites were killed by legal intervention prior to 1978 than whites, but since that time there has been a continuous drop in the number of deaths for non-whites. In the most recent year for which data is available (1992) 87 non-whites died and 216 whites deaths occurred by legal intervention. Studies also show that few women die at the hands of the police. Over a twelve year period (1980 to 1992) 93 women died from legal intervention and 33 of those were African-American. It is

45. *Law Enforcement News,* "How Much Force is Enough?" November 30, 1998, p. 1.

46. *San Jose Mercury News,* "Police Report Shows Frequent Misuse of Guns by Officers," August 15, 1996, A3.

anticipated that in the years ahead more women will die as they become more involved in violent crime.[47]

Table 16–5

Civilian Deaths by Legal Intervention for Five Year Periods and Selected Years

Years	Total Deaths
1972–1977	1,654
1978–1981	1,452
1982–1986	1,275
1987–1991	1,114
1992	14
Total	5,809

Source: U.S. Department of Health and Human Services, Public Health Service, *Vital Statistics of the United States, 1972 to 1992, General Mortality*, Part A., Section 1, Hyattsville, MD. Public Health Service, 1995, pp. 322–389.

Some researchers question the validity of legal intervention statistics suggesting that for numerous reasons there is an under reporting by at least fifty percent. Another interesting statistic is the percentage of civilians who actually die after being shot by officers. Approximately thirty-nine percent of the persons shot by the police in one major city died. At the other end of the spectrum, in another major city, less than one-fifth of the shot civilians were killed. Unfortunately this type of data is not readily available in most cities. While poor data is better than no data at all when determining the number of civilian deaths by legal intervention could be improved in a number of ways. The poor quality of medical diagnoses can be clarified through follow-up investigation where deemed necessary and errors in recording data can be reduced by auditing. Additionally, this data could be recorded for the city in which the event occurred rather than from the county.

A number of experts estimate that in all probability 3,600 individuals are shot at annually by the police. If 600 of these civilians die and 1,200 are wounded it leaves it leaves a large number of individuals who were shot at and missed. In Atlanta in during a five year period the total shots-fired incidents was 267 and of this number civilians 54 were shot non-fatally and 28 were killed. During the same five year period in Houston there were 314 total incidents with persons fired at intentionally. Ninety-four citizens were injured and 54 killed.[48] The population

47. Public Health Service, *Vital Statistics of the United States, 1980–1992*, Volume II, General Mortality, Hyattsville, MD, Department of Health and Human Services, 1983–1995, pp. 220–370.

48. William A. Geller, *Deadly Force: What We Know–A Practitioner's Desk*

of Houston is almost times that of Atlanta, but others things have to be considered such as the policy governing the use of force, and the nature of the crime in each city. These and other factors indicated the complexity of the problem when analyzing the police shootings of civilians. For example, the Houston Police Department police on the use of force is discussed latter in this chapter.

The Shooting and Injury of Police Officers. The hazards of police are real too many officers. The nature of the hazard receiving the most publicity is the death of an officer. Next in line is the number of times officers are assaulted resulting in injury. For example, in 1997 some 49,151 assaults of officers occurred and 13,105 of those officers were injured. Of those assaulted one third were responding to disturbance calls and 19 percent were attempting arrests other than burglaries or robberies. Out of the total assaulted 179 officers were ambushed. Officers were injured primarily by personal weapons, i.e. feet, hands (83 percent), other dangerous weapons, (11 percent), while firearms and knifes were used the least 4.0 percent and 2 percent respectively. Tragically enough many officers are killed accidentally. Out of the 60 who died in 1997 automobile, aircraft and motorcycle accidents were the most frequent which combined for 40 of the deaths. In the same year, 55 officers were killed feloniously. Over the years, fewer officers have been murdered annually. A peak occurred in 1973 when 134 officers died, and the lowest frequency was in 1960 with 28 officers murdered. As indicated in table 16–6, during five-year intervals, the number of officer deaths was the highest from 1973 through 1977 as compared to the most recent period (1993–1997) when 343 officers were killed.

Table 16–6	
The Number Of Officers Murdered for Five Year Intervals from 1963 through 1997	
5 Year Period and Selected Years	**Number of Officers Murdered**
1963–1967	298
1968–1972	488
1973–1977	592
1978–1982	486
1983–1987	369
1988–1992	344
1993–1997	343

Source: Federal Bureau of Investigation, *Law Enforcement Officers Killed and Assaulted, 1963 to 1997*, Washington, D.C., US Government Printing Office, 1964 through 1998, pp. 1–64.

Reference on Police–Involved Shootings, Washington, DC, Police Executive Research Forum, 1992, pp. 523–524.

The reason for the decline is not readily apparent. It could possibly be many factors including improved training, officers are better armed, and they are receiving greater public support. Probably the most important is the increasing use, by officers, of bulletproof vests. It has been suggested that since the introduction of vests, at least 1300 officers have been saved from death or being wounded. There is also a Bulletproof Vest Partnership for fiscal year 1999 wherein the Bureau of Justice Assistance, will provide 25 million for the purchase of vests. At least half of these funds must go to governmental units with fewer than 100,000 residents. Each applicant must match at least 50 percent of the costs.[49] Summarily, about two-thirds of local police departments supplied some officers with protective body armor or the officers were given a cash allowance to purchase the vest (see table 16–7). Of the municipal departments with 100 or more officers 29 percent require the officers working in regular field operations to wear armor while on duty. Overall, about 36 percent of the sheriffs offices require that protective armor be worn by field operations officers. The mandatory wearing of body armor is a critical policy issue in a number of agencies. Some officers' object to wearing it, especially during hot weather, but it would seem that in the interest of saving lives, officers should be required to wear this added protection. This is especially true for those in field operations, traffic, and special operations.[50] During the last decade, of 253 officers wearing body armor when slain, 152 suffered gunshot wounds to the head. Eighty three received gunshot wounds to the upper torso and 18 suffered wounds below the waist. Forty were shot between the panels of the vest or through the arm openings. Fourteen officers died when the body armor was penetrated. In the last year for which statistics are available 15 officers were murdered when wearing protective armor and eight died when shot above the vest.[51]

Table 16–7

Body Armor Supplied/Cash Allowance and Percent Requiring that Body Armor be Worn in Local and State Agencies With 100 or More Sworn Officers

| | | | Type of Agency | |
	County	Municipal	Sheriff	State
Supplied or Cash Allowance				
Armor supplied to all	100%	83%	90%	90%
Armor supplied to some	0	6	6	6
Cash allowance to all	7	14	3	6
Cash allowance to some	0	3	2	4

49. Nancy C. Gist, *The Bulletproof Vest Partnership*, Washington, DC, Bureau of Justice Assistance, January 1999, pp. 1–2.

50. Brian A. Reaves, and Pheny Z. Smith, *Law Enforcement Management and Administrative Statistics, 1993: Data for Individual State and Local Agencies with 100 or More Officers*, Washington, D.C., Bureau of Justice Statistics, 1995, p. xii.

51. Federal Bureau of Investigation, *Law Enforcement Officers Killed and Assaulted, 1997*, Washington, DC, USGPO, 1998, p. 5.

Requiring Body Armor be Worn				
All regular field officers	23	39	41	24
Some regular field officers	17	12	15	24

Source: Brian A. Reaves, and Andrew L. Goldberg, *Law Enforcement Management and Administrative Statistics, 1997: Data For Individual State and Local Agencies*, Washington, DC, Bureau of Justice Statistics, September 1999, p. xvii.

The types of firearms authorized for use by sworn officers has changed considerably during the last decade (see table 16–8). Almost all of municipal police departments, authorize the use of some type of semi-automatic sidearm. The 9mm semi-automatic is the most popular sidearm with 82 percent of the departments authorizing its use. Other authorized types of semi-automatic sidearm include the .45 (38 percent), the 10mm (15 percent),and the .380 (15 percent)[52] During the last five years an increasing number of municipal agencies have authorized semiautomatic firearms with greater fire power.

Table 16–8

Types of Sidearm Authorized in Various Types of Law Enforcement Agencies with 100 or More Sworn Officers

Type of Sidearm	County	Municipal	Type of Agency Sheriff	State
Any Type	88%	98%	94%	96%
10mm	15	15	29	18
9mm	70	82	80	73
.45	27	38	58	35
.380	12	15	20	18

Source: Brian A. Reaves and Pheny Z. Smith, *Law Enforcement Management and Administrative Statistics, 1993: Data for Individual State and Local Agencies with 100 or More Officers*, Washington, DC, Bureau of Justice Statistics, September 1995, p. xii.

Alternatives to Deadly Force. Court decisions and special interest groups have been instrumental in creating an interest in developing less-than-lethal devices. This is especially true for fleeing felons whose deaths have generated more and more restrictive court decisions. Available devices do not allow law enforcement officers to immediately apprehend, control or stop a fleeing felon with less than the use of ultimate force. Nor is there any technology on the horizon that will be a truly effective non-lethal weapon although several are on the drawing board. In larger police department a wide range of non-lethal weapons have been authorized as set forth in table 16–9.

52. *Ibid.*

Table 16–9

Agencies Authorizing (by percentage) the Use of
Non–Lethal Weapons.

Item Description	County	Municipal	Type of Agency Sheriff	State
Baton, Collapsible	36%	49%	64%	53
Baton, Pr–24	48	58	68	53
Baton, traditional	79	64	68	55
Capture net	0	6	1	0
Carotid hold	18	20	16	16
Choke hold	6	4	5	10
Flash/bang grenade	61	57	63	41
Pepper spray	70	69	66	63
Rubber bullet	9	7	12	10
Soft projectile	9	7	10	6
Stun gun	6	14	28	4
Tear gas—personal issue	42	31	35	29
Tear gas–large volume	64	42	41	41
Three pole trip	3	—	0	0

Source: Brian A. Reaves and Pheny Z. Smith, *Law Enforcement Management and Administrative Statistics, 1993: Data for Individual State and Local Agencies with 100 or More Officers,* Washington, DC, Bureau of Justice Statistics, September 1995, p. xii.

It can readily be seen, from the above list, that batons and pepper spray are used extensively. Weapons used less extensively include the capture net, the three-pole trip and the chock hold. In view of the time that some of these non-lethal weapons have been around it appears that the more traditional weapons are in vogue and more recent technological advances are used with less frequency.

Firearms Policy

The question of firearm policy is pivotal to the excessive force controversy. In recent years most departments have taken the position that an officer should exhaust all other reasonable means of apprehension and control before resorting to the use of firearms. On the other side of the coin, police executives have expressed that officers should not unnecessarily, or unreasonably, endanger themselves when confronted with a dangerous situation.[53] For many years the so-called "any felony" policy—essentially, authorized police to use firearms or other means of deadly force to arrest a person suspected of committing a felony prevailed. In some states police were permitted by law to shoot fleeing persons suspected of such offenses as check forgery and auto

53. California Peace Officers' Association, *Officer Involved Shootings,* Sacramento, CA., California Peace Officers' Association, no date, p. 15.

theft. Other states limited the use of deadly force to "forcible" felonies, such as robbery. Another 12 states had no statute at all.[54]

The U.S. Supreme Court in Tennessee v. Garner, 471 U.S. 1, at 9, 1985, defined the justification for using deadly force to prevent the escape of a felony suspect under all circumstances. It held that it is not permissible to use deadly force in all cases. The Court explained, if the officer has probable cause to believe the suspect poses a threat of serious physical harm, either to the officer or others, it is not constitutionally unreasonable to prevent escape by using deadly force.[55] This decision has had tremendous impact on deadly force policies. Agencies have found it necessary to alter policies and train officers, as a means of conforming to the new decision. Like all decisions, it does not solve all the ambiguity in this area, but it clearly prohibits the police from shooting at unarmed, nonviolent, fleeing felony suspects. The Houston Police Department's policy regarding the use of firearms sets forth the general values that must guide an officer's actions. The policy is as follows: The use of firearms is never to be considered routine, is permissible only in defense of life, and then only when all other means have been exhausted. This policy is based on a belief its duty is to protect life. Officers, therefore, are to use firearms only to protect their lives or the lives of others. Since the use of firearms has the potential to endanger life, it should occur only when there is no other alternative. This means officers are to use their firearms only when failure to do so would result in death or serious bodily injury to themselves or others.

The Houston Police Department places its highest value on the life and safety of its officers and the public. The department's policies, rules, and procedures are designed to ensure that this value guides officers' use of firearms.[56]

Rules. The policy stated above is the basis of the following set of rules that have been designed to guide officers in all cases involving the use of firearms:

- Rule 1.   Police officers shall not discharge their firearms except to protect themselves or another person from imminent death or serious bodily injury.
- Rule 2.   Police officers shall discharge their firearms only when doing so will not endanger innocent persons.

54. Community Relations Service, *Police Use of Deadly Force, A Conciliation Handbook for Citizens and the Police,* Washington, D.C., U.S. Department of Justice, 1986, pp. 3–4.

55. John C. Hall, "Constitutional Constraints on the Use of Force," *FBI Law Enforcement Bulletin,* February 1992, Vol. 61, No. 2, p. 27.

56. Community Relations Service, *Principles of Good Policing: Avoiding Violence Between Police and Citizens,* Washington, D.C. U.S. Department of Justice, 1986, citing *Use of Force,* Training Bulletin, Houston Police Department, May 3, 1984 and American Civil Liberties Union, *Fighting Police Abuse– A Community Action Manual,* New York, NY, American Civil Liberties Union, 1997, p. 17.

- Rule 3.   Police officers shall not discharge their firearms to threaten or subdue persons whose actions are destructive to property or injurious to themselves but which do not represent an imminent threat of death or serious bodily injury to the officers or others.
- Rule 4.   Police officers shall not discharge their firearms to subdue an escaping suspect who presents no immediate threat of death or serious bodily injury.
- Rule 5.   Police officers shall not discharge their weapons at a moving vehicle unless it is absolutely necessary to do so to protect against an imminent threat to the life of an officer or others.
- Rule 6.   Police officers when confronting an oncoming vehicle shall attempt to move out of the path, if possible, rather than discharge their firearms at the oncoming vehicle.
- Rule 7.   Police officers shall not intentionally place themselves in the path of an oncoming vehicle and attempt to disable the vehicle by discharging their firearms.
- Rule 8.   Police officers shall not discharge their firearms at a fleeing vehicle or its driver.
- Rule 9.   Officers shall not fire warning shots.

- Rule 10.   Officers shall not draw or display their firearms unless there is a threat or possible cause to believe there is a threat to life or for inspection.[57]

A sound firearms policy, fully ingrained into the value system of a police department can go a long way in reducing the incidence of violence between the police and the community. A good policy builds accountability into police operations and controls discretion. The vast majority of police departments have a firearms policy but the quality of some of those policies leaves a great deal to be desires. The I.A.C.P. has a model policy on the use of force and serves as a positive guide in this volatile area. In the middle of the last decade the US Department of Justice approved a deadly force policy to govern all agencies within the department. It is the first time that a uniform policy was created for federal agencies. The common threads that run throughout the policy are the establishment of an "imminent danger" standard and the reaffirmation of the basic principle that even when an imminent danger exists, deadly force should not be used if to do so would create an unreasonable risk to innocent third parties. It is not sufficient for management to simply expound a policy and then urge officers to do their best. It is important that management commit itself to policy interpretation and application. According to the FBI this not only gives the agents instruction but it also instills confidence that management

57. Lee P. Brown, *Administrative Notice,* Use of Firearms Policy, Office of the Chief, Houston Police Department, May 7, 1984, pp. 2–3, in Community Relations Service, *Principles of Good Policing: Avoiding Violence Between Police And Citizens,* Washington D.C., U.S. Department of Justice, 1986.

has the courage to confront the same issues that the agents must confront on the street.[58]

Liability Issues

Civil liability has always been of concern to police executives, but never to the extent that it is today. In what is now the infamous Rodney King case, Mr. King had sued the city seeking 15 million dollars in damages and a three-week civil trial he received $3.8 million tax free award for medical bills, pain and suffering. It has been reported that the city attorney had suggested that a $800,000 settlement would have been appropriate. Other cases clearly illustrate a trend toward filing law suits against police officers. In

Phoenix ,AZ a jury awarded $45 million to survivors of a double amputee who died while held with a neck hold when officers were trying to subdue him. The jury felt that the police should be accountable to the citizens they serve.[59] In another case, in 1997, two illegal immigrants were beaten by Riverside County (CA) Sheriff's deputies after a freeway chase. TV news helicopters videotaped a deputy shoving a woman face-first on to the hood of a car, then grabbing her by the hair and pulling her to the ground, where she was hit repeatedly. The man was also beaten. The two subjects split an $740,000 award.[60]

The liability for personal injuries or property damage is generally handled under applicable state laws. Section 1983 of The Civil Rights Act, Title 42 United States Code, is the section most commonly used when an officer has deprived someone of their civil rights. These rights include the right not to have life, liberty, or property taken without due process of law. This is a right secured by the 14th amendment to the U.S. Constitution. Additionally there is the right of a person not to be unreasonably seized, a right guaranteed by the fourth amendment.

In the case of City of Canton v. Harris the liability of training was questioned. The court pointed out that in light of assigned duties, the need for more or different training becomes obvious. The inadequacy of training, likely to result in the violation of constitutional rights, may be such that the city policy makers can be said to have been deliberately indifferent to the need. The Court pointed out, the city policy makers know to a moral certainty, their officers will be required to arrest fleeing felons. The city has armed its officers with firearms, in part to allow them to accomplish this task. Thus, the need to train officers in the constitutional limitations on the use of deadly force can be said to be obvious. Failure to do so can properly be characterized as "deliberate indifference" to constitutional rights.[61] Under Tennessee v. Garner,

58. John C. Hall, "FBI Training on the New Federal Deadly Force Policy," *FBI Law Enforcement Bulletin*, April 1996, Vol. 65, No. 4, pp. 25–32.

59. *The Tucson Daily Star*, "Double Amputee's Kin Awarded $45 million in Killing by Phoenix Cop," March 13, 1998, 1B.

60. *San Jose Mercury News*, "Beating Victims Settle Civil Rights Suit," June 21, 1997, 3B.

61. Nugent, *op. cit.*, pp. 3–5.

471 U.S. 1, (1985) a municipality may be liable for failing to have a policy limiting high-risk pursuits to circumstances justifying the risk. Under the City of Canton v. Harris, 489 U.S. 378, 103 L.Ed.2d 412, 109 S.Ct. 1197 (1989), the Court held there was a failure to provide training constraining the application of deadly force.[62]

In addition, to state liabilities, law enforcement can be confronted with Federal civil/criminal liabilities for civil rights. Title 42, US Code, Section 1983, allows individuals to sue for monetary damages when their civil rights are violated. Title 18, US Code, Sections 240 and 241 allow for criminal penalties for criminal violation of civil rights, i.e. misuse of power, abuse of authority. Liability findings have occurred on one or more level. In the Rodney King incident the officers were acquitted in state court and convicted in federal court.

Eliminating or minimizing negligence and misconduct in operation can reduce exposure to liability. This can be done by providing positive training, policies and leadership within the agency. A common theme from litigation is not just weakness in policies and training, but in enforcing policies and documentation of proper training. Effective managers concern themselves with managing risk and liability.[63] Law suits are a reality in law enforcement and in the future the number of suits will increase. Periodically one can find newspaper articles reporting large settlements. In 1988 settlements for the misuse of force, in five cities, ranged from $378,00 to 76.4 million. In a another city, the chief of police banned police pursuits because of more than 10 million dollars in lawsuits over a six-year period. The legal foundation for the suits was a law making local governments liable for injuries and deaths connected with pursuits. The law provided liability held, even if officers were not negligent.[64]

The potentiality for liability from the excessive use of force by officers and high-speed pursuits is significant. Clear and definitive policies must be established in these two important areas. Officers must be trained in the policies and techniques to insure they are clearly understood and applied. Supervisors and managers must constantly evaluate officer performance in these areas. Additionally, the policies and procedures need to be reviewed periodically to conform with legal requirements.

Drug Use and Testing

The testing of employees and applicants for drug use is of recent origin in law enforcement. It is part of the "war on drugs." The specific goal is to have a drug-free workplace, especially for employees who hold

62. Missey K. O'Linn, "The Gaps in Use-of-Force Policies and Training," *The Police Chief,* February 1992, Vol. LIX, No. 2, p. 52.

63. Javier Soto, "Avoiding the Teeth of Liability," *Law and Order,* August 1998, Vol. 46, No. 8, pp. 99–104.

64. Associated Press, "Suits Prompt Omaha to Ban Police Chases." *The Arizona Daily Star,* Thursday, December 12, 1991, A 17.

sensitive positions. Employees also must refrain from using illegal drugs both on and off duty. There is a general feeling that all police employees should be tested. This includes civilians and sworn officers. It also is common to have both mandatory and voluntary testing.

Additionally, drug testing has become an integral component of the screening process when selecting new employees. Within the context of recruiting one of the most difficult tasks has been what to do about the drug-use history of applicants. Generally police departments will reject applicants who have a history of using hallucinogens such as LSD or PCP. On the other hand a one time use of a drug such as cocaine is not necessarily a reason for rejection. The same can be said for the use of marijuana. What's important is the history of drug use and how recent has the applicant used drugs. Usually applicants are rejected if they are currently using drugs. Should an applicant be rejected because they had a juvenile drug experience? How long should an applicant should be drug free is an open question. Is it one year, two years, or ten years. In other words the decision is made case-by-case. Table 16–10 lists the percent of agencies that drug test applicants for sworn positions and the percentage that test probationary officers. It is interesting to note that a relatively high percentage of applicants are tested for drug as compared to those in a probationary position. Additionally, state police agencies use drug testing at a lower rate than other types of law enforcement agencies.

Table 16–10

Percentage of Agencies Testing Applicants and Probationary Officers

	County	Municipal	Sheriff	State
Applicants				
Mandatory testing	70%	67%	66%	53%
Random selection	12	2	3	4
When use is suspected	9	7	4	6
No testing	18	31	32	37
Probationary officers				
Mandatory testing	21%	14	10	2
Random selection	30	18	16	20
When use is suspected	52	46	37	49
No testing	27	38	47	41

Source: Brian A. Reaves and Pheny Z. Smith, *Law Enforcement Management and Administrative Statistics, 1993: Data for Individual State and Local Agencies with 100 or More Officers,* Washington, DC, September 1995, p. x.

Most agencies test employees when there is a reasonable suspicion an employee is using illegal drugs. Normally agencies conducting applicant and random testing do so for marijuana and cocaine. Other departments do additional testing for opiates, amphetamines, and phencyclidine (PCP). There is no consistent rule for how often an agency should test employees. Some test as few as four percent of the employees annually, and others test employees several times a year. In Tucson, AZ newly hired officers must take a drug test and they are also subject to random tests during their 18–month probationary period. Additionally, ten percent of officers assigned to narcotics units are randomly tested each month. There has been discussion to extent testing to all personnel, but this effort has been opposed by the police union.[65] In one municipal agency the testing of officers is in accordance with an agreement between the city and the police union. In this situation testing can only be done when there is a reasonable belief that the officer has used a controlled substance. In another agency an allegation of impairment can result in the administering of tests for alcohol intoxication, being under the influence of drugs or being under the influence of a combination of alcohol and drugs. At the federal level one agency randomly tests five percent of the employees, and another tests 30 percent annually. The percentage of employees tested is a management judgment guided by what will be an adequate deterrent to the use of illegal drugs.

Drug testing is expense. In one agency the collection cost is $41.80 per unit and laboratory analysis was $12.75 per screening. This latter cost escalated to $30.00 per unit for a confirmation with a fee of $50.00 per hour for the services of a medical review officer. In another agency the cost per sample for collection was $29.19, and laboratory analysis was $8.90 per sample. Obviously these costs vary considerably. An agency should carefully screen contracting agencies to find one that can conduct the tests at a reasonable cost. In part, the costs vary and it is a serious consideration when setting up a drug testing program. Some agencies contract with private companies for the collection and analysis of samples and others have a special unit within the police department. The goal of a drug free working place is achievable under a drug testing program. Currently on the horizon are technological developments that represent signal advances over current drug testing that relies on urinalysis. These methods may have advantages beyond cost effectiveness alone. Foe one thing they are less invasive and intrusive. These technologies include hair analysis sweat patches, and saliva testing.[66]

Case Study

Lieutenant Charles Wong

Lt. Wong has been in the Administrative Division of the police department for four years. He worked in the in the training section for two of those years and his most recent assignment has been to

65. *The Arizona Daily Star,* "Drug Tests for Police Possible–Review Board Studying Costs," September 16, 1998, B 1.

66. Tom Mieczkowski and Kim Lersch, "Drug Testing in Criminal Jus-

tice: Evolving Uses, Emerging Technologies," Washington, DC, *National Institute of Justice Journal,* December 1997, pp. 9–15.

recruitment and selection. He has been a member of the department for eleven years and previously worked in patrol and narcotics. He was very successful in both assignments and proved to highly effective when working undercover in narcotics. He made innumerable buys and in his last major case he was seriously wounded although he has made a complete recovery. When working in training he taught investigative techniques and self-defense. He is an expert in martial arts. Additionally, he is bilingual and the Investigations Division will on occasion use him as an interpreter. He has a degree in political science and is currently working part time on a Masters in Business Administration.

In his new assignment he has been asked to revise and update the departmental policy on drug testing. Currently the department has found that an increasing number of applicants have experimented with drugs and he has been asked to clarify and define "experimenting." There is also a question as to whether or not experimenting with marijuana is acceptable and what should be done when applicants have experimented with cocaine or other drugs. Currently, if an applicant has used drugs during the year he or she has applied for a position the application is rejected. It has been pointed out to Lt. Wong that The current policy does not address the problem of officers abusing legally prescribed drugs or over the counter drugs. Additionally, the current policy does not give any consideration to treatment prior to termination. The police union has always opposed the testing of sworn personnel, but it has never taken a position on the testing of applicants for drug use.

If you were Lt. Wong who would you involve in the policy altering process? Would you involve the union? Why or why not? What should be the time period for being "clean" prior to appointment? Define "experimentation." What consideration should be given to treating officers who have voluntarily sought help? Would you involve the police union in the development of the policy? Why or why not?

For Further Reading

Kenneth L. Bayless and Robert Osborne, *Police Management Task Force Report*, Rockville, MD, National Law Enforcement and Corrections Technology Center, September 1998, pp. 1–99.

> This report is the culmination of a task force that provides an assessment of the current techniques and technologies related to pursuits, recommendations regarding technology development and commercialization. It also includes an overview of legal issues related to pursuits and technologies, and recommendations for legislative action. Information for the report was obtained from questionnaires and surveys completed by agencies, line officers, and the general public.

Lawrence A. Greenfeld, Patrick A. Langan, and Steven K. Smith, *Police Use of Force–Collection of National Data,* Washington, DC, Bureau of Justice Statistics, November 1997, pp. 11–38.

> Provides data that allows for estimating, for the first time, the prevalence of all kinds of encounters between the police and members of the public, favorable as well as unfavorable. It was found that the excessive use of force was clearly a small fraction of the number of police encounters. Describes the type of contacts that citizens have had with the police, to include contact without force, contacts with handcuffs only, and contacts with force or threat of force.

Barbara A. Manili, Edward F. Connor III, Darrel W. Stephens and John R. Stedman, *Police Drug Testing,* Washington, DC, National Institute of Justice, May 1987, pp. 1–109.

> This report combines information about technical, legal, and police issues of concern to police agencies that are planning drug test programs or are researching the issues. Describes the major benefits and limitations of drug testing programs. Focuses on testing of police applicants, probationary personnel, and the testing of tenured officers. Of special interest is the recommendations for policy direction of drug testing programs. The report also reviews the role of employee assistance programs.

Joseph E. Scuro, Jr., "Supreme Court Update–Greater Immunity for Officers Involved in Pursuits," *Law and Order,* January 1999, Vol. 47, No. 1, pp. 75–76.

> Describes the decision of the US Supreme Court in Sacramento County v. Lewis (Case No. 96–1337, 63 Cr. L. 245, May 27, 1998). The decision provides greater protection for officers who are engaged in high-speed pursuit. The Court held that high-speed chases that result in fatal accidents or injuries do not violate protected civil rights as provided under the Fourteenth Amendment. Additionally the court held that one must show that the officer intended to harm the subject by initiating the pursuit. Of course there is always the possibility that such cases could be pursued in state courts.

INDEX

References are to Pages